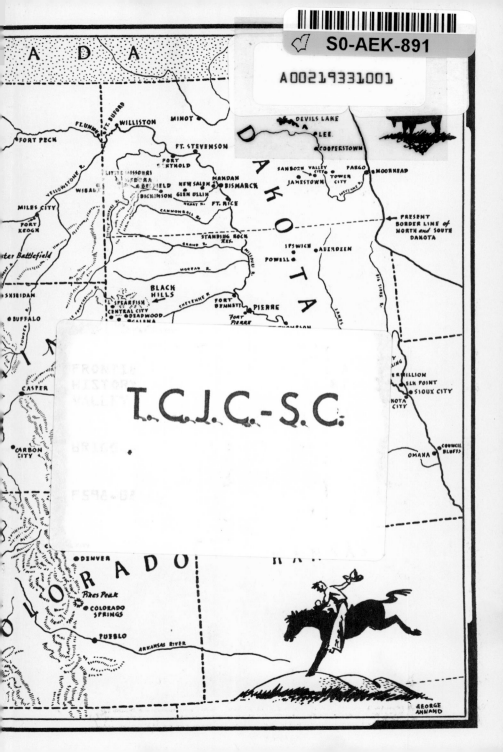

"PIONEERS! O PIONEERS!"

An early settler's thatched log house near Grafton, North Dakota. Courtesy of the Minnesota State Historical Society.

FRONTIERS
OF THE NORTHWEST

A History of the Upper Missouri Valley

By

HAROLD E. BRIGGS, Ph.D.

Professor of History, University of Miami
Coral Gables, Florida

ILLUSTRATED

NEW YORK
PETER SMITH
1950

TO

BOWMAN F. ASHE

PRESIDENT OF THE UNIVERSITY OF MIAMI

A MODERN PIONEER

PREFACE

SOME fifteen years ago I began the study of the section I have termed the Northwest, or the Upper Missouri Valley, which comprises the states of North and South Dakota, Montana, and Wyoming, overlapping into Idaho and northern Colorado. This area has had a common history. Here the northern herd of buffalo made its last stand and the miners hurried from one new find to another in our last golden age. Here men dug ditches to water their newly tilled fields and rode over ranges that stretched away to the horizon. And here to-day the rodeo and the frontier-day celebration, the dude ranch and the wild-western film strive in vain to recapture an era that has gone forever. Historians, too, realizing the impermanency of memories, are trying to keep for the future an accurate record of those colorful years, and to that effort this volume belongs.

A vast variety of material has been covered in preparing the manuscript, and I am indebted to more people than can possibly be named here. Acknowledgments are due R. G. Wellington, formerly professor of history at the University of South Dakota, who suggested this study; to Louis Pelzer, professor of American history at the University of Iowa, who for many years has been most helpful in his criticism and encouragement; to Herbert M. Kellar, director of the McCormick Historical Association, Chicago, who, in addition to allowing me the use of that library, also placed his own personal library at my disposal and made many valuable suggestions; to Everett E. Edwards, editor of *Agricultural History*, Washington, D. C., who allowed me full use of his personal files in the summer of 1936, as well as constantly supplying me with valuable bibliographies and mimeographed material; to

Merrill G. Burlingame, professor of history, Montana State Agricultural College, Bozeman, who gave me the generous use of the notes for his doctor's dissertation in the summer of 1935; to the librarians of the many state historical societies that have extended me courtesies, especially to L. K. Fox, secretary of the South Dakota Historical Society, Pierre; and to my wife, Ernestine Bennett Briggs, for her constructive criticism and assistance in the final preparation of the manuscript for the press. I wish also to acknowledge a liberal grant-in-aid given me by the Social Science Research Council of New York in the summer of 1936 for the purpose of completing the collection of material for this volume, without which its publication would have been greatly delayed.

H. E. B.

CONTENTS

	PAGE
PREFACE	vii
ILLUSTRATIONS	xiii

I

THE FRONTIER OF THE MINER

	INTRODUCTION	3
I.	THE GOLD RUSH TO COLORADO	4
II.	GOLD IN IDAHO	8
III.	THE GOLD FRONTIER IN MONTANA	16
IV.	THE GOLD FRONTIER IN WYOMING	22
V.	THE BLACK HILLS GOLD RUSH	25
VI.	THE SEARCH FOR A NEW GOLD FRONTIER	41
VII.	MINING AND PROSPECTING ON THE GOLD FRONTIER	45
VIII.	TRANSPORTATION AND TRAVEL TO THE GOLD FIELDS	53
IX.	BOOM PRICES IN THE GOLD CAMPS	65
X.	THE CHARACTERS IN THE PAGEANT	71
XI.	THE CALAMITY JANE MYTH	75
XII.	SALOONS AND HURDY-GURDIES	82
XIII.	GAMBLERS AND GAMES OF CHANCE	86
XIV.	CULTURAL LIFE	89
XV.	EDUCATION	98
XVI.	RELIGION	102
XVII.	THE THEATER ON THE MINING FRONTIER	107
XVIII.	JUSTICE IN THE MINING CAMPS	112

II

THE FRONTIER OF THE BUFFALO

	INTRODUCTION	125
I.	BUFFALO EAST OF THE MISSISSIPPI	125
II.	BUFFALO IN THE RED RIVER VALLEY	127

		PAGE
III.	THE BUFFALO RANGE OF THE NORTHWEST	133
IV.	ACCOUNTS OF EARLY EXPLORERS AND TRAVELERS	137
V.	HUNTING THE BUFFALO	140
VI.	PREPARATION OF BUFFALO SKINS	142
VII.	TYPES OF ROBES	143
VIII.	BUFFALO AND THE EARLY FUR TRADE	146
IX.	TRADING FOR ROBES	150
X.	MISSOURI STEAMBOATING AND THE BUFFALO TRADE	154
XI.	DIVISION INTO NORTHERN AND SOUTHERN HERDS	156
XII.	THE SOUTHERN HERD IS SLAUGHTERED	158
XIII.	THE BUFFALO FRONTIER IN THE NORTHWEST	161
XIV.	PROFESSIONAL HUNTERS	171
XV.	BUFFALO BONES	178

III

THE FRONTIER OF THE CATTLE-RANCHER

	INTRODUCTION	181
I.	EARLY CATTLE IN WYOMING AND MONTANA	185
II.	EARLY CATTLE-RAISING IN THE TERRITORY OF DAKOTA	191
III.	THE CATTLE OF TEXAS	195
IV.	THE NORTHERN DRIVE	199
V.	THE NORTHWEST AS A CATTLE AREA	203
VI.	DEVELOPMENTS IN WYOMING	204
VII.	DEVELOPMENTS IN MONTANA	209
VIII.	DEVELOPMENTS IN DAKOTA	211
IX.	A BEEF BONANZA	215
X.	A MEAT-PACKING EXPERIMENT ON THE WESTERN PLAINS IN THE EIGHTIES	228
XI.	ENGLAND AS A POSSIBLE CATTLE MARKET	233
XII.	THE WINTER OF 1886-87	235
XIII.	THEODORE ROOSEVELT AS A CATTLEMAN	246
XIV.	PRICES AND PROFITS	250
XV.	FOREIGNERS AND FOREIGN CAPITAL	253
XVI.	IMPROVEMENT OF RANGE STOCK	259
XVII.	CATTLE ASSOCIATIONS	264

CONTENTS

XVIII. CATTLE ASSOCIATIONS IN ACTION 269
XIX. THE INDIAN MENACE 274
XX. THE CATTLE THIEF 280
XXI. LIFE ON THE RANGE 283
XXII. THE ADVANCE OF THE AGRICULTURAL FRONTIER . . 293
XXIII. THE JOHNSON COUNTY WAR 300
XXIV. THE END OF THE OPEN RANGE 304

IV

THE FRONTIER OF THE SHEEP-RANCHER

INTRODUCTION 309
I. EARLY SHEEP-RAISING IN THE NORTHWEST . . . 313
II. THE EXPANSION OF SHEEP-RANCHING 317
III. PROFITS AND PRICES 322
IV. THE STRUGGLE BETWEEN SHEEPMEN AND CATTLEMEN 327
V. THE SHEEP HERDER 337
VI. HORSE-RANCHING IN THE NORTHWEST 338
VII. HORSE THIEVES 342

V

THE FRONTIER OF SETTLEMENT

INTRODUCTION 347
I. EARLY SETTLEMENTS AND TOWN-SITES IN DAKOTA . 348
II. EARLY SETTLEMENT IN THE VALLEY OF THE RED RIVER
OF THE NORTH 361
III. FACTORS WORKING AGAINST EARLY SETTLEMENT . . 366
IV. FACTORS FAVORING EARLY SETTLEMENT . . . 370
V. DEVELOPMENT IN DAKOTA TO 1870 372
VI. BOOM AND DEPRESSION IN DAKOTA, 1870-1878 . . 376
VII. THE EARLY SETTLEMENT OF WYOMING . . . 392
VIII. THE EARLY SETTLEMENT OF MONTANA 401
IX. IMMIGRATION TO MONTANA, 1870-1880 . . . 405
X. THE DAKOTA BOOM, 1879-1886 410
XI. SETTLEMENT IN MONTANA AFTER 1880 . . . 430

PAGE

XII. SETTLEMENT IN WYOMING AFTER 1880 436
XIII. IMMIGRATION ACTIVITIES 443
XIV. COLONIZATION PROJECTS 454
XV. COUNTY-SEAT FIGHTS 473
XVI. SOME FORGOTTEN TOWNS 477

VI

THE FRONTIER OF AGRICULTURE

INTRODUCTION 485
I. AGRICULTURE IN EARLY DAKOTA 485
II. EARLY AGRICULTURE IN MONTANA 496
III. EARLY AGRICULTURE IN WYOMING 507
IV. BONANZA FARMING IN THE RED RIVER VALLEY . . . 509
V. GRASSHOPPER PLAGUES 522
VI. CLIMATIC HANDICAPS 534
VII. CREDIT AND INTEREST 539
VIII. THE GRANGE IN THE NORTHWEST 544
IX. THE AGRICULTURAL FAIR 555
X. TOWNS AND SETTLEMENTS 564
XI. THE THEATER ON THE GREAT PLAINS 569
XII. LIFE OF THE FRONTIER FARMER 581

BIBLIOGRAPHY 595
INDEX 613

ILLUSTRATIONS

"PIONEERS! O PIONEERS!" . . . . *Frontispiece*

FACING PAGE

SLUICING IN THE GREGORY DIGGINGS 6
HELENA'S MAIN STREET 20
EARLY DAYS OF DEADWOOD 38
BULL-WHACKING INTO THE BLACK HILLS 64
PERSONAGES OF THE FRONTIER 80
THE HURDY-GURDY HOUSE AT VIRGINIA CITY 86
BUCKING THE TIGER 86
ROUGH JUSTICE IN MONTANA 120
BUFFALO ON THE UPPER MISSOURI 134
FORT UNION 148
AN INDIAN BUFFALO HUNT 160
SLAUGHTER ON THE LINE OF THE KANSAS PACIFIC 160
FORTY THOUSAND BUFFALO HIDES 174
"WHERE THE MILLIONS HAVE GONE" 174
A CATTLE DRIVE ON THE MONTANA TRAIL . . . . . . 200.
NOMADS OF THE PLAINS 216
INDIANS DRYING MEAT 216
THE PACKING PLANT OF THE MARQUIS DE MORES 230
THEODORE ROOSEVELT'S MALTESE CROSS RANCH 248
A MONTANA RANCH OF THE SEVENTIES 248
A ROUNDUP ON THE RANGE 266
THE BATTLEFIELD OF THE LITTLE BIG HORN 276
COWBOYS IN TOWN FOR CHRISTMAS 288
A SHEPHERD OF THE MOUNTAINS 312
SHIPPING WOOL ON THE SHEEP FRONTIER 326
A PIONEER LEGISLATURE OF DAKOTA TERRITORY 366
CHEYENNE IN THE BOOM DAYS 394
BANNACK, FIRST CAPITAL OF MONTANA TERRITORY 406
A FREIGHT-TRAIN FERRY ON THE MISSOURI 418
A SETTLEMENT IN THE BAD LANDS 450
A BONANZA WHEAT HARVEST 512

FACING PAGE

GRAIN ELEVATORS DOMINATING A DAKOTA LANDSCAPE 524

THRESHING IN THE FIELDS 538

TRAVELING EXHIBIT CAR OF THE NORTHERN PACIFIC 558

AN EXHIBIT OF NORTHWEST GRAINS 558

VAUDEVILLE ON THE FRONTIER 576

THE COUNTRY EMPORIUM 590

MAPS

PAGE

CHIEF MINING CENTERS 42

BUFFALO RANGE OF THE NORTHWEST, 1876 165

DAKOTA TERRITORY, 1870 375

DAKOTA TERRITORY, 1878 389

WYOMING TERRITORY, 1880 400

MONTANA TERRITORY, 1879 407

DAKOTA TERRITORY, 1885 425

FRONTIERS
OF THE NORTHWEST

He who would wish to see America in its proper light, and have a true idea of its feeble beginnings and barbarous rudiments, must visit our extended line of frontiers where the last settlers dwell, and where he may see the first labours of settlement, the mode of clearing the earth, in all their different appearances. . . .

CRÈVECŒUR, *Letters from an American Farmer*

I

THE FRONTIER OF
THE MINER

MORE than any other phase of American life, mining has presented the spectacle of a pageant. From the time the curtain rose on the carpenter John Marshall, catching the golden flicker of Sutter's mill-race in California, until it descended slowly and unwillingly on Deadwood in the Black Hills of Dakota, the West teemed with the most varied group of adventurers the country ever saw. To men the world over, California in '49 spelled an easy fortune. The rainbow ended in the Far West and the pot of gold was an ample one. The rush to the western gold-fields, lasting almost half a century, more nearly approximated a crusade than anything else America has seen, as thousands hurried to answer the imperious call of the gold empire.

But the nineteenth century, for the United States, was one of exploitation and waste. The country was too impatient to do more than skim the cream from its vast resources. Consequently, the California gold boom of the late forties soon exhausted the deposits that were easily accessible, and gold production declined, leaving hundreds of miners without employment. While some of them turned to farming and ranching, many, afflicted with gold fever, drifted to the north and east in search of new fields. Too, even in the early days of the gold frontier, the miners displayed that strange mania for following new discoveries that characterized the entire period. They have been likened to quicksilver, because of their propensity to scatter in all directions in a promising area, often before the deposits they were working were more than sampled. The decade following 1858 was characterized by the rapid expansion of gold-mining on a large scale into many parts of the Rocky Mountain area, from Arizona and New Mexico on the south, to Washington, Montana, and Colorado on the north.

I

THE GOLD RUSH TO COLORADO

BEGINNING as early as 1697, when a French writer discussed the possibility of "rich mines" in the region west and north of the Mississippi River, rumors of gold in the mountains and other portions of the West had circulated freely and widely. Coronado himself is said to have reached the Colorado country in search of a people who used utensils and implements of pure gold, while from the Spanish settlements on the Rio Grande, impatient and restless explorers visited eastern Colorado and the region drained by the Platte River, and even penetrated parts of the Rocky Mountains. There were rumors throughout the eighteenth and early nineteenth centuries regarding gold in the area that was later to become Colorado.

Among the soldiers of Captain Randolph B. Marcy, who was sent west in 1857 to look into the Mormon situation in Utah, was a man by the name of George Simpson.[1] While on the way south with a detachment of Marcy's troops to obtain supplies, Simpson panned for gold as the party camped for the night on a small stream called Cherry Creek, near Pike's Peak, and struck colors. Continuing their journey the party met a detachment of soldiers carrying despatches from Fort Bridger to whom Simpson showed the gold-dust panned on Cherry Creek, giving a portion of it to one of the men. A few months later, while at West Port, an outfitting point on the Missouri River, the gold created a great deal of excitement. In the spring of 1858, William Green Russell, with a party of experienced gold-hunters consisting of

[1] R. B. Marcy, *Thirty Years of Army Life on the Border* (New York, 1866), pp. 224-49.

Georgians,[2] Cherokee Indians, and men from the border towns of Kansas, crossed the plains to the region of the South Platte and began to prospect for paying diggings. After several weeks of discouraging search over a wide area the party, reduced to twelve men, found gold in paying quantities along Cherry and Dry creeks in the Colorado area and news of the discovery, immediately inflated by border newspapers, spread like wild-fire. Within a few weeks the attention of the nation was directed toward Pike's Peak.

Bankruptcy and unemployment throughout the country, brought on by the panic of 1857, furnished large numbers of people anxious to try their luck at gold-mining. The Colorado region was conveniently located in comparison to California, as it was much closer in distance and there were no mountains or desert lands to cross in making the trip. The advertising of the *Rocky Mountain News*, published at Cherry Creek, and visits of such men as Henry Villard and Horace Greeley, helped to arouse enthusiasm in the East. It has been estimated that about one hundred thousand gold-seekers crossed the plains to the new El Dorado. For a time it seemed to some observers that the whole eastern portion of our country was moving westward in search of gold.[3]

Many of the prospective miners came by boat up the Missouri to the various points of debarkation where they purchased supplies and employed means of transportation varying from hand-carts and wheelbarrows to ox teams for the overland journey. Some said that one "pilgrim" even tried a sail on a light wagon.

[2] Nuggets of gold have been reported discovered in North Carolina as early as 1799, and a quartz vein in the same region in 1831, during which period came America's first gold rush. An even richer find was made in Georgia in 1829 where miners were active until the California gold rush, which drew many of them westward.

[3] Henry Villard, *The Past and Present of the Pike's Peak Gold Rush*, ed. Leroy Hafen (reprint by the Princeton University Press, 1932), pp. 1-37, *passim*; Albert D. Richardson, *Beyond the Mississippi* (Hartford, Conn., 1869), pp. 184-201; Samuel Bowles, *Across the Continent* (Springfield, Mass., 1865), p. 50.

Newspapers continued to print their lurid stories of great fortunes to be made. Towns along the Missouri vied with each other in presenting their merits as outfitting points, one of which stated that there was no reason why any one should remain at home who wished to go, since fifty to seventy-five dollars would pay for an outfit and furnish provisions for several months. As the summer advanced, the fortune-seekers literally swarmed westward, many with the slogan "Pike's Peak or Bust" emblazoned on their wagon covers, and almost choking at times in the dust of what has been called the Great American Desert. There was much hardship, suffering and tragedy, but these did not daunt the seekers of an easy fortune.[4]

Interest was concentrated in the Cherry Creek area and a number of camps grew up at the confluence of this stream and the South Platte River. The towns of Highland, Montana, Auraria, and St. Charles soon developed and joined to form Denver City. But bitter disappointment was to be the lot of a vast majority of those who had accepted the "tall tales" of gold and riches for all in the new diggings. The boom proved to be of short duration since there was not enough free gold to keep the hordes of inexperienced miners at work, and within a few weeks the movement collapsed. Some followed the rumors of other deposits, some settled down to agriculture and stock-raising, while others returned East, disillusioned and true to the last part of their previous slogan, "busted." As they slowly made their way back, they did not hesitate to denounce in bitter terms the humbug of the gold-fields.[5]

On May 6, 1859, John H. Gregory discovered pay dirt, yielding two dollars a pan, in a gulch on the north fork of Clear Creek, some sixty miles north and west of Denver City. Two days later,

[4] *Sioux City Register* (Sioux City, Iowa), May 17, 31, June 14, July 2, 1858; *St. Joseph Gazette* (St. Joseph, Mo.), May 22, 29, June 3, 1858; *Jefferson City Inquirer* (Jefferson City, Mo.), December 4, 1858.

[5] *Rocky Mountain News* (Cherry Creek, Col.), April 23, May 7, 14, 28, August 6, November 3, December 28, 1859; files for 1860-62.

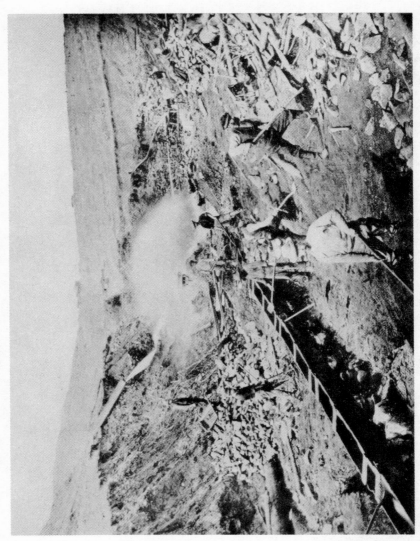

SLUICING
IN THE GREGORY
DIGGINGS

1859. From the
Western Collection of
the Denver Public
Library.

when the story was confirmed, the *Rocky Mountain News* printed an "extra" heralding the news of the rich strike.[6] A stampede occurred that almost depopulated Denver City, business men closing their shops and professional men, including the editor of the camp's only newspaper, locking their offices. Gregory Diggings, where the discovery was made, became the mushroom gold camp of Mountain City, later Central City. Other camps were established in the vicinity and miners flocked in by the hundreds. As the news sped eastward along the trails and among the settlements, there occurred a new stampede of gold-seekers to the Central City region. An eastern newspaper man visiting Gregory Diggings early in June, 1859, found some twenty sluices in operation with most of the miners exultant and hopeful. He reported five thousand people in the camp and hundreds more pouring in daily.[7]

Except for those fortunate enough to discover rich pockets, the outlook in the new camps was soon discouraging. As had been the case on Cherry Creek, the amount of free gold obtainable by placer mining was small. Most of the gold was embedded in quartz, the working of which took expensive machinery and capital. By midsummer there was a second homeward movement of the weary, disheartened miners. An observer reported that even in June there were some who were already discouraged and about to return to the States. A few weeks later the number had noticeably increased, and in contrasting those going out and those coming in, he said: "The new comers going into the mines are sanguine and cheery, walking with elastic step, singing and laughing. But the stampeders turning homeward, convinced that gold digging was hard and unremunerative, left their picks and shovels behind and trudged mechanically with downcast woebegone faces." After spending six weeks in the Colorado mines, he recommended that those who were doing moderately well at home had

---

[6] A copy of the extra is in the State Historical Library at Denver, Colorado.
[7] *Encampment Echo* (Encampment, Col.), December 5, 1935.

better remain there, reminding them that "not more than one man in ten is successful in any mining country." [8]

By the end of 1859 the Colorado gold boom was over, and while new placer finds were made from time to time, mining companies and individuals with capital worked the quartz deposits by bringing in the much-needed machinery, developing gold-mining as an industry. Under this scheme of things, there was little opportunity for large numbers of independent miners, many of whom left the Colorado country for the new placer discoveries as they were made in other areas.

In 1859, while the Colorado boom was at its height, the rich and famous Comstock Lode was discovered in Nevada. Although minor gold activities had been carried on in that region since the early fifties, they had attracted little attention, as they were unable to compete with the mines of California. During the latter part of 1859 and early in 1860 thousands of experienced miners left California and crossed the Sierras because of the promising prospects. Virginia City and Carson City became thriving centers and by the middle of the summer Nevada had almost seven thousand inhabitants.[9]

II

GOLD IN IDAHO

WHILE many rich finds of gold were made in Oregon, the metal was in pockets and small deposits and was soon exhausted. From Oregon the tendency was to move eastward in the search for new discoveries. In the summer of 1860 a significant discovery was made on the south fork of the Clearwater in the Snake River region by Captain E. D. Pierce who, with a small party of prospectors, struck colors on Canal Gulch, a tributary of Oro Fino Creek. Returning to Walla Walla, the headquarters of the

[8] Richardson, *op. cit.*, pp. 198-201.
[9] By 1863, 40,000 miners were reported to be in the Nevada area. *Rocky Mountain News*, May 7, 1859, January 30, 1861.

party, Pierce organized another group that hastened to the new diggings in November, and during the winter of 1860-61 prospectors' holes were sunk, claims laid out and lumber sawed for sluice boxes. More than forty of the claims yielded good returns during the winter and as gold-dust began to arrive in Portland a stampede to the new diggings took place, many of the miners coming from California. Despite the objections of the military authorities, Pierce City was laid out. The number of miners on the ground increased from three hundred in April to more than one thousand in May. As the summer advanced, the rush of gold-seekers caused the camps of Pierce City and Oro Fino to develop into busy mining centers. Within a few months the Clearwater mines were sending more than one hundred thousand dollars in gold-dust to Portland each month.

In 1861 the town of Lewiston was established where the Clearwater joins the Snake and was soon a busy place, with its many pack trains departing for the new camps. There was no more picturesque town in the area, which from a distance looked like a city of white marble, closer inspection, however, revealing that it was in reality a city of tents. Elk City was built to the northward, so named because of the large elk herds that grazed in the vicinity. The beautiful valleys of the region were soon filled with miners, who found it an ideal camping ground, with its luxuriant forests, plenty of grass for grazing, numerous streams, and an abundance of fish and wild game.

The Argonauts of the mining empire could not forget their dream of a Mother Lode. They felt the minor discoveries which so far they had been able to make were only a preface to the riches they were sure existed. Parties of prospectors covered the surrounding country carefully and in the summer of 1861 rich deposits were located on the south fork of the Clearwater in the Elk City district. The camp of Millersburg was established on Miller Creek, where miners were shortly making from seventy-five to one hundred dollars daily. In the fall an exceedingly rich placer discovery was made at the head of Baboon Gulch, at which point the camp of Florence was established, soon becoming one of the most productive camps in the Salmon River country and a point of departure for prospecting parties.

The first winter saw great hardship in the Idaho gold-fields, with the inhabitants snowed in, and food almost non-existent. Physical hardship and discomforts, however, did not daunt the gold-seekers and people came in from all directions. By November nearly two thousand men were reported to be working placers in the Salmon River area, many of whom were said to be making from forty to one hundred and twenty-five dollars a day.[1] In the winter of 1861 there were a thousand men at Elk City, and Florence grew rapidly, while the camps of Pierce City and Oro Fino declined, soon losing more than half of their former population.

The Salmon River diggings, said by some to be even richer than the mines of California, attracted a great deal of attention in Portland, and early in March a stampede occurred, although the Portland newspapers warned that there were still several feet of snow in the area. The arrival of the first pack train at Portland by way of Walla Walla with four hundred pounds of gold-dust stirred many enthusiastic prospectors to action. They hurried to the new fields, large numbers reaching their destination by the middle of May. The stories regarding the richness of the finds continued to circulate, one man being reported to have taken $6,600 from a rich pocket in a single day. Prospectors continued to operate over a large area, and in August, 1862, James Warren made a new discovery south of the Salmon River that was named after the discoverer. Throngs of miners poured into the far-famed Salmon River area from all sides, gold-seekers from California and the Pacific Northwest converging with streams of adventurers from Minnesota, Missouri, Iowa, and Pike's Peak. So many people left Washington and Oregon that, by the middle

[1] *Rocky Mountain News*, November 16, 23, 1861, August 21, 1862.

of the summer, a Portland editor was complaining of the loss of population.[2]

Late in the summer of 1862 rich placers were found in the Boise River region of Idaho where the pine forest furnished timber for sluice boxes and numerous streams contained plenty of water for mining purposes. By the spring of 1863, the usual mad rush was on, and Placerville, Centerville, Pioneer, and Bannack, later known as Idaho City, sprang into sudden and busy existence. By 1864 there were more than sixteen thousand people in the Boise River Basin.[3] In the spring and summer of 1863 groups of miners were active on some of the small streams flowing into the Owyhee River and found gold in paying quantities. As the news spread, more than twenty-five hundred miners rushed to the new diggings. In July, 1863, another exploring party discovered the Owyhee silver mines, around which grew up Boonville, Ruby City, and Silver City. By 1864 the northern camp of Florence was being rapidly depopulated, and while Warren, Elk City, and Oro Fino were still producing, they were not overcrowded. The center of Idaho's mining activity had shifted southward to the Boise Basin, and Idaho City with a population of six thousand was one of the most important centers of the activity.[4]

The Silver City mining district became one of the nation's important silver-producing areas, being surpassed only by the famous Comstock Lode of Nevada. The unique feature of the silver veins of this area was the presence of solid slabs or masses of shining white silver, nearly pure, some of which weighed as much as five

[2] *Portland Daily Advertiser* (Portland, Ore.), June 18, July 9, 1861, July 12, August 7, 1862; files of the *Deseret News* (Salt Lake City, Utah), 1860-62; Wallace W. Elliot, *History of Idaho* (San Francisco, 1884), pp. 64-5. In the summer of 1862, some eastern prospectors on their way to the Salmon River mines were diverted from their course and made important gold discoveries in the western portion of what later became Montana Territory. The Salmon River mines stimulated activity in the Montana area. *Deseret News*, September 23, 1862.

[3] *Idaho Statesman* (Boise, Idaho), May 22, 1932; John Hailey, *History of Idaho* (Boise, Idaho, 1910), pp. 61-76.

[4] *Deseret News*, December 9, 1863.

hundred pounds.[5] The lack of transportation facilities was reme-
died by the completion of the Union Pacific Railroad in 1869,
although the silver ore was of sufficient richness to warrant the
expense of sending it out, even before the arrival of the railroad.
The detailed story of the famous silver mines was chronicled in
the early issues of the *Owyhee Avalanche*, the first daily newspaper in the territory. The Owyhee mining district produced
many ghost cities and Silver City itself has a population to-day
of around one hundred.[6]

To protect the miners from the Indians, who were inclined to
be hostile in the Idaho area, the United States Government erected
Fort Lapwai, twelve miles from Lewiston, in 1862. At a miners'
meeting at Placerville in March, 1863, a company of volunteers
was enlisted under the leadership of a capable captain to patrol
various portions of the area to keep the Indians under control.
In 1863 Fort Boise was constructed by cavalry from Oregon, at
a point not far from Boise City where the Oregon Trail and the
miners' trail to the Boise Basin converged. The erection of this
post marked the end of the trouble between the redmen and the
miners.

In 1866 a party of miners from Montana discovered rich placer
diggings in what shortly afterwards became Lemhi County and
five thousand gold-seekers rushed to the district. Salmon City was
laid out in 1867. Between 1870 and 1880, important quartz-fields
were discovered in that region girdled by the towering Sawtooth
Mountains in what is now Custer County. The famous Charles
Dickens mine was located near the town of Bonanza in 1875, its
fortunate owners crushing out more than one thousand dollars'
worth of gold in a hand-mortar in a single day.

The next gold rush of importance in the Idaho area occurred

[5] Silver, even where the deposits are rich, is ordinarily found in association
with other metals such as copper and zinc. It was only after the ore was assayed
or smelted that the silver content could be ascertained.

[6] *Boise News* (Boise, Idaho), October 6, 1863, January 16, 1864; *Idaho World*
(Idaho City), December 31, 1864, July 6, 13, 1867.

in the Cœur d'Alene Mountains in the northern portion of the territory in 1882 when A. J. Prichard discovered gold on Prichard Creek, a tributary to the north fork of the Cœur d'Alene River.[7] Eagle City, the first mining center, was followed by the camps of Murray, Carbon City, Beaver City, Myrtle, Raven City, and Butte City, all of which became centers of some importance. Eagle City was described in the spring of 1884 as a "tough place." Its buildings, composed of logs and large numbers of tents, were located on lots from which four feet of snow had been removed and piled in the middle of the streets. The place was filled with restless prospectors and miners waiting for the snow to melt so they could start out on their ceaseless search for gold. Packers and transients thronged the stores, saloons and dance-halls and other public places looking for excitement, which apparently they were able to find without difficulty.

A Montana observer in the spring of 1884 said of Eagle City:

There are laborers, stalwart and sinewy fellows. There are gamblers, of that you may be assured. Gamblers of the Bret Harte style, with large hearts, as well as those with slick tricks and who are quick on the draw. The girls are there, too, and more and more of them come every few days. Some of them dress stylishly and wear silks and diamonds, while some dress coarsely and slovenly. Quite a number of them wear men's clothing and walk the streets in garments that would excite the envy of Susan B. Anthony. Boys are here, mere youths not yet out of their teens, yet they come with the rest. A terrible school for lads! There are old forty-niners, men whose hair and beards have silvered in the tireless and persistent search for gold, which will never stop until life closes. There are prospectors living like hermits in lonely gulches. They will share their fare and blankets with a stranger. By

---

[7] A. J. Prichard, the discoverer of the gold, was a freethinker who prided himself on being an infidel, and took delight in explaining his views. He saw in the discovery at Eagle City an opportunity to establish a colony of his liberal friends in a coöperative community where wealth could be divided, and all would be rich and happy. He wrote letters that were widely published and took out claims for many of his friends, who came there from all parts of the country. The "Chosen City," however, soon passed out of the hands of Prichard and his followers, who failed to become rich from their gold claims. Prichard died a few years later, a poor man, in his miner's shack at Murray.

and by rough, hard characters will come, which will include many a bully, cutthroat and scoundrel, but as long as the miners are in a majority, the camp will be all right.[8]

Thousands of placer claims were staked in the Cœur d'Alene area, most of which yielded good wages and some brought in large returns. They did not, however, reach the high production of the Clearwater and Salmon River gold camps, and within a couple of years the rush was over, and many of the miners had departed. Some of the disappointed Argonauts came through Montana on their way to richer fields, and their exodus was described by various newspapers there. The *Helena Daily Herald* of June 19, 1884, said: "The latest news from the Cœur d'Alene mining region is that Eagle City is very dull, and that hundreds of men are there without work or money. Murrayville is a little more lively, but hard times are prevalent throughout the mountains." A month later, the same editor, quoting from the *Dillon Tribune*, said: "The Cœur d'Alene humbug having attracted thousands of fortune hunters and having failed to furnish one twentieth part of them work, Montana is flooded with broke men seeking employment. Many of these stampeders are good miners, too, who, too proud to beg and too high toned to steal rides, have passed through Beaverhead County on foot with their blankets on their backs, retiring to the southern camps of the Rockies from where they stampeded." [9]

The real wealth of the Cœur d'Alene region was established when persistent prospectors discovered rich veins of silver and lead, making it one of the richest districts in the world for those metals. Its mines paid more than forty millions of dollars in dividends within a quarter of a century. The Bunker Hill and Sullivan mine was famous for several decades. Cœur d'Alene and Kellogg became important centers, many of their supplies coming from Spokane, Washington.

[8] *Miles City Weekly Press* (Miles City, Mont), March 22, 1884.
[9] *Helena Daily Herald* (Helena, Mont.), July 17, 1884.

The easiest way of approach to the mines of Idaho was from the west and, as the gold rush gained momentum, miners and men of all classes flocked into the various areas from California, Oregon, Washington, and Nevada. The demand for transportation facilities was far greater than the accommodations. Perhaps the easiest way of reaching the mines was by way of the Columbia River. Miners from California often went by steamer from San Francisco to Portland, where they transferred to the steamboats of the Oregon Steam Transportation Company, which ran to Umatilla or Wallula, where stage lines connected with the various gold camps. Methods of travel after leaving the steamer varied, however, depending upon the needs of the indivdual and his ability to pay. Some purchased supplies and started off on foot, with packs on their backs, stopping at some toll or packer's station to replenish their food supplies. Others combined and purchased a pack-animal. Loading their supplies and provisions on its back, they hurried off. There were regular saddle trains with fare at fifty dollars, payable in advance. The passengers were furnished with a horse and saddle, while the baggage, food and cooking utensils of the party were carried on extra pack-animals. The passengers cooked their own food, while the train master took care of the animals. A strict guard was maintained for the prevention of Indian attacks and horse-stealing. The tolls on a pack-animal for the trip was ten dollars.[10]

The population of the Boise Basin was estimated at from fifteen to twenty thousand in the summer of 1863. Since all provisions had to be brought from either the Columbia River or Salt Lake City, the freighting business was soon extensive. Pack-mules and horses were largely used the first summer, and there was difficulty in bringing in enough supplies to last through the winter. With freight rates ranging from sixteen to twenty-five cents per pound, the packing business proved to be a profitable one. As soon as wagon roads were completed, the rates were cut

[10] *Deseret News*, September 16, 23, 1862, August 16, 23, December 2, 9, 1863.

by 50 per cent, which ruined the small packers. Routes of travel were changed with the completion, in 1869, of the Union Pacific Railroad to Kelton, Utah, which became the supply center for the mines in southern Idaho.

The necessity of bringing in all supplies to the Idaho gold camps by freight wagons and pack trains made prices high. A wagon load of chickens and cats brought into the Boise Basin diggings in September, 1863, sold at a good price, the chickens being disposed of at five dollars each and the cats at ten dollars. The same editor who reported this told of wagons loaded with vegetables arriving from Salt Lake City, and of a large wagon train loaded with flour, bacon, and other produce noted within two days' travel of the Basin: "We hail these harbingers of trade with the Saints with hallelujahs and shoutings, as all our supplies until now have been packed from Walla Walla, Umatilla or Wallula." [11] The prices of supplies varied from week to week, and even from day to day, depending upon the goods available and the price of gold. Prices listed in the local press at Boise City December 26, 1863, were based on gold valued at sixteen dollars an ounce, while those of January 5, 1867, were based on gold at fourteen dollars an ounce and greenbacks worth seventy-five cents on the dollar.[12]

III

THE GOLD FRONTIER IN MONTANA

While it is quite possible that Father De Smet, an early Jesuit missionary, knew that gold existed in the mountains of Montana where he was conducting his religious activities, the evidence is not conclusive. If he had the knowledge, he kept it secret. Various accounts indicate that gold was discovered and reported in 1852 by a half-breed fur trader, François Finlay, sometimes known as

[11] *Boise News*, September 29, 1863; *Deseret News*, August 30, 1863.
[12] *Boise News*, December 26, 1863; *Idaho Statesman*, January 5, 1867.

Benetsee. He is said to have shown the gold to the chief factor of the Hudson's Bay Company post near Flathead Lake, who had grub-staked him. The discoveries were evidently of minor consequence, and the company, not wishing to have its fur business interfered with by a horde of invading miners, doubtless insisted on secrecy and did not encourage further activity on the part of Finlay.[1]

James and Granville Stuart in the spring of 1858 found gold in small quantities on Gold Creek where they were prospecting, and in the spring of 1862 constructed the first string of sluices in Montana where they had previously found gold.[2] The discovery and circulation of information regarding the location of gold in Montana came at a rather opportune time. The Mullan Road was in process of construction,[3] and, in 1859, the Chouteaus of St. Louis contracted to carry annuity goods by steamboat to Fort Benton. Although they did not reach the fort that year, they came close enough that thereafter steamboating was regarded as feasible.

---

[1] P. C. Phillips and H. A. Trexler, "Notes on the Discovery of Gold in the Northwest," *Mississippi Valley Historical Review*, IV (Lincoln, Neb.), 70-7; William J. Trimble, "Mining Advance into the Inland Empire," *Bulletin of the University of Wisconsin*, No. 638 (Madison, Wis., 1914), pp. 16-28; Trimble, "A Reconsideration of the Gold Discoveries in the Northwest," *Mississippi Valley Historical Review*, V; Granville Stuart, *Montana As It Is* (New York, 1865), p. 7; "A Few Items from the West," *Washington Historical Quarterly*, VIII (Seattle, Wash.), 201-2; *Daily Missoulian* (Missoula, Mont.), November 2, 1916; *Miles City Daily Star* (Miles City, Mont.), Golden Jubilee edition, May 24, 1934.

[2] Granville Stuart, "A Historical Sketch of Deer Lodge, County, Valley and City, July 4, 1876," *Contributions*, Montana State Historical Society, II (Helena, Mont.), 121; Trimble, "A Reconsideration of Gold Discoveries," pp. 70-9; Granville Stuart, *Forty Years on the Frontier*, I (Cleveland, Ohio, 1925), 157-229.

[3] Captain John Mullan was appointed by Governor I. I. Stevens of Washington Territory in 1859 to construct a highway connecting Walla Walla, Washington, and Fort Benton, Montana. The road was completed in 1863. The Mullan Road was of vital importance in the Montana gold activities, since in addition to taking care of those coming from the East by the Missouri River and by the northern plains route, it provided an easier entrance into the Oregon and Idaho mining regions than did the Oregon Trail. Many left the Oregon Trail near Corinne, Utah, crossing the easy passes into the Beaverhead and Deer Lodge valleys where gold was later discovered. *Senate Exec. Doc.*, 37th Cong., 3d Sess., No. 43, 138

Another factor favoring the development of the Montana mining areas was their geographic accessibility.[4]

The mining population, always ready to pursue rumors of rich finds, had reached a particularly receptive attitude by 1862. While the discoveries in California, Nevada, Colorado, and Idaho had made large fortunes for a favored few, the less fortunate were still looking for their chance. The Salmon River mines remained in high favor, and were attracting large numbers. On June 24th, a party of sixteen arrived in the Deer Lodge Valley from the Colorado mines bound for the Salmon River diggings. Encouraged by the Deer Lodge prospects, they remained. The next day news came of the arrival of three steamboats at Fort Benton with emigrants, provisions, and mining supplies. On June 29th a party of nine en route from St. Louis to the Salmon River mines, who had come to Fort Benton by steamboat, stopped at Deer Lodge. By July 5th, forty-five miners were reported to be working in the locality.[5] During the late summer large numbers of miners were reported to be arriving, many of whom were bound for Idaho and Oregon. Wagon trains arrived in large numbers from Illinois, Minnesota, Iowa, and Wisconsin.[6]

On July 28, 1862, John White and a party of miners bound for the Salmon River diggings from Colorado made a rich find

[4] Gold was discovered in paying quantities in the Deer Lodge Valley in 1861, Grasshopper Creek or Bannack in 1882, Alder Gulch or Virginia City in 1863, and Last Chance or Helena in 1864. These areas, all of which are located in river valleys, were accessible from the west, south and east. Miners from the Boise Basin, Pike's Peak, and the east found access comparatively easy. J. Ross Browne, *Mineral Resources of the United States* (Washington, D. C., 1868), 505-9; *Owyhee Avalanche* (Silver City, Idaho), January 6, 1866.

[5] *Miners' and Travelers' Guide to Oregon, Washington, Idaho, Montana, Wyoming and Colorado Via the Missouri and Columbia Rivers* (New York, 1865); Stuart, *Forty Years on the Frontier*, I, 211; Stuart, "Historical Sketch of Deer Lodge, County, Valley and City," *op. cit.*, p. 121; *Rocky Mountain News*, May 27, June 14, August 21, 1862; *Deseret News*, September 10, October 15, 1862.

[6] James Harkness, "Diary of James Harkness of the Firm of La Barge, Harkness and Company of St. Louis to Fort Benton by the Missouri River and to the Deer Lodge Valley and Return in 1862," *Contributions*, Montana State Historical Society, II, 352-5; *Deseret News*, September 3, October 29, 1862; *Sioux City Eagle* (Sioux City, Iowa), May 24, June 7, 1862.

on Grasshopper Creek, a tributary of the Beaverhead River and a new gold rush began. A miners' district was established and a frontier town of log huts came into existence under the name of East Bannack. The new camp grew rapidly, increasing from four hundred in October, 1862, to more than a thousand the following April. At that time its name was changed to Bannack City. A rich quartz lode, the Dacotah, was discovered in December, on which a crude mill was constructed, a considerable number of people spending the winter there. Reports of rich yields were widely circulated and miners hurried in from all directions.[7]

True to form the miners in and near Bannack City were on the lookout for bigger and better finds. The lure of new fields and the extreme restlessness of the frontier miner are well illustrated in the events leading to the gold discoveries in Alder Gulch. Dozens of parties panned the streams flowing into the Yellowstone River and its tributaries, one of which located a rich find in the East Gallatin Valley late in May, 1863. They named the stream Alder Creek and after staking out claims for themselves and their friends decided to keep the discovery a secret. The news leaked out, however, and within a month Alder Gulch had attracted most of the loose population of the area and Bannack City was practically deserted. Virginia City sprang up almost overnight and became the chief town in the area. By the summer of 1864, it had a resident population of thirty-five hundred, with a floating population nearly as large. Madison County at this time had 11,493 inhabitants. Within three years Alder Gulch is reported to have produced thirty million dollars in gold, largely from placer mines, ranking it as one of the first, if not the most valuable gulches in the West.[8]

[7] J. H. Morley, "Diary of Life and Events in the Early Gold Camps of Montana," MS, Montana State Historical Society, entries for September 15, October 4, 1862; *Deseret News*, November 19, 1862; *Rocky Mountain News*, June 14, July 12, November 20, December 23, 1862; *St. Cloud Democrat* (St. Cloud, Minn.), November 27, 1862, February 8, 1863.

[8] *Montana Post* (Virginia City, Mont.), July 25, August 5, September 4, 11, 18, October 8, 1864. Nineteen quartz lodes had been tested by September, 1864.

In the summer of 1864 passengers on the overland stages reported long lines of "pilgrims" and freighters on the road to
Virginia City and vicinity. A large amount of machinery for quartz
mills was en route. Late in August a train of one hundred and
fifty wagons arrived from Omaha, Nebraska. During the same
month one hundred buildings were in process of construction and
many persons were taking out as much as fifty dollars per day with
placers. Wages were from six to twelve dollars per day, an abundance of gold making prices high.[9]

The comments of an intelligent observer give a view of the
gulch in the fall of 1863. After giving the location of the four
largest towns, Virginia City, Central City, Nevada City, and
Junction City, within a narrow radius, he said: "The road connecting these cities is bordered with dwellings on both sides all
along. Recalling that only eighteen months ago, this was a howling
wilderness, surely truth is more wonderful than fiction." [10] Another observer, in speaking of Virginia City, said: "The town lies
like a huge serpent, a crooked, irregular strip of log houses wind-
ing for nine miles down Alder Gulch. Every foot of ground along
the creek is staked out and men are busy sluicing out the precious
metal." [11] An Iowa editor printed a letter describing the place in
1864: "We arrived on Sunday, the busiest day in the week. The
streets were densely crowded with pilgrims and miners. Heavily
loaded teams and pack trains were passing up and down the
streets." The main street of Virginia City, made up of a double
row of compact buildings almost a mile in length, contained, in
addition to many other businesses, eight hotels, two churches,
six billiard halls, four or five elegant gambling-houses, three
hurdy-gurdies or dance-halls, several bawdy houses, and innumerable saloons.[12]

[9] Files of the *Montana Post*, July, August, September, October, 1864.
[10] Morley, "Diary," entry for November 12, 1863.
[11] Samuel Bowles, *Our New West* (Hartford, Conn., 1869), pp. 490-520.
[12] *Council Bluffs Eagle* (Council Bluffs, Iowa), September 14, 1864; *Montana Post*, September 18, 25, 1864.

HELENA'S MAIN
STREET

1870. Courtesy of
the Northern Pacific
Railway.

The last of the major gold discoveries in the Montana area was made in the Prickly Pear Valley in the summer of 1864 when John Cowan with a small party made a rich strike in Last Chance Gulch and the town of Helena was established. Favored in location, as well as in resources, it soon became the most important town in the area, displacing Virginia City. It lay directly in line from Fort Benton to Bannack City and Virginia City, being located slightly west of the Madison branch of the Missouri and on the chief route of northwest travel. It was destined to be the last of the boom towns of the Montana region, but its importance was to linger far beyond that of most of its contemporaries.

Several rich gulches opened up in the vicinity of Helena, including Oro Fino, Grizzly, and Nelson's. Quartz was soon discovered, and in December of 1864 the famous Whitlatch Vein was struck, whose yield by 1876 was estimated to have been three million dollars.[13] Stage and freight transportation were soon established between Helena and Salt Lake City and other central points. Montana had a population of 29,500 in 1864 when it was organized as a territory.

The citizens of Helena boasted of living in the "liveliest town west of the Missouri River, if not in the United States."[14] An eye-witness in the fall of 1865 made the following observation:

This town is thriving. The streets are daily crowded with freight wagons either going or returning from Fort Benton. The three daily lines of coaches each loaded with passengers arrive and depart with the punctuality of clock work. Many new stores, warehouses, restaurants and general business places have been constructed in the past few months. Billiard halls, saloons, and other resorts are numerous, all doing a thriving buiness. The crowded bars indicate that there is money in the country and that whiskey can bring it out.[15]

[13] Gilbert Benedick, "Diary of Life in the Gold Camps of Montana," MS, State Historical Library, Helena, Mont., entries for October 8, 10, 14, 1864; *Montana Post*, November 26, December 24, 1864; W. A. Clark, *Contributions*, Montana State Historical Society, II, 51, 112.

[14] *Rocky Mountain News*, January 24, 1866.

[15] *Montana Post*, September 19, 1865.

The Montana mining camps, centering in three major districts around Bannack City, Virginia City, and Helena, were located relatively close together, falling within a circle whose diameter was approximately one hundred miles.[16]

The various gold rushes and mining booms in the West in the late fifties and early sixties caused considerable shifting in population, making certain changes necessary in territorial organization for the purpose of government. The Territory of Dakota, as created in 1861, included what is now North and South Dakota, Montana, and a portion of what is now Idaho and Wyoming. With the Idaho gold rushes, it became obvious that the territorial government located at Yankton, in the southeastern portion of Dakota, would not be able to exercise control over miners in the Rocky Mountain region. The Territory of Idaho was formed in 1863, including what is now Montana and Wyoming. The development of the Montana gold areas led to the creation of Montana Territory in 1864, with its present state boundaries, while Wyoming was shifted back to Dakota. Wyoming Territory was organized in 1868.

IV

THE GOLD FRONTIER IN WYOMING

THE GOLD excitement in Montana overlapped in years a similar boom in Idaho and another of lesser magnitude in Wyoming. Since the early sixties, it had been thought that the whole area included in the headwaters of the Missouri River was rich in mineral wealth. With enthusiasm keyed to such a high pitch, it

[16] In addition to the major mining areas, a large number of other discoveries were made and developed in southwestern Montana. Some of them were: Confederate Gulch on the eastern side of Prickly Pear Valley; Emigrant Gulch and in the Yellowstone Valley in 1865; Copperopolis on the Musselshell River and Lost Horse Gulch in 1866 and Silver and Dry Creeks in 1867. The mad stampede to the Sun River in the winter of 1865 and 1866 is an example of a gold rush in its worst form. The hospitality of the Piegan Indians and the efforts of St. Peter's Mission prevented disaster on a large scale. *Rocky Mountain News,* January 13, 1866.

was only a matter of time before some of the roving prospectors would try their luck in the Wyoming area.[1]

Although gold had not been found in any quantity in the Big Horn area of Wyoming, enough evidences had been discovered to indicate that it might exist there in abundance if searched out. James Stuart led a party of fifteen miners into the Big Horn Valley in 1863 and panned for gold over a wide area during the spring and summer before they were driven out by the Indians.[2] The lure of possibilities led to the organization of another party in the spring of 1864. An outfit of seventy-three men, organized on a military basis, with James Stuart again as captain, left Bannack for the Big Horn country. Most of the party prospected over a wide area until August without locating pay dirt, although the majority of them seemed convinced "that rich mines existed in that country."[3]

The Big Horn country of Wyoming continued for several years to receive the overflow of mining population from the Montana diggings. Indian difficulties along the Bozeman Trail, culminating in the Fort Fetterman massacre of December, 1866, tended to check emigration along that route and to divert part of it, at any rate, to the Wyoming areas, that were rumored at least to yield gold in paying quantities. During the latter part of the decade, miners came into the Big Horn Basin from the south and east rather than from the north.[4]

[1] *Wyoming Industrial Journal* (Cheyenne, Wy.), January, 1903, 171-3; *Sweetwater Miner* (Sweetwater, Mont.), March 17, 24, 31, 1869; Raymond W. Rossiter, "Statistics of Mines and Mining in the States and Territories West of the Rocky Mountains," *House Exec. Doc.*, 41st. Cong., 2d Sess., No. 207, 327. While gold was apparently discovered in the Sweetwater district as early as 1842 by an employee of the American Fur Company, the first organized prospecting was carried on in that region in 1855. In 1861 fifty-two miners who were working placers there were driven away by Indians.

[2] James Stuart, "Journal of James Stuart, Expedition of 1863," *Contributions*, Montana State Historical Society, I, 181-200.

[3] Granville Stuart, "A Memoir of the Life of James Stuart," *Contributions*, Montana State Historical Society, I, 55-7; *Montana Post*, August 5, 19, 1864.

[4] Letter from Colonel Carrington to Major Litchfield, Fort Philip Kearney, July 20, 1866, original in War Department Archives, Washington, D. C.; *Senate Exec. Doc.*, 40th Cong., 1st Sess., No. 33, 16-7.

New mining areas developed in the Wind River Valley and on the divide between the Popo Agie and Sweetwater rivers. The first effective strike occurred there in 1867 and led to the establishment of the mining towns of South Pass City, Atlantic City, and Miner's Delight. Although optimistic reports were circulated, the boom soon expired as the active search for new gold-fields a year or two later suggests the probability that the Sweetwater and Wind River fields were not paying out as well as expected, or that they had absorbed their maximum capacity. The building of the Union Pacific Railroad made it easier to get to the Wyoming mines and by 1869 many people in Cheyenne were again talking about the rich gold deposits that must exist in the Big Horn Mountains.[5] Early in 1870 the Big Horn Mining Association was organized at Cheyenne with the avowed purpose of invading the Big Horn Mountains in search of gold.[6]

During the early spring the association was given wide publicity through the newspapers, some of the press reports indicating that the enterprise had the interest and sympathy of groups a considerable distance from the Wyoming frontier. One Chicago paper stated that two thousand men would participate and that there would be a military escort of five hundred, while another Chicago editor put the number of participating miners at twelve hundred. Reductions in railroad rates were promised and Cheyenne was reported to be willing to furnish the party with a four months' grub-stake. The expedition, consisting of one hundred and twenty men, started May 20th, after promising Federal officials that they would not proceed beyond the Sweetwater. The large number of miners who were expected to join them after they were under

[5] Rossiter, *op. cit.*, pp. 327-30; *Cheyenne Daily Leader* (Cheyenne, Wy.), December 13, 1867, September 12, 13, 14, 1869; *Rocky Mountain News*, November 9, 1868.

[6] Although such action would violate a treaty concluded by the United States Government on April 29, 1868, as well as several other agreements, it seemed to be taken for granted by the local press that the government would not enforce the treaties. *U. S. Public Statutes at Large*, XV, 636; *Annual Report of the Secretary of War*, 1870, pp 61-3.

way failed to materialize and the party was asked by Federal troops to leave the Big Horn country.[7] Before the expedition broke up into factions and finally left the region, a goodly portion of the Big Horn Valley had been prospected. No important finds were made.[8]

The return of the Big Horn expedition marks the end of a period in the mining history of Wyoming. Its failure, however, was attributed to the Indians and the attitude of the government, rather than to the absence of gold. But even while the Big Horn party was assembling, large numbers of miners were leaving the Sweetwater area, and, by the end of 1870, South Pass City was nearly deserted, the once famous Cariso mine [9] was failing to pay expenses, and only two mines were operating at Atlantic City. While there was gold in the Sweetwater, it was not plentiful enough to hold an impatient population. This was no doubt the real reason for Cheyenne's keen desire to make discoveries in the Big Horn Basin. There were spasmodic flurries in Wyoming throughout the seventies and eighties, but before another real boom came the cattle industry had made rapid advances there and absorbed the attention and the capital of the people.[10]

V

THE BLACK HILLS GOLD RUSH

A TRADITION had developed in early times that the Black Hills district was rich in gold. The Sioux Indians are said to have discovered the metal, but knew no method of mining it. According to frontiersmen, the Sioux at different times are reported to have

[7] *Cheyenne Daily Leader*, February 17, 1870.

[8] *Cheyenne Daily Leader*, January 3, 11, February 12, 17, 20, 24, March 8, 14, 15, 1870; Charles Lindsay, *The Big Horn Basin* (Ph.D. Thesis, University of Nebraska, Lincoln, Neb., June, 1930), pp. 77-86.

[9] The Cariso mine was sold for $130,000 at this time. Fifteen thousand was paid down, the balance to be paid in monthly installments. The mine was never paid for; in fact, work in it was discontinued. *House Exec. Doc.*, 42nd Cong., 3d Sess., No. 210, 305-8.

[10] *Cheyenne Daily Leader*, May 28, 1870, January 28, 1871.

had nuggets of gold in their possession, which they exchanged for merchandise at Fort Laramie and at different trading-posts along the Missouri River. Father De Smet, who came early to the Black Hills region, is supposed to have known of the existence of gold there; according to some sources, he was instrumental in inducing the Indians to a policy of secrecy.[1]

That the Black Hills country was prospected for gold almost fifty years before its lawful settlement in 1876 and 1877 has been well authenticated by the discovery of various remains and abandoned "diggings."[2] In 1833 a party of seven adventurers went into the Hills from Fort Laramie. They remained there for about a year and discovered gold. The party was destroyed by Indians and all record of it was lost until 1887 when Lewis Thoen found a stone slab on the top of Mount Lookout near Spearfish. Upon one side of the stone, cut in irregular characters, evidently with a knife, is the following inscription: "Came to the Hills in 1833, seven of us, Doctor Lacon, Ezra Kind, G. W. Wood, F. Brown, R. Kent, William King, Indian Crow, all dead but me, Ezra Kind. Killed by Indians beyond the High Hill. They got all our gold. June, 1834." On the opposite side was cut in similar letters: "Got all the gold we could carry; our ponies were got by the Indians. I have lost my gun and have nothing to eat. Indians are hunting me."[3]

In the summer of 1852 a party of three hundred men, under the leadership of Captain J. H. Douglas, en route from Council Bluffs to the gold-fields of California, arrived at Fort Laramie tired from their long march. While resting from their exhausting trip, a French trapper arrived in camp, and learning of their destination, informed them that gold could be found in the Black

---

[1] "Early Black Hills Expeditions," *Collections*, Nebraska State Historical Society (Lincoln, Neb., January-March, 1922), p. 212; George W. Kingsbury, *The History of Dakota Territory* (Chicago, 1915), I, 861; Doane Robinson, *Encyclopedia of South Dakota* (Pierre, S. Dak., 1925), p. 73.

[2] *Black Hills Telegraphic Herald* (Deadwood, D. T.), May 11, 1878.

[3] The Thoen Stone was for several years on display at the South Dakota Historical Library at Pierre, South Dakota, and is now at Spearfish.

Hills, only a few days journey away. It was finally agreed that thirty of the group should accompany the trapper to prospect the country, and, if gold was found, they were to overtake the main party on the Humboldt River and report. After finding gold in paying quantities, eight of the party hurried on to the main group, leaving the other twenty-two men in the Hills to await the return of their comrades. It was late in November when the delegation of eight caught up with the original group. Since the Indians were hostile, it was deemed unsafe to return and the party went on to California. Those left in the Black Hills were never heard of again.[4]

Early prospectors left many traces of their activities. In 1876 some miners prospecting on Battle Creek discovered an old shaft about ten feet in depth. Sinking the pit about ten feet deeper, they found an old shovel and pick, the handles almost in dust and the iron badly rusted. On the same creek a skull was unearthed, near which was discovered a pair of silver bowed spectacles. Near-by were found a number of prospectors' holes, in some of which trees were growing, as large as eight inches in diameter. An old oak tree over two feet through had been cut down near-by and had almost rotted away.[5] Old stumps bearing ax marks were found in 1877 on an old trail between Rapid City and Galena. Below Deadwood a hatchet was found which showed evidence of having been buried for many years.[6]

Lieutenant James Mullan of the United States Army, with a small party, explored a portion of the Black Hills country in 1853. He reported that he found gold in great abundance, but he was afraid to tell his men for fear they would desert him. Mullan, who had been in the California placer mines, asserted that those of the

[4] *Black Hills Telegraphic Herald*, May 11, 1878; Peter Rosen, *Pa-ha-sa-pah or the Black Hills of South Dakota* (St. Louis, Mo., 1895), pp. 253-5.

[5] *Black Hills Pioneer* (Deadwood, D. T.), June 8, 1876; *Black Hills Tribune* (Crook City, D. T.), August 31, 1876.

[6] *Deadwood Daily Champion* (Deadwood, D. T.), June 2, 1877; *Black Hills Pioneer*, July 13, 1877; *Black Hills Telegraphic Herald*, May 11, 18, 1878.

Black Hills region were superior. In June, 1853, Dr. Ferdinand V. Hayden, a geologist, visited Bear Butte on the eastern border of the Hills, and in 1857 Lieutenant G. K. Warren, accompanied by Dr. Hayden and a military escort, led the first regularly organized military expedition into the Black Hills.[7]

The frontier communities that settled at several points in southeastern Dakota along the Missouri River during the years after the Yankton Treaty of 1859 were interested in the Black Hills. The Black Hills Exploring and Mining Association was organized at the territorial capital of Yankton in January, 1861, headed by some of the leading citizens. A number of public meetings were held during the winter, and membership in the organization came to include half the adult males of the village. While they were not practical miners, most of them were practical frontiersmen, and, when the opportunity for action presented itself, would easily be able to enlist the services of numerous experienced miners who had panned gold in the gulches of California, Nevada, Colorado, and other sections of the west.[8]

In the winter of 1866-67, the Black Hills Exploring and Mining Association, which had become almost extinct after its organization in 1861, was revived under the leadership of B. M. Smith. Widely advertised preparations were made for an expedition to the Black Hills. During the spring of 1867, there assembled at the Yankton rendezvous about one hundred men well armed, equipped and provisioned. Many of them were ex-soldiers of the Civil War, and their tents made an orderly village on the banks of the Missouri. While some of the new association members came from different portions of the country, most of them were from Dakota and Nebraska, coming largely from the settlements along the Missouri River. Early in June the impatient party was thrown

[7] Kingsbury, op. cit., I, 873. An expedition led by Captain W. F. Raynolds skirted the northern slopes of the Hills in the summer of 1859.

[8] Yankton Weekly Dakotian (Yankton, D. T.), July 27, 1861; Sioux City Tribune (Sioux City, Iowa), August 10, 1861; Rocky Mountain News, April 5, 1865.

into great consternation by a letter from General W. T. Sherman virtually forbidding the invasion of the Sioux country. After a week or more of discussion, the larger part of the members decided to disband, some of them, however, remaining in the territory awaiting more favorable times.[9]

Late in November, 1867, Captain P. B. Davy, an experienced frontiersman, arrived in Yankton from the Montana gold-fields and announced his plan of conducting an exploring and prospecting expedition to the Black Hills in the spring. Yankton was to be the rendezvous and starting-point of the party to be recruited during the winter months in Minnesota and adjoining areas. In April, Colonel D. S. Stanley, in command of the Dakota Military District, stopped the assembled party from entering the Indian country.[10] There was no further attempt to launch an expedition from Yankton until interest was revived by the Custer expedition of 1874.[11]

The edict forbidding encroachment upon Indian territory, while temporarily delaying the exploration of the Hills country, served to intensify popular interest in the matter, and gradually sentiment came to favor the opening of the region to settlement. This was caused in part by the innumerable reports afloat regarding the mineral wealth of the country. The stories were often ingeniously made to fit the situation and to give the proper coloring. An example is reprinted from a St. Paul newspaper by a Yankton editor in April, 1871.[12] A Sioux Indian of the Oglala band, while trading at Fort Laramie, told about a hunting trip into the Black Hills. He had shot a badger near its hole, and, upon going to get the animal, found the ground covered with small gold nuggets which it had dug out in making its nest. He filled his buckskin bag

[9] All the correspondence regarding the expedition, including a letter from Secretary of War Stanton, is printed in Kingsbury, *op. cit.*, I, 863-74; *Sioux City Tribune*, June 23, 1867.

[10] *Sioux City Tribune*, April 24, 1868; Kingsbury, *op. cit.*, I, 871-3.

[11] A. T. Andreas, *Historical Atlas of Dakota* (Chicago, 1884), pp. 22-8.

[12] *Yankton Weekly Dakotian*, April 20, 1871, reprinted from the *St. Paul Pioneer Press* (St. Paul, Minn.), April 5, 1871.

and started for Fort Laramie. On the way he met a small band of Brule Sioux whom he told of his find. The account, instead of surprising and pleasing them, threw them into a terrible rage. They took his gold and clothes, and, after giving him a severe beating and killing his horse, told him if he reported finding the gold, they would kill him. They said that the whites would never be allowed to enter the country. The effect of such stories upon the public mind can easily be imagined.

The Black Hills gold fever and agitation had reached nearly every part of the United States by 1872, and it was apparent that sentiment was growing throughout the country favoring the cession of the region from the Indians. From all appearances, the time was near when the proclamations of civil and military authorities would be disregarded. Expeditions were forming as far east as Massachusetts, and were determined to explore and develop the valuable mineral resources of the Black Hills country that were of little value to the Indians. So acute had the situation become by the spring of 1872 that Major-General W. S. Hancock, commanding the Department of Dakota and the Northwest, was attempting to counteract the wild gold stories and to allay the growing popular feeling by engendering doubt as to the existence of gold in the Black Hills in paying quantities.[13] On April 6, 1872, Edwin S. McCook, Secretary and Acting Governor of the Territory of Dakota, issued a warning proclamation in strong language against the violations of treaty stipulations with the Indians.[14] Gold-seekers found on Indian lands were to be promptly arrested.

The event that intensified popular feeling and interest in the Black Hills was the Custer expedition of 1874. Acting under orders from General P. A. Sheridan, General George A. Custer

[13] *Yankton Weekly Dakotian*, March 28, 1871; Letter dated at St. Paul, March 26, 1871, quoted in Kingsbury, *History of Dakota Territory*, I, 874-5.
[14] *Yankton Weekly Dakotian*, April 16, 1872. The proclamation said in part: "The government will use as much of its civil and military force as may be necessary to remove from the territory all persons who go there in violation of law."

left Fort Abraham Lincoln early in July with a corps of scientists and a force of twelve hundred men. He returned to the fort on August 22nd and reported definitely the presence of gold in paying quantities. This information created intense excitement and started the great gold rush of 1874 to 1877.[15] The chief gold discoveries of Custer were in the placers in the eastern portion of the Hills. At last the Black Hills country had been invaded and explored, and the dream of miners and adventurers in the Northwest for twenty years proved a reality.

In the meantime, certain developments had taken place at Sioux City. Largely through the efforts of Charles Collins,[16] editor of the *Sioux City Times,* there had been organized in February of 1872 the Black Hills Mining and Exploring Association of Sioux City. Among those actively interested in the company was Thomas H. Russel, an experienced frontiersman, who had been in the gold-fields of Colorado, and had been attracted to Sioux City by the editorials of Collins and Daniel Scott, editor of the *Sioux City Journal,* which drew many adventurers to the area. The twofold dream of Collins, an Irish-American, was to drive out the Indians and appropriate the golden wealth of Dakota for the white man, and to free Ireland from the yoke of England. He wanted to found an Irish colony in Dakota Territory, taking advantage of government homesteads, and Congress was induced to pass a bill permitting a colony corporation. However, the very realistic dangers of pioneer life in the territory were too evident to most of the members of the Fenian committee who traveled

[15] *Senate Exec. Doc.,* 43rd Cong., 2d Sess., No. 32, 10-19; *Sioux City Weekly Times* (Sioux City, Iowa), August 15, 1874; *Harper's Weekly,* September 12, 1874, 753.

[16] Charles Collins was an ardent Fenian who, in 1869, conceived a scheme for the establishment of an Irish-American empire on the upper Missouri River to await a favorable opportunity to invade Canada. His plan was presented to a Fenian convention at St. Louis and rejected. Collins then turned his efforts to a scheme for the settlement of the Black Hills. During the spring and summer of 1872, he published in his paper a series of sensational articles depicting the wonders of the Black Hills, especially stressing the possibility of finding gold. *Sioux City Weekly Times,* March 6, 1875.

through the area, and in spite of a minority report favoring the project, Collins saw the region must be settled by other emigrants than the Irish.

In their schemes to settle the Dakota area and to develop its mineral resources, Russel and Collins paid little heed to the Indian treaty of 1868, which gave the area to the Kiowa, Sioux, and Dakota tribes. Their bold advertising, carried by Russel as far to the south as Kansas City, attracted the attention of the military authorities, who ordered the association to disperse or be arrested. The leaders, however, did not give up their plans, although they discontinued issuing pamphlets or holding meetings. In May, 1874, before the departure of Custer's expedition, Charles Collins and Russel were planning a new project for the invasion of the forbidden land. Within three months, according to the *Times,* communication had been received from three hundred men who desired to go into the Hills. While Custer was still in the region, their representatives had gone to Chicago and enrolled as many as eleven thousand men who were anxious to go to the new Golconda.[17]

The extensive publicity given the project soon caused the military authorities to warn the party not to enter the Hills. Although the leaders publicly announced that the project had been given up, they apparently had no intentions of abandoning their proposed invasion of the gold regions. A meeting of those interested was held in the rooms of the Irish Literary Society, at which time fifty men signed up for the expedition. Hundreds of letters were reported to be coming in daily, and, according to one observer, the excitement at this point was intense: "No less than one hundred frontiersmen, all of whom had had service in the mountains and on the plains, were anxiously awaiting the departure of the expedition." On September 3, 1874, it was reported that two tents, each capable of holding fifty persons, had been pitched on

[17] *Sioux City Weekly Times,* March 6, 1875. The number supposed to be actually enrolled was no doubt greatly exaggerated.

Prospect Street to house the gold-seekers who could not be accommodated at the hotels.[18]

The first civilian expedition, consisting of twenty-eight persons, including one woman, Mrs. Annie Tallent, left Covington, Nebraska, opposite Sioux City, on October 16, 1874. Their wagons were placarded "O'Neill Colony" to give the impression that they were bound for a settlement that was being established in the Elkhorn Valley. Their six wagons, drawn by oxen, passed at the rate of fifteen or twenty miles a day beyond the edges of the area of the O'Neill colony and on into the desolate and dangerous land where Indians were a constant threat to the white traveler. It was a difficult journey, routed as it was through the Bad Lands. The daily fare of coffee, beans, and bacon was meager and depressing. Russel had accompanied the party, which chose John Gordon and Ephrim Witcher as leaders, after it had got beyond the settlements. Gordon, who was familiar with the country, acted as guide. The party, while receiving many warnings of hostile Indians from travelers and surveyors along the way, encountered only one group of the red men, who proved to be peaceful Cheyennes, and went quietly on after receiving gifts of food and tobacco. The route had been largely chosen so as to avoid troops as well as Indians. At last the party came in sight of the great purple mountains, rising sharply from the plains, and on December 28, 1874, reached French Creek, two or three miles from Custer's abandoned diggings, having lost two members of the group on the way, one by desertion and the other by death.

[18] *Sioux City Weekly Journal* (Sioux City, Iowa), September 3, 1874; *Sioux City Weekly Times*, August, 29, September 3, 1874; *Yankton Press and Dakotian* (Yankton, D. T.), August 20, 27, 1874. At this time the Sioux City and Yankton papers began to call attention to both places as outfitting centers for Black Hills expeditions. One Sioux City business firm advertised a complete outfit consisting of a rifle, revolver, flour, salt, ammunition, blankets, cooking utensils, a pick, shovel and gold pan, all for one hundred dollars. Full equipment for a party of six was advertised at five hundred dollars. The opinion was expressed that the government would not interfere, although it had warned people to stay out. The press urged, however, that no one should start without receiving orders from Collins or Russel. *Yankton Press and Dakotian*, September 3, 10, 17, 31, 1874; *Sioux City Weekly Times*, September 5, 1874.

They constructed a stockade of upright logs sixteen feet high and built seven cabins within the enclosure. After obtaining a small amount of gold by prospecting, Gordon and Witcher left on February 2nd for Sioux City.[19] In the meantime, the government searched out the party and compelled it to leave. The fate of the expedition discouraged further attempts to send out large prospecting parties from Sioux City to the Hills in 1875.

Though many miners succeeded in evading the troops and entering the Hills,[20] the government would not consent to their remaining there. However, the flood of interest in the Dakota region was engulfing the entire country and could not be held back much longer. Early in August, 1875, about six hundred miners were forced to leave the area. Others continued to enter, however, some of whom were sent back and returned by circuitous routes and hid in the numerous gulches where they often prospected without being discovered. Some were held prisoner for short periods and then sent out. A single issue of a Yankton newspaper in May, 1875, mentioned the arrival of several parties who had been compelled to leave the mining regions and listed thirty-five hotel arrivals, most of whom were bound for the mines, representing the states of Texas, Illinois, Nebraska, Minnesota, Iowa, Wisconsin, and Colorado.[21] At the same time, people were entering the area by way of Sioux City, Iowa; Cheyenne, Wyoming; and Bismarck and Pierre in the Territory of Dakota.[22]

While the government was assiduously endeavoring to keep miners out of the Black Hills, it was also engaged in definitely ascertaining the resources of the region, as well as trying to con-

[19] A Yankton editor on March 11th announced the arrival of the two men who reported rich finds. They told that it was possible to make twenty-five dollars a day in spite of the winter weather. *Yankton Press and Dakotian*, March 11, 1875.

[20] *Iowa Register* (Des Moines, Iowa), April 12, 1875; files of the *Yankton Press and Dakotian*, May, June, 1875.

[21] *Yankton Press and Dakotian*, May 19, 1875.

[22] Files of the Sioux City, Cheyenne, Bismarck, and Pierre newspapers all indicated some activity. Yankton, however, on the Dakota Southern Railroad was, during the gold activity, the most important point of departure.

summate treaties with the Sioux which would allow white occupation of the area. Walter P. Jenny, a noted geologist, was instructed by the Commissioner of Indian Affairs to investigate the mineral wealth, climate, and natural resources of the Hills area. He reported gold in paying quantities in various parts and large numbers of miners already at work, with others journeying there from all directions.[23] In September, 1875, the Allison Peace Commission met with certain of the Sioux tribes at the Red Cloud agency. After nine days of discussion, the conference broke up without coming to any agreement and the failure to draw up a treaty was followed by withdrawal of all military opposition to the occupancy of the Black Hills. There immediately began a rapid rush of gold-seekers to the region, as many as fifteen thousand miners assembling there during the fall and winter.[24] Representatives of every trade and profession made headlong haste to be the first to reach the new gold-fields, using every known means of conveyance, and going either as individuals or as members of a party. In less than a year, the wilderness of the Black Hills was the scene of a populous and busy life.[25]

But this invasion was not carried on without danger and bloodshed. The Indians, restless and hostile after the failure of the Allison Peace Commission, feared the loss of their hunting-grounds as military protection was withdrawn and miners began flocking to the Hills. They went on the war-path in 1876 and a year and a half of bloody conflict ensued. The outstanding event of the war was the battle of the Little Big Horn on June 25, 1876. General George A. Custer, who two years before had been sent by the government into the Hills to report on gold, and his entire

[23] *Senate Exec. Doc.*, 44th Cong., 1st Sess., No. 51, 4-9; *Yankton Press and Dakotian*, July 2, 9, 16, 1875.
[24] *Sioux City Weekly Journal*, October 21, 1875; *Yankton Press and Dakotian*, September 25, October 9, 1875.
[25] Annie D. Tallent, *The Black Hills* (St. Louis, 1899), pp. 115-7; *Yankton Press and Dakotian*, files for 1875 to 1877; *Bismarck Daily Tribune* (Bismarck, D. T.), files for 1875 to 1877; *Sioux City Weekly Journal, Sioux City Weekly Times, St. Paul Pioneer Press, Omaha Daily Bee* (Omaha, Neb.), and *Cheyenne Daily Leader* carry considerable news regarding the gold rush.

command were wiped out. Of all the officers who served on the upper Missouri, he was the one whose career was to become a tradition throughout Montana and the Dakotas.

Arrangements were finally made whereby the Sioux Indians gave up all claims to the Black Hills and the region was opened for settlement on February 28, 1877.[26] While Indian hostilities had not stopped migration to the gold-fields of the Black Hills, they had had a retarding effect. The Sioux made things lively for the unprotected treasure-seeker and the newspapers contained many references to Indian attacks and their tragic results. Travelers returning from the Hills reported that many miners were leaving the region because of Indian raids. But, while a few left, many more were entering in spite of the danger. How many of the Black Hills adventurers fell victims to the hostile Sioux will never be known, but it was no doubt a considerable number. But even Indian troubles were not enough to discourage the ambitious gold-seekers, and they continued to go into the widely advertised region in increasing numbers.[27]

The first mining district formed in the Black Hills was organized on French Creek May 29, 1875, and was called the Cheyenne Mining District. Rules and regulations regarding mining claims were drawn up in considerable detail.[28] Before the miners left the Hills in August, 1876, under General Crook's

---

[26] Robinson, *Encyclopedia of South Dakota*, p. 74.

[27] *Sioux City Weekly Journal*, April 27, September 8, 1876; *Sioux City Weekly Tribune*, September 12, 1876, April 13, 1877.

[28] Every United States citizen was given the right to hold a placer claim of twenty acres, but no holder of a claim was allowed to empty his sluices or tailings or deposit strippings upon any land or claim of another without permission. Every miner had the right to make a ditch through the land adjoining his own for the purpose of drainage, provided he did not cause damage to such adjoining claim or claims. Every miner was allowed the right to hold 1,500 feet of a claim on quartz ledges, with all the depths, spurs, angles or accretions and 150 feet of service land on each side of the crevice of said claim. Eight persons were allowed to hold 160 acres for mining purposes. Claims were to be recorded within ten days from date of discovery and each claim was to be represented every thirty days from May first to November fifteenth of each year. The recorder was allowed one dollar for recording the certificate. *Yankton Press and Dakotian*, June 24, 1875.

proclamation, they found time in the intervals of their mining labors to lay out a town and organize a local government. A site was selected in the valley of French Creek, a natural center for travel and transportation through the eastern section of the Hills.

Every man in the Cheyenne mining district was interested in the town; a commission was appointed, streets were laid out and named, lots surveyed and numbered, and everything went well until the question of naming the town was raised. A general meeting was called which was about evenly divided between Northerners and Southerners. The former were agreed to call the place "Custer City" in honor of General Custer, while the latter were unanimous on "Stonewall" as the proper name. Debate ran high, and, from words, the two factions very nearly came to blows, weapons being brandished freely. After much discussion, the matter was left to the ballot, and the judges of the vote finally pronounced the name of the town to be Custer City.[29]

Gold was discovered in Deadwood Gulch in the late autumn of 1875 and the following spring saw the arrival of many miners. The town of Deadwood was laid out April 26, 1876, and a provisional town government was organized. In spite of the fact that the country had not been formally opened to settlement and Indian scares and depredations were common, miners flocked in, and in less than a year Deadwood grew from a few log cabins to a town of seven thousand inhabitants. Beaver had been so busy in the gulch that often good locations lay under water, and prospecting was difficult. The gulch was only wide enough for one street and the town was built along it, with mountains rising on either side. During this time the gulch from Gayville to Crook City was staked out and located by new-comers, and the towns of Central City, Gayville, North and South Deadwood, Fountain City, Chinatown, and Cleveland grew rapidly. Lead City began its history in the spring of 1876, when gold was discovered in the surrounding hills and gulches. A few cabins were constructed

[29] "The Black Hills," *Motor Travel* (August, 1927), p. 22.

and their occupants were engaged in placer mining. People flocked in during the summer, and all placer claims in the various gulches were soon taken. Prospecting for quartz began, and the Emanuel brothers discovered the famous Homestake Mine. Little could be done with the ore until a mill could be constructed. The first quartz mill, which had twenty stamps, went into operation April 15, 1877, and another was started in July. Lead City, which had heretofore been nothing but the scattered cabins of prospecting miners, became, during the summer of 1877, one of the largest towns in the Hills. Spearfish, fourteen miles northwest of Deadwood, near the foot of Crow Peak, was located in April, 1876, and a town-site association laid out the town in May. During the summer it developed into a good-sized village.[30]

The Deadwood press recorded the rapid growth and development of the town. Gold-seekers poured in and hastened to corral their wagons or pitch their tents on the first suitable location they could find. Glowing reports were common; placers yielded fabulously and quartz brilliant with gold was passed around to arouse even wilder hopes. Speculation in town lots amounted to a furore and real estate was in great demand. Boughton and Berry's sawmill was kept in continuous operation, and an amateur carpenter could almost command his own price.[31]

Saloons multiplied rapidly, and gambling went on day and night, hurdy-gurdies and houses of prostitution being open at all hours. C. H. Wagoner established the first hotel in Deadwood, the Grand Central, and it was speedily followed by the I.X.L. Both houses did an enormous business from the start, and it was considered a luxury to be able to occupy a chair in the office during the night. All sorts of business enterprises were started; doctors, lawyers, and druggists came into the mining towns in large numbers. The first theater was opened on July 22, 1876. The building was enclosed by four walls, but had a dirt floor covered with saw-

[30] *Black Hills Pioneer*, June 8, 1876.
[31] *Ibid.*, July 11, 1876.

EARLY DAYS OF DEADWOOD

Harper's Weekly, 1876.

THE FRONTIER OF THE MINER 39

dust and a canvas roof. The years 1876 and 1877 were characterized by much lawlessness and a considerable number of men
lost their lives in the frequent quarrels. The town was full of
gamblers, and shooting was a common pastime.[32] This general
development was characteristic of the mushroom communities
in the western mining regions of the period.

Captain John G. Bourke, who was in the Hills in the autumn
of 1876, stated that Crook City, Hill City, and Custer City and
other places through which he passed were more substantially
built than was Deadwood, and better situated for expansion. But
Deadwood, at that time, was the metropolis of the Hills, although
most of the distance from Crook City to Deadwood was lined on
both sides with ditches and sluice boxes where gold-bearing gravel
was being worked. Captain Bourke was amazed at the marvelous
exhibition of energy shown on all sides:

We walked along the main street and looked in the stores, which were
filled with all kinds of articles necessary in a mining district: clothing,
heavy and light hardware, tinware, mess pans, camp kettles, blasting
powder, blankets, saddlery, harness, rifles, cartridges, wagon grease,
rubber boots, garden seeds, dried and canned fruits, sardines, yeast,
lamps and candles, and many other things, all of which had been
transported overland for two hundred and fifty miles, loaded down
the shelves. The medium of exchange was gold dust, and each counter
displayed a pair of delicate scales, while each miner carried a buckskin
pouch containing the golden grains required for daily use.[33]

In the spring of 1878 the editor of the *Lead City Telegraph*
gave a literary description of the general activity throughout the
gold-field:

In all parts of the Hills the sound of pick and spade cause the air to
resound with the music of Midas. Innumerable towns spring up like
mushrooms on a summer's night, while placer and quartz mines develop with almost incredible rapidity. Rough board shanties are the

[32] *Black Hills Pioneer*, August 8, 29, September 5, 12, 19, 1876, January 2,
1882; *Black Hills Daily Champion* (Deadwood, D. T.), March 30, 1878.
[33] John H. Finerty, "Deadwood in 1876," *Motor Travel* (November, 1927),
pp. 17-8.

chief architectural feature of the new "Cities" which swarm with people of all kinds.[34]

But the busy mining towns of the Black Hills, with their mixed and adventurous population, were far from being stable and permanent, and, as was the case in other gold booms, often deteriorated as rapidly as they had developed. The collapse of Custer City, the pioneer town of the Hills country, shows how quickly a thriving mining town could go to pieces. Custer City, in the early spring of 1876, was a place of almost six thousand people. The news of rich discoveries in Deadwood Gulch late in May started a stampede and as many as one thousand people left Custer City in a single day. Within a few weeks, the population of the place had diminished to less than one hundred. The fourteen hundred log cabins were gradually torn down and used for fuel. In the fall, however, the population began slowly to increase and the next spring was estimated at about four hundred. Its inhabitants continued at about that number until the autumn of 1878, when the population diminished again during a stampede. By actual census, taken September 5, 1878, there were fifty-seven persons living in the pioneer mining town of Custer City: thirty-seven men, eleven women and nine children.[35]

A reliable correspondent, writing from Deadwood October 12, 1877, said:

Custer City, the first camp in this country, and, at one time, quite a city, is almost deserted, and Castleton, on Castle Creek, is meeting with the same fate. Rapid City, on Rapid Creek, is still there, but the miners in that vicinity are not getting anything better than "grub stakes." In fact, the industry, population and trade of the Black Hills country are nearly all centered about Deadwood, Gayville and Central City within a radius of ten miles. The population of this area is about 12,000, a good deal less than in midsummer. It will no doubt remain about the same during the winter. There are still many out-

---

[34] *Lead City Telegraph* (Lead City, D. T.), March 31, 1878.
[35] Finerty, "Custer's Black Hills March of 1876," *Motor Travel* (December, 1927), pp. 13-5.

lying camps in different directions and perhaps a population of 5,000 to 6,000 scattered through them. The principal large towns are Deadwood with a population of about 4,000; Central City with 1,500; Gayville, 1,200; Lead City, 1,000; while Lancaster City, Pennington and Galena together have about 2,000.[36]

The peak of the gold rush was reached in the spring of 1877, and soon the rapid influx of gold-seekers was materially reduced. The cause was largely the shift of emphasis from placer to lode or deep vein mining and the taking up of claims to the extent that there were few available to new-comers by the summer of 1877. W. H. Wright, special correspondent for the *Sioux City Weekly Journal*, writing about the Hills June 4, 1877, said: "Immigration to the Hills has about ceased. Those coming in with freight trains say that there are few on the road." The Yankton and Bismarck papers for the summer of 1877 took little notice of the decline in numbers going into the area, but made many references to the transportation of heavy mining machinery and the installation of quartz mills in the various gold camps.[37]

VI

THE SEARCH FOR A NEW GOLD FRONTIER

AFTER the Big Horn expedition in 1870, enough activity was maintained in Wyoming to keep alive hopes that portions of the territory contained gold. Railroad surveys noted its presence, while ambitious prospectors were active in spite of Indian hostilities, reports of the scalping of miners being frequently matched by rumors of rich strikes. Adjustment of Indian difficulties, successful gold-mining in the Black Hills of Dakota, together with optimistic reports of gold in the Big Horn Mountains, created a new interest in possible rich gold-fields in Wyoming in

[36] *Appleton's Annual Cyclopedia and Register of Events* (New York, 1877), pp. 245-6; *Report of the Deadwood Board of Trade* (Deadwood, D. T.), 1878, p. 10.
[37] *Sioux City Weekly Journal*, June 21, 1877; files of the *Bismarck Tribune*, and the *Yankton Press and Dakotian*, summer and autumn, 1877.

1877.[1] Early in that year extensive preparations were made at various railroad points for what was predicted to be a great stampede. The town of Rawlins, anxious to become a center of activities, circulated posters and advertising material booming the Big Horn country as "the real aurora for gold-seekers." It was reported that three hundred experienced miners and mountaineers would leave Rawlins early in April. Horses and provisions were

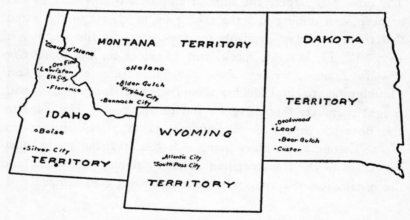

CHIEF MINING CENTERS

advertised at rock-bottom prices. "Reliable data," wrote a Cheyenne editor early in May, "settles the question of gold deposits in the Big Horn Basin beyond all doubt." Tables of distances were published, together with detailed descriptions of routes.[2]

During the last part of May and the first part of June some two hundred miners crossed the Powder River at Fort Reno and headed for the mountains, while another party numbering slightly more than one hundred left Fort Reno about the middle of June. The groups were made up for the most part of overflows from

[1] J. H. Willard, who spent the greater part of the winter of 1876-77 in the Big Horn Valley, reported a find that he claimed netted him three dollars a pan. He was said to have sent $20,000 in gold-dust to St. Louis in the spring of 1877. Willard also reported rich quartz deposits. *Cheyenne Daily Leader*, June 10, 13, July 2, 1877.

[2] *Cheyenne Daily Leader*, May 2, 1877.

the Black Hills and other areas where opportunities were not as great as they had been, and of roving miners ever on the lookout for new strikes. In contrast to the indiscriminate crowds that rushed to the Black Hills, these men were generally old miners thoroughly armed and carrying sufficient provisions for several months. But the Big Horn stampede of 1877, boomed and advertised as it was, failed to locate gold in sufficient quantities to be worth working, and the enterprise ended in dismal failure.[3]

In August, 1890, word came to Cheyenne and Sheridan that an enormously rich strike had been made in the vicinity of Bald Mountain and that prospectors were taking out twenty-five dollars to the pan in free gold. The news reached Sheridan late in the afternoon and a mad rush occurred, many packing their outfits and heading for the diggings during the night. During the next few months, a very thorough and systematic search for gold was made in the gulches and canyons around Bald Mountain. While operations were held up by a heavy snowfall in October, claims were staked out and the miners waited eagerly for spring. Wyoming newspapers were more optimistic than ever.[4]

The spring of 1891 saw a resumption of activity in the Bald Mountain region. The Fortunatus Mining Company was organized and installed a quartz mill costing a quarter of a million dollars. Placing the heavy machinery for the crusher and stamp mill on the top of a mountain at an altitude of eight thousand feet was no easy task. After carefully widening the trails, long strings of bull teams slowly pulled the low wagons loaded with machinery to the summit. In the meantime, a few miles from Bald Mountain a typical mining town had sprung into existence. Two long rows of log houses lined the single street and trains of freight

[3] *Cheyenne Weekly Leader,* June 18, 21, 1877; *Billings Weekly Gazette* (Billings, Mont.), June 21, 28, August 14, 21, 1877; Lindsay, *The Big Horn Basin,* pp. 235-40.
[4] "There is no longer any doubt that there is plenty of gold in the Big Horn Mountains," wrote an editor in the fall of 1890. *Billings Weekly Gazette,* October 23, 1890.

wagons carried provisions from Sheridan up the mountainside. Stores, saloons, and dance-halls were soon a part of its social and commercial life. It was confidently expected that Bald Mountain City would become as important as Deadwood or Virginia City in their boom days.[5]

Meanwhile, another Wyoming area was opened up in the Kirwin district at the head of Wood River. Miners rushed in and several mining companies were organized, representing considerable capital from the East.[6] But the new gold-fields of Bald Mountain and the Kirwin district did not pay an adequate return on the investment and had to be abandoned. It was estimated that the Fortunatus Mining Company lost at least half a million dollars in the Bald Mountain region. But even after this, it was difficult for the newspapers of Wyoming to admit defeat. A despatch to an Omaha paper in 1896 pointed out that, while the cattle industry was receiving considerable attention at the expense of mining, there must be rich gold-fields in Wyoming, since there were rich mines all around it. There was the Homestake Mine in the Black Hills on the east, the Montana mines on the north, the mines of Idaho on the west and the Colorado gold-fields on the south. "Lying in the very heart of this immense district and with the same chain of mountains running through her, Wyoming should be the richest of them all." [7]

But prospectors continued to dig for gold in the Big Horn country, and, while they were able to find some of the coveted metal, it was hardly enough to pay for the trouble of digging. At almost any time after the boom of the nineties, miners could be found in the mountains of Wyoming with gold-dust and nug-

[5] *Billings Weekly Gazette*, September 24, October 8, 22, 1891.

[6] The first ore sent out from the Kirwin district was taken from the Bryant claim in 1897 and was carried out of the mountainous area on pack-mules, a distance of about fifteen miles, and then was freighted to Billings, Montana. The first car, when analyzed at Omaha, is reported to have averaged sixty ounces per ton in silver, six dollars in gold and some lead. Lindsay, *op. cit.*, p. 243.

[7] *Omaha World-Herald* (Omaha, Neb.), July 15, 1896.

gets in small buckskin bags ready to exhibit as evidence of the richness of the region. However, the deserted mines on Bald Mountain with their rusting machinery, and the abandoned town close by with its dilapidated shacks with their caved-in roofs, told the other side of the story.[8]

VII

MINING AND PROSPECTING ON THE GOLD FRONTIER

THE FIRST gold secured in most of the mining camps of the Northwest was by placer mining. The golden dust was sometimes seen in the form of small flakes called colors; sometimes in larger particles about the size of grains of wheat; and, once in a while, in bright lumps or nuggets. This first layer of wealth, lying close to the surface and easily accessible, required practically no capital and the simplest of tools for removal. In the early days of gold-mining, the first claims were staked along the wet diggings on the rivers, where at flood season the waters rose over the gravel bars, only to recede later, leaving their riches. Placer came originally from the Spanish *plaza*, meaning a place. The miners rhymed it with "passer."

The gold-bearing gravel was carefully washed out by use of a pan, the free particles of gold collecting at the bottom. Gold-dust and shot gold consisting of solid bits or nuggets were thus obtained. As miners worked along a stream, there would be little conversation, for every man was intent upon his own claim. The pick, shovel, and pan were the first tools used by the early prospectors. The pan, made of sheet-iron or tin, looked much like a bread pan, and often a miner would use his gold pan for both purposes.

As miners came into the various diggings in larger numbers,

[8] *Big Horn County Rustler* (Basin, Wyo.), March 27, April 10, 24, 1908; *Wyoming Stock Grower and Farmer* (Cody, Wyo.), August 29, September 5, 1908; *Wyoming Industrial Journal*, August, 1909.

rockers and sluice boxes were used, enabling them to work far more gravel than with the pan, although the same principle was involved. The rocker was constructed somewhat like an old-fashioned cradle, with a piece of sheet-iron punched full of holes fastened where the slats of the cradle would have been. Two men usually worked together on the rocker, and while one poured water and rocked the machine, the other threw dirt on the sheet of iron. The gold, falling through the holes, was caught behind cleats on the bottom of the rocker, while the coarse dirt was washed away by the water.[1]

Where water and fall could be utilized, wooden troughs or sluice boxes ten to twelve feet long, about twelve inches wide and ten inches deep, were used with transverse slats, called "riffles," nailed to the bottom. Mercury or quicksilver was placed in the bottom to collect the dust and shot gold. Often a number of sluice boxes were built at once and placed end to end or in "strings." The boxes were filled with earth and a current of water run through them.

A further modification of the sluice box was the use of hydraulic power, which necessitated considerable construction work and equipment.[2] The prospector turned strong streams of water, shot through nozzles, against the sides of the hills or rivers, and thus tore great holes in the earth, which later crumbled so that the loose dirt could be freed from the gold in sluice boxes.

[1] A miner, who, with four others, established the Palmer's Gulch Mining District in the Black Hills in the spring of 1876, made the following observation: "One Sunday in March, 1876, we made a fairly good strike about a quarter of a mile up from our cabin, and decided to make a rocker. We procured our lumber at Berry's mill, which had been established at Hill City. In a month, our party had rocked out about $1,000 each in dust, carrying the gravel to the creek bank in fifty pound flour sacks." G. W. Stokes and Howard Driggs, *Deadwood Gold* (New York, 1926), pp. 55-7.

[2] At various camps "ten-dollar diggings" were frequently advertised for sale, which meant that a man working a string of six sluices, with fair fall and ample water, could make ten dollars a day. Four men picking and shoveling, one man forking and another in the tailrace, might make sixty to seventy dollars per day. *Black Hills Weekly Times* (Deadwood, D. T.), January 15, 1877; *Black Hills Daily Champion*, June 2, 1877; *Montana Post*, April 15, 22, 29, 1865.

While the pay dirt in shallow diggings was made accessible by stripping, in many of the rich fields of Montana [3] and the Black Hills the pay stratum was often deeply buried, necessitating shafts and drifting which required the services of an expert miner. Good drifters were always in demand at wages from three to four dollars a day higher than ordinary labor. In this type of work, the skill and knowledge of the old California miner were held in high regard. But even with the skill of experienced miners, early mining procedure was wasteful. Most of the men in the mining areas were there to make as much money as possible as quickly as they could. They moved from place to place, working the ground hastily, and could not be expected to work carefully a mine that paid only wages. In the second place, the expenses of the miner in remote places, involving long tedious transportation, were so great that only rich gravel could be profitably worked. The early mines were therefore skimmed, and the waste was enormous.[4]

But even if the miners had been careful, the rocker and sluice system of mining was wasteful at the best. Weather conditions made sluice-box yields vary, as in early spring and late fall mercury is sluggish and does not attract gold readily. It was estimated that the most careful miners only secured about 65 per cent of the gold when using the sluice box. Miners without funds often panned the refuse in the tailrace to procure dust with which to purchase food, and Chinese often worked over the camps after the miners had taken the cream, or after the flush times were over.[5]

Because of the early exhaustion of placer gold, its wasteful methods, and the lack of stability of the placer camps, the more substantial miners and business men concentrated their attention on quartz. Gold and other metals were often found in rocks and

[3] Much of the pay dirt in Last Chance Gulch at Helena, Montana, was buried beneath from twenty to sixty feet of dirt and rocks.

[4] Browne, *Mineral Resources of the United States*, p. 95.

[5] More work of this sort was carried on after the boom periods than is commonly thought. William J. Trimble, "A Reconstruction of Gold Discoveries in the Northwest," *Mississippi Valley Historical Review*, V, pp. 94-5.

ledges, buried deeply under the surface of the earth. These ledges, often called lodes, were eagerly located and developed in Montana, in the Black Hills, and even in Wyoming. The mining camps that appeared in the areas of quartz mining were, as a rule, more permanent than those in the placer regions.

The simplest machinery for working quartz was the arrastra, originally a Mexican invention.[6] The remains of those old arrastras may be found in many of the gulches of the Northwest to-day. Their use required neither capital nor labor, since the owner could dig his own rock one day and reduce it the next.[7]

The arrastra, however, was too crude for the enterprising and ambitious miner to use any length of time, and he set to work at once to construct mills, in spite of enormous obstacles. The first quartz mill in Montana, constructed in November, 1862, was located in the Bannack diggings in connection with the Dacotah Lode. The mill was described by a pioneer as follows:

An overshot wheel, twenty feet in diameter, is placed on a shaft eighteen feet long with large pins in it for the purpose of raising the stamps that are fourteen feet in length and eight inches square. They are strapped with iron on the bottom and worked into a box lined on the sides with copper plate galvanized with quicksilver, so as to catch the gold as the quartz is crushed and clashed up the sides of the box. There is an opening on one side of the box with a fine screen in it, through which the fine quartz and fine gold pass and run over a table covered with copper.[8]

More elaborate mills were constructed, as outside capital was brought in, and the introduction of heavy expensive machinery to develop the quartz changed the unstable placer mining com-

[6] The arrastra (or arrastre) consisted of a circular area paved with stones, with a post in the middle, to which was attached a sweep. A mule or horse was attached to the sweep and dragged a block of granite fastened to it over the quartz that was distributed within the circle.

[7] Browne, *op. cit.*, p. 21.

[8] J. F. Campbell, *Six Months in the New Gold Diggings* (Helena, Mont., n.d.), p. 35; W. T. Mendenhall, *History of Gold and Silver Mining in Montana* (Helena, 1891), p. 6.

munities to highly organized capitalistic and stable towns, and represented what may be called the second stage in quartz development. Early in the summer of 1865, thirteen quartz mills were on their way to Virginia City.[9] A Helena editor wrote June 17, 1867: "From all information we have been able to obtain, we estimate that there will be over a million and a half dollars worth of mining machinery brought into Montana during the coming season." The same editor told of the organization of the Plymouth Gold and Silver Mining Company of Montana, with a capital of one million dollars, while the St. Louis and Montana Gold and Silver Mining Company voted to invest $100,000 in heavy machinery.[10]

On October 12, 1877, it was reported from Deadwood in the Black Hills of Dakota Territory that methodical work had been going on for some time toward the development of quartz mines, which were termed "prominent" and prophesied to become the permanent industry of the Hills. The gulch or placer mines were said to have been exhausted. It was estimated that by the following summer there would be as many as one thousand stamps in operation. The yield of the quartz mines for the year was put at about $1,500,000, while $1,000,000 had been obtained from placer mining.[11]

An observer, fascinated by the process of reducing gold quartz in a mill, described the process:

The quartz was first broken into fragments the size of apples by sledge hammers, and then shoveled into feeders which brought it under the large iron stamps weighing three hundred to eight hundred pounds and which, rising and falling sixty times per minute with thunder and

[9] *Montana Post,* August 5, 1865.
[10] *Helena Weekly Herald* (Helena, Mont.), February 28, June 12, 17, 1867; Mendenhall, *op. cit.,* pp. 29-32. The participation of outside capital in Montana mining is shown in the charters granted to mining companies by the first territorial legislature. *Session Laws of the Territory of Montana,* 1864-1865, pp. 558-68.
[11] *Black Hills Daily Champion,* October 12, 1877; *Appleton's Annual Cyclopedia* (1877), pp. 245-7.

clatter, made the building tremble as they crushed the rock to wet powder. Silent workmen ran the pulp through the settling tanks, amalgamating pans, agitators and separators, refuse materials passing away and quicksilver collecting the precious metal into a mass of shining malgam soft as putty. This goes into a fire retort, where it leaves the quicksilver behind, and finally into molds where it comes forth in bars of precious metal.[12]

Prospecting, as a general rule, was carried on by small organized parties of five or six men, although at times the groups were larger. Each party, if possible, included some experienced miners from California or other fields. After careful preparations as to supplies, horses, arms, and mining equipment, a group might range over a wide area of mountain valleys and canyons, studying the geology of the country and prospecting where indications were good. When colors of sufficient richness were found to warrant working, the next step was to lay out the camp and stake out claims.[13] In case of a narrow canyon or gulch, the claims would extend over the flat portion from hill to hill, and were ordinarily one hundred feet in width.[14] If the flat were wider, the claims might be from 100 to 250 feet square. The claims were usually numbered up and down from the discoverer's. The man who located the find was entitled to one claim as discoverer and one by preëmption, while late comers were only entitled to a preëmption claim. A miner could generally purchase one additional claim. A man could have holdings in more than one district and on different kinds of placers. While the mining camps themselves were scattered and isolated, each one was laid out on the order of a town and was comparatively concentrated.[15]

Having staked out claims, the discoverers of new fields, because

[12] Richardson, *Beyond the Mississippi*, p. 501.

[13] The discoveries in Alder Gulch in the spring of 1863 averaged $2.40 to the pan and went to $150 for a single day's work for three persons. Henry Edgar, "Diary," MS, Montana State Historical Society, p. 139.

[14] Grizzly Gulch, just back of Helena, Montana, was narrow and nearly nine miles in length. The claims extended across the gulch.

[15] Trimble, "Mining Advance into the Inland Empire," pp. 87-96.

of lack of supplies or fear of the Indians, were generally compelled to return to some camp or trading center. Although pledged to secrecy, the news invariably leaked out. Friends for whom claims had been staked out were told, and a stampede occurred. Day-laborers, constituting an important part of mining camp population, threw down their tools and joined the rush. They put their money, if they had any, into an outfit, or they might even go into the new field without one. The big consideration was to be first on the ground. Merchants and packers joined in the rush, for the man who arrived with the first well-loaded train in the new camp was bound to make a fortune. Picks and shovels were thrown aside, claims deserted, the miners hurrying with all speed to the stores, literally besieging them for supplies. Prices immediately went up, and the masses of jostling, excited and optimistic miners hurried to the new diggings. In a short time, all of the available mining ground was taken, a district organized and rules formulated for the new camp.[16]

One of the most important district rules was the time required for work in holding a claim. Ordinarily one day out of seven during the working season was sufficient, although some camps required two days when they were first laid out.[17] The holder of the claim could hire the work done or could do it himself, as he wished. After the working season, the claim might be "laid over" for the winter season, as determined by the district meeting. During the slack period, the miner did not have to be in camp and some miners returned home for the winter, where they could live more cheaply, or life was more attractive. Still, the mining camps were far from deserted during the winter months. Since a considerable proportion of the population remained and occupied themselves in sawing lumber, building sluices, drifting, and digging

[16] Good examples of stampedes are the rushes from Virginia City and other places to Dry Creek, Silver Creek, and Prickly Pear in Montana in 1864. *Montana Post*, September 3, 1864.

[17] Biven's Gulch in Montana required two days work when it was first laid out.

shafts. A Montana editor in September, 1865, made the following observation: "A large number of prominent citizens are leaving for the East to spend the winter and to enjoy the fruits of their labor at home. Yet more are coming in than are going out." [18]

J. H. Morley, who visited the early camps of Idaho and Montana, has left an account of a typical miner's cabin:

To the left of the stage road leading to Idaho City stands a log cabin, ten by twelve feet in size, the roof of a porch extending eight feet from the front, a pile of pitch wood at the left of the door; over the wood hangs a fore and hind quarter of beef. Under the same porch is seen a hand sled for sledding wood or articles from town. We open the door and go in. On the left of the room is stored any amount of provisions, over which are fixed two bunks, one above the other. To the right of the fireplace stands a small table, on which are piled books and papers and many other small articles too numerous to mention, and still to the right is a dry goods box nailed on the wall for a cupboard, which is filled with all kinds of cooking traps. On the right side of the room is the window, one pane of glass constitutes its size, under which is placed the dining table. The right hand side of the room is ornamented with a large mirror and pictures; among them is seen Abraham Lincoln and his secretary.[19]

The staple foods of the camps were beans, bacon, bread, and coffee, with few fresh vegetables. A visitor to the Montana goldfields in the spring of 1869 described his dinner, obtained in a restaurant in Helena, as consisting of "doughnuts green and poisonous with saleratus, suspicious looking eggs fried in grease, and rusty bacon, intolerably fat." [20] The lack of fresh vegetables and potatoes caused many miners to suffer from the dreaded scurvy. An Idaho pioneer told how potatoes carried on the backs of packers for twenty miles through the deep snow were sliced and put in vinegar and eaten raw as a remedy for scurvy. So great were the demands in the surrounding Idaho gold camps for garden prod-

[18] *Montana Post*, September 23, 1865.
[19] Morley, "Diary," entry for May 22, 1863.
[20] *Helena Weekly Herald*, May 13, 1869.

ucts grown in the Payette Valley that green corn and cucumbers sold for two dollars a dozen and green onions could be disposed of at one dollar per dozen. Oranges sold in one of the early camps for eighty cents each.

VIII

TRANSPORTATION AND TRAVEL TO THE GOLD-FIELDS

THE INFLUENCE of the western mines upon the public mind was great. Eastern and middle western newspapers, often containing maps of the Far West with suggested routes, warned of evils to be avoided on the road, gave vivid descriptions of mining life, printed letters from miners in the gold-fields, and announced the occasional arrival of the precious metal. The activity of capitalists in organizing mining companies, together with the mania for speculation in mining stock, helped to keep interest high.

The movement of population over the plains to the mines was constant. Included in the stream were those who were influenced by difficulties growing out of the Civil War. Dangers and disorders in the border states, opposition to the draft, and desertions from both the Northern and Southern armies, helped to populate the mining camps of Colorado, Idaho, Montana and Wyoming. Glowing reports of rich agricultural lands, incomparable climate, and the great gold discoveries called the attention of the world to the new El Dorados.[1]

Sioux City, on the Missouri River, was located at a strategic point to observe the migrations to the western gold-fields. Files of the Sioux City newspapers for the early sixties are filled with accounts of this activity. An editor late in 1859 reported that "gold fever is alarmingly prevalent in the cities of the Mississippi Valley and the excitement is spreading eastward." "The gold ex-

---

[1] Emerson D. Fite, *Social and Industrial Conditions in the North During the Civil War* (New York, 1910), pp. 33-40.

citement is intense," wrote the same editor in 1860. "The roads leading to the mines are alive with emigrants, some with teams, some footing it, some pushing wheelbarrows and some harnessed like mules to hand carts, all bound for the mines. Most of them will be disappointed, but they are bound to go. Many miners are going by way of the Missouri River and steamboats are loaded with passengers bound for the mines." [2]

Except for the beginnings of agricultural activity in the southeastern portion of the Territory of Dakota, the principal movement of the frontier line of settlement in the Northwest during the sixties was in the mining regions on the eastern edges of the Rocky Mountains. Starting with the migration of gold-seekers to Colorado during the Pike's Peak gold rush, there was a steady and continuous movement of population to the westward. Gold-seekers and their supplies went into the mining camps by several different routes. The southern route, from Omaha or St. Joseph on the Missouri River, by way of Denver and Salt Lake City to the Montana and Idaho fields, was popular, and covered a distance of about nineteen hundred miles.[3] In 1864 it was estimated that 75,000 people, 22,500 tons of freight, 30,000 horses and, mules, and 75,000 cattle left Omaha on their way to the gold camps of the Northwest, and authorities agree that at least 150,-

---

[2] *Sioux City Eagle*, January 22, February 19, April 9, 1859; *Sioux City Weekly Press*, files for 1859-60; *Sioux City Register*, May 18, 1861. The files of the *Council Bluffs Eagle* and the *St. Paul Weekly Pioneer and Democrat* (St. Paul, Minn.) for the period contain many references to the gold-fields.

[3] While there were several routes leading into the gold-fields from the south and east, the one over which a large number passed was known as the Bozeman Trail. The road turned north from Fort Laramie to Fort Reno on the Powder River, past Fort Phil Kearney, on the Little Piney, skirting the Big Horn Mountains on the east and north, to Fort F. C. Smith on the Big Horn River. Crossing the Big Horn, it turned westward, crossing Clarke's Fork and the Yellowstone River to Bozeman City on the Gallatin River and then north again to its terminus at Virginia City. Another route began at Salt Lake City and went northward via Fort Hall to Fort Lemhi on the lower Salmon River, and to the gold diggings of Deer Lodge and the Bitter Root Valley. *Deseret News*, September 17, 1862; "Report of Major General John Pope, Commander of the Department of Missouri, to the War Department for 1865," *House Exec. Doc.*, 39th Cong. 1st Sess., 10-4.

ooo emigrants left the various Missouri River towns by the routes passing through Kansas and Nebraska.[4]

In the early spring of 1859, a daily stage line had been established between Leavenworth, Kansas, and Denver, with stations from ten to twenty miles apart. Within a year a hundred stage-coaches and a thousand mules and horses were in use on the route. The stage fare from Leavenworth to the mountains was one hundred dollars, with short distance tariff at twenty-five cents a mile. Most of the emigrants, however, went by private conveyance and by day the trails were white with wagons, and at night the sky was filled with the smoke of a thousand camp-fires. Some emigrants hauled their supplies in hand-carts, while others carried them in packs on their backs. Some consumed their provisions before a third of the journey had been accomplished, and had to be fed by friends or by those who were better supplied. Large numbers took an unexplored route by way of the Smoky Hill River, where grass and water were lacking and fearful suffering occurred. The various roads were lined with mining tools, clothing, cook stoves, furniture, and almost all articles imaginable, thrown away to lighten the loads of the travelers. Grass was so scarce at times that it was necessary to feed flour to the exhausted stock to keep them from starvation. But undaunted by the withering heat of summer and the blizzards and biting cold of winter, this restless population, imbued with the spirit of the frontier, pressed steadily and courageously on to seek for gold.[5]

Major-General Pope, in a letter written from St. Louis in February, 1866, said:

People in incredible numbers continue to throng across the great plains to the rich mining territories, undeterred by the seasons, by hardship and privations, or by the constant and relentless hostility of the Indian tribes. Notwithstanding the unusually severe weather which has pervaded the whole region west of the Mississippi during the

---

[4] *Idaho World*, February 3, 10, 1866; Fite, *op. cit.*, pp. 38-40.
[5] Richardson, *Beyond the Mississippi*, pp. 400-507.

present winter, the stream of people crossing the great plains seems
to have been nearly as continuous and determined as during the summer months. For several hundred miles along the routes to . . . Colorado
and Montana, the hospitals of the military posts are filled with frost-
bitten teamsters and emigrants whose animals are frozen to death and
whose trains, loaded with supplies, stand buried in the snow on the
great plains. Notwithstanding these bitter and discouraging experiences and the eminent danger of like, if not worse results, trains of
wagons still continue to move from the Missouri River and to pursue
the overland routes to the mining regions.[6]

Another overland approach to the gold-fields of the Northwest
was one variously known as the Dakota route, the Northern
Plains route, or the Montana-Minnesota route. Beginning at St.
Paul, Minnesota, it went by way of Fort Abercrombie and Fort
Wadsworth to Fort Rice on the Missouri River and thence by that
valley to Fort Union and Fort Benton and on to Fort Walla
Walla.[7] This route received considerable publicity in 1862 through
the first expedition of Captain James L. Fiske, who was detailed by the United States Army to organize and guide the people
in the northern Mississippi Valley who wished to migrate to the
gold camps of Idaho and Montana.[8] The interest of the people in
Minnesota in the gold-fields enabled Captain Fiske to secure another party in 1863,[9] but a third expedition in 1864 was turned
back at Fort Rice because of Indian difficulties.[10] In preparation

[6] "Report of Major-General Pope," *op. cit.*, pp. 3-15.
[7] A second northern route was from Fort Snelling or St. Cloud in Minnesota
to Sioux Falls, Dakota, by way of Fort Ripley and to Fort Pierre on the
Missouri River. From that point it went westward by way of the Big Cheyenne
River along the north base of the Black Hills, thence by the Big Horn Mountains
and the upper Yellowstone to Bannack and Virginia City. Another route sometimes followed was by way of the Missouri Valley and Niobrara River along
the south side of the Black Hills to the Powder River and thence to the mining
regions. "Report of Major-General Pope," *op. cit.*, pp. 4-6.
[8] *House Exec. Doc.* 37th Cong., 3d Sess., No. 80, 3-36.
[9] Report of Captain J. L. Fiske of His Late Expedition to the Rocky
Mountains and the Gold Fields of Idaho," *House Exec. Doc.*, 38th Cong., 1st
Sess., No. 45.
[10] Captain James L. Fiske, "The Overland Expedition of 1864," MS and
photostat copy in the library of the Minnesota Historical Society; original in the
War Department Archives, Washington, D. C.

for a fourth overland party, Captain Fiske prepared a pamphlet, twelve pages in length, giving high praise to the western country and announcing the plans of the expedition which was to leave St. Cloud late in May, 1865. It was reported that as many as two thousand people and one thousand wagons would make the trip. The fare was to be one hundred dollars a person, each of whom would be allowed to carry fifty pounds of baggage. A family with its own wagon and provisions could join the expedition for the small amount of ten dollars.[11] A Virginia City newspaper on August 19, 1866, said: "Captain Fiske, with an emigration train of twelve hundred families, is now enroute for the Yellowstone country near the mouth of the Big Horn River. He is now past Fort Union."[12] Numerous other expeditions left Minnesota during the sixties, one led by a Captain Davy attracting considerable attention because of Indian difficulties. It arrived safely at Fort Benton late in September, 1867.[13]

The water route by way of the Missouri River was a popular means of getting to and from the gold-fields, although the uncertainty and dangers of navigation caused by low water at times restricted its use. As railroads were constructed to various key points on the Missouri, the southern terminus of trade was steadily pushed to the northward. In 1859 it reached St. Joseph, Missouri, and in 1867 when the Chicago and Northwestern line was constructed to Council Bluffs, that frontier outfitting settlement became the emporium of Missouri River trade. It advanced to Sioux City, Iowa, when the Illinois Central arrived there in 1870. Until the gold discoveries in Idaho and Montana, beginning in 1862, the main river traffic on the Missouri was the transportation of supplies, troops, and Indian annuity goods to the posts of the

[11] Fiske, "Fourth Expedition from St. Cloud, Minnesota, to the Gold Fields of Montana," pamphlet in Minnesota Historical Library (St. Paul, 1866); *St. Cloud Democrat* (St. Cloud, Minn.), January 11, 18, 1866.
[12] *Montana Post*, August 19, 1866.
[13] "Report of the Secretary of War, 1868," *House Exec. Doc.*, 40th Cong., 3d Sess., p. 3; *Helena Weekly Herald*, January 17, September 26, October 3, 1867.

Northwest, and the shipment of furs on the downward journey. The impetus given to river traffic is well illustrated by the increase in the number of steamboat arrivals in the vicinity of Fort Benton in Montana, the head of navigation. Out of a total of one hundred and fifty arrivals in the decade 1860-70, all except twelve are recorded for the last five years. The years 1866 to 1869 marked the high tide of Missouri River traffic with 31 arrivals at Fort Benton in 1866, 39 in 1867, 28 in 1868 and 24 in 1869. In 1865, 1,000 passengers, 6,000 tons of merchandise, and 20 quartz mills arrived at Fort Benton by steamboat. In 1867, the number of passengers had increased to 10,000 and freight to 8,061 tons. With passenger fares at $150, and freight rates at from five to ten cents a pound, profits must have been good.[14]

But in spite of the profits obtainable, the dangers and difficulties of Missouri River steamboating were many. Of the 2,300 miles between St. Louis and the head of navigation, 1,300 miles of the distance were little known to river navigators. The trip took about a month and it was necessary to lay up at night because of snags and sandbars. Wood for the engines was expensive and often hard to obtain on the upper reaches of the river, while barricades and guards were needed against Indian attacks. There were also delays and losses due to low water and accidents.

Many miners returned to the States from the gold-fields in the fall, when the steamboat season was over, by means of mackinaw boats. In September, before the approach of winter, successful Argonauts who had made fortunes, and those who had failed to find gold and were discouraged, returned to the States. Thronging to Fort Benton and other places along the river, the miners constructed large numbers of broad flat-bottomed boats with square sterns for the trip down the river. They were roughly built and were either sold for lumber or abandoned at the end of the

---

[14] H. M. Chittenden, *The History of Early Steamboat Navigation on the Missouri River* (New York, 1905), II, 418; *Contributions*, Montana State Historical Society, I, 317-27.

journey. While the boats were supplied with oars and sails, they relied largely upon the current of the river to carry them to their destination. Day after day they pushed off with crews of from ten to thirty, according to size, some going singly and others in flotillas. Making as much as a hundred miles a day under favorable circumstances, they soon arrived at Sioux City, some of them going as far at St. Louis.[15] In September, 1865, six hundred passengers were reported to be waiting at Virginia City in Montana for a fleet of mackinaw boats to leave the mouth of the Yellowstone Canyon for the States.[16] It was estimated by a reliable authority that as many as two hundred mackinaw boats carrying more than one thousand two hundred passengers left Fort Benton annually.[17] After 1870 there was a marked reduction in the use of the Missouri River as one of the main highways of migration and trade to and from the mines.

Fort Benton, the important entrepôt of the gold-fields, to which the steamboats struggled and unloaded their freight and passengers, was a small frontier village not far from the old fort of the American Fur Company. The levee of the river landing was piled high with merchandise of every possible description to be transported to the interior camps. There were barrels and cases of liquor, sacks and crates of provisions, boxes of clothing and drygoods, cases of mining tools, and great quartz mills ready to be loaded into freight wagons, while large piles of buffalo-robes and hides were waiting to be loaded on the steamboats for the downward journey. Warehouses were jammed to their doors with goods and the safes of the town were filled to their utmost capacity with gold-dust left there for safe-keeping. The streets were thronged with men of every nationality and description. There were miners

[15] Bradley Journal, "Effects at Fort Benton of the Gold Excitement in Montana," MS, Vol. II, Contributions, Montana State Historical Society, VIII, 128-30; Chittenden, op. cit., II, 130, 275-6, 379-91; J. M. Hansen, The Conquest of the Missouri (Chicago, 1909), p. 64.
[16] Montana Post, September 10, 1865.
[17] Bradley Journal, op. cit.

and prospectors, fur traders and buffalo hunters, desperadoes, traders, merchants, clergymen, Indian agents, soldiers, and speculators, an exuberant array of frontiersmen.

Steamboat and freight transportation met at Fort Benton in the sixties, in part as a result of the work and plans of John Mullan in the construction of a road to the gold camps. Travel and work on the Mullan Road is indicated in 1862 in the journal of James Harkness on a trip from Fort Benton to the Deer Lodge Valley. After crossing the Little Prickly Pear River and following it northward, he recorded on July 15th: "At the foot of the mountains we found four trains trying to cut a road and helped them until noon." July 16th: "It is noon now and we have made but two miles this morning. The road is filled with other trains and we cannot get ahead of them." Three days later the party met three different groups returning to Fort Benton from the gold-fields.[18] Late in September, 1866, a Montana editor, writing regarding transportation activities, said: "A reliable party informs us that 2500 men, 3000 teams of horses and 20,000 oxen and mules were employed this past season in carrying freight from Fort Benton to the mining towns of the Northwest." [19]

As the various mining centers were established in the Northwest, pack trains penetrated to the remote golds camps of Idaho and Montana from Walla Walla and Portland. Packing was a business that required skill and strength as the trails were often steep and rocky and difficult to follow. As roads were improved, and bridges and ferries constructed, the tinkling bells of the pack trains were replaced by the "gee-haw" of the bull-whacker and the crack of his whip as the long trains of heavily laden wagons drawn by oxen moved slowly over the mountain trails. In the sixties, large amounts of goods were brought in from California. San Francisco battled with St. Joseph and St. Louis in com-

[18] Harkness, "Diary," pp. 351-2.
[19] *Montana Post*, September 29, 1866; H. A. Trexler, "Missouri and Montana Highways," *Missouri Historical Review*, XII, 80.

petition for the trade of the gold camps. Her goods were excellent in quality and were well adapted to the use of the mining population and her mining machinery and woolen clothing were particularly in demand. An Idaho editor writing in October, 1865, made the following observation: "Three-fourths of the great wagon trains penetrating these gloomy forests and skirting the dreary deserts with the rising sun in their eyes are Californians." But as the Missouri River came into use, the eastern trade centers obtained an advantage over the Far West that the latter was never able to overcome.[20]

Virginia City soon became the center of Montana trade. Late in September, 1864, a wholesale firm there, advertising in the *Montana Post*, announced that they had on hand the following commodities, which indicated the heavy freighting at that early date: 500 boxes of tobacco; 250 barrels and cases of liquor; 1,500 sacks of flour; 500 pounds of ham; 400 cans of lard; 50 bags of sugar and 100 kegs of nails.[21] Arthur J. Dickson, a Montana pioneer, described Virginia City early in September, 1864:

Of the four mining towns in the gulch, Virginia City was destined to lead in importance. It consisted of an orderly village of neat log and frame buildings nestled in a sheltered basin, where a tiny stream fed by a series of springs reached Alder Creek from the north through a tangle of alder and willow. The streets were lined with bull trains and pack animals. From the farther diggings, buckskin clad miners with beards and flowing hair hiked in for supplies which they carried away in great packs strapped to their backs. Strings of donkeys loaded with everything from groceries to lumber took the steep trails into the hills. Merchants were busy at their counters or replenishing their stocks from the freight wagons hurrying in from the south while the pass was still open to travel.[22]

[20] *Idaho World*, October 14, 1865, February 3, 1866; Richardson, *op. cit.*, p. 507.
[21] *Montana Post*, September 24, 1864.
[22] Arthur Jerome Dickson (ed.), *Covered Wagon Days, A Journey Across the Plains in the Sixties and Pioneer Days in the Northwest*, from the private journals of Albert Jerome Dickson (Cleveland, Ohio, 1929), pp. 172-3.

On December 17, 1864, five hundred freight teams, loaded with supplies, were reported to have been laid up between Salt Lake City and Virginia City on account of heavy snows.[23]

It has been said that between seventy-five and one hundred thousand persons visited Virginia City in 1864, of whom probably four-fifths returned to the States.[24] The Society of Montana Pioneers in 1899 made a careful survey of 1,809 early settlers whose records indicated that they came into the gold camps of Montana before 1865. Of these, 1,474 gave their route of travel. The division was thus: 61 came by the northern route across Dakota; 111 came in by way of the Pacific coast and 1,302 came in either by the Missouri River to Fort Benton or the overland southern route by way of the Oregon Trail.[25] As to incoming freight, it has been estimated that about one-fifth of the supplies were brought into the camps of the Northwest by way of Oregon and California; one-fifth by the overland route through Kansas and Nebraska; and three-fifths by way of the Missouri River and Fort Benton.[26] While large numbers of gold-seekers returned to the States by the latter route, many who had exhausted their resources trekked back as best they could. John Buchanan, editor of the *Montana Post*, reported that early one morning in October, 1864, he found an old dilapidated wagon with mules to correspond in front of his office, with the following sign displayed on the wagon cover: "Passioners to Omihaw."

The relative importance of Virginia City as the center of Montana transportation declined with the establishment of the new mining camp at Helena. The settlement was well situated for trade between Fort Benton and the gold areas farther west, and later became the territorial capital. The editor of the *Helena Weekly Herald* in November, 1868, gave a description of its activity as a trade center: "Since the storm has subsided, our

[23] *Montana Post*, December 17, 1864.
[24] *Contributions*, Montana Historical Society, I, 279.
[25] Trexler, *op. cit.*, p. 68.
[26] Richardson, *op. cit.*, p. 412.

streets are a perfect jam and our business houses are doing a lively trade. Helena is the commercial center of Montana and is a jobbing center for outside camps. We notice among the shipping, goods marked Fort Benton, Virginia City, Fort Ellis, Bannack City, Musselshell, Philipsburg, Cable City and Leesburg."

The arrival of the Northern Pacific Railroad at Bismarck on the Missouri River in the Territory of Dakota in 1873 made it an important terminus for river trade and when gold was discovered in the Black Hills in 1876, the Northwestern Express, Stage and Transportation Company established a freight and stage line between that point and the Hills. In March, 1876, Bramble, Miner and Company, wholesale grocers and millers at Yankton, the territorial capital, announced plans for the opening of a freight line to the new gold-fields. At about the same time Charles T. Campbell and John Dillon established stage connections to the Hills by way of Fort Pierre and later added facilities for carrying freight. Cheyenne, Wyoming and Sidney, Nebraska, both on the Union Pacific Railroad, soon became important points of approach to the Black Hills from the west and south. While the Black Hills gold rush was at its peak from 1876 to 1881, Bramble, Miner and Company of Yankton employed three hundred men and used two thousand yoke of oxen on their freight line and the capacity of their wagon trains was seven hundred tons of weight.[27]

One of the important aspects of early communication before government mail service was established was the development of express and letter carrying by private parties or companies. The prospector and "pilgrim" in the gold camps, long distances from their former homes and friends, were anxious for news and letters and were willing to pay liberally for their delivery. Hardy express and letter carriers delivered the longed-for messages from

[27] *Bismarck Daily Tribune,* files for 1876-1881; *Yankton Press and Dakotian,* March 11, June 11, 1876; files of the *Cheyenne Daily Leader,* 1876-1880; *Rocky Mountain News,* August 7, 1878; "The Black Hills of Dakota" (Deadwood Board of Trade, 1881), pp. 11-2.

Walla Walla, Portland, and other western points to the miners in the Idaho and Montana camps for a dollar each. Hinckley's Express in Denver delivered mail from the East and South to twenty thousand miners in the mountains, while the Central Overland and Pike's Peak Express carried passengers and mail the 656 miles from St. Joseph on the Missouri River to Denver, the fare being $75, exclusive of meals. "Every seat is filled," reported an observer, "and on the days an armed messenger carried 40 to 50 thousand dollars in gold dust every passenger is vouched for as a motley crowd gathers to witness the stage's departure after the heavily laden mail bags are loaded." Stage and mail connections were established by Ben Holladay from Salt Lake City with the camps to the northward, fare from Atchison, Kansas, to Helena, Montana, being $450 in 1866, exclusive of meals, which increased the cost at least $150 more.

Local mail and stage connections were established between the various Montana camps and with sister camps in Idaho. Many private toll roads, ferries, and bridges were constructed and many were chartered by the territorial legislature of Montana that were never built or were only built in part. There was a good deal of opposition to excessive toll charges and when Governor Ashley in his message of 1869 recommended that some of the charters be revoked, he pointed out that a team going from Helena, Montana, to Corinne, Utah, and return, paid as much as forty dollars in tolls.[28]

Although the postal department of the United States Government refused to furnish mail facilities to the Black Hills in Dakota until the area had been officially obtained from the Indians, private mail connections were immediately established with the Union Pacific Railroad to the south. H. T. Clarke and his two brothers of Omaha, Nebraska, who were interested in the stage and freighting business, constructed a toll-bridge over the North Platte River, which made possible a short cut from Sidney, Nebraska, to the

[28] *Message of the Territorial Governor of Montana*, 1869.

BULL-WHACKING INTO THE BLACK HILLS

Courtesy of the Adams Memorial Hall Museum, Deadwood, South Dakota.

gold region. Seeing the need for mail accommodations, they organized Clarke's Centennial Express in the fall of 1876 and
opened post-offices in all of the leading gold camps in the Black
Hills. Two trips were made on horseback each way every week.
While the toll-bridge and the freight and stage business were
successful, the mail service of the Centennial Express was unprofitable because of the heavy expense for riders, horses, and
feed in proportion to the amount of mail carried. When the
Black Hills area was ceded to the government by the Sioux Indians on March 1, 1877, the Post Office Department immediately
granted mail contracts and Clarke's Centennial Express went out
of business.[29]

IX

BOOM PRICES IN THE GOLD CAMPS

WITH the mining settlements located as they were, long distances from centers of production, with transportation difficult
and expensive and subject to weather and seasonal handicaps as
well as to dangers from Indian attacks, price levels for commodities were necessarily high. In the early years, prices in the camps
of Idaho and Montana were almost as high as they had been during the gold boom in California. Wholesale prices for standard
commodities in August, 1864, at Virginia City, the early center
of trade in the area, were as follows: St. Louis flour (made from
winter wheat), $28.00 per hundred pounds; Salt Lake City flour
(made from spring wheat), $24.00 per hundred; and corn-meal,
$19.00 per hundred-pound sack. The price per pound of various
articles was: sugar, $.65; cheese, $.85; dried peaches, $.65; dried
apples, $.40; soda-crackers, $.40; lard, $.50; bacon, $.50; sauer-
kraut, $.30; coffee, $.40; ranch butter, $1.20; tobacco, $2.00; tea,

[29] H. T. Clarke, "Freighting to the Black Hills," Nebraska State Historical
Society *Collections*, 2d Series, V, 305-10; *Black Hills Herald* (Custer City,
D. T.), August 23, September 14, 1876, January 3, 17, February 20, 1877;
Black Hills Pioneer, February 10, 17, March 3, 1877.

$2.25. While fresh vegetables and fruit were scarce, and at times impossible to obtain, potatoes were quoted at $.20 a pound and green apples were priced at $.75. Belcher's Golden Syrup sold for $6.00 a gallon and coal-oil was available, but scarce, at $7.00 a gallon. By October, 1864, coal-oil was quoted at $8.50 a gallon, increasing to $10.00 within a few days, and by November was selling at $12.00. In September, 1865, George Gohn of the "Bull's Head Meat Market" in Virginia City purchased twenty small hogs at a cost of $1,650.[1]

During the winter of 1864-65, there occurred a serious shortage of flour in the Idaho and Montana settlements, due largely to the tying-up of freighters by a series of heavy snows. The *Montana Post* at Virginia City reported on October 29th that flour had gone up four dollars on the hundred-pound sack that morning. By February, St. Louis flour was selling for $80.00 per bag and in small amounts sold for $1.00 a pound. In the badly isolated settlements of Idaho, flour is said to have sold for as high as $5.00 a pound. The shortage, together with the tendency to speculate and hoard flour for even higher prices, brought the matter to a crisis in Virginia City in April. The population was badly upset and bread riots were threatened unless some action was taken. A public meeting was called at Leviathan Hall and after passing rather drastic resolutions against the hoarding of flour for speculation, when the population was in danger of starvation, a committee was appointed with authority to search out all flour that had been hidden. A standard price was set which was about half the previous figure and twelve pounds was sold to each person who wished to make the purchase. Other food commodities were also high, potatoes selling the last part of April at $.45 a pound. The arrival of freight wagons with flour and other foodstuffs early in May soon brought prices down to normal. The development of local agriculture and the improvement of freight connections soon

[1] *Montana Post*, August 27, September 3, 17, October 17, November 5, 19, 1864, September 3, 1865.

made food and other articles more reasonable in price. In November, 1866, various commodities sold in Helena in the Territory of Montana as follows: St. Louis flour, $15.00 per hundred; cornmeal, $10.00; bacon, $.38 a pound; lard, $.42; ham, $.48; cheese, $.50; nails, $.20; dried apples, $.30; and coal-oil sold for $3.00 a gallon.[2]

While some of the miners going into the Black Hills in the seventies took supplies with them, which they purchased from merchants along the way, most of them, in the early period of the gold rush, outfitted at Yankton, the territorial capital of Dakota, on the Missouri River. The early miners were compelled to take extra supplies with them, since they were obtained with difficulty in the Hills until the government withdrew its opposition to settlement, as a treaty with the Indians was being negotiated. Prices at Yankton in the spring of 1876 were reasonable, a considerable number of gold-seekers who outfitted there signing a statement to that effect. Flour was listed at $2.50 per hundred pounds; sugar at $10.00 a hundred; beans, $2.00 per bushel; coffee, $.25 a pound; bacon, $.15; lard, $.15; and tea, $1.00 a pound, with other food prices in proportion. In the early months of the Black Hills stampede, prices were about the same as in Montana, although they soon reached a level that was relatively lower since the Hills were much closer to centers of production. Farmers of the area were soon raising crops and selling their produce to miners. In January, 1879, cabbage was for sale on the Deadwood market at $.05 a pound; potatoes, $.04; butter, $.10; corn, $.06; eggs, $.50 per dozen; and flour at $7.50 a hundred.[3]

To the mines of the Idaho area around Florence City, commodities were brought in from Walla Walla by pack trains in good weather and were packed in on the backs of men in the

[2] Files of the *Montana Post*, winter and spring, 1864-65; *Helena Weekly Herald*, November 15, 29, 1866.
[3] *Yankton Press and Dakotian*, May 27, June 7, 1876; *Black Hills Weekly Times* January 29, 1879; *Black Hills Pioneer*, June 8, July 11, 1876.

winter. In the spring of 1862, a miner paid the following prices for a bill of supplies at Florence City: [4]

Beans	$1.25 per pound	
Flour	1.00 " "	
Coffee	1.25 " "	
Salt	.25 " "	
Nails	1.00 " "	
Sugar	1.50 " "	
Bacon	1.25 " "	
Beef	.25 " "	
Bar of soap	3.00	
Paper of saleratus	6.00	
Gallon of whiskey	25.00	

During the era of high prices there was a tendency for merchants and freighters to take large amounts of goods into the camps during the summer months, when transportation facilities were at their best, and to glut the market with goods, bringing a marked reduction in prices. During the late fall, winter, and early spring there might be a shortage of necessities, sufficient to cause actual suffering and want. A letter from Virginia City, dated June 10, 1864, said, in part: "I am at last here, after an almost unheard of journey from Salt Lake City. The market is already overstocked with all kinds of goods and if I get cost for what I brought out I will do well. I can buy staples here almost as cheap as in Denver or Salt Lake City." [5] Within six months flour was selling in Virginia City for $1.00 a pound and other foodstuffs were not obtainable at any price. Prices in the Wyoming gold-fields were not as high as in the Montana, Idaho, and Black Hills regions, since railroad facilities were made available there comparatively early with the building of the Union Pacific Railroad. During the rush to the Big Horn Valley in 1877, flour, bacon, and other

[4] Bowles, *Across the Continent.*
[5] *Rocky Mountain News,* July 6, 1864; *Deseret News,* June 8, 15, 29, July 6, 1864.

supplies were advertised at Rawlins, Wyoming, at "rock bottom prices." [6]

In the era of high prices, the cost of commodities other than food was ruinous. The government and stage companies paid from $10 to $12 a bushel for corn and $75 to $100 a ton for hay. The charge for a box of matches was $1.00 and a saddle that was worth $15 in St. Louis cost $100 in the gold camps. A miner paid $28 for enough cotton ticking to make a mattress and pillow, which he stuffed with grass. Rents were said to be higher in Helena, Montana, in 1867 than on Broadway in New York City. Deadwood, wedged in as it was between two ledges, experienced a real estate boom in 1876 and 1877. Log buildings with false fronts rented for from $200 to $550 a month and lots in the rocky gulch sold for $125. The Helena items in the *Montana Post* of July 29, 1865, carried the following announcement: "Tom White has reduced the price of a bath to $1.50 and states that he is determined to bring the rate down to the lowest possible figure." A sawmill in Bevin's Gulch, ten miles from Virginia City, sold its lumber for $150 per thousand feet in 1865 and 1866, the price dropping to $50 and $60 two years later. Belting for the mill was almost worth its weight in gold. The proprietors purchased 80 feet of 6-inch two-ply belting in 1865 at a cost of $600. Miner's wages were $10 a day paid in gold, which was worth $15 an ounce.

Hotels in the early mining camps reaped rich profits, charges running as high as $5.00 per night for a bed, with the privilege of sleeping in a chair in the office costing $2.00. A pioneer arriving in Bannack in the fall of 1864 made arrangements with a hotel proprietor for accommodations at a weekly charge of $40 in advance. He found that what he had paid for was not a room, in fact, not even a bed, but only a place to sleep on blankets on the dirt floor in the corner of the hotel office. Another traveler arrived in Helena and was assured by the hotel proprietor that he could have a room. After paying the clerk $5.00 in advance, he was led

[6] Poster printed in Omaha, 1877.

to a room in which there were four beds, three of which were each occupied by two sleepers while the fourth had only one occupant. Half of bed Number 4 evidently was supposed to be his "room." Many of the so-called hotels were constructed of logs or rough lumber with canvas roofs and paper or muslin partitions. Most of them had cots and bunks arranged in rows in large rooms.

Prices for meals varied from $1.00 up, depending upon what was ordered. At the Mountain House, not far from Florence in the Idaho area, in the spring of 1862, a meal consisting of hard bread, bacon, and black coffee, was priced at $3.00. At Deadwood, late in 1876, at the various restaurants and eating-places, a meal of beans, bread, and coffee cost $1.00, while one of beans and potatoes was priced at $1.25; second-class hash was on the menu at $1.25, while first-class hash was $1.50. "Ham and eggs" was $2.50 and the quality of the eggs was not guaranteed. In 1864 N. P. Langford paid $36 a week for board at the Gibson House in Helena. The price, however, was reduced to $20 when the flour shortage was over. In Virginia City, when flour was the scarcest, many boarding-houses and restaurants posted signs: Board with bread at meals, $32 per week; board without bread, $22; board with bread at dinner, $25.[7]

The register and records of the California Hotel, opened at Nevada City in the Territory of Montana on October 16, 1864, of which Louis Bahr, formerly of New York City, was proprietor, reveal much information. Board by the week was $12.50, while board and lodging were priced at $15.00. Lodging accommodations consisted of a cot in a large bunk-room. Single meals were $1.25. There was a bar connected with the hotel and, from the accounts kept, whiskey played as important a part as food. Ordinary whiskey was $.25 a drink, with the better grades at $.40 and $.50, the cheaper grade apparently being the more popular. An A. J. Gower was a guest at the hotel for three weeks, the records indicating charges of $37.50 for board and $35.00 for

[7] *River Press* (Fort Benton, Mont.), November 23, 1881.

liquor. Credit evidently was liberally granted; one guest running a bill of $188.50, of which he paid $84.75, leaving a balance of $103.75 that was never paid. He partook of from five to twenty-six drinks of whiskey at the bar daily. Bad accounts were transferred to the back portion of the book, designated as the "morgue." One man's account amounting to $78.75 was among the "dead," after which was written in a firm hand: "Gone to Iowa." As to whether or not he ever came back, there is no record.[8]

After the early stampedes, prices became more stable and were lower. The Crystal Hotel in Helena, Montana, on May 14, 1867, was advertising board and room at $8.00, while lodging without meals in the bunk-room was 50 cents a night. Single meals were $.75, while à la carte orders were priced at $.50 for oyster stew, $.60 for steak and the same for several other items.[9]

X

THE CHARACTERS IN THE PAGEANT

IF THE PHASE of American life which is called the mining frontier can be likened to a pageant, surely it deserved the term richly in the colorful array of human beings who flocked into the gold-fields. We might call the play *The Golden West;* the specific location "The Northwest"; and the characters "The World and His Wife." For while, as a rule, men did not bring their families, but left the period of peaceful home life for the time when they should have made their fortunes, women, too, came into the new El Dorado.

In surveying the general make-up of the population in the diggings, certain characteristics stand out rather prominently. It was heterogeneous, including men of every possible type and nationality. In the various camps, the Southerner, Northerner,

---

[8] Register and account book of the California Hotel, Montana State Historical Library, Helena, Mont.

[9] *Helena Weekly Herald,* May 14, 1867.

Easterner and Westerner mingled, each somewhat amused at times at the others' "lingo." There was a large preponderance of men, and those men, as a rule, were quite young. Only youth would hazard the long hard journey across the plains, and even after arriving, the activities were rough and hard, and of such a nature that only youth could survive and make itself a part of the mining community. The average age has been estimated to have been about twenty-five, with only a few over thirty-five. While there were dance-hall girls and prostitutes, there were also some respectable women, who, in certain camps, made up an appreciable number. Apparently more attention has been paid to the women of questionable standing than to those of the other type. Many travelers and observers tell of encountering women, some of whom were dressed in men's clothing, but, as Richardson puts it, "all were of the wretched class." [1]

The inhabitants of the mining camps were much the same. There were grizzled forty-niners, who had panned for gold in California, miners from Australia, diamond-hunters from Brazil and South Africa, and Mexicans dressed in the gaudy colors popular south of the Rio Grande. There were tarheels from the Carolinas, English farmers ruined by high rents and low returns from their land, close-fisted Scotsmen, light-hearted Irishmen, and the enthusiastic German whose blue eyes sparkled as he talked of the golden future. There were sallow and worried merchants, eager-eyed speculators, gentlemen in reduced circumstances, worn and harassed clerks, and followers of the various professions. There were gamblers and toughs from the slums and water-fronts of American cities, outlaws and renegades from the frontier, as well as large numbers of honest workmen and farmers from the villages and cities to the south and east. It was indeed a strange mixture of humanity, a motley crowd who hurried into the mining

---

[1] Richardson, *Beyond the Mississippi*, p. 200. Maggie Bixbie, a well-known prospector, is reported by the Black Hills newspapers from time to time. *Black Hills Weekly Times*, May 27, 1877.

regions of the Northwest with bare hands and high hopes to dig for gold.

Among the thousands of gold-seekers, scarcely two men could be found who were dressed alike. All types of clothing were represented, from buckskin to broadcloth. Many wore their native costumes, while among the Americans the red or blue flannel shirt, high boots with a wide variety of colored tops, buckled-up trousers, broad-brimmed slouch hats, and heavy cloaks or pea-jackets prevailed. The Missourian, with his white wool hat and corduroys and red woolen shirt trimmed with blue anchors, added variety. There were men dressed in the height of fashion and others who had no objection to being seen in the most ragged of garments. No man was judged in the mining camps by his dress. Hardened women, richly dressed, mingled with the crowd, apparently proud of being recognized as of dubious character, but determined to share the golden harvest.

The Chinese played some part in the advance of the miner's frontier in the Northwest. They were to be found in most of the camps, although forewarned, as a rule, to keep away as long as the claims were productive. While not as proficient in the use of machinery as the white miners, their patience and industry enabled them to extract a great deal of gold from the abandoned claims. They also operated restaurants and laundries. There was a feeling of hostility toward them because of their alleged lowering of living standards. It was said that they could live on as little as twenty-five cents a day, their food consisting of rice, bread, and skunk-cabbage. They were looked up as inferiors by the whites and were discriminated against, attacks and outrages sometimes being inflicted upon them. It is difficult to estimate their numbers in the rapidly shifting mining population. One writer puts the number in the Montana gold camps in 1869 at eight hundred.[2]

[2] *San Francisco Daily Bulletin* (San Francisco, Cal.), May 19, 1865; June 23, 1866.

Some of the Orientals came directly from China, although most of them probably came from California. They were usually brought into the camps in small groups by a Chinese contractor who provided the outfit and paid expenses. The Yong Wo Company operated in Idaho and Montana. A Virginia City editor late in 1872 under a news-heading "Chinese Slavery in Montana" said: "The system is in full operation here. Most of the Chinamen who come to Montana are coolies owned and controlled by Chinese in California. A healthy young Chinese is marketed for from 400 to 600 dollars while one of extraordinary ability is worth 800 to 1,000 dollars." [3] During the Black Hills stampede, an observer in Cheyenne, Wyoming, in the spring of 1877 said: "John Chinaman still continues to arrive here and depart for the Hills as quietly as the Arabs. He will work the played out claims and make them pay long after the white man has left." [4]

Early in 1866, the territorial legislature of Idaho passed a law requiring every Oriental operating claims in the gold-fields to pay a tax of five dollars a month. The law was so drawn that if the tax was not paid promptly, the property could be sold on three hours' notice. Although the law was later declared unconstitutional, the tax was collected and the Chinese operators were frequently robbed by fake tax-officials. Chinese in Montana were taxed by a law that required all male persons operating a laundry to pay fifteen dollars a quarter. Governor Ashley declared the tax oppressive and unjust. Although the yellow man ordinarily attended strictly to his own business and was quite unoffensive, feeling became so keen in some of the camps at times that race riots took place and the Chinese population was compelled to flee to the Hills. While every race and nationality were represented in the mining population, very few Negroes migrated to the camps.

[3] *Montanian* (Virginia City, Mont.), December 29, 1872.
[4] *Cheyenne Daily Leader*, April 23, 1877.

XI

THE CALAMITY JANE MYTH

MARTHA JANE CANARY, commonly known as Calamity Jane, has become a legendary figure of the mining-camp era in the Northwest. Since her death in Deadwood in 1903, and particularly in recent years, she has been depicted by numerous writers [1] and even in moving pictures, as a picturesque and romantic border character, a "heroine of the plains," having most of the qualities of the good Samaritan and of a feminine Robin Hood. She is, as a well-known historian familiar with her life and activities has said, "almost in the class of Paul Bunyan and of old Hugh Glass." [2] It is obvious that much has been said and written about this woman by those who have had little knowledge of Calamity Jane herself or of the period in which she lived. Many of the stories are pure fabrications and have little or no historical basis. Apparently many of the tall tales that have developed had their origin in a little leaflet, "Life and Adventures of Calamity Jane," written by herself in 1896 for publicity purposes when she was on exhibition in various dime museums. Written many years after her active life on the Plains was over, it was thoroughly embued with the frontier characteristic of exaggeration.

The principal facts regarding her early life have been fairly well established. In her leaflet account she claims to have been born in Princeton, Missouri, May 1, 1852, the eldest of six children. Her mother, Charlotte Canary, was a coarse, good-looking woman who drank, smoked, and cursed in public, while her father, Robert Canary, was an amiable young farmer of very ordinary

[1] Duncan Aikman, *Calamity Jane, The Lady Wildcat* (New York, 1927); Estelline Bennett, *Old Deadwood Days* (New York, 1935); Edna La Moore Waldo, *Dakota* (Caldwell, Idaho, 1936); Lewis F. Crawford, *Rekindling Campfires* (Bismarck, N. Dak., 1926); Frank L. Wislack, *Wild Bill Hickok* (New York, 1926); *Sunset Magazine*, July, 1922; *Literary Digest*, November 14, 1933.
[2] Paul C. Phillips, "The Life and Adventures of Calamity Jane," *Frontier and Midland* (Missoula, Mont., Summer, 1936), p. 314.

ability. According to one story, he had picked up his wife in an Ohio "bawdy house" and had married her to reform her, a task at which he apparently had little success.[3] The father and mother quarreled constantly, and it is said that the citizens of the little frontier town of Princeton were somewhat shocked at the bold auburn-haired Charlotte, who flirted so openly. The family migrated to Montana during the gold rush of 1865, and the myth of Calamity Jane had its genesis very soon after.

There are various stories regarding the activities of the Canary family after arriving in Montana. One is that the father died and Martha Jane and her mother laundered clothes in the gold camp at Blackfoot. Another is that her father and mother were divorced or separated and Charlotte started a brothel, becoming Madame Canary, calling her place the "Bird Cage." A third account states that the mother married a second husband and moved to Salt Lake City. According to Jane's account, she and her stepfather left Blackfoot in the spring of 1866 after the death of her mother. They went to Salt Lake City, where the stepfather died in 1867. At any rate, it seems generally agreed that Martha Jane was in Salt Lake City in 1867.

After spending some time in various portions of Wyoming, Jane relates in "Life and Adventures of Calamity Jane" of following the grading camp of the Northern Pacific Railroad until 1870, when she joined the army of General Custer as a scout at Fort Russell, going from there to Arizona on a military campaign against the Indians. It was at this time that she started to wear men's clothing. She had many adventures as an army scout, was sent on numerous dangerous missions, and said of herself: "I was considered the most reckless and daring rider and one of the best shots in the western country." Located at Fort Sanders, Wyoming, until the spring of 1872, she was ordered to the Mus-

[3] Some say that Martha Jane was born in Ohio and came to Princeton as a child. There is also a difference of opinion as to the year of her birth, several writers putting it at 1850.

selshell country during the Nez Percé war, the campaign lasting until the fall of 1873. It was at this time that she claimed to have been christened Calamity Jane by a Captain Egan, after she had saved his life in an Indian ambush. Later she was ordered to the Black Hills with troops sent to protect the miners from the Sioux Indians while the area was under controversy. She wintered at Fort Laramie, and, if she had not been confined to the hospital at Fort Fetterman after a long and dangerous mission as a bearer of despatches, during which time it had been necessary to swim the Platte River, she might have been in the Battle of the Little Big Horn in which Custer's command was wiped out.

She claims to have met J. F. (Wild Bill) Hickok at Fort Laramie in June, 1876, and that they came to Deadwood together. Within a few months, according to her booklet, Calamity visited every camp within a radius of a hundred miles, and rode a pony express between Deadwood and Custer City, a distance of fifty miles and one of the most dangerous routes, on which many riders were killed and robbed. "Being a well-known rider and a good shot," she says, she was not molested. She was in Deadwood when Bill Hickok was shot by the desperado, Jack McCall, and upon hearing the news started looking for the murderer. She tells of finding him in Shurdy's butcher shop, and grabbing a meat cleaver, made him throw up his hands. She "would have killed him on the spot," but had left her gun and belt hanging on the bedpost in her room. Calamity remained in Deadwood until the spring of 1877, during which time, according to her tale, she saved the Overland Mail between Cheyenne and Deadwood from being robbed, and nursed the sick in an epidemic of smallpox and black diphtheria, and in the fall of 1877 helped the Seventh Cavalry construct Fort Meade and the town of Sturgis. She prospected for gold in 1878 and drove bull teams for Fred Evans, as a bull-whacker, between Fort Pierre and the Hills in 1879. During the next few years she covered much of the West, took a homestead, ran a wayside inn, and finally located in Texas in 1885 where she married, living there until 1889. She then ran a hotel in Boulder, Colorado, until 1893, and after another period of travel, arrived again in Deadwood in October, 1896, after an absence of seventeen years.

The above information comes from her own account of her life and much of it, at least in its interpretation, must be regarded as a fabrication of her imagination. She probably visited the various places as indicated, but in a far different capacity than that claimed in her booklet. A modern psychologist would find much of interest in the glamour with which Jane, in her later years, overlaid the drab adventures of her youth, when her only claim to fame was her absolute lack of respectability.

Soon after her arrival in Deadwood, Calamity joined Al Swearengern's mining camp burlesque at the Gem Theater, but was dismissed for improvising lines and for action that was objectionable to her employer. She signed a contract with Kohl and Middleton, operators of a string of dime museums, who thought their public might be interested in seeing a woman scout and Indian-killer. Dressed in a suit of buckskin and with two well-polished guns in her belt, she appeared in the Palace Museum in Minneapolis, later going to Chicago, St. Louis, and Kansas City. She gave a brief lecture on her career and sold her autobiography, but failed to make a success of her new position, because she objected to the attitude of the sight-seers and their jokes at her expense. In the summer of 1901 a show company employed Calamity Jane for the Pan-American Exposition at Buffalo, but here, too, she was a failure, and after a drunken fight, Buffalo Bill paid her fare to Billings, Montana.

During the pathetic last years of her life, she went from place to place in Montana, sold souvenir portraits of herself and panhandled drinks, small change and hand-outs. A newspaperman who interviewed her early in 1902 found that she could not be induced to talk unless well primed with liquor, and even then would only mumble in a mechanical way the stilted lines of her autobiography. She became ill at Bozeman, Montana, and being without friends or funds spent a week in the Gallatin County poor-house. Late in the fall of 1902 she returned to Deadwood ill, worn out by her hard and careless life, dressed in an old shabby coat, the cheapest of hats, a frayed and faded skirt and broken shoes. While her old hang-outs refused to take her in, some friendly Deadwood citizens paid for her drinks, food, and lodging. She replenished her stock of scout pictures, that were becoming difficult to sell, and had a few drunken carousals. She died in a miners' boarding-house in the gold camp of Terraville, in the Black Hills. Her funeral, held at the Methodist Church in Dead-wood, was well attended, and no mention was made of her ir-regular life. A curious crowd followed the funeral procession to the Mount Moriah Cemetery where she was laid to rest beside Wild Bill Hickok.

The crowded and colorful account written by Calamity Jane and later expanded by various writers may seem plausible as long as one remains unfamiliar with the area in which she spent her life, and with the details of its history. But the closer one comes to the actual scenes of the heroic performances she claimed, and the more opportunity one has of examining contemporary records, the less stock can be placed in her personal story. Most of her experiences as recounted, are outside the realm of possibility, and no contemporary will vouch for them. To one who is at all familiar with the United States Army during the period, with its discipline and standards, the claim of Calamity Jane to being a scout and Indian-fighter is absurd and ridiculous. If she went with the vari-ous military expeditions mentioned, she certainly did not go as a soldier or scout, but was smuggled away in a wagon train by bullwhackers, most of whom knew her.

There are also many details of her scout and Indian expe-riences that are unsound geographically, and the story of being christened by Captain Egan as Calamity Jane has many dis-crepancies. Her only traceable relation with Egan was when she laundered his uniform, while he remembered that he ordered her and another woman off the reservation because of their bad influence on the men. It is true that it was during these years that she acquired the name that was so well-chosen, but as to where or why, there is no accurate record. Bill Nye, the humorist of the *Laramie Boomerang*, said it was because "hard luck and Martha Canary always went hand in hand." Jane no doubt was in the Black Hills during the early gold rush, but the stories of scouting and carrying messages have no foundation. About the only chance she had of being with the commands of Generals Custer, Crook, or Terry was to hide away in their wagon trains, an inglorious but possible adventure. She often wore men's clothing, no doubt in order to travel more easily through the West, and was able to dress very successfully in such attire because of her appearance, which contemporaries described as very mannish.

One of Calamity Jane's claims to fame was that she had been the sweetheart of Wild Bill Hickok, and that they came to Deadwood together from Fort Laramie in 1876. The friends of Hickok have always resented the association of his name with that of the notorious Calamity. Frank J. Wilsack, in his book dealing with the life of Hickok, is of the opinion that Hickok was not a paramour of Jane's, and that they did not come to Deadwood together, although it is possible that Hickok knew her. In her old age, Calamity denied the sweetheart episode and told Ellis T. Pierce, who interviewed her in Livingston, Montana, in 1901, that the Hickok story was a lie.

Much has been made by writers of the Calamity who was a big-hearted woman of the frontier, who always helped others, nursed the sick, and looked after the poor. The gold camps tended to neglect their sick in the hurly-burly of fortune-seeking, and there is not much real evidence to prove the tender-heartedness of Calamity Jane. The debunking historians would not deny her a kind heart, one of them being willing to admit that she might have sat up with a sick miner if she could have kept sober long

WILD BILL HICKOK

CALAMITY JANE

SITTING BULL

BUFFALO BILL

PERSONAGES OF THE FRONTIER

enough. At the time of the so-called smallpox epidemic, Calamity Jane was hailed before the Justice of Peace court for robbing a drunken miner of thirty dollars. While some writers say she took the money to keep some of the other girls from getting it, and that it was used to pay the hospital bill of a poor sick girl who was broke, any perusal of the evidence leads to the conclusion that the services of Calamity as a good Samaritan in looking after the sick have been grossly exaggerated.

Jane no doubt shocked Deadwood soon after her arrival in 1876 and there was much written about her in the local press. A citizen who objected to the amount of space devoted to her wrote a letter of protest which was printed in the *Deadwood Daily Champion* in November, 1877. It said in part: "As far as her solid merit is concerned, she is a fraud and a dead give away. A hundred waiter girls or mop squeezers in this gulch are her superior in everything. She strikes out and lays around with a lot of bull-whackers or road agents like an Indian squaw. But everybody in the Hills knows her, largely through newspaper accounts that have made her famous. Her form and features are not only indifferent but are repulsive. It makes me tired to see so much written about such a woman." A newspaper item in the *Black Hills Daily Times* for September 24, 1878, bore out the above contentions and read as follows: "Calamity Jane was a passenger by the outgoing Bismarck coach last evening. Her destination is not known by this reporter but she probably went down to see the boys in blue." A citizen of Deadwood who knew her well in the Black Hills said some years later: "She was a common harlot, large and mannish looking, profane and obscene, whose boast was that she never went to bed sober as long as she had a cent in her pocket." Doane Robinson, for many years secretary and historian of the South Dakota Historical Society, who knew Calamity Jane and collected considerable historical material concerning her life and activities, said: "She was a woman low down even in her own class. Her fame was almost entirely outside the Hills. She was a prostitute of the commonest variety, so vulgar and coarse that she was rarely welcome even in the dives around Deadwood."

When Jane died in 1903, she was in her early fifties but looked twenty years older. The winters and summers she had followed the hard life of the Plains had left her a "worn out strumpet, vile and disgusting." But despite her appearance and her life, she was Deadwood's own, and it did not desert her. She still is an integral part of the miner's frontier and while one can place little credence in her own accounts, she will always remain the personification of those hardened and adventurous women who, since time immemorial, have followed the advance of the various frontiers.

XII

SALOONS AND HURDY-GURDIES

DRINKING was very common in the early mining camps, as liquor was regarded as one of the necessities of life by the average miner or prospector. Places where drinks were dispensed were almost innumerable. In addition to the regular saloons, every hotel, gambling-house, and billiard hall had its bar, while many dance and concert halls derived most of their income from the sale of drinks. A prominent variety house in Idaho City carried this announcement in the local press: "Good music, plenty of whiskey and cigars and the prettiest girls in town." [1] Saloons and drinking establishments were important as social centers for the miners and were about the only places in camp where a stranger could find free companionship. There apparently was no stigma whatsoever connected with getting "decently drunk." Whiskey was the favorite drink and was usually taken straight, at one gulp, followed perhaps by a chaser of water. The purity of the liquor at times may have been questionable, since many observers speak of the "villainous concoctions" that were sold. Some of the

---

[1] *Idaho World*, March 25, 1865.

saloons were operated by honest men, but many owners and their bartenders did not hesitate to dispense with the scales and to take goodly pinches of dust from the extended pouches as the customers approached the last stages of intoxication.

Late in February, 1867, there were fourteen saloons, three billiard saloons, and three wholesale liquor establishments operating in Helena, Montana, and in 1878 a directory of the same place indicates twenty-two places where liquor was retailed, and three breweries.[2] In the spring of 1877 a Deadwood newspaper carried advertisements of seven saloons, ten combination places where drinks were sold, and two wholesale liquor houses.[3] Saloons often had interesting and colorful names, some of which were The Eldorado, The Happy Hour, The Miner's Delight, The Nugget, The Exchange, and The Magnolia.

The amount of liquor used in the gold camps was apparently enormous. A government official coming to Fort Benton on one of the early steamboats in the spring of 1866 told of the great piles of barrels and cases of intoxicants waiting to be loaded for transportation overland to Helena and Virginia City. The books and records of Davis, Sperling and Company of Virginia City show how important liquors were in their sales. A typical purchase was recorded on October 27, 1869: one case of bitters, $17.50; four and one-half quarts of whiskey, $22.50; one pair of blankets, $15.00. The register and records of the Gibson House in Helena indicate that the whiskey bills of the patrons were large, one guest taking as many as thirty drinks daily. Vigorous young men of the type found in the boom towns evidently could drink enormous amounts without ill effects, but the evils attendant on hard and continuous drinking were by no means absent.

The story is told of two travelers on their way to the Colorado gold-fields late in May, 1859, who stopped at a stage station not far from Denver City. Being hungry, they looked around for a

[2] *Helena Weekly Herald*, February 27, 1867.
[3] *Deadwood Daily Champion*, April 23, 1877.

place to obtain food. On a creek crossing beside the road, they saw a small tent bearing a sign "Groceries" in large letters. Possessing keen appetites, they awakened the melancholy merchant who was sleeping soundly between two whiskey barrels. After making inquiries about food and finding the merchant did not have what they wanted, they finally asked the man what he did have. "I have sardines, pickled oysters, smoking tobacco, and, stranger, I've got some of the best whiskey you have ever seen since you was born," was the answer.[4]

Wherever miners congregated, the bottle was present, a typical statement being: "After the whiskey flask went around, we breakfasted." In a combination saloon and gambling-house in Helena was posted the following sign: "Don't forget to write home to your dear old mother. She is thinking of you. We furnish paper and envelopes free, and have the best whiskey in town." Many saloons installed reading-rooms and museums to attract patrons.

Along with the saloon and gambling-house, and often operating in combination with them, was the hurdy-gurdy or public dance-house. Occupying a large room or hall, with a well-stocked bar at one end, an orchestra at the other, and good-looking young girls available for dancing, the hurdy-gurdy was an established institution in the gold camps and a very popular place of amusement and recreation for the miners. While there was no entrance fee and no charge for dancing, the patron, at the end of each dance, was supposed to take his partner to the bar and buy her a drink. Whiskey was fifty cents a glass, so each dance cost the miner a dollar, half of which went to the proprietor and the other half to the girl. The shorter the dances, the more revenue for the owner. The places were open most of the night and although a certain decorum was publicly preserved, these crude and informal establishments, catering as they did to the rougher elements of the population, and operated under circumstances and conditions conducive to excessive drinking and general immorality, were often

[4] Richardson, *Beyond the Mississippi*, pp. 161-2.

severely criticized and were soon in more or less disrepute among the better elements of society.

While the various mining-camp editors were not generally reformers and ordinarily had little to say about the accepted activities of the camps, there appeared in the press from time to time some reference to the hurdy-gurdy. Early in October, 1864, an editor of Virginia City, in commenting upon events, said: "Hurdy-gurdy dance houses are now all the go and one of the main places of amusement among the boys. There are four in full blast in Virginia City and the same number in Nevada City and from the patronage they receive, we infer that money is plentiful." [5] At Summit City, a camp not far from Virginia City, a public meeting was held on January 6, 1865, at which a resolution was passed to the effect that the hurdy-gurdy houses were injurious to the welfare of the community and that every effort should be made to maintain peace and harmony there. About the same time a Helena editor severely indicted the hurdy-gurdy by saying: "Great crowds are in attendance nightly at these places of nocturnal amusement where between bad whiskey and the wiles of the wantons, the sophisticated and unsophisticated are fleeced with unerring regularity." On September 21, 1866, the *Virginia Post* published a letter of complaint, part of which said: "Why don't you pitch into that infernal nuisance on Jackson Street called by some a dance hall? I live a few doors away and every night my rest is broken by shouts of drunken prostitutes and their partners. Sometimes the tumult lasts until morning. Fights are constant and profane and obscene language prevail." While hurdy-gurdies must not be confused with houses of prostitution, it is reasonable to conclude from contemporary evidence that a goodly percentage of the dance-hall girls were lax in their morals. Judging from the newspaper comments, dance-hall girls of German nationality were the most popular. The general sentiment toward the girls of this popular rendezvous is well expressed in the following verse:

[5] *Montana Post*, October 8, 1864.

Bonnie are the hurdies O!
The German hurdy-gurdies O!
The daftest hour that e'er I spent
Was dancing with the hurdies O!

Brothels or houses of ill fame were to be found in every mining camp of any size, although local editors seldom mentioned them, apparently taking their presence for granted. Activities of wanton women, however, became so flagrant and open in Deadwood in the Black Hills of Dakota in 1878 that the editor of the *Deadwood Times* wrote an editorial pleading for the regulation of the social evil by licensing such places, as was successfully being done in Cheyenne, Wyoming, not far away. He went on to say: "A monthly fine or license fee not only replenishes a depleted city treasury, but has a most salutary effect in driving women of the street out of town or into the house of a responsible Madame." [6]

XIII

GAMBLERS AND GAMES OF CHANCE

GAMBLING was perhaps the master passion of the miner, and along with the saloon, dance-hall, and brothel were the ever-present games of chance. They went on day and night and in every camp could be heard the well-known cry: "Make your game, gentlemen, make your game." While some of the operators of gambling establishments were no doubt "clever villains," many of them were honest men who refused to tolerate crooked playing of any kind. But even in the best places the patron knew when he went into a game that there was a percentage against him. There were certain games, however, that were regarded as unfair and the territorial legislature of Montana passed a law declaring some of them illegal. Those enumerated in the law were three-card monte, thimble-rig game, patent-safe game, black and red, two-

[6] *Deadwood Daily Times*, April 28, 1878.

THE HURDY-GURDY HOUSE AT VIRGINIA CITY
Albert D. Richardson, *Beyond the Mississippi*, 1867.

BUCKING THE TIGER

A faro game at Cheyenne, Wyoming. *Frank Leslie's Illustrated Newspaper*, 1877.

card box at the fair, and the strap game. The law was not always enforced, however, and in the other territories almost anything went.

Faro was probably the squarest and the most popular game played in the camps. It was considered respectable and dignified, the percentage for the house was usually less, and the player had some chance of winning part of the time. A faro bank lay-out consisted of a pack of cards in a metal box exposing the face-card. On the table or faro board were painted the cards of the deck, from the ace to the king. The player bet by placing his chips on the card chosen to win or lose and the dealer slipped off the top card, exposing the one underneath that decided the result. A considerable number of players could be accommodated in a game, each bet involving the turn of one or two cards. A miner wishing to enter a faro game, or "buck the tiger," as it was sometimes called, handed his buckskin poke of gold-dust to the dealer, who placed it in a rack containing twenty to thirty compartments. A slip was placed in the rack with the poke each time chips were purchased, the cashier or barkeeper figuring them up when they were cashed in at the end of the game. There was sometimes loss of dust in handling and it was a common sight early in the morning, to see small boys or bummers gathering up the sweepings of the saloons and gambling-houses, from which they extracted the dust.

For those who preferred other games of chance, there was three-card monte, and rondo, a game in which the player, using eight small balls, attempted to roll an even number into a pocket in a pool-table. A dice game called chuck-a-luck was also popular and in the larger places there were roulette wheels and the Chinese game of fan-tan. Some of the games combining skill with luck were stud and draw poker, euchre, and whist. Every possible type of confidence game was used, including loaded dice, marked cards, and the famous shell game. The average three-card monte table in a gambling-house was figured to bring in at least one hundred dollars a day.

There were many well-known gamblers in the Northwest, some of whom were Allen Hankins, a notorious Chicago gambler who operated a house in Virginia City during the early gold boom, and Jack Hensley, who with his wife, the famous Josephine Hensley, better known as "Chicago Joe," operated a variety theater and gambling-house in Helena that was celebrated throughout the West. There was Dan Floweree, owner and manager of the popular Exchange Saloon and Gambling House in Helena. He conducted a high-class place, that was straight and honest and was noted for its poker games involving big money.

In the Black Hills were to be found such well-known gamblers as Wild Bill Hickok, California Jack, Johnny Otis, and Bedrock Tom. One of the best-known gamblers and faro dealers on the miner's frontier was Alice Tubbs, better known as Poker Alice. Coming to America from England as a small girl, she is said to have graduated from a southern woman's college, later marrying Frank Duffield, a mining engineer, who worked in Colorado until his death by an explosion. Taking up gambling in order to support herself, she married W. G. Tubbs, a professional gambler of good reputation, and together they made the mining camps of the West. It is reported that she broke the faro bank at Silver City, New Mexico, cleaning up six thousand dollars in one night. She became a familiar figure in Helena, Virginia City, Denver, and Idaho City, finally coming to Deadwood during the Black Hills rush. There she dealt faro for Bedrock Tom, usually working the "graveyard shift" from midnight until six in the morning when life was most hectic and the miners plunged most wildly. She smoked long black cigars and became a famous Deadwood character. Whenever she make a stake, she went to New York to spend it and, like most gamblers, spent her last years in poverty.

The professional gambler, quiet of manner and soft of tongue, was often the best-educated individual in the camp. He dressed expensively and neatly in linen and broadcloth. He was entertaining in conversation, seldom lost his temper, and never drank while playing. He was a good loser and could play his last dollar and watch the cards come up without flickering an eyelash. As a Deadwood editor once said, "Professional gamblers seldom commit suicide unless it's a woman." Most gamblers and keepers of gambling-houses were open-handed to those that were down and out. A miner once made this observation: "If I were broke I'd rather ask a gambler for a lift than anyone else." The early mining camps knew few social distinctions, and if a man was on the level and played the game fairly, he could earn his living by digging gold or playing poker, with no one caring which. The search for gold attracted the bold and aggressive individual whose chances of making a worth-while find were never more than one to ten. The gold-seeker, therefore, was playing a long game of chance himself and had much in common with the man who played the green cloth.

XIV

CULTURAL LIFE

THE MOBILE population of the gold camps, consisting largely of men, a majority of whom were of the laboring class, leading a life of hard physical toil, with poor food and bad living conditions, and with interesting companionship and mental stimulus reduced to a minimum, was badly in need of relaxation. This it often secured by a liberal patronage of the saloon, gambling-house, hurdy-gurdy, and brothel. The inhabitants, coming as they did from various portions of the country and of the world, many of them of good family, bringing with them the habits, customs and thinking of their former homes, were compelled to adopt a code of morals and a philosophy reconciling their previous backgrounds with their new conditions and circumstances of life. Standards of behavior are relative, making the moral status of the mining frontier difficult to appraise, and placing it beyond the range of generalization. Much depends upon what the observer is looking for, and his point of view. It would be difficult to apply the standards of conduct that prevailed in the older areas of the United States to the new communities appearing in swift succession on the mining frontier. There one found much profanity, the miner being inclined to curse almost unconsciously. There was much reckless-ness and debauchery on the part of certain groups. Drinking and gambling were more or less taken for granted, and a man's stand-ing was not affected by either. The commercially amorous woman plied her trade with the sanction of the populace. Life in the mining camps was turbulent and crude because of the circum-stances which created it, and there was no disgrace in personal combat in the early years, nor even in murder, provided both parties had engaged in the encounter willingly and no unfair ad-vantage was taken.

The rough side of mining life has probably been overempha-sized, or perhaps the scene has failed to receive a proper balance because of lack of attention to the stable elements and activi-ties of the camps. There is much evidence to indicate that the comparative wildness of the western communities, as observed by some, was less apparent to its contemporaries than it has been to later generations. Samuel Bowles, editor of a newspaper in puri-tan Massachusetts, writing in 1865 while on a trip through the West, said, "I see less drunkenness: I see less vice here in the towns of the border and the Rocky Mountains than I see at home in Springfield."[1] An Englishman who visited Denver in 1867, after commenting upon the gambling-houses and much "fast life," praised the respectability and decorum of the citizens and reported the place as orderly as any town he had ever been in.[2] A. K. McClure, a well-known traveler, affirmed the report in 1869.[3]

The more superficial travelers and observers were inclined to report the unusual and abnormal features of life in the mining camps. The society in many ways was crude, and often unattrac-

[1] Bowles, *Across the Continent*, p. 50.
[2] John White, *Sketches from America* (London, 1870), pp. 313-4.
[3] A. K. McClure, *Three Thousand Miles Through the Rockies* (Philadelphia, 1869).

tive, while there were individuals who were violent, sordid, and obnoxious in their actions. The appearances of many made it easy for the observer to misjudge them. A minister of the gospel, A. M. Hough, connected with the early Methodist church in Montana, while on the way with a friend from Helena to Prickly Pear to conduct religious services, was compelled to stop over night at a place called Daly's Ranch, where he and his companion slept in a bar-room. They witnessed much drinking, gambling and profanity. The minister had not been in Montana long, and as he looked over the rough group, many of whom wore long beards and were armed with knives and revolvers, feared for his life. He later said, "I did not know the miners as I do now, or I would have known that I had nothing to fear." At bedtime, when the minister read a few verses aloud from the Bible, profanity ceased, there was respectful silence, and a few miners knelt as the brief service was ended with prayer.

While an examination of the local press reveals various reports of crime, vice, and debauchery, and of the exploits of ruffians, such accounts are infrequent. There were many good men in the camps and newspaper evidence of stability was not lacking. An Idaho editor in the gold district of the Boise Basin in describing the holiday season of 1864 said: "Christmas here was a decided success. The town was filled with miners and the day passed quietly and pleasantly without disturbances of any kind." [4] On July 6, 1867, another editor of Idaho City, in commenting on the town's Fourth of July celebration, observed that the city government was quite effective and that "rogues and rioters had little show." [5] Many such accounts were to be found in the various gold camp newspapers. The editor of the *Montana Post* of Virginia City, writing in June, 1865, describing the mining population, said: "The outstanding characteristics of our people are enterprise, restless activity and contempt of danger and privation.

[4] *Idaho World*, December 31, 1864.
[5] *Boise News*, July 6, 1867.

Hospitality is general and unaffected. There is a sort of rough, though genuine, courtesy much in vogue among Montanians that makes them excellent companions in danger or hardship." [6]

As a whole, the mining population possessed many admirable qualities and a certain chivalry toward women was noticeable. Contemporary records may be searched in vain for accounts of outrages committed upon white women by miners, although women were present in all the gold camps. One miner journeyed from Central City, Colorado, to Bannack City in Grasshopper Gulch, Montana, in the summer of 1863. In his diary he told of an offer of two hundred and fifty dollars per month to tend bar in a saloon and billiard hall in the new Montana diggings. He made the following comment: "I do not intend to sell whiskey for a living. There may be money in it, but I don't like the business and the associations connected with it." [7]

The cultural life of the stable population in the mining camps of the Northwest was interesting and vigorous, especially in the larger places where considerable numbers of substantial business and professional men gave it support. The majority of settlements had literary, lyceum, or library associations that gave public programs consisting of essays, lectures, debates, musical numbers, and short plays, often repeating them in near-by camps. The editor of the *Montana Post* on December 31, 1864, recorded the holding of a "terrific debate" by the library association on the subject: "Resolved, that the Love of Woman has had more influence upon the Mind of Man than the Love of Gold." Virginia City also boasted a Young Men's Literary Association that scheduled regular meetings with commendable programs. The first issue of the *Helena Herald* in the autumn of 1866 [8] carried an announcement of a mass-meeting to organize a lyceum association. One of its early musical and literary offerings included on

[6] *Montana Post*, June 28, 1865.
[7] N. W. Webster, "Journal," MS, Montana State Historical Society, entry for October 22, 1863.
[8] *Helena Weekly Herald*, November 15, 1866.

the program a series of songs by Mr. Bartlett, a local member who opened the exercises with a song of his own composition, "Oh, Sweetheart of Mine." According to the report, this "delighted all lovers of music and elicited repeated applause." The program closed with the song, "Roses Are Falling One by One." There was also a one-act play and an essay on the Constitution of the United States, "scholarly and eloquent, showing an accurate knowledge, and just appreciation of the merits, defects and dangers of our type of government." A discussion period was scheduled at the end, in which those present were allowed to participate. This program was open to the public, cards of admission selling for one dollar. A lecture club was organized at Idaho City in November, 1864, and an active literary society was holding meetings in Denver early in 1865.[9]

Many of the miners were men of education who were interested in good books, magazines, and other reading material. J. H. Morley, one of the early gold-seekers at Bannack City, told in his diary of ordering books and magazines from Salt Lake City and of reading the novels of Sir Walter Scott to his companions during the long winter evenings.[10] Library associations were popular and active in the mining towns, giving programs to raise money and sponsoring the collecting of books for general library use. A local book-store in Idaho City was operating a circulating library of some two thousand volumes in the various Idaho camps as early as 1866, a local newspaper carrying the following statement: "Books and newspapers are much cheaper and better companions during the long winter evenings than are likely to be met with in the streets or barrooms of the city. Patronize the library." [11] The library association at Helena was exceptionally active, raising several thousand dollars during its early years for books and magazines. Practically all of the larger mining camps had some

[9] *Idaho World*, November 12, 1864.
[10] Morley, "Diary," entry beginning September 21, 1862.
[11] *Boise News*, October 6, 1863.

facilities for the loaning or renting of books, magazines and newspapers at moderate charges. The *Helena Herald* of November 15, 1866, carried an advertisement of "Fenton's Saloon and Reading Room."

One of the most popular means of recreation in the gold camps was dancing and it was made use of by all classes. The more stable male population, not being satisfied with the hurdy-gurdy dance houses and the crude and rough variety halls, organized their own dancing clubs, holding informal dances at frequent intervals, at which attendance was restricted to actual members and to those who held cards of admittance, given or sold only to close friends. Numerous balls were held on Thanksgiving, Christmas, New Year's, and St. Patrick's Day, and according to newspaper reports, must have been well attended and thoroughly enjoyed. The editor of the *Boise News* of Idaho City on October 13, 1863, announced that the Pioneers, a local organization, would hold their first annual ball at Magnolia Hall that night. It was expected to be the "grandest affair of the kind that ever took place in the territory." The grand Fourth of July ball held at Boise City in 1865 had more than seventy-five couples in attendance and the music was said to be excellent. The party was "hugely" enjoyed, many of those in attendance "deserving special compliments for their taste and elegant toilets." [12] The Excelsior Dancing Club was organized at Helena, Montana, November 15, 1866, holding its first dance late in December.

In Deadwood in the Black Hills mining area of the Territory of Dakota in 1876, a group of respectable young men, most of whom were bachelors, were dissatisfied with the dancing facilities offered by the Melodeian, Bella Union, and Gem variety halls. They organized a dancing club, using considerable care in their choice of members. The first dance, held in the dining-room of the I.X.L. Hotel, was claimed by some to be the first polite social affair held in the camp. The dance had just begun with a quad-

[12] *Ibid.*, July 8, 1865.

rille when a "painted lady" pushed her way rudely into the room, and announced in a loud voice that her "man" was there, and that she had as much right to attend the "high-toned affair" as he. She challenged the floor committee to put her out. Before she could be ejected, the dance broke up in confusion. The club dances continued throughout the winter, and the man responsible for the disturbance did not make his appearance again. Even mining camp society learned early to apply indirect methods of control.[13] A deadwood editor reporting the New Year's ball of 1877 said: "The New Year's ball at the General Custer House was a more recherché and brilliant affair and one of the most enjoyable gatherings ever assembled here. The beauty and gallantry of Deadwood and surrounding localities were well represented." [14]

There were amateur theatricals in many of the camps, a home-talent performance being advertised to be held at Parker's Hall in Virginia City on the evening of October 22, 1864. There were traveling phrenologists, ventriloquists, magicians, and bell-ringers, who made the camps at intervals, and there was a demand for traveling lecturers. Prize-fights and wrestling bouts were popular and were patronized by all classes. In September, 1864, Joe Riley and Tom Foster fought twenty-six rounds for a purse of seven hundred and fifty dollars at Nevada City in Montana, Riley winning the bout.[15] On New Year's Day Con Orem and Dalsey Marley of New York fought for the championship of Montana. An Idaho editor early in August, 1864, announced that a circus was scheduled to show at Idaho City and hoped that it would be liberally patronized. It was back again for the Fourth of July the following year, so it had evidently proved successful. The Great Western Museum and Circus made many of the mining camps in the Northwest in the spring and summer of 1867.

[13] Bennett, *Old Deadwood Days*, pp. 254-5.
[14] *Black Hills Pioneer*, January 6, 1877.
[15] *Montana Post*, September 10, 1864.

According to the advertising, it was "the greatest moral show of the age, with a menagerie containing the greatest congress of animals, birds and reptiles on earth." [16]

There were horse-racing and cock-fighting and dog fights, with prizes running into the hundreds of dollars. There were checker and whist tournaments that were well attended, with the admission fee at one dollar. Ice and roller skating, sleighing and coasting parties were popular, with contests of various sorts keeping interest keyed to a high point. The sliding club of Placerville, Idaho, challenged the club from Idaho City whose sled, the "Wild West" won over her opponent's entry, the "Flying Cloud." [17] Gymnastic organizations were active, the Keystone Gymnastic Club of Virginia City giving a well-attended program in May, 1865. Many of the camps had bands and musical organizations. The *Montana Post* of Virginia City in the fall of 1864 carried an advertisement announcing that W. C. Waugh's Brass and Quadrille Band was prepared to furnish music for processions, parties, dances, concerts, serenades, or for any affair where a band or orchestra was needed. [18] Raffles were held with prizes ranging from five hundred dollars on down to much smaller sums. A lottery of gold nuggets was held at one of the billiard halls in Helena, in the summer of 1865. More than four hundred tickets were sold at ten dollars each, and the drawing for the two nuggets, one valued at $2,073 and the other at $110, was made August 13th. Bath-houses were constructed at various points where there were medicinal springs for pleasure-seekers and invalids, one of the most popular being located close to Idaho City. An excellent bathing-pool was also constructed there that was filled during certain seasons and on holidays. Dancing schools were well patronized, as were singing schools during the winter months.

[16] *Helena Weekly Herald,* July 17, 1867.
[17] *Boise News,* February 2, 9, 1864; *Idaho Statesman,* December 20, 1864.
[18] *Montana Post,* September, October, 1864.

Each of the larger camps had its aristocracy or "400," although there would probably have been objection to the term. Dinner parties were held, at which tables were conventionally set with fine linen, cut glass and silver, china, candles, and flowers, and the guests were served with wine, roast bear or buffalo meat, and other foods. These groups had their own gatherings at which they enjoyed piano music and singing, had picnics, rode horseback, played tennis and held sleighing, skating, and porch parties.

Although far removed from cultural centers, a vigorous cultural interest was prevalent. There were meetings in homes and business places to discuss questions of the day. Interesting conversations took place in the business place of George Chrissman at Bannack City and W. G. Pfout's Merchandise Emporium in Virginia City, where the topics were not only current problems, but also points of philosophy, religion, history, and the classics. Of the resourceful and intelligent men who had thronged to the gold camps, many were doubtless above the average. They were well educated, and were eager to build a mental, as well as a physical life on the mining frontier.

Fraternal orders or lodges, with their idealism of brotherhood, pushed westward with the advance of the frontier. They constituted an important tie of unity and stability as members of the same secret societies became known to each other and chapters were formed in the camps. By 1866 there were strong Masonic organizations in Idaho City, Placerville, Pioneer, and Boise City, in the Territory of Idaho, and at Helena and Virginia City in Montana. Some observers claimed that Masonry played a considerable part in the establishment of law and order in the mining centers of the Northwest. While such influence is difficult to estimate, it is no doubt true that some of the leaders in the law enforcement movement were members of that order. Masonry later became strong in the Black Hills mining area.

Another active organization in the gold camps was Fenianism, local chapters of which were formed in many of the mining centers. There were very strong units of this organization at Virginia City, Helena, Idaho City, and Owyhee. Editorials appeared in the local press from time to time on Fenianism and on January 3, 1867, the Lyceum Club of Helena, Montana, held a well-attended debate on the subject: "Is it Policy for the United States to encourage the Fenian Organization in its efforts for the Liberation of Ireland from the British Rule?" On Saint Patrick's Day in 1869 more than twelve hundred members paraded at Helena and Fenian feeling apparently reached its high point.[19]

The Odd Fellows and Good Templars were active in the various camps. The early lodges took charge of funerals of members and participated in the social and charitable activities of the communities. They gave balls and dances and held benefits and fairs to raise money for their projects. A ball conducted by the Masonic lodge at Idaho City late in 1864 brought in more than thirteen hundred dollars and was described by the local press as "the most brilliant affair ever witnessed in Idaho."[20]

XV

EDUCATION

ALTHOUGH children were not numerous in the mining camps, and provisions for education at public expense lagged, as families gathered in the various towns there arose a demand for educational facilities and contemporary records indicate the early establishment of private or subscription schools. Three subscription schools were in operation in and near Idaho City in the autumn of 1863, one of which had as many as twenty-one pupils. The tuition

[19] The plan of the Fenians was a simultaneous uprising of the Irish in England, Ireland, and Canada for Irish liberty and an invasion of Canada by members in the United States, who were to render assistance in the movement. The organization was active in the Middle West with strong centers at Chicago and Sioux City, Iowa. The Fenians in Idaho and Montana had in mind the possible invasion of British Columbia. *Idaho Weekly Statesman*, April 22, 29, May 6, 1866; *Idaho World*, May 28, June 4, 1866; *Helena Herald*, January 5, 1867.

[20] *Idaho Statesman*, December 29, 1864, April 22, 1866; *Idaho World*, December 31, 1864, May 28, 1866.

charge was one dollar per week. In the fall of 1864 schools were opened in Boise City, with a Mr. and Mrs. Savage conducting a "select school." When Mr. F. B. Smith reopened his day and night school, a local editor called attention to his lessons in penmanship, specimens of his "chirography" being on display for examination. In October, 1864, a school was opened in Boise City that gave special instruction in French and drawing, in addition to the common branches. A Professor Newell held a singing school two times a week at the American Hotel in Idaho City that seemed well attended, and two dancing schools were opened at Boise City. A Mrs. S. E. Robinson was employed to teach a public school at Florence and had six pupils. A census taken of Boise County late in 1864 gave a total population of 15,000 inhabitants, of which 13,500 were men, 1,000 women, and 500 children. J. R. Crittenden was appointed Superintendent of Public Instruction for Idaho Territory in December, 1864, and his first official report indicated that the territory contained 1,239 pupils of school age and three public school-houses.[1]

In the Montana and Dakota gold-fields the development of schools was about the same as in Idaho. A Miss Dunlap was operating a subscription school at Nevada City in the fall of 1864, and a Miss Darling, niece of Governor Edgerton of Montana, was operating one at Bannack. The editor of the *Montana Post* late in October, 1864, printed the following announcement: "We are glad to inform our readers that Professor Thomas J. Dimsdale has opened a school on Idaho Street. A school is essential to a community like ours and parents and guardians are urged to send their children."[2] The next week the editor wrote again on the subject of education. There was apparently some attempt on the part of the citizens of Virginia City to get a building equipped as

[1] Files of the newspapers of the Territory of Idaho. According to the census of 1870 there were 25 schools in Idaho, 21 of which were public. Of the 33 teachers employed, 23 were male and 10 female. There were more than 1,200 pupils in attendance and expenditures had almost trebled over 1866 *U. S. Census Report for 1870*, Compendium, pp. 495-6.

[2] *Montana Post*, October 27, 1864.

a school-house. The editor spoke highly of the efforts of Professor Dimsdale and suggested that he should be employed to teach the school. The project evidently failed, as Dimsdale, on October 10th, was advertising his subscription school in the local press with tuition at $1.50 a week. The following week a visitor wrote a pleasant description of the school, where the pupils were reported to have been "studious, courteous and obedient." The professor was operating a singing school on two evenings a week, beginning at seven o'clock.[3]

In October of 1867 the *Helena Herald* gave a report on educational progress in that area. There were four schools in operation, only one of which was receiving aid from the county. There were five teachers employed, and 132 pupils enrolled. The school operated by Mr. and Mrs. Stone, called the Academy Hill School, had seventy pupils, and while charging a tuition fee of $1.50 a week, expected to reduce it commensurate with the amount of aid that the county would give. A school in the Methodist Church had thirty pupils and the other two had twenty-seven and fifteen respectively.

No sooner had the gold-seekers begun prospecting and digging in the gulches of the Black Hills than schools were established. The *Black Hills Pioneer* early in 1877 carried an advertisement to the effect that a Mrs. John Callison would open a subscription school for three months on Whitewood Creek, parents being "respectfully solicited to enroll their children with her for advancement." Tuition was $1.00 a week. The editor, in referring to the advertisement, said: "We are pleased to call the attention of our readers to this announcement of Mrs. Callison, who is a lady of rare accomplishments. The need of education is growing in Deadwood."[4] The editors of the various newspapers on the mining frontier were interested in schools and education. As a rule, they were free in their comments and were often critical of

[3] *Ibid.*, November 3, December 10, 17, 24, 1864.
[4] *Black Hills Pioneer*, January 6, 1877.

the alleged public indifference to education and to the improvement of schools supported by public taxes. Religious organizations apparently played a very minor part in the support of early
education in the mining camps of the Northwest.

There were at least three attempts made in the early years to
establish schools whose educational offerings included subjects
more advanced than those in the common-school curriculum. In
October, 1864, a Miss F. A. Call and a Mrs. M. J. Pefferlie
announced through the press that they would open a school in
Boise City where they would offer special instruction in French
and drawing to those who desired it, in addition to work in the
common branches. In the spring of 1867 the Boise Valley Seminary was opened in the Baptist Church building at Boise City.
There were five teachers, Reverend H. O. Hamilton, principal, and
his wife, assistant principal. In addition to the common branches,
their offerings included work in vocal and instrumental music,
penmanship, Greek, Latin, French, Spanish, and Italian. The first
term of twelve weeks began April 15, 1867, and it was announced
that boarding arrangements would be included the second term
should it be warranted by the enrollment. The tuition charge was
$5.00 per month for the common branches and $6.00 per month
for each advanced subject. The project must have failed, since
the next year two of the teachers were conducting a school in the
Baptist Church building.

In Virginia City in August, 1865, the editor of the *Montana
Post* announced the arrival of Professor J. B. Patterson, a graduate of Lafayette College, Easton, Pennsylvania, with ten years'
experience as a teacher, who would open a public seminary where,
in addition to the common branches, there would be offered
courses in the German language, vocal music, and in "the higher
branches of an English education." There is no record of the
result of the project.

One of the difficulties confronting teachers of both private and
public schools in the mining camps was the scarcity and the wide

diversity of textbooks. There were few textbooks offered for sale and the ones brought in by parents, who came from all the states of the Union, differed widely. Some of the common books in use were Webster's *Blue Backed Speller*, Ray's *Arithmetic*, and McGuffey's *Readers*, whose selections of "dignity and grace" from the pens of such notables as Shakespeare, Byron, and Wordsworth were studied diligently for the moral lessons involved, as well as for the practice in reading, Wilson's *Readers*, Green's *Introduction to English Grammar*, Hooker's *Physiology*, and a *Comprehensive Geography* by Shaw and Allen. Another popular series was one by Quakenbos, which included books on grammar, composition, rhetoric, physiology, as well as a United States history. The pedagogical procedure of memorization was stressed, the repetition of pages of material by rote being considered a worthy accomplishment. When school opened in Virginia City in the fall of 1864 the only textbooks available for sale were a few copies of Webster's *Blue Backed Speller*. These were soon exhausted at a dollar a copy.

Many of the buildings erected for school purposes were used as social and religious centers as well as for education, thus becoming the scene of mining camp recreation and fun, pious sermons and Sunday-school classes, as well as of class recitations.

XVI

RELIGION

No SOONER had miners and prospectors established their locations than representatives of organized religious bodies appeared to look after the spiritual needs of the new communities. While there was some coöperation and a reasonable amount of support on the part of local inhabitants, much of the impulse and motivation of missionary work came from the older and more densely settled portions of the country.

In the summer of 1863 Archbishop F. N. Blanchet of the

Roman Catholic Church sent two priests, I. Mesplie and A. Z. Poulin, to the Boise Basin of Idaho and within six months they had established churches at Idaho City, Placerville, Centerville, and Pioneer. Their first church was dedicated on November 15, 1863, the other three being completed in time for the celebration of Christmas mass. The Protestant churches were also active in the Idaho area, two ministers by the names of Gift and Kendall holding services there in the summer and early fall of 1865, at Idaho City. Resident work began when Charles S. Kingsley, representing the Methodist Church, came from Portland, Oregon, in November, 1863. The local press announced that he would preach at ten-thirty the following Sunday in Union Hall. "The house will be made warm and comfortable for ladies and children," promised the paper. By spring Kingsley had succeeded in constructing a church building that would seat between four and five hundred people. In the summer of 1864 Michael Fackler, representing the Episcopal Church, arrived at Boise City and by September, 1866, a building 40 feet by 22 feet had been constructed and opened for services. Reverend H. O. Hamilton arrived at about the same time and preached in saloons, tents, and store buildings until he could raise money for the building of a church.

In Montana in 1864 the Episcopal, Methodist, Congregational, Baptist, and Presbyterian churches were active from the first. The dedication of the first Methodist church in Montana was chronicled late in October, 1864, by the following announcement in the local press: "Providence permitting, the first Methodist Episcopal Church of Montana Territory will be dedicated at Virginia City to the worship of God. A general attendance of all lovers of Zion is invited." [1] The building was constructed of split logs, with a dirt roof and had windows of white muslin cloth. The pastor was the Reverend A. M. Hough. Reverend G. F. Smith of the Presbyterian Church and Bishop Tuttle of the Episcopal Church

[1] *Montana Post*, October 29, 1864.

were active in the early years of the Montana gold rush. Sometimes, as in the case of the Presbyterian minister, G. F. Smith, and Reverend Jonathan Blanchard, president of Wheaton College in Illinois, representatives of the various religious groups were sent out by eastern missionary societies to look over the needs of the gold-fields.[2]

The Reverend G. F. Smith arrived in Bannack in June, 1864, losing his trunk on the way. He later said, "I was in my first parish eighteen months with no books except my small English Bible, without notes and comments, and I had the most intelligent and wide awake congregation I ever ministered to." Board was so high that he erected a rude log cabin and prepared his own meals. The work of the Episcopal Church in Montana was well begun by Bishop Daniel S. Tuttle, who preached at Virginia City, Deer Lodge, Missoula, Butte, and Bozeman, with his headquarters at Helena. He lived in a rude cabin, into which the snow drifted through crevices when the thermometer was twenty below zero. There were no church buildings and he was compelled to hold services in saloons or stores, often using a dry-goods box as a pulpit.[3] Reverend Hough reported preaching in a saloon in the Prickly Pear Valley where he was given a gracious welcome by the proprietor, but when he asked a saloon-keeper in Nevada City for permission to use his place of business, he was told he could have it any evening of the week except Sunday, as business was briskest on that night.

The first "sky pilot," using a term sometimes applied by the miners, to come to the Black Hills area was probably the famous character "Preacher Smith," who came from a small Connecticut town where he had been a Methodist minister, to bring the gospel to the gold camps of Dakota. He arrived in Deadwood in the summer of 1876, coming into town with a freighting outfit.

[2] Hailey, *History of Idaho*, p. 117.
[3] Daniel S. Tuttle, "History of the Episcopal Church in Montana," *Contributions*, Montana Historical Society, V, 289-324.

During the week he worked at manual labor at whatever tasks he could find, living frugally and quietly in a log cabin. He preached in the street on Sunday, in Deadwood and in the other gold camps of the vicinity. On Sunday, August 20, 1876, while on his way to Crook City to preach, he was killed by Indians, and his body was brought to Deadwood and buried in the cemetery that was to become famous as the last resting-place of Wild Bill Hickok and, many years later, of the notorious Calamity Jane.

The first record in the local Black Hills press of a church service was dated January 6, 1877, and announced a morning and evening service with Sunday-school to be held the following day in a building "directly opposite the steam sawmill in Deadwood." The Congregational Church was apparently the pioneer church, not only in Deadwood, but in all the Black Hills, and the Reverend L. P. Norcross, who came to Deadwood in November, 1876, was its first minister. He held his first services in a carpenter shop. By July, 1877, the local organization had succeeded by hard work in raising sufficient money for the construction of a church. It was an unattractive frame building, painted a dull gray, whose crude temporary belfry housed the bell from an old Missouri River steamboat that had been presented to the congregation by Captain Beard. Father Lonergan of the Catholic faith celebrated the first mass in Deadwood one Sunday morning in May, 1877. The Congregational Church was used by the ministers of all denominations, with the various services arranged so as to avoid conflict in time. The Reverend A. C. Dill, the Congregational pastor in Deadwood in the early eighties, was the object of criticism and comment when he began to teach the neglected Chinese population English and to give them religious instruction. His pastorate was followed by that of the dignified and steadfast Alexander McConnell, who shocked even hardened Deadwood when he went to the "place" of Hattie Bell, madame of one of the most notorious houses of prostitution in the Black Hills, at her request in order to extend to that "wicked and unchristian woman" a few words of comfort as she lay upon her death-bed. The Reverend R. H. Dolliver of the Methodist Church at Deadwood adopted the policy of reserving the three back rows of pews in his church for the gamblers, loafers, and outcasts, who slipped unobtrusively into their places as the first hymn was sung, often leaving just before, or as, the benediction was being delivered.

The pioneer clergymen in the gold camps of the Northwest were compelled to sacrifice much, and were obliged to live a life involving great risk, privation, and danger in order to minister to their congregations of miners. The actual church membership in the early mining camps was never very large, although considerable financial support was given by non-members. Bishop Tuttle, in describing his experiences in the Montana area, said, "Many people who were not churchmen or churchwomen cast their lot with us and heartily, loyally and generously supported our work." The miners who attended services were generous in their contributions to the collection plates, which were often gold pans. Drawing out their buckskin pouches, they either poured out a quantity of gold-dust on the plate or took out a pinch between the thumb and forefinger, the latter amount being worth from twenty-five to fifty cents.

The church played an active part in social matters, often raising funds for religious and charitable purposes by balls, fairs, benefits, and parties. A circus gave a benefit performance for the Catholic Church at Idaho City in August, 1864, and a short time later another religious body served a "bounteous supper" priced at $1.50, with ice-cream and cake available to those who desired lighter refreshments. Churches gave plays and fairs which were liberally supported by the local communities.

While the majority of the mining population did not belong to a church and probably did not conform to the requirements of any denomination, the average miner had a peculiar attitude toward religion. He may have scoffed at the idea of belonging to a church, but he was seldom sacrilegious. While he was respectful

toward religion and toward ministers, he was often satisfied to
view the church from a distance and not identify himself with any
organized creed. Numerous contemporary accounts show the emo-
tional feeling which seemed prevalent among the population on
the mining frontier toward the church. When the church bell in
Deadwood rang on Sunday morning, many miners, working at
their claims, were accustomed to remove their hats and stand with
bowed heads until the sound died away. In the early days of
Deadwood's history, before the establishment of the variety houses,
a crude "song and dance" music-hall was short on talent. The
management, as a last resort, located a second rate singer who rendered a group of hymns, including "Sweet Spirit," "Hear My
Prayer," "Consider the Lilies," and "I Know That My Redeemer
Liveth." The act became immediately popular with the miners,
who paid a generous admission and showered the stage with gold.[4]

XVII

THE THEATER ON THE MINING FRONTIER

ONE of the cultural ties binding the motley population that poured
into the gold camps was the theater. The miners were keenly
interested in theatrical entertainment of all sorts and gave it their
hearty support. They patronized the early offerings of the dance-
halls, gambling-houses, saloons, and variety theaters. They welcomed visiting circuses, magicians, elocutionists, ventriloquists,
acrobats, variety troupes, and stock companies.

The earliest and crudest form of stage entertainment ordinarily
presented was that of the hurdy-gurdy or dance-hall type. Serving
as a rendezvous along with the saloon, gambling-house, and brothel
for recreation and amusement, the early frontier dance-hall often
staged mixed shows of singing, dancing, and high-kicking acts
to attract patrons. While some of the establishments had a small
stage, many of them had only a movable platform upon which

[4] *Cheyenne Daily Leader*, January 1, 1876.

at various intervals crude and rough vaudeville acts were presented.[1]

During the period when the mining camps were developing,
the variety theater was in general favor throughout the country,
and soon became popular among the hard-working, hard-playing
population on the frontier. Some of the variety theaters were not
far removed from the hurdy-gurdy, but most of them emphasized
their theatrical offerings, often staging plays along with their
mixed entertainment. Scores of such playhouses rang up their
curtains in the boom towns of the mining camps, their lives frequently being as brief as they were merry. Traveling dramatic
companies, with their actor-managers, played the boards in many
of the gold towns with a wide and varied offering of well-known
plays, often remaining in one place for several weeks. While many
of them played in the variety houses, some of them built their own
theaters at central points and followed regular circuits.[2]

Many of the early variety theaters were constructed and operated on about the same plan. On one side or near the entrance was
a bar. If gambling was allowed, the tables were on the other side
and the elevated stage was in the rear. On the sides above the
gambling tables or the bar were galleries, divided into compartments, some of which were made into curtained boxes in which
drinks were served by attractive young girls. At the close of the
usual variety bill or play, if a dance-hall was operated, the wooden
seats were removed and the girls in the show and others employed
by the management danced with the patrons. There was no
charge for dancing, but after each dance the gentleman was expected to take his lady to a bar or to a booth and buy her a drink.
Bottled beer was served in the booths at a dollar a bottle, and
what passed for champagne at five dollars, while drinks were dis-

[1] *Avant Courier* (Bozeman, Mont.), January 10, 1878; *Helena Herald*, October 13, 1867.
[2] Arthur H. Quinn, *A History of the American Drama, to the Civil War*
(New York, 1923), pp. 368-92; *Montana Post*, January 14, 1865, September 15,
21, 1866.

pensed at the bar at from twenty-five to fifty cents, profits from the
sale of liquor reimbursing the management for its free music and
dance floor. The band was instructed to play the dance through
as quickly as possible so as to add to the revenue of the owner.

No sooner had the mining camps of Montana been established
than contemporary records indicate the presence of variety troupes,
home-talent performances, and regular stage plays in abundance.[3]
Early in December, 1864, the Montana Theater was opened in
Virginia City.[4] During 1865 and 1866 this theater offered tri-
weekly performances that included variety bills interspersed with
a considerable number of plays. A new variety house called the
Melodian was opened in 1865.[5] In 1867 the Langrishe Stock Company, under the actor-manager, J. S. Langrishe, established a
theater in Virginia City, appearing there for several weeks twice
a year. Of the many actor-manager stock companies playing legitimate drama in the Northwest in the sixties and seventies, by far
the most active and important was that of Langrishe. Coming from
San Francisco, where he had operated a theater in the fifties, he
and his accomplished wife followed the recoil of the miner's frontier eastward, and opened theaters in Denver, Central City, Virginia City, Helena, White Pine, and Bear River, later going to
Cheyenne. During the Black Hills gold rush, they established
themselves at Deadwood and Central City in the Territory of
Dakota. The company followed a regular circuit, appearing in each
of their theaters from two to four weeks twice a year. The
Langrishe theaters were real playhouses, presenting legitimate
drama, with no dance-hall, bar, or gambling-room attached, and
their doors were never open on Sunday.[6] They attracted the
better type of people, who would not frequent the variety theaters.

[3] *Montana Post*, August 27, September 3, 10, 1864.
[4] *Ibid.*, October 1, 8, 17, November 29, December 10, 17, 23, 31, 1864.
[5] *Ibid.*, June 10, September 16, 23, October 7, 14, 21, 1865.
[6] *Rocky Mountain News* (Denver, Col.), November 12, 1860, April 24, 1861;
Encampment Echo, December 5, 1935; *Salt Lake City Daily Herald*, March 11,
1871; *Deseret News*, July 1, 1863; *Salt Lake City Daily Tribune*, January 4,
1878; *Denver Post*, January 23, 1860, September 23, 1865; *New Northwest*

After the discovery of gold in Last Chance Gulch and the establishment of the new mining camp of Helena, Virginia City declined in importance and Helena became a theatrical center. Leviathan Hall was opened late in 1865 and early in 1866 the People's Theater was established over the Montana Billiard Saloon.[7] In October, 1869, A. J. Sawtelle, an actor-manager of his own troupe, opened a theater in Helena that was active throughout the seventies and early eighties.[8] The best-known variety theater in Helena was the one owned and operated by Josephine Hensley. Although her theater was small, it was constructed in the general style of the combination place, consisting of saloon, gambling-house, and theater.[9]

After the Black Hills gold rush, a large floating population led to the establishment of the theater in Dakota Territory. During the boom Deadwood was the theatrical center of the region and is said to have had more places of amusement than any other town of its size in the United States. Except for some crude song-and-dance programs presented on a makeshift stage at the Melodian Saloon and Gambling Hall, the Bella Union was Deadwood's first variety theater. Constructed as a combination establishment with seventeen curtained boxes facing the stage, it was housed in a log building. Its first seats were wooden slabs fastened to stakes driven into the ground. During the early weeks general admission was $2.50, with reserved seats at $5.00. It had the first piano used in the Hills, an old-fashioned square instrument brought in from Bismarck on the Missouri River by bull

(Deer Lodge, Mont.), February 9, 1876; *Helena Herald*, October 3, 1867, November 12, 1868, August 28, 1869; *Black Hills Daily Times* (Deadwood, D. T.), July 2, 24, 1878; *Cheyenne Daily Leader*, January 2, 1869.

[7] *Owyhee Avalanche*, November 11, 1865, February 23, 1866, March 13, 1867; *Helena Herald*, November 12, 1868; *Madisonian* (Madison, Mont.), June 1, August 2, 1876, July 19, 1877; *Montana Post* (Helena items), July 24, December 11, 1865, January 27, 1866.

[8] *Helena Herald*, October 7, 1869, August 22, September 2, 9, 1878; Program of Sawtelle's Theater, September 27, 1879.

[9] *Daily Independent* (Helena, Mont.), October 26, 1899. Many references to this theater are found in the various Helena newspapers.

train, the trip taking almost two months. Packed to its doors from the opening night, the Bella Union, in its three and a half years of existence, developed a somewhat disreputable name, but presented fairly good variety bills.[10]

Of the many variety houses that came and went in Deadwood Gulch in the hectic seventies and eighties, the Gem, owned and managed by A. E. Swearengen, and famous even in the roaring mining-camp days for its iniquity, was the longest-lived and perhaps the best-known theater of its kind in the West.[11] In the early evening a brass band played outside on the balcony to drum up a crowd. The musicians went inside at eight o'clock, after which the variety show began with singing, dancing, banjo-players, burnt-cork comedians, and high-kicking ladies. The Gem contained living quarters for the girls who worked there, and the careers of its young actresses were strenuous ones. They often increased their incomes by resorting to prostitution, and suicides among them were frequent.

Among the stock companies that played in the mining camps were the Denver Dramatic Troupe, the Boston Company, the John A. Stevens Company, the J. W. Carter Dramatic Company, and the better-known Langrishe, Hasenwinkle, and Katie Putnam players. Each theatrical company needed an extensive repertoire, for frontier audiences were constantly shifting and required a variety of entertainment. Bills were changed daily, each with a full play and an afterpiece. The companies were not large, actors frequently being required to take several parts in a single play. The maintenance of order in the mining theaters catering to a rough population made up largely of men must have tested the courage, as well as the ingenuity, of many a manager.

[10] *Cheyenne Daily News*, January 11, 1876; *Bismarck Daily Tribune*, March 27, 1876; *Black Hills Pioneer*, June 8, 1876, January 6, 15, February 24, March 3, May 26, 1877, February 6, 1878; *Black Hills Daily Times*, January 15, March 3, April 4, 1877; *Black Hills Daily Champion*, June 2, 1877; *Black Hills Weekly Times*, January 6, February 12, 26, 1877, June 1, July 24, 1878; *Lead City Telegraph*, March 31, 1878; "The Black Hills," *Motor Travel*.

[11] Bennett, *Old Deadwood Days*, pp. 105-39.

When one considers the large number of variety bills, the numerous farces and afterpieces presented with the legitimate plays, it is apparent that the preference of the frontier population was decidedly in favor of comedy. In the field of the legitimate drama, the situation was reversed, the preference being divided between sentimental melodrama and tragedy. Some of the more popular plays, judging from the number of times they were presented, were *Camille, East Lynne, The Lady of Lyons, Rip Van Winkle, La Tour de Nesle, Richelieu, The Two Orphans, Uncle Tom's Cabin, Hazel Kirke, Black Eyed Susan, Led Astray, The Octoroon, Joshua Whitcomb, Our American Cousin,* and *The Old Curiosity Shop.* Although Shakespearean productions were not emphasized, *Richard III* and *Othello* were popular, and *The Merchant of Venice, Macbeth,* and *Hamlet* were occasionally offered.

The variety-theater period in the gold camps was a colorful one, with its constantly changing playhouses, its devil-may-care attitude and its absence of outstanding theatrical figures. It was dominated by the actor-manager, who owned his company and often built his theaters. In its crudeness and vigor, it was an integral part of the life of the mining camps. In its contrast between variety programs and the legitimate plays that were popular all over the country, it brought to attention again the twofold character of the population that had invaded the gold frontier—the rough miner who had early forsaken civilization to follow the call of the gold coast of California and the more effete Easterner who had come to Montana and the Dakotas to make his fortune, or, in some cases, to practise his profession.

XVIII

JUSTICE IN THE MINING CAMPS

THE MINING TOWNS of the Northwest drew on the population of many others like them which had known a brief existence. Nat-

urally, the men who depended on what they could take by force
and skill from those who dug for gold, or ran pack trains to bring
in needed provisions, hurried to every new digging. Wherever
treasure was most abundant appeared the worst and the greatest
number of desperadoes.

The gold-fields of the Northwest had hardly been opened when
bands of outlaws, taking advantage of the lack of regular courts,
flocked to the various districts, robbing stage-coaches, especially
those carrying gold, stealing horses and cattle, and murdering
miners. The groups were so well-organized that if a judge, jury,
or miners' association attempted to punish a member, the "gang"
would immediately carry out brutal revenge on those who had
brought the culprit to justice. Towns and often whole areas were
terrorized to such an extent that often there was no attempt at
punishment. In some camps outlaws and ruffians became so numerous that the miners found it necessary to form Vigilance Committees. One of the unique features of the procedure of these
committees was that the action to be taken was decided upon
before the criminal was arrested. Conviction was swift and sure
and the penalty was usually the "end of the rope," or, as it was
sometimes called, "stretching the hemp." The sign of the Vigilantes was left on the body. There were no jails and the criminals
were so fearless and ruthless that definite and quick action was
essential. Often one punishment by a Vigilance Committee was
all that was needed to frighten the remainder of a gang out of
the territory. When local and territorial laws and courts became
effective, these popular tribunals came to an end.

In 1861 the most infamous of outlaws in the Northwest, Henry
Plummer, a Connecticut Yankee, came to Lewiston, Idaho, where
he quickly gathered about him a gang of desperadoes. Outwardly
respectable, he was afraid of no crime, and with his friends followed the mining frontier as it shifted. Plummer arrived in
Lewiston with a woman who was supposed to be his wife, and
the two were quickly accepted by the casual society of the town.

Deserting the woman, who had left a husband and several children to accompany him west, he soon became the acknowledged leader of a band of robbers, murderers, and gamblers. Both in New England and in California young Plummer had committed numerous crimes and he made good use of his knowledge in the mining towns. The Plummer gang had a rendezvous on each of the two main highways leading into Lewiston, and it was not safe to attempt to take treasure into or out of the town. The citizens were virtually terrorized, as stores were shot up and owners killed without any one daring to punish the criminals. Plummer went to Florence to observe movements of gold in and out of that camp. After a particularly daring robbery to secure money for goods brought in by a pack train, two of the masked bandits of the Plummer gang were recognized, followed, and seized by the owners of the gold, and imprisoned. Morning found them swinging in the breeze. This punishment appeared to free the area from the fear which had allowed the gang to operate with such impunity, for the rest of the criminals hastily left for the Montana mines.

Plummer's men followed the various bonanzas as they appeared in the Northwest. In 1862 the leader, accompanied by his friend, Jack Cleveland, came to Bannack, where the former made many acquaintances who soon became stanch allies, not suspecting the real character of the new-comer. Cleveland was soon recognized as a rogue, and Plummer, fearing that his friend would tell of his earlier escapades, planned to kill him. Managing a quarrel, Plummer killed Cleveland, pleading self-defense, and was acquitted. Then he was afraid that his old friend had told the sheriff, who had taken care of the dying man, of his former life, and so planned another murder. Finally he maneuvered the sheriff, Crawford, into such a situation that the two were forced to shoot at each other, but neither was seriously injured. Crawford was afraid the gang would revenge the injury Plummer had suffered, and fled to the States. For more than a year Plummer's band of a hundred road-agents terrorized the locality around Bannack, with spies in every store and saloon, sending out stage-coaches with secret marks that only the bandits would recognize, and wearing a certain sailor's tie-knot as identification.

As soon as gold was struck in Virginia City, the gang, known as "The Innocents," crowded into the new camp to prey upon the miners. So carefully had Plummer maintained his false status that few suspected his past record and he was made sheriff. He married, moved into a beautiful house, and lived an outwardly dignified and respectable life. When he wished to leave town to help carry out a raid, he had a member of the gang notify him that there was a silver deposit on which an opinion was desired. Plummer inspected numerous "silver deposits." Finally his neighbors began to clamor to be let in on the silver strikes, and to be told their location. Plummer refused to give any information. One man, more curious than the rest, followed him on one occasion, and stopped overnight at the same place Plummer had been overheard to mention as his destination. The man went to bed, and during the next few hours saw one after another of the gang come in and retire. Another robbery had been successfully staged, but it was the last one which Plummer was able to manage in this area. A young boy had been held up about the same time by bandits and had seen the mask of one blown aside, recognizing the face beneath it as Plummer's. He had told his story, and this, together with what the man had seen in the inn, convinced Bannack that Plummer was really the head of a notorious band of outlaws. Numerous atrocities had been committed in the area, and as one by one they were traced to Plummer's band, the citizens' anger slowly rose, until the organization of the Vigilantes wiped out more than twenty members, including the leader, and banished others.

The steps in the organization of a Vigilance Committee are shown in the files of the early Montana newspapers, which present an excellent study in frontier justice as carried out in the mining camps of that western territory. The first issue of the *Montana Post* at Virginia City, August 27, 1864, reported the robbery of the overland stage between that place and Salt Lake City, while passing through Port Neuf Canyon. Four robbers stopped the coach, taking twenty-seven thousand dollars in gold-dust from four passengers who were on their way to the States. "This business is commencing a little early," commented the editor, "and prompt measures should and will be resorted to to stop these daring outrages." On October 29th the stage was stopped and robbed by twelve men who riddled the coach with bullets, killing a soldier riding with the driver. The same paper announced the discontinuance of the passenger and express line between Virginia City and Salt Lake City, because of the activity of road-agents. "If nothing is done to bring these agents to the rope, times will be rougher than last winter," observed the editor. On July 22, 1865, another stage robbery was reported in Port Neuf Canyon, in which four men were killed and three badly wounded. Gold valued at sixty thousand dollars was taken and the passengers and driver were brutally treated. On August 26, 1865, the Salt Lake City coach was attacked about twenty-five miles from Virginia City in Cedar Canyon by four men on foot, with blackened faces. One of the drivers was killed at sight, his partner escaping. On September 16th another robbery was reported not far from Diamond City, and others were staged near Helena and other Montana mining centers.[1]

On September 23, 1865, the *Montana Post* printed the following warning:

To whom it may concern; whereas divers foul crimes and outrages against persons and property of the citizens of Montana have been lately committed and whereas the power of the civil authorities, though exerted to its fullest extent, is frequently insufficient to prevent their commission and to punish the perpetrators thereof. Now this is to warn

[1] *Montana Post*, September 16, 1865; *Helena Weekly Herald*, November 15, 29, December 20, 1866, January 30, September 19, December 12, 1867, May 21, 1868.

and notify all whom it may concern that a vigilance committee composed of the citizens of the territory have determined to take the matter in their own hands and to inflict summary punishment upon any and all malefactors in every case where the civil authorities are unable to enforce the proper penalty of the law. The practice of drawing deadly weapons, except as a last resort for the defense of life, being dangerous to society and in numerous instances leading to affrays and bloodshed, notice is hereby given that the same is prohibited and will be summarily dealt with. In all cases the committee will respect and sustain the action of civil authorities. This notice will not be repeated and will remain in full force and effect from this day. September 19, 1865. Vigilance Committee.

The committee was forced to almost immediate action. The *Montana Post* of September 30, 1865, said:

On Monday morning the beams of the rising sun fell upon the stiffened corpse of Johnny Cooke, a thief, swinging in the morning breeze. The Vigilantes had left a label on this pickpocket. The criminal, Johnny Cooke was a thief and rough from "the other side," whether Boise or California, we do not know. He worked in both these training camps of road agents, robbers and desperadoes of the West, and was probably a graduate of both places. The climate of Montana is unhealthy for criminals and Helena seems to be particularly so.

On Wednesday morning of the same week two men were found hanging from a hay frame over the corral of the slaughter-house up the gulch. On the back of one of them, John Morgan, was the notice of the Vigilantes, penciled with the inscription: "Road Agent Beware." The name of the other man was John Jackson, alias Jones. The bodies were cut down and brought into town by the sheriff and his posse, and were decently interred in the new burying-ground the afternoon of that same day. Several instances of theft and horse-stealing were mentioned as having been carried out by these men. "A good name is better than precious ointment," declaimed the local press. Another account in the same paper mentioned two other men found dangling in the air "without labels" near the Prickly Pear toll-gate about fifty miles from Confederate Gulch, and it commented, "The way of the Transgressor is hard."

Another man was found the following Tuesday morning on the same tree, with no label to tell the cause of his death. It was ascertained that his name was Kirby and that he hailed from Boise. The paper remarked that "the good people of Helena have a way of doing these matters of necessity with a quiet determination which is praiseworthy."

On November 4, 1865, the editor published a severe criticism from the *Carson Appeal* (Nevada) on lynch-law in Montana:

The last *Montana Post* mentions in a flippant manner that three men were found swinging in the breeze. No one knew or cared who they were. "Just little matters of necessity." We look upon such a transaction as a greater crime than that committed by the executed. . . . The people of Montana must aid or compel their law officers to do execution upon the bodies of criminals, if they would have honest men fill up the territory.

The *Montana Post* answered by saying:

Upon general principle the majority of a community can be justified in taking the law into their own hands. It has been necessary here. Circumstances alter cases. Our vigilance committee is not a mob. . . . Until justice can be reached through the ordinary channels our citizens will be fully protected against these evil desperadoes, even if the sun of very morning should rise upon the morbid picture of a malefactor dangling in the air. Protection through the open courts if possible, but protection anyway is the prevailing sentiment of the honest people of Montana, of all creeds and factions.

The apparent inability of the law to maintain justice caused the citizens of Argenta to take matters into their hands. The Vigilantes organized there December 28, 1866, composed of twenty of the best men of the town. The desperadoes in the area were asked to "read and reflect." A warning was issued through the *Montana Post* which notified "all whom it [may] concern that crime must and will be suppressed; and to that end all offenders will be summarily dealt with and punished. . . ." There was so little evidence of any activity on the part of the Vigilantes that their warning must have been heeded.

The first issue of the *Helena Weekly Herald* appeared on November 15, 1866. A close examination of the early files indicates that, while there was the usual amount of crime which invariably accompanied mining activities, the problem of maintaining order was not as serious as in the earlier years. The sheriff and his deputies appeared able to fulfill the duties of their offices unassisted, although for several years there were scattered incidents in which an aroused citizenry took justice into their own hands. The *Helena Herald* for May 21, 1868, reported the Vigilantes at work in Dale City, where three desperadoes were hanged and one was shot, and on May 5th it had reported activity in Lannon, a mining camp. The *Helena Daily Gazette* for May 1, 1870, described the hanging of A. F. Compton and Joseph Wilson by the outraged citizens for the shooting and robbing of an old man, George Lenhart. The vicious crime called forth action by an irate community. "Over a thousand citizens gathered in the court house square, chose a chairman and organized a people's court to investigate the charges against the accused of murder and robbery and to pass judgment accordingly." The chairman announced that the purpose of the meeting was to deal justly with certain parties suspected of foul play. The Federal judge of the district protested emphatically against the irregular procedure and advised the townspeople to let the law take its course. The judge's advice was voted down and a special committee of twelve reliable men was chosen to hear the evidence and determine the verdict, which was "guilty." The chairman then asked the crowd to decide what to do with the prisoners. The quiet assembly made the expected answer: hang them by the necks until dead. This was apparently the last episode of frontier justice by citizens in this territory.

The problems of the Idaho and Montana mining frontiers were repeated in the Black Hills area. No sooner were the mining camps of Deadwood Gulch and the surrounding region occupied than criminals of various types made their appearances. The Black Hills press gave a contemporary record of what went on in the camps and also recorded the activity of stage-robbers. A Crook City paper in June, 1877, reported that the Cheyenne stage-coach had been held up at Hat Creek, Wyoming, by two men who had concealed themselves in the grass and sprung out in front of the stage. They had gone through the passengers and the treasure box. The news-item ended with the following comment: "This savors of the days of Robin Hood and the more recent exploits of the road agents who harrassed Ben Holladay's Overland stages. The drivers in this case are to be particularly blamed for allowing themselves to be so easily caught." [2]

On June 28th the Deadwood coach, bound for Cheyenne, was stopped near the Cheyenne River. The treasure box was blown up and the passengers relieved of their belongings. Twelve armed men with sawed-off shot-guns conducted the robbery. They sent word by the driver to the manager of the stage line to furnish them with a pair of scales the next time, as they disliked dividing the dust with a tablespoon. A Black Hills newspaper for July 14, 1877, contained the following observation: "We have again to repeat the hackneyed phrase, 'the stage has been robbed.' Three miles below Battle Creek, four masked men took over the treasure box, robbed the passengers, rifled their baggage, and after taking a drink all around and wishing the passengers and driver a pleasant journey, packed their booty on their horses and started off at a loping gallop." [3] On July 28th the stage-coach bound for Pierre was held up at the water-hole near the Cheyenne River and in September and October of 1877 several other robberies were reported, after which the Black Hills editors earnestly plead that some action be taken against such lawless gangs as were operating in the area.

[2] *Black Hills Herald*, June 16, 1877.
[3] *Deadwood Daily Champion*, June 28, July 14, 1877.

ROUGH JUSTICE IN MONTANA
"Hangman's tree" at Helena, 1870.

On September 3, 1877, the Cheyenne and Black Hills Stage Company offered one thousand dollars reward for the capture of the agents who had robbed their stage on July 28th near the crossing of the Cheyenne River. In 1878 the robberies continued, but action was taken by the community. The famous "Robbers' Roost," with its organized band of robbers and horse-thieves, was discovered in March, and some of the outlaws were driven out of the country, while others "stretched hemp." In the summer of 1878 an armored treasure coach was constructed to take shipments of gold-dust out of the Hills. A contemporary newspaper on July 11th said, "A bullet proof coach, lined with three-fourth inch steel, is being manufactured for the Deadwood-Cheyenne road." Observed a Montana editor: "It will carry an eight hundred pound burglar proof safe to which the driver does not know the combination. There will be port holes for rifle shooting. The coach will carry no passengers and will have four armed guards, two on the inside and two on horseback ahead. With a coach of this pattern it looks as if the road agent problems were solved unless the knights of the road supply themselves with flying artillery." Some three weeks later a Cheyenne editor, upon the arrival of the armored treasure coach, said: "The iron clad coach arrived from Deadwood yesterday. The road agents didn't care to tackle it." [4]

The famous Deadwood coach made several trips carrying its treasure box filled with gold bullion, until the day it arrived in fancied security, attended by only one man, at the stage station in Cold Springs Canyon, in a wild and remote district. The station attendant had been held up and tied just before the arrival of the coach. The driver threw his lines to the ground, and he and the messenger who was outside were about to alight when the hold-up occurred. The driver was shot but the messenger escaped. The treasure box was opened with a pick, and forty-five thousand dol-

[4] *Butte Miner* (Butte, Mont.), June 11, 1878; *Cheyenne Daily Sun* (Cheyenne, Wy.), July 3, 1878.

lars was taken. The story is told that one of the road-agents was left lying in the road, and was so infuriated at his comrades' desertion of him that he gave the names of the other men involved, most of whom were captured and sent to the penitentiary. The greater part of the bullion was later recovered.

Black Hills editors began to demand action against stage-robbers. One of them wrote:

Stage robberies are reaching a crisis. At frequent intervals ever since treasure has been carried out of the hills to the East, road agents have interrupted coaches going out by the Cheyenne route and have not only robbed the treasure safe, but have rifled the pockets of the passengers and violated the United States mails. An iron clad coach was built and it has been robbed and the Cheyenne and Black Hills stagecoach company is offering $5,000 reward for the arrest and conviction of the highwaymen.

Organized action was taken and the number of robberies tended to decrease. On October 3, 1878, a local posse headed by Ed Cook surrounded a band of desperadoes some thirty miles from Fort Pierre. They slipped away in the darkness and the officers set off in pursuit. Two days later the *Black Hills Daily Times* reported that two men of the gang had been found dead, where the posse had hanged and left them. The bodies were left to "swing as a warning to others of the same ilk." [5] With the increasing stability of the courts and activity of official guardians of law and order, crimes grew fewer in number.

There is, of course, a short and ugly word for the act by which the Vigilantes maintained order in the Northwest. That word is lynching, and it is peculiarly American, found almost alone on the American frontier, and disappearing when the early period came to an end,[6] and the Vigilance Committees, their work over, dis-

---

[5] *Black Hills Herald*, files for 1878; *Black Hills Daily Times*, October 3, 5, 11, 16, 18, November 15, 1878.

[6] Lynching as known in the southern United States, is, of course, different in character, and consequently the above comments are devoted entirely to that on the western frontier.

banded. On the frontier, where every man arrived almost as he had first come into the world, with a future, but no past, especially if he wished to forget what he had been or done, all sorts of characters lived. There was the professional man who wished better economic opportunities where competition was less because there were fewer of his kind, the minister or teacher who saw a field for his service, the business man, trader, or merchant who knew that there would be a sure and steady demand for food and clothing, and also the thief, robber, or murderer who saw new wealth to exploit. Usually, since human nature rarely changes overnight, these last continued their wrong-doing, and while, like Plummer, they often succeeded in getting into the good graces of their fellow-settlers and sometimes rose to positions of authority, in the end they were frequently left to "stretch hemp." Courts and codes of law were far away from the little western settlements, and punishment had to be certain and swift, for there were few jails, and little time left from the onerous task of making a living to build them.

In Owen Wister's *The Virginian*, one of the characters, Judge Henry, gives the reasoning of the Westerner who condoned lynching:

"... the ordinary citizens," said the Judge. "... They are where the law comes from, you see. For they chose the delegates who made the Constitution that provided for the courts. There's your machinery. These are the hands into which ordinary citizens have put the law. So you see, at best, when they lynch they only take back what they once gave. ... in Wyoming the law has been letting our cattle-thieves go for two years. We are in a very bad way, and we are trying to make that way a little better until civilization can reach us. At present we lie beyond its pale. The courts, or rather the juries, into whose hands we have put the law, are not dealing the law. They are withered hands, or rather they are imitation hands made for show, with no life in them, no grip. They cannot hold a cattle-thief. And so, when your ordinary citizen sees this, and sees that he has placed justice in a dead hand, he must take justice back into his own hands where it was once at the beginning of all things. Call this primitive, if you will. But so far from being a *defiance* of the law, it is an *assertion* of it—the fundamental assertion of self-governing men, upon whom our whole social fabric is based. . . ."

The Judge admits that lynching is terrible. " 'But,' he says, 'so is capital punishment terrible. And so is war. And perhaps some day we shall do without them. But they are none of them so terrible as unchecked theft and murder would be.' " [7]

Either secretly or openly, Vigilance Committees, under various names, existed all through the West. But as soon as the civil government proved its ability to function adequately, they were quietly dissolved. Through the various frontiers, however, they had protected the miner and the rancher, the settler and the farmer, and whatever personal feeling the reader may hold toward the institution of lynching, the facts undoubtedly prove that in a period when the machinery for maintaining order and security was either entirely missing or too weak to serve, the committees were a necessity.

[7] Owen Wister, *The Virginian, a Horseman of the Plains* (New York, 1922), pp. 435-6. Quoted by special permission of The Macmillan Company, New York.

II

THE FRONTIER OF
THE BUFFALO

IN THE GENERAL drama of the westward movement, buffalo, or bison, have played an important part. As the various types of frontier moved across the United States these animals were a distinct asset, in fact, often life itself, to the Indian, the fur trader, the explorer, the miner, the soldier, and the settler. Buffalo trails guided them, fresh and cured buffalo meat was indispensable as food, buffalo chips warmed them and cooked their monotonous fare, buffalo-robes were used for clothing and sold to gain wealth, while, as a last offering, buffalo bones helped many homesteaders to live until their farms became productive. The buffalo helped to build railroads and contributed to their early prosperity by the stimulation of freight transportation and passenger traffic.

I

BUFFALO EAST OF THE MISSISSIPPI

WHILE early records indicate the presence of buffalo in the eastern portion of the United States, their range, except in the Georgian lowlands, seldom extended eastward beyond the fall-line. As explorers and frontiersmen crossed the Appalachians in their westward trek, they followed paths or traces left by buffalo. The famous Cumberland Road and other overland routes across the mountains into the Middle West, as well as the north and south trails of the various warring Indian tribes in that area, were made first by the hoof marks of buffalo. As the animals traveled, they invariably found their way to salt-licks or springs, which were carefully indicated on early maps of the trans-Appalachian country to guide hunters and trappers.[1]

By the middle of the eighteenth century there is evidence that wanton and wasteful slaughter had already thinned the buffalo in the region of the Blue Ridge Mountains and was tending to force them west. On March 15, 1750, Thomas Walker, a well-known traveler, stopping to purchase corn for his horses at a famous salt-lick in western Virginia where there was a small settlement, observed that the lick, which had been one of the best places for game in that region, would have been of far greater advantage to the inhabitants if the buffalo had not been killed off for diversion. General Daniel Harmar, at Fort Washington in Ohio, wrote to a friend in 1790 inviting him to come west for a visit as they could afford him an abundance of buffalo and venison. Buffalo had been exterminated in Pennsylvania by 1800 and by 1802 the last of them had been killed in Ohio.[2]

In Kentucky the early settlers were reluctant to take up agriculture since a living could be made so easily with a gun. John Filson, the well-known frontiersman, told that he had heard a hunter assert that he had seen as many as a thousand buffalo at Blue Licks in a single herd before they had been killed so wantonly by the first settlers. In 1805, Thomas Ashe told of the experiences of an old buffalo hunter who killed more than six hundred at one time for their skins that were worth but two shillings each, and, after the slaughter, had been compelled to leave the place until the following season in order that the carcasses might decompose or be devoured by animals and birds. Ashe reported meeting a

---

[1] W. T. Hornaday, "The Extermination of the American Bison," *Annual Report of the United States National Museum*, II (Smithsonian Institution: Washington, D. C., 1887), 373-87; W. H. Bogart, *Daniel Boone and the Hunters of Kentucky* (Boston, 1874), *passim*.

[2] James Hall, *The Romance of Western History* (Cincinnati, Ohio, 1857); A. T. Goodman, "Buffalo in Ohio," *Western Reserve Historical Society Tract* (Cleveland, Ohio, January, 1877), *passim*; E. Douglas Branch, *The Hunting of the Buffalo* (New York, 1929), pp. 61-2.

settler who claimed to have killed as many as two thousand buffalo.[3] Cane-breaks and undergrowth around creeks and salt springs
were fired and the animals shot as they came out, piles of carcasses often becoming so foul as to drive herds away from the
salt-licks. By 1810 there were no buffalo left in Kentucky and
they ceased to range east of the Mississippi.[4]

II

BUFFALO IN THE RED RIVER VALLEY

IN THE SUMMER of 1800, Alexander Henry, an employee of the
Northwest Fur Company, led a party of voyageurs and Indian
hunters on a trading expedition to the forks of the Red River of
the North. He constructed a trading-post at the point where the
Park River enters the Red River because the salty content of the
water at that place attracted buffalo and other game. By late August the plain of the river was filled with buffalo migrating to the
southward, while in September great herds of the animals were
grazing on the plain below the camp. By the middle of January
the herds were beginning to move slowly back toward the north,
and the plain and the ice-bound river at times were black with
them. Early on the morning of January 14th, Henry was awakened by the bellowing of buffalo and after locating himself to advantage for observation, he recorded: "The ground was covered
at every point of the compass, as far as the eye could reach, and
every animal was in motion. All hands attacked with a running
fire, which put them to a quicker pace but had no effect in altering
their course. . . . They passed at full speed until nine o'clock when
their numbers decreased and they kept further off in the plain."

[3] This is a large number when one considers the relative scarcity of buffalo
in this area as compared with the trans-Mississippi West. Theodore G. Grieder,
The Influence of the American Bison or Buffalo on Westward Expansion
(Master's Thesis, University of Iowa: Iowa City, Iowa, 1928).
[4] John Filson, *Kentucke* (reprint of the 1784 edition: Louisville, Ky., 1929);
John M. Brown, "The Kentucky Pioneers" (*Harper's Monthly Magazine*,
LXXV, June, 1887).

The next day he reported: "The plains are still covered with buffalo moving slowly northward," and, on the sixteenth, an entry noted the passing of some lagging old bulls, the last of the herd, some of the "lone scabby ones" taking shelter in the woods where they were harassed by the dogs from the post. For some time from twenty to thirty herds were counted daily feeding on the plains, seeking refuge in the woods in stormy weather, but returning to the grass when the storm or cold abated.[1]

Henry broke camp early in May and sent to Grand Portage, the headquarters of the company, five thousand pounds of pemmican and thirty-one buffalo-robes. During the summer of 1801, he constructed a permanent post on the Pembina River and for the next eight years the Northwest Fur Company depended upon Henry for a part of its pemmican. Although the main emphasis at this time was on beaver, the lower Red River department, which contained from four to eight posts, sent one hundred and fifty buffalo-robes to headquarters during the next seven years, one hundred of which came from Henry's post.[2] From 1800 to 1808 the Northwest Company used approximately 21,250 pounds of pemmican and ten tons of grease, dried meat, tongues, and humps from the lower Red River area, while the Hudson's Bay Company also obtained large quantities of buffalo products from the Red River Valley.[3]

Early in the eighteenth century Thomas Douglas, the fifth Earl of Selkirk, a member of the board of directors of the Hudson's Bay Company, secured a large grant of land which included most of the Red River Valley and decided to establish a colony of Scotch Highlanders in the area. In 1812 a settlement was made two miles below the confluence of the Red and Assiniboine rivers.

[1] Manuscript Journals of Alexander Henry and David Thompson, ed. Elliott Coues (New York, 1897), I, 160-75.
[2] To show the relative importance of the various furs: the Northwest Fur Company in 1805, a typical year, received from all its posts: 77,500 beaver skins, 51,250 muskrat, 40,440 marten, and 1,135 buffalo-robes.
[3] Manuscript Journals of Alexander Henry and David Thompson, I, 169.

Until they could develop agriculture, they maintained themselves largely by hunting the buffalo that roamed the plains within a few miles of their lonely little settlement. As they migrated southward for the winter buffalo herds that grazed near the banks of the Saskatchewan in summer visited the area around the Little Pembina River that joins the Red River not far from the present boundary of Minnesota. The Indians assisted the inexperienced Highlanders in establishing a camp at that point consisting of a storehouse and cabins surrounded by a palisade. Buffalo were numerous and during the winter the hunters remained in Pembina, which became the regular hunting-ground of the Selkirk colonists.

The settlement had hardly been established when controversy began with the fur traders. The Northwest Fur Company, alarmed at the planting of a permanent colony in the midst of the buffalo range, feared the extermination of the buffalo herds and the destruction of the beaver streams. The settlement promptly announced that it would not allow traders to remove pemmican and other supplies from their land, and when the Northwest Company refused to abide by the decision, Governor MacDonnell, acting for the colony, seized six hundred bags of pemmican.[4] The bloody and discreditable "Pemmican War," thus begun, continued until the merging of the Northwest Fur Company and the Hudson's Bay Company in 1821. Realizing the importance of the buffalo, the colony organized a "Buffalo Wool Company" as a speculative venture and distributed samples of their cloth in London and in other European centers. More than thirty thousand dollars was raised by subscription and the sale of stock. The bubble soon burst,

---

[4] Pemmican was made by pounding dried strips of buffalo meat into a flaky mass and pouring over successive layers of the shredded meat an equal amount, or a little less, of melted tallow. Buffalo fat was far more palatable and digestible than that taken from domestic cattle and oxen. The pemmican was packed in bags of buffalo skin, making a compact, nutritious food that would keep indefinitely and became the standard fare of the fur trader. The bags of pemmican as prepared by the Northwest Fur Company weighed ninety pounds, fifty pounds of which were beef and the rest tallow.

however, as the cost of producing the cloth was too great.[5] The versatile settlement then shipped four hundred thousand pounds of buffalo tallow to England by way of Fort York. No further shipments were made, since high transportation costs absorbed the profits.[6]

Hunting parties of Selkirk farmers, French-Canadian fur hunters, and half-breeds, often numbering as high as four hundred, journeyed each June to Pembina in their wooden Red River carts.[7] It has been estimated that from 1821 to 1840 the hunters of the Red River settlement in their annual hunts killed more than six hundred and fifty thousand buffalo. This Pembina buffalo hunt was one of the most unique and picturesque events in the buffalo country of the Northwest. While it was considered an annual affair, in some years more than one trip was made to the bison country to the west. Men, women, and children joined the excursion. In 1840 there were 1,630 people connected with the hunt and 1,210 carts were used in the trip. There were certain requirements as to equipment, each man being supposed to have a draft-horse or ox for his cart and a special horse for "running" the buffalo. The hunters took great pride in their excellent horses, which they kept in the best of condition.

The Pembina hunt of 1840 started about the middle of June. As soon as the party assembled, a council was organized and Jean Baptiste was chosen as chief or president of the hunt. Ten cap-

---

[5] C. H. Lee, *Long Ago in the Red River Valley* (St. Paul, Minn., 1880), pp. 10-37; C. C. Andrews, *Minnesota and Dacotah* (St. Paul, Minn., 1856); Louis W. Wood, *The Red River Colony* (Toronto, Ont., 1920), pp. 27-56; Alexander Ross, *The Red River Settlement* (London, 1856), pp. 42-68.

[6] *First Annual Report of the Minnesota Commissioner of Statistics*, 1859, pp. 25-7.

[7] The Red River carts were two-wheeled vehicles, made on somewhat the same pattern as the country carts of France, except that no iron was used in their construction. The wheels were large, about five feet in diameter, and three inches thick. There were four spokes in each wheel, each being placed perpendicular with no bending out. The felloes were fastened to each other by tongues of wood and the hubs were thick and strong. The box, fastened together by wooden pegs, would hold about a thousand pounds of freight. A Red River cart is on exhibit in the historical museum at Bismarck, North Dakota.

tains were elected to assist the president, each of which had ten soldiers under his orders. Guides were also appointed to take turns in supervising the travel and the making of camps. The camp flag was in charge of the guide for the day, who hoisted it as the signal for raising camp in the morning and set it in the ground as the signal for the evening pitching of tents. The camp was formed at night in the shape of a great circle with the thills of the carts turned toward the center, stock and horses being placed inside this barricade.

The council established rules or laws regulating the hunt that were strictly followed. No buffalo were to be run on Sunday; no party or group was to fork off or lag behind without permission; nor was any person to run buffalo or shoot at them until the general order was given; and each captain was to patrol the camp and keep guard with his men. For the first violation the offender had his saddle and bridle cut into pieces; for the second offense the coat was taken from his back and cut into strips; and for the third he was formally and publicly flogged. Stealing, even to the value of a sinew, was not tolerated.

On the morning of the chase, a herd of buffalo having been located on the plains not far from Fort Union the day before, the hunters broke camp early, and after Mass had been said by the priest they were drawn up in line for their last instructions. They cautiously approached the herd and when they were near enough to attack, the president gave the signal by yelling "Ho!" and four hundred well-mounted hunters rode headlong toward the herd, causing the several thousand buffalo to gallop away in rapid motion. Each hunter picked his quarry and approaching the animal at full speed, kept pace with him for a short distance and fired at close range, his horse stepping aside as the shot was fired. The hunter then reloaded his gun as he rode and picked another bison. The shifting and zigzag attack lasted for more than an hour, during which time those with the swiftest horses brought down ten or twelve buffalo while those with ordinary mounts killed three or four. After the kill the animals were skinned and the meat and robes were packed in wooden carts whose squeaking wheels carried them slowly to Pembina.[8]

The camp killed about 3,500 buffalo, from which were made 375 bags of pemmican and 240 bales of dried meat. Since 750 buffalo would easily have produced that amount, only the tongues and humps were taken from many of the animals, the rest being left for the wolves and crows. Buffalo were abundant, and waste, that outstanding characteristic of most western buffalo hunts, was obviously present.[9]

The famous Red River trail was opened in 1844 when a number of Red River carts brought furs and buffalo-robes to St. Paul. By 1856 Pembina had become well established as the Canadian base and by 1858 six hundred carts came to St. Paul bringing goods valued at approximately two hundred thousand dollars, two-thirds of which were estimated to consist of furs and buffalo products. Just what part of the furs carried was made up of robes and articles produced from the buffalo is hard to say. That it must have been a goodly portion is apparent when we note that the failure of the "buffalo crop" in the winter of 1858-59 caused a considerable decrease in the amount of goods carried that spring, and when the United States Government levied a duty of 20 per cent on buffalo robes and 30 per cent on moccasins, the Red River trade soon declined to almost nothing.[10]

The result was the extermination of the buffalo in that area, the very thing that had been feared by the Northwest Fur Company. After 1847 there were no large herds of buffalo in Mani-

---

[8] Alexander Ross, "Adventures of the First Settlers," *Early Western Travels*, ed. R. G. Thwaites (New York, 1897), Vol. VII.

[9] J. L. Coulter, "Industrial History of the Valley of the Red River of the North," *Collections*, State Historical Society of North Dakota (Bismarck, N. Dak.), III, 189-203.

[10] "The Red River Oxcart Trade," *The Record* (Fargo, N. Dak., August, 1895), pp. 6-8; Coulter, *op. cit.*, p. 552; Lee, *Long Ago in the Red River Valley*, pp. 26-7; J. Wesley Bond, *Minnesota and Its Resources* (St. Paul Minn., 1853), p. 332.

toba, northern Minnesota, or northeastern Dakota,[11] while hunters
had carried the destruction westward from the Red River settlement to the Qu'Appelle and the Saskatchewan rivers. The Cree
Indians of the Plains, whose country was in the vicinity of the
headwaters of the Qu'Appelle, two hundred and fifty miles west
of the Red River, decided in council in 1857 that because of the
rapid destruction of the buffalo upon which they fed, they would
no longer allow white men or half-breeds to hunt or travel
through their country except for the purpose of trade.[12]

III

THE BUFFALO RANGE OF THE NORTHWEST

THE WESTWARD advance of the buffalo frontier was slow and
gradual, keeping just beyond the fringe of civilization until the
final drive was made against them on the plains of the Northwest.
While great herds ranged over much of the area west of the
Mississippi River in the early nineteenth century, the settlement
of the fertile area between the Missouri and Mississippi rivers
had, by 1825, driven most of the buffalo beyond the Missouri as
far north as the area that later became the Territory of Dakota.
As the herds were slowly driven westward, the development of the
Oregon Trail and the California gold rush divided the bison of
the West into the northern and southern herds, leaving the highways bare except in the months when the animals were moving
north or south. The buffalo were soon driven from the vicinity of
those lines of travel, thousands being wantonly slaughtered annually. Increase in travel, the opening of portions of the land to

[11] The westward line of advance of the buffalo, like that of the other frontiers,
was very irregular. Reports show that there were buffalo in considerable numbers
within fifty miles of St. Paul, Minnesota, as late as 1856 and that they were
common around the headwaters of the Des Moines and Cedar rivers, on both
sides of the Minnesota and Iowa boundary, as late as 1845. There are records of
buffalo in Iowa as late as the sixties. J. A. Allen, *American Bison, Living and
Extinct* (Cambridge, Mass., 1876), pp. 140-3.
[12] Branch, *Hunting of the Buffalo*, pp. 82-3.

settlement, and, finally, the construction of the Union Pacific Railroad brought about a wider separation of the herds, the buffalo retiring further and further each year.[1] It is in the northern herd, the center of whose range included Wyoming, Montana, and portions of Dakota, that we are primarily interested.

The area of the Northwest, much of which later became the grazing ground of vast herds of cattle and sheep, made an ideal range for buffalo. From the plains of the upper Missouri, somewhat more rugged than those to the south and east, the region extends westward through the Black Hills and Bad Lands of western Dakota through Wyoming and Montana to the Rocky Mountains. The area consisted of prairies, river valleys, sand dunes, jagged rocks, pine-covered ridges and hills, barren and stony buttes, some in chains and some isolated, much of which was covered with sage-brush and bunch-grass, including thickets of plum, and buffalo-berry bushes and trees of ash, box-elder, elm, and cedar. The short nutritious "buffalo grass," cured on the stem during the dry months of July and August, made excellent feed, while light snow-falls, high rate of evaporation, and high winds permitted winter grazing on the naturally cured hay.

The great Missouri with its branches, the Yellowstone, Little Missouri, Cannon Ball, Milk, Musselshell, Marias, and the Big Horn, furnished the bison with plenty of water. During dry periods, with many of the smaller streams dried up, pools of water from some of the creek beds were available, and "buffalo wallows" are still to be seen in various parts of the region. The presence of alkali soils and salt lakes in the western portion, together with the salt springs in parts of the Dakotas, made it unnecessary for the bison to travel long distances for salt as they had to do in some sections. Such was the buffalo range of the Northwest.[2]

---

[1] Allen, *op. cit.*, pp. 144-5; Ernest Thompson Seton, "The American Bison or Buffalo," *Scribner's Magazine*, XL (October, 1906), 385-406; Hornaday, "Extermination of the American Bison," p. 501.

[2] G. A. Batchelder, *A Sketch of the History and Resources of Dakota Territory* (Yankton, D. T., 1870), p. 38; S. S. Visher, "The Geography of South Dakota,"

BUFFALO ON THE UPPER MISSOURI

Maximilian, Prince of Wied, *Reise in das Innere Nord-America*, 1839-41.

The folklore of the Plains Indians all had one fact in common, the importance of the buffalo in the culture of each tribe. Likewise, the common myth existed of great numbers of the shaggy bison coming each spring out of large openings like caves to the south. The Indians thus explained to themselves the fact of the annual migrations of the buffalo and also a second fact which later made them such an enticing object of the hunt to the white man—that they traveled and fed in herds.[3]

The general movements or migrations depended somewhat upon weather and climatic conditions and could not definitely be determined. Ordinarily the movement was southward with the approach of winter and northward in the spring, the seasonal shifts varying from two hundred and fifty to four hundred and fifty miles. As long as the buffalo of the western regions roamed at will, the general movements north and south did not extend to the limits of the range. There were perhaps two major regional migrations in the Northwest. The herds that grazed during the summer months in the Saskatchewan country moved southward with the coming of winter into Montana and those that grazed on the ranges of Montana and northern Dakota in the summer migrated into Wyoming, southern Dakota, Nebraska, and northern Colorado. The migrations of the southern herds were less organized and less methodical than those of the northern herds. It was the latter that brought forth comment from travelers on the buffalo ranges of the Northwest.[4]

Except for size and gregariousness, the buffalo had few qualities that fitted it for life on the plains. It was clumsy and slow of gait and was described by practically all observers as a stupid ani-

---

Report of the State Geologist, 1916-18 (Vermillion, S. Dak., 1918), pp. 133-5; Collections, State Historical Society of North Dakota, I, 153-80; Walter Prescott Webb, The Great Plains (New York, 1931), pp. 10-44.

[3] Buffalo did not graze in closely packed groups or herds, but were scattered over the prairie in small bands of twenty to two hundred in a bunch with fifteen to a hundred yards between bunches. Generally speaking, all of the buffalo within a range of ten to fifteen miles might belong to the same herd.

[4] Hornaday, op. cit., pp. 388-91; Branch, Hunting of the Buffalo, pp. 3-4.

mal. It was not much afraid of sound and had poor eyesight. While it had a rather keen sense of smell, that ability was not of much use except when approached on the windward side. When the winter storms descended, the herd huddled together, each animal trying to get to the warm inside, the constant moving and pushing making for protection against the cold winds and snow. Often by spring the buffalo were hungry, but seldom did they succumb to the rigors of the plains winter. Every spring many buffalo were drowned, as the migrating herds pushed out on the thin ice of lakes and streams. Travelers and observers in the upper Missouri country noted that streams were filled at times with their dead bodies. The Stinking Water, a small river in Wyoming, no doubt received its name from the stench that came from the decaying bodies of buffalo mired in the mud. Indian camps often had to be abandoned when the odor became too offensive.

From early July to late September was the rutting season for buffalo, at which time the various herds came together and there was much confusion, bellowing, and fighting. The calving season came late in the spring, the cows generally leaving the bulls at the time, but returning as soon as the buffalo calves were able to be with the herd. The bulls protected the calves from attack by wolves and coyotes until they were able to look after themselves. Gray wolves and coyotes prowled around the buffalo, waiting with patience until a calf strayed or an animal became sick or wounded and left the herd. The coyotes were upon him in a minute, ready to do justice to a meal of juicy meat. The gray wolf, larger and stronger, would hold them off until he had satisfied his appetite, after which he would retire, leaving the coyotes to finish the meat or pick the bones. Crows and vultures hovered above the spot, swooping now and then to seize a fragment. These animals and birds cleaned the carcass of many a buffalo slaughtered for his hide and part of the meat.

IV

ACCOUNTS OF EARLY EXPLORERS AND TRAVELERS

FROM the buffalo ranges of the Northwest came numerous accounts of the great herds that grazed there during the early
years of exploration and settlement. The first travelers or explorers to leave records of their observations in this area were
Lewis and Clark, authorized in June, 1803, to conduct an expedition from the mouth of the Missouri River to the Pacific Coast.
Advised by Jefferson to make detailed observations of the wild
life of the Northwest, their journals make many references to
buffalo herds as seen on the various ranges, as hunted by the
Indians, and as used for food by trappers and explorers. Beginning their voyage up the Missouri in the middle of May, on
August 25th, while near the mouth of the Vermillion River in
what is now southeastern South Dakota, their journal reported:
"Numerous herds of buffalow were seen feeding in various directions." On September 21st, "numbers of buffalow elk and goats"
were seen feeding on the plains, while thirty days later Clark
wrote: "I observe near all gangues of buffalow, wolves, and when
the buffalow move these animals follow, and feed on those that
are killed by accident or those that are too pore or fat to keep
up." [1]

After wintering with the Mandan Indians in what is now North
Dakota, the party pushed on westward, making frequent references to the herds of bison that roamed the plains. At the mouth
of the Yellowstone the journal noted: "The buffalow now appear
in vast numbers." When they arrived at the mouth of the Musselshell they saw fewer and fewer until they reached the mountains,
where they saw practically none. On May 17, 1805, at a point
some one hundred and twenty miles above the mouth of the Milk
River, Lewis wrote: "Buffalow are not as abundant as they were

[1] *Original Journals of the Lewis and Clark Expedition, 1804-1806*, ed. R. G.
Thwaites (New York, 1904-5), I, 206, 221-3.

some days past." The last one killed by the party was found about fifty miles above the Great Falls of the Missouri River, well within the foot-hills of the Rocky Mountains. Three days later, Lewis wrote: "We have seen no buffalow since we entered the mountains." They observed, however, that buffalo no doubt wandered a considerable distance beyond the Three Forks of the Missouri, since buffalo bones and chips were discovered on the upper waters of the Jefferson.

On the return trip the explorers separated, Lewis coming by way of the Missouri, while Clark followed a more southerly route, the two parties meeting at the mouth of the Yellowstone. Far up in the mountains in the vicinity of what is now Beaverhead County, Montana, Clark observed old buffalo paths and heads and on July 30, 1806, at a point just east of the present city of Livingston, Montana, reported that they at that time seemed to be entering the buffalo country. On August 29th, he reported seeing "a greater number of buffalow than I have ever seen before at one time. I must have seen near 20,000 of those animals feeding on the plain." [2]

John Bradbury, the intrepid traveler, near the present site of Bismarck, North Dakota, on June 22, 1809, wrote: "On a plain four miles across, covered in every part with herds of buffalo feeding, I counted seventeen herds aggregating upwards of ten thousand." [3] George Catlin, the artist, while traveling up the Missouri, told of meeting an immense herd crossing the Missouri River near the mouth of the White River. They surrounded the boat and the river was filled and, in parts, blackened by the enormous numbers. [4] Captain John C. Frémont, "the pathfinder," stated: "At any time between the years 1824 and 1836 a traveler might start from any given point, south or north in the Rocky Mountains, journeying by the most direct route to the Missouri

[2] *Journals of Lewis and Clark, op. cit.*, II, 41-2, 235-9, 276, 300, V, 249-79.
[3] "Bradbury's Travels in the Interior of America," *Early Western Travels*, ed. R. G. Thwaites (Cleveland, Ohio, 1904), V, 140.
[4] George Catlin, *The North American Indian* (London, 1876), II, 13.

River, and during the whole distance his road would always be
among large bands of buffalo, which would never be out of his
view until he arrived almost within sight of the abode of civilization." [5] The statement of Frémont is supported by the personal
experience of Mr. Kipp, one of the principals of the American
Fur Company, who in August, 1843, in traveling from Traverse
Bay to the Mandan Nation in Dakota, "passed through herds of
buffalo for six days in succession."

While many travelers and explorers who crossed the plains
have left stories of the great numbers of bison that ranged the
West, few have left estimates that are definite. It is very difficult,
in fact, practically impossible, to judge with any degree of accuracy the total number of buffalo on the plains of the West at
any particular time or period. A well-known writer in this regard
has said: "Of all the quadrupeds that have ever lived upon the
earth, probably no species has ever marshaled such innumerable
hosts as those of the American bison. It would have been as easy
to count or to estimate the number of leaves in a forest as to
calculate the number of buffaloes living at any given time during
the history of the species previous to 1870." [6]

The northern herd was especially difficult to estimate, since the
territory was little traveled and not readily accessible. It did not
group together to make extensive migrations as did the southern
herd, as it stood the cold weather better than the southern herd
could withstand the heat of summer, and moved only a few miles
north or south during the change of seasons. During the period of
migration, the northern herd was widely scattered and divided
into small groups. David Hilger, a well-known Montana pioneer, while driving a bull team from Minnesota to western Montana in 1867, wrote that his party encountered "thousands upon
thousands of buffalo." [7]

[5] John Charles Frémont, *Memoirs of My Life* (New York, 1887), I, 219.
[6] Hornaday, "Extermination of the American Bison," p. 387.
[7] David Hilger, "Overland Trail," *Contributions*, Montana State Historical
Society, VII, 263.

Hornaday and Dodge, both well informed on the subject of buffalo, discounted the early estimates as to numbers that reach into the many millions. In 1870, Colonel Richard Irving Dodge estimated the number of buffalo along the Arkansas River at four million, which he thought more likely to be below the truth than above it. Hornaday, in attempting to determine the number in the southern herd in 1870, stated that there were "at least three millions, and most estimates place the total higher than that." [8] It is true that by 1870, great inroads had already been made upon the herds, especially those of the southwest, although it had not at that time assumed the aspect of a general slaughter. In 1870, a fair estimate would apparently have been that there were around four million buffalo south of the Platte River and probably one and one-half million north of it.

V

HUNTING THE BUFFALO

BUFFALO, found in such large numbers on the ranges of the Northwest, played an important part in the economy of the Indian of that region, who utilized every portion of the animal. He used the meat, dried or fresh, for food; the skins for clothing, for beds, and for covers; the hides to make leather and the hair to make cord and cloth; and buffalo dung for fuel. The war shield of an Indian brave was made from two thicknesses of the neck of a buffalo bull which was tough enough to turn the bullet of an ordinary rifle. Choice robes served as gifts from one chief to another and as peace-offerings or tribute between the various tribes. Products of the buffalo were traded for prize articles brought in by neighboring tribes for barter. As early as 1738 the Assiniboines were trading commodities received from the Hudson's Bay Company with the Mandans, whose ability to make artistic articles from buffalo products was superior to their

[8] Hornaday, op. cit., pp. 391, 493.

own. Traders of the American Fur Company in 1810 found the Snake Indians, in a region where no buffalo were to be found, clad in buffalo-robes for which they had traded salmon to hunting tribes. The Bannack Indians traded buffalo meat and robes to the Nez Percés for horses.[1] General Isaac Stevens, Governor of Washington Territory, writing in 1854, stated that the Blackfeet Indians, numbering about ten thousand, lived almost exclusively on buffalo meat, killing at least one hundred and fifty thousand of the animals each year.[2] In fact, the basis of culture of the Plains Indian was the buffalo, and this was clearly recognized by the United States Government when it later deliberately encouraged its destruction.

Methods of hunting the buffalo employed by the Indian tribes varied, the oldest and simplest probably being the "surround" or "approach" as it was sometimes called. When a herd of buffalo was reported to the chief, the braves armed themselves and made ready. They formed a large circle a considerable distance from the buffalo, fully surrounding them. The windward side of the circle was usually formed last. The hunters then gradually closed in on the herd and as they came close enough to be smelled by the buffalo, the hunters yelled and tossed their robes, inducing the animals to run in a circle. Gradually closing in, they often slaughtered a whole herd without a single one escaping. Great heaps of bones observed by early explorers were no doubt remains of these "surrounds." Another method was the use of a trap into which the buffalo were slowly driven. One side might be the vertical line of a cliff or bluff, while the other sides, six to eight feet in height, were made of rocks, logs, and brush. Some of the tribes of the Northwest constructed enclosures on the open prairies, using decoys dressed in skins around the opening. When the animals were inside the trap was closed. Some of the northern tribes living along the Missouri River killed buffalo in large

[1] Branch, *Hunting of the Buffalo*, pp. 86-7.
[2] Hazard Stevens, *The Life of Isaac Stevens* (New York, 1901), II, 105.

numbers by driving them over a cliff. Several such slaughters were noted by the Lewis and Clark expedition.

Another favorite method of hunting commonly practised by the Indians was that of "running," in which the hunters, riding horses along with the herd, placed themselves alongside various buffalo and killed them with rifle or pistol, or with bow and arrow, or by the use of the lance. A practiced and skilful rider, well mounted, might kill five or six or even more animals in a single chase. With a well-trained horse, it was possible to get close enough to a buffalo to actually touch it with the hand. The horse ran without guidance, turned as the buffalo turned, and leaped aside as the arrow twanged or the gun was fired. It took a good horseman to remain in the saddle and to load his rifle or get another arrow ready while continuing the chase. The real danger in the "running" method was from rough uncertain ground and badger and coyote holes.

VI

PREPARATION OF BUFFALO SKINS

AMONG the Indians it was the task of the squaws to prepare the robes for market, as the fur traders did not buy untanned skins. By hard and incessant labor, one squaw was capable of preparing ten robes in a season, although two or more often worked together on the heavier ones. The skin was first treated with a mixture of ashes and water to loosen the hair. The next step was to spread the skin on the ground with the flesh side uppermost and stretch it by means of wooden pegs driven in the ground through small slits cut in the edge of the hide. The squaws then worked, using scrapers made of sharp stones or buffalo bones, to free it from every particle of flesh. It was sometimes reduced as much as one half in thickness during the process. When the fleshing had been satisfactorily accomplished, the skin was kept thoroughly moistened with a solution of water and buffalo brains for about ten days. Once each day the robe was taken up and thoroughly rubbed and grained; after which the skin was smoked, which made it pliable and soft even after it had been wet. There seems to have been no definite amount of time spent on a skin, the squaws working until the robe was in acceptable condition.

While the actual dressing of the robes was carried on in about the same way among the different tribes, they varied somewhat as to details and in the character and type of robe produced. The Crow Indians had the best reputation for making fine robes in the upper Missouri country, and their ability to prepare extra high-grade skins was commented on by several early explorers and travelers and was generally recognized among the fur traders. Occasionally a robe was painted and decorated, which greatly enhanced its value, but as a rule the Indians kept the decorated robes for themselves. There was a certain amount of rivalry among the various tribes as to robe quality, as well as competition as to numbers obtained. It is impossible to estimate with any degree of accuracy the number each tribe produced. Between 1830 and 1840 the Crows are said to have made about five hundred packs of robes, ten to the pack, while the Sioux and Blackfeet, being more numerous, are said to have produced a good many more, and smaller tribes in proportion to their numbers and the availability of buffalo in the regions in which they lived.

VII

TYPES OF ROBES

THE ROBES that were taken in the Northwest divided themselves into different kinds, depending upon their quality, traders keeping a keen watch for the more valuable ones. The most rare and, therefore, the most valuable of all robes was that of the white buffalo. The Mandans and Crows valued it for ceremonial rather than commercial purposes and a white robe would bring from ten to fifteen horses. After three or four years' use, it was left exposed to the weather to deteriorate under rain and wind. There is record of a Mandan chief giving ten horses, a gun, some kettles, and other articles for a white robe, and on the Montana range in 1882, when enormous numbers of buffalo were slaughtered, only one white robe was included among the lot and it sold for two hundred dollars.[1]

The "beaver robe," the fur of which was extremely fine and the color of beaver, was also rare and therefore valuable. The skin had to be carefully prepared since, when taken, it contained a large number of coarse hairs that had to be removed, leaving the soft silky fur underneath. Fur traders estimated that not more than one robe in ten thousand would be classified under this type. The "blue robe" was also comparatively scarce and in demand, the fur of this type being long and fine and of a definite bluish cast. James McNaney, a robe-buyer in the Dakota and Montana region in 1882, found only one "beaver robe" and twelve "blue robes" in his purchases for the season, which amounted to twelve hundred robes. He sold the first for seventy-five dollars and the other twelve for sixteen dollars each. The "black robe" of the mountain buffalo, sometimes called the "black and tan robe" because of its coloring, was quite valuable, though far more common than the other special types mentioned. The ordinary buffalo-robe was light tan in color, and was sometimes called the "buckskin robe." While the price varied according to quality, a good robe of this type was worth about three dollars and a half in 1882.[2]

While buffalo meant life itself to the Indians of the western plains, they often meant as much to the pioneering white man who went into the Northwest in the early part of the nineteenth cen-

---

[1] "Maximilian, Prince of Wied's Travels in the Interior of North America, 1833-54," *Early Western Travels*, ed. R. G. Thwaites, XXII, 354; Hornaday, "Extermination of the American Bison," *op. cit.*, pp. 444-5; Merrill G. Burlingame, "The Buffalo in Trade and Commerce," *North Dakota Historical Quarterly* (July, 1929), pp. 273-4.

[2] E. T. Seton, *Life Histories of Northern Animals* (New York, 1909), p. 256; Hornaday, *op. cit.*, p. 444; Burlingame, *op. cit.*, p. 274.

tury to explore, trade, trap, hunt, and travel.[3] That Lewis and Clark were dependent upon the buffalo for food is amply indicated in their journals. Early in 1805 at the Great Falls portage on the upper Missouri River, Lewis wrote: "Some hunters were sent out to kill buffaloe in order to make pemecon to take with us and also for their skins which we now want to cover our baggage in the boat and canoes when we depart from hence. The Indians have informed us that we should shortly leave the buffaloe country after passing the falls; this I much regret for I know when we leave the buffaloe that we shall sometimes be under the necessity of fasting...." Alexander Henry in January, 1801, in the valley of the Red River of the North, wrote: "My winter stock of provision is complete, all good fat buffalo meat, and my men have little to do."[4] Between October, 1806, and January, 1807, Zebulon M. Pike, the famous army explorer, told of the killing of eighty buffalo and explained that in the intervals between hunts they were often short of food.

The expedition of S. H. Long, which carried only enough supplies to supplement the meat they expected to find, was worried and often went without sufficient food when no game was at hand. Like Pike, Long carried supplies of jerked meat in regions where buffalo were not abundant and at one time ate buffalo meat that was evidently diseased in order to ward off starvation. The extent to which buffalo were utilized in the forts of the fur companies is indicated by a statement from Prince Maximilian of Wied, who said, "Fort Union alone consumes from 600 to 800 buffaloes an-

[3] Father Marquette, writing in January, 1675, told of the importance of the skins of wild cattle to the Illinois Indians and of trading tobacco to them for buffalo-robes. La Salle, in carrying out the orders of the French king to develop the industry of "buffalo wool," wrote him a letter in 1682 in which he spoke of the large number of buffalo killed each year in Ouisconsing (Wisconsin). Father Poisson, another Jesuit, writing from the present state of Arkansas in October, 1727, told how a Canadian trapper and his partner the year before had brought to New Orleans 480 tongues of buffalo that they had killed during the winter.

[4] *Manuscript Journals of Alexander Henry and David Thompson*, ed. Coues, I, 170.

nually and other forts in proportion."[1] The value of the bison to the Plains traveler is amply verified by Josiah Gregg in his famous work, *The Commerce of the Prairies*. The buffalo was of vital importance to the larger governmental reconnaissance expeditions, that were generally organized on the basis of not being hampered by the carrying of many extra supplies. "Except for buffalo," reported W. H. Emory, "game is very scarce. The buffalo where they range may be relied upon to support a column of several thousand men, but their range is uncertain."[2]

VIII

BUFFALO AND THE EARLY FUR TRADE

ALTHOUGH the fur trade grew rapidly in the early nineteenth century in the Northwest, few buffalo-robes were handled until after 1815.[3] A conservative estimate of the buffalo-robes obtained on the Missouri between 1815 and 1830 was 26,000 each year, purchased at an average price of $1.50 and sold for about three dollars each.[4] That the yearly return of buffalo-robes, however, often reached large numbers, is shown by the records

[1] "Maximilian, Prince of Wied's Travels in the Interior of North America," *op. cit.*, XXII, 382.

[2] W. H. Emory, "Notes on a Military Reconnaissance from Fort Leavenworth in Missouri to San Diego in California," *Senate Exec. Doc.*, 30th Cong., 2nd Sess., III, No. 7, 14.

[3] The fur trade in the Northwest may be roughly divided into three periods influenced largely by conditions at St. Louis, the center of its activity. The first period 1764-1808, at which time it was largely under French and Spanish control, was followed by the second, 1808-1860, which was one of exploitation by large American fur companies that pushed their way into the Northwest, bringing down the Missouri River to St. Louis unprecedented amounts of valuable furs. During these two eras the trade was mostly in the smaller furs, buffalo-robes becoming important after 1815. In the third period, 1860-90, the trade in smaller furs declined until it almost disappeared and the trade in robes shifted to buffalo hides. It was during this period that the buffalo were most viciously attacked and the great herds finally exterminated. Isaac Lippincott, "A Century and a Half of the Fur Trade at St. Louis," *Washington University Studies*, III, Part II, No. 2 (St. Louis, Mo., 1916), 206-16.

[4] "Report of Thomas J. Doughery, Indian Agent at the Upper Missouri Agency, October 25, 1831," *Senate Exec. Doc.*, 22nd Cong., 1st Sess., II, No. 90, 53.

for the port of New Orleans for 1825, which indicated that 184,-000 robes were received. Dropping to 77,400 in 1826, rising, however, to 134,000 in 1827, the peak was reached in 1828 with the arrival of 199,870 robes. The returns for 1829 were 159,870, dropping to 30,610 in 1830. The returns after 1830 for a number of years did not exceed 30,000 and on several occasions fell below that number.[5]

The decline in number of the beaver, mink, otter, and other valuable types of fur-bearing animals in the early thirties, together with various changes in fashions, caused more attention to be directed to the hunting of the buffalo. John Jacob Astor, who had forecast the decline of the beaver trade, sold the northern department of his company to Ramsey Crooks and his associates, and the western department with its headquarters at St. Louis to Pratte, Chouteau and Company. It was not long before buffalo-robes exceeded in bulk all other furs combined in the business of the various fur companies and occasionally surpassed them in value. The heavy robes and hides of the buffalo necessitated different methods and tactics from those required by the smaller pelts, and with the development of Missouri River steamboating a number of permanent trading-posts were established to facilitate their collection.

With the change of method, the old type of trapper became less in evidence and the fur trade was left to agents among the Indians and to buffalo hunters who connected themselves with the various forts or lived with the Indians. When Colonel Frémont left the valley of the South Platte on one of his expeditions and could not find any one sufficiently acquainted with the region at the base of the Rockies to serve as a guide for his party, he made the following observation: "The race of trappers who formerly lived in these recesses have almost entirely disappeared." The German physician and traveler, Wislizenus, in observing the last summer rendezvous for trappers in 1839, said: "The Indians had for trade

[5] Lippincott, *op. cit.*, pp. 219-20.

chiefly tanned buffalo skins, moccasins, thongs of buffalo leather or braided buffalo hair and fresh or dried buffalo meat. They had no beaver skins." [6]

The American Fur Company constructed a number of fur trading-posts along the upper Missouri River, the largest and best equipped being Fort Union at the mouth of the Yellowstone. Built in 1828 by Kenneth Mackenzie, it united the fur routes of the rivers and mountains, and from there supplies were taken to the smaller forts where traders bargained for robes, or making it their headquarters, traveled among the Indians collecting robes. On March 20, 1834, Charles Larpenteur reported the arrival of two traders at Fort William, one with sixteen packs of robes and a few wolf and fox skins, while the other, who had been sent among the Crows, brought in thirty packs of buffalo-robes and one pack of beaver. The results of the winter's labor at Fort William totaled "one hundred packs of buffalo-robes, five of beaver, six of wolf and one of fox and rabbit." [7]

As trading declined in the spring months, the robes were brought to Fort Union for shipment down the river. On April 2, 1835, Larpenteur reported the arrival of D. Lamont and traders from Fort Assiniboine with 4,200 buffalo-robes, thirty-seven dressed cow skins, twelve dressed calf skins, 450 salted tongues, 3,500 pounds powdered and 3,000 pounds dried buffalo meat. On April 24, 1835, "Mr. James Kipp arrived at Fort Union from Fort McKenzie with the results of the season's trading which included 9,000 robes and 390 buffalo tongues." In 1841 Fort Mackenzie sent 2,100 packs of buffalo-robes to Fort Union and in 1847 one of the best seasons' returns included 20,000 robes. [8] At the various fur-trading forts buffalo meat was the common staple

[6] F. A. Wislizenus, *A Journey to the Rocky Mountains in 1839* (St. Louis, Mo., 1912).

[7] Charles Larpenteur, *Forty Years a Fur Trader of the Upper Missouri: the Personal Narrative of Charles Larpenteur, 1833-72*, ed. Elliott Coues (New York, 1898), I, 62, 69, 79.

[8] Bradley Journal, "Affairs at Fort Benton," *Contributions*, Montana State Historical Society, I, 233, 244, 256.

FORT UNION

Maximilian, Prince of Wied, *Reise in das Innere Nord-America*, 1839-41.

of food, and at the larger posts such as Laramie, Union, and Bridger, regular buffalo hunters were employed whose sole duty was to keep the post supplied with meat.

An official of the American Fur Company in 1843 estimated the total number of robes traded annually for the preceding ten years by the various companies as follows: American Fur Company, 70,000 robes; Hudson's Bay Company, 10,000 robes; other companies, probably 10,000 robes. In addition to the robe trade, there was an extensive trade in tongues and tallow. In 1848 the number of buffalo tongues sent to St. Louis had reached 25,000 and the number of robes had reached 100,000. Fort Benton, on the upper Missouri, developed as a rendezvous for traders and Indians, 2,000 robes being collected there as early as 1834. By 1841 the annual collection had risen to 20,000 robes and from then until the outbreak of the Civil War the average number of robes sent yearly from Fort Benton was 20,000. Kansas City became important in the robe business, 70,400 robes being received there in 1857 and 55,000 pounds of buffalo meat.

In the autumn of 1858, William T. Hamilton left Walla Walla on a trading expedition among the Blackfeet Indians in the Montana area. On October 18th, his journal stated: "On Marias River just down from the fork of the Sun River, at a camp of Piegans, I traded for 120 robes and two parfleches full of dried buffalo tongues." On October 24th: "Traded for 55 robes with the Blackfeet." October 25th he "traded for 42 robes with the Crows at a Piegan camp." Hamilton started back on November 7th having secured 237 good buffalo-robes, as well as some excellent marten and fisher skins.[9]

[9] William T. Hamilton, "A Trading Expedition Among the Indians in 1859 from Fort Walla Walla to the Blackfeet Country and Return," *Contributions*, Montana State Historical Society, III, 62-114.

IX

TRADING FOR ROBES

IN THE EARLY days of the fur trade in the upper Missouri country, there was little competition among the various fur companies, each of which obtained a monopoly over a certain region and established permanent forts and posts at central points. As the fur companies and the forts declined in importance, traveling traders went from village to village with their outfits, negotiating for furs and buffalo-robes. The methods of trading employed varied greatly with the different tribes, the fur company, and individual traders. Whether the Indian came to the fort with his furs and friends, or whether the trader came to the village, the red man loved to linger over the bargain and to be entertained as the terms of exchange were considered. The type and extent of entertainment were therefore about as important as the values attached to the robes and goods. It has been said by many observers, however, that the longer the Indian delayed the closing of the deal, the less he received for his furs. Manuel Lisa was one of the best-liked traders in the Northwest, but even he could bargain to his own advantage. The well-known traveler, John Bradbury, who accompanied him on a trading expedition in 1809, told of stopping at an Arikara village where negotiations were opened to bargain for some buffalo-robes. While the chiefs did not wish to hurry the process, they set the price expected as thirty loads of powder and lead per robe. The next day, after twenty-four hours of entertainment, during which time presents had been distributed and whiskey used rather freely, the deal was consummated on the basis of twenty loads of powder and lead for each robe.[1]

Among the various articles in the stock of a Missouri River fur-trader were tobacco, blankets, blue and scarlet cloth, fire steels, files, arrow-points, brass wire, tacks, leather belts, silver ornaments,

---

[1] "Bradbury's Travels in the Interior of America," ed. Thwaites, V, 132.

axes, hatchets, shells, beads, knives, and guns. Some of the items in an order sent by Pierre Chouteau to an English firm for goods to be used in trade in the winter of 1840-41 were as follows: 6,000 pairs of French blankets; 300 guns; 300 butcher knives; 9,000 pounds of blue and white chalk beads; 500 pounds of "Pidgeon Egg Beads"; and a quantity of colored cloth.[2] The Indians also came to value the coffee, sugar, salt, flour, and pepper offered by the traders.

One of the chief articles, however, used by the fur companies and individual traders in obtaining furs and robes from the Indians was whiskey and alcohol. After being prohibited by government Indian agents, it was smuggled into the Missouri River region in great quantities and for years an alcohol still was secretly operated at Fort Union. Indians had a keen liking for intoxicants of almost any type and the traders took full advantage of their weakness, many travelers and observers of the Indian trade severely indicting them for their ruthlessness in using it. "Whiskey was one of the chief articles," wrote a critic. "Four gallons of water were added to each gallon of alcohol and a pint of the stuff was traded for a buffalo robe worth five dollars."[3] Some traders even increased the ratio, as Larpenteur, a well-known trader, at one time obtained 210 excellent robes from a camp of Cree Indians for five gallons of whiskey and a small quantity of beads and trinkets.[4]

Some of the robe buyers added other things than water to their liquor, which by the time it reached the Indian must have been a concoction that the distiller would have had difficulty in identifying. An early Montana pioneer, familiar with the buffalo trade in all its details in that area, gave a formula by which some of the liquor used was made:

[2] Letter from Crooks to Chouteau, August 15, 1840, papers of the American Fur Company, Item No. 9,207, quoted in Branch, *Hunting of the Buffalo*, pp. 99-100.
    [3] *Prose and Poetry of the Livestock Industry of the United States* (Kansas City, 1905), p. 292. Statement by James P. Beckwith.
    [4] Larpenteur, *Forty Years a Fur Trader*, ed. Coues, I, 190.

1 quart of alcohol
1 pound of rank black chewing tobacco
1 handfull red peppers
1 bottle Jamaica ginger
1 quart black molasses
water from the Missouri River ad libitum
Mix well and boil until all the strength is drawn from
    the tobacco and peppers.[5]

The value of robes was not fixed and depended upon the time of year, quality and excellence of tanning, the shrewdness of both trader and Indian, and the number of presents and the amount of whiskey the trader was willing to distribute. For the staple products that were also sold to white settlers, hunters, and traders, monetary units were used. Prices established for those commodities in 1833-34 were as follows: salt, sugar, and coffee, $1.00 a pint; pepper, $2.00 a pint; while flour sold for $.25 a pint. There was apparently no attempt to apply monetary values to robes and even when the Indians were told that a robe was worth a ten-dollar bill, it was figured that since seven pounds of sugar filled a trading-cup ten times both sides preferred to deal in cups rather than in monetary terms. A standard formula used for years in the Northwest was:

10 cups of sugar make one robe;
10 robes make one pony;
3 ponies make one tepee.[6]

Another trick frequently resorted to in trading with the Indian was that of giving quantity rather than quality. If an Indian could obtain several desirable articles in exchange for one, in his reasoning he had got the better of the bargain. Under this philosophy a good exchange price for a robe might be a cup of sugar, a yard of calico, some red paint and a string of beads. A plug of tobacco

[5] Peter Koch, "Life on the Musselshell in 1869 and 1870," *Contributions,* Montana State Historical Society, II, 298.
[6] Hamlin Russell, "The Story of the Buffalo," *Harper's Monthly Magazine,* LXXXVI (April, 1893), 162-3.

might be thrown in for good measure should the robe happen to be an extra nice one.[7]

James H. Bradley in his journal told of a standard employed whereby blankets and clothing of different colors, but identical in quality, were traded for various numbers of buffalo-robes. The formula followed was nine and seven robes for two kinds of striped blankets; six robes for a red blanket; five robes for a purple one; and three robes for a white one; eight robes for a red coat trimmed with gold or silver lace, and six robes for a blue coat trimmed with white or red braid.

At the fort or camp, as the robes were obtained by the trader, they were arranged in lots of ten or twelve and bound firmly together into bales or packs by means of a rude press. Little attention was ordinarily given to quality except to distribute those that were exceptionally good or bad through the various bales. The packs were then transported to the central fort or down the Missouri River to headquarters.

In the thirties Pierre Chouteau and the American Fur Company worked in close coöperation in order to dispose of their robes. In the spring of 1835 Ramsey Crooks wrote to Chouteau saying that orders had already been taken for the entire robe crop of the next year, even if it would amount to 36,000 or more. It was agreed that their inferior summer skins should be disposed of by including one in each pack of twelve skins. It was also agreed that the selling price should be $48.00 a pack and that calf skins should be priced at $2.50. It was decided that it was best to keep the price moderate and divide their robes among a considerable number of buyers in order to create competition, keep prices down and insure the consumption of robes on hand, leaving the market clear for the next year's crop.

The slaughter, however, continued to outdistance the market. Pratte, Chouteau and Company were compelled to carry over a

[7] Lyman E. Munson, "Pioneer Life on the American Frontier," *Journal of American History*, I (1907), 117.

surplus of 23,000 robes into the season of 1838. Crooks estimated that the year's trading would bring at least 51,000 new robes on to the market, which, together with the 9,500 robes remaining in the hands of rival fur companies, would make nearly 85,000 robes to be disposed of. It was necessary to hold back all defective robes and in spite of the efforts to sell those on hand, the surplus continued to accumulate. In the summer of 1840, 67,000 new robes were thrown on the market.

In the early forties, Ramsay Crooks made an attempt to develop a market for buffalo-robes in Europe, several packs being sent to a fur dealer in Hamburg in the winter of 1841-42. Although wide publicity was given their arrival and statements of their possible uses, the auction was poorly attended and the highest bid was less than actual cost. Some of the robes were then sent to Leipzig to be considered for a possible Russian and Polish market, but there, as in Hamburg, the price was too high to recommend them to military authorities as possible material for coats, carpets, and service covers, domestic sheepskin being much cheaper than the imported robes. Some of the first shipment were disposed of when the price declined in 1843-44, but the number purchased in Europe was never very large.[8]

X

MISSOURI STEAMBOATING AND THE BUFFALO TRADE

WITH the development of steamboat traffic on the upper Missouri River, buffalo-robes and products became important articles of transport. The steamboat *Yellowstone* on its first trip to Fort Tecumseh, later called Fort Pierre, returned to St. Louis in July, 1831, with a full cargo of buffalo-robes, furs, and peltries, including ten thousand buffalo tongues, and when it left Fort Union on July 23, 1832, on its second trip, it carried several hundred packs

[8] Branch, *Hunting of the Buffalo*, pp. 101-2.

of buffalo-robes.[1] In August, 1842, seven vessels from the Yellow-- stone River arrived at St. Louis consigned to the American Fur Company, carrying twenty thousand buffalo-robes.[2] On July 16, 1850, Joseph La Barge, captain of the steamer *St. Ange,* arrived at St. Louis with 674 packs of buffalo-robes and on June 2, 1851, the steamer *Alton* arrived loaded with robes and was followed about two months later by the *St. Ange.* In June and July of 1852, three steamers arrived with furs and robes, including the faithful *St. Ange* carrying 1,305 bales of robes and 959 loose ones.

By 1853 the custom of floating robes down the river from the upper forts to Council Bluffs on rafts and flatboats eliminated in part the difficulties encountered by steamboats with shoals, snags, and bars when the water was low. Early in June, 1853, the steamers *El Paso* and *Highland Mary* arrived from Council Bluffs with close to 1,200 bales of robes and early in June the *Banner State* arrived with 1,218 bales of buffalo-robes and 31 bags of tongues.[3] An Indian interpreter on the upper Missouri of more than twenty-five years' experience estimated in 1857, when an agent for the American Fur Company, that the trade in robes at Fort Benton was 3,600 bales; Fort Union, 2,700 to 3,000 bales; Fort Pierre, 1,900 bales; and at Forts Clark and Berthold, 500 bales each, or a total of 75,000 robes, which he estimated to have been an average yearly amount during the period.[4] That number is well in line with the yearly estimates of other contemporaries.

[1] Chittenden, *History of Early Steamboat Navigation on the Missouri River,* I, 90, 187-8.
[2] *Niles Weekly Register* (Baltimore, Md.), LXIII, August, 1842, 16.
[3] *Missouri Republican* (St. Louis, Mo.), June 2, 9, July 16, 30, 1851, June 13, 29, July 14, 1852, June 9, July 6, 1853. The files of the *Missouri Republican* and other St. Louis newspapers record considerable activity in robes and buffalo products in the fifties and sixties. *Western Journal and Civilian,* LX (St. Louis, Mo., n.d.), 48.
[4] Statement of F. F. Gerard, quoted in "Maximilian, Prince of Wied's Travels in the Interior of America," ed. Thwaites, XXII, 188. A complete record of the number of buffalo robes handled by traders at Fort Benton from 1834 to 1861 is found in the Bradley Journal, *Contributions,* II, 121-2.

The Missouri River was used as a means of getting buffalo hides and robes to market as late as 1880, as is indicated by an editor of Sioux City, Iowa, in the spring of 1881:

Most of our citizens saw the big load of buffalo hides that the "C. W. Peck" brought down last season, a load that hid everything about the boat below the roof of the hurricane deck. There were ten thousand hides in that load, and they were all brought out of the Yellowstone on one trip, and transferred to the "C. W. Peck." How such a load could have been piled upon the little "Terry," not even the men on the boat appear to know. It hid every part of the boat, barring only the pilot house and the smoke stacks.[5]

XI

DIVISION INTO NORTHERN AND SOUTHERN HERDS

As LINES of prairie travel developed, the buffalo moved far enough away from the various routes to make general killing difficult and unprofitable. Emigrants on the Oregon Trail and gold-seekers on their way to California caused the buffalo to congregate in great herds on the northern and southern ranges, leaving the area along the main lines of travel without buffalo except during the periods of seasonal migrations. The party of Howard Stansbury, on its way to explore and survey the basin of the Great Salt Lake in the summer of 1849, traveled forty-four days from Fort Leavenworth and were well up in the valley of the Platte River before they killed their first buffalo. The shift of the herds to the northward is evidenced by the report of the Stevens expedition in the summer of 1853. After crossing the Cheyenne River they observed large herds of buffalo, estimated by some of the party to number as many as half a million.

While large numbers were being destroyed for meat, robes, and sport, as long as the buffalo ranged more or less out of reach of the white hunter it would have taken many years for extermina-

[5] *Sioux City Journal,* May, 1881, quoted in Hornaday, "Extermination of the American Bison," p. 502.

tion to have been accomplished. There were, however, certain developments taking place that would eventually cause its immediate destruction and the most important of those factors was the construction of the railroads. Railroads not only made the buffalo range accessible but furnished a ready means of transporting its products to market. In the process of extermination, most of the animals were killed for the purpose of making money, and that was only possible after railroads had brought eastern markets within reach of the field of production.

As the rails of the Union Pacific Railroad penetrated into the Territory of Wyoming in 1867, the construction crews and floating population making up the ever-shifting railroad towns satisfied their husky appetites in part on steaks, stews, and other delicacies from the buffalo brought in by hunters whose rifles helped to diminish the herds that ranged the plains. In 1867, when Major Powell traveled the Union Pacific to its terminus, which at that time happened to be Cheyenne, he reported having seen only one live buffalo on the entire trip, an old bull wandering aimlessly near the mouth of the Platte River.

The completion of the Union Pacific in 1869 finished the division of the buffalo of the West into two distinct bodies: the northern herd, whose numbers were estimated at about one and a half millions, and the southern herd, estimated variously at from four to five millions. The northern herd ranged in general through the northern half of Wyoming northward to the Canadian border and from western Dakota westward to the Rockies. In 1869 and 1870 the Musselshell in south central Montana was in the heart of the buffalo country. "In March, 1870, I traveled from the Musselshell to Fort Browning on the Milk River," wrote Peter Koch, an early settler in the Territory of Montana,[6] "and for a distance of forty miles I was not out of easy rifle range of buffalo. On the Musselshell, it was not uncommon to shoot bulls from the

[6] Koch, "Life on the Musselshell," *Contributions*, Montana State Historical Society, II, 142.

doors of our cabins, and during the rutting season we were frequently kept awake at night by incessant pawing, bellowing and fighting."

XII

THE SOUTHERN HERD IS SLAUGHTERED

No SOONER had the golden spike been driven completing our first transcontinental railroad than a southern extension later called the Kansas Pacific, and another road, the Atchison, Topeka and Santa Fe Railroad with its various branches, opened the way into the heart of the southern buffalo country, literally cutting the southern herd into pieces by rendering every portion of its range easily accessible. Hunters poured onto the range.[1] Hunting was carried on winter and summer, many hunters in their keen desire to make money taking only the skins, not stopping to utilize the meat or other products. The frontier towns, including Dodge City,[2] Wichita, and Leavenworth, did an enormous business selling guns and supplies to hunters. Camps were established along the banks

---

[1] William F. Cody, as official hunter for the construction gang of the Kansas Pacific Railroad, is reported to have killed 4,280 buffalo in fifteen months. William F. Cody, *The Life of Buffalo Bill by Himself* (Hartford, Conn., 1879); Branch, *Hunting of the Buffalo*, p. 142.

[2] Dodge City, Kansas, in the heart of the buffalo country in the southwest, is a notable example of a frontier town centering its early activity around the buffalo trade. Hardly had the railroad reached that point when the trade in buffalo products began, a box-car used as an office until a depot could be constructed. Dozens of cars were loaded with hides and meat for eastern markets that had come in loaded with food, ammunition, and supplies for hunters. The streets of the town were lined with great creaking wagons bringing in and unloading meat and hides and reloading with supplies for hunters on the buffalo range. Robert M. Wright of Wright, Beverly and Company, the most prominent firm in the buffalo trade in that area, in whose warehouse and yards it was no uncommon sight to find from sixty to eighty thousand hides and robes, said, "Charles Rath and I shipped more than two hundred thousand buffalo hides and robes, the first winter the Atchison, Topeka and Santa Fe reached Dodge City (1872) and I think there were at least as many more shipped from there, besides two hundred cars of hind quarters and two cars of buffalo tongues." Robert M. Wright, *Dodge City, the Cowboy Capital* (Topeka, Kan., 1913), pp. 77, 140-1; John R. Cook, *The Border and the Buffalo* (Topeka, Kan., 1907), pp. 116-7. In 1878 it was estimated that 120 cords of baled buffalo hides were stacked at Dodge City. Hornaday, "Extermination of the American Bison," pp. 493-5.

of the rivers and streams where the buffalo were shot down by the thousands as they came to drink.

Trains going west were full of excitement and anticipation on reaching the buffalo country, often stopping to allow the passengers to shoot from the car windows. It was said that the trains ran so close to the buffalo in the first few months that one could almost touch them as they passed. The buffalo did not learn to fear the railroad, and often ran for miles parallel to the tracks. Sometimes the herds would try to cross the tracks, and, after a few trials on the part of the trainmen in running through such a multitude of buffalo, the engineers learned to give the animals the right of way. Engines were thrown from the tracks and sometimes trains were overturned by the force of the stampede. The whistle and bell of the train, used to frighten away the animals, only served further to enrage them. Besides running trains for the benefit of passengers who wanted to enjoy, in safety and comfort, the sport of buffalo-hunting, the crews of construction groups building railroads into the West were dependent on the bison for meat. Buffalo hunters, engaged for each construction gang, were well paid because the range of the buffalo and that of the Indian had become the same, since the western trails were so well traveled and were deserted alike by animals and red men. Buffalo Bill (William Frederick Cody) gained his title and his fame by virtue of his career as a buffalo hunter during the construction of the Kansas Pacific.

While emigrant trains of wagons seldom stopped to hunt buffalo, unless they needed meat, because of the loss of time involved, something in the sight of the great herds of bison, easy targets in their fat sleekness, often roused their excitement until it seemed impossible to refrain from killing the beasts until the last one was beyond reach of their rifles. Many a fine horse, weakened already by an unaccustomed fare of grass instead of grain, was sacrificed in the buffalo chase. As the tide of emigration swelled westward, the buffalo retreated until, where before the plains had appeared black with the vast herds, not one animal was to be seen. The slaughter was heaviest from 1871 to 1875 and by 1880 buffalo were virtually gone in the Southwest.[3]

As early as 1868, John F. Meline, who was riding horseback across the prairies, saw evidences of terrific slaughter: "The road is a perfect buffalo Golgotha ... a place of skulls, where in 1857 there had been large numbers grazing." [4] Another observer, writing in 1873, described the withdrawal of the herds from the railroads and the ruthless extermination. "We saw few live ones ... but whole catacombs of the dead," wrote J. H. Beadle. "For twenty miles in one place the sight is awful ... about the stations are skins piled in great heaps to dry for market." [5] An account of the activities on the southern range dated in 1874 stated: "On the south fork of the Republican River, on one spot were to be counted 6,500 carcasses of buffalo from which the hides had been stripped. The whole plains was dotted with the putrifying remains of buffalo." [6] The Atchison, Topeka and Santa Fe Railroad carried 459,-453 buffalo hides and robes over its lines from 1872 to 1874 and it is reported that other railroads in the southwest carried at least twice as many more, making a total in the three years of 1,378,-359.[7] It was estimated by Hornaday that approximately three and one half million buffalo were killed in the southwest in 1872, 1873, and 1874.[8] The declining numbers of buffalo is indicated also in the reports of the various Indian agents in the southwest. The Indians of the Kiowa Comanche agency sold 70,400 robes to

[3] W. E. Webb, *Buffalo Land* (Philadelphia, 1876), p. 316.
[4] John F. Meline, *Two Thousand Miles on Horseback* (New York, 1868), p. 281.
[5] J. H. Beadle, *The Undeveloped West; or Five Years in the Territories* (Philadelphia, 1873), pp. 436-7.
[6] J. A. Allen, *American Bison, Living and Extinct*, p. 178.
[7] Hornaday, *op. cit.*, p. 479.
[8] Hornaday summarized the numbers killed in the three years indicated as follows: killed by professional white hunters, 3,158,730; Plains Indians, 390,000; settlers and mountain Indians, 150,000; making a total of 3,685,730. Hornaday, *op. cit.*, p. 501. Dodge estimated the numbers killed on both the southern and northern ranges during the same years as about five million. R. I. Dodge, *Our Wild Indians* (Hartford, Conn., 1882), p. 295.

AN INDIAN BUFFALO HUNT

Maximilian, Prince of Wied, *Reise in das Innere Nord-America*, 1839-41.

SLAUGHTER ON THE LINE OF THE KANSAS PACIFIC

Richard Irving Dodge, *The Plains of the Great West*, 1877.

traders in 1876; 64,500 in 1877; 26,375 in 1878; and 5,068 in 1879.[9]

In the seventies, packers became interested in buffalo meat, which became popular in the East as a novelty, and there was a considerable demand for buffalo tongues.[10] Many butchers in the West sold buffalo meat as domestic beef to those who did not know the difference and buffalo entrees were on the menus of all western hotels and eating-houses. Hindquarters were selected carefully, cut into three pieces, sugar-cured, smoked and sewed into canvas, and shipped to eastern markets where they sold at excellent prices. Buffalo hides were used for leather, and tanneries were built, one of the larger ones being that at Greeley, Colorado, where tens of thousands of hides were baled and stacked for shipment. Prices, good at first, went as low as seventy-five cents a hide and buffalo meat sold as low as half a cent a pound, as hunters in wagons, on horseback, and on foot swarmed onto the buffalo range.[11]

XIII

THE BUFFALO FRONTIER IN THE NORTHWEST

AFTER the Civil War there had been located at strategic points on the plains of the Northwest and near the foot of the Rocky Mountains, a number of military posts to whose garrisons was assigned the task of watching the Indians and protecting emigrants and other travelers. Some of the more important military establishments were: Forts Benton, Shaw, Peck, and Missoula in the Territory of Montana; Randall, Berthold, Bennett, Buford, and Union in the Territory of Dakota; and Laramie, D. A. Russell,

[9] *Annual Report of the Commissioner of Indian Affairs*, 1879, p. 65. Early in 1874 John A. Lessig reported 2,000 hunters in camps along the Rickaree River waiting for buffalo. *Denver News*, January 15, 29, 1874.

[10] It was not until 1870 that private business concerned itself with the enormous profits to be had from the great buffalo herds that roamed the plains of the West. By 1871 the buyers of hides and meat were eager to pay cash to the hunter for every animal he could kill.

[11] Branch, *Hunting of the Buffalo*, p. 154.

and Bridger in the Territory of Wyoming. In the years from 1865 to 1870, there had collected at the various forts and minor military garrisons, fur-trading posts, mining camps, and other frontier settlements, a considerable number of soldiers, freighters, trappers, traders, miners, gamblers, and bad men, who, with the emigrants on the trails and a few scattered ranchers and frontier farmers, made up the white population of the Northwest. Over this area roamed large herds of buffalo that furnished food, clothing, shelter, and wealth to the sparse Indian population as well as to many of the white inhabitants.

In the sixties and seventies there occurred in the Northwest a series of developments that were greatly to hasten the final slaughter of the large herds of buffalo that grazed on the ranges of that area. The Indian was gradually forced to the westward and placed upon reservations, cattle and sheep ranchers began to move their herds into the rich grasslands and there occurred an advance of the agricultural frontier into the promising valleys of the Missouri and its tributaries. It was generally understood that it would be impossible to keep the Indian on reservations as long as there were buffalo available,[1] nor could the rancher and frontier farmer occupy the lands of their choice in any numbers if they were to be subject to Indian attacks. The construction of the Northern Pacific Railroad through the very heart of the grazing grounds of the northern herd made possible the destruction of the buffalo, which

---

[1] It has often been said that the United States Government was interested in the rapid extermination of the buffalo herds that served as a basis for the independent existence of the Indian. As long as there were buffalo in eastern Montana, western Dakota, and northern Wyoming, it was impossible to keep the Indians of those regions on their reservations. Although the Indian Bureau authorized Indian agents to issue hunting "passes" to the various tribes, it was really officially sanctioning what would in most cases have been done anyway. Some writers claim that the military officers at the government forts furnished free guns and ammunition to buffalo hunters. If that sort of thing went on, it was done without official sanction by the War Department. In a congressional debate in 1872, James A. Garfield, a representative from Ohio, made the assertion that the Secretary of the Interior had said he would rejoice as far as the Indian was concerned when the last buffalo had been killed. *Congressional Record*, 43rd Cong., 1st Sess. (1874), pp. 107-9.

was essential should the movements mentioned be carried out. The invention of the Sharp's accurate breech-loading rifle with telescopic sights, and an increased demand for buffalo products, facilitated the final slaughter.

The end of the Civil War brought to the West many ambitious young men, eager for any enterprise that promised profit and adventure. Some of them engaged in scouting for the United States Government, others in freighting and in the Indian trade, and not a few became buffalo hunters. In the sixties, as miners and prospectors invaded various portions of western Montana and northern Wyoming, the eastern and southern halves of the Territory of Dakota were cleared of buffalo as the Indians were crowded westward onto reservations. Robe-takers were active among the Indians and the slaughter for food and robes slowly drove the buffalo north and west where they joined the northern herd. So few buffalo remained in southwestern Dakota in 1874 that the Custer expedition of that year saw none between Bismarck and the Black Hills.

The Northern Pacific Railroad crossed the Red River of the North from Minnesota into Dakota at Fargo early in 1872 and slowly advanced westward through the Indian lands of the territory, under military protection against the hostile redskins. The track was completed to Bismarck on the Missouri River early in June, 1873, where it received the buffalo-robes that came down the Missouri and Yellowstone rivers. Construction was brought to a halt by the panic of 1873. Railroad activity was resumed in 1878, the road being completed to Sentinel Butte near the Montana line in 1880, and the following spring continuing west. In 1881 the road was constructed as far west as Glendive and Miles City and soon had penetrated the plains area to the Rockies.[2] The building of the Northern Pacific caused a rapid advance of agri-

[2] E. V. Smalley, *The History of the Northern Pacific Railroad* (New York, 1883), *passim; Fargo Times* (Fargo, D. T.), March 8, 1879; *Bismarck Daily Tribune*, Immigration number, January 1, 1884.

culture and ranching in the Northwest, but also made the northern herd accessible and furnished transportation for buffalo hides, and so rendered inevitable the speedy destruction of the great herds, setting the stage for the enactment of the last scene in the drama of the buffalo frontier.

In the sixties and seventies, while the slaughter of the southern herd was being carried on, there is much evidence to indicate that many buffalo were being killed in the Northwest, but as long as they were killed largely for their robes, there was little material decrease in their numbers. The *Cheyenne Daily Leader*, in the spring of 1869, reported buffalo traders active near Fort Laramie and in the Powder River country.[3] In western Montana, collectors of buffalo-robes were active around Helena in 1870 and 1871.[4] Although in the early seventies there were hundreds of thousands of buffalo slaughtered for their hides and robes on the northern range, in 1875 they were seemingly as numerous as ever along the upper Missouri and its branches. In that year, from 50,000 to 100,000 robes were sent east from the northern area, not counting those that were sent from Canada.[5] In the summer of 1875, the I. G. Baker Company of Fort Benton, Montana, shipped out around 20,000 robes and the T. C. Price Company of the same place handled about 25,000. In 1876 the Baker Company increased its number to 75,000.[6]

In 1876 N. J. David of Minneapolis, Minnesota, for many years a buyer of furs in the Northwest, was of the opinion that there were at least a half million buffalo within a radius of a hundred miles of Miles City. The first shipment of buffalo killed by white men was made that year and the statistics of the Northern Pacific show that approximately fifty thousand robes and hides were received at Bismarck from the area between there and Miles

[3] *Cheyenne Daily Leader*, March 12, 20, 1869.
[4] *Helena Weekly Herald*, December 25, 1870, January 4, 1871.
[5] Hornaday, *op. cit.*, p. 502.
[6] *Benton Record* (Fort Benton, Mont.), February 1, August 7, 1875, August 24, 1876.

City, Montana.[7] In 1877 a Fort Benton editor reported immense herds of buffalo in that area and near the mouth of the Marias River, and the Crow Indians were reported to be gathering a rich crop of robes. The editor went on to say: "This source of wealth to the Indians promises to play out in a few years. Five years ago vast herds of these animals made their camping grounds on the Missouri covering an area of several hundred miles along the

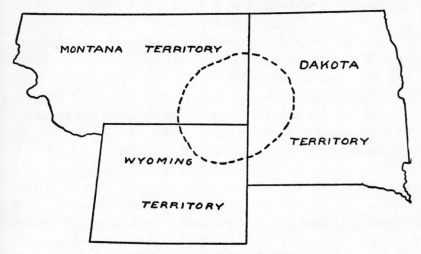

BUFFALO RANGE OF THE NORTHWEST, 1876

stream between the foot of the mountains and Fort Peck, but now there is scarcely one to be seen east of the Marias."[8] The *Avant Courier* of Bozeman on the edge of the mountains in western Montana reported activity in buffalo products during the seventies. On October 1, 1875, there were large supplies of dried buffalo meat for sale in the mining camps and on February 18, 1876, much activity in the robe business was reported in the Yellowstone country for the past year. On January 11, 1877, several fine lots

[7] Burlingame, "Buffalo in Trade and Commerce," *North Dakota Historical Quarterly*, p. 78.

[8] Quoted from the *Benton Record*, in the *Yankton Press and Dakotian*, March 1, 1877.

of robes were being purchased and the outlook for the buffalo season was optimistic. Thirty-three thousand buffalo hides were shipped out of Bozeman during the spring and summer of 1880.[9]

In the spring of 1879 the professional hunters who had been following and slaughtering the buffalo herds in the southwest for seven or eight years suddenly discovered that the southern herd had ceased to exist except for a few thousands scattered over the sage-brush area to the southward. In 1879 and 1880, many of the old professional hunters shifted their activities to the Northwest and cordons of buffalo hunters began closing in on the northern herd. With the building of the railroad through western Dakota and into Montana, there developed a demand for buffalo hides that could be taken through the summer months without exposure, preparation and delay, eliminating the hardships connected with the taking of robes during the winter months. In 1880, the first shipment of green untanned hides was made out of the Northwest. As long as the northern buffalo herds were only killed for their robes, they did not decrease very rapidly, but when they began to be killed for their hides, a most indiscriminate slaughter began that did not stop until the herds were wiped out.[10]

In 1879 and 1880, as the Northern Pacific advanced westward toward the Montana line, thousands of buffalo were killed in Montana and shipped by river to Bismarck[11] or to the western

[9] *Avant Courier*, October 1, 1875, February 18, 1876, January 11, 1877, July 22, 1880; *Helena Daily Herald*, January 11, 1877.

[10] *Avant Courier*, July 22, 1880; *Helena Daily Herald*, July 28, 1881. Robes were taken during the winter months, when the fur of the buffalo was in best condition, and were used chiefly for coverings and coats; hides were taken largely during the warmer months when hunting was easier, and were used for leather articles.

[11] J. N. Hanford, traffic manager of the Northern Pacific, writing to W. T. Hornaday in September, 1887, stated that in the years 1876 to 1879 inclusive there were handled yearly at Bismarck on the Missouri River in the Territory of Dakota, at that time the western terminus of the road, from three to four thousand bales of robes brought down by river steamer. About half of the bales contained ten robes while the other half contained twelve. He stated that the amount of buffalo meat shipped over the N.P. was never large. The bulk of the meat was left on the prairie and was not of sufficient value to pay the cost of transportation.

terminus of the road to be carried to the East. Granville Stuart, a well-known Montana pioneer, in describing the events of 1879 and 1880 in the Territory of Montana said: "The bottoms are literally sprinkled with the carcasses of dead buffalo. In many places they lie thick on the ground, fat and the meat not yet spoiled, murdered for their hides which are piled up like cordwood all along the way.... Probably ten thousand buffalo have been killed in this vicinity this winter. Slaughtering the buffalo is a government measure to subjugate the Indian."

The merchants of the little towns along the railroad were not slow to take advantage of the boom in hunting, many of them becoming wealthy by advancing outfits of guns, ammunition, and supplies to buffalo hunters on ordinary credit arrangements or on a stated percentage of the hides taken. An editor of Miles City, Montana, in January, 1880, reported that more than one hundred of the town's citizens were out hunting buffalo for the hides, which were reported to be worth $1.50 each. "One firm alone in this city already has on hand more than four thousand hides and many other houses have almost as many. There is much difficulty and expense by travelers in following roads along the Yellowstone valley as the trails are totally obscured in some places by immense herds of buffalo." [12]

In 1881 and 1882 the Northern Pacific line was extended westward and shipping points increased, reaching as far west as Terry and Sully Springs in Montana. Dickinson, located immediately east of the Bad Lands in the western portion of the Territory of Dakota, became one of the main outfitting and shipping points for buffalo hunters on the Northern Pacific. Wagon trains unloaded vast piles of green hides for shipment. The Indian agency at Standing Rock, located southwest of Dickinson, extended every hospitality to buffalo hunters and encouraged the Sioux warriors to join in the hunt, disposing of their hides to the professional

---

[12] In 1880 the shipment of dry and untanned hides taken during the summer months commenced. *Yellowstone Journal* (Miles City, Mont.), January 17, 1880.

hunters. Hides were worth from $2.00 to $3.50 each. The criminal waste that had characterized the destruction of the southern herd was not as pronounced in this area. For every one hundred hides carried to market, it was estimated that they represented not more than one hundred ten buffalo, while in Kansas ten years before, they would have represented at least two hundred.[13]

From 1881 to 1884 buffalo hunters were very active in the Northwest along the line of the Northern Pacific Railroad and the number of buffalo killed was enormous. Professional hunters followed the herds northward just as harvesters later followed the grain-cutting season from the south to the north. The Frazier brothers were professionals and had one of the largest hunting outfits operating in Montana and Dakota. The year 1881 was an important one on the range. An editor of Sioux City, Iowa, in the spring of that year, stated that competent authorities were estimating the number of buffalo-robes and hides to be shipped out of the Yellowstone country to be at least 100,000, and two firms were already reported to be negotiating for the transportation of 25,000 each. The previous year about 30,000 had come out of the Yellowstone country, less than a third of what was then awaiting shipment. In the spring of 1881 it was estimated that at least 75,000 dry and untanned buffalo hides came down the river as far as Bismarck to be shipped east by railroad.[14]

The season of 1881 and 1882 was perhaps the biggest on the northern buffalo range. The great triangle formed by the Missouri, Yellowstone, and Musselshell rivers was a favorite hunting-ground, and those streams with their tributaries were lined with the camps of buffalo hunters. An editor of Helena, Montana, reported on July 28, 1881, that more than 200,000 buffalo hides had been shipped out of that region during the past winter, and the *Billings Herald* and the *Glendive Times* both carried infor-

---

[13] *Helena Daily Herald*, July 28, 1881, May 27, 1883.
[14] *Sioux City Journal*, May 6, 9, 14, 19, 24, 1881; Hornaday, "Extermination of the American Bison," p. 502.

mation of range activity.[15] By 1882 it was estimated that there were at least 5,000 white hunters and skinners on the northern range, to say nothing of the Indians whose sentinel camps extended northward to the Canadian border. H. F. Douglas of Glendive, Montana, bought thousands of buffalo hides in the summer and fall of 1881, most of which came from animals killed in Montana and western Dakota. During the fall and winter of 1881-82, his firm was said to have shipped out more than 250,000 hides. Isaac P. Baker, a Missouri River steamboat captain, stated that he carried more than 250,000 hides secured from hunters and Indians on his steamboats during those years. On one trip in June, 1882, the steamer *Rosebud*, of which he was captain, brought 10,000 hides to Bismarck. Joseph Dietrich operated a meat market in Bismarck from 1881 to 1883 and sold large amounts of buffalo meat to his patrons. He secured his meat from the Clifford brothers, professional hunters whose headquarters were located at Sully Springs in Montana.[16]

During the fall and winter of 1882-83 the slaughter continued on the northern range, although the number taken was probably smaller than the previous season. When winter began the main herd, consisting of about 75,000 buffalo, moved from the Yellowstone region toward the north and was wiped out. One small band escaped and fled to the rough land above Dry Creek, a tributary of the Missouri, and a small herd of about two hundred found

[15] *Helena Daily Herald*, July 28, 1881; *Billings Herald* (Billings, Mont.), June 23, 1881; files of the *Glendive Times* (Glendive, Mont.), spring and summer of 1881.

[16] Files of the *Bismarck Tribune*, 1881-83; files of the *Glendive Times*, 1882-85; *Yankton Press and Dakotian*, August 14, 1883. Between 1918 and 1928 Lewis F. Crawford, superintendent of the North Dakota Historical Society at Bismarck, North Dakota, collected a large amount of valuable material on the subject of ranching and other phases of early Dakota and Montana history by collecting letters and diaries and interviewing many of the old cattlemen and settlers who were still living. Through the courtesy of Mr. Crawford, the writer was allowed to use the material collected by him on two visits to the Historical Library at Bismarck: one in the summer of 1927 and the other in the spring of 1928. References to this material are cited as Crawford's *Notes*. L. F. Crawford, *Notes:* Interviews with W. F. Douglas, Minneapolis, Minnesota; with Joseph Dietrich, Bismarck, North Dakota.

shelter in the Bad Lands west of the Musselshell.[17] As the hunting season opened in the fall and winter of 1883-84, a small herd was reported grazing between the Black Hills and Bismarck. The *Helena Daily Herald* on January 3, 1884, printed the following statement: "The last of the great herds of buffalo on the American continent is now grazing on the Badlands south of the Yellowstone, between the Powder and the Little Missouri Rivers."[18] Another Montana editor on January 10, 1884, reported the situation as follows: "The only buffalo herd of any considerable size in this region is now wintering in the Badlands country of the Little Missouri west of Fort Gates. The buffalo is nearly gone."[19] Granville Stuart said of the last herd: "It is surrounded by a line of fire. The Sioux Indians compose part of that line and the white hunters the other. It is anticipated that by spring the herd will be entirely destroyed or scattered out in little bands in secluded places." The various predictions were right. The white hunters struck first and destroyed most of the herd, while the remainder was set upon by Sitting Bull and his warriors who, within two days, wiped them out.

Buffalo hunters organized their outfits for the regular spring hunt in 1884 and started for the buffalo range. They found only a few scattered bulls as they traveled westward through the decaying carcasses of the last year's kill. Robe and hide buyers along the railroad were disappointed in the spring and summer of 1884 and only enough hides were collected at Dickinson to make up part of a carload. It was the only one shipped east that year and was the last shipment of buffalo hides made by the Northern Pacific Railroad.[20]

[17] *Helena Daily Herald*, January 3, 10, 17, 26, 1883; files of the *Dickinson Press* (Dickinson, D. T.), 1883.

[18] The various newspaper accounts estimated this herd as numbering from 10,000 to 75,000. The first figure is probably closer to being correct.

[19] *Mineral Argus* (Lewiston, Mont.), January 10, 1884.

[20] *Dickinson Press*, May 6, 1883; *Medora Badlands Cowboy* (Medora, D. T.), November 13, 1884; *Mandan Weekly Pioneer*, Immigration edition, January 1, 1884; files of the *Bismarck Daily Tribune*, 1881-84; Branch, *Hunting of the Buffalo*, pp. 218-20.

Ralph Finger and Miles Vineyard, two homesteaders of the Heart River country in western Dakota, spent the fall and winter of 1883-84 on the buffalo range and killed only 235 animals, which was considerably less than their ordinary kill. They worked part of the time with Ben and Joe Gatling, who were located on neighboring homesteads. They hauled most of their hides to Beckett and Foote, who operated a buying camp for an eastern firm near Eagle's Nest and Grand River, three miles north of the Cave Hills in the northwestern corner of what is now South Dakota. They reported that most of their kill that season were bulls, as the herds had been well worked over by earlier hunters who picked the cows out of the herds because their hides were of greater value.

Cowhides, when dried, averaged about fifty pounds each and sold on the range in 1883-84 at from $.03 to $.04 a pound, while bullhides, averaging 120 pounds, sold for $.013. The hunters, stated Finger, seldom saved any more of the meat than the hams, humps, and tongues, and sometimes none at all. They hauled some of their meat to Dickinson but most of it was sold to buyers who followed the hunters. They received $.03 a pound for cow meat and $.015 for bull meat. Buffalo steaks, tender and juicy, could often be bought for as little as $.02 a pound. The meat and hide of the average buffalo cow brought the hunter about five dollars. Finger and his homesteading partners hunted on the range up to the close of January, 1885, but found few buffalo after the winter of 1883-84.[21]

XIV

PROFESSIONAL HUNTERS

WHILE methods of hunting the buffalo, as employed by white hunters, varied, as long as sport was an element in the process,

[21] Crawford, *Notes:* Interviews with Isador Bireau, Ralph Finger, Miles Vineyard, Bismarck, N. D.

shooting them from the back of a horse galloping at the edge of the herd was by far the most popular. However, when skin-hunting reached a point where it was conducted on a wholesale basis and became strictly a business proposition, this method could not be used effectively, since the number killed was definitely limited, the carcasses were widely scattered and the buffalo herds might be stampeded out of the country. The favorite method, and the one largely used later, was "still" hunting, where the hunter would get a "stand" and shoot from behind cover. The hunter, after locating a herd and carefully looking over the ground, would cautiously approach the buffalo from the leeward side. Within a reasonable distance, from fifty to one hundred and fifty yards, the hunter would find a comfortable position, get a rest for his gun, adjust the sights and start shooting. He tried to shoot the leader first, after which he picked off the buffalo on the outside and those that were inclined to wander away. Large kills were often made in this manner. Colonel Dodge counted one hundred and ten carcasses in a semicircle, killed by a single hunter from one spot in less than an hour.

The hunter used the well-known Sharp's .55-caliber rifle or buffalo gun. It weighed fourteen pounds and is said to have been one of the most accurate guns ever manufactured. It would kill at fifteen hundred yards and a good hunter could make every shot bring down a buffalo. The vital spot was the heart and the hunter prided himself upon his ability to hit it. In a "stand" care had to be taken not to fire the gun fast enough to heat the barrel, as this might cause it to expand. Some hunters carried two rifles, allowing one to cool while the other was in use. The careful hunter as a rule loaded his own shells. There was ordinarily little danger from the buffalo, although now and then a wounded bull might charge the hunter, who needed steady nerves and the ability to shoot quickly and straight to finish the animal in time. For its size and bulk, the bison was surprisingly agile and had been known to gore a horse to death that did not move quickly enough to get out of its way. At times when buffalo broke from a "stand" the hunters gave chase on horseback.

While the Northwest had some very able buffalo hunters, it apparently did not produce any with the reputation of Charlie Rath, or of Frank Carver who won the championship of the southwestern prairies, and because of his ability to shoot accurately from horseback was given a position with a circus, where he delighted his audiences with his skill, while in the saddle, in breaking glass balls thrown into the air. Probably the most famous hunter in the northern area was Vic Smith, whose exploits on the buffalo range brought from a Dickinson editor in the spring of 1883 the following comment: "Vic Smith, the champion buffalo hunter of the northern ranges, came in today with his partner, J. W. Anderson, who have several thousand buffalo to their credit since last fall." Early in August "the famous hunter" was again in town but left for the range within a few days after obtaining supplies.[1]

After the buffalo were killed came the skinning. Some hunting outfits employed regular skinners who were paid by the month, or from twenty-five to thirty cents a hide, while others worked on the basis of shares. A good skinner could take care of fifty buffalo a day, if the carcasses were conveniently located and fairly close together. Some of the larger organizations used horses to facilitate the work. The skin was split the length of the animal, and loosened about the head, legs and tail. Ropes were then fastened to it and a team of horses pulled the skin from the body. The hides were then taken to camp, where they were stretched and staked out to dry and were scraped free from flesh. One buffalo skinner in describing his work said: "We then had stretched and dried two thousand three hides, nine hundred and two of which I had skinned, and was so accredited. This was an average of twenty-two buffalo a day for forty-one days. At twenty-five cents per hide I had earned $225.00." [2]

[1] *Dickinson Press*, May 6, August 11, 1883; Crawford, *Notes:* Interviews with Miles Vineyard and J. W. Anderson, Bismarck, N. D.
[2] John R. Cook, *The Border and the Buffalo*, pp. 116-8.

Hunting parties came to be highly organized, making provision for division of labor. Some of the party did nothing but shooting, others did the skinning, while others stretched and staked out the skins. A typical outfit consisted of four to five wagons, the driver of one acting as camp watchman, stock-tender, and cook, while the other drivers did the skinning and work on the hides. As a rule the hunter furnished the wagons, animals and supplies, the pay of his helpers being determined by the number of buffalo killed. The money obtained from the hides and meat was ordinarily divided into two equal parts: one went to the hunter, who paid all expenses from his part and the second was split into as many shares as there were drivers and skinners. No buffalo hunter with a "top notch" reputation would stoop to the degrading task of skinning the animals he shot. It was a matter of caste, and not necessarily of laziness.

Parties were organized and fitted out to remain in the field for weeks and even for months, often constructing a "camp" in a locality where buffalo were plentiful. They carried with them all necessary supplies for the hunt and camp except meat. The hunter usually purchased his outfit on the basis that he would kill one hundred buffalo a day, and would sell the meat and hides for from three to five dollars an animal, depending upon size and quality. While one good hunter and four skinners could dispose of that number daily, there were very few outfits that did so as the traits of the game, methods, and difficulties of hunting usually combined to hold down the average daily kill to below fifty.[3]

Dickinson, in the Territory of Dakota on the Northern Pacific Railroad, well toward the Montana line, was close to the center of activity in the last years of the northern buffalo hunting. The *Dickinson Press* therefore gives one a good idea of activities on the buffalo range. On August 18, 1883, it mentioned that a herd of buffalo was seen within ten miles of town. "This has been a great place for buffalo hunters during the past year," wrote a

[3] Crawford, *Notes:* Interview with R. Finger and W. F. Douglas.

FORTY THOUSAND BUFFALO HIDES

Ready for shipment in the yards of Rath & Wright, Dodge City, Kansas, 1877.
Collection of N. H. Rose.

"WHERE THE MILLIONS HAVE GONE"

Painting by J. H. Moser, 1888. Courtesy of the United States National Museum.

settler, "and there have been about 250,000 buffalo hides shipped from here this spring. Sixty buffalo were killed not over thirty miles from here the other day. One man shot them in two hours." On September 15th, several hunters from Dickinson were on the range, and a week later a small herd was reported within a mile of town. On October 6, 1883, said the *Press*, "about five hundred Gros Ventre Indians passed through here on Monday on their way to the buffalo range. They camped overnight just outside the town." November 3rd, the following item appeared: "Several hunters came in this week, who report buffalo as scarce." And on July 12, 1884, the editor wrote: "C. D. Cope of Philadelphia recently returned from a trip west and reports the bison almost gone. The Dakota herd numbers only seventy-five thousand, while the Montana herd is now the object of relentless slaughter. These bands are about all that is left of the countless millions that once roamed the Plains."

Some idea as to the number of hides handled at Dickinson may be gained from the same newspaper during the summer of 1883. Early in May William Cooper of Bozeman, Montana, had purchased 20,000 hides at his Dickinson warehouse. During the last week in May 3,000 hides came into Dickinson in two days. On June 9th, thirty-one wagons loaded with buffalo hides came into the town from the range, and about 4,000 were delivered at the warehouses that week. Eight ox-teams came in on the evening of July 4th with 1,300 hides. The decline in the number of hides handled is indicated by a news item April 5, 1884: "Beckett and Foote brought in hides and furs Thursday. They had the skins of 1,000 deer and antelope, 400 coyote and 200 buffalo hides." [4]

In marketing the immense numbers of buffalo-robes and hides, there developed in the United States several large companies having branches in western cities whose organizations handled the bulk of the trade. The J. and A. Moskowitz Company of New York, with offices in Chicago, between 1876 and 1884 handled a

[4] *Dickinson Press*, files for 1883-84; *Avant Courier*, May 29, 1883.

total of 246,100 robes and hides valued at almost a million dollars. The prominent New York firm of Joseph Ullman, with offices at St. Paul, was also quite active. Perhaps the strongest company on the northern range in the seventies was that of I. G. Baker and Company of Fort Benton in the Territory of Montana. This firm was gradually driven out of business, however, in the last years of the buffalo slaughter, by the large numbers of private parties and small companies that came into the northern range. In 1876 the I. G. Baker company shipped 75,000 robes out of Fort Benton; in 1880 the number was 20,000, falling to 5,000 in 1883 and to none at all in 1884.[5]

The prices paid for robes and skins varied with the type and quality and with the general supply and demand. In 1869 buffalo hides to be tanned for leather were valued on the St. Louis market at $16.50 for a bale of ten first-class hides, $12.50 for a bale of second-class hides, and $8.50 for a bale of third-class hides.[6] Joseph Ullman in 1881 handled 14,000 hides at an average cost of $3.50 and 12,000 robes at $7.50. In 1882 the same company purchased between 35,000 and 40,000 hides at the same price as the year before and about 10,000 robes at $8.50. In 1883 hides and robes were purchased at a slight advance over the quotations of 1882. In 1884 the Joseph Ullman concern bought approximately 8,500 hides and in 1885 their purchases amounted to practically nothing. A general estimate of prices paid buffalo hunters from 1880 to 1884 was: cowhides, $3.00; bullhides, $2.50; yearlings, $1.50; calves, $.75. The cost of getting the hides to market brought the cost of cowhides up to an average of $3.50 and others were increased in proportion.[7]

In 1886 William T. Hornaday, chief taxidermist for the National Museum, was sent on an expedition by the Smithsonian

---

[5] Burlingame, "Buffalo in Trade and Commerce," p. 79.
[6] Theodore R. Davis, "The Buffalo Range," *Harper's Monthly Magazine*, XXXVIII (January, 1869), 163.
[7] Letter from Joseph Ullman to Hornaday, November 12, 1887. Quoted in Hornaday, "Extermination of the American Bison," p. 440.

Institution to obtain specimens of buffalo or bison. It was with difficulty that twenty-five specimens were found, some of which were mounted, while of the others only parts were preserved. Careful investigation at that time revealed that there were in the United States between three and four hundred buffalo, eighty-five of which were living in the wild state. In 1889 it was estimated that there were 541 live bison in the country and in 1902 E. A. Hitchcock, Secretary of the Interior, reported 1,143, of which 968 were pure-blooded animals and 175 mixed bloods.[8]

With the disappearance of the buffalo, the Indians of the Northwest were either supported by the government or eked out an existence, with some government aid, by farming, living precariously and squalidly as they tried to raise crops. One writer estimated that 25 per cent of the Piegan band of Indians died of starvation in the winter of 1883-84 due to the driving of the buffalo from the Blackfeet country and their extermination. While these figures may be exaggerated, this is typical of what happened among the various Indian tribes to a greater or lesser degree.[9] In 1887, Hornaday estimated that there were about fifty-five thousand Indians being supplied with food by the government, all of which had formerly been dependent upon buffalo. The typical frontier attitude is voiced by an early settler who said: "With the end of the buffalo, the Indian depredations were over. They lived on buffalo and came in and murdered our women and children. After the buffalo were gone the government had no trouble in keeping them on their reservations, and the range was soon settled by thrifty farmers and ranchmen."[10] To-day the buffalo are gone, the Indians are dependent and the plains are settled— the end has been accomplished. Whether or not it justified the

[8] *Senate Doc.*, 57th Cong., 1st Session, XXX, No. 445, 1; Hornaday, *op. cit.*, 525-9.
[9] Henry Inman and W. F. Cody, *The Great Salt Lake Trail* (New York, 1898), p. 307.
[10] John Clowd Jacobs, "The Last of the Buffalo," *World's Work*, XVII (January, 1898), 1098-1100.

means and whether the government might not have accomplished its objective by greater care and control are questions regarding which there is bound to be a considerable difference of opinion.

XV

BUFFALO BONES

AFTER buffalo hunting was over, there developed a traffic of some importance in the bones that were thickly strewn over certain portions of the west Missouri country. Large numbers of them were hauled to the railroad and river towns by small ranchers and farmers, who were badly in need of cash. They were shipped east where they were used as fertilizer and as carbon for use in the refining of sugar. Indians, as well as whites, gathered them, often building fires to burn the grass, making it easier to locate and collect them. Great stacks of bones, from ten to twelve feet in height and often a quarter of a mile in length, consisting of hundreds of tons, were piled along the railroad tracks for shipment. A man could gather a wagon-load in a short time, which, when taken to market, was worth seven or eight dollars.

The first mention of buffalo bones appearing in the *Dickinson Press* was on May 24, 1884. "The buffalo bone business is beginning to boom in this vicinity, and several loads have been brought in during the week. We understand that the business will be entered into on a large scale during the present season and will give employment to quite a number of men." On June 14th, an advertisement stated that Beckett and Foote wanted one thousand tons of buffalo bones, while on June 28th two outfits came in with bones, one consisting of twenty-seven yoke of oxen and another of thirty-four yoke, owned by Arthur Johnson and Peter Bland from Deadwood in the Black Hills. The Deadwood party loaded with freight for the return trip. Many bones were also delivered at other stations on the Northern Pacific, as well as in towns on other roads.

One writer said of the bone business:

As late as 1886, overland travelers saw at many of the stations between Jamestown in the Territory of Dakota and Billings in Montana Territory, immense heaps of bones stacked alongside the Northern Pacific tracks awaiting shipment. In 1885 a single firm shipped more than two hundred tons of buffalo bones from Miles City, Montana. The valley of the Missouri River and its tributaries was gleaned by teamsters who gathered bones from as far back as one hundred miles, often hauling them to the river for shipment. One operator who had eight wagons gathering bones for him sold crushed bones in bags to a fertilizer company in Michigan for $18 a ton, and uncrushed bones at $12.[1]

In three weeks' time in the summer of 1884 one hundred carloads of buffalo bones were shipped from Ipswich, in Dakota Territory, and Fred Stoltz, a bone buyer at Minot in the northern part of Dakota, purchased large amounts in 1884 and 1885, at one time having on hand as many as five hundred carloads stacked up and standing along the tracks awaiting shipment. Traffic in the bones of the buffalo continued until those near the railroads had been gathered. In the dry years of the late eighties, when the frontier farmers had nothing to sell, some of them hauled bones long distances to obtain small amounts of cash in order to keep their families from starvation.[2]

With the removal of the bones of the buffalo from the plains and valleys of the Northwest, the history of the buffalo frontier was ended, and, while it was not a romantic story, it wrote a fitting climax to a century of wasteful conquest carried on with a ruthlessness typical of the frontier and of America in the nineteenth century.

But even while the hunters were mercilessly slaughtering the rapidly diminishing and broken herds of buffalo on the plains and Bad Lands drained by the upper Missouri River and its tribu-

[1] Hornaday, op. cit., p. 446.
[2] Blunt Advocate (Haynes County, D. T.), June 14, 1884; files of the Miles City Weekly Times, 1884; Dickinson Press, May 16, 1885.

taries, small ranchers and cattlemen from the East and South were locating ranches amid the rich grasslands where the buffalo had formerly fed. All that was required of an ambitious ranchman was to select a suitable location beyond the range of other cattlemen, construct a few log buildings and drive in his herds. The story of the frontier of the cattleman is colorful and full of action and will be the theme of the next section.

III

THE FRONTIER OF
THE CATTLE-RANCHER

IN THE WESTWARD movement of the frontier across the
United States, ranching, or the raising of live stock on a considerable scale, has always been an important industry. It was
possible to obtain cheap pasture on the unoccupied and unclaimed
lands, and, when the lack of transportation facilities made the
growing of crops otherwise unprofitable, to feed the grain and
corn produced to stock, which were disposed of by driving them
to market. The early settlers on the Atlantic seaboard brought cattle with them from their European homes, and as their stock increased in numbers and the land in the various settlements
increased in value, the owners of the larger herds moved westward
where they fattened their cattle for markets in the eastern settlements. There they remained until permanent settlers cleared the
land and planted crops, after which the ranchers moved on again.
Thus, as the agricultural frontier pushed westward, it has usually
had what may be called a "pastoral fringe," a narrow band or
border on its outer edge occupied largely by those who devoted
their energies to grazing. While they kept ahead of the permanent agricultural settlements, they were always held back
from penetrating very far into the wilderness by the danger of
Indian attacks.

In the early decades of the nineteenth century the frontier of
the rancher crossed the Alleghenies and large herds of cattle were
raised in Kentucky and Ohio and driven to the markets of Louisville and Cincinnati. As this area became more thickly settled
and agricultural lands increased in value, cattle-raising on a large

scale shifted westward again, and the process was repeated in Indiana and Illinois, St. Louis and Chicago becoming the central markets. The next shift was to Missouri and Iowa, where the industry was at its height in the forties. While the better settled areas improved their stock and placed a greater emphasis on dairying, they still fattened and marketed their surplus cattle for beef. That phase of the business, however, became less and less important, since they could not compete in the production of beef cattle with areas of cheap or free land farther to the west.

By 1830 the most western point of the American frontier, that line of continuous settlement containing two or more inhabitants to the square mile, had reached the Big Bend of the Missouri River, where its turbid waters, flowing toward the south, turn sharply and flow eastward to the Mississippi. From that point the north and south wings of the frontier line bent backward rather sharply toward the east. The advanced line of western settlement hesitated at the Big Bend of the Missouri for more than two decades while the areas to the north and south gradually filled in as new states were formed in the upper valley of the Mississippi and in the lower South. The frontier town of Independence, Missouri, established in 1831 at the tip of the advancing wedge, was known in the thirties and forties as the "Gateway to the West." The vast plains region between the western line of settlements and the Rocky Mountains was probably best known to the average American as "Indian country" or the "Great American Desert."

Fur traders, operating from their posts along the Missouri River and its branches, combed the area for furs, and in their efforts to expand their activities, penetrated well into the valleys and passes of the Rocky Mountains. Each spring they brought downstream in great keel-boats the fruits of their labors, unloading the pelts at St. Louis. This great area was looked upon by the Federal Government as the permanent home of the Indian and even the eastern tribes at this time were being requested to give up their old tribal lands and to take reservations beyond the western line of settlement, where they might live as they pleased unmolested. The United States Army, in its efforts to protect the frontier in the early decades of the nineteenth century, had established military posts or forts at strategic points, their garrisons being instructed to keep a watchful eye on the Indians and to aid and protect explorers, emigrants, and other travelers. Over the plains roamed immense herds of buffalo, whose flesh and skins provided the necessities of life for the sparse Indian population, as well as for the scattered whites.

At the western settlement of Independence was being enacted a scene that embodied all the color and action of a frontier pageant. Fur traders, explorers, Indian agents, travelers, soldiers, missionaries, and emigrants stopped there on their way up the uncertain waters of the Missouri or passed through the dusty streets of the town in their great covered wagons. Those traveling overland to the Columbia River country stopped to outfit or replenish their supplies before starting across the trackless Indian country to the Platte, which they followed to the Sweetwater and on to South Pass, discovered in the early twenties by Ashley, the fur trader, and on to the Columbia River and Oregon. Wagon trains loaded with "yankee goods" made their way to the southwest bound for Santa Fe where they could be sold for high prices.

During the westward movement, the missionary had been wont to follow the frontier of the explorer and fur trader and in the movement to Oregon, the sequence ran true to type. In 1834, the Methodist Church sent out two missionaries who established themselves in the valley of the Willamette River not far from the headquarters of the Hudson's Bay Company at Vancouver. In 1835 the American Board of Foreign Missions sent out the vigorous Marcus Whitman who located in central Oregon. Both parties sent back glowing accounts of the excellent climate and the richness of the land. It was not long before the new region was being discussed in lyceums and on the lecture platform. Joint occupation of the area with England, provided for by treaty, was still in effect and the possibility that this desirable area might be taken from our traditional enemy aroused added interest. The financial panic of 1837 worked many hardships and furnished groups of population in the older settled areas, restless and poor, who were not only willing but anxious to try their luck in Oregon. By 1840 the Jesuits under Father De Smet had established a mission in the Bitter Root Valley on the eastern edge of the Rocky Mountains in the western portion of what later was to become the Territory of Montana.

The growing interest in Oregon caused the Federal Government to send John Charles Frémont to that area in 1842 on an expedition of exploration, and the same year it was induced to send out Dr. Elijah White to the Oregon settlements as sub-Indian agent and magistrate. His party, consisting of one hundred and thirty persons and eighteen Pennsylvania wagons, was the first formally organized group of settlers to make the trip. In the decade that followed there gathered each spring at the rendezvous at the bend of the Missouri, as the pastures were becoming green, groups of pioneers who organized and made ready for the long trek to the fertile lands of Oregon. Estimates of numbers vary but conservative opinion puts the number that made the trip in 1843 at 1,000, increasing to 3,000 in 1845 and to between 4,000 and 5,000 in 1847. In the spring of 1847 the harassed Mormons, giving up hope of finding a safe place in the States where they might practise their religious beliefs unmolested, began to move from their winter quarters in Iowa to the valley of the Great Salt Lake. In 1849 the news of the discovery of gold in California aroused the nation almost to a state of frenzy, and set the whole frontier in motion as thousands of gold-seekers flocked westward in a wild stampede. The early cattle business of the Northwest began as a result of the needs of the emigrants as they slowly made their way to Oregon, Salt Lake City, or California, the first herds being brought together to meet their demands.

The thousands of emigrants that crossed the plains in the two decades before the Civil War stirred into activity the various traders in the fur country of the Northwest, whose business had suffered a serious decline with the passing of the boom period of the fur trade. By the time the great wagon trains had reached the road leading up the North Platte, they were in need of food and their animals were tired and foot-sore. Some of the pioneers had been ill-advised as to how to stock provisions and others had been held up and robbed by roving bands of Indians, but even those who had started out well supplied and who had avoided robbery were out of many things and oftentimes in want. These groups of pioneers in search of new homes and fresh opportunities were good customers of the traders and bought to the limit of their resources.

I

EARLY CATTLE IN WYOMING AND MONTANA

THE SCATTERED traders were quick to see the possibilities and sought out favorable locations where they could sell to advantage their stocks of coffee, sugar, flour, bacon, beans, powder, and shot, brought in by pack train from the Oregon settlements. Flour sold readily at one hundred dollars for a hundred-pound sack, giving a good margin of profit to the trader. Fort Bridger became one of the central trading points as early as 1845. There was also need for assistance in crossing rivers and streams where a slip or a misstep meant disaster. At strategic points along the North Platte, Sweetwater, and other streams, ferries and bridges were constructed where the emigrant might cross for a liberal fee.[1] As travel increased over the emigrant roads, grass for grazing became so scarce that it would not support the cattle and horses and it

[1] William K. Sloan in his autobiography tells of a toll-bridge across the North Platte, about twenty miles north of Fort Laramie, where the owner collected $40,000 in tolls during the single season of 1853. The cost of constructing the bridge was about $5,000. *Annals of Wyoming*, IV (Cheyenne, Wyo., 1926), 246-7.

was necessary to obtain hay. Road stations were established whose owners cut the wild hay along the various streams, dispensing it to the needy emigrants at prices varying from $.50 to $1.50 per hundred pounds.[2] Last but not least was the business of selling or trading fresh stock to the travelers for their worn-out and foot-sore animals, enabling the emigrants to continue their journey. The ratio of the transaction was usually two weary and trail-worn animals for one rested and in good condition. Many of the Oregon and Mormon emigrants who took dairy stock with them for use on their new farms were compelled to dispose of them for a few dollars or a few pounds of bacon or coffee, rather than abandon them to starve on the trail. The first herds of cattle in the North-west developed from bands of live stock collected at the various ranches by traders along the emigrant trails. Granville Stuart, one of the earliest settlers in the Montana area, reported several herds in 1858, one of which numbered six hundred head, and was owned by a man named Grant who was trading along the road from Fort Hall,[3] and Horace Greeley on his journey to the West in 1859 reported several former fur traders with good-sized herds of cattle doing a prosperous business along the trail.[4] Freighting companies were active in the Northwest. Alexander Majors of the freighting company of Russell, Majors and Waddell, while haul-ing a consignment of government freight to Fort Laramie in the fall of 1854, reached the place in November, too late to return with his ox teams to Missouri. He wintered three hundred head of cattle in what later was to become Wyoming, grazing them on the plains near Fort Laramie and they came out in the spring in good condition.[5] The same firm of freighters was reported to have

[2] *House Exec. Doc.*, 39th Cong., 2nd Sess., No. 23, pp. 5-6.

[3] F. W. Warner, *Montana Territory and Business Directory* (Helena, Mont., 1879); Stuart, *Forty Years on the Frontier*, II, 97-8.

[4] Horace Greeley, *An Overland Journey from New York to San Francisco in the Summer of 1859* (New York, 1860), pp. 194-5.

[5] Letter of Alexander Majors to the editor of the *Cheyenne Daily Sun*, printed May 1, 1884. *Annual Report of the Commissioner of Agriculture* (Helena, Mont., 1870), pp. 303-10.

wintered fifteen thousand head of freight stock in the Wyoming area in 1857-58.

As the herds increased in numbers and forage became scarce along the trails, some of the owners began to drive their cattle to the north and to winter them in the sheltered Beaverhead, Stinking Water, and Deer Lodge valleys in what later became western Montana. The Jesuits at their mission at St. Ignatius kept stock, their herd numbering as many as a thousand head in 1858. In addition to the small herd for his own use at his fort, Major John Owen in 1860 imported three hundred head more from Oregon which he disposed of to the Flathead Indians.[6] The edict of the leaders of the Mormon Church early in 1857 ordering all Gentiles to leave their territory caused many local traders to hurriedly exchange their goods for stock which they drove out of the country, most of them going north into the mountains of western Montana for safety. When General Albert S. Johnston, who was assigned the task of quelling the Mormon uprising, detailed a small party to go into the mountain valleys to the northward to buy beef for his soldiers, they found herds of cattle but the ranchers refused to sell, as they did not care to deliver them in the Mormon territory. A contract was finally drawn up in the Deer Lodge Valley for three hundred head of stock at ten dollars a hundred pounds live weight. The ranchers, however, must have lost their courage, as the cattle were never delivered.[7] Thus, toward the close of the fifties, the cattle industry had made a start in the Northwest and it had been well demonstrated that stock could be wintered on the ranges of that area. If it were to expand beyond the stage of mere beginnings, there must be better markets than were as yet available. The time was ripe for the crea-

[6] Conrad Kohrs, "Autobiography," dictated by him at Helena, 1885, in Montana State Historical Library; *The Journals and Letters of Major John Owen*, ed. Seymour Dunbar and Paul C. Phillips (New York, 1927), II, 218-23, 264-7.

[7] Ernest Staples Osgood, *The Day of the Cattleman* (Minneapolis, Minn., 1929), pp. 13-6; Kohrs, *op. cit.*; "Annual Report of the Secretary of War, 1859," *House Exec. Doc.*, 35th Cong., 2d Sess., II, Part II, No. 2, 68-70.

tion of a greater demand for beef, which in this case was to be a local one.

In the autumn of 1858 gold was discovered on Cherry Creek, some two hundred miles south of the Oregon Trail, and in the spring of 1859 the Pike's Peak gold rush was well under way, as thousands of gold-seekers hurried into the diggings to make their fortunes. By winter, twenty-five thousand miners were reported to be located in the Colorado gold camps. There was a demand for beef and the miners were willing to pay a good price for their roasts and steaks. Small bands of cattle were driven in and sold, no doubt some of which came from herds of Mexican cattle to the south. Some of the gold-hunters, failing to make a strike and being without funds to get back to their former homes, started to raise vegetables and stock to sell to the miners who continued to arrive in ever-increasing numbers. The *Rocky Mountain News*, published at Cherry Creek, on April 23, 1859, when the gold rush was getting well under way, printed an article, "Farming and Stock-raising versus Gold-Digging," in which the editor recommended that some of the many prospectors who were failing to locate paying placer claims could farm or raise cattle and make more money than many of the miners, as prices for those commodities were high.

J. W. Iliff, sometimes called the first "cattle king" of Colorado and Wyoming, came to the gold-fields in 1859 and failing to make a "strike" started to raise vegetables near the settlement that later was called Denver. With the money made in this way, he located a small store on the old California and Oregon Trail, not far from where Cheyenne, Wyoming, was later located and started to sell goods and trade for cattle. It was not long before he had a herd large enough that he could begin selling beef to the gold camps to the south. J. D. Henderson and Edward Creighton also started herds of cattle and before the Civil War there were a considerable number of ranches scattered over the Colorado and Wyoming areas that sold their finished stock to the miners and to the freighters who hauled goods into the various camps.[8]

As the frontier of the miner advanced north and east from California into Oregon, Idaho, and finally into the western portions of Montana, rich gold camps were established at Bannack City, Virginia City, and Helena, where there were soon thousands of miners to be fed, and prices were even higher in these remote camps than they had been in Colorado. A worn-out ox could be purchased for sixty to seventy-five dollars which sold when slaughtered for twenty-five to thirty cents a pound. The small ranchers located in the area surrounding the new gold camps were soon selling their cattle and enlarging their herds, while disappointed miners, attracted by good profits, went into the cattle business. The mining camps grew rapidly and soon created a demand that could not be supplied locally and was felt in Oregon, California, and southward in Wyoming and Colorado, along the Platte, and even in the settlements of Missouri, Kansas, and Texas.

Captain J. L. Fiske, on his second expedition to the Montana gold-fields, arrived at Morgan's ranch in the Prickly Pear Valley on September 18, 1863, and reported cattle ranging over most of the valley. A few days later in the Beaverhead Valley, he told of the ranch of John Grant and his father, who owned a herd of several thousand cattle with which they were supplying beef to the mining camps of Bannack and Virginia City. Conrad Kohrs worked in a butcher-shop at Bannack, and finally started a shop of his own in Helena in the spring of 1865 which he called the "Highland Market." Cattle were scarce and Kohrs borrowed several thousand dollars and purchased a large band of stock, paying only part of the money down and the rest as he marketed the beef. He soon had his cattle paid for and enlarged his herd. The Stuart brothers also had a large herd of cattle.[9] Several early issues of

[8] W. B. Graham, "Cattle Ranches of the Far West," *Fortnightly Review*, XXVIII (1880), 453; W. A. Baillie-Grohman, *Campfires in the Rockies* (New York, 1884), pp. 351-4.

[9] Kohrs, *op. cit.*, p. 16; Stuart, *Forty Years on the Frontier*, I, 130-56.

the *Montana Post* at Virginia City gave a glowing account of the possibilities of the cattle business in that area, and on December 26, 1867, a Helena newspaper told of a fine bunch of cattle that had been driven in from Deer Lodge and sold to the local butchers.[10]

Cattle had become numerous enough in Deer Lodge County in the Territory of Montana by 1866 that difficulties regarding range regulations caused the territorial legislature to pass an act granting the county commissioners authority to define the various types of range and to regulate their use for the general welfare. The act was repealed at the next session of the legislature since it violated the right of the Federal Government to control the public lands.[11] Cattle in the vicinity of the Montana mining camps increased rapidly, and in 1868, five years after the discovery of gold in Alder Gulch, the nine organized counties of the territory reported 10,714 oxen and 18,801 other cattle. Four years later the stock cattle had increased to about seventy-five thousand and the oxen declined in number as horses and mules took their place in freighting.[12]

In 1867 the rails of the Union Pacific Railroad were gradually laid through Wyoming and the construction camps with their large numbers of laborers, as well as the floating population of riffraff and camp-followers, were in need of meat. While Buffalo Bill, the well-known buffalo hunter, and others of the same profession furnished large amounts of buffalo meat to appease their appetites, there was also a keen demand for beef, and the ranchers and cattle-raisers of the Laramie plains of Wyoming and the surrounding country had a better market for their beef than in the gold camps of Colorado and distant Montana.[13] The early issues

[10] Files of the *Montana Post*, 1864-65; *Helena Weekly Herald*, January 10, December 12, 26, 1867.

[11] *Session Laws of the Territory of Montana*, 1866, 2d Sess., pp. 35-6; 3d Sess., p. 83.

[12] Osgood, *Day of the Cattleman*, p. 21.

[13] While great herds of buffalo roamed the plains and valleys of the Northwest and contemporary newspapers of the mining camps frequently refer to such

of the *Cheyenne Leader* contained many references to stock-raising and the activity of the cattlemen in Wyoming. The first issue of the *Wyoming Tribune* on November 20, 1869, described at some length the development of the cattle industry and called attention to the large numbers of cattle that were fattening on the Laramie plains and in the vicinity of Cheyenne. On November 27th, it described the possibilities of cattle-ranching thus: "Millions and millions of cattle can be successfully reared and fattened upon the plains of Wyoming with little expense save the time of the herdsmen. Cows can be purchased in Texas or western Kansas for a trifling consideration and the expense of driving them to this territory is not large. A small amount of capital thus invested would serve to secure the owners within five years a handsome competency." The stock of Wyoming increased rapidly and by 1870 it was estimated that there were in the territory 36,472 head of cattle, no doubt a conservative figure.

II

EARLY CATTLE-RAISING IN THE TERRITORY OF DAKOTA

IN THE MEANTIME, what had been happening on the plains and in the river valleys to the eastward in the extensive region that had become the Territory of Dakota in the spring of 1860? The first settlers that migrated westward into the Big Sioux and Missouri valleys of this territory brought cattle with them, and in the days of early settlement they were a mainstay in all of the pioneer communities of the area. During the periods of drought and grasshopper scourges that were so numerous in the first years of settlement, the frontier settlers depended almost entirely upon cattle for their support, and had it not been for this source of food,

---

herds and to the sale and transportation of robes and hides, there was apparently little buffalo meat consumed in the camps. The miners and other population evidently preferred beef.

many families would have been compelled to leave their home-steads.[1]

The early pioneer farmer in southeastern Dakota, fully realiz-ing the importance of stock, combined the raising of cattle and farming operations. The nutritious native grasses, cured to hay during the dry months of late summer, the presence of much un-settled land allowing free and unlimited pasture, the light snow-fall of the average Dakota winter, and the ability of stock to travel many miles to market or to shipping points, gave grazing a distinct advantage over cereal farming. The vast unsettled stretches of country favorable to the cattle industry were, for the agriculturalist, menaced by prairie fires and grasshoppers. The cost of transporting crops long distances, in many cases, was almost prohibitive, or, at the best, greatly reduced the profits, while drought with the variable and uncertain rainfall made farming alone a more or less precarious occupation in many of the early settled portions of Dakota.

Notwithstanding these factors, the live-stock business, involving a considerable investment as well as various improvements in buildings and fences, did not develop rapidly as a separate in-dustry. Mixed farming in which stock-raising occupied a promi-nent place proved more profitable than either cereal farming or the raising of stock alone. Therefore, the joint occupations of agriculture and stock-raising became important and underwent a slow and steady development in the area east of the Missouri River in the sixties and early seventies before that region was served by railroads. The Indian agencies and military posts of the territory were excellent markets for beef not needed by the towns or the farms. Cattle-raising became very profitable and capital in-vested in it often brought a return of 50 per cent per annum.[2]

[1] *Sioux Falls Democrat,* July 2, September 3, November 8, 1859; *Yankton Weekly Dakotian,* June 6, 1861.

[2] *Yankton Weekly Dakotian,* June 6, 1861; Visher, "Geography of South Dakota," p. 115; John R. Brenan, "Conditions and Resources of Southern Dakota" (Sioux City, Iowa, 1872), p. 11.

James A. Foster of Yankton, a prominent resident in the territory, writing concerning ranching in 1870, said:

The raising of stock is and has been since the first settlement of the territory a very remunerative business. The nutritious grasses of our prairies cause cattle to thrive and fatten easily, so that a poor animal, in any of the numerous herds of Dakota, is an exception, and very fat cattle the rule. . . . Capital invested in livestock usually brings a return equal to fifty percent of the amount invested. Farmers usually put up large quantities of hay at an expense of about two dollars per ton which they feed to their stock in winter as occasion requires. Sometimes the winters of Dakota are so mild that herds of cattle run out all winter and provide their own food. . . . Some farmers have sheds and stables for cattle in winter, but (these) are the exception and not the rule.[3]

Another early settler of Yankton, writing in 1870, also stressed the importance of the cattle industry and its opportunities in Dakota. He told of a young man who a few years before had left a store in the East and come to southeastern Dakota with three hundred dollars in cash, and turned his attention to cattle-raising. In 1870 he had a herd of three hundred that were worth from forty to seventy dollars each.[4] According to the census of 1870 there were in the Territory of Dakota 56,724 head of neat cattle. Of that number 12,467 were on farms, the balance being owned by men who followed stock-raising as a business. The *Yankton Weekly Press* early in February, 1871, listed twenty-one men in that vicinity who kept cattle as their means of income and who owned from fifty to three hundred head.

The demand for cattle at the various Dakota military posts and Indian agencies was greater than the local supply and some were driven into the territory from the outside. In the summer of 1869 H. H. Larned drove a herd of cattle from Sioux City, Iowa, to Fort Rice, Dakota, to be used by the soldiers there for beef. The

[3] J. S. Foster, *Outline of the History of Dakota and Immigrants' Guide* (Yankton, D. T., 1870), pp. 91-2.
[4] Batchelder, *History and Resources of Dakota*, pp. 29-30.

herd was driven through northeastern Nebraska and up the east side of the Missouri River. The profits of the contract are said to have amounted to $4,700.[5] On July 13, 1871, a herd of one hundred and fifty cattle crossed the Missouri River at Yankton. They were a part of a herd that had been driven from Minnesota to Fort Thompson where four hundred and fifty head had been left. The remainder of the herd had been driven to a point opposite Fort Randall where several head were lost in attempts to get them across the Missouri River. The cattle were finally driven down to Yankton where they were ferried across. They were then driven up to Fort Randall on the Nebraska side of the river. C. H. Pay of Minnesota was the contractor and had sent six hundred head to Fort Stevenson, another Dakota fort. "The cattle were in excellent condition after their long hard drive," said a Yankton editor, "which speaks well for the quality of our Dakota grasses."[6]

The influx of miners into the gold camps, the movement of great trains of freight wagons carrying supplies to the various frontier settlements, military posts, and Indian agencies of the Northwest, together with the increased activity and traffic across the plains that went with the construction of the Union Pacific Railroad, taking place as they did between 1860 and 1870, tended to upset and disturb the stability and isolation of the Indian tribes that had characterized the previous decade. Some of the tribes became restless and hostile and the danger of Indian attack forced the army to protect the routes of travel and the new communities by the construction of additional forts and the detailing of heavier garrisons in some of the older ones. These military posts with their hundreds of soldiers furnished good markets for beef, while the cavalry horses needed hay. Contracts for these commodities were granted to local cattlemen and ranchers. In 1871 the newly established Fort D. A. Russell near

[5] Crawford, *Notes:* Interview with H. H. Larned, Sentinel Butte, N. Dak., June 21-30, 1921.
[6] *Yankton Weekly Press*, July 19, 1871.

Cheyenne was paying a contract price of $8.35 a hundredweight for live cattle to the ranchmen on the Laramie plains and along the Platte and was also paying good prices for hay, which must have netted the ranchers an excellent margin of profit. Other important military posts in Wyoming after the Civil War were Forts Laramie and Bridger. In the Territory of Dakota some of the more important garrisons were located at Forts Randall, Berthold, Union, Bennett, and Buford; and in the Territory of Montana at Forts Benton, Shaw, Peck, and Missoula.[7]

By the close of the sixties there had developed on the plains of the Northwest and in the valleys of the upper Missouri River country, herds of cattle of considerable size whose owners were making excellent returns on their investments by supplying the local mining camps, military posts, and railroad construction camps with beef. While they had demonstrated the practicability of wintering stock on the open ranges of the north, they soon saw that if they were to utilize the enormous resources of the Northwest by the expansion of this pioneer industry, they must have a supply of cheap cattle with which to stock the open ranges, markets to take care of the increase, better railroad connections with the East,[8] and the removal of the Indian barrier in certain areas. The first step in the process was to obtain range stock and for that part of the story we must turn our attention briefly to the southern state of Texas.

III

THE CATTLE OF TEXAS

THE CATTLE industry began in Texas when the early Spanish settlers brought in their long-horned cattle that, under favorable

---

[7] Forts in the Northwest, during this period, changed quite rapidly. They were often constructed, garrisoned, and abandoned so quickly that lists mean but little. They were sometimes regarrisoned for short periods as the needs of the frontier required.

[8] While the building of the Union Pacific Railroad gave ranching in the area many advantages, it was not readily accessible for the northern portions of the cattle ranges under consideration.

conditions of range and climate, increased rapidly. Some of them escaped from their owners and roamed the great unoccupied areas unbranded and unattended and became the so-called "wild cattle" of Texas. While large numbers of the early settlers going into Texas from the United States were cotton-farmers, they took some stock with them, including a considerable number of milk cows which in time mixed with the Spanish stock and developed good-sized herds. The liberal land policy of the Spanish, and later of the Mexican Government, offered concessions to those engaged in ranching and when Texas came into the Union as a state, this policy was continued. The industry grew, as the expense of raising cattle was small since they lived the year around on free range. Many of the oxen used in freighting on the western plains came from the ranges of Texas.

The chief problem of the Texas cattleman, however, was that of markets. Beginning in 1837 and 1838 small herds were driven into the interior towns where they were sold for beef. The first drive was made to New Orleans in 1842, a place which soon became the main market for Texas cattle. They were usually driven to Shreveport, from which point they were shipped down the Red River to their destination. Others were loaded on boats at Galveston and other gulf ports and sent to Mobile and Cuba. There is record of a herd numbering some fifteen hundred head being driven to Missouri in 1842, and in 1846 Edward Piper drove a herd of one thousand to Ohio where they were fattened and sold at a good profit. There was a drive to California in 1850 and in 1856 a herd reached Chicago. Unfortunately, as Texas cattle began to move into the North, there occurred an epidemic of "Texas fever" among stock along the roads over which the cattle passed, and large numbers of the local stock died. Groups of farmers in southwestern Missouri held protest meetings and organized to turn back the cattle from Texas. The feeling and action of the northern farmers were sufficiently strong to check the drives from the South by 1858.

Stock multiplied rapidly on the Texas plains, increasing from 100,000 head in 1830 to 330,000 in 1850 and then jumping to more than 3,500,000 in 1860, which is no doubt a conservative estimate for that year, one investigator coming to the conclusion some years later that the number should have been 4,500,000. At any rate, the increase was enormous and as one writer has recently phrased it, cattle must have "virtually swarmed over portions of the Texas plains." [1]

During the period of the Civil War the cattle of Texas were neglected, although a few herds were delivered to the Confederate armies. But even that outlet was stopped when the Union Army took over the Mississippi River. Breeding went on, however, and the Texas longhorns increased in numbers, and calves and young stock went unbranded and often unclaimed. When the Texas soldiers returned to their homes at the close of the war they found large numbers of fat cattle running loose, or obtainable for almost nothing. The economic condition of the state and its inhabitants spurred them into activity, in order that they might revive their fortunes. The fact that Texas cattle, purchased at from three dollars to ten dollars a head, might be sold in the North at from thirty to forty dollars was something to merit serious consideration.[2] A few thousand head delivered at the right place might mean a fortune. In the two decades following the Civil War a flood of cattle moved into the plains country of the North and Northwest and did not cease until the eastern markets had reached a point of saturation and the ranges of the plains region were filled to overflowing.

It is estimated that approximately 260,000 cattle started north

[1] *U. S. Census Report for 1870*, III, 341; *U. S. Census Report for 1880*, III, 965-6; *Prairie Farmer* (Chicago), July 14, 1866, p. 23; *Yearbook of the Department of Agriculture* (1870), pp. 348-50; Edward Everett Dale, *The Range Cattle Industry* (Norman, Okla., 1930) ch. 1; J. M. Hunter, ed., *Trail Drivers of Texas* (Nashville, Tenn., 1925), *passim*.

[2] In 1867 a fat steer worth $9.46 in Texas was worth on the average of $32.83 in Missouri, $38.40 in Kansas, $46.32 in Nebraska, and even more in Chicago and eastern markets. *Annual Report of the Secretary of Agriculture* (1867), pp. 108-10.

in 1866, most of which were headed for Sedalia, Missouri, the most western point on the Missouri and Pacific Railroad. Only a few of those that started, however, actually reached their destination or a place where they could be marketed. Inexperienced drivers, Indian dangers, quicksands and swollen rivers, prairie fires, stampedes, and opposition by white thieves and outlaws all served as serious handicaps. In southern Kansas and Missouri the trail drivers were attacked by armed mobs who did not hesitate to use violence as they whipped and sometimes killed the cowboys. While some of those making the attacks were no doubt sincere in being afraid of the Texas fever, the motive of many was robbery.

The person most responsible for the establishment of a point of contact for the Texas cattlemen and northern buyers and place of shipment to eastern markets was J. G. McCoy, who, with his brothers, had been dealing in live stock in Illinois. It was through his activity that Abilene, Kansas, on the Kansas Pacific Railroad became the first cow-town of the West. This railroad, connecting with the Hannibal and St. Joe, gave marketing facilities to Chicago. The number of cattle arriving at the new center increased from 35,000 in 1867 to 350,000 in 1869, jumping to 700,000 in 1871, which was the peak year of the Texas drives. In 1872 the Texas cattle center shifted to the Kansas towns of Wichita and Ellsworth and the number dropped to 350,000.[3]

Many of the cattle driven to Abilene in the sixties were shipped to the East by rail to be sold, while others were purchased and driven to various points to be fattened before being put on the market. Some were driven to the ranges of Colorado and Wyoming, the influx there being stimulated by the construction of the Union Pacific Railroad in 1868 and 1869. Some few even filtered into the mountain valleys of Montana and Idaho. The beef of

---

[3] Joseph G. McCoy, *Historic Sketches of the Cattle Trade of the West and Southwest* (Kansas City, 1874); *U. S. Census Report for 1880*, Statistics of Agriculture, pp. 965-75.

these early Texas cattle, often butchered before they had been
fed or fattened for market, was probably tough and not any too
savory, but, according to some observers, it was good enough for
factory laborers, reservation Indians, drunken and dissipated
soldiers at the army posts, and the "paddies and chinks" who were
the "gandy-dancers" on the railroad construction crews.[4] By the
early seventies more and more of the Texas cattle were brought to
the ranges of the Northwest that were ready and waiting to receive them.

IV

THE NORTHERN DRIVE

THE JOURNEY from Texas to the northern ranges with a herd of
longhorns took from four to six months and as the movement
gained momentum the driving of large herds of cattle uptrail
was reduced to a science and costs brought down to a minimum.
Herds varied considerably as to size, and experience soon taught
the drover that from twenty-five hundred to three thousand head
was perhaps the most convenient number for a long drive.[5] While
herds of five or six thousand head were sometimes taken northward, they moved slowly and were handled with difficulty. A herd
of more than three thousand was apt to prove unwieldy, while
two thousand or less required about the same amount of expense
as did a larger number. A trail party for a drove of twenty-five
hundred usually consisted of from ten to twelve men, including
a manager or captain, eight or ten cowboys, and a cook. The
manager and the trailers were furnished from four to six horses
each, the cook taking charge of food and equipment in a supply

[4] *Cheyenne Daily Leader,* May 21, 1868, April 15, May 5, June 19, 1869;
National Livestock Journal (Chicago, Ill.), I, October, November, December,
1870.
[5] The inspector at Trail City on the Arkansas River reported 57 herds crossing the stream from June 9 to July 20, 1886, varying in size from 3,300 to 70
head. There were only five herds of less than 1,000 head, fifteen numbered
between 1,000 and 2,000 and five contained 3,000 head or more. The other 32
herds varied between 2,000 and 3,000 head, averaging around 2,500. Dale, *op.
cit.,* p. 62.

wagon drawn by four horses or mules. Sometimes a boy was employed to look after or "wrangle" the horses. Some herds were
taken north by professional drovers who purchased them on
several months' credit and sold them in the northern markets.
Many Texas cattlemen, however, drove their own herds or sent
them northward under a trusted trail boss.

Before starting the long trek, the cattle were marked with the
"road brand." Horses for the trailers were provided by the owner,
while the cowboy supplied his own saddle and blankets. Wages
for competent cowhands were $30 to $40 per month with the
cook's pay running somewhat higher, while the captain or trail
boss, who was responsible for the cattle, received a monthly salary
of from $100 to $125. The herd was moved slowly and carefully
during the first few days in order that they might become accustomed to the trail and they were watched carefully at night.[1]
After a few days they would make a steady pace of from twelve to
fifteen miles a day, stopping at night to rest. The necessity of
watching the cattle with great care until they were used to the
road was carefully observed because a herd that stampeded or became frightened early in the drive was apt to cause trouble the
whole trip. Night-guard was divided into three shifts.

After breaking camp early in the morning the cattle were
allowed to graze as they moved slowly on their way. Scattering
out, they moved along at a good rate of speed until the stop
was made for dinner. The cook, driving ahead, stopped at a place
designated by the boss where there was water. The cattle were
scattered loosely along the stream for a couple of hours to rest,
and the drive was resumed, the cook establishing a night camp
with his chuck wagon at a place chosen by the trail captain. On
the trail two men known as lead drivers or point men rode on
opposite sides of the herd a trifle in advance, but not directly in

[1] Evidently procedure during the first few days varied, as there are records
of those who started their cattle off at a rather rapid rate at first that they
might become tired and more docile.

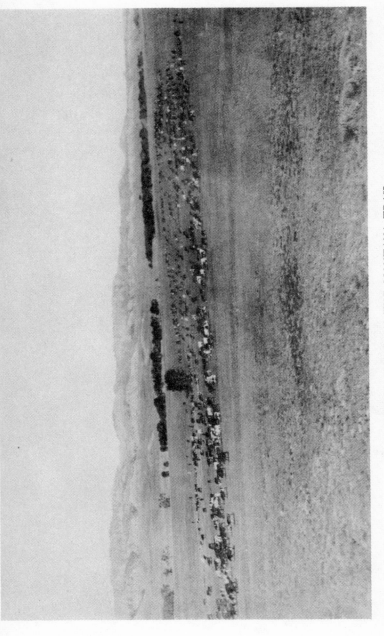

A CATTLE DRIVE ON THE MONTANA TRAIL

Approaching the Niobrara crossing of the Powder River, 1886. L. A. Huffman photograph.

front, as the cattle resented being hemmed in. Behind the point men at frequent intervals came other cowboys known as flank drivers. The slow and lame cattle followed along in the rear, and being located at the end or "drag" was a disagreeable position because of dust and the difficulty of keeping the backward animals with the herd. The success of the drive depended to a large extent upon the ability and experience of the point men, whose job was to control the leaders of the drove. The foreman, chuck wagon, and the "horse wrangler" and his horses had no regularly assigned places. At times, when water or grass was scarce, the entire outfit might be pushed and not infrequently the weaker animals were trampled to death as the herd rushed for water.

The cowboys were alert and watchful as there were many obstacles to overcome. There was danger of Indian attacks. Streams had to be forded, and there were quicksands and spring floods. There was always difficulty in getting the herd started across large streams, the leaders being induced only by hours of prodding and urging to enter the water. This accomplished, the rest usually followed and the crossing was made with little difficulty unless the leaders became frightened by the swift stream or something on the other bank. They would then turn and swing in a circle and it was necessary for the cowboys to ride into the mass of struggling cattle and turn the leaders toward the shore. Often a rider was thrown from his horse and was compelled to swim ashore or to ride a steer's back or to make land by holding the end of one's tail.

One of the most dreadful occurrences that could happen on the drive was a stampede, especially at night. The cattle were grouped together on a small plot of ground and the cowhands guarded them, working in three shifts during the night, with two or three on watch at a time. They rode slowly around the herd and sang to the cattle, often using profane language to some sacred air. Human company and music seemed to give the cattle a feeling of security. The drivers had to watch also for cattle-thieves and for wild animals. A dark stormy night was exceedingly dangerous and a larger guard was placed on duty when a storm broke. A sudden flash of lightning with a crash of thunder might start the herd in a mad stampede. The cowboys had to turn the leaders and get the cattle to milling and quiet them down. This was difficult to do and several miles were often traveled before they were able to control the herd again. The pony was guided by instinct and what little he might be able to see by flashes of lightning. Out of the darkness would often come the horrible scream of a mangled horse as it carried its rider over a cut bank to certain death.

After a stampede the cowboys gathered for a check-up on personnel and although they joked in a flippant way as their comrades came drifting in, there was, underneath their outward manner, a serious anxiety for the safety of the group. Upon ascertaining that some one was missing, the search for the body began. Some were found trampled to death by cattle when their horses stumbled, or at the foot of a cut bank or a cliff, buried beneath heaps of carcasses. There was an awkward silence as the body was carefully prepared for burial. The funerals of those who died on the trail were crude and simple. The body, wrapped in a saddle blanket, was lowered into the open grave, followed by an embarrassed pause as each puncher no doubt wished for the ability to say something appropriate for the occasion. The tension was broken when one of them took the shovel and slowly covered the body with loose dirt. The grave was carefully covered with rocks to keep out marauding animals, and the hardened trail drivers, cloaking their deeper feelings with silence, rode away to their work.

In 1884, Colonel Ike T. Pryor of San Antonio, Texas, moved fifteen herds of cattle from southern Texas to the Territory of Montana and gave an estimate of the cost of the drive. It required 165 men and 1,000 saddle-horses. Each herd averaged 3,000 head and required eleven men, including the trail captain. Monthly expenses, including wages and food, averaged about $500, not counting the money invested in horses. The cattle were ordinarily driven from 300 to 450 miles per month. Pryor estimated that he could move 3,000 head as many miles for $3,000. The losses en route would run about 3 per cent. Other estimates as to driving costs vary from $.75 to $1.25, depending on the destination.[3] After the cattle were delivered, the men were paid off and returned to Texas, sometimes going back with the wagon and equipment for another drive.

v

THE NORTHWEST AS A CATTLE AREA

THE TERRITORIES of Wyoming, Montana, and Dakota, with their great expanse of plains region, their river valleys, and their mountain slopes, were well fitted for large-scale ranching. The region was abundantly watered, while its thickets of small trees and bushes along the river valleys and deep bedded creeks afforded natural shelter for stock and its mesas and buttes broke the force of the winter winds. The plains were covered with nutritious buffalo-grass which cured on the stem during the dry months of July and August and made an excellent winter feed. The dryness of the atmosphere caused the snow to be blown off the hillsides, exposing the dry grass and facilitating winter grazing.[4] Evidence of its ability to support great herds of cattle is pointed out by many writers in the fact that it had once been the feeding-grounds of immense herds of buffalo and the often-repeated story of the government trader, E. S. Newman, is cited as the first practical demonstration of the fattening qualities of the grasses of the Northwest and the possibilities of cattle wintering on the open range. Newman, bound for Utah with a wagon train of supplies, was overtaken in November, 1864, by bad weather on the Laramie

[3] George W. Sanders, *Trail Drivers of Texas* (1920), pp. 332-3; *Montana, Its Story and Biography*, ed. Tom Stout (Chicago, 1921), I, 393; Joseph Nimmo, *The Range and Ranch Cattle Business of the United States* (Washington, D. C., 1885), pp. 154-5.
    [4] *Report of the Commissioner of Agriculture*, 1871, pp. 100, 441.

plains of Wyoming and being unable to proceed farther, prepared a winter camp and turned his oxen out to die. In the spring he found them not only alive but in better condition than when he had turned them loose. In 1869 a similar experience occurred at Fort D. A. Russell near Cheyenne, when a herd of Texas cattle were driven there in the fall to supply the garrison with beef. Scattered by a violent snow-storm, they were not seen again until the following spring when they were rounded up in excellent condition.[1] While such stories no doubt made good copy for newspapers, magazines, and pamphlets for advertising purposes, the fact that cattle could be wintered on the open ranges of the Northwest had been known to local ranchers for years, and with the development of better marketing facilities and a supply of cheap cattle, they were waiting for an opportunity to try it out on a large scale.

VI

DEVELOPMENTS IN WYOMING

WYOMING, because of its location and the building of the Union Pacific Railroad, was the first portion of the Northwest to absorb Texas cattle in large numbers. Some of the early herds to arrive in the Wyoming area came by way of Colorado [2] and were brought in during the winter of 1867-68 by the cattle firm of Goodnight and Loving. J. W. Iliff met the trail drivers in southern Colorado

[1] Robert C. Morris, *Internal Commerce of the United States* (Bureau of Statistics: Washington, D. C., 1889), pp. 805-6.

[2] During the late sixties and early seventies the eastern portion of Colorado became the corridor to the range farther north. Although the farmers and ranchers at first opposed the bringing in of Texas cattle, and turned them back by armed force, the opposition was soon overcome by possible profits in shipping Texas cattle to eastern markets or by acting as stockers for Wyoming, Montana, and Idaho. By 1869 a million cattle were said to be grazing within the borders of the Territory of Colorado, more than half of which were to be found between Denver and the Wyoming border. In 1870 the governor of the territory was extolling the great advantages of ranching in the area and told how its herds had increased from 60 to 80 per cent since cattle had started to come in from Texas, and there was room for unlimited expansion. *Cheyenne Daily Leader*, June 19, 1868; *Annual Report of the Territorial Governor of Wyoming to the Secretary of the Interior*, 1870.

and drove the cattle to Wyoming in midwinter. A Cheyenne editor reported the arrival of a large Texas herd in that vicinity in February, 1869, and in May announced the sale of a thousand head to a local meat-dealer at five cents a pound live weight. The same editor, commenting upon the season of 1871, reported that the number of cattle in that area had more than doubled since 1869, while another observer stated that Wyoming absorbed more than seven thousand head of Texas cattle in 1870. In 1871 the influx of cattle was rapid, the Snyder Brothers alone bringing in fifteen thousand head in ten herds, and Edward Creighton, J. W. Iliff, Coe and Carter, Taylor and Gaylord, Latham, Keith, and Barton, and others had herds of from three to sixteen thousand head. In 1873, Silas Reed, Surveyor General of the Territory, said, "Large herds of cattle are found along every stream and valley and public confidence has been established in the cattle business in spite of the severity of the winter storms." [2]

With this excellent beginning, and with the outlook as optimistic as it was in the early seventies, ranchers and territorial officials wrote letters and published reports designed to advertise the cattle industry in the area. One Wyoming rancher wrote a letter that was widely printed, urging his brother to come to the territory and enter the cattle business, where he might soon become rich. The letter told how the rancher had invested about eight thousand dollars five years before and had made a profit each year that exceeded his original investment. Cattle prices were reported to have increased from $4.80 per hundredweight in 1863 to $8.10 in 1868.[3] In spite of the unfavorable business conditions of the early seventies, the process of stocking the Wyoming ranges went on unabated, the number of cattle increasing from 90,000 in 1874 to 450,000 in 1879.

[2] *Report of Silas Reed, Surveyor General of Wyoming Territory, to the Secretary of the Interior,* 1871-72, Part I, 295; *Annual Report of the Commissioner of the General Land Office,* 1873, p. 247.
[3] James Brisbin, *The Beef Bonanza, or How to Get Rich on the Plains* (Philadelphia, 1881), pp. 69-71.

In 1877 Robert E. Strahorn published a book at Cheyenne designed "to advertise to the world the large opportunities of Wyoming." While he admitted that he in no way wished to imply that the territory did not have mineral wealth, he did wish to point out "the sure and unlimited possibilities of stock-raising." In one place the author gave information and figures secured from the books of an "experienced and dependable stockman of Cheyenne" over a three-year period. The man had invested $16,800 and the net profit for the three years was $32,200. He pointed out that Texas yearlings could be purchased at almost any railroad point in Wyoming at a cost of $7.40 per head and two-year-olds for $12.00 each. A ranch could be bought within two days' drive of the railroad for $1,500 with necessary buildings and corrals thrown in. First-class herders could be employed for a wage of $32.50 per month, and a herd of a thousand cattle could be handled at a cost of $1.75 a head. If the owner wished to run a herd of five thousand, he could reduce the cost to $1.40 and if he wished to try ten thousand, the cost could come down to $1.00. "It is also reliably stated," said Strahorn, "that such stock-growers as J. W. Iliff, who graze 25,000 head, figure their expense down as low as 65 to 75 cents a head per annum." [4] While some of these figures are a bit difficult to accept, they are repeated in the report of the territorial governor, William Hale, to the Secretary of the Interior a few years later. [5]

While the ranges were being stocked by the long-horned herds from Texas, the packing-houses of Swift and Armour were working on a plan whereby the slaughtering of cattle might be concentrated at a few central points and dressed beef sent out to the surrounding areas in refrigerator-cars. The idea of stock-yard companies, commission firms, and meat-packing establishments was soon to lay a new basis for the future development of the meat

[4] Robert E. Strahorn, *The Handbook of Wyoming and Guide to the Black Hills and the Big Horn Basin* (Cheyenne, Wy., 1877), pp. 27-32.
[5] *Report of the Territorial Governor of Wyoming to the Secretary of Interior,* 1883, p. 25.

industry. The Union Stockyard Company of Chicago was organized in 1860 and was ready to receive large numbers of cattle
from the West as soon as they were available. As the ranges of
the Northwest became stocked, Kansas City was soon in a position to make a strong bid for a part, at least, of the trail cattle.
A large stock-yard was constructed there in 1870 and Texas cattle
dominated the market. In 1872 stock-yards were established at
St. Louis.[6]

The first shipment of stock from the Territory of Wyoming
occurred in the summer of 1870. Prices for both work stock and
beef cattle were extremely high, due in part to the European demand brought on by the impending war. One H. B. Kelly, who
was filling a government contract for wood and hay, sold his
oxen on the local market for seventy dollars each. The figures
given by Governor Thayer to the General Land Office for cattle
shipments show that the number of cars of cattle shipped over the
Union Pacific Railroad increased from 286 in 1873 to 1,694 in
1877. Union Pacific cars carried twenty head. The largest number of shipments were made from Rock Springs, Rock River,
and Cheyenne. Freight charges to Chicago in 1879 varied from
$250 a car at Green River in the western portion, to $138 at Pine
Bluffs in the eastern part of the territory. The prices paid in 1876
for trail cattle averaged thirteen dollars for two-year-old steers
and sixteen to seventeen dollars for three-year-olds.[7]

[6] Rudolph A. Clemen, *The American Livestock and Meat Industry* (New
York, 1923), p. 6; *Kansas City Daily Times* (Kansas City, Mo.), January 1,
1880. Stockyards were established at Omaha, Nebraska, in 1884, and at St.
Paul and Denver in 1886 to provide the necessary points of concentration to
handle the rapidly expanding cattle industry.

[7] *Cheyenne Daily Leader*, May 24, 1870, July 11, 1876; *Cheyenne Daily
Sun*, January 3, 1884. In spite of the high freight rates and a large shrinkage
from the long haul, it was possible to make a good profit. Texas cattle could be
bought at a reasonable price and the Chicago market was beginning to pay
better prices for the heavy well-conditioned western cattle. One must discount,
however, some of the local accounts of profits. The statement, for example, of
Governor Thayer that the yield per head to the rancher in 1877 was $30 is
perhaps too strong. *Message of the Territorial Governor of Wyoming*, 1877, pp.
10-11.

In commenting upon the range-cattle business of Wyoming in 1877, the territorial governor said, "These cattle have literally raised themselves for market. They have been out on the ranges during the whole of the winters without shelter and without feed from the stack and have been prepared for slaughter almost without cost, save the expense of gathering them in and shipping them. Winter grazing in Wyoming, so long doubted, has come to be an accomplished fact." [8]

From the many local and territorial reports it is apparent throughout the early period that the ranges of Wyoming were generally regarded as more or less of a middle ground in the cattle business. The territory was not a place to breed cattle but a place to graze and fatten them for market. The early herds were made up largely of young steers and the profits derived came mostly from the flesh they could put on after being purchased and put out to graze. It was some time before heifers in any considerable numbers were added to the Wyoming herds and breeding became the accepted procedure.[9] In this regard, in 1872 a territorial official stated:

The success of stock-growing in this region has caused Cheyenne to become a stock-market of large and growing importance. The great herds required for Utah, Nevada, Idaho and Montana markets are brought here from Texas and sold to dealers west of this point. Mr. Bush, who lives at the old stage ranch, at the crossing of Rock Creek, has recorded nearly 100,000 head of cattle that have passed west this season along the old stage road across the Laramie plains.[10]

By 1879 the best eastern and southern ranges of Wyoming, most of which were within easy driving distance of the railroad and on streams of water, had been occupied by more than a quarter of a million cattle. The northern and western portions of the territory, however, had as yet been untouched. The cattlemen of

[8] Report of the Territorial Governor of Wyoming, 1877.

[9] Lindsay, Big Horn Basin, p. 94.

[10] Annual Report of the Commissioner of the General Land Office, 1872, p. 259.

the territory had been active for about ten years and their winter losses under the open-range system had never been more than 3 to 5 per cent. They felt that they knew what to expect and were confident in their outlook. By the close of the seventies and the beginning of the new decade they were ready for the final expansion.

VII

DEVELOPMENTS IN MONTANA

THE DEMAND for cattle in the stock-growing regions of southwestern Montana grew out of the mining activities in those areas and coincided in time with the early Texas drives.[1] Small herds of southern cattle were driven to these out of the way places to meet the local demand for beef. The first Texas cattle to reach Montana was a herd of six hundred driven by Nelson Story up the Bozeman Trail to the Gallatin Valley in 1866. They had been purchased in Dallas and were readily disposed of, as the gold-miners in the Montana gulches were hungry for beef. In the spring of 1871, the editor of the *Montana Post* announced that eight hundred Texas longhorns were due to arrive at Virginia City in October. There is record the same year of another herd being driven to the Sun River district northeast of Virginia City, and the frontier of the Montana cattle country at the time. Ford and Dunne drove a herd to the Sun River in 1871 and about the same time Kohrs and Bielenberg established a ranch there, later becoming one of the largest cattle outfits of the area. They are said to have branded nearly five thousand calves in 1879.

In 1875 it was reported by the Surveyor-General of Montana

[1] It seems that cattlemen were skeptical of taking their stock so far north, fearing that the change in climate from the South would be disastrous. Experience soon proved that there was little difference between the winters of the Territory of Montana and those of Wyoming and northern Colorado and that winter losses due to weather conditions were in most cases no greater. The numerous ravines, small canyons, and sheltered valleys afforded much protection from storms, while the tendency of the snow to drift gave opportunity for cattle to feed on the plains during the winter months. *Annual Report of the Commissioner of Agriculture*, 1871, pp. 431-47.

that numerous herds of cattle were coming into that territory from Oregon, Texas, and Colorado. In 1878 Granville Stuart noted that D. S. G. Floweree of Helena had purchased one thousand head of stock in Oregon and expected to range them on the Sun River.[2] In 1879 an emigrant on the way from Kansas to Washington Territory came upon a drove of three thousand cattle in northeastern Oregon that was on its way to Montana.[3] In the last few years of the seventies several thousand head of cattle from Washington and Oregon were driven into Montana. As the force of the early invasions was felt, many of the older stockmen moved their herds into the less crowded areas to the north and east. Miles City was founded in 1877 and in 1878 became the metropolis of the eastern Montana cow country. In 1878 T. C. Power of Fort Benton and several colleagues drove eighteen hundred cattle into the Judith Basin and started the Judith Cattle Company. The *Rocky Mountain Husbandman* in December, 1875, estimated that there were ten thousand cattle in the Musselshell Valley and in February, 1879, the same publication placed the number of cattle in Meagher County at sixty thousand. In 1878 and 1879 several herds were located south of the Yellowstone. The range north of that stream and east of the Musselshell was the last to be stocked, much of the area north of the Missouri being Indian country.[4]

Ranching in Montana during the seventies did not expand and develop on a very large scale, the main handicap being the lack of railroad connections and outside markets. The local market decreased as a change from placer to deep-vein mining occurred, and there was a shift from the use of oxen to horses and mules in freighting, and the early boom in the cattle industry came to a close. As some cattle continued to come in, the Montana ranchers found their herds increasing far beyond the local needs. As early

[2] Stuart, *Forty Years on the Frontier,* II, 98.
[3] J. Orin Oliphant, "The Cattle Trade from the Far Northwest to Montana," *Agricultural History* (April, 1932), p. 73.
[4] Nimmo, *Range and Ranch Cattle Business of U. S.,* p. 57.

as 1874, a Deer Lodge newspaper placed the surplus in that vicinity at seventeen thousand head, chiefly four- and five-year-olds, which could be purchased for ten dollars each. A few ranchers, in their eagerness to get rid of their surplus, made drives to the Union Pacific Railroad, a distance of about four hundred miles. Small profits were sometimes made, but it was too uncertain to become a regular practice.[5]

The Montana stockman did not develop the open-range system in the late sixties and early seventies, as did his Wyoming colleague. His early activities, restricted to the hills and mountain valleys, compelled him to keep his cattle within comparatively small areas. Under these circumstances it was necessary to feed and look after his herds during the winter months. But as he began to move eastward into the open country of central and eastern Montana, he gradually discarded his old methods and learned the technique of the open range.[6]

VIII

DEVELOPMENTS IN DAKOTA

As EARLY as the summer of 1871, Texas cattlemen were driving their herds into that portion of the Territory of Dakota along the Missouri River to be used by military posts and Indian agencies. The *Yankton Weekly Press* of July 26, 1871, lists ten Texas stockmen that were making drives to Dakota. In the summer of 1874 a herd of two thousand Texas cattle crossed the Missouri River at Niobrara, Nebraska, to be taken to the Dakota Indian agencies to be slaughtered for beef.[7] Leo Tucker of Yoakum, Texas, tells of driving a herd of Texas cattle to Yankton, the territorial capital: "In 1874 with John May and Joel Bennett we left Bovine, Texas, in February with three thousand head. We

[5] *New Northwest*, May 23, 1874; *Cheyenne Daily Leader*, July 6, 1876; *Helena Daily Independent*, January 25, 1879.

[6] Osgood, *Day of the Cattleman*, pp. 88-9.

[7] *Yankton Press and Dakotian*, August 13, 1874.

went to Norfolk, Nebraska, on the Missouri River, where the cattle were to be delivered to Millett and Mayberry. They offered us $1,000 extra if we would deliver them across the river to Yankton, Dakota. We swam them across seventy-five at a time, the boys using three canoes and fighting them in the face with water to keep them from angling across." [2] Texas cattle were delivered at regular intervals to the various military posts and Indian agencies in Dakota throughout the seventies and eighties, as that demand existed throughout the territorial period.

Until 1875 no cattle were raised in the territory west of the Missouri River. The Black Hills area was Indian country in the great Sioux reservation. There is evidence, however, that the possibilities of the area as a cattle-producing region were fully realized. T. O. Dore of Yankton, writing in the early seventies, said: "The attractions of a country to make it desirable for the raising of stock must be various and manifold. There must be plenty of good nutritious grasses, sufficient natural shelter against storms and inclement weather, and an abundance of clear spring water. These three most necessary requisites are found in and about the Black Hills." In June, 1875, a short editorial appeared in the *Yankton Press and Dakotian* extolling the excellent facilities of the Black Hills region for both cattle and sheep ranching. That the Black Hills was especially adapted to stock-growing was reported by W. P. Jenney, the government geologist in charge of an exploring and scientific expedition to that region in the late summer and early fall of 1875. He closed his comments on possible ranching in the area with these words, "It constitutes the great future wealth of this region and its value can hardly be over estimated." [3]

With the discovery of gold in the Hills in paying quantities in 1875, some of the people going there to look for the precious

[2] Hunter, *Trail Drivers of Texas*, pp. 712-6.
[3] W. P. Jenney, *Official Geological Report Submitted to the Secretary of the Interior*, November 11, 1875, pp. 2-3.

metal took cattle with them. In 1876 the rapid increase in miners and prospectors created a demand for meat and dairy products and several small droves of cattle were taken there for that purpose.

The Park Ranch Company [ran an advertisement in a Black Hills newspaper] is now prepared to herd stock on their ranch on Bear Butte Creek, three and one-half miles from Crook City and six and one-half miles from Deadwood. Good grazing and water and five men are in charge. Good corrals for night use and it is impossible for Indians to run off the stock. Terms: per month, $3.00; per week, $1.00; for delivery, $.50. Ten percent charged for selling and returns promptly made. McKay and Smith, Crook City, August 3, 1876.[4]

Among the first ranchers to locate in the Black Hills were Erasmus and John Deffebach, who located a small herd in October, 1876. By butchering cows that cost them between fifteen and twenty-five dollars each, they were able to dispose of the fresh beef for one hundred to one hundred and twenty-five dollars for each animal. They brought several herds into the Hills from Wyoming and Nebraska during the next two years, selling them to butchers at good prices. In the fall of 1878 they located a ranch near the mouth of the Belle Fourche River, about one and one-half miles from where the town of Belle Fourche now stands. They ran mixed cattle and in season made weekly deliveries of beef to Lead, Deadwood, Central City, and other gold camps in the Hills where the large number of transients and miners created a steady demand for fresh beef.

With the abrogation of the treaty previously made with the Sioux Indians and the official opening of the Black Hills to settlement on February 27, 1877, a new field of operations was presented to the cattlemen of the Northwest. Included in the area opened for settlement was the region from the Platte River to the Yellowstone, and from the confluence of the Belle Fourche and Cheyenne rivers to the Big Horn Mountains, which constituted an

[4] *Black Hills Tribune,* August 31, 1876.

excellent grazing district. It contained valleys rich in native grasses, abundantly watered, and so effectively sheltered that stock could easily subsist by grazing throughout the entire season. Stockmen hastened to take advantage of the opportunity and flocked into the newly opened area in large numbers with herds varying from a few hundreds to several thousand. In December, 1878, one hundred thousand cattle were reported in the Black Hills region, many of which had been driven in from Texas. Most of them were in that part of the territory enclosed by the forks of the Cheyenne River.[5] Probably the first large herd of cattle to be located in the southern portion of the Black Hills was one of from two to three thousand head located in the vicinity of Rapid City by Gregory and Pease who drove them in from Colorado in 1878. Another herd of from three to four thousand head was located near Rapid City by James Wood about the same time.

Late in 1879, a Deadwood newspaper gave a résumé of what was happening:

The country north and east of Belle Fourche is rapidly being filled up with herds of cattle, many of which have been driven from Texas and Oregon. They are rolling fat and we are assured that they will need neither hay nor shelter during the coming winter. Last year the percent of loss from exposure was less than in Montana, Wyoming or Colorado. Large herds are now on their way from the south and west and before another year passes Dakota, or at least this portion of it, will be one of the great stock sections of the west.[6]

Stock in the Hills area increased 80 per cent in 1880 and 100 per cent in 1881, in which year one hundred thousand head were marketed. The Black Hills Live Stock Association was organized in the spring of 1880,[7] and on January 1, 1881, reported a mem-

[5] *Black Hills Weekly Pioneer* (Deadwood, D. T.), January 1, 1882; Visher, *op. cit.*, 117.
[6] *Black Hills Daily Times*, December 1, 1879.
[7] The first advertisement of the Association, which includes the brands of some of the members, appeared in a Rapid City newspaper on November 13, 1880. *Black Hills Journal* (Rapid City, D. T.), November 13, 1880.

bership of fifty-two, with headquarters at Rapid City. Statistics compiled by P. B. McCarthy, treasurer of the Association in the winter of 1881-82, gave sixty ranchers or cattle companies with a total of 264,200 head of stock. Their holdings were estimated to include 75 per cent of the cattle in the Black Hills vicinity. The average value was nineteen dollars per head.[8]

IX

A BEEF BONANZA

THUS by the late seventies open-range ranching had made a good start in portions of the Northwest, although its expansion into northeastern Wyoming, central and eastern Montana, and northwestern Dakota was being delayed since that region was still Indian country and had no railroad connections with the East. Until the Indian barrier could be removed and access to eastern markets made possible by the completion of the Northern Pacific Railroad, its development into a cattle country was impossible. The great possibilities of the region as an open range, however, were fully appreciated by those interested in the cattle business.[9]

Although the battle of the Little Big Horn in 1876 and subsequent events made eastern Montana, northeastern Wyoming, and northwestern Dakota comparatively safe from hostile Indians, the region was not officially evacuated until 1880 and 1881, when the tribes were gradually moved to the Standing Rock Reservation in Dakota.[10] In 1880 the Northern Pacific Railroad, held up at Bismarck, Dakota, since the panic of 1873, began construction westward, meeting the western division at Gold Creek, Montana, in 1883. The Union Pacific, spurred into activity by the possibilities of the cattle business in western and central Montana, began

[8] *Black Hills Daily Times,* December 1, 1879, January 21, February 14, 1880; *Black Hills Journal,* January 1, 29, April 13, May 21, 1881; *Black Hills Weekly Pioneer,* January 1, 1882.

[9] Jenney, *op. cit.,* pp. 2-5; *Black Hills Weekly Pioneer,* January 1, 1882.

[10] *Miles City Weekly Press,* June 4, 1881; *Cheyenne Daily Leader,* May 12, July 7, 11, 1876.

building northward from Corinne, Utah, in 1877 and crossed the Montana line in 1880.[3]

By the early eighties prospects were bright indeed for the stockmen of Wyoming, Montana, and Dakota and the stage was set for the great boom period in the cattle industry. The removal of the Indian barrier and railroad construction opened up an enormous area of unsettled country, admirably fitted for open-range ranching and made possible in this northwest region one of the most dramatic episodes of frontier history.

A forecast of the future traffic in cattle over the Northern Pacific was obtained in the autumn of 1879 when more than two thousand head of Montana steers arrived in Bismarck from the upper Yellowstone Valley. After the drive of over seven hundred miles they were loaded into stock-cars and shipped to Chicago. A St. Paul editor, commenting upon the significance of the event, said: "These are forerunners of the immense cattle trade the Northern Pacific will have as it moves westward into Montana. It is possible that these northern ranges will even compete with those of Texas in their vast herds of cattle." As the tracks were laid beyond the Missouri River, into eastern Montana, thousands of cattle were driven to meet the advancing road and loading chutes were often constructed as soon as the rails were laid.[4]

General conditions in the early eighties were ideal for the development of the great cattle boom. The financial depression of the seventies was over and capital, both domestic and European, was available at reasonable rates of interest. Western steers sold in the Chicago market for high prices and could be finished on the western cattle ranges at a small cost. Advertising, often extravagant, played an important part. The Black Hills gold rush and the Indian hostilities of 1876 and 1877 attracted attention and many an Easterner who came west to find gold remained to raise

[3] *Bismarck Weekly Tribune*, June 12, 1880, July 21, 1883; *Helena Daily Independent*, March 10, 17, 1880.

[4] *Bismarck Weekly Tribune*, September 9, 1879, October 4, 1880; *Helena Daily Herald*, September 18, 1879, quoted from the *St. Paul Pioneer Press*.

NOMADS OF THE PLAINS

Cheyenne Indian children and tavois. L. A. Huffman photograph.

INDIANS DRYING MEAT

Photograph by W. H. DeGraff, courtesy of Mrs. Robert W. Smith.

cattle. He wrote to his friends of the wonderful opportunities in the cattle country, a region made familiar to the people of the East by the campaigns of Custer, Crook, and Miles.[5]

Territorial newspapers were optimistic in their accounts, while eastern papers, particularly live-stock and farm journals, printed letters and articles of observers, and editorials telling of the wonders of this new land. A conservative eastern editor writing in 1882 said: "In the region traversed by the Northern Pacific lie boundless, gateless and fenceless pastures of the public domain, where cattle can be grown and fattened with little operating expense save that of a few cowboys, some corrals and a branding iron. There a poor man can grow rich while a rich man can double or even treble his capital." [6] The *Breeders' Gazette* in 1883 told how a steer worth five dollars at birth could run on the plains and crop grass on the public domain for four or five years at scarcely any expense to the owner, and could then be sold on the market for forty-five to sixty dollars.[7]

As a result of these conditions, the period from 1880 to 1886 was marked by an enormous expansion of the ranching business, a sharp increase in the amount of capital invested and overcrowding of the ranges. During these years the demand for cattle on the ranges of Wyoming, Montana, and Dakota was greater at times than the available supply. In addition to the Texas longhorns that were brought in by the thousands, cattle were moved northward out of Colorado in large numbers and some were brought in from Washington, Oregon, and northern Idaho.[8] More significant, however, than the enormous influx of Texas stock, and the drift from Colorado and the far northwest, was the shipment of young breeding stock and stock steers from the farms of Wisconsin, Minnesota, Michigan, Illinois, Iowa, and Missouri. While the

---

[5] John Clay, *My Life on the Range* (Chicago, 1924), pp. 149-57; Stuart, *Forty Years on the Frontier*, II, 150-9.

[6] *Cincinnati Gazette* (Cincinnati, Ohio), July 7, 1882.

[7] *Breeders' Gazette*, IV (Chicago, Ill., September 27, 1883), 421.

[8] *Annual Report of the Public Land Commission*, 1879, pp. 295-305.

scramble to stock the northern ranges was at its height, eastern feeders found it more profitable to sell their young cattle to western cattlemen at the high prices then prevailing than to fatten them for market themselves. The eastern stock, commonly known in the West as "pilgrims" or "barnyard cattle," were crowded into westbound stock trains or driven to the ranges in large numbers. From 1882 to 1884 there were probably as many cattle shipped west as were received in the East. In 1884 the Northern Pacific Railroad is said to have brought almost one hundred thousand head of "pilgrims" into the Dakota and Montana areas and to have taken about seventy-five thousand head of range stock to the Chicago market.[9]

Although some eastern and western cattle were brought into Wyoming during the boom period, by far the larger portion of the range stock came from Colorado and Texas. Wyoming stockmen went down the trail in 1879-80, buying up herds as they came up from the south, for their new ranges along the Powder, Tongue, and Upper Cheyenne rivers. They even trailed some of the southern herds into Montana where they were purchased to be taken to the Musselshell and Yellowstone valleys or to fill the vacant ranges occasioned by the driving of cattle to meet the Northern Pacific Railroad.[10] Between 1880 and 1886 every available bit of range in central and northeastern Wyoming was occupied with a startling rapidity. In many of the counties the increase between 1880 and 1883 was more than 500 per cent. Many large cattle companies were organized. In 1883 twenty companies, capitalized at more than twelve million dollars, were incorporated under the laws of the territory.[11] The membership of the Wyoming Stock Growers Association increased from 267 in 1883 to 363

[9] Nimmo, *Range and Ranch Cattle Business of U. S.*, pp. 182-3; *Rocky Mountain Husbandman* (Great Falls, Mont.), January 15, 1884; *Medora Bad Lands Cowboy*, November 13, 1884 files of the *Bismarck Daily Tribune* and *Dickinson Press*, 1880-1886.

[10] *Rocky Mountain Husbandman*, August 28, 1879.

[11] *Cheyenne Daily Sun*, March 9, 1884; *Annual Report of the Territorial Governor of Wyoming to the Secretary of the Interior*, 1886.

in 1885, at which time its members owned some two million head of stock.[12]

In the eighties the more remote grazing sections of Wyoming filled up at a remarkable rate, the Big Horn Basin being a case in point. There were no cattle in the area in 1878, and by 1884 it was completely stocked, the largest number of outfits locating there between 1880 and 1883. Many of the ranches established in these years were of the larger type. The first ranch in the Big Horn Basin was that of Charles Carter who, in December, 1879, chose land sixteen miles southwest of where the town of Cody, Wyoming, was later founded. The Carter, or "Bug" outfit, as it was called, played a prominent part in the range history of the Big Horn area. In 1880 Captain Henry Belknap placed a large herd in the same vicinity and the same year Otto Franc located his famous Pitchfork outfit on the Greybull River, which, when at its largest, numbered approximately twenty-five thousand head, and became one of the best-known ranches in the western part of Wyoming. At about the same time Angus J. McDonald built his Quarter Circle Y ranch on Gooseberry Creek some twenty miles south of the site of Meeteetse. His band of cattle is said to have numbered twenty thousand.

In the eastern portion of the Basin Henry T. Lovell located on the Big Horn River in 1880, and by 1883 was operating three ranches, his ML brand probably representing the largest cattle ranch in the eastern part of the Big Horn country. N. P. Noble brought in another large herd from the south in 1880, and the M— (M bar) established in 1881 by Robert A. Torrey was said to have run as many as fifty thousand cattle. Its policy was to absorb smaller herds that were located close to it. In 1882 the Big Horn Cattle Company, managed by Milo Burk and representing English capital, was established in the Tensleep region.[13]

[12] Osgood, *Day of the Cattleman*, pp. 120-1; Clay, *op. cit.*, pp. 250-1.
[13] Lindsay, *Big Horn Basin*, pp. 98-105; *Billings Weekly Gazette*, May 10, 1888; C. G. Coutant, "Notes of an Unfinished History of Wyoming," MS, Montana State Historical Library.

Open-range ranching had become well established in the Black Hills district in southwestern Dakota in the late seventies. During the boom period Dakota received more Texas stock than did Montana, a good many of which were absorbed in the Hills district. While some eastern cattle were taken into the southwestern portion of the territory, by far a larger part of the "pilgrims" were distributed in the areas to the north. In 1882 the drives from Texas into the Black Hills were estimated at 100,000, jumping to 250,000 in 1883. It was announced by the Black Hills Live Stock Association in the spring of 1884 that there were 500,000 head of cattle in the Black Hills district and that as many as 200,000 head had been marketed in 1883. By November of 1884 the total for the Hills region was put at from 700,000 to 800,000.[14]

Although a few scattering ranches were located in the region immediately north of the Black Hills in the late seventies, the west central and northwestern portions of Dakota were not occupied by cattlemen until the extension of the Northern Pacific Railroad from Bismarck in 1880.

In 1881 Hiram B. Wadsworth and W. L. Hawley from Minnesota shipped in about two hundred head of stock and located the Maltese Cross ranch on the Little Missouri River not far from the mouth of Little Cannon Ball Creek. Joseph and Sylvane Ferris and A. W. Merrifield came to the railroad station of Little Missouri in the heart of the Bad Lands in 1881 to engage in hunting buffalo. The Northern Pacific was just beginning to operate in this region and the Ferris brothers and their friend came out on one of the first coaches that was fastened to a construction train. They found Jerry Paddock and Howard Eaton already at the little frontier station, which had gained a rather unsavory reputation as a rendezvous for gamblers, saloonkeepers, lewd women, and toughs during the construction period. Merrifield and

[14] "Report of the Black Hills Live Stock Association, 1882-84"; *Black Hills Pioneer*, extra edition, March 17, 1884; *Spearfish Record* (Spearfish, D. T.), March 5, 1884.

Sylvane Ferris were employed by Wadsworth and Hawley to run their cattle on shares. This was probably the first ranch of importance to be established in northwestern Dakota.

A few scattered ranches owned by small pioneer cattle outfits had been located in the Little Missouri region by the end of 1882. There were A. C. Huidekoper, the Eaton brothers of Meadville, Pennsylvania, and the Rumsey brothers of Buffalo, New York. As yet the southern cattlemen and other cattle companies of the West, with their vast herds, had not penetrated the Little Missouri Bad Lands, although they had sent out some of their old cowhands to look over the new ranges and to spy out the best places for new ranches. Reports had no doubt been made, as it was rumored late in 1882 that some of the Texas outfits had cattle on the trail bound for the new area. By 1883 everybody had supreme faith in the cattle industry and southern cattlemen were hurrying their herds northward, while others were coming in from the west and east.[15]

The Northern Pacific Railway reached Gold Creek, Montana, in 1883, where it met the western division, thus connecting the East and the West. This was an important event in the ranching industry in northwestern Dakota and northern and eastern Montana, since it made possible the filling in of those areas with stock and provided shipping facilities for marketing. Texas herds were driven into the Dakota Bad Lands in 1883 in considerable numbers. The large herds of southern cattle caused the small ranchers of the area so much trouble that the territorial legislature of Dakota in 1883 passed a bill prohibiting Texas cattle east of the Missouri River.[16]

In 1883 Pierre Wibaux came west from Roubaix, France, and located his headquarters just over the Dakota line at Wibaux [17] on the Northern Pacific. He owned only one hundred and sixty

[15] Crawford, *Notes:* Interviews with Sylvane M. Ferris, Dickinson, N. Dak.
[16] *Session Laws of the Territory of Dakota*, 1883, pp. 227-30.
[17] Called Mingusville until 1896, when it was changed to Wibaux.

acres of land where his "White House" was built, but he claimed all the range between the Little Missouri and the Yellowstone rivers north of the railroad. He located his W-B ranch-house on the Little Missouri in Dakota at the mouth of Cherry Creek, a bull camp on Charbonneau Creek, and line camps on Bennie Pierce and Spring creeks. The ranges for the W-B ranch extended from the Yellowstone on the west to the Little Missouri on the east, being equally in Montana and Dakota. From 1883 to 1887 he ranched on a small scale, running about eight hundred head of stock, which he secured from both the southern and western ranges.[18]

In 1883 J. R. Tower and J. Gudgell established the O-X ranch on Little Beaver Creek not far from the Little Missouri. Their ranch buildings were on the present site of Marmarth, North Dakota, where they ran from twenty to thirty thousand cattle. About seven miles to the north, on the Little Missouri, were the headquarters of the Three Sevens (7-7-7) ranch, operated by the Berry-Boyce Cattle Company of New Mexico. They owned a maximum of thirty thousand head of cattle and also operated the P-K horse-ranch on Elk Creek about nine miles north of Beaver Creek. Their foreman was a Texan by the name of William Follis. Both the O-X and the 7-7-7 outfits drove their cattle from Texas. The next large ranch to the north was the H-T owned by A. C. Huidekoper, with headquarters on Deep Creek about twelve miles west of the later town of Amidon. Huidekoper ran some cattle but his main ranch-stock was horses. He owned several townships of land, being the only large outfit of the early days in this area that owned its range.

Going down the Little Missouri from that point, the next ranch of any size belonged to Theodore Roosevelt. Roosevelt came to Medora in September, 1883, on a hunting trip and was accompanied on the expedition by Joseph Ferris. While on the trip he

---

[18] Bertha M. Kuhn, "The W-B Ranch on the Missouri Slope," *Collections*, State Historical Society of North Dakota, V (1923), 157-60.

became interested in stock-raising and on his return purchased the Maltese Cross herd of cattle from Wadsworth and Hawley. The cattle were placed in charge of Sylvane Ferris and A. W. Merriweather and moved to Chimney Butte ranch, eight miles south of Medora. He bought several hundred head more that fall and the next year established the Elkhorn ranch, about twenty-five miles north of Medora. Roosevelt bought eastern cattle, mostly cows, and finally had about three thousand head on both ranches. The brand used on the first ranch was the Maltese cross cut on the left hip and right side, while that of the second was an elk horn cut on the left side and a triangle on the right. William Sewall and Wilmot Dow managed the Elkhorn ranch for Roosevelt, who visited these ranches twice a year, taking an active part in the round-up and all phases of general ranch work, remaining one year until Christmas.[19]

During 1883 and 1884 cattle came into the Little Missouri country so rapidly and so many ranches were established that only a few of the larger ones can be mentioned. The Reynold brothers of Albany, New York, later of Texas, established the Long X ranch north of Dickinson on Cherry Creek, a tributary of the Little Missouri. Thomas and Arnette established the Circle H ranch with about twenty-five thousand head, with headquarters a few miles west of the inland post-office of Fayette and twenty-five miles north of Belfield. Badger and Green had the largest outfit in the eastern part of the new cattle range at their Riverside ranch, south of Mandan. The Eaton brothers ran two outfits, one called the Custer Trail ranch and the other the Badger Cattle Company. Their main buildings were located north of Roosevelt's Elkhorn ranch.[20]

Dakota newspapers of 1883 to 1886 are filled with accounts

[19] Crawford, *Notes;* Kuhn, *op. cit.,* pp. 158-9.
[20] Crawford, *Notes:* Interview with Sylvane Ferris; *Dickinson Press,* January 3, 1885; University of North Dakota *Newsletter* (Grand Forks, N. D., October 22, 1927); *Theodore Roosevelt, an Autobiography* (New York, 1916), pp. 95-100.

of the beef bonanza. The *Dickinson Press* in the summer of 1883 announced the arrival of train-load shipments from Iowa and Minnesota, and as late as October 6th stated that "Howard Eaton, a Little Missouri rancher, passed through town with a herd of 2,500 cattle driven from Minnesota." On May 3, 1884, the same editor told of two Texas cattlemen with a herd of seven thousand looking for a location. During the spring and summer of 1885 hundreds of train-loads of eastern stock came into Dakota by way of Dickinson, Bismarck, and Pierre, the *Bismarck Journal* in April announcing that the Northern Pacific had contracted to bring forty thousand head of cattle to Dakota from Washington Territory.[21]

In 1886 the large eastern shipments to Dakota points continued, those received at Pierre being even larger than in 1885. Among the many items in a Pierre newspaper concerning cattle, the following show what was occurring. On April 8, 1886, W. C. Fairbanks, a wealthy Minnesota cattle-dealer, was in town looking over contracts involving eight thousand head of stock. On the morning of May 13th a special train of stock arrived, followed by three more late in the evening. On June 3rd C. A. Sturgis was in town awaiting a shipment of cattle from the East to be taken to his ranch on the upper Cheyenne River. A train-load of cattle had arrived during the night and two hundred cows from Minnesota passed westward in the morning on their way to the Black Hills, while two local ranchers were reported to have started from Texas with a large herd of cattle. Large numbers of Texas and western cattle were no doubt coming into Dakota in 1885 and 1886, although statistics are not available as to the number. A Bismarck editor reported in September, 1886, that the Reynold brothers, a large Texas firm, had brought up nine thousand head and located them on the Dakota ranges during the summer.[22]

[21] *Dickinson Press*, files of 1883-86; *Bismarck Saturday Evening Journal*, April 25, 1885.
[22] *Pierre Weekly Free Press* (East Pierre, D. T.), April 8, May 13, June 3, 1886; *Bismarck Saturday Evening Journal*, September 15, 1886.

It was estimated that in 1880 Montana contained 250,000 head of stock, including dairy cattle and work oxen, with the central and eastern areas of the territory practically unoccupied. By the fall of 1883 the number had increased to about 600,000 and the central and eastern ranges were rapidly being taken over.[23] As in the northwestern portion of Dakota, the early eighties was a period of large companies. In 1881 Scott and Hanks brought to their ranges on the Tongue and Powder rivers a herd of almost 20,000 head. They were purchased in Nevada and driven to Montana in one of the biggest drives ever made in the area. In 1882 E. S. Newman of the Niobrara Cattle Company drove in 13,000 head of Oregon cattle, locating them in the east central part of Montana, not far from the Wyoming line. The stock agent of the Northern Pacific Railroad reported the shipment of 41,700 cattle into Montana from the East in 1883, 13,000 of which were unloaded at Miles City and 12,000 at Billings.[24] The winter of 1883-84 saw the western and southern portions of the Montana area rather closely stocked, including the grasslands south of the Yellowstone in Custer County. There was still unclaimed range, however, in the Judith Basin and in the area north of the Yellowstone and south of the Indian reservation.

The climax to the cattle boom as far as the incoming cattle are concerned came in 1884, when more Texas cattle were driven north than in any other season since 1874, large numbers being shipped by railroad to such points as Ogallala, Nebraska; Pierre, Dakota; Cheyenne, Wyoming, and then driven on the Montana ranges from the point of debarkation. In addition to the cattle moved in from Texas, there were large numbers removed from Indian territory and from Colorado and other south central states. The Northern Pacific brought in large numbers of cattle from Wisconsin, Minnesota, and Iowa, the numbers billed for Montana, according to some estimates, running as high as 100,000,

[23] Stuart, *Forty Years on the Frontier*, II, pp. 187-8.
[24] *Yellowstone Journal*, December 6, 1883.

as many as 12,800 being unloaded at Glendive in a single day. The Concord Cattle Company of Concord, New Hampshire, brought in eight thousand head and the New York Cattle Company six thousand head to Miles City in April. While the importation of western cattle seems to have fallen off in 1884, Joe Scott of Scott and Hanks brought in six thousand head from Nevada and another herd of five thousand head from the Porcupine range in Idaho.[25]

A Texas live-stock journal estimated the drive out of Texas in 1885 to have been 385,000, of which a possible hundred thousand reached the Montana ranges. The year 1885 saw a revival of importations of Pacific Coast stock, some forty thousand coming into Montana from the West, with a like amount coming in over the Northern Pacific from the East. Heavy buying on the part of Montana stockmen was reported in Washington, Oregon, and northern Idaho early in 1886, and with cattle coming into the eastern and central ranges from almost all directions, it is exceedingly difficult to draw conclusions as to numbers. Drives from Texas were not especially heavy, the largest being that of the Home Land and Cattle Company who brought in ten thousand Texas yearlings. Although general bad conditions on the southern ranges tended to force additional stock into the northern drives for that year, shipments from both the East and West were heavy. The years 1884-85 saw a general movement of Montana stock toward the northern portion of the territory, the editor of the *River Press* at Fort Benton in September, 1885, estimating that at least fifty thousand head had crossed the Yellowstone River near Miles City and moved northward. They were reported to have been the larger outfits. By 1886 the ranges of Wyoming, Montana, and Dakota had reached a point of saturation.[26]

[25] *Yellowstone Journal*, March 1, April 5, 19, 26, July 26, 1884.
[26] *Yellowstone Journal*, November 21, 1885, September 4, 1886; *Miles City Weekly Press*, files for 1882-84; *Rocky Mountain Husbandman*, January 15, 1884; *Glendive Times*, April 26, 1884; *Wyoming Daily Sun* (Cheyenne, Wyo.),

Good profits made in the early years of the boom attracted eastern and European capital and large cattle companies became common. Many pioneer ranchers were induced to sell their holdings to the large promoters or to exchange them for capital stock in a newly organized company able to furnish additional funds for further expansion. This rapid increase of large companies often composed of eastern and European stockholders resulted in all the weaknesses common to absentee ownership, while the evils that accompany an era of inflation and speculation were present. In spite of warnings by western newspapers, cattle companies were often organized with little else to recommend them than attractive stock certificates.

The price of cattle reached its peak in May, 1882, when the best steers sold on the Chicago market for $9.35 per hundred. There was a rapid decline, especially in the lower grades, from $4.25 in April, 1883, to $1.00 in the fall of 1886.[27] The numerous cattle establishments, anxious to expand, began to bid against each other in the purchase of young stock and cows, and prices went up. Freight rates remained constant. Faced with sagging prices and increased expense, but anxious to pay dividends, the large ranchers adopted a dangerous policy. They sold more beef than their calf crop and the purchase of young stock would warrant, thus reducing their capital in order to show a large yearly earning.[28]

The cattle operators of the Northwest, faced with the problem of increasing costs of production with a general decrease in prices

January 3, 1884; *Breeders' Gazette*, IV, 297; Oliphant, pp. 69, 74, 79; R. S. Fletcher, "The Hard Winter in Montana, 1886-87," *Agricultural History*, IV (October, 1930), 123-30; R. S. Fletcher, "Eastern Montana Cattle Range Industry," MS in office of Everett E. Edwards, editor of *Agricultural History* (U. S. Dept. of Agriculture: Washington, D. C.).

[27] "Report on the Transportation and Sale of Meat products," *Senate Exec. Doc.* No. 829, 221-2; *Medora Bad Lands Cowboy*, November 25, 1886; *Bismarck Weekly Tribune*, October 6, 1886. Both papers contained surveys of beef prices.

[28] The Prairie Cattle Company of Dakota in 1883 sold 21,448 head of stock, while their calf brand showed 28,207, leaving a margin of 7,000 head for winter losses in a herd of about 100,000. Clay, *My Life on the Range*, pp. 131-5.

received for their finished stock, began to seek relief. They made every possible effort to secure better service and cheaper transportation rates with improvement in methods of marketing, but were unable to cope with the railroads, packers, and commission merchants. Failing in these efforts, they resorted to other schemes and experiments for the solution of their difficulties, two of which are deserving of our attention: the meat-packing experiment of the Marquis de Mores, and the plan to ship western range steers direct to England where meat prices were higher than in our markets.

X

A MEAT-PACKING EXPERIMENT ON THE WESTERN PLAINS IN THE EIGHTIES

THE DEVELOPMENT of the refrigerator-car in the late seventies led to the idea in the boom period of establishing slaughterhouses and meat-packing plants on the "high plains" as a means of solving the stockman's problems. The plan seemed reasonable and promised to free the rancher from commission men and packers, as well as cutting the heavy costs of transporting live stock to eastern markets. "The day will come," prophesied a Wyoming cattleman in 1883, "when a living bullock will only be seen in the circuses of Chicago, when dressed beef will be a home industry and the evils of transportation, commission men and packers will be eliminated."[1] Such an experiment was put into operation in the northwestern portion of the Territory of Dakota from 1883-86 and is connected with the romantic yet pathetic story of the activities of a Frenchman of noble birth, commonly known as the Marquis de Mores.

M. Antoine de Volombrosa, Marquis de Mores, son of a French duke, member of the Orléans family and son-in-law of a New York millionaire, L. A. (Baron) von Hoffman, arrived at the picturesque frontier town of Little Missouri, Territory of Dakota,

[1] *Cheyenne Daily Sun*, April 8, 1883.

early in April, 1883. Pierre Wibaux of Roubaix, France, who had located a large cattle ranch in the eastern portion of Montana in 1882 was a friend of the Marquis and had no doubt influenced his coming. The plan of the Frenchman, who had plenty of capital at his disposal, was to raise cattle and sheep and slaughter them on the range, shipping the meat in refrigerator-cars directly to eastern markets. The waste in transportation would be cut and the price of meat would be lowered to the consumer. Preparatory to the establishment of his ranch and meat-packing plant, De Mores purchased twelve thousand acres of land to be used for range and hay.[2]

Little Missouri, located 624 miles west of St. Paul on the Northern Pacific Railroad in the western part of Dakota, not far from the west bank of the Little Missouri River, was in the midst of the open range country and the shipping point of several large cattle outfits. Although containing less than one hundred inhabitants at the time of the arrival of De Mores, its reputation was not of the best. With its population of buffalo hunters, cowboys, trappers, gamblers, and cattle rustlers, it was classified by railroad men as the "toughest town on the Northern Pacific."[3]

The Marquis immediately began the construction of a large residence at Little Missouri known as the "chateau" or "castle." When the rough population of the village intimated that it had no room for his plant, he founded his own town on the east side of the river, calling it Medora after his wife. A complete meat-packing establishment was built in the fall of 1883 with a maximum capacity of three hundred beeves daily, and employing about two hundred men. It was equipped with the very latest machinery, including a newly invented blood-drying machine which alone cost $10,000. A large hotel was constructed called the "De

---

[2] *Bismarck Weekly Journal*, July 11, 1883; *University of North Dakota Newsletter*, October 22, 1927.

[3] Crawford, *Notes*; Lewis F. Crawford, superintendent of the State Historical Society at Bismarck for several years, collected a great deal of valuable information on De Mores and on ranching. Through the courtesy of Mr. Crawford, the author was allowed to use the material.

Mores," and a special clubhouse for his workmen containing a small theater, billiard tables, bowling-alleys and lounging-rooms. A stage line carrying passengers and express was established between Medora and Deadwood in the Black Hills, a distance of 215 miles.[4]

The packing company, incorporated under the title of the Northern Pacific Refrigerator Car Company, constructed branch slaughter-houses at Miles City and Billings, Montana, with cold-storage plants scattered across the continent at New York, Chicago, Milwaukee, St. Paul, Duluth, Helena, and Portland. An editor of Mandan, Dakota, writing in the spring of 1884, described the Medora enterprise:

The town of Medora on the east bank of the Little Missouri River has grown rapidly during the past few months, by far the most important buildings belonging to the Northern Pacific Refrigerator Car Company of which the Marquis de Mores is president. An immense slaughtering establishment has been erected with branch houses at Billings and Miles City in the center of the cattle ranges of Montana. The disposal of dressed beef will be secured through cold storage houses extending from Portland on the Pacific to New York on the Atlantic and Winnepeg on the North. The cold storage houses will keep the meat in prime condition until it can be sold in the local markets.[5]

A. T. Packard, editor of the *Medora Bad Lands Cowboy*, describes the progress of the project in the spring and summer of 1884.[6]

The Associated Press broadcasted the plans and accomplishments of the energetic Frenchman, and people flocked to Medora to work or to observe, much to the discomfort of Little Missouri across the river. But that was his only victory. The whole plan, so reasonable in theory, was a complete failure in practice, while

[4] *Dickinson Press*, July 7, September 22, October 18, 1884; Lewis F. Crawford, "Marquis De Mores and His Prairie Adventure," radio talk, Bismarck, N. Dak., April 13, 1927; *Medora Bad Lands Cowboy*, November 13, 1884.

[5] *Mandan Weekly Pioneer*, Immigration edition, January 1, 1884.

[6] *Medora Bad Lands Cowboy*, November 13, 27, December 18, 1884.

THE PACKING PLANT OF THE MARQUIS DE MORES

Medora, Dakota Territory, 1886. Courtesy of the North Dakota State Historical Society.

the lack of business judgment on the part of De Mores hastened its collapse. He invested heavily in steers at high prices, to find when he sold the meat that he had paid too much. He then purchased large herds of cows at low prices and slaughtered them before he learned that cow meat was not salable on the market. At one time he purchased twelve thousand head of sheep, many of which were too old to sell readily as dressed mutton.

Competition with the large packing companies was keen and he could furnish the consumer only grass-fed beef, which was not readily disposed of. His plant could be operated but five or six months of the year as cattle could only be slaughtered in the summer and fall. During the months in which the plant was idle his organization broke down and his overhead was too great for his volume of business. When butchers refused to buy his meat, the undaunted Marquis opened dozens of local shops, selling direct to the consumer, and organized a coöperative company to buy up the meat retailers. The packing-plant was in operation about two and one-half years, losing steadily all the time. In the autumn of 1886, the father-in-law of De Mores, who was backing the enterprise, visited Medora, and it was decided to close the plant and save what was possible from the ruins.[7] The losses of the company were heavy, amounting to approximately $1,500,000. The Marquis and his family left their Medora home for Paris in the spring of 1887.[8]

The De Mores lived in "grand style" while at Medora, bringing a touch of the aristocracy of France to the little frontier town. The "chateau" was finely furnished and more than twenty servants were employed about the household. Two dining-rooms

[7] Part of the land was purchased by Theodore Roosevelt, whose two ranches, the Maltese Cross and Elkhorn, were located in the vicinity of the Little Missouri River in September, 1883. *Dickinson Press*, November 24, 1886.

[8] *Mandan Daily Pioneer*, October 24, November 13, 1886, April 4, 1887; Crawford, *Notes; Dickinson Press*, November 24, 1886. The Marquis de Mores was killed in Egypt in 1898 while acting as a special agent for the French Government in the famous "Fashoda Affair." *Bismarck Saturday Evening Journal*, August 21, 1898. Madame de Mores returned to Medora for a short visit in 1903. *Mandan Daily Pioneer*, October 8, 1903.

were maintained, while the family employed a private doctor, a butler, coachman, gardener, laundress, general caretaker, as well as several chambermaids and cooks. The Marquis had his valet, while four special maids were employed for his wife and two children. When traveling the Marquis always rode in his own private railroad car, which, when not in use, stood on its special switch by the company's offices. When the family left Medora, they took very little with them and for many years their home stood as it was left, with furniture, dishes, saddles, children's toys, and clothing, and twenty leather trunks packed with the gowns and personal belongings of Madame de Mores.[9]

The packing-plant and buildings at Medora were not disposed of after the return of the Frenchman to his native land. In 1908 the plant in which the machinery still stood, as on the day it was closed twenty-two years before, was burned to the ground. All that remains to-day is a two-hundred-foot brick chimney, which stands as a monument to the dreams and visions of the Marquis de Mores. He was adventurous and visionary, but did not hesitate to back his visions with money. His ideas were not practical but his business dealings were honorable. Neither the nature nor the location of his enterprise was favorable to success, and his ventures were doomed to failure from the beginning. But in spite of this, his very boldness won the admiration, if not the approval, of the big-hearted and open-minded men of the frontier. Boundless energy, enthusiasm, confidence, and courage were all his. The element apparently lacking was judgment.

But the experiment of the Marquis de Mores was not the only meat-packing enterprise to be attempted in the Northwest. Two men by the names of Hough and Dustin from Lincoln, Illinois, constructed at Miles City during the summer of 1886 a large and comparatively costly abattoir with refrigerator-houses. The plant was destroyed by fire early in July and was rebuilt, sending out its first shipment of dressed beef in October. The loss by fire

[9] Crawford, radio talk, *op. cit.*

was evidently too heavy a blow for the new corporation. The obituary of the company is to be found in the *Yellowstone Journal* for November 20, 1886, which briefly but tersely said, "The slaughter house and machinery of the late Miles City Dressed Beef Company was yesterday insured for the benefit of the creditors in the name of the Sheriff of Custer County."

XI

ENGLAND AS A POSSIBLE CATTLE MARKET

IN 1884 a group of western cattlemen, still anxious to combat the railroads and the Chicago commission houses, formulated a plan of shipping unfinished steers direct to England to be fed for market. While cattle had been exported from the United States to England as early as 1868, they had come largely from the Middle West, as the English had never cared for the grass-fed product of the western cattle ranges. In the eighties England was obtaining her feeders, or "store cattle" as they called them, largely from Ireland, where they were usually purchased as yearlings and fed for two years before being slaughtered. If cheap mature western steers could be delivered in England and fed a few months, they would be ready for market. A bullock of fair quality brought about $9.50 a hundred in England. If $3.00 or even $3.50 were allowed for transportation, there was still $6.00 left for the rancher on his range. The originator of the plan is said to have been Moreton Frewen, an Englishman who managed the Powder River Cattle Company of Wyoming. The plan was pushed by its advocates with enthusiasm in good boom style, although some of the conservative stockmen questioned it in the discussions that took place in the "Cheyenne Club." Here was a plan, the proponents said, that would bring immediate returns and would force the railroads and commission merchants to make concessions. They talked of using the ranges of the West as a breeding-place for "lean cattle" that would be fattened and used in England, with good profits to the American rancher. The cattle could be shipped to Duluth over the Northern Pacific, and from there to Montreal by Canadian lines, where they would be loaded on cattle-boats for England.[1]

The one obstacle to the plan was the fear of pleuro-pneumonia that had developed in the eastern states, causing the English Privy Council to prohibit the importation of cattle from the United States except under strict regulations that included quarantine and slaughter within a few days at the point of debarkation. This might, however, be turned to the advantage of the western ranchers since the ranges of Wyoming and adjacent territory were sufficiently isolated from the East and it was within the authority of the Privy Council to exempt from their regulations localities that were free from the disease. As the proposition was discussed, it was looked upon by many as fantastic, as they could not see how the farmers of either England or Canada could benefit from it. The probability seemed that it would do them harm. The idea that it might be used as a means of compelling the railroads, packers, and commission men to be more reasonable caused many to withdraw their opposition. The plan no doubt commended itself to those who wished additional English capital to promote the cattle bonanza and may have been attractive to a few who in some way sensed that the cattle boom was about to collapse.

At any rate, the powerful Wyoming Stock Growers Association chose Moreton Frewen, who had good connections in England, to present the proposition to the English Privy Council. He went to England in the summer of 1884 and appeared before the representatives of the English Government and other prominent Englishmen interested in cattle-raising. He was introduced by the chairman of the group as representing the Governor of Wyoming, "a territory west of Lake Michigan." Frewen presented his proposition and explained how the territorial governor of Wyoming could quarantine against pleuro-pneumonia and fore-

---

[1] *Breeders' Gazette*, April 10, 1884.

stall any danger of the disease starting among its herds. He claimed that he had discussed the matter with Canadian officials who had indicated that they would be glad to coöperate in the plan. The English Government told Frewen that they would consider the idea but would take no action until the Canadian officials had been consulted. Canada refused to accept the plan, and the appearance of Texas fever on the ranges of the Northwest in 1884-85 gave them sufficient excuse to veto tactfully a project which would have been detrimental to the Canadian stock-raiser. The plan was impractical since neither the British nor Canadian farmer could hope to benefit by it, and their governments could hardly be expected to sponsor the opening of their doors to floods of cheap cattle when their markets were already too low. The scheme, when considered from all angles, was a wild one but was pursued with an optimistic egotism characteristic of the frontier.[2]

XII

THE WINTER OF 1886-87

By 1885 two points are clear regarding the open-range cattle business in the Northwest. In the first place, it was ceasing to be a frontier industry, while in the second it was falling a victim to overexpansion. Although ranching continued to have a frontier environment with the danger, hardship, and isolation of earlier years, it was coming to be largely controlled by company officers in eastern cities. Although the small operator had not disappeared, it was more and more difficult for a man of limited means to remain in the business. Finally, in the scramble for profits resulting from speculation and inflation, the industry had expanded to a point far beyond the margin of safety. Hundreds of thousands of cattle were thrown upon already overstocked pastures or pushed into areas where grazing was poor. While some forward-looking

[2] *Breeders' Gazette*, September 18, 1884; files of the *Cheyenne Daily Leader*, summer and fall, 1884.

companies had attempted to establish their business upon a sound economic basis by purchasing lands to serve as grazing grounds, in 1885 the industry as a whole still rested upon the open range. While little attention was paid to its dangers in the early eighties, many cattlemen were beginning to realize that the system was more and more insecure as time went on.

Cattle-raising under the open-range system, dependent as it was upon weather conditions, had always been recognized as hazardous.[1] Each spring losses were counted and the rancher felt relieved if fortune was with him. Somewhat of a gamble under normal conditions, the throwing of hundreds of thousands of young eastern stock upon an already overstocked range greatly increased the risk. The "pilgrims," as they were called, were far more valuable than southern or western cattle, and exhibited a dangerous tendency to stand around in the winter waiting to be fed, instead of rustling as did the other stock. They were far less able to stand the rigors of a hard winter, making the dangers of winter losses correspondingly greater. The millions of dollars invested in cattle in the face of such risks as these shows how far the spirit of wild speculation had been carried. A series of fortunate years with the chance of making large sums of money caused old cattlemen, whose experience should have taught them better, to plunge as madly as the new-comers.

The winter of 1880-81 had been quite severe on the northern ranges and losses had been heavy in central Montana and in parts of Wyoming. The Black Hills Live Stock Association reported a loss of only 8 to 10 per cent, mostly "through" stock.[2] The following winters were mild and the losses of 1880-81 were soon forgotten as the boom gained momentum. There was little snow on the plains of the Northwest during the winter of 1884-85 but

[1] The editor of a stock journal in 1885 commented upon the fact that spring had always brought a feeling of uneasiness on the cattle ranges of the Northwest. *Northwestern Live Stock Journal* (Cheyenne, Wy.), March, 1885.

[2] *Black Hills Weekly Pioneer*, January 1, 1882; "Report of the Black Hills Live Stock Association," 1882, pp. 1-2.

it was extremely cold. The *Medora Bad Lands Cowboy* for January 29, 1885, reported that four cowboys of the Hash Knife ranch had been frozen to death in the recent storm. It had also been reported to the editor at the same time that three men of the Three Sevens outfit had suffered a like fate but when the paper went to press the report had not be‿n confirmed. Feed was good, however, on the ranges of the Northwest and few cattle were lost.

The winter of 1885-86 was warm with little snow, and Montana, Dakota, and Wyoming range stock came through with little loss. When the news arrived, however, of the enormous losses in western Kansas and Colorado the better-informed and more conservative cattlemen became uneasy and realized that only sheer luck had saved them. A special meeting of the Montana Stock Growers Association was held at Miles City in April, 1886, and was well attended by stockmen from both Wyoming and Dakota. The problem of overstocking was discussed at length, but eastern and southern cattlemen who had contracted heavily for the coming season, enthusiastic over the small losses of the past winter, refused to act.

Frank Wilkeson, experienced in the cattle business on Kansas ranges some years before, wrote in April, 1886, about the same time the stockmen were in session at Miles City:

In the summer of 1885, up to September eighth, the Northern Pacific Railroad carried 68,860 young cattle from the east into Montana and western Dakota. Many thousands have been driven in and other thousands have been carried in by other railroad companies. But let a hard winter come with heavy snows and a succession of blizzards. Then how will the cattle fare, especially the through Texans? I answer, just as they did in Kansas in the winter of 1871-72 when the losses ranged anywhere from sixty to eighty percent. And if the coming winter should be as severe as Indian traders tell me they have seen it in the Yellowstone and upper Missouri Valleys, the toughened range stock will be decimated before spring.[3]

[3] *Harper's Monthly Magazine*, LXXII (April 12, 1886), 794-5.

The summer of 1886 was dry and warm. Hot winds swept across the plains and valleys of the Northwest, checking the growth of the grass and shriveling what did manage to grow. Creeks and springs went dry and by the first of June stockmen were moving their herds to places where water was obtainable. Conditions in central and eastern Montana were even worse than in Dakota and Wyoming, and during the first part of August the *Mandan Pioneer* reported that Montana stockmen were driving their cattle into Dakota and Canada to keep them from starving.[4] With Texas, western and eastern cattle arriving during the summer, conditions that were already bad became more serious. According to various contemporaries, one element making the drought more dangerous was the collapse of beaver dams. The larger creeks in earlier days were enabled to hold water to better advantage because of the numerous beaver dams built at frequent intervals along their courses. By 1886 and even before, the beaver had been largely trapped out and the dams were "letting go," causing many creeks to dry up more quickly. This, together with an extremely dry season, caused intense aridity, prairie fires often burning the grass not already dried out and killed. By the end of September feed available on the ranges was sufficient to sustain but a small part of the cattle located there.

To make matters worse the price of cattle was low in the fall of 1886, grass-fed native steers being worth from $3.00 to $3.40 per hundred; grass-fed Texas steers, $2.75 to $2.80; medium cows, $1.25 to $1.65. Although a good many cattle were shipped to eastern markets, the low price, together with the poor condition of the stock, caused a considerable decrease in the number

---

[4] *Mandan Weekly Pioneer*, August 12, 1886; *Pierre Daily Free Press*, June 12, 1886. Many Montana cattle were driven north into Canada, where grazing land was leased from the government. In August, 1886, 40,000 head left Dawson and Custer counties. By September it was estimated that 250,000 head of Montana cattle had been driven into Canada. *Stock Growers' Journal* (Miles City, Mont.), August 12, September 22, 1886. Some ranchers in Wyoming and Montana tried to forestall disaster by boarding out small herds of their weaker stock in the agricultural sections. *Cheyenne Daily Sun*, December 8, 9, 1886.

that would have been shipped out under normal conditions, thus making conditions worse on the overcrowded ranges.[5]

In addition to all this, indications in the fall of 1886 pointed toward a hard winter. The beaver that were left are said to have piled up abnormal quantities of saplings for winter food and the bark of the younger cottonwood trees was thick and tough. The native birds, showing a marked uneasiness all through the fall, bunched much earlier than usual, while the wild animals were said to have been growing unusually heavy coats of fur. The arctic owls came early and the wild-fowl began to migrate southward fully six weeks before their usual time. From all indications Nature was preparing for what was to follow, but aside from a few old plainsmen, proficient in nature's lore, little attention was paid to these warning signs.[6]

A Black Hills newspaper in October sounded a note of warning: "Judging from the tone of livestock papers throughout this region, there is well grounded apprehension among the stockmen that there is a hard winter ahead of them, which is likely to be attended with a great loss of stock. The unusual drought in Texas has brought in many extra cattle. The season has been dry here, also, and there seems to be far more cattle than there is feed."[7] Late in the fall, at a meeting of the Little Missouri Stock Growers Association, it was decided that the ranges were badly overstocked in that round-up district and that in the future the ranch hands there would refuse to work with new outfits running either cattle or horses. This action came too late to be of any value, as the winter was already settling in and the stage was fully set for the enactment of the disastrous finale.[8]

The story of the calamitous winter of 1886-87 has been told

[5] *Medora Bad Lands Cowboy*, November 25, 1886; *Bismarck Saturday Evening Journal*, August 28, September 15, October 6, 1886.
[6] Crawford, *Notes*; Herman Hagedorn, *Roosevelt in the Badlands* (New York, 1921), pp. 431-2; Lincoln Lang, *Ranching With Roosevelt* (Philadelphia, 1926), pp. 239-40.
[7] *Black Hills Weekly Pioneer*, October 7, 1886.
[8] *Bismarck Daily Tribune*, December 9, 1886.

many times. It closed down upon the Northwest fully six weeks earlier than usual, holding the cattle ranges in its iron grip for more than four months, relaxing at last only to leave ruin and desolation in its wake. The first storm began on the Dakota ranges on the evening of November 4th and before midnight the temperature had fallen very low. In a few days a terrible blizzard was sweeping the entire Northwest. The fine dry snow packed into the coulées and depressions and covered the river bottoms. The blizzard finally spent itself but the extreme cold continued. Then followed blizzard after blizzard, with the temperature often dropping to forty degrees below zero. This continued throughout the months of November, December, and January, the snow becoming four or five feet deep on the level with drifts of monstrous size. With what little grass there was buried under successive layers of snow, it is easy to foretell results.

The files of the *Bismarck Daily Tribune* for the winter gave an approximation of what was going on. About the middle of December a herd of more than a thousand antelope, the largest ever known, was reported roaming the Bad Lands between Medora and Belfield in search of food, and James Parsons, a rancher near Minot in the northwestern part of the territory, had lost a thousand head of stock in the last storm. On December 14th the town of Glen Ullin on the Northern Pacific reported that it was in winter quarters and that its public school had been closed for the season. The weather report in the *Pierre Free Press* for December 2nd said that Monday had been the worst day ever experienced in the town. During a period of twenty-four hours there was rain, sleet, snow, and extreme cold. On December 9th, the thermometer registered twenty-five degrees below zero in the Black Hills, while on December 30th it was announced that another severe storm had swept Dakota and that thirteen thousand cattle north of Deadwood in the Black Hills were in dire straits for lack of feed. On January 13th there was three feet of snow on the level in the Black Hills and on February 2nd, 1887, occurred a storm that was reported to have been the most severe of the whole winter. On March 10th, J. H. Lenhart of Mandan reported that out of a herd of one hundred and seventy-five cattle all but fifteen had been found dead. He had put up a hundred tons of hay and had fed it until it was exhausted.[9]

The Wyoming and Montana newspapers gave about the same account. Stuart, in writing of the extremely cold weather in Montana, said, "The thermometer dropped to twenty-two degrees below zero, then twenty-seven degrees, then thirty degrees and on the night of January 15 stood at forty-six degrees below zero." One of the best statements as to general conditions during the winter is furnished by a Bismarck editor writing on February 11, 1887:

There is serious apprehension that there will be an appalling loss of human lives in Montana and western Dakota. Snow began falling early in November and there is more on the ground than for ten years. Most of the stage roads are entirely closed up and trains are running at irregular intervals, some being four or five days apart and the supply of fuel is becoming almost exhausted. The snow is drifted to enormous depths and should another protracted storm occur it is believed that hundreds would succumb to its terrors. As it is, more people have frozen to death this winter than for a quarter of a century. The cold has been intense. Reports are coming in from the ranges of Dakota, Montana and Wyoming of the large losses of cattle owing to the scarcity of feed and insufficient protection from the severe weather. Losses already reach eight to twenty percent and it is not overdoing it to say that in event of the snow lying on the ground for four weeks longer the loss will reach from fifty to seventy-five percent.[10]

Under these conditions the new stock, Texas "dogies" and "pilgrims" from the East or Northwest, unacclimated, and often foot-sore and weak from a long trek, were in no condition to withstand the blizzards and extreme cold. They crowded into the coulées and creek beds and other sheltered places and froze to

[9] *Bismarck Daily Tribune*, November-April, 1886-87; *Pierre Weekly Free Press*, December 11, 1886.
[10] *Dakota and Burleigh County Settler* (Bismarck, D. T.), February 11, 1887.

death or were smothered by the drifting snow. The native stock, with their heavier coats, better able to withstand the cold, hung on a little longer. They kept moving and fed as best they could on sage-brush and cottonwood twigs. The gaunt and bony animals, resembling living skeletons, collected around the ranch-houses, often gnawing at the tar-paper on the buildings, until they were too weak to stand any longer. They died by the thousands and tens of thousands, often piled one upon another in the more sheltered places, the wolves and coyotes taking a goodly toll of the weakened animals that became stuck or imprisoned in the drifts of snow.

The winter was one of tragedy and suffering among the ranchers themselves. Many cattlemen left their ranch-houses during a storm and never returned. Women and children lost their way between the stable and house, in some cases freezing to death within a few yards of their own door-steps. In early March a "chinook" began to blow, loosing the icy grip of winter and melting the snow at a rapid rate. Within a few days the creeks and rivers were overflowing and were carrying countless dead cattle downstream amid cakes of ice and debris. One writer, describing the Little Missouri River, tells how the stream spewed forth the carcasses of cattle in untold thousands, and "one had only to stand by the river bank for a few minutes and watch the grim procession ceaselessly going downstream to realize in full the depth of the tragedy that had been enacted within the past few months." [11]

As the weeks went by and the snow slowly disappeared, the ranchers were able to ascertain the extent of their losses. They hoped against hope during the spring round-up, but as the reports gradually dribbled in, the stockmen of the Northwest who had been running cattle on the open range saw that they were ruined. The coulées and sheltered places were found packed with dead

[11] Crawford, *Notes;* files of the *Bismarck Daily Tribune* and the *Mandan Daily Pioneer.*

cattle, and men during the round-up would ride at times for a whole day without seeing a single living animal. Where hundreds of thousands of cattle had grazed the previous autumn, there remained only a few emaciated, skeleton-like survivors, mostly steers, with frozen ears, feet, and tails and often so weak they could hardly stand. As the summer advanced the bodies that had not been carried away by the high water gradually dried up and only piles of grass-covered bones were left. By late summer it was not the remains of the dead cattle that told the tale, but the few live ones that were left. Joseph Scott, president of the Montana Stock Growers Association, at the annual spring meeting in 1887, expressed the opinion that, had the winter continued for twenty more days there would have been little necessity of an Association.

Losses on the different ranges of the Northwest varied, as did losses of individual ranchers in the different regions. General conclusions and estimates for the whole area are therefore difficult to ascertain. Gregor Lang, whose ranch was in the Little Missouri country of Dakota not far from that of Theodore Roosevelt, started the winter with three thousand head and came out in the spring with four hundred. Lovell, a prominent Wyoming stockman, estimated that at least half of his herd died of exposure and starvation. Beckwith and Quinn, in the Big Horn Basin of Wyoming, had hardly enough cattle left in the spring to operate a round-up outfit. Alex Swan, one of the "cattle kings" of Wyoming, who in the spring of 1886 had twenty-nine thousand fat cattle for which he is said to have been offered a million dollars, in the June round-up had nine thousand cattle to meet $350,000 of liabilities, and went into bankruptcy. Another Wyoming rancher told of seeing his cattle mill together and die by the thousands, their bodies almost covering a stretch ten miles long. His losses amounted to practically 100 per cent. Nelson Story of Bozeman, Montana, put his losses at two-thirds and Conrad Kohrs of western Montana claimed that his losses were 50 per cent. The Home Land and Cattle Company of Montana lost more than four thousand head out of a herd of six thousand.

As is usually the case in most catastrophes, there were those who were favored by the gods of fortune. George B. Baxter, a Wyoming cattleman of the Big Horn valley, told a unique story of how he escaped disaster by obeying a lucky intuition. He and his foreman moved his herds to the foot-hills just as winter set in. There the high winds, alternating with the heavy snow-storms, kept the ridges bare during most of the winter. Quite fortunately, the range where his cattle were located had not been used for two years, which added materially to the amount of grass available. Baxter claimed to have branded more calves in the spring of 1887 than usual, while his neighbor who had kept his cattle on the regular range branded four hundred in comparison to three thousand the year before.[12]

The local press was quite reluctant to face the facts and to admit the full extent of the losses. The *River Press* of Fort Benton, Montana, in the summer of 1887 came to the conclusion that losses in the territory varied from 50 per cent or more in the Yellowstone and Musselshell regions, to 40 per cent in the Shonkin and Judith Basin areas, and even less in the Sun River country. These estimates are far too conservative and a Dakota editor, growing impatient with the tendency to underestimate the extent of cattle losses, came out in an editorial to the effect that it was about time the ranchers of the Northwest were facing the facts. He estimated the losses for the open-range area to have averaged 75 per cent.[13] With many authenticated records of losses running as high as 90 to 95 per cent a conservative estimate of the average loss for the whole area would be from 75 to 80 per cent.

Many of the large companies went into the hands of the receiver in the summer of 1887 and disposed of the remnants of

[12] Lindsay, *Big Horn Basin*, p. 133.
[13] *Mandan Daily Pioneer*, July 23, 1887.

their herds as their creditors demanded payment. Every marketable animal was sold and in some sections the heavy shipments
during the summer and fall practically cleared the range. More
than seventy thousand head were shipped from the Wyoming
area alone.[14] Cattle were sold on the Chicago market for as low
as $2.50 per hundred pounds, ranchers often closing out stock for
forty dollars a head that they had paid thirty dollars a head for
three years before. Most of those who remained pared down their
herds to what they considered a safety point, while a few, more
courageous than the rest and with more financial backing than the
average, bought up the surviving cattle at low prices and waited
for better times. They realized that only the strongest and best
cattle had survived, most of which were steers, and at a low price
they were an excellent investment.

Pierre Wibaux of the famous W-B ranch was one of these who
hung on, and is said to have borrowed considerable sums of money
in France to finance his activity. He purchased twenty thousand
head from the Running Water Land and Cattle Company in
1887, and in 1889 bought ten thousand head from the Powder
River Cattle Company at $18.50 each.[15] Prices for Texas cattle
were quite low at this time, three-year-olds being sold for ten
dollars to fourteen dollars a head in 1887-88. While they were
brought on to the depleted ranges in conservative numbers, business in Texas cattle was active. The Home Land and Cattle
Company bought fifteen thousand head in 1887 and the Hash
Knife outfit purchased six thousand. They continued to come in
during 1888, and in 1889 at least 150,000 head were brought
into Montana alone. Some of them continued to come in during
the nineties. In July, 1891, a large herd of Texas yearlings was
delivered at the Fort Benton stock-yards at thirteen dollars a
head, all expenses paid.[16]

[14] *Cheyenne Daily Sun*, November 1, 1887.

[15] *Rocky Mountain Husbandman*, September 15, 1887; *Yellowstone Journal*,
May 28, 1887, May 29, 1889.

[16] *River Press* (Fort Benton, Mont.), July 29, 1891.

The hard winter eliminated most of the "cattle barons" and those that remained were obliged to develop more scientific methods, to give up hopes of enormous profits and to be satisfied with reasonable returns. The economic depression of the early nineties made the recovery of the cattle business a slow process. With the "beef bonanza" gone, outside capital, as a rule, was not interested, and where it was, utmost caution was demanded. Then, too, the ranchers themselves had lost their earlier confidence, and refused to take many chances. The catastrophe of 1886-87 demonstrated to cattlemen, both large and small, the dangers of open-range feeding and overexpansion, and adjustments were made. Large herds were no longer turned loose without shelter to graze and drift where they willed. Herds were smaller and were kept under careful control, shelter being provided for the weaker animals and hay cut for emergency feeding.[17] Low prices continued throughout the nineties and proved a serious handicap to the recovery of the cattle industry.

XIII

THEODORE ROOSEVELT AS A CATTLEMAN

To MANY students of history, perhaps the most glamorous name among those of the ranchers of the Northwest in the eighties and nineties is that of Theodore Roosevelt. In common with other cattlemen, his losses were heavy in the disastrous winter of 1886-87, and although he kept his ranch until 1900, he seldom visited it after 1887. His losses for the whole period, including interest on his investment, amounted to at least seventy-five thousand dollars. While he participated in an active way in the affairs of his ranch, at one time serving as round-up captain for the

[17] The manager of a large cattle outfit on the Powder River in Montana shipped in 12,000 pounds of grass seed in the spring of 1887. In 1888 the company put up 1,200 tons of hay; 3,600 tons in 1892 and 14,000 tons in 1904. This is typical of the nineties in the ranching areas of the Northwest. Clay, *My Life on the Range*, pp. 221-3.

Little Missouri district, and no doubt would have welcomed profits, it seems reasonable to say that running cattle in western Dakota was not primarily a business with Roosevelt and the results and effects of his ranching experience can hardly be evaluated in terms of money.[1] He arrived at Medora, a little frontier settlement in the northern Bad Lands of western Dakota in September, 1883. At the time of his arrival, he was a pale, slender, shy young man, twenty-five years of age and in bad health. When he left in the summer of 1887 he was strong and healthy, with the constitution of an athlete.

Roosevelt, like many others from the East, first came to hunt, but, fascinated by the western country and its opportunities for self-expression and development, he remained and invested in a cattle ranch. Later, as he grew more enthusiastic and gained greater confidence in the country and its people, he purchased a second ranch. At the time of Roosevelt's arrival, the Northern Pacific Railroad had just come through from Bismarck, and Little Missouri and Medora on opposite sides of the Little Missouri River were typical boom towns or construction camps. They both had bad reputations and as one observer stated, "while Little Missouri was a God-forsaken place, Medora was even worse."[2] Although Medora had all the characteristics of a typical frontier settlement, in many ways it was not an ordinary place. A town of less than one hundred inhabitants, representing as it did men of all kinds and classes, it was indeed a human mosaic. There was the Marquis de Mores, a French army officer and capitalist, with his cousin, Count FitzJames, who were operating a ranch and a packing-house. Associated with them in the packing enterprise

[1] Between September, 1884, and July, 1885, Roosevelt invested $82,500 in his ranching venture. By 1891 his books show a flat loss of $23,556, at which time he invested $10,000 more in the enterprise. Between 1891 and 1900, when he closed out, he made a profit of $3,264. His loss for the whole period, not counting interest, was a little more than $20,000. Allowing for a very reasonable rate of interest on money invested, for the period 1885 to 1900 the losses of Roosevelt amounted to a considerable sum. Hagedorn, *Roosevelt in the Badlands,* p. 482.

[2] Crawford. *Notes:* Interview with Sylvane Ferris.

were two brothers, Henry and Edgar Haupt, sons of a West Point graduate and a well-known military engineer. There was H. H. Gorringe, a retired navy man, who with an Englishman, Sir John Pendar, and A. S. Hewitt, later one of Roosevelt's New York political opponents, was promoting a ranch company. There was Pierre Wibaux, a shrewd Frenchman, owner of the W-B ranch to the westward. He was the son of a wealthy textile manufacturer of Roubaix, France, and had been educated at home and in England. There was A. T. Packard, editor of the *Medora Bad Lands Cowboy* and a graduate of the University of Michigan. A. C. Huidekoper was there, a Harvard graduate and member of an eastern family of wealth and culture. Associated with him were his two nephews from Boston. There were Howard Eaton, manager of the Badger Cattle Company, and C. B. Richards, founder of the Hamburg-American Steamship Line. There were scions of English nobility who had come to hunt, one of whom was Laval Nugent, son of a member of the House of Lords. There was Gregor Lang and also D. K. Wade, sometimes called "Deacon" Wade, a former designer of stoves from Pittsburgh. Add to the above group the usual men of the frontier—plainsmen, buffalo hunters, cowboys, trappers, gamblers, cattle rustlers, and outcasts, many of the latter probably fugitives from justice—and one has a fair picture of the society into which Roosevelt was plunged in the fall of 1883.

The life that Roosevelt led while on the cattle ranges of the Dakota Bad Lands could not have been without powerful effect upon the future President. He learned the virtues of life in the open, gained self-confidence, became self-reliant, and learned the value of making prompt decisions, all of which stood him in good stead in later life. He gained the respect of the common cowboys and men of the frontier, as well as of the men of ambition, wealth, and culture with whom he worked and associated. He learned of the needs, hopes, and desires of the various classes of people with whom he came in contact. Many of the qualities displayed by

THEODORE ROOSEVELT'S MALTESE CROSS RANCH

Medora, Dakota Territory. Photograph by W. H. DeGraff,
courtesy of Mrs. Robert W. Smith.

A MONTANA RANCH OF THE SEVENTIES

Benders Ranch near Miles City. L. A. Huffman photograph.

Roosevelt in public life are those that are also typical of the frontier. Ranching in western Dakota was to Roosevelt more of a spiritual than a financial adventure.[3]

In his autobiography, Roosevelt gives an account of his experiences in the Dakota Bad Lands:

It was a land of vast silent places, of lonely rivers, and plains where the wild game stared at the passing horseman. It was a land of scattered ranches, of herds of longhorned cattle, and of reckless riders, who unmoved looked into the eyes of life or death. In that land we led a free and hardy life, with horse and with rifle. We worked under the scorching midsummer sun, when the wide plains shimmered and wavered in the heat; and we knew the freezing misery of riding night guard around the cattle in the late fall roundup. In the soft spring-time the stars were glorious in our eyes each night before we fell asleep; and in the winter we rode through blinding blizzards when the driven snow burned our faces. There were monotonous days, as we guided the trail cattle or the beef herds, hour after hour, at the slowest of walks; and minutes or hours teeming with excitement as we stopped stampedes or swam the herds across rivers treacherous with quicksands or brimmed with running ice. We knew toil and hardship, hunger and thirst, and we saw men die violent deaths as they worked among the horses and cattle or fought at evil feuds with one another; but we felt the beat of hardy life in our veins, and ours was the glory of work and the joy of living.[4]

In a speech made at Sioux Falls, South Dakota, September 3, 1910, Roosevelt said, "I can never sufficiently express the obligation I am under to the Territory of Dakota, for it was here I lived a number of years in a ranch-house in the cattle country, and I regard my experience during those years when I worked and lived with my fellow ranchmen on what was then the frontier as the most important educational asset of my life." [5]

[3] A. T. Volweiler, "Roosevelt's Ranch Life in North Dakota," *Quarterly Journal of the University of North Dakota*, IX, No. I (October, 1918), 31-49.
[4] Roosevelt, *Autobiography*, pp. 94-5. Quoted by special permission of Charles Scribner's Sons, New York City.
[5] *Sioux Falls Argus Leader*, September 4, 1910.

XIV

PRICES AND PROFITS

THE ACCOUNTS of such writers as Brisbin, Baillie-Grohman, and Strahorn as to possible profits to be made in the cattle industry in the Northwest in the seventies and early eighties are apt to appear to the average reader as pure fabrication. A careful analysis of the figures and facts involved, however, indicate that while their statements may have been somewhat too optimistic on certain points, they were by no means products of the imagination. During those years there was plenty of money to be made in the stock business. With good stock cattle available on the range at prices ranging from $10 to $20 a head and the actual cost per year of fattening steers for market running $1.50 per head or under, counting labor, supplies, equipment, and interest on the original investment, the actual cost of production was low.[1] Under the circumstances rapid expansion was encouraged.

Market prices for cattle were high. Early in 1880 western native stock and common cattle were listed in Chicago at $4.00 to $5.50 per hundredweight, while in 1881 common cattle and shippers were quoted on the Chicago market at $4.85 to $6.10, with feeders and butchers at $4.00. The peak was reached in 1882 when good to choice shipping cattle were quoted at Chicago at $5.90 to $6.90, with fancy steers even higher.[2] Beef contracts for Indian reservations and army posts were lucrative. In 1882 T. C. Power of Helena, Montana, was granted a contract to provide 500,000 pounds of beef to the Indians of Standing Rock Agency, south of Mandan in the Territory of Dakota, at $4.65 per hundred pounds live weight. Figuring the average steer to weigh 1,200 pounds, the contract brought about $55 a head to the owner. In this case there was little cost for transportation and

[1] Nimmo, *Range and Ranch Cattle Business of the U. S.*, pp. 20-1.
[2] *Omaha Daily Republican* (Omaha, Neb.), February 14, 19, 1880; *Omaha Daily Bee*, September 28, 1881, September 4, 18, 1882.

practically no loss in weight. With stock animals selling at $20 a head profits were high indeed.[3]

In 1883 Dan Floweree of Helena sold steers on the Chicago market for $5.80 per hundred. His cattle, averaging over 1,400 pounds each, brought him more than $80 a head. His expense of marketing involved an overland drive to Billings, Montana, and freight rates from that point to Chicago at about $7.00 a head. A local editor estimated his profit to have been at least 50 per cent and that it might possibly run as high as 100 per cent. The Marquis de Mores in August, 1883, purchased 500 head of beef stock from the Concord Cattle Company for his packing plant at $4.50 per hundred. If they averaged 1,200 pounds, the price received was approximately $54 each, delivered at Medora, Dakota, involving practically no expense for transportation.[4] The average price paid for range cattle in Chicago in 1883 was $4.70 per hundred.

Large profits began to react on the price of range stock and the price advanced in 1884 and 1885 to $30 per head and even higher. In 1885 and 1886 the market price of beef decreased rapidly and the average for the latter year in Chicago was $3.30 or around $40 a head. Add to the original cost $6.00 or $7.00 freight charges, $1.00 to $1.50 a year for two or three seasons' herding expense, with interest on the money involved, and it is easy to see that there was little profit. One of Roosevelt's partners took a train load of stock to Chicago in 1886 and was compelled to sell them at a price he estimated to be $10 below actual cost. The losses for the last two years of the boom probably about balanced the excessive profits of the early eighties.

The business of raising cattle on the open range involved other risks or obstacles that included Indians, cattle thieves, disease, wolves, grasshoppers, poisonous weeds and plants, and blizzards

[3] *River Press*, April 27, 1882. The Prairie Cattle Company announced a dividend of 42 per cent for 1882. *Breeders' Gazette*, July 10, 1884.
[4] *Rocky Mountain Husbandman*, December 26, 1884; *Yellowstone Journal*, August 11, 1883.

and regular winter losses. Although losses because of Indians
were rather irregular and declined in the eighties, in various
sections of the range in the earlier period they were sometimes
serious. While winter losses were low at times in 1880-81, they
ran as high as 10 to 15 per cent. Dangers from poisonous plants
during the dry season were serious.[5]

With large numbers of cattle thrown on the market after the
winter of 1886-87, the price of beef went down to an extremely
low point. With a temporary upward movement in 1888 the price-
curve for the nineties showed a definite downward trend. Wyoming cattlemen were badly discouraged in the spring of 1889,
when the editor of the *Cheyenne Daily Sun* in April wrote that
eastern markets were the worst he had ever seen. Fancy steers were
quoted at $5.00 per hundredweight in December, 1890, while
Chicago quotations in the fall of 1893 were as low as $2.85. In
Omaha, range cattle were quoted from $1.50 to $3.30 while corn-
fed steers were priced there at $4.50.[6] The only suggestion made
by the various stock journals was to curtail shipments until prices
went up, which would hardly have done much to improve conditions as it could only mean the glutting of the market when they
were shipped. Then, too, most of the ranchers needed liquid capital and were often compelled to sell. "Hold Your Cattle," appeared in the head-lines of the *Stock Growers' Journal* of Miles
City, Montana, in August of 1893, "If you cannot Hold all, Hold
all You Can and as Long as You Can." Four years later, the
same editor was still worried about the market and the weak
prices which were becoming common.[7]

In spite of low profits and other obstacles, there was some
money being made in the cattle business after the winter of 1886-
87. The Benton and St. Louis Cattle Company was organized in

[5] *Yellowstone Journal,* June 15, 29, 1882, February 10, 17, March 31, 1883,
July 4, November 14, 1885; *River Press,* November 30, 1881.
[6] *Cheyenne Daily Sun,* April 2, 16, 1889, December 2, 1890; *Omaha Daily
Bee,* files for October, 1893; Lindsay, *Big Horn Basin,* pp. 139-41.
[7] *Stock Growers' Journal,* August 5, 1893, July 17, 1897.

1882, capitalized at $500,000, at which time it purchased five thousand head of stock. It later increased its capital to $600,000 and made one addition of stock to its herds by 1902. Although it suffered a 40 per-cent loss in 1886-87, the company paid an annual dividend after the first year which amounted in twenty years to $980,000, and at the same time built up a herd of twenty thousand cattle and purchased eleven thousand acres of land.[8] The Wyeth-Brown Cattle Company, founded in 1886, over a period of twelve years made profits amounting to more than $220,000, which constituted a fair return on the money invested.[9]

XV

FOREIGNERS AND FOREIGN CAPITAL

THE NUMBER of cattle exported from the United States to the British Isles before 1875 was small, the main reason being that the British consumer was accustomed to the very best grade of beef, demanding a heavier and fatter type than was produced on the western plains. In about the middle of the seventies, however, the corn-belt region of the central United States, where some attention had been placed on stock improvement, began to send cattle and beef to England to compete with the domestic product. Part of the animals exported had been shipped from the plains of the West to the Middle West where they had been fattened for the English market. Having read and heard various stories of the great Texas herds, the unlimited free range of the West, of railroad construction, and the development of the great cattle market of Chicago and of other centers, the English Government and stock-raisers became alarmed lest the imported American beef might drive their own out of the market. At the same time these activities had attracted the attention of European capital.

---

[8] *River Press*, May 26, 1902; Fletcher, "Eastern Montana Cattle Range Industry," ch. iii. Part of the holdings of the company were in Canada.

[9] *Yellowstone Journal*, April 19, 1904.

In 1878 the *Scotsman,* a leading Scotch newspaper, sent James MacDonald to visit the United States to investigate the cattle business and resources of the West, and to inform the British farmer and the general public as to the possible dangers of com petition and opportunities for investing capital. In 1879 the Royal Agricultural Commission of Great Britain sent two special representatives, both members of Parliament, to make an investigation of the cattle industry here.

Both reports concerning possible competition were to the effect that there was little to fear since American beef, especially that of the West, was inferior in quality to the English product and was therefore not a source of danger. Their reports on the matter of investment were very favorable and stated the possibilities of high returns on money. With the cost of keeping a fair-sized herd for twelve months running as low as $1.50 a head and in some cases even lower, there were profits to be made as high as 20 to 30 per cent. This announcement made a deep impression on the British public, as profits of that size were more than the thrifty Scotch and English could withstand and an interest in American ranching that constituted almost a craze swept Great Britain and the Continent.[1] Many Europeans with surplus capital, despairing of conditions in their home countries and lured by the glowing accounts of the ranching industry in the United States, migrated to America to try their fortune at cattle-raising on a large scale. In the

---

[1] *U. S. Census Report for 1880,* Volume on Agriculture, p. 966; William Trimble, "Aspects of the Surplus Food Production in the United States," *Annual Report of the American Historical Association for 1919,* p. 232; *Annual Report of the Secretary of Agriculture,* 1876, p. 312; *Agricultural Gazette,* London, England, January 29, 1877. This keen interest had no doubt been stirred up in part by the wide publicity given to ranching and "beef bonanzas" in the American and European press. Newspapers were filled with articles of this type: "The Merry Roast Beef of England is giving way to American Beef," *Chicago Times* (Chicago), March 11, 1880; Strahorn, *Handbook of Wyoming and Guide to the Black Hills and Big Horn Basin;* Brisbin, *Beef Bonanza, or How to Get Rich on the Plains;* Henry Latham, *Trans-Missouri Stock Raising; the Pasture Lands of North America* (Omaha, Neb., 1871); Baillie-Grohman, *Campfires in the Rockies* (London, 1884). Such publications as these were widely read and there were many others.

late seventies and early eighties cattle companies were organized throughout Great Britain and in some of the Continental countries in wholesale fashion, and many people who did not come to America invested their money in the various companies and awaited bountiful returns.[2]

The Scots, being exceedingly thrifty and aggressive speculators, soon became active in the cattle business. W. J. Menzies organized the Scottish-American Investment Company as early as 1872, which, with the Scottish-American Mortgage Company, sponsored several of the more important Scottish cattle enterprises. They borrowed money from various local investment corporations at low rates and loaned it out in the United States and Canada at 6 to 8 per cent to be used in the cattle business. These and other small firms turned eagerly to the new field of investment and were responsible for some of the large cattle organizations that functioned in the Northwest during the cattle boom. Some of the larger companies backed by Scottish capital were the Wyoming Ranch Company, Limited, that controlled 2,500,000 acres of grazing land in Sweetwater and Carbon counties in Wyoming, the Swan Land and Cattle Company, capitalized at more than four millions of dollars under the leadership of A. H. and Joseph Swan, the Matadore Land and Cattle Company with two and a half million dollars invested in southwestern Dakota and in Montana, the Powder River Cattle Company of Wyoming, and the Western Ranches, Limited, often called the V V V outfit, that operated in the Black Hills area near Deadwood on the Belle Fourche River. In addition to the larger companies there were many individual Scotchmen who operated on their own accord,

[2] This was not the first instance of foreign investment in western or frontier enterprises in America. Part of the capital used to construct the western railroads was obtained from the sale of large blocks of securities to English, German, and Dutch investors. Millions of acres of public lands had been purchased by European land companies and held for speculation or settled by various colonizing schemes. After the close of the Napoleonic wars in 1815, England became the chief capital-exporting nation of the world. The London Financial Association and the International Financial Society formed in 1863 seems to have been among the first of the British investment trusts.

good examples being Gregor Lang, whose Dakota ranch lay in the Little Missouri country some eighty miles north of Theodore Roosevelt's, and John Clay who came to America in 1874 as agent for various Scotch interests and who became an active figure in ranching circles.[3]

There were also many Englishmen interested in the raising of cattle on the ranges of the Northwest during the boom period. Some of them were men of considerable wealth and were attracted to the cattle business in America for a number of reasons. Some had their interest aroused while on hunting trips, some came to investigate gold-mining and remained to raise cattle on the open range, while others came as a matter of adventure to seek their fortunes in "the land of opportunity." Among the prominent Englishmen were Sir John Pendar, who operated a ranch in the Dakota area; Lord Dunraven, the Marquis of Tweeddale, the Duke of Sutherland, and Sir John Leslie Kaye, the last four having interests in Wyoming and Montana. Captain Henry Belknap established a sizable ranch in the Big Horn Basin of Wyoming and Frank Cooper had a large herd on Rock Creek. Robert Marsh and Jack Williams ran herds on the Laramie plains, and Moreton Frewen and his brother were managers and promoters of the Powder River Cattle Company. Most of the English operators in southern and central Wyoming were prominent in the "Cheyenne Club" at Cheyenne. The Carlisle Cattle Company was an important English company operating in Wyoming.[4]

In addition to the Scotch and English ranchers in the Northwest in the late seventies and eighties were a number of Conti-

[3] *Foreign Relations of the United States,* 1879, I, Part I, No. 54, 463-6; W. B. von Richthofen, *Ranching on the Plains* (New York, 1885), p. 55; Clay, *My Life on the Range; Miles City Daily Star,* Golden Jubilee edition, May 24, 1934, sec. 3.

[4] Statistics as to the amount of English capital invested in stock-raising and the number of Englishmen concerned in management and ownership of cattle ranches are difficult to obtain. A New York newspaper in the spring of 1884 estimated that one-sixth of all the herds on the northern plains were owned by English capital. *New York Sun,* April 6, 1884, quoted in F. L. Paxson, "The Cow Country," *American Historical Review* (1917), p. 74.

nental Europeans who became active and interesting figures in the cattle business. Among the outstanding Germans were Otto Franc, whose Pitchfork brand became famous in northern and western Wyoming, and who purchased his first herd in Montana in 1880 and located it in the Greybull River in the Big Horn Basin, and Charles Hetch, another German who operated a ranch in the Cheyenne area. Two outstanding Frenchmen in Wyoming were the Count de Dorey and Victor Arland, while perhaps the most interesting were De Mores and Wibaux.

Money of the European cattle companies was often invested in a careless manner, with little or no investigation, herds being bought on "book count" at relatively high prices. Dividends were often declared on the basis of book profits, while slipshod methods and careless management under absentee ownership were common. The hard winter of 1886-87 ruined most of the European companies, many of which closed out their herds and left the country. Clay doubts that any of them really made any money at the business.[5] Foreign owned and managed cattle companies were never popular with the local ranchers and settlers, who resented the intrusion of the "cattle kings" or "barons," as they called them, from abroad and were quite critical of their activities, often being openly hostile to their holding and controlling land. In a report made before the House Committee of Congress on the Public Lands in the summer of 1884, it was noted that thirty-two alien firms and individuals, mostly Scotch and English, held the title to or controlled almost twenty-two million acres of land in the cattle country. At the next session of Congress in 1885-86 a bill "to prohibit aliens and foreigners from acquiring title to or owning lands within the United States of America" was introduced but failed to receive serious consideration.[6]

The territorial legislature of Montana, becoming worried over the influx of foreign capital and its influence on the ranges, passed

[5] Clay, *op. cit.*, p. 80.
[6] *House Exec. Doc.*, 48th Cong., 2d Sess., No. 267, 46, serial 2304.

a law in February, 1885, designed to prevent the commercialization of the cattle industry by that group. The law provided that any corporation made up of foreigners and any corporation in which 20 per cent of the capital stock was held by foreigners could neither acquire, hold, or own any real estate within the territorial limits. It was not strictly enforced, and many foreign cattle companies, ambitious to extend their activities, began to get possession of considerable portions of the open range.[7]

While an attempt to evaluate or measure the influence of foreigners in the cattle business of the Northwest is a difficult task, it seems fair to conclude that their influence was probably out of proportion to their numbers and the amount of capital invested. The Northwest is marked to-day by towns established and named by foreign cattlemen: Medora, North Dakota; Wibaux, Montana; and Roubaix, South Dakota, being some of the best examples. Foreigners were influential in the introduction and development of better grades of stock; they were active in the organization and work of the various stock associations, and they played some part in the establishment of the Bureau of Animal Husbandry within the Department of Agriculture at our national capital. They were ambitious, courageous and progressive, and willing to try out new ideas, thereby instilling new spirit into ranching operations. It will be remembered that it was the French De Mores who experimented with a slaughter-house on the cattle range, and Moreton Frewen, the Englishman, who sponsored the idea of shipping cattle direct to England to be fed a few months and finished for market. While both schemes failed, they indicate the character of some of the men from abroad. It was Pierre Wibaux who borrowed half a million dollars to invest in herds after the disastrous winter when hundreds of others were closing out and leaving the country. The foreign ranchers also aided in giving a cosmopolitan character to the cattle country and contributed much to the cultural interests and

[7] *Compiled Statutes of Montana,* 1887, sec. 31, 594.

activity of the ranchers. They were active members of the well-known "Cheyenne Club" at Cheyenne, Wyoming, and of other cultural groups that existed during the cattle boom on the plains of the Northwest.[8]

XVI

IMPROVEMENT OF RANGE STOCK

As soon as cattle began moving onto the ranges of the Northwest, there was evidence of serious efforts on the part of various groups of ranchers to develop a good beef stock, capable of withstanding the hardships of the open range. The early herds came largely from Texas, Oregon, Washington, and Utah, representing several types of cattle. The Mormon stock, influenced by a strong Shorthorn strain, were not primarily beef cattle, but were dairy cattle and heavy milkers. However, when bred with Durham or Hereford bulls, the result was an offspring rather well adapted for beef purposes. While a considerable percentage of the early Texas stock driven on to the ranges of Wyoming and Montana were steers to be finished for market, large numbers of Texas cows were included in the herds as the northern drives increased in numbers. The cows from Texas were poor milkers but were noted for their ability to rustle for themselves and their offspring. Also, as the herds were on their way northward from Texas, the cows were influenced by mixing with Shorthorn blood from the fine herds of Missouri and Kentucky that tended to produce an excellent beef animal. The stock cattle from Washington and Oregon combined the good qualities of both Utah and Texas cattle without further breeding, which is one of the reasons for their popularity on the ranges. While the predominating influence

[8] Charles M. Hager, "Cattle Trails of the Prairies," *Scribner's*, XI (May, June, 1892), 732-42; "Where Beef Comes From," *Lippincott's Magazine* (November, 1879), pp. 573-80; Kuhn, "The W-B Ranch on the Missouri Slope," *Collections*, pp. 159-61; Clay, *op. cit.*, p. 181; Clara M. Love, "History of the Cattle Industry in the Southwest," *Southwestern Historical Quarterly*, XIX (April, 1916), 12-5.

in the early years of range activity in Wyoming was Texan, that
of western Montana was largely from the herds of the Mormons
and the far Northwest.

The earliest evidence of attempts at stock improvement comes
from western Montana, where as early as 1870 there is record
of five Durham bulls being brought in by the ranchers. They
were purchased in Omaha, Nebraska, and shipped to Ogden, Utah,
from which point they were driven northward.[1] Other shipments
of blooded stock are recorded in the early seventies and there
seems to have been considerable activity in high-grade Durham
bulls, a local newspaper in the early winter of 1871 reporting the
selling at auction in Helena, Montana, of a prize Durham bull
for $1,885.[2] The legislature of the Territory of Montana, anxious
to encourage the bringing in of pure-bred cattle to the area,
passed a law in 1871 providing for the exemption from taxation
for one year after their arrival of all blooded stock of English
and American registry.[3] James Brisbin tells of the cattle firm of
Poindexter and Orr starting in 1872 with five bulls and eight
heifers of the Shorthorn variety, brought in from Canada, from
which they built up in the seventies a herd of thoroughbred cattle
located near Watson in Montana. They believed that blooded
stock-breeding would develop into one of Montana's greatest
interests.[4]

The older cattlemen of Montana and to a certain extent of
Wyoming offered serious objections in the seventies to their ranges
being considered as a feeding-ground for the finishing of Texas
cattle for market. They early argued that a steer bred on the
northern ranges was superior to one driven from Texas and that
they brought a better price on the market when sold. Texas cattle,
largely of Spanish or Mexican descent, had long slender legs,
light flanks, a bony frame, and a large head with long sharp horns,

[1] Stuart, *Forty Years on the Frontier*, II, 34.
[2] Quoted in the *National Live Stock Journal*, December, 1871.
[3] *Session Laws of the Territory of Montana*, 1871, chap. xc.
[4] Brisbin, *Beef Bonanza*, pp. 163-94.

measuring at times from four to five feet from tip to tip. This last feature made them hard to ship by railroad. The Texas steer, when placed on the northern range, grew and fattened reasonably well and attained a weight of 650 to 950 pounds. Unimproved American cattle grew larger and fattened better and were worth from $.50 to $1.00 per hundred more on the market than Texas cattle of similar age. Graded cattle fattened much more readily and their flesh was of better quality than that of ordinary stock and sold for $1.00 to $1.50 per hundred more. The northern cattlemen found it to their advantage to raise their own young stock and grade up their herds.[5] The early ranchers of western Montana were proud of their beef stock and did not hesitate to defend it against the incoming Texans. Conrad Kohrs, writing in 1874, after making a shipment of beef to eastern markets over the Union Pacific said: "We marketed some magnificent cattle. My native three-year-olds weighed 1,300 to 1,350 pounds on the Chicago market, far outweighing the triple wintered Texan."[6]

As cattle from Texas gradually spread over the plains of the Northwest, various ranchers, realizing the importance of improving their herds, began almost immediately to purchase breeding animals from the corn belt and even from abroad. The purchase of breeding stock gradually gained momentum, reaching its peak at the time of the cattle boom. After the hard winter of 1886-87, it declined, but by that time the quality of the stock had been greatly improved, and eventually it was as high as or perhaps even higher than the average in many of the farming states to the east.

During the latter part of the seventies the demand for Durham stock declined, and Herefords and Shorthorns began to supplant them for breeding purposes. The demand for Shorthorns seems to have occurred first, and by the early eighties had reached con-

[5] Edward W. Perry, "Texas Cattle," *First Annual Report of the Bureau of Animal Husbandry for the Year 1884*, p. 255; *Fourth and Fifth Reports of the Bureau of Animal Husbandry for 1887-88*, pp. 339-41.
[6] Kohrs, *Autobiography*, pp. 1328-9.

siderable proportions. Among the more important additions were the placing of two hundred thoroughbred Shorthorns on their range on the Musselshell in Montana by the Ryan brothers in 1884. The same year the Niobrara Cattle Company put two hundred high-grade animals into their herds, securing them from the finest stock of Kentucky, and Moreton Frewen imported forty-eight thoroughbred Shorthorns from Sussex, England. In 1885 the Judith Roundup Association of Montana purchased one hundred high-grade Shorthorn bulls and placed them on their range, and the Shonkin Stock Association placed sixty on theirs, while Conrad Price added fifty to his herd. Shorthorn cattle, finely bred and accustomed to a certain amount of pampering and protection afforded by the farming methods of the eastern states and in England, did not do as well as the ranchers thought they might when left to shift for themselves. Attention was therefore turned to other blood.

As early as 1878 at the stock show in Chicago some attention had been attracted to the Hereford breeds, which, it was claimed, were suitable for the ranges because of their thick hides and their ability to travel and rustle for themselves on the open range. Some of the early important additions of Hereford bulls and cattle were made in Montana by the Grinnell and Montana Cattle Companies in 1882, and in 1883 there was established a Hereford Breeding Farm in the vicinity of White Sulphur Springs, Montana, whose stock was recorded in the American Herd Book for that year.[7] The Wyoming Hereford Association was organized in 1883 with A. H. Swan of the Swan Cattle Company as president and George Morgan as vice president.[8] While a good many Herefords were brought onto the ranges of the Northwest prior to the hard winter that killed so many cattle, they were not as numerous as the Shorthorns. The Herefords, however, were easily acclimated, and when mixed with other stock there were formed certain com-

[7] *Rocky Mountain Husbandman,* October 4, 1883.
[8] John M. Hazelton, *History and Handling of Hereford Cattle* (Kansas City, 1925).

binations that became almost ideal for range hardiness and beef qualities.

Experiments were also made with the Aberdeen Angus, an interesting article appearing in the *Medora Bad Lands Cowboy* early in 1885 in praise of their qualities. While various cattle companies placed a good many of them on their ranges they never rivaled the Shorthorn or Hereford in popularity.[9] The cattle from the far Northwest kept coming in throughout the period, adding stock of good grade in large numbers.[10]

There were present certain handicaps and obstacles to herd improvement that were combated with difficulty. Wherever there were large numbers of Texas longhorns, those who put money in blooded cattle found their investment threatened. Since the owners of cheap low-grade Texas cattle enjoyed the same privilege of running their cattle on the open ranges as those who owned high-grade stock, the latter found his increase graded down by the presence of scrub bulls. The territorial legislature of Wyoming as early as 1873 attempted to eliminate this outside breeding influence by passing a law imposing a fine upon any owner who allowed a "Texan, Cherokee, or Mexican Bull" to run at large.[11] In Wyoming and Dakota the problem of clearing the range of low-grade bulls was left to the local associations and was never satisfactorily worked out. Another problem in addition to that of quality was one of quantity, as various cattle companies were inclined to use a smaller number of male animals than their herd warranted and by so doing imposed on those about them.

[9] Many of the large cattle companies tried stock of all types in their experiments to find a desirable combination. The Swan Cattle Company was among the first to put considerable numbers of Shorthorns on its ranges and A. H. Swan at about the same time was made president of the Wyoming Hereford Association.

[10] *Medora Bad Lands Cowboy*, January 29, 1885; files of the *Yellowstone Journal, Rocky Mountain Husbandman, Cheyenne Daily Leader*. In 1885 the number of blooded stock recorded in the Territory of Montana were 174 Shorthorns, 120 Aberdeen Angus, 38 Herefords, and 31 Holstein-Friesians. Perry, *op. cit.*, pp. 339-48.

[11] *Session Laws of the Territory of Wyoming*, 1873, 3d Sess., 223.

XVII

CATTLE ASSOCIATIONS

The average cattleman of the Northwest owned very little of the land upon which his cattle grazed. He could not afford to buy it, and since he was not allowed to lease the public domain, the usual procedure was to find as large an unoccupied area as possible away from neighbors, locate a ranch, and claim the surrounding land as his "range." He sometimes obtained the land upon which his ranch-house and buildings were located by filing on it under the various land laws and at times had his cowboys and friends file on additional land for him. Sometimes, in order to control the water supply, he bought small tracts but even then his actual holdings were not great.

His cattle did not remain on his "range" at all times; in fact, there was little or no effort to force them to do so, and fences were almost unknown on the open ranges until after the boom, with boundary lines indefinite. As additional cattle were moved into the area and the range filled up, there was an intermingling of the stock of the various owners in the vicinity and coöperation among the ranchers was imperative. Some of the objectives of coöperative effort, in addition to the regulation of the range, were the establishment of regulations regarding brands and marks, the round-up, mavericks, control of bulls on the range, and the protection of cattle from Indians, thieves, wild animals, and disease. While activities of this sort are ordinarily controlled by either the local or Federal Government, in the case of the cattleman neither was able to function effectively. While the various territorial legislatures passed laws regarding the cattle industry, it had no organization with which to enforce them over a wide area with only a scant population. The Federal Government, even had it had jurisdiction, was too far away, was uninformed as to facts, and was too much immersed in other affairs to be of much use to the rancher. The cattleman, therefore, was obliged to take the matter into his own hands and create his own organizations that he might attain his objectives.

There is evidence of live-stock associations in the range areas as soon as ranching had become established there, and their numbers and influence increased as the industry grew. The various associations were of two types: local or district organizations, and larger general associations that included all or most of a territory or state.[1] In the early seventies, as herds of Texas cattle moved northward in larger and larger numbers, local cattlemen through whose holdings the drives were made began to feel the need of organization. Their cattle were often picked up, or joined the herds, and were thus lost to their owners. After a good deal of discussion by ranchers and the local press, a group of Colorado stockmen met at Denver on January 19, 1872, to work out some form of protective organization. All cattle-raisers from adjacent areas were asked to attend and there were sixteen delegates from Wyoming present. General plans were laid for the conduct of a spring round-up, and the problems of the suppression of theft and the regulation of brands were carefully discussed. A few months later a second organization was formed called the Southern Colorado Stock Growers Association, which was too far south to have much effect upon Wyoming.[2]

But even before Colorado ranchers had taken action, a local organization was perfected at Cheyenne, the first of its kind to be organized in the territory. On October 28, 1871, a group of local ranchers, including several men active in the freighting business, met at Cheyenne to discuss methods of protecting their cattle.

---

[1] Although the various general associations were ordinarily named after the state or territory in which they were located, there was no effort to limit membership to one unit. The close connection of the interests of the stockmen and overlapping holdings caused many of the large ranchers to join several associations, and associations were always liberal in their invitations to those outside, both for membership and attendance.

[2] *Report of the Denver Board of Trade*, 1871; *Cheyenne Daily Leader*, January 6, 13, 20, 26, 1872, January 6, 21, 1873.

They organized the Wyoming Stock Graziers Association and called a regular meeting for November 14th. They discussed at some length the need of more stringent laws against the stealing of cattle and the possibilities of getting the territorial legislature to take action on the matter. It is apparent that nothing definite was accomplished as there is no evidence in the local press of any further meetings of this association.

In the fall of 1873 a few Wyoming cattlemen,[3] engaged in range herding in the vicinity of the North and South Platte rivers and their tributaries, gathered at Cheyenne to discuss the possibility of group action on matters regarding their mutual welfare. A chairman was chosen and a committee appointed to formulate rules and by-laws for an association, and a resolution was passed giving in some detail the conditions and circumstances out of which had developed the need for an effective organization. On November 29, 1873, the Laramie County Stock Growers Association was organized at Cheyenne. There was to be a regular meeting the first Monday of each month and an annual meeting the first Monday in April. The only requirements for membership were the ownership of stock and the payment of a fee of five dollars. Monthly dues were to be fifty cents. Sixteen members were recorded at this first session. The following May there was conducted the first organized round-up in Wyoming held under a foreman appointed by an association.[4]

By 1874 membership had risen to twenty-five and the organization grew rapidly in size and influence. Some idea as to its expansion is indicated by the creation of two round-up districts in 1876 and four in 1878. In 1879 the name of the organization was changed to the Wyoming Stock Growers Association, which soon became the most powerful organization of its kind in the Northwest. In 1881 all local organizations in the territory, as well

---

[3] Eleven men are said to have attended this first meeting.

[4] *Cheyenne Daily Leader*, November 19, 26, 1873, April 25, May 2, 1874; Osgood, *Day of the Cattleman*, pp. 119-20.

A ROUNDUP ON THE RANGE

Courtesy of the Montana State Historical Society.

as those in Montana and Dakota, were asked to join them. Delegates from Rapid City and Deadwood in the Black Hills of Dakota attended the annual meeting of that year. By 1883 the organization had a membership of 267 which increased to 363 in 1885, and to 401 in 1886. A perusal of its membership roll in 1886 shows thirty-one members from Nebraska, twenty-one from Dakota, twenty-one from Colorado, and ten from Montana, with members from fourteen other states and territories included on its list. The association controlled more than two million cattle, two hundred thousand horses and several hundred thousand sheep. The property and holdings of its members were said to be valued at one hundred million dollars. It was the largest organization of its kind in the world.[5]

As ranching developed in the western portion of the Territory of Montana, an attempt was made to organize in that region. In December, 1873, a group of stock-growers met at Virginia City and issued a call for a meeting of the ranchmen of Madison County, to convene the following month. The meeting was held and the *Weekly Montanian* of Virginia City gave its purpose as that of considering and discussing the problem of protecting winter ranges from summer grazing, disposition of stray cattle, rules and regulations regarding brands and marks, better protection against cattle thieves, and the achieving of unified action among the stock-growers as well as the possibility of taking measures to secure legislation at the forthcoming territorial assembly was also discussed. No permanent organization was formed.[6] No further action was taken until 1879 when, at a meeting at Helena early in January, James Fergus, one of the oldest and most influential of the stockmen, urged the formation of a cattleman's association. The Montana Stock Growers Association was organized February 19, 1879, at Helena with twenty-two members.

[5] *Minute Book of the Wyoming Stock Growers Association*, 1886, pp. 5-21; *Annual Report of the Territorial Governor of Wyoming to the Secretary of the Interior*, 1886, II, 1022; Osgood, *op. cit.*, pp. 120-1.
[6] *Weekly Montanian*, January 15, 1874.

Local communities were urged to organize their own organizations and active units were formed in Madison, Lewis and Clark, Deer Lodge, Gallatin, and Chouteau counties. Two of the outstanding local organizations were the Eastern Montana Stock Growers Association, organized at Miles City, October 12, 1883, and the Shonkin Stock Association, formed in Chouteau County in July, 1881. A meeting of the Yellowstone Roundup Association is recorded in the *Mineral Argus* in April, 1884, while the Sun River Association was organized in 1883. The Montana Stock Growers Association held a meeting of reorganization in an attempt to combine the whole territory in one association. Eleven of the fourteen counties were represented and delegates were chosen to attend the meeting of the Eastern Stock Growers Association at Miles City. On April 3, 1885, the two major organizations consolidated in a meeting at Miles City, at which time it was arranged that the spring meeting should be held the third Monday in April at Miles City and the fall meeting the third Monday in August at Helena. At this meeting the name of Theodore Roosevelt was proposed for membership by the Marquis de Mores. The membership included practically all of the large cattlemen in the territory, as well as many of those in western Dakota, northern Wyoming, and adjacent parts of Canada.[7] Reaching its high point of membership in 1887, the Montana Stock Growers Association declined in influence and importance in the late nineties, with a membership of less than two hundred in 1898, after which it gradually revived.

The Black Hills Live Stock Association was formed at Rapid City in the Territory of Dakota in the spring of 1880, the first advertisement of the organization appearing in the *Black Hills Journal* on November 13, 1880. The Black Hills district, as reported by the association, included the area north of the Hills

---

[7] Clay, *My Life on the Range*, pp. 117-207; Hagedorn, *Roosevelt in the Badlands*, pp. 222-3; *Sun River Sun*, August 7, 29, 1884; *Mineral Argus*, April 24, December 4, 1884.

proper to about the present line between North and South Dakota. By 1884 its membership had increased to well over a hundred and there were five hundred thousand head of cattle ranging the district and two hundred thousand head had been marketed the year before.[8] As ranching activities extended to the north and northeast into the Bad Lands and along the Northern Pacific Railroad, the distance between the new areas and the Black Hills Association was too great and there was need of another organization. The *Medora Bad Lands Cowboy* for December 4, 1884, carried a published notice signed by Theodore Roosevelt asking all cattlemen along the Little Missouri River to meet at Medora for the purpose of organizing an association whereby the cattlemen of that area might protect their common interests. Roosevelt had called the meeting after discussing the need of coöperation with several of the ranchers of the area. A general meeting of stockmen was held at Roberts' Hall in Medora at eleven o'clock on Friday, December 19, 1884, at which time the Little Missouri Stock Growers Association was organized and Theodore Roosevelt was chosen president.[9]

XVIII

CATTLE ASSOCIATIONS IN ACTION

THE GENERAL policy of the open range in the Northwest was fixed largely by the various stock associations. They formulated rules, many of which were made into statute law by the territorial legislatures; they caught and prosecuted criminals, regulated and policed round-ups; in fact, regulated and controlled every phase of range activity. Much of their work was indirect or extralegal in nature. An excellent example of this type of activity was in their control of the range, which is well exemplified in the Conrad

---

[8] *Black Hills Weekly Pioneer*, March 17, 1884; *Black Hills Journal*, April 14, 1884.

[9] Hagedorn, *op. cit.*, pp. 222-3; *Yellowstone Journal*, April 17, 1886; *River Press*, April 21, 1902.

case in the area north of the Yellowstone in Montana, in 1885. The facts may be briefly stated. J. H. Conrad of the Conrad-Price Cattle Company moved six thousand head of stock from the company's ranges near Fort Benton into the regions east of the Musselshell where they were located on grazing lands claimed by the Niobrara Cattle Company. The leading cattlemen of the north Yellowstone country met at Miles City November 5, 1885, and unanimously adopted a resolution condemning Conrad for trespassing on land previously occupied by the Niobrara Cattle Company, stating that such action was unfair and injurious to the best interests of the country and that they would refuse to recognize or to work with such an organization or to handle its cattle. A local newspaper a few days later, in commenting on the case, said, "To the uninformed, it implies nothing, but to those acquainted with the harmonious workings of the range interests and the mutual dependence of each on the other it means plenty." [1] J. H. Conrad moved the cattle of his company back to his own range.

As large numbers of cattle were turned out to graze on the public domain of the Northwest, there was bound to be an intermingling of stock and there was soon a need for some means of identification. The marking and branding of cattle is by no means peculiar to the West, as it has been used consistently by stockowners as the frontier has advanced across the United States. The early legal enactments of the territorial legislatures of Wyoming, Montana, and Dakota regarding stock identification were duplications of the laws of the older states. In the first sessions of the legislatures of both Montana and Wyoming, provision was made whereby each owner of cattle was required to adopt a distinctive brand to be recorded with the county clerk. Punishment by both fine and imprisonment was provided for any one who knowingly used a brand already recorded or who defaced a brand. Provisions

[1] *Yellowstone Journal*, September 7, 1885, February 13, 1886; *River Press*, November 18, 1885.

were made for the handling of stray stock and for the effective prosecution of cattle rustlers.[2] If ranching had continued on a small scale over a limited area, legal provisions such as these would have been sufficient for the needs of the industry.[3]

Round-up practices developed out of the needs of the cattle industry on the open range, and were conducted according to rules and laws established and enforced by the cattle associations as well as by the territorial legislatures. As cattle became numerous on the ranges there was a great deal of intermingling among the herds, and if each of a dozen or more outfits was allowed to go through the region rounding up its own calves and branding them, there would be little opportunity for the cattle to rest and graze. It also gave opportunities whereby overzealous cow-punchers of the early branders could pick up mavericks and strays for his outfit or for himself. One general round-up conducted under well-defined rules was inevitable as time went on.

The first steps in the direction of establishing rules and regulations for a general round-up in Wyoming occurred in 1874 when the Laramie Stock Growers Association appointed a committee to compile a set of rules for the conduct of a general round-up. The rules were drawn up and evidently were not strictly enforced, since those cattle-owners who refused to coöperate and continued to work the range for their own stock were severely condemned by a resolution of the Wyoming Stock Growers Association in 1879, which recommended at the same time that action be taken by the territorial legislature. A law was passed that year laying down the general plan, the details of the procedure to be left to

[2] *Session Laws of the Territory of Montana,* 1864-65; *Session Laws of the Territory of Wyoming,* 1869. George R. Wilson, a pioneer cattleman of the Musselshell country, began to brand his cattle in the early seventies, using two red-hot iron bolts tied together, which was later registered as the Two Dot brand. *River Press,* October 30, 1907.

[3] On several occasions there was agitation to stop the branding of cattle and substitute some other method of marking that would do less damage to the hide. *Yellowstone Journal* on January 31, 1885, made a strong plea for a change, stressing the point that an unbranded hide was worth at least a dollar more than one that had been branded. *Medora Bad Lands Cowboy,* December 18, 1884.

the association. The territory was to be divided into convenient districts and there were to be two general round-ups each year: one in the spring for the branding of calves, and one in the fall to brand any cattle missed in the spring but primarily to cut out the stock for fall shipping. The dates and details of the two round-ups were to be established by the association. All legal branding was to be under the supervision of the round-up foreman and heavy penalties were provided for any violations of the law.[4]

The following round-up arrangements for 1881 were made at Cheyenne by the Wyoming Stock Growers Association at its meeting on April 4, 1881:

Roundup number one shall begin at Fort Laramie on May 23, shall proceed up the south side of the Laramie River to the mouth of Sabile Creek, up the Sabile to the Black Hills divide; thence to the head of the Chugwater; down the Chugwater to Kelly's ranches; thence to the head of Richard's Creek; down said creek to its mouth; thence to Houston's Creek; thence to Bear Creeks, up said Bear Creeks to their head; thence to the telegraph road where it intersects Horse Creek; thence up said Horse Creek to Horse Creek Lakes; thence to the head of Pole Creek and down Pole Creek to the telegraph road; thence across the country to Big Crow Springs; thence up Big Crow Creek to its head; thence across to the bend of Lone Tree Creek; thence down Lone Tree Creek to Charles Terry's ranch; thence to Jack Springs and thence to Box Elder. James Lane, W. H. Hackney, Foremen.[5]

The next step making the round-up more effective was the working out of a scheme of representation, which while never entirely satisfactory was not improved upon during the open-range period. The plan provided that each owner or company should choose one or more representatives to accompany the round-up outfits in those areas in which his cattle might be found. Theodore Roosevelt in one of his articles describing his life on the range tells of

---

[4] *Session Laws of the Territory of Wyoming*, 1879; *Compiled Statutes of Montana*, 1887, sec. 110.

[5] *Minute Book of the Wyoming Stock Growers Association*, April 4, 1881.

accompanying the Little Missouri round-up in Dakota as a representative.[6] The system of accrediting representatives used made it possible for unprincipled cowboys to accompany the round-up as representatives of well-known companies when they were really representing themselves. This sort of action became so common that the association made a rule that a charge of fifty cents a day would be levied upon any outfit for each cowboy following a round-up to which he did not belong. The purpose of this was to induce the cattle companies and the round-up groups to check the representatives. The spring round-up sometimes lasted until October. It was seldom over on one end of the range before the fall round-up was ready to begin on the other. The fall round-up was primarily for cutting out beef for shipment but some branding was done, chiefly of the calves missed by the spring round-up and the late calves.[7] Various systems of dividing the cost of the round-up were used, depending to some extent upon the association. The expense was often pro-rated among the owners, according to the number of calves branded. This system is said to have been used first by the Shonkin Stock Association of Montana.[8] The more common plan was to require one rider for a certain number of cattle. The minutes for the round-up meeting at Fort McGinnis for that area in 1883 indicate that every rancher with a thousand cattle or less was to furnish one rider and a rider for every additional thousand. The alternative to this was a charge of two dollars a head for each calf branded.[9]

As large shipments of cattle began to move out of the Northwest, the problem of inspection arose. There was the matter of stray cattle becoming mixed with the shipments and also the

[6] Roosevelt, "In Cowboy Land," Outlook, CIV (May 10, 1913).
[7] Late fall and winter calves were undesirable as it has been estimated that three-fourths of them died. Bulls were prohibited on the ranges between December and July. When breeding became the accepted procedure on the northern ranges, each rancher was required to furnish five bulls for every one hundred two-year-old heifers and to keep them on the range only during the breeding season.
[8] River Press, July 19, 1882, May 9, 1894.
[9] Stuart, Forty Years on the Frontier, II, 177-8.

possibility of non-owners sending out cattle belonging to some other outfit. Then there was the matter of protecting the herds from contagious diseases. The stock associations took over the work and inspected the cattle both at the shipping point and at the destination. In 1882 the Wyoming Stock Growers Association found 1,465 strays, valued at sixty-six thousand dollars, among the various shipments. Proceeds from the sale of strays were returned to the association, which turned the money over to the rightful owners of the cattle. When ownership could not be established, the money became the property of the association. For the year ending March 21, 1887, nearly two hundred thousand cattle were inspected at the railroad points in Wyoming and 3,437 strays reported. During the spring and fall of 1889 the number of head inspected had risen to approximately three hundred thousand. Dakota and Montana were also active in the work of inspection, watching closely the shipping points along the Northern Pacific. Inspectors established at central points of debarkation such as Chicago, Omaha, and St. Paul were paid from a joint fund provided by Montana, Wyoming, and Dakota associations. Another phase of association work was that of providing detectives who occupied practically all ranges, usually coöperating with the county officials.[10] Judging from the correspondence carried on with various association headquarters, some of these detectives must have been busy.

XIX

THE INDIAN MENACE

INDIAN hostilities were a serious handicap to the early cattle industry in Wyoming, beginning as early as 1862 and 1863. There was more trouble in 1864 and 1865 and again in 1867, ending in a treaty in 1868 whereby reservations were set aside for their

[10] *Annual Report of the Governor of Wyoming Territory to the Secretary of the Interior*, 1889, pp. 584-85; *Minute Book of the Montana Stock Growers' Association*, 1889, p. 27; *Statute Laws of Montana*, 1888.

exclusive use. Indians not only stole cattle in these early years, but they often murdered the attending cowboys. But Indians on reservations also caused trouble. Within the boundaries of Wyoming were to be found the Shoshone and Arapahoe reservations, while just across the border in the Territory of Montana lived the Cheyenne and Crows, and in the Territory of Dakota were to be found the aggressive Sioux. The various tribes were often granted the privilege of leaving their lands to hunt buffalo, and wandered over the country killing cattle for food, as it was often easier to stampede a herd of cattle and kill what they wanted than it was to stalk buffalo. Governor Warren reported that the Indians often shot young calves for mere pleasure, taking choice bits of the meat for food.[1] One of the main reasons for the organization of the Laramie County Stock Growers Association was to prevent Indian depredations.

Wyoming cattlemen suffered rather heavily from marauding Indians throughout most of the seventies, but did not suffer as badly in the period after the Sioux War in 1875-77 as did the cattle-owners in Montana. In the early eighties the ranchers who moved their cattle into the Tongue and Powder rivers country when it was opened were harassed by hunting parties who killed their stock. In 1883 the officers of the Wyoming Stock Growers Association reported incontrovertible evidence that ranchmen on the ranges of Powder River, the Belle Fourche, Cheyenne, and Little Missouri rivers were often visited by parties of Indians who begged from them, and sometimes by parties who robbed them. The previous winter there had been cases where Indians, prevented from returning to their reservations by heavy falls of snow, lived upon cattle. With the rapid growth of the Wyoming Stock Growers Association and the gradual but effective expansion of the activities of the Indian Bureau in its attempts to solve the problem, attacks on cattle began to diminish and in 1885 the governor of the territory said, "The Indian has also been provided for and

---

[1] *Annual Report of the Secretary of the Interior*, 1885, II, 1174.

now property in Wyoming is believed to be as safe from theft as in the most favored location." [2]

In the early seventies Montana cattlemen were having their Indian difficulties also. In 1873 a battle was fought between the Indians and white men in the vicinity of the Yellowstone River and guerilla warfare continued thereafter until 1876, when several serious battles were fought in the eastern part of the territory. It was in this campaign that General Custer and his entire detachment of five hundred troops were massacred by the Sioux Indians led by Sitting Bull. The battle was fought in the valley of the Little Big Horn, near what is now Fort Custer in Big Horn County, Montana. After this the government took stringent measures and moved the Sioux Indians out of Montana and other Indians were required to remain on their reservations for a time. The area north of the Yellowstone was thrown open to settlers and stockmen.

Indian raids continued, however, some of which were recorded by General Philip H. Sheridan, Commander of the Military Division of Missouri, in 1879:

March 1, 1879, Several head of stock were stolen by Indians, from McDonald and Dillon's ranch near Powder River, Montana. March 4th, twenty-three head of stock were stolen from Countryman's ranch near the mouth of the Stillwater. March 28th, Indians attacked two white men near the mouth of the Big Horn Basin, killed one named H. D. Johnson and wounded the other, named James Stearns. The Indians committing these depredations were ascertained as Sioux from the north with a few Nez Perces. [3]

In the early eighties the Indian reservation in northern Montana, covering some twenty million acres of the best grazing land in the territory, was occupied by less than three thousand Indians.

[2] *Annual Report of the Territorial Governor of Wyoming to the Secretary of the Interior*, 1883, II, 608-9; *Annual Report of the Secretary of the Interior*, 1885, II, 1175.

[3] P. H. Sheridan, *Record of Engagements with Hostile Indians Within the Military Division of Missouri, 1868-72* (Chicago, 1882), p. 97.

THE BATTLEFIELD OF THE LITTLE BIG HORN

Photograph by W. H. DeGraff, courtesy of Mrs. Robert W. Smith.

While the fact that ranchers were not allowed to occupy this territory was in itself a sore spot with the various cattle companies who were looking for fresh pastures, the situation was made worse when buffalo and wild game became scarce on the reservation and it was necessary for the government either to feed the Indians or allow them to leave the reservation to hunt. In 1881 a remnant of the northern buffalo herd was in the area between the Yellowstone and Missouri rivers just east of the Musselshell. In 1881 and 1882 bands of Indians carrying passes issued by the Indian Bureau left their agencies to look for buffalo. While they were supposed to have been under military supervision, most of them were never seen by their escorts after they left their reservations. As they made for the buffalo range they left many carcasses of cattle along the various routes traveled, many of them being shot by the Indian braves as they rode along to test out their rifles.[4]

The cattlemen of the Shonkin area in Montana were so alarmed at the daring thefts of cattle going on there that they organized the Shonkin Cattle Association for self-protection. At the first meeting it was recommended by unanimous resolution that force should be used against the Indians if necessary. In 1882 and 1883 the various local stock associations of northern and central Montana sent out small bodies of cowboys to patrol the ranges and to break up camps of Indians and force them back on their reservations. The plan was quite successful, although in the local press from time to time there appeared accounts of running fights in which cowboys, as well as Indians, were killed.[5] The Eastern Montana Stock Growers Association in 1883 petitioned the Secretary of the Interior, recommending that the Indians of the cattle regions be furnished with sufficient supplies that it might not be necessary for them to depend upon stolen cattle for food. The petition made it quite clear that the cattlemen felt that the

---

[4] *Session Laws of the Territory of Montana*, 1881, 12th Sess., pp. 131-2; *River Press*, August 8, 15, 1881; *Rocky Mountain Husbandman*, September 4, 1884.

[5] Files of the *Rocky Mountain Husbandman*, 1882-83.

provisions for Indian maintenance were entirely insufficient and
that the only recourse of the red men was cattle, as buffalo and
other wild game were becoming scarce.[6] The national convention
of cattlemen at St. Louis in November, 1884, passed a resolution
to be sent to Congress stating that Indians should be better treated
by the government and that they should be rigidly restricted to the
limits of their reservations.[7]

A. C. Huidekoper, later operator of the Custer Trail Cattle
Company in the Little Missouri River country, while on a hunting
trip in western Dakota with some friends in 1881, stopped at Fort
Yates near the Standing Rock agency and has left a description
of a government issue of beef rations to the Indians:

At the time we were at the fort, the government issued relief rations
to the Indians in the form of cattle on the hoof. It was as barbaric a
sight as one can imagine. On ration day the six thousand Indians collected on a plain west of the fort. The beef was placed in a big corral
close by. As the quartermaster called the name of a chief, he stepped
out, followd by his tribe and the Indian agent counted them. Sometimes
the agent would say to the chief, "Too many," and the chief would
reply, "More since last count." The beef allotted to the chief were
then run out of the chute into the open and certain bucks on horseback were turned loose to kill the steers. It was pandemonium; rifles
cracked, the bucks yelled, and the squaws and children screamed. As
fast as a steer was down the squaws were on him with their ripping
knives, cutting him open and dragging out the entrails and eating
them. They smeared themselves and their children with blood and
looked and acted like fiends. This was repeated until the issue was
completed. Then the fires were lighted and the gorge commenced. It
lasted several days. Then the tribes trailed back to their camps to exist
until the next ration day. During the gorge the tom-tom sounded night
and day; the bucks raced their ponies and gambled and the squaws
slaved.[8]

---

[6] *Rocky Mountain Husbandman*, April 19, May 3, 1877; Stuart, *Forty Years
on the Frontier*, II, 154-6, 220-1; *River Press*, April 27, August 17, 1881;
Yellowstone Journal, March 22, 1884.

[7] Nimmo, *Range and Ranch Cattle Business of the U. S.*, p. 108.

[8] From a manuscript written by A. C. Huidekoper of Meadville, Pa. Used at
the office of L. F. Crawford, state historian, Bismarck, N. Dak., April, 1928.

There seems to be some difference of opinion regarding the seriousness of Indian attacks on range cattle in the eighties. As the United States Government made more liberal provisions for supplying the various tribes with food, no doubt many a white cattle-thief laid the blame of his depredations on the Indian, even going so far at times as to disguise himself as one. The average cattleman had little consideration for an Indian and was ready to blame him for losses whether the proof was adequate or not. The average cow-puncher did not consider it wrong to take anything an Indian had if he could use it, and many individual ranchers assumed the attitude that "the only good Indian was a dead Indian." On March 27, 1880, the *Yellowstone Journal* of Miles City, Montana, in the heart of the cattle country, printed the following statement, which is typical of western newspapers during the period: "The Indians of the Crow reservation are dying at the rate of seventy a day from measles and scarlet rash. If all the Indians in this country could be thus afflicted the Indian problem would soon be solved."

Another serious menace to cattle at times were wolves, which became so vicious in Montana in the early eighties that the territorial legislature placed a bounty of one hundred dollars on each one taken. The law was fairly effective and in 1884 five thousand wolfskins were brought in, and about the same number the following year. At the close of the eighties the act was repealed and the wolf menace again became serious. There were reports of large losses in 1894 and as the situation became desperate, wolves and other animals were often poisoned by placing strychnine in beef carcasses, and when bounties were high a group of men made their living as "wolf hunters."

XX

THE CATTLE THIEF

OF THE MANY problems confronting the cattlemen of the North-west, there was none that caused him more constant trouble than that of the stock thief or cattle rustler. Because of the nature of ranching, covering as it did great areas with little opportunity of direct control, it was easy for rustlers to carry on their work. These parasites of the cattleman's frontier infested the whole area, stealing both horses and cattle. Sometimes they flogged the herders until they agreed to abandon the cattle, they stampeded herds, altered brands, drove off small bunches of stock, branded young stock, and killed cattle, peddling the meat to local constitutents. Often a local cowboy branded strays and the young stock of various ranchers, laying the foundation for a herd of his own. When he was ready to claim the herd, he might sell his brand under a legal bill of sale to some buyer not too particular from whom he purchased his stock.

Early in the development of ranching on the northern plains, diligent efforts were made to eliminate the stealing of cattle. In the fall of 1875 the territorial legislature of Wyoming passed a law making it illegal to buy or sell stock without a bill of sale, and people engaged in the slaughter of cattle were required to keep complete records of all animals killed and from whom they were purchased. Everybody with live stock was required to have a brand which must be recorded in the office of the county clerk and it was illegal to brand cattle between February 15th and the beginning of the general spring round-up. There were severe penalties for changing brands and liberal rewards were offered for the apprehension of those stealing cattle. Butchers were required to keep all hides at least seven days for possible inspection, while others killing stock had to keep the hides for three weeks.[1]

[1] Lindsay, *Big Horn Basin*, p. 113; *Compiled Statutes of Wyoming*, 1887, sec. 4094-6, 4125-9.

No phase of cattle-stealing worried the stockmen of Wyoming quite as much as that of local cowboys starting herds of their own by branding the young stock of their employers or of neighboring cattlemen for themselves. That temptation was apparently hard to resist on the part of the individualistic cowhands and became so common that the stock associations began to look upon brand-owning cowboys with suspicion. There was some agitation early in the Wyoming Stock Growers Association not to allow them to own herds and to refuse to employ those that did. In the spring of 1883 at the regular meeting the secretary of the association, speaking in behalf of the powerful executive committee, criticized rather severely the matter of cowboys stealing cattle from their employers and the fact that many of them had herds of their own. "I refer," he explained, "to the starting of brands by men who have no cattle or means to buy any." [2] In the fall of 1883 arrangements were made for the preparation of a "black-list" of cowboys who branded for themselves, to be circulated among the members of the association, and no man on it was to receive employment from them. If a cowboy was caught using the branding-iron, he was to be discharged and no other rancher was to employ him. It was also agreed that members were not to allow their help to put small bands of cattle with the large herds.[3] As to the results of these efforts we have no positive record, and no doubt some association members continued to employ cowhands who built up brands of their own.

In the meantime the territorial legislature was working out possible statutes to govern branding and the operation of the round-up. Another act of the association at its autumn meeting in Cheyenne in 1883 was to recommend a more stringent law regarding the branding of mavericks and details of the round-up, which was acted upon by the legislative body in 1884. But in spite of strict legal regulations, the secretary reported many mav-

[2] *Minute Book of the Wyoming Stock Growers' Association*, April 9, 1883.
[3] *Ibid.*, November 9, 1883.

ericks unsold and large numbers of irregularities. Several cattle-men were called before the executive committee of the association to explain their actions, on different occasions. However, the trouble encountered by the association in Wyoming in early years with rustling cowhands was simple compared to what it had on its hands when the "nester" or small farmer appeared on the scene a few years later.

Without doubt there were many sections in the Northwest in which rustlers were highly organized and at times may have had some of their numbers holding various county offices to facilitate their activities. While cattle-stealing was serious on all portions of the range at times, it probably was never quite as bad in Montana and Dakota as it was in the northern and central parts of Wyoming. The legislative regulations in Montana were quite similar in content to those passed in Wyoming, while in Dakota more dependence was placed on the work of the associations than in detailed acts by the legislature. In areas where courts were organized, reasonable efforts were ordinarily made to take care of those accused of cattle-stealing by the regular civil authorities. Legislative statutes, however, were difficult to enforce and often became dead letters, while prompt action at times seemed imperative to the cattle fraternity. They, therefore, took action into their own hands and serving as judge, witnesses, and jury, passed judgment on the accused. When the evidence was positive, they served also as executioner, using a convenient tree and a stout rope to bring the case to a speedy end. Therefore, as in the mining areas, early law and order were administered on the cattle ranges by local Vigilance Committees who hanged some of the more vicious thieves or compelled them to leave the country.

There are many contemporary records of the activities of cattle and horse thieves on the ranges of the Northwest and the work of Vigilance Committees in their attempts to curb them. The *Helena Herald* for January 11, 1867, told of the killing of Jim Wallers, alias J. P. Staley, a cattle thief who had been operating in the Gallatin Valley. The *Cheyenne Leader* for July 11, 1868, reported the activity of cattle raids on the North Platte and in October of the same year reported a vigilance organization at Laramie to curb the work of cattle rustlers. In 1881 the cattlemen took matters into their own hands in Custer County and in Judith Basin when they rounded up a group of cattle killers, tried them before a jury of ranchmen, found them guilty, and gave them twenty-four hours to get out of the country.[4] In the early years it was estimated that the Vigilance Committees of Montana disposed of seventy-five thieves, among them being the most notorious and troublesome in the country. Some of them were allowed a limited time in which to leave the territory, but others were not given that opportunity. In one hanging, thirteen rustlers against whom the evidence had been definite and conclusive were hanged from a bridge, their bodies being found the next morning by workmen. "Purification by hemp," as it was called by a Montana editor, brought about a marked reduction in the stealing of stock on the ranges in the eighties.

XXI

LIFE ON THE RANGE

THE CATTLEMEN of the Northwest came from all parts of the world and from every state in the Union. They came from every class of society and represented almost every possible profession and occupation. A study of a group of fifty-six Montana stockmen in relation to their previous homes revealed fourteen from foreign countries, four from Canada, and the rest from fifteen different states in the Union. The states with the largest number of representatives were Kentucky and Missouri, with five each; New York and Tennessee, each with four; Pennsylvania with three; and two each for Minnesota and Michigan. The former occupation of seventy-nine Montana ranchers showed the following distribution:

[4] *River Press*, March 9, 1881; *Yellowstone Journal*, September 3, 1881.

eighteen miners, ten farmers, eight traders and freighters, five railroad hands, three soldiers, three clerks, three hunters and trappers, three steamboat hands, two grocers, two lumbermen, two iron molders, two saloonkeepers, with fourteen other occupations with one representative each, including a lawyer, a sheep herder, and a school-teacher. Only four of the group had been previously engaged in the cattle business before coming to Montana.[1]

The cattlemen engaged in large-scale ranching may be divided into two more or less distinct groups: the investors who put their money into the enterprise and probably never saw it, and the managers or actual bosses who were on the ground and operated the ranch. The managers as a class were able men and received good salaries for their services. In the spring of 1885 the *Yellowstone Journal* carried an advertisement of a New York investment company that was offering a salary of $7,500 a year for a man to handle a ranch on the western range.[2] While no doubt in most cases the "lure of large and easy profits" was a motivating force, the spirit of adventure and the attractiveness of the frontier brought many to the western ranges. Where cattlemen came into a locality with enthusiasm but no training for the new occupation they had chosen, there were enough experienced trail drivers and cowboys to overcome the lack of experience of the owner, and to carry the various enterprises along without disaster.

The ranch-houses of the cattle companies, made of logs and often roughly constructed, with rude corrals and outbuildings, while not especially attractive from the outside were usually comfortable and well furnished inside. The ranch-house of an English rancher near Bozeman in western Montana is described in a letter written home to friends by his wife, who was visiting her husband for a few months. She reported that there were only two fireplaces in their ranch home, one in the drawing-room and the other in her husband's den. The other rooms were heated with

[1] Fletcher, "Eastern Montana Cattle Range Industry," MS, chap. i, 45.
[2] *Yellowstone Journal*, April 4, 1885.

stoves and it was a full-time job for one man in the winter to supply the wood.[3] Many of the ranch-houses had pianos, libraries, and were well supplied with magazines. Granville Stuart on his Montana ranch had a library of three thousand volumes and subscribed to all the leading newspapers and magazines. James Fergus at his ranch on Arnell's Creek had another excellent library and Roosevelt had a good collection of books. The ranchmen and their families, when they were not in the East, exchanged dinners and met at the different houses for social gatherings where books and magazines were exchanged and current affairs discussed. The ranches of Huidekoper, Roosevelt, and Wibaux were centers for the leading cattlemen of the Little Missouri area in Dakota.

In Wyoming the social life of the ranching communities did not lack cultural and educational aspects. At the "Cheyenne Club" in Cheyenne, Wyoming, the élite of the cattle country of that area gathered for its social functions. They ate well served food and drank excellent liquor as they made business deals and discussed politics and the problems of the day. Laramie City was another focal point for the Wyoming ranchers on the Laramie plains, many of whom were Englishmen of culture and wealth.

From the very first, the annual meetings of the cattle associations served as social as well as business and educational gatherings. There were lectures, music, and parades, and a generous passing-out of free tickets to theaters and variety halls. In Cheyenne those attending the meetings of the Wyoming Stock Growers Association were given tickets to the Museum and Variety House of James McDaniels, or the popular Gold Room of J. W. Allen where they observed the freaks, stuffed birds and animals, or heard a program of dancing and music. Or, if their tastes were more genteel, they may have seen the well-known J. S. Langrishe troupe of legitimate players present *The Lady of Lyons, Camille* or *The Merchant of Venice.* When the Black Hills Stock Growers Association met at Rapid City or Deadwood, there is abundant

[3] Anonymous, *A Lady's Ranche Life in Montana* (London, 1887), p. 27.

evidence in the local press to indicate the members were well entertained.

The convention meetings of the Montana Stock Growers Association in 1885 were particularly attractive from the standpoint of social activities. In Miles City at the spring meeting there was a cowboy parade, and a special program at the Skating Rink, which served the "cowboy capital" as a center of amusement and entertainment. The convention was always invited as a body to the famous "roast pig banquet" given by the Miles City Club. The roasted meat of young pigs, washed down by the excellent liquor furnished in liberal quantities, was always a high point in the activities of the convention. At Helena in the autumn of the same year the Board of Trade of the city presented complimentary tickets to all visiting members of the association for the play *Only a Farmer's Daughter* at Ming's Opera House. President Bryan, in making the announcement at one of the association sessions, requested that members accompanied by ladies mention the number of tickets needed.[4]

Much has been written about the American cowboy, in which he has usually been depicted as a romantic, glamorous figure of the hero type or as a drunken, card-playing rounder with many of the characteristics of a desperado. But the cow-puncher of the open range country was neither of these. He was an average Westerner dressed for utility and comfort and not for picturesqueness, whose traits of character and habits of action were largely conditioned by the work he followed and the kind of life he was compelled to lead.

The life of a cowboy was hard, monotonous, and often lonely. For months at a time he neither slept in a bed or under a roof. During the round-up period he arose at three o'clock in the morning, and at the call of the cook to "come and get it," ate his break-

---

[4] *Stock Growers' Journal*, April 20, 1905; *Minute Book of the Montana Stock Growers' Association*, 1885, pp. 56-7; files of the *Helena Herald* and *Yellowstone Journal*, 1880-88.

fast of corn-dodgers, saleratus biscuits or sour-dough bread with bacon or salted sow-belly, beans and black coffee, squatting or standing near the chuck wagon holding his tin plate and cup in his hands, after which he spent twelve or fifteen hours in the saddle under a blistering sun. During the winter months he rode the line, hunted wolves in the bitter cold or loafed at the lonely ranch-house, where about the only recreation was card-playing, varied at times by practical jokes or the telling of "tall tales." He had access to few magazines, books, or papers, and was practically without cultural influences.

Some of the outstanding characteristics of the cowboy were physical courage, ability to endure hardship and exposure, mental alertness, and skill as a horseman and in the use of the lariat. He was famed for his ability to ride bucking bronchos and spent most of his waking hours in the saddle. He thoroughly disliked walking and objected to work except while on horseback. To the cowboy one man was as good as another and he firmly believed in a philosophy of perfect equality. Some of the English and European ranchers found difficulty in adjusting themselves to the theory and more than one rancher complained that the main trouble with "hired help" was that they expected to be treated as "one of the family, to eat with you and to sit in the drawing-room." The newly arrived wife of an English rancher in western Montana wrote in a letter to her London friends of committing a serious social error when a farm woman delivered some butter at the ranch-house: "She was very much offended when I met her in the kitchen and did not ask her to come into the parlor." [5]

There was in the cowboy a strong element of the "showoff," so characteristic of other types of frontiersmen. He liked to make an impression on others, either by his action or his dress, and perhaps the matter of living up to his reputation may have played some part. The cowboys, when in groups, carried on a good deal of rough and crude play and were fond of extravagant or smutty

[5] A Lady's Ranche Life in Montana, op. cit., letter dated November 10, 1885.

stories. They thoroughly enjoyed harassing a "tenderfoot," a favorite procedure being to shoot off his hat, or a cigarette or glass of liquor out of his hand. Physical courage ranked high with the cowboys, in whose lives it was of paramount importance. If a man showed evidence of cowardice or fear, his life was rendered miserable by the punchers. No cowboy could afford to allow himself to be bullied and any one looking for trouble among a group of them was likely to find it. Often he paid far more than he could afford for clothing, sometimes spending one hundred dollars or more for a saddle and twenty-five dollars for a hat or a pair of boots. An observer in the West for the first time, traveling over the Northern Pacific on her way to western Montana, told of the train stopping at Dickinson in the Territory of Dakota, its advent being a signal for a salvo of revolver shots from a group of men on horseback "called Cowboys, wearing broad brimmed hats, blue shirts and funny leather leggings with fringes down the side." [6]

The cowboy relaxed after months of hard and monotonous toil by visiting the important cow towns along the railroads or inland settlements that developed at strategic points as places of rendezvous on the open range. There he drank enormous quantities of whiskey and other liquors, gorged himself with food, played roulette, faro, black Jack and poker in the gambling establishments, and visited the houses of prostitution and the dance-halls, until his accumulated wages were spent. The process usually took from one to three days. Then with his purse empty, his head swollen, half-sick and perhaps a bit ashamed of himself, he rode slowly back to the ranch to work until he had earned enough for another spree. [7] Townspeople as a rule saw very little of the cow-

[6] *Ibid.*, p. 5; *Dickinson Press*, October 13, 1885.
[7] Cowboys in some localities, after spending their money, would go to a store and ask to purchase clothing and other necessities on credit on condition that they pay for them on their next arrival in town. If a cowboy kept his promise, he repeated the process, which always left him in debt to the local merchant. "Jawbone credit," as it was called, was not always granted and might be withdrawn should the puncher fail to pay the storekeeper before he started on his spree.

COWBOYS IN TOWN FOR CHRISTMAS

Drawing by Frederic Remington. *Harper's Weekly*, 1889.

hands except when they were in town and at that time many of them were living at a rapid pace. It was these few hours spent in the saloons, gambling-houses, and dens of vice that gave the cowpuncher his bad reputation and brought him in disrepute. Of course, as in the case of all groups, there were both good and bad cowboys. Frontier population has always had its "dregs" or "scum," and very unfortunately that portion of the group is more or less conspicuous. There were no doubt many stable cowboys but they were not in the limelight and as a rule were not patrons of the saloons, gambling-houses, or brothels.

The area under consideration might well be said to have had two "cowboy capitals": Cheyenne, Wyoming, and Miles City, Montana. Conventions of the various stock associations were held in these towns and it was the ambition of most of the pleasure-seeking cowboys to visit them, if only at long intervals. As early as 1871 a local newspaper was advertising Cheyenne as "the Magic City of the Plains" and the center of a cattle region two hundred miles wide.[8] By 1873 it had fifteen saloons, and numerous gambling establishments, dance houses and variety halls and was spoken of in the local press as the "Cowboy Mecca." [9] Laramie City and Rawlins, also on the Union Pacific Railroad, became important cowboy centers and, like Cheyenne, were infested during the early years by "toughs" and "hanger-ons" who followed the construction camps and new railroad towns. In the spring of 1869 a local editor made the following observation regarding Rawlins: "The vigilantes on Tuesday night cleared the town of all prostitutes and loafers. They tore down the houses of some prostitutes and ordered them and their pimps to leave town." [10]

Early in 1877, as a result of military operations against the Indians in the Northwest, a fort was constructed at the junction of the Yellowstone and Tongue rivers. On the opposite side of the

[8] *Cheyenne Daily Leader*, September 2, 1871.
[9] *Ibid.*, February 3, 24, 1873.
[10] *Wyoming Weekly Leader*, April 24, 1869.

Tongue in June, 1877, there developed a collection of shacks and tents which served as a beginning for Miles City. Cattle had been moving into this area for some time and there gathered at this point in 1877 a motley population made up of cowboys and cattlemen, buffalo hunters, deserters from the army, the backwash from the Black Hills gold camps, gamblers, dive-keepers, all laying the foundation for what was to become the metropolis of the cow country of eastern Montana.[11]

A Bozeman newspaper gave a description of Miles City early in 1878, at which time it was reported to have one hundred and fifty houses and to be the "metropolis of the Yellowstone Valley." The editor went on to say:

Saloons are numerous in the "cowboy capital" and are to all appearances well patronized. Gamblers are here in plenty, plying their vocations and that great institution of upper Montana, the hurdy-gurdy house, is in full blast and is crowded nightly with all classes and conditions of men. Let us enter such an establishment any evening. On one side of the room is a bar and an orchestra, while on the other side are tables with faro banks and other games presided over by gamblers of the better class who apparently are the only unconcerned persons in the room. Close examination will show, however, that their glittering eyes take all in and every person is scanned and weighed and their probable calling arrived at by the experienced judges of human nature. Occasionally a song from an amateur or professional lends variety to the music. No one is barred from entrance here and the solid men of the city and the "soiled doves" often jostle each other in the crowd. At the entrance to the club rooms in the rear the smiling and polite doorkeeper may inform us that "no one is admitted this evening, gentlemen," which means that large amounts of money are changing hands and privacy is desired. . . .

A few steps up Front Street and the sound of music again falls upon our ears, which on close inspection proves to come from a house, the sides of which are canvas. Here is a dance hall, or, in Montana parlance, the hurdy-gurdy house. "Honor to your partners" and "all

[11] Miles City was named after General Nelson Miles, the Indian-fighter. *Miles City Daily Star*, Jubilee edition, May 24, 1934; *Avant Courier*, August 3, 1877.

promenade to the bar" follow each other in quick succession. Here, too, all is peaceful. Eight or ten saloons are likewise crowded and in all of them games of faro and monte are running but in all good nature prevails. The law of Miles City is supreme without a vigilance committee.[12]

Cowboys looking for excitement found it in the theaters, saloons, gambling establishments, and dance-halls. While a variety theater was operated in connection with the well-known Grey Mule Saloon, during the early period the Cosmopolitan Theater with John Chinnick as manager was the first important playhouse in Miles City. Entrance to the theater proper was through the saloon portion of the building where the patron was waited upon by a bevy of barmaids who sold drinks while the performances were on.[13] With the construction of the Northern Pacific Railroad to Miles City in the early eighties, the arrival of the usual group that followed the construction camps looking for an easy means of livelihood unsettled the more or less stable life of the town, until in 1883 the citizens arose in a body, and after a number of hangings, drove the drifters out of the community.

The cow towns on the railroads, however, were not sufficient to take care of the amusements and recreation of the puncher fraternity and local social centers or small inland towns and settlements developed at convenient points to answer a vital need. A. J. F. Corbett and Victor Arland abandoned the ranching business in northern Wyoming and established the inland town of Arland consisting of a store, post-office, saloon, and what passed for a hotel. There were a dance-hall and, as in most frontier rendezvous, lewd women who operated houses of ill-fame, or served as barmaids and dance-hall girls.[14] These places afforded days and nights of relaxation for the cowboy, tired and jaded from weeks and often months of work in the saddle. There he allowed his

---

[12] *Avant Courier*, January 3, 10, 1878.

[13] *Miles City Daily Star*, Jubilee number, May 24, 1934.

[14] *Big Horn County Rustler*, December 23, 1910; *Wind River Mountaineer* (Lander, Wyo.), March 4, 1896.

emotions free vent and with his friends and colleagues often
"painted the town red." There was another cowboy rendezvous
south of Arland at Meeteetsee in Wyoming and there were others
scattered over the open-range area, all more or less alike. There
were killings and disorder in the saloons and dance-halls as
drunken cowboys ran amuck, for whiskey did not make for frontier
stability. Sometimes there was trouble on the range and in the cow
camps as the cowboys got into fights or abused their horses. A
writer on the Big Horn Basin tells of an unpleasant episode in
which a cowboy of the Pitch Fork outfit killed the cook at one of
the camps, after which he turned his gun on others and was shot
down by another member of the outfit.[15] The hard life of the
range was not one that made for pleasant, veneered emotions.

The drunkenness, gambling, and horse-racing became problems of sufficient seriousness to cause discussion at the meetings of
the cattle associations. As early as 1887 the Wyoming Stock Growers Association threshed the matter out in one of their meetings
and action was taken against such practices. They went on record
opposing the carrying of arms at round-ups as productive of trouble,
and prohibited drinking, gambling, and horse-racing on the range.
While the decision was probably never effectively enforced, at least
it stood as a weight on the side of law and order.[16]

Since the days of the open range the cowboy has been one of the
dominant figures in the literature of the West and as J. M. Carey
of the Wyoming Stock Growers Association said, "There is a
charm and romance about the life of a cowboy during this period
that will live as long as history." [17]

[15] *Wind River Mountaineer*, September 10, 13, 1897; Lindsay, *Big Horn Basin*, pp. 131-2.
[16] *Members of and By-Laws of the Wyoming Stock Growers Association*, 1887.
[17] J. M. Carey, "Early Days of the Cattle Business," speech, *Proceedings*, Wyoming Stock Growers Association (1915), p. 69.

XXII

THE ADVANCE OF THE AGRICULTURAL FRONTIER

WHILE the cattle boom was developing on the ranges of the Northwest in the late seventies and early eighties, the line of frontier settlement was advancing into the plains area west of the Missouri River. It made rapid advances into Nebraska and into the Territory of Dakota. A slight boom that began in 1868 ended in 1873, and the period from 1873 to 1877 was one of pronounced economic depression throughout the East and Middle West. The winter of 1874-75 had been somewhat severe and grasshoppers appeared in enormous swarms in the midwestern regions in 1874-76. By 1877 conditions began to improve and the Black Hills gold rush paved the way for the Dakota boom of 1878-86. During those years much of the Territory of Dakota was settled and what a few years before had been an almost uninhabited expanse of prairie, became a fairly populous region soon to be divided and admitted into the Union as two states.

The causes for the boom were numerous. The abundant moisture which had prevailed for several years suggested a humid climate, while extensive railroad expansion furnished transportation facilities to the various sections. Extensive advertising was carried on by the railroads, colonizing associations, land and town-site companies, and territorial boards of immigration. Another potent factor was the rapid occupation of much of the more desirable land farther east and its gradual rise in price, accompanied by an increase in taxes. Liberal immigration laws were bringing Europeans to our shores in large numbers, and capital was available at this time for reasonable business ventures.

Settlement into the Dakota area was rapid in the early eighties, the population of the territory increasing from 135,177 in 1880 to approximately 210,000 in 1882 and to about 330,000 in 1883. In 1884 there were eight land-offices operating in Dakota, and the Bismarck office recorded 2,563,543 acres filed upon. By 1887 there was no free land left in twenty-two Dakota counties and nine others had only twenty-five hundred acres each, most of which was undesirable. In 1885 there were 415,610 inhabitants living within the territory and by 1890 that number had increased to more than a half million.

This rapid advance of the frontier of settlement made up largely of agriculturalists was bound to have its effect on the cattle country. Contemporary newspapers of the ranching area give ample evidence of the activity of home-seekers. In the late seventies in southwestern Montana small ranchers were settling down to agriculture, often selling their cattle to the large operators. They purchased land in the rich valleys, fenced it, and planted their crops. By 1879 the newspapers of western Montana indicated that many local herds were being driven to the Musselshell and Yellowstone areas. If the local farmers kept cattle, their herds were small and they practised close herding with winter feeding. In the Smith River Valley of central Montana the same development occurred a few years later.

In western Dakota and in southern and eastern Wyoming the granger farmers began coming in during the middle eighties, at about the time the cattle boom was ready to break. They took up their homesteads on the public domain, choosing the desirable locations near water, plowed their lands and fenced their farms. They cared nothing for range rights and range customs; they were entitled to their free farms by law and were prepared to hold them against all comers. The Fremont, Elkhorn and Missouri River Railroad, a branch of the Chicago North Western, crossed the line into Wyoming in 1886 and reached Douglas on the North Platte the next year and in 1890 the Black Hills was supplied with railroad facilities.[1]

The land laws of the United States were designed primarily for the benefit of the home-owner, to bring the lands of the public

[1] Henry V. Poor, *Manual of Railroads of the United States*, 1868-1902, pp. 842, 886.

domain under cultivation, and to promote settlement. Under the Homestead, Preëmption, Timber Culture, and Desert Land acts, it was possible for an individual to obtain 1,140 acres of land. Many cattlemen took advantage of the laws, using the land that was legally supposed to be used for cultivation for grazing purposes, and after utilizing their own rights had their agents or employees acquire title to large tracts, afterwards purchasing or taking over the land themselves. This illegal procedure was openly practised in Wyoming, Montana, and Dakota. An indication as to how common the practice was is evident when in 1883 the Territorial Governor of Wyoming in his report to the Secretary of the Interior said, "The greatest source of encouragement to men of moderate means desiring to engage in cattle-raising in Wyoming arises from that feature of the policy of the United States government by which it encourages its citizens to acquire title to the public lands." He goes on to show that under the land laws it was possible to acquire title to 1,140 acres of land: [2] 160 under the Homestead Act, 160 under the Preëmption Act, 160 under the Timber Culture Act and 640 under the Desert Land Act. One Wyoming rancher after taking a homestead persuaded eight men to act as his agents and secured title to five thousand acres. A letter dated June 21, 1885, sent to the General Land Office, told of a band of cowboys coming to a land-office in Wyoming to make final entry on land that they stated openly was for their employer.[3]

Beginning as early as 1872 there were various complaints registered by the commissioner of the General Land Office in his reports to the Secretary of the Interior of the malfunctioning of the land laws on the cattle ranges where large tracts had been monopolized by cattlemen through fraudulent entries. With the passing of the Desert Land Act the violations became even more flagrant,

[2] *Report of the Territorial Governor of Wyoming to the Secretary of the Interior*, 1883, p. 7.
[3] *Annual Report of the Commissioner of the General Land Office to the Secretary of the Interior*, 1886, pp. 69-70, 87.

many of the worst offenders being in Wyoming. With the election of Cleveland as president of the United States in 1884, William A. J. Sparks was appointed to the post of commissioner of the General Land Office and he went to work to eliminate some of the fraud in connection with the administration of the land laws. He suspended final action on all Desert Land Law entries until they could be investigated for fraud. In Wyoming alone 350,000 acres were returned to the government and some attempt was made to administer the laws in a proper manner.

In the early eighties another development was taking place that was also illegal. As the range was becoming crowded and there was a tendency for settlers to come in, many of the large cattle companies began to erect fences around that portion of the public domain that they claimed by custom and priority rights. This movement took place largely between 1880 and 1885. Complaints and requests for relief were sent to the Land Office in large numbers and the matter was investigated, the Secretary of the Interior advising that prospective settlers cut fences that barred them from land on which they wished to homestead or settle. The matter became so serious that in 1885 a law was passed doing away with illegal enclosures and authorizing President Cleveland to see that such obstructions were removed. Laramie County, Wyoming, was one of the most serious offenders and in 1886 contained ten cattle companies that had illegal enclosures, the Swan Land and Cattle Company being reported to have one hundred and thirty miles of illegal fences.[4] After the Law of 1885 legal action was often taken and illegal fences began coming down.[5]

Worried by the attitude of the Land Office, the cattlemen decided upon a new means of obtaining grazing lands. At the national cattle convention in St. Louis, November 17-22, reso-

---

[4] *Rocky Mountain Husbandman*, April 12, 1883.
[5] Most illegal fencing was eliminated by the law but it did not disappear entirely. Patents for barbed wire and for a machine to manufacture it were taken out in 1874. By 1880 at least forty thousand tons were produced, the amount tripled by 1890. Osgood, *Day of the Cattleman*, pp. 190-1.

lutions were adopted to be sent to Congress asking that cattle-men on the ranges be granted long-term leases to large tracts of land to be used for grazing purposes. Congress refused to act on what it declared to be class legislation. In the meantime, Commissioner Sparks of the Land Office began to work against the large cattle operators—"cattle barons," he called them—favoring the idea that the public lands in the plains region should be used to provide homes for poor men. His office and the Democratic administration encouraged the taking up of the public lands for agricultural purposes and thousands of Americans, as well as numerous immigrant farmers from western Europe, took the government at its word and went west to get their free quarter-sections. The *Northwestern Livestock Journal* and other loyal papers of Cheyenne ridiculed Sparks and his idea of homes for poor men in the cattle country, but large groups of granger farmers were drifting into western Nebraska and into Wyoming. In the year 1884 there were 3,592 homesteads, 1,294 desert claims and 1,371 timber-culture claims filed on in the Territory of Wyoming. The settlers continued to come and by 1887 and 1888 the situation was serious. They were ridiculed by the local press as "ignorant gangs of continental paupers with innumerable ragged kids," who were often carried through the first winter by food and beef contributed by some generous-hearted ranch foreman.

By 1888 they were migrating into Wyoming in large numbers and along the line of the newly constructed railroad, Germans, Swedes, and Russians were coming in at the rate of fifteen families a day in the spring of 1888. Several small farming settlements were established, of which Lusk and Douglas were good examples.[6]

When the homesteaders took their claims they chose the best sites, often near water, and plowed up the land and practised mixed

[6] *Cheyenne Daily Leader*, April 21, May 23, 25, 1888; *Cheyenne Daily Sun*, March 25, 31, 1888. The interests of the large cattleman and those of the homesteader were so unlike that there was little hope of them living side by side without trouble.

farming with cattle-raising. They complained that their small bands of cattle were absorbed by the great cattle companies who even branded them in the spring round-up. They also claimed that every possible effort was made to discourage and intimidate them. They sent many letters to the Land Office complaining that the cattlemen were doing everything in their power to obstruct settlement. On the other hand, the cattlemen had their legitimate grievances against the homesteaders. The latter would often settle in small groups and plant their crops. Since wire for fences was expensive and they had little money, and wood was scarce, they didn't bother to abide by the territorial laws, and later, the state laws, requiring that all crops be fenced. They plowed a furrow around the edge of their land and when cattle crossed it they shot them and had beef for their hungry families. When the cattlemen protested, nothing was done and the killings continued. The manager of a large cattle company wrote to the secretary of a stock association in the spring of 1887 offering bitter objections to the promiscuous killing of cattle by granger farmers. Large numbers of cattle were found dead from gunshot wounds. As the settlers increased in numbers, it was almost impossible to obtain a bill from a grand jury against a farmer. To make bad matters worse, President Cleveland appointed an "anti-stock" governor in 1887 for Wyoming. Feeling between the two groups became more tense. The manager of one of the large cattle companies in the Big Horn Basin wrote his ranch foreman, who evidently had been having some trouble with the farmers, to "turn a cold shoulder on land grabbers" and not to allow them to remain on the ranch for more than twenty-four hours at a time, and not to feed them or their horses.

In the meantime cattle rustlers, taking advantage of the trouble between the two groups, became active, arousing the Wyoming Stock Growers Association, which was already sensitive at the charge brought against it of obstructing settlement, and was worried at the increased number of farms in the range area. At this time it was also observed that cattle thieves and rustlers were becoming extremely bold. Local associations held long sessions discussing the rustling menace. In March, 1889, the news arrived in Cheyenne of the lynching of three members of a cattle-rustling gang in Colorado. A homesteader and his son were arrested near Cheyenne in July, 1889, for roping some cattle that had strayed on to their farm. They were charged with cattle rustling but were finally allowed to go free. That same summer there were several hangings of cattle thieves in Carbon County, without the formality of a trial. Among them were two notorious characters, James Averill and Ella Watson, who was sometimes known as "Cattle Kate." [7]

The impression was gradually created by this type of episode that the country was full of cattle thieves and the cattlemen were inclined to blame the granger farmers for most of the acts. Many observers maintain that there were in reality only a few rustlers in the country and they were as apt to be found among the cattlemen as among the grangers. The center of cattle-stealing gradually came to be identified with the northwestern part of the state, where the association reported that thieves were thick but were hard to catch. Once in a while one would be shot and would be reported as a granger. Apparently many of the killings in the out of the way places on the range had nothing to do with cattle-stealing. Rustling gangs were reported to be highly organized and to be operating with the coöperation and consent of the county officials. No doubt many granger farmers talked too much, even bragging about shooting cattle and sitting on grand juries that boasted of never indicting a cattle rustler, while on the other hand many cattlemen made indiscreet remarks to the effect that there were "too many people and not enough cattle in Wyoming." [8]

[7] *Cheyenne Daily Sun,* April 2, 7, 10, February 19, March 6, July 13, 1889; *Big Horn County Rustler,* September 15, 1911.
[8] *Cheyenne Daily Leader,* July 12, 1892.

XXIII

THE JOHNSON COUNTY WAR

JOHNSON COUNTY acquired the reputation of being the center of operations of the rustlers, and for this reason the ensuing conflict was popularly called the "Johnson County war" or the "war of invasion." The *Denver Republican* and the *Denver Times* took the side of the cattlemen against the farmers and rustlers, suggesting on several different occasions that unless the state did something about the situation, the cattlemen would have to act for themselves. The *Denver Times*, early in April, carried this statement, "The cattle dealers' organization has determined to exterminate the gang of cattle rustlers that have been playing havoc among the herds of the northern portion of Wyoming."[1]

In the fall of 1891 the Wyoming Stock Growers Association made ready to save the range cattle industry from the small rancher, farmer, and rustler. They made their first attack through the Live Stock Commission that they dominated. In October, 1891, they ordered inspectors to hold all cattle of certain brands that were on their prepared list of rustlers. They were instructed to disregard all bills of sale held by the owners of cattle so branded, as rustlers and grangers were working together. The suspected cattle were to be sold by the inspectors and the money held by the Live Stock Commission.[2] The cowhand who had a few cattle to sell and was suspected of rustling, the farmer, and the small rancher were all hit by this action. They were brought before a board decidedly in favor of the large cattleman to prove that they were not rustlers and their cattle had not been stolen. The burden of proof thus was put upon the accused, which was out of line with the theory of American justice. The action aroused public opinion and was inclined to bring the honest rancher and farmer to a point

[1] Quoted in the *Cheyenne Daily Leader*, April 8, 1892.
[2] 16,306 cattle were taken over and 5,238 head were sold. *Minute Book of the Wyoming Live Stock Commissioners*, p. 6.

where they sympathized with the rustler. The local press, which had always before backed up the powerful organization, took the popular side and began to criticize the association and large ranchers for their un-American attitude, and the *Cheyenne Daily Leader* of March 23, 1892, printed a strong editorial on the intolerance of the association and its attempts to ride ruthlessly over the weaker groups.

In November, 1891, matters came to a head in Johnson County when two men who were accused of rustling cattle were shot from ambush. Two large cattle outfits in the area were thought to have been responsible for the murder and a United States deputy marshal, who had been employed as an inspector, was suspected of doing the killing. He was arrested but was released by the sheriff when he was able to furnish an alibi. Crowds gathered in Buffalo, the county-seat, and threatened to do violence unless some action was taken. Things quieted down, however, and by spring the farmers and small ranchers of Johnson County were holding the Stock Growers Association responsible for the murders and severed all connections with it and the State Board of Live Stock Commissioners. About fifty men took over the town of Buffalo, and, receiving the coöperation of the county officials, proceeded to hold their own round-ups, paying no attention to the rules of the association.[3]

The big cattle outfits, faced with the problems of low prices, small profits, and the increased expense of hay for winter feeding, feared for their existence as they observed the invading farmer restricting their ranges and blocking their water supply. Surrounded by opposition, the once powerful Wyoming Stock Growers Association, so long monarch of the territory, refused to give way without a struggle and was ready, if necessary, to resort to force to keep control in its own hands.

The regular meeting of the association was held at Cheyenne on April 4, 1892, and forty-three members answered the roll-call.

[3] *Cheyenne Daily Leader*, February 24, 1892.

Routine business was conducted and a resolution was passed sanctioning the address of J. H. Hammond, president of the Wyoming Live Stock Commission, made a few days before, challenging the Wyoming cattlemen who had risked their lives against Indian attacks and had faced many hardships to build up the state and the cattle industry, not to give way before the cattle thief, but to defend themselves, exterminating him, if need be.[4] The association adjourned after a one-day session.

But even while the association was in session, preparations were being made for action on the part of the stockmen. There was activity in the railroad yards as several cars were quietly loaded and the following afternoon a special train arrived from Denver. Late that evening, April 5th, a train consisting of a passenger-coach with blinds closely drawn, three stock-cars loaded with horses, a flat-car loaded with wagons and camping equipment, and a caboose left for Casper, Wyoming. On board were about twenty-five Texas cowboys picked up in Denver, some twenty cattlemen, a physician, and a correspondent of the *Chicago Herald*. The members of the party were armed with revolvers and Winchester rifles. All details had been carefully worked out and the plan proceeded smoothly.[5] A Denver newspaper, apparently having some information regarding the expedition, spoke of "the important mission the mysterious train" had to perform. It told of a gang of outlaw cattle thieves operating in the northwestern portion of Wyoming with great herds of stolen cattle in its possession, whose activities must be curbed.[6]

Reaching Casper just before daybreak the party of horsemen, accompanied by their wagons, started northward, led by guides who were well acquainted with the region. They were directed by the foreman of the Western Union Beef Company to a ranch-house on the north fork of the Powder River where two alleged

---

[4] *Minute Book of the Wyoming Board of Live Stock Commissioners*, p. 9.
[5] *Cheyenne Daily Leader*, April 12, 1892.
[6] Quoted from the *Denver Sun* by the *Cheyenne Daily Leader*, April 8, 1892.

rustlers were located. They surrounded the ranch-house and, cap-
turing two trappers who had spent the night there, killed the other
two occupants, supposed cattle thieves, and moved on to the
ranch-house of the Western Union Beef Company, where they
spent the night and obtained fresh horses, heading for Buffalo the
next morning where they expected to make a surprise attack. In
the meantime their killing of the two men and the activity at the
ranch-house had attracted the attention of some farmers who had
given the alarm. Hearing that a large party of citizens and
farmers from Buffalo was coming to meet them, they barricaded
themselves against attack in the ranch-house where they had
spent the night. They were soon surrounded and it looked as if
more blood would be shed.[7]

News of the danger of the expedition reached Cheyenne and
frantic telegrams were sent to President Harrison, requesting that
he order troops sent out from Fort McKinney to establish law
and order. On April 13th three companies of Federal cavalry
arrived on the scene and they appeared none too soon, as the
besiegers had constructed a movable platform or "Go Devil"
carrying powder and dynamite and were about to close in on the
cabin.[8] Forty-six men surrendered, including some of the most
prominent members of the association. The governor, fearing
violence, had the prisoners brought to Cheyenne where charges
were preferred against the whole party. Feeling was so strong in
Johnson County that there was fear that the cattle of the larger
ranch companies would be slaughtered. Cattlemen were badly
frightened and appealed to President Harrison, who ordered all
unlawful assemblages to disperse by August 3, 1892.[9] Good judgment prevailed and arrangements were made for Johnson County
to take over the prisoners with the understanding that they should
not be tried in that county. No trial was ever held, as Johnson

[7] *Cheyenne Daily Leader*, April 13, 14, 1892.
[8] *Ibid.*, April 13, 1892.
[9] James D. Richardson, *Messages and Papers of the President* (Washington, D. C., 1899), IX, 290.

County was bankrupt and unable to stand the expense. Then, too, it was doubtful that an unprejudiced jury could have been obtained within the state and in the meantime two of the most important witnesses had disappeared.[1] Since the district court at Cheyenne had no right to force the county to pay the expenses and hold the trial, the cattlemen and Texans were dismissed and the "Johnson County war" was over.[2]

XXIV

THE END OF THE OPEN RANGE

MANY of the large cattle companies in northern Wyoming liquidated their herds in the fall of 1892 and by the spring of 1893 the ranges were cleared. A letter from one of the ranchers to the association tells of the process. "We shipped everything last year [1892] that we could find in all our brands. . . . I do not believe we have twenty-five head left. . . . Windsor, Kemp and Company cannot have more than 200 head in the old Powder Company brands and the Big Horn Company both put together."[3] Some of the large interests moved out, and the ones who remained cut down the size of their herds and increased their acreage of hay. Cattle herds decreased in size but increased in numbers. From 1886 to 1896 cattle in Wyoming decreased from 900,000 to 300,000 and their valuation shrank from $14,651,125 to $3,732,-558.[4] Governor Brooks of Wyoming in 1905 said, "To-day our cattle are owned by 5,000 different stockmen and farmers, instead of a few hundred outfits."[5]

---

[1] The two men who had spent the night in the cabin with the two murdered men were charged with selling whiskey to the Indians and were taken to Omaha, where they were probably kidnapped.

[2] *Cheyenne Daily Leader*, April 29, 1893.

[3] Letter of Fred Hesse to H. J. Ijams dated May 31, 1893; letter file of the Wyoming Stock Growers' Association.

[4] William A. Richards, *Message to the Fourth State Legislature*, January 12, 1897.

[5] *Message of the Governor to Eighth State Legislature*, January 11, 1905.

In Montana and Dakota the break-up of the range cattle business took place without a struggle, due to the fact that the cattle industry was never as important there as in Wyoming. Mining and agriculture were strong enough in those areas to keep ranching from domination. By 1903 practically all of the cattlemen of eastern Montana were making provisions for winter feeding. As a rule, only part of the stock was fed, in most cases for about six weeks. There was no attempt to fatten them for the spring market, but it was recognized that winter-fed cattle had a distinct advantage.[6] By 1900 there had occurred a marked decline in the size of Montana herds, and by 1905 the small ranchers had taken the place of the range cattlemen and "corrals and sheds were superseded by bars and stables." According to the Custer County assessment records of 1900 there were located in the county 76 herds of over 500 head each, and 244 herds of from 20 to 500 head. In 1905 there were only 25 herds with more than 500 head, the number of small herds increasing to 334. In 1908 the figures for herds of over 500 was 22, while the number of those from 20 to 500 amounted to 498. The passing of the Harris Cattle Company is indicative of what was taking place. Started by Franklin Harris in 1881 as a small rancher, in 1899 he added to his greatly increased holdings the cattle of the old Continental Land and Livestock Company and the following year purchased the twenty thousand head in the herd of Creswell and Day. By 1903, however, the dogs and aggressive herdsmen of the small farmer and the sheepman had so encroached on his range that it was decided to sell all marketable stock and to move the remainder southward into western Nebraska. This action closed out the H U, the Continental and the Day and Creswell brands, three of the greatest companies of the open-range days.[7] In 1902 the annual meeting place of the Montana Stock Growers Association was

[6] *Yellowstone Journal*, August 3, 10, 17, 24, 1895; *River Press*, September 2. 1897; *Montana Stockman and Farmer*, Miles City, Mont., January, 1897.
[7] *Billings Daily Gazette*, July 31, 1903.

changed from Miles City to Helena and as the agricultural frontier advanced eastward, open-range ranching was gradually eliminated. In the Little Missouri country where the herds of Roosevelt, Wibaux, and De Mores and others had ranged, by 1902 the dogs of the settlers were making it impossible for the old range outfits to operate.

The legislature of the Territory of Dakota as early as 1885 enacted a statute requiring western stockmen to fence in and keep their live stock under control, or else to stand liable for any damage inflicted by them.[8] As early as 1887 Dakota ranchmen were beginning to feel seriously the pinch of the wire fences that were erected by the immigrant settlers under government protection around their newly homesteaded farms and of the statute making the owners of cattle liable for trespass. They were compelled to submit to the new order of things, and the days of the open range when grass and water were "as free as air" to all comers were at an end. One powerful factor in the driving out of the cattle outfits was the coming of the sheep rancher, and after the sheepman and the small rancher had helped to close out the large rancher, they found that their interests, too, needed adjusting. As the range cattle industry disappeared from the Northwest, the part played by the sheepman in its elimination remains to be told, and will be the theme of the next part.

Although the picturesque days of the great cattle outfits and of the open range had passed, never to return, ranching continued to be an important industry in the Northwest. The cowboy still rode the restricted ranges of western Dakota, Montana, and Wyoming, remembering the free and easy days of the open range,

[8] The first "Herd Law" in the Territory of Dakota was passed in 1870-71 and was amended at the next session of the territorial legislature to apply to meadowlands. It was amended again in 1881 to make it more effective. The region west of the Missouri River was exempt from such laws until 1885 when a strict "Fence and Herd Law" was passed which included the western counties. *Session Laws of the Territory of Dakota*, 1870-71, pp. 63-9; 1872, 56; 1881, 68; 1885, pp. 245-6.

when great herds wandered at will over the prairies. Ever hopeful
and optimistic, he still sang the ranchman's song:

> In saddle or in camp at home,
> I fear not fortune's change.
> My wealth the branded herds that roam
> The green wastes of my range.
> Oh, who more independent, free,
> And care exempt than I?
> Not he that sails upon the sea,
> Or scales the mountain high.
> I laugh and sing, give fancy wing,
> And let the world go by.
> The saddle is my throne,
> The vast wild herds my vassals tried.
> The lariat's unerring cast,
> My mandate undefied.
> My spurs were won by stubborn deeds,
> That ne'er a blush can bring.
> No other right or sanction needs,
> The carefree cattle king.
> And joy brims up the stirrup cup,
> As this the song I sing.[9]

[9] *Medora Bad Lands Cowboy*, November 13, 1884.

IV

THE FRONTIER OF
THE SHEEP-RANCHER

WHILE sheep were brought into the English colonies from the mother-country during the colonial period, the development and expansion of the industry was held up by the restricted market for wool, which was limited to household demands. Following a slight improvement in the wool market immediately after the American Revolution, there occurred a depression in the wool business in 1793 that lasted for a period of fifteen years, the most noteworthy development during those years being the introduction of the Spanish Merino into the country in an effort to improve sheep breeds.[1] Trade restrictions in the years leading up to the War of 1812 caused wool-growing to become a commercial enterprise, as woolen mills increased in numbers and there occurred an expansion of household manufacturing of woolens.

Because of the peninsular campaign of the Napoleonic Wars, the Spanish authorities were anxious to dispose of their best flocks to save them from being taken by the French and to secure ready money. Between April 1, 1810, and August 31, 1811, nearly twenty thousand Spanish Merinos were landed in the United States, some of the first ones selling for as much as one thousand dollars a head, the price soon dropping to one hundred to three hundred dollars. Although the War of 1812 temporarily stimu-

---

[1] The Spanish Merino first appeared in the United States in 1793 when William Foster smuggled two ewes and a ram out of Spain, bringing them to Boston from France. L. G. Connor, "A Brief History of the Sheep Industry in the United States," *Annual Report of the American Historical Association* (1918), I, 93-102.

lated the wool market and woolens industry into a mushroom growth, a depression had set in by 1815 which caused a stagnant sheep and wool market until the early twenties, when it gradually began to improve.

By 1830 there were in the United States between twelve and thirteen million sheep and in the period 1830 to 1837 the woolen mills of the country more than doubled their output, the keen demand for wool causing the sheep industry to assume new form, as small flocks designed largely to furnish wool for home use changed to an emphasis on larger flocks among the farmers who lived in outlying districts or on the frontier. Except for slight setbacks caused by the panics of 1837 and 1857 the sheep industry made rapid progress in the United States and, between 1840 and 1860, the center of wool production shifted decidedly westward.[2]

Because of the life habits of sheep, the relative non-perishability of wool and its low cost of marketing, sheep-raising has been well adapted to regions remote from centers of population and has been favored as a frontier enterprise. While the pioneer aspects of the industry tended to pass away as communication and transportation improved, the above factors, with the ability of sheep to adapt themselves readily to a wide range of climatic conditions, to go several days without water, and to thrive on shrubby and weedy types of forage, made it possible to keep them in regions that would not otherwise have been utilized.

Prior to 1840 the West had produced its wool largely for local needs and very little of its clip reached eastern markets. At the same time the movement of population westward during the late thirties and forties tended to strengthen the local market and it was some time before there was any considerable surplus for eastward shipment, except from the earlier settled areas in the Ohio Valley. Low prices for agricultural products and the high cost of transportation in the forties worked definitely against agricul-

[2] Frederick A. Buechel, *The Commerce of Agriculture* (New York, 1926), p. 376; Connor, *op. cit.*, pp. 130-7.

ture and favored sheep-raising in the West. The price of wheat
and flour in New York from 1840 to 1846 averaged nearly 40
per cent lower than from 1836 to 1839. In Chicago wheat was
generally less than $.60 a bushel and in 1843 sold for $.20; while
hogs in Cincinnati in 1842-43 sold for $1.75 to $2.50 per hundred
pounds and beef brought $2.25 to $3.25. Prices in Chicago were
about the same. It cost $.20 a bushel to ship wheat from Buffalo
to New York City by way of the Erie Canal, while a pound of
wool could be transported from Illinois to Boston for between
$.02 and $.03 cents. With wool varying from $.23 to $.53 a
pound according to quality, the price of one pound would carry
nine to twenty pounds to market. It was profitable to grow wool
two hundred miles from a shipping point when a team of horses
could haul one thousand dollars' worth to market.[3]

Another factor favoring sheep-raising in the West was the
difference in wool production costs. From 1840 to 1860 the estimated cost of keeping sheep in the West was only about half as
great as in the East. This was due to the low cost of range stock,
the small expense of herding, and lower land values, grass and
water often being free.[4] In the early forties sheep increased
rapidly in the region west of the Allegheny Mountains, and the
cheaper western wool was shipped to the Atlantic seaboard in
sufficient quantities to offer serious competition with that of the
East. In the late forties and early fifties there was a general shift
of the sheep industry into the middle western states. This shift
to the westward was accompanied by a partial abandonment of
the enterprise in the eastern states and its gradual and general
adaptation in the West, rather than by a rapid increase in the
total number of sheep. Between 1846 and 1850 thousands of
sheep were slaughtered in the eastern states [5] for their pelts and

[3] *Niles Register*, XXIX, 166, XXXIII, 155, XXXVI, 399, LXIV, 254; *Report of the Secretary of the Treasury*, 1836, p. 306.
[4] *Report of the Secretary of Agriculture*, 1862, pp. 303-4.
[5] Large numbers of sheep were sacrificed in Ohio in 1844-50 because of a
temporary shortage in feed and a slump in wool prices. *Prairie Farmer*, X, 37.

tallow, or sold in droves to rendering plants. There was a shift of emphasis in the East from the wool-producing type of sheep to the mutton type.

Against certain handicaps, the sheep industry advanced into the West slowly. Eastern sheep were acclimated in the West with difficulty, some estimates being that as many as 50 per cent driven into the prairie states from the East died the first year. While 50 per cent may have been somewhat high, there were heavy losses, due in part to carelessness, lack of shelter, and poor feed. The price of other agricultural products was on the upward trend, the average price of farm products other than wool averaging 32 per cent higher from 1847 to 1859 than in the seven preceding years. There also occurred a decrease in the general cost of transportation, that on grain being greater than on wool. There was also a tendency to substitute other farm activities for sheep, one of the more important being dairying. The wool clip of the United States in 1840 amounted to 36,000,000 pounds, increasing to 52,500,000 in 1850, and to 60,250,000 in 1860. Part of this increase in wool production is accounted for by the increase in the average weight of the clip per head. It was a trifle under 2 pounds in 1840 and was 2.5 pounds in 1850, increasing to 2.6 pounds in 1860. From 1850 to 1860 the number of sheep east of the Allegheny Mountains declined from 7,900,000 to 6,500,000 or nearly 22 per cent.[6]

During the first half of the decade between 1860 and 1870 there occurred a rapid increase in the number of sheep in the United States, caused by the increased demand for wool brought on by the Civil War. The industry made a rapid advance in the West where free pasture was plentiful and little capital was necessary to make a start, other than that needed for the actual purchase of sheep. Following a sharp slump in wool prices at the close of the Civil War, the sheep business was back to normal again by 1870, and following that year the outstanding charac-

[6] *Report of the Secretary of Agriculture*, 1862, pp. 303-34.

A SHEPHERD OF THE MOUNTAINS

Courtesy of the Montana Wool Growers Association.

teristic of the sheep industry was its further shift westward into the area of cheap land. The total number of sheep in the United States increased from 28,478,000 in 1870 to more than 42,000,000 in 1880. The figures for the West show an increase from 4,666,000 to 18,233,000 for the same period.[7]

I

EARLY SHEEP-RAISING IN THE NORTHWEST

DURING the early years of the development of the cattle industry in the territories of Dakota, Wyoming, and Montana, the sheep industry, while not as important, developed along with it, sheep being brought in from the south and west.[8] The area, with its dry atmosphere, nutritious grasses, coulées, and ravines affording shelter, was as well, if not even better suited, for sheep as for cattle. The sheep industry producing wool and mutton, with its ability to utilize inferior range lands and offering opportunity for men of small means, lying close to good foundation stock, gradually gained momentum, even promising to rival the cattle business in certain areas. The sheep industry in the Northwest began and continued on a different basis than in the East. In most cases it was adopted as a sole or major enterprise, on a ranching basis, with flocks of from two to five thousand.[9]

[7] In 1890 the total number of sheep was 40,876,000, with 19,203,000 in the West, while in 1900 the figures were 36,853,000, of which 23,669,000 were in the West. These figures include the Pacific Coast area as well as the region east of the Rocky Mountains. *U. S. Census Report for 1900*, V, 708; *Report of the Secretary of Agriculture*, 1870, p. 48.

[8] Sheep were driven into western Montana and Wyoming from Oregon and California, while New Mexico on the south was drawn on also for foundation stock. By 1869 two million sheep were reported within the limits of the Territory of Colorado, more than half the number being located in the northern area between Denver and the Wyoming boundary. *Denver Tribune*, April 13, 1869; *Cheyenne Daily Leader*, June 19, 1868, April 15, 1869; *Annual Report of the Commissioner of the General Land Office*, 1869, p. 153; Connor, *op. cit.*, pp. 137-40.

[9] *U. S. Census Report for 1880*, III, 991. Some early cattlemen ran both cattle and sheep, herding the sheep on the rocky and sparsely grassed areas. Alvin T. Steinel, *History of Agriculture in Colorado, 1858-1926* (State Board of Agriculture: Denver, Col., 1926), pp. 140-50.

Sheep appeared on the assessment lists of Montana as early as 1866, and on those of Wyoming in 1870. With the completion of the Union Pacific Railroad across southern Wyoming in 1869, herds of sheep were moved rapidly into the Laramie Plains area around Cheyenne. In that year J. S. Maynard shipped a large herd of fine-wooled Merinos to Cheyenne over the Union Pacific. By 1870 a good start had been made as in the census report for that year Wyoming was listed with 6,409 sheep, 6,000 of which were in Carbon County, and Montana with 2,204 head, 1,400 of them being in Beaverhead County. Wyoming reported a wool clip of thirty thousand pounds.[3]

Sheep from California, Utah, Oregon, New Mexico, and Nebraska arrived on the ranges of Montana, Wyoming, and in the Black Hills area of Dakota in considerable numbers during the seventies. Poindexter and Orr, cattle ranchers, located a flock of 2,467 on Blacktail Deer Creek, Montana, in 1871, driving them in from California, and Robert Ford and Thomas Dunn located a flock on the Sun River.[4] A Montana editor, writing late in 1875, reported the arrival of a flock from Oregon, brought in by the Seaborn brothers of the lower Smith's River Valley, Meagher County. "These gentlemen started early and have spent the summer on the road traveling slowly, their sheep in consequence are in good condition to stand the change of climate."[5] The same editor, writing a few months later, in the spring of 1876, reported that "Messers Crombaugh and Burt are so well pleased with the manner in which their sheep have wintered on Smith's River Valley that they have decided to drive 15,000

---

[3] *Butte Miner*, Holiday edition, January 1, 1889, p. 105; *Cheyenne Daily Leader*, June 24, 1869; *Annual Report of the Commissioners of the General Land Office*, 1869, p. 153; Osgood, *Day of the Cattleman*, p. 189; Steinel, *op. cit.*, p. 146; *U. S. Census Report for 1870*, volume on Industry and Wealth, pp. 196-7, 284-5.

[4] *Rocky Mountain Husbandman*, April 2, 1885; *Report of the Commissioner of Agriculture*, 1871, pp. 431-47; Maude E. Felter, *The Beginnings of the Range and Ranch Business of Montana* (Master's Thesis, Dept. of History, University of Iowa: Iowa City, Iowa, 1924), p. 14.

[5] *Rocky Mountain Husbandman*, December 2, 1875.

head from their ranches near Red Bluffs, California, to Montana this season." [6]

The first herd of sheep to be located on the Yellowstone in eastern Montana was brought in in the fall of 1876 by J. G. Burgess. The herd of fourteen hundred was located on the present site of Miles City. Another flock numbering slightly over one thousand was brought in by George M. Miles in the fall of 1877, who reported that the increase had been sufficient to pay costs, leaving the wool clip as a profit. The Montana Wool Growers Association was formed at Helena, September 20, 1876.[7] In 1878 John Healy of San Francisco, agent for a California company, established a depot at Helena for the grading and buying of wool.[8]

While small lots of sheep were brought into southern Wyoming from the south and west in the late sixties, sheep-ranching as an industry did not develop until the early seventies. At that time E. M. Post and James A. Moore were important sheepmen in the vicinity of Cheyenne. Extensive sheep ranches were located in the Big Horn Valley and in the valley of the North Platte. In the Black Hills area of Wyoming were two large herds, one numbering twenty-seven hundred on Oak Creek and one of some four thousand on Sun Creek.[9] The Laramie County Stock Growers Association, including both sheep and cattle ranchers, was organized in 1873 with ten members. In 1879 the name was changed to the Wyoming Stock Growers Association. Its object as stated in the by-laws was "to advance the interests of stock-growers and dealers in live stock of all kinds within the territory." [10]

The pioneer farmers of the Territory of Dakota in their early

[6] *Ibid.*, April 6, 1876.

[7] *Rocky Mountain Husbandman*, October 10, 1876, June 14, 1877; *Butte Daily Miner*, Holiday edition, January 1, 1889; M. S. Alderson, *History of Bozeman, Montana* (Bozeman, 1882), p. 71.

[8] *Helena Independent*, February 19, 1878.

[9] *Cheyenne Daily Leader*, January 16, 1874, November 3, 7, 1876; *Annual Report of the Territorial Governor of Wyoming to the Secretary of the Interior*, 1878, Part I, 1131.

[10] *Proceedings*, Wyoming Stock Growers Association, 1915, p. 61; *List of Members, By-Laws. etc., of the Wyoming Stock Growers Association*, 1886, p. 21.

practice of mixed farming introduced sheep into the southeastern portion of the territory. Newton Edmunds, former governor of the territory, located a small herd on his farm near Yankton in the late sixties. The census of 1870 reported 1,901 sheep in the territory, most of which were in the southeastern area.[11] Sheep were not introduced as a range enterprise in the Territory of Dakota until after 1878, and even then the Black Hills area was the only section where sheep-ranching developed extensively. Among the early sheep ranchers in the Black Hills were J. D. Hale, who located a flock of three thousand on Morris Creek in 1879, and William Lewis, who drove in a flock of more than two thousand on Box Elder Creek the same year. Several smaller herds were scattered through the hills region of Dakota.[12] In 1880 about fifteen thousand head were driven into the Black Hills, eight thousand coming from Wyoming and seven thousand from Nebraska. The total number of farm and range sheep in Dakota was 85,244, of which 23,143 were located on ranches in southwestern Dakota.[13]

In 1880 the Territory of Wyoming contained a total of 450,225 sheep, 364,082 of which were located in the southeastern portion, 75,564 in the western area and 10,579 in the northeast. It was estimated that approximately 40,000 head had been driven or shipped out of the territory that year, while 96,000 had been brought in. Montana reported 279,277 sheep in 1880, 138,877 of which were in the central portion of the territory, with 88,691 in the western area. In 1878 one company drove 30,000 head into Montana from California. In 1880 a total of 136,500 were brought into the territory, of which approximately 72,000 came from California.[14]

[11] *Sioux City Weekly Journal,* October 5, 1868; *Yankton Weekly Dakotian,* September 14, 1869; Foster, "Outline of History of Dakota," pp. 26-7; *U. S. Census Report for 1870,* Volume on Agriculture, p. 66.
[12] *Black Hills Weekly Pioneer,* January 1, 1882; *Yankton Press and Dakotian,* November 24, 1879, February 19, 1880.
[13] *U. S. Census Report for 1880,* III, 67.
[14] *U. S. Census Report for 1880,* III, 59-84. Sheep could be purchased in

While some of the early sheep ranchers ran their sheep on an open-range basis, the general policy followed was to keep hay for emergency feeding. An English traveler writing in 1883 made the following observation: "Sheep are delicate animals as compared with cattle and horses and of course cannot be allowed to run wild as other stock. But if properly handled, with hay for winter feeding, the rancher will get more profit out of his three to five thousand sheep than from the same money invested in cattle." [15]

II

THE EXPANSION OF SHEEP-RANCHING

WHILE railroad construction and the removal of the Indian barrier [16] opened up an enormous area of unsettled and unused country and set the stage primarily for the great cattle boom of the eighties, the sheep industry expanded and developed also. Indeed, general conditions in the early eighties were as ideal for the development of the sheep industry as for cattle. The financial depression of the seventies was over and capital, both foreign and domestic, was available at reasonable rates of interest. Range sheep were plentiful and cheap, while free range lands could easily be obtained, offering opportunities for men with little capital. Many small cattlemen, unable to compete with the large-scale cattle industry as it developed, went into sheep-ranching.

California for from $1.50 to $2.00 per head. A drive took two years, the wool clip practically paying expenses. They were driven in by the thousands in the late seventies and early eighties.

[15] Major W. Shepherd, *Prairie Experiences in Handling Cattle and Sheep,* (New York, 1885), pp. 3-4.

[16] The region was officially evacuated in 1880 and 1881, when the tribes were gradually moved to the Standing Rock reservation in Dakota. The Northern Pacific Railroad arrived at the present site of Miles City early in 1882. It reached Billings in August of that year and met the western extension at Gold Creek, Montana, fifty miles west of Helena in 1883. The Union Pacific Railroad began constructing a line northward from Corinne, Utah, to Garrison, Montana, and crossed the Montana line in 1880. A branch line was then extended from Garrison to join the Northern Pacific at Butte. *Cheyenne Daily Leader,* May 12, July 7, 11, 1876; *Miles City Weekly Press,* June 4, 1881, April 14, August 7, 1882.

The Indian hostilities of 1876 and 1877, followed by the Black Hills gold rush, attracted attention to the Northwest. While extravagant claims were made for cattle-ranching during the boom period from 1880 to 1886, writers were also pointing out the advantages of sheep in the Northwest. R. H. Clendenning of Martindale, Montana, writing in October, 1879, gave a glowing account of the success of his sheep ranch that he had owned less than a year. He reported taking in more than four thousand dollars on a five-thousand-dollar investment.[2] Regular yearly profits of from 25 to 35 per cent on investments were reported in the Yellowstone Valley in 1880-81.[3] A reliable observer writing in 1881 described portions of Wyoming and Montana as a "sheep-grower's paradise" where wool could be produced as cheaply as any place in the world, and which soon would be famous for its flocks and wool. He reported average profits of from 25 to 30 per cent per year, some sheepmen making as much as 60 per cent on their investment.[4] An English traveler in Montana and Wyoming in 1884 reported numerous advantages for the sheep rancher: "Men with small capital will find it more profitable to keep sheep than cattle as there is a steady demand for fine wool and mutton."[5]

A Black Hills editor, writing in January, 1882, reported a rapid increase in sheep in that region after 1878, listing ten ranchers with from two to six thousand head in 1881, while more than eight thousand head had been brought into the Hills area that year. The total number of sheep in the Hills district on March 17, 1884, was reported as eighty-five thousand, Lawrence County having almost two-thirds of the total.[6] The Marquis de Mores, the French nobleman who established a meat-packing establishment

[2] *Rocky Mountain Husbandman,* October 10, 1879.
[3] *Climate, Soil and Resources of the Yellowstone Valley* (St. Paul, Minn., 1882), pp. 70-75.
[4] Brisbin, *The Beef Bonanza,* chap. viii, 93-131.
[5] Shepherd, *op. cit.,* pp. 4-8, 20-7.
[6] *Black Hills Weekly Pioneer,* January 1, 1882; *Turner County Herald* (Hurley, D. T.), May 10, 1883, March 17, 1884.

at Medora, Dakota, as an experiment in 1883, wishing to sell mutton to his clients, began to run sheep on shares for his plant among the ranchers near Medora in the spring and summer of that year. According to some accounts, he handled as many as twelve thousand head in this way. The plan collapsed with the failure of the packing enterprise in 1885.[7]

A Montana editor in the spring of 1884 estimated the number of sheep in the territory at 524,440, with a wool clip of 2,637,000 pounds,[8] while a Montana almanac estimated the number at 362,776 in 1882, 465,667 in 1883, and 593,896 in 1884.[9] In 1886 J. P. Woohlman, the territorial auditor, reported 968,298 sheep.[10] The number of sheep in Wyoming Territory in 1886 was estimated at 875,000.[11] By 1881 the number of sheep assessed in Montana Territory exceeded the number of cattle. Meagher County, the leading cattle county in that year, was the leading sheep county as well. In Wyoming by 1884 sheep predominated in the western counties of Uinta, Fremont, and Sweetwater and were important in the other counties of the territory.[12]

After the disastrous winter of 1886-87, cattle-ranching as an open-range enterprise broke down completely in the Northwest. Many large cattle companies went into the hands of the receiver in the summer of 1887. In some sections heavy shipments during the summer and fall practically cleared the range, and many of those who remained pared down their herds to what they considered a point of safety. The difficulties of the cattle business were further intensified by declining prices and the pressure of granger farmers and sheep ranchers.[13]

As the cattlemen moved out, sheepmen moved in their herds

[7] *Medora Bad Lands Cowboy*, November 13, 20, 1884; *Mandan Weekly Pioneer*, Immigration edition, January 4, 1884; *Dickinson Press*, July 7, 1886.
[8] *Rocky Mountain Husbandman*, March 20, 1884.
[9] *Anaconda Standard Almanac* (Anaconda, Mont., 1894), p. 80.
[10] *First Annual Report of the Montana Bureau of Agriculture, Labor and Industry*, 429.
[11] Osgood, *Day of the Cattleman*, p. 230.
[12] Ibid., pp. 189, 230, 233.
[13] *Rocky Mountain Husbandman*, March 17, 1887.

to many ranges that were no longer capable of supporting herds of cattle. In fact, many portions of the Northwest were better suited to sheep than to cattle, since there was considerable rough inferior range land, wide areas of which were covered with salt sage, distasteful to cattle, that sheep would crop with relish the entire winter, keeping in good flesh. While some of the cattle operators had been gradually shifting to sheep even before the hard winter,[14] many of them now went into the sheep business. One rancher, in describing the process, said, "As most of our neighbors moved out and left us, sheepmen moved in on our lands and were often hard to handle." [15] Gibson and Carpenter, pioneer cattlemen of Montana, after heavy losses in the winter of 1886-87, sold the remnants of their herds and crossing the Missouri River, entered the sheep business, and soon became the largest sheepmen in that section of the territory.[16] T. N. Howell, coming into Wyoming from California in 1888, located a sheep ranch on the Stinking Water River and by 1892 was running ten thousand head of sheep. "Ours used to be a great cattle country," observed Otto Franc, a former "cattle king," "but it is mostly sheep now and they are driving the cattle out. I used to run 20,000 cattle on my range, now I run 1,200." [17]

In the decade from 1886 to 1896 cattle herds in the Northwest increased in number and decreased in size, the owners depending more upon winter feeding and less upon the open range. During the decade the number of cattle in Wyoming decreased from 900,000 to 300,000, the valuation shrinking from $14,651,125 to $3,732,558.[18] The sheep in the territory increased from 875,000

[14] Clay, *My Life on the Range*, pp. 222-4.
[15] The Warren Livestock Company, whose herds at first were largely cattle, by 1884 had only 3,000 head of cattle and horses and nearly 25,000 sheep. In 1889 it had 2,500 cattle, 2,000 horses, and 90,000 sheep. It owned all the water in the boundaries of the land it controlled and its meadows were securely fenced. *Report of the Secretary of Agriculture*, 1889, p. 267.
[16] *Report of the Helena Board of Trade* (Helena, Mont., 1887), pp. 31-2.
[17] *Billings Gazette*, July 18, 1899.
[18] William A. Richards, *Message to the Fourth State Legislature of Wyoming*, January 12, 1897.

in 1886 to 3,327,000 in 1900, jumping to 4,580,453 in 1909.[19]
In 1898 the number of cattle and sheep reported in Big Horn
County, Wyoming, was 32,605 and 55,489. Two years later, according to a reliable report, there were 21,810 cattle in the county,
while the number of sheep had increased to 387,014.[20]

The decline in cattle was not so marked in Montana in the
years following 1886, but the increase in sheep was equally
apparent. In 1886 the assessment lists showed 663,716 cattle and
968,298 sheep. By 1893 the figures were 570,931 for cattle and
2,254,527 for sheep, while by 1900 the figures were 678,528
and 3,552,527. North and South Dakota, reporting 136,413
and 238,448 sheep in 1890, listed a total of 958,000 in 1900, of
which 507,000 were in the Black Hills area of South Dakota.[21]

The early sheep in the Southwest and Pacific regions came
from a combination of the degenerate mongrel coarse-wooled
Mexican breed, a survival of early Spanish importations, with the
later long-wooled common sheep of Spain and with some of what
were called Spanish Merino. The flockmasters of these areas
gradually improved their herds with Merinos, most of which
were brought in from the older wool-growing sections of the
United States. Early sheep brought into the Northwest were
Mexican stock from Colorado and New Mexico, modified and
improved by Merino grades driven in from California, Oregon,
and from the East.[22] In 1870 it was estimated that more than
80 per cent of all the sheep in the United States were Merino or

[19] *First Annual Report of the Montana Bureau of Agriculture, Labor and
Industry*, pp. 429-35. These figures based on assessment rolls vary somewhat
from those given in the *U. S. Census Report for 1900*, V, ccii-cciii, 466-7.

[20] W. D. Pickett, *Big Horn County, State of Wyoming* (1898), p. 17.

[21] *Anaconda Standard Almanac*, 1894, p. 80; *U. S. Census Report for 1890*,
III, pp. 591, 621-2; *U. S. Census Report for 1900*, V, ccii-cciii, 446-67.
The development of the sheep industry reached its high point in the United States
in 1885, after which there was a gradual decline in numbers. The rapid increase
in the West offset the pronounced decline in other areas. The number of sheep
in the United States decreased from around 43,000,000 in 1884 to less than
37,000,000 in 1900. The increase for the West for the period was approximately
4,500,000. Connor, "Brief History of the Sheep Industry in the U. S.," p. 139.

[22] Connor, *op. cit.*, pp. 119-24; *U. S. Census Report for 1900*, V, ccii-cciii.

Merino grades.[23] By 1880 more than nine-tenths of the sheep in the Northwest approximated more or less closely the Merino standard, and three-fourths of the sheep in Wyoming Territory were bred from the original Mexican ewes crossed with Merino and, to a less extent, with Cotswold rams. In Montana Territory the sheep were a mixture of Merino and, to some extent, Cotswold and Southdown bred on the original Mexican stock.[24]

III

PROFITS AND PRICES

THE DECREASE in the number of sheep in various sections of the country and the decline in the price of wool, together with the rapid increase in urban population, better transportation facilities, and the development of the refrigerator-car, caused a shift of emphasis to mutton types to meet the growing demand. There was an appreciable increase in mutton rams in the range country of the Northwest immediately following the period of low wool prices that began in the middle eighties. The shift was especially rapid after 1893. From 1900 to 1910 the tendency to increase the mutton breeds was marked. In 1900 30 per cent of the flocks in the range country of the Northwest were of the mutton type. By 1910 60 per cent of the rams and 30 per cent of the ewes were of mutton breeds.[25]

The weight of wool clip per fleece in the United States increased from about two pounds in 1840 to three pounds in 1860 and by 1870 had reached an average of nearly four pounds. Although the average clip of the early herds in the Northwest was

[23] The excellence of the Merino lay in the fineness of its wool, the weight of each individual fleece, the animal's ability to endure extreme cold, its unequaled docility and its ability to exist on the coarsest food. The Merino does not deteriorate easily, the offspring frequently surpassing the parent stock. *U. S. Census Report for 1900*, V, ccii-cciv.

[24] *Ibid.*

[25] *Breeders' Gazette*, December 30, 1915; E. A. Carman, H. A. Heath and John Minto, *Special Report on the Sheep Industry* (U. S. Department of Agriculture: 1892), p. 87.

not high, it increased rapidly as emphasis was placed upon the Merino type. A Wyoming editor, describing activities in the Cheyenne area in 1881, said, "Mr. E. M. Post is quite an extensive sheep grower. His herd is made up of Mexican sheep which he is crossing with the Merino. The wool of the Mexican breeds is coarse and averages less than three pounds per fleece. The cross-breeds shear on the average three pounds each, the first year the wool being of a much better quality. The second year they will run from four to five pounds per fleece." [2] The average wool clip in the United States in the middle eighties was approximately seven pounds per fleece. In 1900 Montana reported 4,383,568 fleeces and 30,437,829 pounds of wool, averaging about seven pounds per fleece; Wyoming reported 3,390,571 fleeces averaging about eight pounds per fleece; South Dakota averaged a little more than six pounds; while North Dakota averaged about six and one-half pounds per fleece.[3]

The great majority of sheep were shorn once a year, usually in June. The shearing was ordinarily done without previous washing, and dipping usually followed. At first extra men were employed for shearing, who often received as much as eight to ten cents per fleece. As sheep-ranching expanded in the Northwest, bands of shearers began to come in from New Mexico and Colorado and sheared for five cents and sometimes for as low as three cents per fleece. "The shearers are a strange lot," said Brisbin, "and are every year becoming more numerous. They cut a fleece with marvelous rapidity and want little else than their food and clothing. They stroll in bands hunting sheep to shear and there appears to be a strange fascination about their nomadic life. Sheep shearing is now a regular business . . . and there are now men who do little else for a living." [4]

[2] *Cheyenne Daily Leader*, September 14, 1881; Brisbin, *The Beef Bonanza*, pp. 130-3.
[3] *U. S. Census Report for 1900*, V, 679-684.
[4] Brisbin, *op. cit.*, pp. 118-20; *Cheyenne Daily Leader*, May 28, June 9, 14, 1870, June 24, 1880, July 23, 1881.

Wool prices, after slumping in the late sixties, advanced considerably in the early seventies, after which occurred a steady decline lasting until the late nineties, interrupted only by a temporary rise in the early eighties. The average price per pound in the eastern markets for fine, medium, and coarse wool for the five-year period ending in 1875 was $.516, $.506 and $.457. For the ten years 1887-97 the same grades averaged $.261, $.294 and $.248 per pound, while from 1897 to 1907 the price averaged $.305, $.323 and $.292 respectively.[5] A Montana editor in the late nineties made the following observation: "There is as much optimism among sheepmen as there was among the earlier cattlemen and wool prices make sellers happy."[6]

During the seventies much of the wool from the Northwest was shipped to eastern markets from Cheyenne, Wyoming. After the extension of the Northern Pacific Railroad through Montana many of the sheepmen of northern Wyoming trailed their sheep into Montana to avoid freighting the wool.[7] T. N. Howell and Son moved their flocks for this reason and by 1892 were running ten thousand head of sheep within easy freighting distance from Billings. By the end of the nineties Billings had become one of the largest wool markets in the West. In June, 1899, the local paper was full of announcements of large wool clips being sold there. David Dockie from the Greybull River sold 50,000 pounds while the Newton Brothers, James F. Howell, Taylor and Hogg, and R. B. Heritage marketed shipments of from 20,000 to 35,000 pounds.[8]

Estimates of annual losses among range sheep where hay was

[5] The greater part of this last increase in price was due to the tariff of 1897, which followed three years of free wool under the tariff of 1894. For the three years 1895-6-7 the price was $.191, $.211 and $.19. Other factors influencing price were the increase in value of general farm products other than wool, better transportation facilities, and lower freight rates. Connor, "Brief History of the Sheep Industry in the U. S.," pp. 145-50.

[6] *Billings Gazette*, June 30, 1899.

[7] *Rocky Mountain Husbandman*, January 17, 1877.

[8] *Billings Gazette*, April 14, 1892, June issues, 1899.

kept for emergency feeding vary from 7 to 10 per cent. The average loss among adult sheep during a term of years was 9 per cent. Causes of losses other than those due to changes in the price of wool and mutton were poisonous plants, predatory animals, snake bites, straying from the herd, and occasional protracted drought or unusually severe spring and winter storms. Scab was the most prevalent disease and caused a great deal of damage to both sheep and wool. Scab was brought in by trail sheep and was treated by dipping. H. F. Galen, a Montana sheep grower, drove thirty-five hundred sheep to his ranch from Nevada in the fall of 1876. He leased twenty-five hundred of them to the Smith brothers on Crow Creek, whose experience with sheep was rather limited, and the herd took the scab. Out of a lamb crop of twelve hundred almost eight hundred died and the whole flock produced only seven thousand pounds of wool. The flock was dipped in a solution of lye and tobacco which cured them.[9] Grub in the head and dropsy were also sources of limited losses.[10]

Losses were often heavy where the industry was conducted on an open-range basis and hay was not kept for emergency feeding. The winter of 1879-80 was the most severe ever experienced and losses from late spring storms when the sheep were in poor condition were large. More sheep were lost after March 15th than during the winter because of the lack of new grass. Losses were especially heavy among emigrant and diseased sheep. In Meagher County, Montana, where the open-range system was used to a considerable extent, losses were estimated as high as 80 per cent, while Gallatin County in the same territory, where many sheepmen kept hay, reported losses of only 10 per cent.[11] A Black Hills editor writing early in 1882 said: "Last winter's (1880-81) experience with sheep was not encouraging in the Black Hills area

[9] *Rocky Mountain Husbandman*, June 24, 1877.
[10] *U. S. Census Report for 1880*, III, 63; Buechel, *Commerce of Agriculture*, pp. 388-9.
[11] *Helena Daily Herald*, April 19, 1880; *Rocky Mountain Husbandman*, May 8, 1880.

of Dakota and Wyoming. Deep snows, low temperatures and the lack of hay caused losses of more than twenty percent." [12] The winter of 1881 and 1882, however, proved more disastrous to the sheep business than the previous one had been. Losses of as high as 50 per cent were reported in certain areas of the Black Hills.[13]

Profits in sheep-ranching, depending, of course, to some extent upon the prices of mutton and wool, were rather high. There were many ranchers and observers who felt that sheep, if properly handled, with hay for winter use, would make more profit for the rancher than the same amount of money invested in cattle. Statements of annual profit vary from 25 to as high as 60 per cent on money invested. R. B. Rumsey of Laramie Plains, Wyoming, for three years reported a net profit of 35 per cent. E. M. Post of Cheyenne reported a net profit of 60 per cent for a year on the money invested.[14] Willard Clark of Clark and Company, located eighteen miles from Laramie City, Wyoming, stated that in three years he could clear a herd and ranch worth twelve thousand dollars. While many of the reported profits were no doubt exaggerated, sheep-ranching in the Northwest, located as it was close to cheap foundation stock, with possibilities of free range, gave good returns on money invested.[15]

As a rule, early sheep ranchers, starting off as they often did

[12] *Black Hills Weekly Pioneer*, January 1, 1882.

[13] *Ibid.*, May 21, 1883; *Turner County Herald* (Hurley, D. T.), May 10, 1883.

[14] Statements of net profits for a single year may be very misleading since losses and misfortunes the following year could greatly reduce the percentage. Profits averaged over a period of years give a more accurate picture of the business.

[15] William H. Sutherlin, "Montana as an Agricultural Country," Holiday edition of *Butte Daily Miner*, January 1, 1889; *Rocky Mountain Husbandman*, April 6, 1876, January 18, June 14, 1877; Brisbin, *The Beef Bonanza*, pp. 114-5; Shepherd, *Prairie Experiences in Handling Cattle and Sheep*, pp. 3-7. The average sheep ranch with a herd of five thousand sheep had an outfit investment somewhat as follows: 640 acres of land at around $800; buildings and fences, $1500; equipment in vehicles, harness, tools, etc., $750; horses and dogs, $750; sundries, $200, making a total of $4000. Add to that five thousand sheep at $2.00 to $3.00 each and the investment amounted to from $14,000 to $18,000. In addition in most cases were several thousand acres of "free range."

SHIPPING WOOL ON THE SHEEP FRONTIER

The last of the bull teams, delivering 96,000 pounds of wool to the railroad at Big Timber, Montana, 1892.
Courtesy of the Montana Wool Growers Association.

with a small amount of cash, were careless about their buildings. A Mr. Merriam of Colorado Springs, Wyoming, writing in 1881, stated that he could start a suitable herd with range provided, for from five hundred to one thousand dollars. He would, of course, have to build his own stables, corrals, and ranch-house.[16] An English traveler, writing in 1883, made the following observations regarding the general appearance of sheep ranches:

The usual ranches have poor buildings built of logs joggled together at the ends. They are very inferior and seldom have more than two rooms, even one room is common. The ready excuse offered for not improving his home is that it is temporary, though the man and his family may occupy it for several years. The stable is a mere shed, with walls of thin poles badly put together. Some of the ranches have better buildings, with substantial houses, with adequate stables for horses and sheds for sheep.[17]

IV

THE STRUGGLE BETWEEN SHEEPMEN AND CATTLEMEN

THE STEADY growth of sheep-ranching and the final shift of emphasis from cattle to sheep in the Northwest did not occur without a struggle, as keen feeling and prejudice between sheepmen and cattlemen existed from the first. As early as 1874 Joseph McCoy reported that conflict between the two groups was being waged in Colorado and Wyoming and that definite sides were being formed on the question as to whether or not the sheep or cattle industry should control the future of the West.[18] Cattle-owners resisted the increasing number of sheep because of the gradual overcrowding of the range, and because they claimed that the sheep not only killed the grass on their own range, but ruined the ranges over which they traveled. Cattle, it was said, were satisfied with crop-

---

[16] Brisbin, *op. cit.*, pp. 114-5.
[17] Shepherd, *op. cit.*, pp. 20-2.
[18] McCoy, *Historic Sketches of the Cattle Trade of the West and Southwest*, p. 379.

ping the grass to the crown, while sheep took the crown with the stock and left only the roots. What they did not eat they tramped down, often leaving the ground practically bare. Aside from the actual destruction of the range, sheep were accused of rendering the range valueless by an offensive odor which caused cattle to refuse to graze or drink on ranges crossed by them. Such were the grievances, real or fancied, of the cattlemen against the flock-masters.[2]

Since the "free range" belonged to the government, sheep-owners felt that they had had as much right to use it as did the cattlemen, and accordingly grazed their flocks over its wide areas, paying little attention to ranges claimed by cattlemen to be theirs because of priority rights and customs.[3] While each considered the other the aggressor, it was usually the cattleman who took the initiative in attempting to eliminate or at least restrict the activities of the sheepman, whom he considered an intruder. As a rule, both cattle and sheep associations deprecated strife and at various annual meetings constant references were made to the subject, cattlemen insisting that raids on sheep camps were made on individual responsibility and against the counsel of the organization.[4] Public

[2] *Wyoming Industrial Journal* (Cheyenne, Wyo.), November, 1900; Grace Lillian Marner, *The Range and Ranch Business in Wyoming, 1870-90* (Master's thesis, University of Iowa, Dept. of History: Iowa City, 1922), pp. 40-5; Felter, *Beginnings of the Range and Ranch Business in Montana, passim;* Steinel, *History of Agriculture in Colorado, 1858-1926,* pp. 147-52.

[3] Eastern Wyoming suffered considerably from these "loafer flocks," as they were sometimes called.

[4] Early organizations of ranchmen in the Northwest made no distinction between cattle and sheep owners, admitting both to membership. As antagonism developed between the two groups, the sheepmen withdrew and formed organizations of their own. The Montana Wool Growers Association was organized in September, 1877, while meetings of sheepmen are recorded in Wyoming in the eighties. Dakota sheepmen apparently had no association of their own, but were often members and attended meetings in the other two areas. County sheep associations were quite common in Wyoming and were active. *Helena Daily Herald,* September 19, 1877; *Rocky Mountain Husbandman,* September 24, 1877; *Cheyenne Daily Leader,* September 24, 1880, June 13, 1882; *Black Hills Weekly Pioneer,* January 1, 1882, March 17, 1884; Strahorn, *Handbook of Wyoming and Guide to the Black Hills and Big Horn Basin,* pp. 27-35; *Members and By-Laws of the Wyoming Stock Growers Association,* 1887.

sentiment on the ranges of the Northwest in the early years was prejudiced against the sheep-owner and strongly in favor of the cattleman. While this feeling was not always openly expressed, there invariably occurred an undercurrent of covert antagonism against the sheepman, accompanied by a feeling of sympathy for the aggressive cattle-owners.

Edward W. Smith of Evanston, Wyoming, giving testimony before the Public Lands Commission in behalf of the cattlemen, said:

Cattle and sheep ranges are held by suffrage and custom. There is now a law in the territory which prevents trespassing upon unoccupied ranges near settlements, but away from settlements the shot-gun is the only law; and sheep and cattlemen are engaged in constant warfare. The sheepmen are generally the aggressors. Their sheep destroy the grasses and the cattle will not graze on their land. If stock-growers could obtain absolute control of the ranges under United States law, the value of herds of both cattle and sheep would be materially increased . . . and peace and quiet would supersede the present turmoil.

A. T. Babbit, testifying before the same group, said, "Cattlemen usually respect one another's claims and rights, sheepmen are the aggressors." [5]

One writer quotes a cattleman whose testimony was expressive of the keen feeling against sheep ranchers: "The sheep herder is the worst blot on the state. He is no good and does much harm. . . . He fits out his wagon with a Mexican and a dog and several thousand sheep and away they go like an Egyptian scourge, eating the grass down to the ground and in sandy soils tramping it down so there are great regions where bunch grass once grew knee high, but where the country is now bare as a desert." [6] The commissioner of the general land office in 1898 reported that "next to

[5] "Report of the Public Lands Commission," *House Exec. Doc.*, 46th Cong., 2d Sess., XXII, No. 46, 548-50, 558. Edward W. Smith was a member of the firm Beckwith, Quin and Company, who were bankers, merchants, and cattle-dealers of long standing at Evanston, Wy.

[6] Ralph Julian, *Our Great West* (New York, 1893), pp. 368-70.

330 FRONTIERS OF THE NORTHWEST

fires, sheep grazing was found to constitute the most serious difficulty to be considered in administering certain of the reserves." [7]

In the eighties and nineties there occurred in Wyoming a series of struggles between sheep and cattlemen, often so prolonged and bloody as practically to constitute "range wars." Attacks on herds of sheep were numerous and were often made against flocks in charge of Mexicans, newly arrived immigrants from Ireland or Scotland, or farm boys from the East, employed by the owners of the sheep, who were seldom with their herds. These herders as a rule knew nothing of the range feuds between the cattle and sheepmen. They were not generally informed by their employers of the dangers of the work, since it was difficult to get good herders under the unfavorable circumstances. Ignorant oftentimes of the cattleman's opposition, the herder would take his flocks to the best grazing lands he could find in the vicinity. If they happened to be on a range claimed by a cattle rancher, the flockmaster might shortly receive word that another herder was missing. The newspapers as a rule carried very little news of the deaths of herders, as the sheepmen were not especially anxious to have the stories known, and the cattle-owners responsible for the murder certainly were not going to advertise it. Only the more serious tragedies were published, and for many of these a single short paragraph was the amount of space given by the local press.[8]

Thousands of sheep were poisoned, clubbed to death, or had their throats cut. Flocks were driven over cliffs, and on various occasions large herds were driven from southern Wyoming into Colorado. The herders were held while the sheep were killed and were warned not to return. Groups of cattlemen armed and sent out scouts to locate the sheep camps. The sheepmen recruited forces to combat them but were usually overcome. Herders were often bound to trees while their sheep were killed and many of the

[7] *Annual Report of the Commissioner of the General Land Office*, 1898, XIV.
[8] For examples *see Cheyenne Daily Leader*, January 4, 5, August 4, 1887, July 2, 1907.

trails leading from Wyoming were strewn with carcasses of dead sheep.[9] The struggle not only meant loss of animals but often involved that of human lives. The mountain gorges and plains of Wyoming contain the bones of many a sheep herder who was murdered at night as he slept in his isolated wagon or tent and the evidence hidden as the camp was burned or the body thrown into some deep valley or chasm. Along the roadside on the north fork of Buffalo Creek, eighty-six miles northwest of Casper in the Big Horn Mountains, is the lonely grave of a sheep herder whose life was staked and lost in the struggle over the range. At the head of the rock-covered mound is a weather-beaten board, perhaps a foot long and six inches wide, upon which is carved with a pocket-knife: L. Henderlight, died June 17, 1904.[10] This grave and others not so well marked stand as symbols of the bloody struggle that took place in the sheep and cattle country of Wyoming.

One reliable writer states that in the years from 1893 to 1903 three scores of men were killed and five times that number were wounded in the conflict that extended pretty well over the state.[11] "Despised and rejected of men" might well have been applied to the flockmasters of Wyoming as far as the cattlemen were concerned.

In Montana adjustments between the two interests were made without a serious struggle. This was due to the fact that the cattlemen had never occupied the prominent position in Montana that they had in Wyoming. The mining and agricultural interests were far too strong to allow such domination, and, second, the

[9] Love, "History of the Cattle Industry in the Southwest," pp. 12-5; McNeeley, "Conditions of the Livestock Industry of Colorado and Wyoming," *Sixth* and *Seventh Annual Reports of the Bureau of Animal Husbandry, 1889-90,* pp. 438-40; Steinel, *History of Agriculture in Colorado, 1858-1926,* pp. 147-52; *Cheyenne Daily Leader,* files for 1885-1900; *House Exec. Doc.,* 50th Cong., 1st Sess., No. 232, 230-3.

[10] Coutant, "Notes of an Unfinished History of Wyoming."

[11] Love, *op. cit.,* pp. 15-6; W. H. Ogden, "The Toll of the Sheep," *Everybody's Magazine,* XXIII, pp. 263-348.

presence of newly opened Indian country in northern and eastern Montana made it possible for the open range to continue for some time undisturbed by the small farmer and small rancher. The local press in western Montana gave information regarding the rapid growth of the sheep industry in that area and told how sheep gradually crowded out many of the big cattle outfits without serious trouble or bloodshed. A Helena editor in the summer of 1870 wrote: "Sheep husbandry is making rapid strides in western Montana. In 1870 there were no sheep in the territory and now there are at least 200,000, nearly 50,000 being driven in last summer." [12] An editor in the Judith Basin of Montana, writing late in 1883, said: "Two years ago this region was a wilderness. Now almost every valuable location is taken up. It seems that here, as elsewhere in Montana, sheep are in fact crowding out large bunches of cattle. Within the past two years at least 30,000 sheep have been brought into a section where there are about 25,000 head of cattle." [13]

Brooks and Hilger, who ran both sheep and cattle in the Judith Basin, when interviewed by a Helena editor in December, 1883, were of the opinion that in a very short time cattle-owners would be forced to remove their herds to other sections as sheep would monopolize their ranges:

All sheepmen are now making permanent locations. They erect sheds, fences, cut hay and make other improvements, thus providing both food and shelter for their flocks. Large bands of cattle flourish best in those sections where the country is open to trail travel. Only in this way can they obtain water. The gradual appropriation of choice locations by sheepmen will make cattle raising on the present system so precarious as to entail such heavy losses that soon the large herds of cattle will be broken up as a measure of safety. [14]

By the spring of 1885 there were two sheep associations in the Judith Valley and it was reported that more than a million pounds

[12] *Helena Daily Herald*, August 14, 1879.
[13] *Mineral Argus* (Maiden, Mont.), December 20, 1883.
[14] *Ibid.*, December 20, 27, 1883.

of Montana wool had been exported by way of the Missouri River.[15] By 1902 an attempt was made by the Montana Stock Growers Association to move its headquarters from Miles City in eastern Montana to Helena in the western portion of the state, on the grounds that sheepmen were taking over many of the ranges of eastern Montana. The association decided by a close vote to continue its meetings in the eastern part of the state.[16] While sheep had increased rapidly in numbers in the Black Hills area of Dakota in the eighties and nineties, the sheepman was never enough of a competitor with the cattle operator to cause serious trouble.

The feeling between cattle and sheepmen was keen in southern Idaho, and came to a head in that area when the cattle ranchers claimed that the sheep growers were encroaching on their territory, objecting strenuously and even threatening the use of force. On February 16, 1896, two sheep herders were found shot to death in their wagon in Shoshone Basin in Cassia County. They had been dead several days, their sheep were widely scattered over the range, and their dogs, starved to the point of emaciation, were found tied to the wagon. Jack Davis, an employee of a large cattle outfit and known in the locality as "Diamondfield Jack," was suspected of the crime and was brought to trial for the murder. Although Davis had been seen in the area where the men had been killed and had evidently made numerous threats to kill sheepmen, the evidence was largely circumstantial and the authorities could produce no witnesses who had actually seen the shooting. However, the incriminating facts and circumstances were sufficient to cause the jury to find the defendant guilty of murder and he was sentenced to be hanged. The influence of the cattlemen who had worked hard for the acquittal of Davis, together with the lack of definite and conclusive proof, caused the sentence to be

[15] *Billings Herald*, October 13, April 26, 1884; *Mineral Argus*, March 6, 1885.

[16] Osgood, *Day of the Cattleman*, p. 255; *Stock Growers' Journal*, April 17, 1902.

changed to life imprisonment and later he was pardoned. The feeling of both sides was intense and the sheep group was much incensed at the turn of events.[17]

In the Northwest during the late nineties the passing of the large-scale cattle operator was accompanied by a rapid increase in the number of small ranchers, granger farmers, and sheepmen. The small-scale cattleman was often a farmer who had curtailed his agricultural activities to go into the cattle business. The governor of Wyoming in 1905 recognized the change, which was by that time complete in that state: "To-day our cattle are owned by 5,000 different stockmen and farmers instead of by a few hundred outfits." [18] The increase in number of cattle and sheepmen during this period necessitated the eventual adjustment of differences between the two groups. The process of adjustment was much more difficult in Wyoming than in Montana and the Dakotas, and was accompanied by a second period of conflict and bloodshed.

The cattlemen of the upper Shoshone River Valley in Wyoming in the spring of 1901 organized a Stockmen's Protective Association and discussed the matter of a division of range between the cattle and sheep interests. The general opinion seemed to favor a division of territory with the establishment of a "dead line" over which sheepmen should not be allowed to come. Threats were made at the time by both sides but no serious outbreak occurred. For the next two years the smoldering fires of hard feeling were restrained although there was danger of an outbreak at any moment.[19] Early in 1903 the possibility of the President of the United States appointing a special committee to investigate and to determine the respective rights of the two groups was widely discussed.[20]

[17] C. J. Brosnan, *History of the State of Idaho* (New York, 1935), pp. 240-1.
[18] *Message of Governor of Wyoming to the Eighth State Legislature,* January 11, 1903.
[19] *Wyoming Industrial Journal,* June, 1901.
[20] *Dakota Republican* (Vermillion, D. T.), January 13, 1903; *Thermopolis Record* (Thermopolis, Wy.), January 23, 1903.

Early in February, 1903, a band of men, armed and masked, attacked a large sheep camp in the Big Horn Valley. They killed or scattered the sheep and murdered the herders. This was the signal for the outbreak of a "range war" in Wyoming which lasted for nearly six years.[21] While the struggle was quite general throughout the grazing area, the conflict was keenest in the eastern and north central portions of the state. Bands of masked and armed horsemen terrorized various areas, shooting owners of flocks and their herds without warning. Sheep camps were burned and herds were dynamited or rim-rocked.[22] The climax of the struggle came at a time when the sheep industry was at its peak. In 1909 Wyoming was estimated to produce more wool and mutton than any other state in the Union.[23]

In April, 1909, a camp on Spring Creek in the Big Horn Basin, containing five thousand sheep belonging to two wealthy sheepmen, Joseph Emge and Joseph Allemand, who had been warned to stay out of the valley, was attacked after nightfall by about twenty armed men wearing masks. The owners of the herd and one herder were killed before they could surrender, the camp wagons were burned and the sheep slaughtered. The affair caused much excitement and the National Wool Growers Association said it was ready to subscribe $20,000 to back a prosecution. Several county associations offered $1,000 each.[24]

A grand jury took testimony and was in the process of deliberation when one of the witnesses committed suicide, leaving several letters which implicated a number of prominent cattlemen in the

[21] The controversy between cattle and sheepmen attracted considerable attention and was discussed in current periodicals. Examples of articles are as follows: R. S. Baker, "The Tragedy of the Range," *Century Magazine*, August, 1902; Charles Mickelson, "War For the Range," *Munsey's Magazine*, December, 1902; E. P. Snow, "Sheepmen and Cattlemen," *Outlook*, April 1, 1903.

[22] Lindsay, *Big Horn Basin*, pp. 232-3; Marner, *Range and Ranch Business in Wyoming*, pp. 45-50; *Dakota Republican*, February 17, 1903; *Thermopolis Record*, February 6, 13, March 11, 1903, June 4, 11, 25, 1904.

[23] *Wyoming Industrial Journal*, October, 1909.

[24] *Wyoming Industrial Journal*, May, 1909; *Big Horn County Rustler*, April 9, 16, 30, 1909; Lindsay, *op. cit.*, p. 233.

attack. Seven arrests were made early in May, one of the men
being George Sabin, owner of the Bay State ranch. After two of
the suspects turned state's evidence, the other five accused pleaded
guilty and were given penitentiary sentences of from three years
to life. The whole affair, promptly and ably handled by the civil
authorities, had a wholesome effect upon the range struggle. It
showed that public sentiment was on the side of law and order
and that crimes committed on the public range would be punished. After 1909 range difficulties in Wyoming rarely assumed
serious proportions.[25]

One who reads of the struggle between the two grazing groups
is apt to wonder why the sheepmen did not fight back by using
the same methods as were used against them. The answer is that
the cattlemen were in control and dominated the legislature, controlled the courts and intimidated grand juries and witnesses. The
sheepmen knew that to fight the cattlemen meant to fight the law
and they patiently waited until they were stronger in numbers
and sentiment had tended to shift to their side. By 1909 they
were well organized and were no longer willing to turn the other
cheek after being struck. They had a national association with
headquarters at Cheyenne and numerous local organizations. They
were able to influence elections at the polls and to influence the
makers of state laws. Their organizations offered liberal rewards
for those who molested their herds and their herders, and county
sheriffs and prosecuting attorneys did their best to win them. They
also allied themselves with the farmers against their common
enemy and the lawless opposition of the cattlemen gradually
ceased.[26] But just as the sheepman, with his plodding but determined methods, gradually crowded the cattleman back on the
range, another industry developed which slowly put an end to
large-scale sheep-ranching. Dry farming was responsible for a

[25] *Big Horn County Rustler*, May 7, 13, 27, 1909; *Denver Republican*, November 13, 1909; *Wyoming Industrial Journal*, November, 1909, June, 1910;
Lindsay, *op. cit.*, pp. 233-4.
[26] *Cheyenne Daily Leader*, April 6, 1909.

change in certain parts of Wyoming and other sections of the Northwest. Farming of this type meant smaller flocks and put an end to promiscuous grazing. It necessitated a change in procedure and methods.

V

THE SHEEP HERDER

WHILE much has been written regarding the cowboy and his activities, little attention has been paid to the man who tended the herds of sheep and he is far from being a glamorous figure. In fact, the general attitude toward a keeper of the flocks has been that he is a kind of freak, with some mental affliction, or he wouldn't be following the occupation. A writer on the subject of sheep recently pointed out that there are two theories regarding sheep herders: that herding sheep for six months will make any man crazy, or that he must have been "off balance" for that length of time to have been in a frame of mind to have considered such an occupation. The same writer tells of how an old Scotch herder from the sheep country of Montana compared the attitude toward a flockmaster in the hills of Scotland with the American attitude on the ranges of the West. As the herder brought his animals down from the Scottish hills to the valleys in the late autumn months, the observers would comment upon the noble shepherd bringing down his flock, while in the West a similar situation would bring forth an observation on the cracked herder bringing in his band of "woolies." [1]

Many stories have been told on the sheep herder and always at his expense. In the winter of 1884 a Montana editor in the heart of the sheep country told of an interview with a typical sheep herder. He first described the herder as a "queer freak of nature about forty years old with a full bearded face. His actions were premeditated and his steps were slow and deliberate and the

[1] Archer B. Gilfillan, *Sheep* (Boston, Mass., 1936), pp. 3-8.

appearance of the man's face was of a person in deep thought."
He was accompanied by his dog. The conversation ran as follows:

Editor: Hello, there. How are you?

Sheep herder: I've got all the black ones.

Editor: Pretty cold out to-day?

Sheep herder: I'd rather have two hundred and fifty sheep of my own
than two thousand on shares.

Editor: How far do you call it to Maiden?

Sheep herder: Here, Shep, round them up. (He sends dog after the
imaginary sheep.)

Editor: Well, I guess I'd better be going. Good-by.

Sheep herder: They have better sheep in Scotland.

After the editor was off a good distance, the herder shouted after
him: "I'll bet the tariff on wool will be raised next year." [2]

A sheep herder led a nomadic life, as a band of sheep would
consume the grass within a reasonable distance of a sheep camp in
four or five weeks, depending upon the condition of the range.
Then the herder with his wagon or pack horse moved on to fresh
pastures, accompanied by his ever-faithful dog. No doubt too
much emphasis has been placed on the queer and peculiar traits
of the sheep herder. The ones who remained after the first hard
winter were as a rule a rather select group, faithful to their employers and seldom deserting their flocks. In fact, they often risked
their lives during heavy storms to save their herds from danger.

VI

HORSE-RANCHING IN THE NORTHWEST

GROWING out of the local needs of cattlemen on their ranches and
of the transportation companies for freight and stage lines, some
emphasis was placed on the raising of horses in the Northwest in
the seventies, increasing in importance in the eighties. Many
ranchers raised horses in connection with their cattle and sheep

[2] *Mineral Argus,* February 28, 1884.

activities in sufficient numbers to satisfy their own needs. Brisbin, writing on the subject in 1881, said, "Horse growing on the plains has hardly been established as a business; nevertheless, something has been done, and the results show that it can be made immensely profitable." [1] In the late seventies several horse ranches were established in the southern portion of the Territory of Wyoming, two of the more important being those of Creighton and Alsop, and T. A. Kent. The former outfit, beginning with three hundred brood-mares of California stock, soon had a good-sized herd of yearlings, two- and three-year-olds, which it sold at a good profit. T. A. Kent also used California mares and purchased twenty stallions of good blood weighing from 1,200 to 1,650 pounds, at an average cost of seven hundred dollars each. Kent experimented by changing stallions and mixing blood in order to produce riding horses for the cattlemen, as well as racing and draught types. The base stock for most of the horse ranches were the tough wiry type spoken of by some as "American bronchos." Although close herding was followed, with little emphasis on feed or shelter, the horses and colts seemed to be fat and in good condition most of the time. By the close of the eighties there were large numbers of horse ranches in Wyoming, English outfits being especially active on the Laramie Plains.

In the seventies, horse-ranching began in western Montana, which later became one of the most important horse-producing areas of the West. Nelson Story, one of the early horse operators in the western part of the territory, started in the upper Yellowstone country in 1876 with two hundred head of California mares and soon had a herd of thirteen hundred horses. He sold large numbers of young horses each year at from fifty to seventy-five dollars each and would give buyers their choice of the herd at one hundred dollars a head. [2] One Edward Curly in three years claimed to have made $45,000 profit from an investment of

---

[1] Brisbin, *The Beef Bonanza,* pp. 130-45.
[2] *Ibid.,* pp. 140-5.

$48,000. In 1877 there were several horse ranches in the vicinity of Deer Lodge and the local press carried many references to their activities. The *Rocky Mountain Husbandman* for June 14, 1877, reported W. E. Larabie of Deer Lodge having a fine horse ranch with excellent animals, and J. S. Pemberton, who was specializing in race-horses, with a herd of several hundred head. J. N. York had just purchased a stallion from him for twelve hundred dollars. An advertisement in the same issue gave the prices for Pemberton's stallion service at fifteen, twenty and forty dollars. A Bozeman paper a week later described the formation of a joint stock association capitalized at $50,000 with shares at one hundred dollars each. County Treasurer M. C. Cannon was sponsoring the corporation, which planned to raise and deal in blooded horses.[3]

In 1877 the Territory of Montana was reported to have 26,466 horses valued at $851,674, which had more than doubled by 1880, Gallatin County alone having 8,033 head. C. E. Williams of Helena had a horse farm of fine blooded animals and there were fifteen other horse ranches in that vicinity dealing in blooded horses. An editor in western Montana, writing in January, 1881, said, "The breeding of horses in the territory is becoming an important factor in our stock interests. Very few horses are as yet sold out of the territory and we are unable to gather any reliable statistics; however, we may place the yearly increase at 12,000, valued at $1,300,000." [4] In the fall of 1885 there were several Englishmen operating horse outfits in the vicinity of Moreland, Montana, a small town on the Northern Pacific about eighteen miles from Bozeman. The wife of one of the ranchers, who was visiting her husband, in writing back to her friends in London, said, "All the Englishmen out here have been to call. I have had a visitor every day and sometimes two." [5] She described the process of branding colts: "They were driven into the corral or

---

[3] *Avant Courier*, June 21, 1877.
[4] *Helena Daily Herald*, January 1, 1881.
[5] *A Lady's Ranche Life in Montana*, letter dated October 27, 1885.

sort of yard generally round, with a fence seven feet high made of strong poles laid one on top of the other between very strong posts. Then the colts were lassoed by the front feet and thrown. One man jumped on their heads to keep them down while the other held their forefeet off the ground with a lasso and a third branded them." The best horses were kept near the ranch for fear of horse thieves. There appeared to have been a good deal of activity in the buying and selling of horses, her husband going to Oregon to purchase a large drove of horses for possible sale in the eastern market, but he found the price too high and came back without them.[6] In 1888 the editor of the *Montana Live Stock Journal* made the following observation: "Eastern Montana is fast coming to the front as one of the best horse raising countries of the world." [7]

Horse-ranching developed slowly in the Territory of Dakota, during the early period, and like sheep- and cattle-ranching, was limited to the western portion of the territory. A. W. Merrick, editor of the *Black Hills Pioneer* of Deadwood, in his report on ranching of January 1, 1882, said of horses, "It is very difficult to estimate the number of horses in the Black Hills as there are no exact records. The number is not large as the principal ranges for them are within the Wyoming line. A reasonable estimate would be about 7,000 but the number is rapidly increasing. They are principally 'half breeds' of the quality most desirable on the frontier." In 1884 there was a tendency to improve breeding in the Black Hills district by bringing in high-grade Clydesdale and Norman stallions. C. D. Germain and Thomas Jones were the leaders in this work. Horses on the range, however, were greatly mixed, and those from Oregon, Texas, California, Colorado, and

[6] *Ibid.*, letters dated November 2, 10, 23, December 2, 23, 1885, January 2, 26, May 11, July 12, 1886.

[7] *Montana Live Stock Journal* (Miles City, Mont.), June 28, 1888. The number of horses reported for Montana jumped from 44,416 in 1879 to 99,843 in 1884, 160,940 in 1890, and 184,187 in 1893. *Anaconda Standard Almanac*, 1894, p. 81; *Report of the Helena Board of Trade*, 1887.

other areas rustled side by side and all seemed to thrive. In 1885 there were 11,084 horses west of the Missouri River, 9,112 of which were in the Black Hills region.[8]

A. C. Huidekoper started a horse ranch in 1883 on Deep Creek in the Little Missouri region, which he stocked largely from Sitting Bull's war ponies captured near the Canadian boundary, many of them still showing bullet marks received in the battle of the Little Big Horn. Horses came through the hard winter of 1886-87 fairly well, and several bankrupt cattlemen immediately saw the possibilities of horse-ranching as a permanent business. Huidekoper purchased the old Logging Camp ranch and organized the Little Missouri Horse Company. By the end of the eighties horse-ranching had developed into an established industry in the Black Hills and Little Missouri districts of Dakota. The Little Missouri Horse Company became almost famous for its fine horses. Huidekoper raised horses of many breeds, from full-blooded Percherons to polo ponies.[9]

VII

HORSE THIEVES

Horses were needed on the ranges of the Northwest and since they were quite valuable, from the very beginning there was about as much trouble with horse thieves as with cattle rustlers. Outside of using the branding-iron to obtain cattle dishonestly, it was perhaps easier to steal horses than cattle. They could be moved rapidly over long distances and were more easily disposed of. A horse thief was in even greater disrepute in the range country than a stealer of cattle. The contemporary press of the area under consideration contained many accounts of the despised horse thieves.

---

[8] *Report of the Secretary of the Interior for the year ending June 30, 1885,* Vol. II, 979; *Black Hills Weekly Pioneer,* March 17, 1884; *Turner County Herald,* May 10, 1883.

[9] *Bismarck Weekly Tribune,* November 6, 1885; *Mandan Pioneer,* August 12, 1886; files of the *Bismarck Tribune,* 1886-88.

Like cattle rustlers, they often worked in groups or gangs and would terrorize a locality until they were killed or driven away by organized action on the part of the ranchers. Evidence of such is apparent in an announcement by the *Yellowstone Journal* in the autumn of 1880, "The body of a man was found hanging on a tree near the Smith fork of the Judith River with a card marked 'Horse Thief' pinned on his coat."[1] While horse-stealing was present in all parts of the Northwest, it was probably worse in Montana than in the other territories, largely because horse-ranching was more prominent there.

When horse-stealing became serious enough to arouse organized local action, it did not ordinarily take very long to exterminate it, after which the local organization would disperse and there would be little trouble until another outbreak. The Judith Basin country had been relatively free from cattle thieves for several years, when in the spring and summer of 1884 horse-stealing became so common that the editor of the *Mineral Argus,* published at Maiden, Montana, took up the matter in its columns, urging that horse thieves be hanged or driven out of that area.

The issue for June 4, 1884, carried an editorial to this effect: "From every side come reports of horses stolen and action must be taken. Not long ago a poor man near Maiden lost thirteen horses in one night. It is time a lesson should be taught this class of criminals and the most speedy and safe cure is to hang them as fast as captured. An organization should be formed without delay." Nothing further was said in the local press until June 13th when it was announced that a horse thief had been captured and killed. He was supposed to have been connected with a daring band of thieves operating in the Judith Basin area.[2] On June 26th a horse thief was shot at the Lavina crossing of the Musselshell when he attempted to run off some horses. On June 27th a half-breed was hanged at Judith Landing for horse-stealing. He had

[1] *Yellowstone Journal,* October 9, 1880.
[2] *Madisonian,* June 13, 1884; *Mineral Argus,* June 12, 1884.

acknowledged his guilt. "A rope was swung over the branch of a large cottonwood tree at 2 P.M. on June 27th with a regular hangman's noose and the thief must have died quickly of strangulation. He was captured, tried, and executed in fourteen hours. His body was cut down the next day at ten A.M. and buried," reported the *Mineral Argus*.[3] Then followed an editorial on "Horse Thieves" by the editor:

Horse thieves must go. Mankind is blessed with a liberal amount of patience. At last the depredations of the numerous horse thieves in this portion of the territory have reached a point that to stockmen is beyond endurance. To a man they are determined to exterminate this class of culprits. Last week we chronicled the shooting of two and this week we publish the hanging of another at Clagget placarded on the back with the words "Horse Thief" as a gentle yet persuasive hint to the rest of the fraternity. Though for several years Montana has been afflicted with horse thieves and cattle killers, at no time have they been so numerous and displayed the bravado that has characterized their raids during the past few months. They have carried on their deviltry with a high hand. They often when captured have been freed rather than killed because of the lack of evidence. If the riders and cowboys take the law in their hands and annihilate the scoundrels, they will save the taxpayers money.

The *Argus* for July 10, 1884, told of Sam McKenzie, a half-breed, found hanging to a tree on the morning of the 4th, one mile below Fort Maginnis:

McKenzie has been suspected for sometime and the committee has been waiting to catch him and for the opportunity to raise him from the ground after the prevailing fashion, and thereby check the career of one of the despicable class that infests the territory in every section. Who the parties were that took the law into their own hands on the night of the third we have no knowledge. It is sufficient to say they did their work with neatness and dispatch. At last account the body was still hanging from a limb with a card attached bearing the words "Horse Thief."

---

[3] *Mineral Argus*, June 26, July 3, 1884.

On July 24th the *Mineral Argus* printed a telegram from the captain of the steamer *Benton* dated July 23rd, received at Fort Maginnis, and stating that the bodies of seven men had been found hanging to a tree at the mouth of the Musselshell. On July 31st: "Burying parties are quite numerous. The crop of horse thieves is falling off from the trees." August 7, 1884: "The roundup of horse thieves down the Missouri, so far as we can get at the inside view, will teach respect for lawful ownership of cattle and horses." On August 28th, Granville Stuart was advertising that there were sixty-nine head of horses recovered from horse thieves awaiting identification. The issues of the *Argus* for September 11th and 30th both carried announcements of the hanging of horse thieves, after which, for some time, the local press was again quiet regarding the problem. Evidently the primitive justice which the frontier editor had so warmly, if unlawfully, encouraged had accomplished its purpose.

V

THE FRONTIER OF
SETTLEMENT

FROM early colonial times until the end of the nineteenth century the frontier line of settlement in the United States shifted steadily westward. It crept slowly over the fall-line, crossed the Allegheny Mountains into the Ohio Valley, and by 1850 had penetrated into the valley of the Mississippi. From 1850 to 1860 the center of population in the United States moved westward faster than in any other decade. During that period a steady stream of immigrants poured into the Mississippi Valley. The state of Illinois alone gained 200,000, and the population of Iowa increased from 192,214 to 674,915. There was also a rapid increase in population in the states and territories along the upper course of the Mississippi, as prairie lands were cut up into farms and forests were hewn down to make way for civilization.

The settlement of Minnesota is an excellent example of the rapid growth in the upper Mississippi country. In 1845 it was a desolate and inaccessible region, and in 1849 its population was probably less than five thousand. After territorial organization in 1849 its development was very rapid. In 1851 twenty-eight million acres of land belonging to the Sioux Indians in Minnesota and Iowa were ceded to the United States and thrown open to settlement. Chicago and Rock Island were connected by railroad in 1854 and two years later the Sault Sainte Marie Canal was opened. Thus Minnesota was made easily accessible, and there was a rapid influx of immigrants. In 1857 the population of the territory was 150,000, which was thirty times as large as it had been in 1849. When the people of Minnesota sought admission as a state in 1858 their request was granted, and within two years there was a population of 172,023.

In March, 1861, the wild stretch of country west of the new state of Minnesota was organized as the Territory of Dakota. That organization was the natural consequence of the rapid westward expansion of the fifties, as concomitant with the movement of settlers into that region there had come a growing demand for an organized government. The character and extent of settlement in the Dakota area in pre-territorial days is deserving of brief consideration.

I

EARLY SETTLEMENTS AND TOWN-SITES IN DAKOTA

WITH the surge of population into the trans-Mississippi West, town-site promotion became a popular form of speculation as land companies and individual land jobbers sought choice pieces of public domain where water-power might be utilized and for other reasons towns would be likely to develop. This so-called "boom in town lots" began in parts of the Middle West about 1854. Such practices were common throughout the upper Mississippi Valley, and Sioux City, Iowa, was a hot-bed of this speculative activity. Each week steamboats, chartered and operated by the various land and town-site companies, came up the Missouri River from Sioux City and other points. The trips were advertised in glowing terms, and hundreds of excursionists crowded the boats. At least a half-dozen towns were laid out on the Nebraska side of the Missouri between Sioux City and the Niobrara, and town lots were readily sold at comparatively high prices.

Pictures were circulated showing steamboats moored at the town levee, taking and discharging their cargoes and passengers. Many of the towns were elaborately planned on paper as to streets, buildings, and all details, when in actuality there was nothing there except a few log shacks. These methods enabled town-site agents to sell their beautifully engraved stock certificates almost as rapidly as the printing-presses could furnish them. This state of "boom" extended into Dakota, where, prior to territorial organization, there was considerable activity on the part of various land and town-site companies. Many paper town-sites were laid out on land secured at $1.25 per acre and sold to the gullible public at prices from $2.00 to $10.00 a lot. Points for towns and mill-sites were located everywhere but usually few permanent improvements were made. Many a town or city was established by nailing a tin plate to a tree or post and marking the name of the new settlement upon it..

Although many of the enterprises were no doubt carried out with the definite idea of fleecing the public, it is only fair to say that a great number of individuals organized companies and located towns sincerely believing that their locations were destined to become thriving and populous cities. They had the optimistic and hopeful spirit of the West, which saw the country, not as it was, but as it would be some day in the future. In the period just prior to the Civil War, when this speculative mania was at its height in the lower Mississippi Valley, several towns were located in the attractive valleys of the Missouri, Big Sioux, Vermillion, and the Red River of the North, within the area that was later to become the Territory of Dakota.[1]

After the treaty of Traverse de Sioux in 1851, the first land in this area was opened to settlement. It embraced a tract between the Big Sioux River and what was later the western boundary of the state of Minnesota, extending from the northwest corner of Iowa northward to the west shore of Big Stone Lake. In the same year the territorial legislature of Minnesota included that area as part of Dakota County.[2]

---

[1] *Sioux City Journal*, August 20, 1914; Visher, *Geography of South Dakota*, pp. 133-4; George W. Kingsbury, *A History of Dakota Territory* (Chicago, Ill., 1915), I, 97-8; Clement A. Lounsberry, *Early History of North Dakota* (Washington, D. C., 1919), p. 230.

[2] Charles J. Kappler, *Indian Affairs and Treaties* (Washington, D. C., 1904-

350 FRONTIERS OF THE NORTHWEST

In the latter part of the summer of 1856 Dr. J. M. Staples
of Dubuque, Iowa, while on a tour of the upper Mississippi region, obtained a copy of Nicollet's *Travels in the Northwest in
1839*. In it was a description of the Big Sioux River, which the
Indians called "Te-hau-kas-an-date," or the "Thick Wooded
River." Staples, much impressed by Nicollet's graphic description
of the Big Sioux region, became afflicted with the speculative fever
that was running high at the time and decided to organize a land
or town-site company to secure desirable locations in that area.
Within a few weeks he had succeeded in organizing the Western
Town Company, which was largely made up of business men
from Dubuque.[3]

In September, 1856, Ezra Millard and David S. Mills were
employed by the Western Town Company to go in quest of the
remarkable falls on the Big Sioux River and to make a town-site
claim of 320 acres contiguous to it. Upon their arrival at the desired point a band of Indians warned them to move on. The two
men returned to Sioux City, but Mills went back in a few weeks
and located a personal claim upon which he built a small cabin.
In May, 1857, a group employed by the Dubuque company arrived and took 320 acres of land bordering the falls for town-site
purposes. They named their location Sioux Falls.[4]

At the same time Minnesota was about to become a state and a
group of enterprising business men and politicians at St. Paul were
not slow to understand that with the admission of Minnesota, a
new territory would eventually be formed from the region lying

13), II, 437; *Session Laws of the Territory of Minnesota*, 1853, p. 34; *Council
Journal of Territorial Legislature of Minnesota*, 1853, pp. 57, 93, 98, 107,
115-9; *House Journal of Territorial Legislature of Minnesota*, 1853, pp. 185,
187, 201, 202, 207.
   [3] Dana R. Bailey, *History of Minnehaha County* (Sioux Falls, S. Dak., 1899),
pp. 10-1; M. K. Armstrong, *History and Resources of Dakota, Montana and
Idaho* (Yankton, D. T., 1866), pp. 32-3.
   [4] Foster, *Outline of History of Dakota*, pp. 7-8; *Sioux Falls Argus Leader*
(Sioux Falls, S. Dak.), June 17, 1919. Mills' cabin was on Brookings Island.
He claimed to have resided there an entire year, but Kingsbury, who made a
careful study of the records, is of the opinion that he probably left during the
winter months. Kingsbury, *op. cit.*, I, 98.

beyond its proposed western line. Consequently on May 23, 1857, a group of land speculators organized the Dakota Land Company at St. Paul to secure all the feasible town-sites in the region west of the proposed Minnesota line and to make improvements at the most eligible of them. At one of these points they hoped to locate the capital of the possible territory. This would enable the members of the company to secure for themselves and their friends the various county and territorial offices and public contracts, as well as to make a goodly sum from the sale of lots.[5]

In June, 1857, the Dakota Land Company decided to begin its proposed activities in the Big Sioux Valley and to carry out its rather extensive plans. A body of men representing the company traveled from St. Paul by steamboat to a point on the Minnesota River,[6] where they divided into three parties and pursued their journey overland to the Big Sioux country. The contingent, headed by Alpheus G. Fuller, arrived at the falls on the Big Sioux River about the 20th of the month and was greatly surprised to find that the Western Town Company had already located Sioux Falls town-site. The St. Paul party, however, decided to make the best of the situation and selected 320 acres immediately adjoining that of the other company, naming their location Sioux Falls City.

The second group of the St. Paul party, headed by Franklin J. Dewitt, struck the Sioux River farther down and located the town of Flandreau, and the third group, led by S. A. Medary, established a town north of Flandreau which was named after the leader. Sioux Falls was to be the initial point of the company's operations. The representatives decided by common consent that the new territory, as soon as it could be organized, should be called "Dakota" and that Sioux Falls City should be the capital. They then returned home, leaving two men in charge of the interests

[5] *St. Paul Pioneer and Democrat* (St. Paul, Minn.), June 3, 1857; *Session Laws of the Territory of Minnesota*, 1857, p. 191; Lounsberry, *op. cit.*, pp. 215-6.
[6] Probably New Ulm, Minnesota.

of the company. Five men were on the ground in charge of the Dubuque company's holdings.[7]

In July the Indians became threatening and insisted that the whites should leave at once. Greatly outnumbered and unprepared to resist, the men abandoned the town-site. The Indians made no attempt to harm them and seemed glad to get rid of them without resorting to arms. On August 23, 1857, the Dubuque party returned with nine men, armed and provisioned to hold the site selected. They brought a sawmill and other equipment and began the erection of several buildings. Although the Indians annoyed them by running off their stock, no effort was made to drive them away. Early in the fall several men representing the Dakota Land Company arrived and both companies kept men on their locations during the winter. They erected a blockhouse near the Island for protection against the Indians.[8]

In accordance with the plans of the Dakota Land Company, the territorial legislature of Minnesota created Big Sioux, Midway, and Rock counties with Sioux Falls City, Medary, and Flandreau as the respective county-seats.[9] In 1858 a few settlers arrived and the Dakota Land Company located several new town-sites. Although the number of settlers was not large, A. G. Fuller was appointed by the county commissioners of Big Sioux County as a delegate to Washington in an attempt to secure recognition for the proposed territory.[10]

Early in the summer of 1858, a band of about one hundred Yankton Indians appeared at Medary and demanded that the place be evacuated at once.[11] The Indians, who had destroyed all

[7] Andreas, *Historical Atlas of Dakota*, p. 96; scrapbook owned by Franklin Taylor (Vermillion, S. Dak.), I, 20; Bailey, *op. cit.*, pp. 11-12.

[8] *Sioux Falls Argus Leader*, June 17, 1919; Armstrong, *op. cit.*, pp. 33-4; Bailey, *op. cit.*, pp. 12-3.

[9] *Session Laws of the Territory of Minnesota*, 1857, *Extra Session*, p. 67; *Council Journal*, pp. 51, 53, 72; *House Journal*, pp. 59-62.

[10] "The First Organized Government of Minnesota," printed letters and documents, Minnesota Historical *Collections* (1859-98), pp. 115-6; Andreas, *op. cit.*, p. 95.

[11] A portion of the Yanktonnaise tribe had refused to recognize the treaty of

the improvements of the settlers in that portion of the valley, burned the buildings at Medary and sent word to Sioux Falls City that the thirty or forty people there must leave the country.[12] After holding a council of war it was decided to remain and fight. Preparations were immediately made for a siege by building a fortification of logs and turf around the buildings of the Dakota Land Company, which they called "Fort Sod."

A letter written by James M. Allen, who was at Fort Sod during the summer, to his father, dated June 17, 1858, gave an account of what occurred:

We are in a state of excitement at the present time. Last Sunday a half-breed, who had been acting as interpreter at Medary, reached here, stating that one hundred lodges of Indians (Yanktonnaise) had arrived at the place and ordered our townsite people away. Mr. Dewitt was at first inclined to fight them, but his men, a dozen or so in number, thought the odds were against them and refused to do so.

The consequence was that the Indians forced all hands out of the houses and took what provisions they wanted and burned every building down. Dewitt and the men have all gone to the agency or to St. Paul. The Indians sent word by the half-breed for us to leave the country forthwith and that they would be down here in the course of a week and drive us out.

The letter continued with the story of a settlers' meeting and the construction of a fort on the location of the Dakota Land Company. It consisted of a perpendicular wall eighty feet square, ten feet high, and two feet thick, built of sod and logs. A deep ditch surrounded the exterior base, and port-holes were arranged every few feet in the wall. There was also an interior platform to stand upon in case of an attack. Mrs. Goodwin, the only woman at the fort, made a large flag out of flannel shirts and the stars and stripes was soon waving over Fort Sod.

cession made with the Sisseton and others, claiming that the Big Sioux Valley belonged to the whole Sioux nation, and that no tribe or group of tribes had the authority to cede it without the consent of all.

[12] *Sioux Falls Democrat*, November 8, 1859.

We are on a military footing [Allen wrote], have organized into a company and have sentries and scouting parties on guard duty day and night. All told, we number thirty-five for defense, not including the woman who can shoot as well as anyone.... All the troops in this section of the country [Forts Randall and Ridgely] are on the Mormon expedition, and the result is that the settlers are left to protect themselves.

The news of this Indian difficulty will travel all over the country, and we cannot expect any more immigration this way before next spring; and from all accounts there are large numbers enroute here to settle in the Big Sioux Valley, who will turn back. I fear immigration will be retarded for several years.[13]

The Indians, learning of the preparations for the defense of Sioux Falls, did not make an attack and soon abandoned their hostile expedition. No further trouble was experienced with them until the Minnesota massacre in the summer of 1862. The incident, however, tended to make the settlers extremely nervous and uneasy, and the fort was maintained at Sioux Falls throughout the summer. A few new immigrants dribbled in, but many of the settlers, fearing another outbreak, left the country.[14]

S. J. Albright, a member of the Dakota Land Company, established a newspaper at Sioux Falls in the summer of 1859. The first issue of the *Sioux Falls Democrat* was printed July 2, 1859, and although the first few numbers contained largely political news, some of the later issues gave considerable information regarding settlement. On September 3rd a number of prospective settlers were reported to have been in town during the month looking for locations. "They seldom leave the valley to look further," remarked the editor. On November 9th it was announced that an M. K. Armstrong of High Forest, Minnesota, had paid a visit to the Falls while the editor was absent, in search of a location for himself and prospective settlers from Minnesota. It was also reported that "since our last issue we have added to the

[13] Bailey, *History of Minnehaha County*, pp. 14-5.
[14] *Sioux Falls Democrat*, January 28, 1860.

subscription list of the *Democrat* 143 paying names." Several families had arrived from Dubuque, Iowa, and had made permanent locations, while many settlers were said to have been on the road. "Many of these are business men," stated the *Democrat*, "and will give great aid to the future development of the capital and to Dakota in general."

The third annual report of the Dakota Land Company described its activities from August 1, 1858, to October 1, 1859, during which time six town-sites had been selected and laid out in the Big Sioux Valley. Considerable work had been done to improve the various towns. The company had been quite active in sending out exploring expeditions for the purpose of getting new locations.

The last exploring party sent out by this company [stated the report] was in charge of Bradley and Smith. They left St. Paul in June, and have ere this [15] planted the flag of the Dakota Land Company on such valuable sites as may be found from the mouth of the Sioux to old Fort Lookout on the Missouri, and on the James, Vermillion and Wanari rivers. They have sounded for the points to which steamers may run, and there also have commenced the nuclei of towns. Their movements will be seconded by the more timid adventurers, and the way being paved, a lively immigration will follow. As soon as settlers begin to come in large numbers, Dakota will be granted a permanent territorial government.

There were about one hundred and fifty stockholders in the company at the time the report was rendered, forty or fifty of whom lived in the territory and as many more in St. Paul. They had active representatives in half the states of the Union who were doing their best to attract settlers to their various locations.

It is the policy of the company [the report added] to grant land and to sell lots to actual settlers at reasonable prices, and to render substantial aid to all enterprises that may promise good to southwestern

[15] The meeting at which this report was rendered was held in St. Paul, October 1, 1859.

Minnesota and eastern Dakota. Nothing has as yet been put on the
market by the company, but anyone wishing to establish himself at
these towns has only to call at the office of the company in St. Paul,
or on the agents in the territory, where liberal inducements will
always be held out.[16]

The political aspirations of the Dakota Land Company to establish a provisional government with Sioux Falls City as the territorial capital failed to materialize.[17] Settlement at that point was
continuous down to the serious Indian trouble of August, 1862,
although the number of settlers was not large.

During the latter part of the fur-trading period, several French-
Canadian "voyageurs" or "cordellers" formerly employed by the
various fur companies on the Missouri River had married Indian squaws and settled on small farms along the Missouri lowlands and in the Big Sioux Valley. Ferries were established at
river crossings and small mercantile establishments opened for
business. In the spring of 1856 General W. S. Harney selected
the site for the military post at Fort Randall which on its completion became an important link in the chain of military forts
designed to protect the advancing settlements. The first garrison
was located at Fort Randall in the spring of 1857. Paul Paquette,
who had settled on the Big Sioux River in 1854, began in 1856
the operation of a rope ferry on the Sioux City and Fort Randall
wagon road to meet the demand for improved crossing facilities
created by the construction of the new fort.[18]

In 1857 a rope ferry was established across the Vermillion
River by A. C. Van Meter, a squaw-man who was employed by
the United States Government to carry mail from Sioux City to
Fort Randall. In the early part of May, 1857, William P. Lyman

[16] *Sioux Falls Democrat*, November 8, December 15, 1859, January 28,
1860.
[17] The election of 1860 really spoiled the plans of the company. They tried
to get recognition before Buchanan went out of office and the Republican
Administration came in.
[18] Batchelder, *Sketch of the History and Resources of Dakota Territory*,
pp. 3-5; Kingsbury, *History of Dakota Territory*, I, 27.

and a group of colleagues established a ferry and a trading-post on the James River near the Sioux City and Fort Randall military trail. They were employed by Frost, Todd and Company, a mercantile association holding a permit from the United States Government to engage in traffic with the Indians at various points along the Missouri. The little party of frontiersmen spent the winter at the post, hunting, trapping, and cutting cabin timber. In March, 1858, George D. Fiske, an employee of Frost, Todd and Company, camped at the point where the town of Yankton was later located and established a trading-post there. The party then moved on to a point ten miles above called "Smutty Bear's Camp" where they erected another post.[19]

In the spring of 1858 the Upper Missouri Land Company was organized at Sioux City by J. B. S. Todd,[20] D. M. Frost, and others for the purpose of taking possession of the town-sites along the Missouri River. By using their license to establish trading-posts, they would be able to select desirable town-site locations while the region was still Indian country and not open to settlement. During the summer and fall of 1858 various posts were located in the Missouri Valley between Sioux City and Fort Pierre. According to the statement of an observer passing through this region in 1860 on government business, Frost, Todd and Company or the Upper Missouri Land Company had constructed posts or cabins at the following places: Sioux Point on the Missouri, nearly west of the Big Sioux crossing, near the later town of Elk Point; Hall's Point, about half-way between Elk Point and Vermillion; at the Vermillion crossing; at the James River crossing; at Yank-

[19] *Dakota Republican* (Vermillion, D. T.), June 16, 1879; Anna M. Goetz, *The History of Yankton County to 1886* (Master's thesis, University of South Dakota, Vermillion, S. D., 1927), p. 3.
[20] Captain Todd was a cousin of Mrs. Abraham Lincoln. He was on duty at Fort Pierre as Captain of Company A, Sixth U. S. Infantry, but resigned September 16, 1856, to become sutler (military post trader) at Fort Randall. He was manager of D. M. Frost and Company of Sioux City and of Frost, Todd and Company in Dakota. Both organizations were interested in the store and trading businesses.

ton; at Smutty Bear's Camp; and twenty miles west of Yankton at Bon Homme.[21]

Thus, even before the formal relinquishment of the soil by the Indians, a thin line of settlement had established itself along the Missouri River from Sioux City to Fort Randall. Practically all of those who resided there were hunters, trappers, or licensed traders, many of whom had Indian wives. These people were allowed to occupy Indian lands without being molested. But all were not traders or squaw-men, as a few adventurous and intrepid pioneers had entered the wilds and built cabins in the Indian country before the proposed Indian treaties were consummated and the land thrown open to settlement.

In the spring of 1858 a group of men at Sioux City, aware of the ambitions of the Upper Missouri Land Company, decided to locate a town at some point on the Missouri that might later become a metropolis. The party left Sioux City in March, 1858, advancing up the Missouri Valley on the Nebraska side. They halted a few miles below the present site of Yankton and crossing to the Dakota side decided to establish a town there. Twice driven out by the Indians, they were finally advised by the military authorities to leave until the land was opened to settlement. The representatives of the Upper Missouri Land Company, being licensed traders, were allowed to remain.[22]

A small party from Dodge Center, Minnesota, under the leadership of John H. Shober, a man of energy and ability, while *en route* to the gold-fields of Colorado, crossed the Missouri River at Sioux City in the spring of 1858 and continued their journey, following the south bank of the river as far as Bon Homme Island.[23] Favorably impressed by the land on the other side of

[21] *Sioux City Register*, May 17, 1858; Taylor scrapbook, pp. 23-4; Kingsbury, *op. cit.*, I, 120-1. Kingsbury is the only writer who mentions a post at Bon Homme.

[22] *Sioux City Register*, June 12, 1858; Foster, *Outline of History of Dakota*, p. 9.

[23] Bon Homme Island in the Missouri River is said to have received its name from a young man who was captured by the Indians about 1830. After his release

the Missouri, they crossed over and camped, finally deciding to abandon their expedition to the gold-fields and to settle there. They squatted upon Indian land, erected their log cabins, and planted crops with all the confidence of true frontiersmen.[24]

During the late fifties the spirit of speculation and the desire to take advantage of opportunities offered in a new territory were strong in many eastern and middle western states. Various interests and groups of individuals worked hard at Washington to secure the relinquishment of the Indian title to the land between the Big Sioux and Missouri rivers. The increasing demands for public lands was supplemented by the reasonable argument that the safety of the Minnesota and Iowa frontiers demanded that the Indians be brought under control in reservations near military posts.

Early in 1858 the United States Government, yielding to insistent demands, took steps to secure the cession of certain Indian lands. The negotiations resulted in a treaty with the Yankton and Ponca Sioux at Washington, April 19, 1858. The tribes were to cede to the government all their lands between the Missouri and Big Sioux rivers except a reservation of about four hundred thousand acres lying along the Missouri above Chouteau Creek, in what later became Charles Mix County in Dakota Territory. The lands ceded, watered by the Big Sioux, Vermillion, and James rivers, were the choicest portions of the Sioux nation's holdings. The Indians were to move to their new reservation within a year after the treaty was ratified.

Pending the ratification of the treaty a considerable number of squatters came in and located their farms, and as time went on more and more log and sod cabins dotted the bottom lands of the various river valleys. The Indians viewed this trespass with

he located a cabin on the island and lived there until his death in 1848. He was famous for his hospitality to both whites and Indians and was known in the area as the "good man" or "*bon homme.*" After his death the island was called by that name. Kingsbury, *op. cit.*, I, 121-2.

[24] Kingsbury, *op. cit.*, I, 121-3; Andreas, *Historical Atlas of Dakota*, p. 96.

much disfavor and the licensed traders were annoyed. Upon appeal to Washington the government sent orders to the military authorities at Fort Randall to eject all white settlers on Indian land and to destroy their improvements; licensed traders, their employees, and white squaw-men excepted. The ejected settlers were allowed to return when the treaty was finally ratified and proclaimed early in 1859.[25]

While there was some misunderstanding regarding the clause giving the Indians one year to remove to their agency that resulted in ill feeling, there was no bloodshed and the red men formally withdrew July 10, 1859.[26] As soon as the Indians were removed, several hundred prospective settlers who had encamped on the Nebraska side of the Missouri, awaiting the opening, crossed over and within a few weeks the towns of Yankton, Meckling, Vermillion, and Bon Homme were laid out. The town-site owners placed their lands on the market and encouraged settlement. Many business men and laborers located in the settlements and others took up farms in the surrounding areas. The town-site of Wanari was established a few miles south of Bon Homme in the summer of 1860, its name being changed to Springfield two years later. Meckling and Gayville were laid out in the summer of 1860 between Vermillion and Yankton, and Elk Point was located a few miles south of Vermillion in the fall.[27]

Scandinavian settlers from northeastern Nebraska sent favor-

[25] *Report of the War Department to the Secretary of the Interior* (Washington, D. C., 1858); *Yankton Press and Dakotian*, January 1, 1879. The Yankton treaty that had been signed on April 19, 1858, was ratified February 16, 1859, and proclaimed February 26th. Kappler, *Indian Affairs and Treaties*, II, 586-90.

[26] It would seem from the clause in the treaty that the intention was to give the Indians ample time to collect their effects before removing to their new home, but that they were no longer to exercise any authority to restrain settlement or to prevent the improvement of the country. The one-year clause ceased to be a bone of contention after July 10, 1859, although hundreds of Indians took advantage of it and returned to their favorite camps on the James and Vermillion rivers in the fall and early winter of 1859-60 where they fished and trapped. Kingsbury, *op. cit.*, I, 140-1.

[27] *Session Laws of the Territory of Dakota*, 1862, pp. 242-50; Foster, *op. cit.*, pp. 6-7.

able reports concerning Dakota to their friends and relatives at
Koshkonong Prairie, Wisconsin, which resulted in a group of
Norwegian farmers with their families, household goods, and
farm implements in fifteen wagons leaving there for Dakota,
May 20, 1859. While some of the party settled in Nebraska, most
of them settled in the western part of what later became Clay
County in Dakota, in the fall of 1859 and spring of 1860.[28] By
1860 there were also small settlements opposite Fort Pierre and
Fort Randall and west of the Missouri River near the Ponca
agency. The settlers at those points were engaged in contracting
cattle and agricultural products for the soldiers and the Indians.
Each of the little pioneer communities on the frontier of Dakota
at this time had been established independently and, since transportation facilities were not available, had little to do with the
others. The only attempt at concerted action had been in the upper
Big Sioux Valley, where it had failed.

II

EARLY SETTLEMENT IN THE VALLEY OF THE RED RIVER OF THE NORTH

By THE TIME the Territory of Minnesota was organized, a fairly
large settlement existed south of the international boundary line
in the valley of the Red River of the North. In 1850 the Pembina
district had a population of 1,134,[29] and in 1852 H. H. Sibley, in
a government report, said, "Pembina is the name of a settlement
on our side of the British possessions, and contains upwards of a
thousand souls, principally persons of mixed Indian and white
blood. These people are active and enterprising, hardy and intrepid, excellent horsemen and skilled in the use of arms. They

[28] *Dakota Republican*, January 16, 1879; *Yankton Weekly Dakotian*, July 27, 1861.
[29] *U. S. Census Report for 1850*, pp. 1006-7. The population as given included both sides of the river.

subsist by agriculture and the chase of the buffalo." [2] St. Joseph was a small settlement thirty miles west of Pembina village on the Pembina River.

The treaty of Traverse de Sioux of 1851 provided for the cession of the lands east of the Red River between Lake Traverse and the Buffalo River to the United States. During the summer of 1851, before the treaty had been ratified, there had been a general influx of white settlers into the Indian country. They took claims along the east bank of the Red River of the North, and began locating town-sites, cutting timber, building log cabins, and erecting mills. A. C. McLean, Indian agent at Saint Peter, Minnesota, in his report of September, 1852, said, "At the commencement I used all my efforts to prevent this state of things and to induce the white population not to occupy the land until it could be done lawfully. But the current of immigration became irresistible, and the country is virtually in the hands of the white population. Treaty or no treaty, it will be occupied unless opposed by a stronger force than is now here to dislodge them." [3]

The Red River country received a great deal of advertising from the early town-site boom on the Minnesota side of the river, but aside from a small fur business and a small amount of lumbering, the location of town-sites was the most important activity during the early fifties. Throughout the history of the American frontier the white population has always tended to extend its settlements beyond the line provided for by treaty, and to encroach upon the Indian lands. It was not long, therefore, before settlers and town-site companies were active on the west bank of the Red River of the North in what was later to be included in the Territory of Dakota. [4]

[2] "Sibley Correspondence 1849-54," MS, Minnesota Historical Library, St. Paul, Minn., section for 1851-52. A United States Customs House had been established at Pembina in 1851 with a resident revenue agent. *U. S. Public Statutes at Large*, IX, 510.

[3] *Senate Exec. Doc.*, 33rd Cong., 2nd Sess., No. 658, 349.

[4] Bond, *Minnesota and Its Resources*, p. 329; Andrews, *Minnesota and Dacotah*, p. 89.

Pembina County was established by the territorial legislature of Minnesota in 1856,[5] and in 1857 there occurred two events that were of considerable importance in the development of the Red River Valley. During that year the Hudson's Bay Company abandoned York Factory and completed arrangements with the Secretary of the Treasury of the United States whereby an extensive trade for that company and the Selkirk colony could be carried through its territory by way of Minnesota and the Red River Valley.[6] Another event of equal significance was the location and building of Fort Abercrombie, in the heart of the Red River country. The construction of this post on the eastern border of what later became the Territory of Dakota was largely on account of its location near the head of navigation of the Red River and its proximity to the northern Indian tribes. The mail came to Fort Abercrombie from the western forts and was sent weekly by the quartermaster's team to St. Cloud, Minnesota, from where it was forwarded to St. Paul.[7] The western army posts in turn received their mail from the East by way of Fort Abercrombie.

William H. Moorhead and a group of St. Paul men in the summer of 1856 organized a company to lay out town-sites in the Red River Valley. The party located several towns on the Minnesota side of the river and did some reconnoitering on the west side of the valley, but there is no record that any towns were located there. In July, 1858, a number of men from Red Wing, Minnesota, located a town-site about seven miles south of where Fargo was later established, called East Burlington. The party spent the winter at another town-site called Lafayette, about eighteen miles north, which had been established by a party of men from St. Paul. Another town was located a short distance south of Lafayette called Dakota City. At the same time George

---

[5] *Session Laws of the Territory of Minnesota*, 1856, p. 115; 1858, pp. 157, 183.

[6] Lee, *Long Ago in the Red River Valley*, p. 37.

[7] *Proceedings of the Red River Valley Old Settlers Association*, 1897, pp. 22-7; *Sioux Falls Democrat*, December 15, 1859.

W. Northrup was holding a nameless town-site about a mile north of Lafayette, and a town called Banning's Point was later established between Dakota City and Lafayette. Georgetown was located in 1859 by James McKay for the Hudson's Bay Company, and a warehouse, store buildings, and shops were erected. A few settlers gradually drifted in, and by the time of the Indian outbreak in 1862 there were thirty men employed at Georgetown. The number of people connected with the various town-sites was not large, and only a few pioneer farmers were scattered along the valley in the late fifties.[8]

The first surveys in Dakota were made by two government surveyors, James Snow and Stephen Hutton. In the summer of 1859 these men surveyed and marked the eastern boundary of what was to become the Territory of Dakota from Big Stone Lake to the Iowa line. During the same season a contract was let by Warner Lewis, the United States Surveyor-General, at Dubuque, Iowa, to run townships in southeastern Dakota extending west to the Vermillion River. Part of the work was done during the fall of 1859. In the spring of 1860 Congress appropriated fourteen thousand dollars to be expended on surveys by the Dubuque Land Office and Lewis was persuaded to spend the entire amount in surveying the newly acquired public lands in southeastern Dakota. A contract was given two surveyors, James Bell and Henry Darling, who with a party left Dubuque late in the summer of 1860. They ran all township lines between the standard line and the Missouri River and in addition subdivided two fractional townships at Yankton, two at Vermillion, and one at Elk Point. With these surveys the preëmptors were enabled to adjust their claims.[9]

In 1860 the total white population of the region subsequently

[8] *Proceedings of the Red River Valley Old Settlers Association*, 1897, pp. 26-35; Lee, *op. cit.*, p. 102; *The Record* (Fargo, N. Dak., July, 1896), p. 13.
[9] *Annual Report of the Commissioner of the General Land Office*, 1860, pp. 18-9, 79-80, 1861, 93-8; J. H. Goodfellow, "Early Surveys in Dakota," *South Dakota Historical Collections*, V, 362-3.

included in the Territory of Dakota was 4,837 with the largest settlements located as follows: [10]

Between Big Sioux and Big Stone Lake	44
Between Red River and Big Sioux	198
On the Big Sioux	34
On the Red River	54
Pembina	1,606
Sioux Falls City	36
Vermillion	226
Yankton Agency	353

By 1861 settlements had become definitely established along the Missouri, Big Sioux, Vermillion, and James rivers and there was a tendency for those frontier communities to expand. But as yet, however, these pioneer districts lacked laws and local government, without which they could not hope to develop to any great extent. No doubt the greatest need of the Dakota settlements at this time was the organization of a territorial government.

Following a period of activity on the part of the pioneer settlers at Sioux Falls, Yankton, and Vermillion, a bill creating the Territory of Dakota was signed by President Buchanan on March 2, 1860, and President Lincoln appointed the territorial officers, choosing William Jayne of Springfield, Illinois, his friend and former physician, as governor. He arrived in Dakota late in May and selected Yankton as the territorial capital. One of the first acts of the governor was to order the taking of a territorial census. There were four districts reported with a total population of 2,402. The Vermillion and Big Sioux districts contained settlements at Brule Creek, Bottom and Clay Creeks, Elk Point, Big Sioux Point, Vermillion, Yankton, and Sioux Falls, with a total of 1,140 inhabitants. The western district reported settlements at Bon Homme, Hamilton, Fort Randall, and the Ponca and Yankton Indian agencies, with a total of 759 settlers, while the Red River district, embracing Pembina, St. Joseph, and adjacent set-

[10] *U. S. Census Report for 1860*, Volume on Population, p. 550.

tlements, reported 603. Yankton was the largest settlement with a population of 287, while Vermillion ranked second with a total of 265. In the fall of 1861 there were eleven post-offices operating in the territory.[11] The first session of the legislature of the Territory of Dakota, which met March 17, 1862, enacted a law defining the boundaries of sixteen counties and actually organized Union, Clay, Yankton, and Bon Homme counties, all on the eastern border of the territory.[12]

III

FACTORS WORKING AGAINST EARLY SETTLEMENT

SETTLEMENT in the Territory of Dakota was retarded by the Civil War, the Indian outbreak that accompanied it, and a general fear of drought and grasshoppers. The Homestead Act, which later was of great significance, had little immediate effect since there was still much good government land available farther east and there was a lack of cheap transportation facilities between the Dakota settlements and the more settled portions of the East. By the time of the Indian troubles in 1862 southeastern Dakota had a few feeble settlements strung along the Missouri and Big Sioux valleys. It should not be considered unusual that a large number of these frontier people, anxious for the security of their families, decided to seek a home where there was likely to be greater safety. It was estimated shortly after the stampede of August and September, 1862, that the territory lost at least one-half of its farming population, some writers putting the number at three-fourths. Nor do Indian troubles tell the whole story, for

[11] *U. S. Public Statutes at Large*, XII, 139-40; *Report of the Territorial Governor of Dakota to the Secretary of the Interior*, 1861, pp. 4-5; M. K. Armstrong, "The Burning Issue of 1859," *Monthly South Dakotan*, IV (Yankton, S. D., 1901), 73-4.

[12] *Session Laws of Territory of Dakota*, 1862, pp. 1-156. The first legislature seemed to expect that the settlement of the newly organized territory would be rapid. Although the boundaries of sixteen counties were defined at the first session in 1862, up to 1871 only six counties had been organized.

A PIONEER LEGISLATURE OF DAKOTA TERRITORY

In the session that located the capital in 1862. Moses K. Armstrong, *The Early Empire Builders of the Great West.*

crop failures due to drought and grasshoppers were a serious handicap. It is a wonder that with all the discouragements that faced them, any settlers remained at all, much less that new settlers were difficult to attract to the Territory of Dakota.

The military authorities at this time opposed settlement, and many of the officers openly discouraged the Dakota settlers. Some of the prominent army men even advised them to leave the country and to give up their lands to the Indians. During the early period, limited facilities for communication and transportation added greatly to the hardships of the settlers. Although steamboat traffic had existed on the Missouri River since the early fur-trading days and had been greatly increased after the discovery of gold in the Idaho and Montana country, the steamers made few local stops, as there was a scarcity of good landings. During drought periods steamboat traffic was far from dependable.[1]

Throughout the middle sixties the number of settlers migrating to the West to take claims was not large, and the Union Pacific Railroad, with its empire of lands granted by the government, and with plenty of financial backing, was an opponent far too formidable for Dakota to combat. That enterprising corporation carefully combed the country to secure people for its lands, and even went to Europe to secure settlers. The Sioux City newspapers continued numerous advertisements in which the Union Pacific Company offered liberal concessions to prospective settlers, and its representatives were active in the vicinity, while other less powerful railroad companies worked in the same direction.[2]

In addition to the efforts of the land-grant railroads, the states of Minnesota and Iowa at this time were only meagerly settled, and home-seekers from the eastern states, even when headed for Dakota, were often beset by tempting opportunities presented by the people and immigration agents who were endeavoring to obtain settlers for their vacant acres. In this way Dakota's immigra-

[1] *Yankton Weekly Press,* February 1, 1871.
[2] *Sioux City Weekly Journal,* January 21, 1865.

tion was retarded, and the territory received but a handful of those who were migrating westward.

As a rule the new-comer to Dakota who had resisted the temptations and blandishments presented by the citizens of the neighboring states, and finally reached the territory, had an interesting story to tell of the methods employed by Dakota's neighbors to dissuade immigration from going to the eastern part of that area. The information was often given that Dakota was no place for a white man to live, as nothing fit for the subsistence of civilized people could be grown on the arid plains of that territory. It was depicted as a land of perpetual drought in summer and terrible blizzards in the winter. If a farmer was fortunate enough to obtain the promise of a good crop, the grasshoppers were sure to devour it, before it could be harvested. Even potatoes were not safe from the ravages of the gluttonous insects, according to various tales, as they would dig into the ground to consume the tubers. Stories of Indian outrages were common, and the redskins were said to be constantly brandishing their tomahawks and scalping the settlers, and it was told that "nearly all dead people in the territory could be found without their scalp-lock." Sioux City citizens would often inform parties of immigrants headed for Dakota that the Great American Desert would be found just west of the "Jim River." [3]

Iowa and Minnesota newspapers and other eastern journals took particular pains to herald these things to the world. The worst effects of the drought and grasshoppers had been observed by the various companies of Iowa troops who were members of General Sully's second expedition against the Indians and by those stationed at the Dakota forts. These men naturally told what they had seen, and their stories certainly were not favorable to settlement. In addition to the accounts of outside people, many of the discouraged settlers who abandoned the territory, while passing through the settlements to the East, told pitiful stories of the perils

[3] Taylor scrapbook, I and II.

they had encountered and of the privations they had endured. The newspapers were quick to seize upon reports of this sort, and articles appeared under various headings: "Another Survivor of Plague-Stricken Dakota Reaches Town" or "Another Dakota Pioneer Tells His Story." Then would follow a tale, often exaggerated, concerning Indians, drought, grasshoppers, and general suffering, frequently embellished with an account of a blizzard told the narrator by a "poor Dakota cripple who had lost both legs and an arm during one of the winter storms." As late as 1866 George Catlin, a writer of some note, stated that the Dakotas were a part of that region known as the Great Plains, "which is and ever must be useless for civilized men to cultivate." [4]

There also existed at this time in the minds of many early settlers and of those living farther east grave apprehensions regarding the timber supply of Dakota. It was generally believed that the small patches of timber that fringed the rivers would soon disappear and there would be a lack of timber for fuel and cabins. The pioneer settlers in regions remote from the timbered streams were often forced to live in sod shanties and to resort to the burning of prairie hay for fuel. This was no doubt an important factor retarding settlement in the Dakota area.

These various adverse factors could mean nothing but stagnation for Dakota during the period from 1862-67. The inactivity and lack of immigration are well illustrated by the population in the Big Sioux Valley, which in 1868 was less than it had been in 1859. The valley was entirely deserted from September, 1862, until May, 1865, when Fort Dakota was erected at Sioux Falls. In 1866 a few farmers returned. Bon Homme, the most western of the permanent settlements, with a population of two hundred in August, 1862, was deserted until early in 1868. [5] The popula-

[4] Kingsbury, *History of Dakota Territory*, I, 338; Foster, *Outline of History of Dakota*, p. 23; John I. Faris, *Seeing the Middle West* (Philadelphia, 1923), p. 74; files of the *Sioux City Weekly Journal*, 1865-68.
[5] William Chamberlain, "Sod Shanty Days," *Monthly South Dakotan*, III, 78-9.

tion of Lincoln County, which had been several hundred in 1862, numbered thirty-three persons on January 1, 1869. Although Elk Point had been incorporated in 1862, it did not have a store until 1866.[6]

IV

FACTORS FAVORING EARLY SETTLEMENT

IN SPITE of the many adverse conditions which reacted against settlement in the Territory of Dakota during the early sixties, there were some factors which tended to favor immigration to that area. There were those in the territory, even when conditions were at their worst, who would not admit that the climate and soil of Dakota made it unsuited for agriculture. Surveyor-General Hill at Yankton, in his report to the Secretary of the Interior in 1862, spoke favorably concerning the soil and climate of Dakota and throughout the period of adversity refused to change his mind. He held that the cultivation of the soil would bring an increase of moisture, and urged the planting of groves as an additional means of attracting and conserving it. He stood for the natural advantages of Dakota and championed the territory when it was sadly in need of friends. He insisted that Dakota would develop into a farming community and advocated his ideas and theories on the platform and through the leading eastern newspapers to which his position gave him access. He had an ardent co-worker in the person of Governor Newton Edmunds, and these two men, realizing, as did most of the pioneer settlers, that the first great need of the territory was a large population,[7] did everything within their means to secure it.

The Homestead Act awakened a strong sentiment throughout

[6] R. L. Polk and Company, *Gazetteer for Minnesota and Dakota* (Detroit, Mich., 1881).

[7] Hill, *Annual Report of Territorial Governor to the Secretary of the Interior,* 1862; *Messages and Documents of the President of the U. S.,* 1862-63; pp. 91-2. Prior to his appointment as Surveyor-General of Dakota, Mr. Hill had been a president of the Michigan State Agricultural Society and had attracted considerable attention by his lectures and articles on practical farming.

the United States favorable to the occupation of western public lands. The liberal provisions of the law appealed to the poor man, and soon movements were on foot in various parts of the country to organize groups of people or colonies to emigrate in bodies to the West and locate wherever soil, climate, and natural advantages offered the most favorable inducements. Such an organization was formed at Syracuse, New York, March 7, 1863, called the "Free Homestead Association of Central New York." The purpose of the association was to get away from the overcrowded East, where farmlands were too high in price for the man of ordinary means to find a satisfactory location, and to settle there in a body.

With the close of the Civil War and the consummation of the Indian treaties of 1866 had come an increased feeling of security from the red men. That feeling had been further stimulated by the various military expeditions into the Indian country and the construction of forts along the Dakota frontier. Beginning with a fairly good crop in 1867, those of 1868 to 1870 were exceptionally good, and the citizens of the territory in writing to their eastern friends were able to give glowing descriptions of the country. Another reason for the boom in settlement in the Far West was the rapid occupation of government land in Iowa. After the Civil War, great numbers of homesteaders, including many discouraged soldiers from the Union Army, migrated westward into Iowa and took up land. As a result of that movement the unoccupied land of that state became scarce, and the emigrants from the East began to look toward Dakota as the nearest and most practical place for locating a homestead.

In 1868 the Sioux City and Pacific Railroad was completed and Sioux City was connected with the East by rail, thus placing a railroad within four miles of the eastern line of Dakota and bringing the territory within two days' travel of Chicago. The influx of settlers was also promoted during the period by improvements in local transportation facilities. Early settlers had kept ferries on the larger streams between Sioux City and Yankton, but in 1868 the various streams were bridged at the expense of the Federal Government. Shortly after the arrival of the railroad at Sioux City, a daily stage was established to Yankton, and in the same season Yankton and Sioux Falls were connected by mail stage. In 1865 Congress had appropriated eighty-five thousand dollars for the opening of three wagon roads through the Territory of Dakota to the western mining districts, the construction of which facilitated transportation in the territory.[2]

Real-estate and land agents were very active during the late sixties and Dakota was widely advertised. Another factor influencing the boom was the excellent financial condition of the period. Prices for articles purchased by the farmer were not high and his products brought a fair price. Labor of all kinds was at a premium, which enabled many of the homesteaders to work for others part of the year and thus get started themselves. Taxes were not heavy and as a rule did not exceed 1 per cent of the assessed valuation. Because of low taxes and a good rate of interest paid for money, many wealthy men in the eastern states sent their money to Dakota for investment.

V

DEVELOPMENT IN DAKOTA TO 1870

In spite of the hard times and many handicaps, a few settlers had come to Dakota in 1866 and there was a tendency for the existing settlements gradually to expand. Governor A. J. Faulk in his message of December 4, 1866, made an ardent appeal for

2 *Sioux City Weekly Times,* June 3, 1869; *U. S. Public Statutes at Large,* XIII, 516-7; Foster, *op. cit.,* pp. 35-6. Chicago was connected with the Atlantic coast by rail in 1853, and by 1855 railroads reached the Mississippi River. Chicago and Sioux City were connected by railroad in 1868 by way of Council Bluffs. The connection was made in 1870 by two lines directly across the state of Iowa. Sioux City became a railroad terminal because it was located on the outside of the great bend of the Missouri River, which was not easily bridged. The Big Sioux River was not crossed until 1872.

practical measures to promote immigration. A year later he said: "I have heretofore expressed unbounded confidence in our natural advantages, the salubrity of the climate and the inexhaustible fertility of the soil of Dakota. Others from abroad are also beginning to realize these important truths. Within the last twelve months, it has been estimated that the population of the territory has more than doubled by immigration." Lincoln County was organized on December 30, 1867, by the territorial legislature. The harvest of 1868 was bountiful, and Minnehaha County was organized January 4, 1868, while Union, Clay, Lincoln, and Yankton counties all received many new settlers. Careful estimates placed the population of the territory at ten thousand by the end of 1868 and it was claimed that the number of settlers had doubled during the year.[1]

The year 1869 was the most prosperous in the history of the territory. There was a large increase in population and a great deal of building and other improvements occurred in the towns and farming settlements. Vermillion was the only land-office in the territory at this time, and its records show that 186 claims were taken in May and 300 in the month of June.[2] Practically all of the new arrivals settled in the six counties of Minnehaha, Lincoln, Clay, Yankton, and Bon Homme, a few, however, entering Turner and Hutchinson counties. Although the villages along the Missouri bottom all showed a considerable increase in population, Yankton's growth was the greatest, amounting to one hundred during the year. There were hundreds of arrivals at the Yankton hotels each month, as they were the rendezvous or headquarters of the eastern parties who came to "spy out the land" or to begin business ventures.[3]

[1] *Message of the Territorial Governor of Dakota*, December 7, 1868, pp. 1-3; *Session Laws of Territory of Dakota*, 1867-68, p. 126; Foster, *op. cit.*, p. 40; Kingsbury, *op. cit.*, I, 504.
[2] The Springfield and Pembina land-offices were created May 5, 1870.
[3] *Sioux City Weekly Times*, June 3, 1869; *Yankton Weekly Press*, May 27, August 24, 1870.

There are few Dakota newspapers available for this beginning boom period, and outside papers paid little attention to Dakota affairs. The following bits of Dakota news are taken from the *Sioux City Weekly Times,* during the summer of 1869. June 3rd: "Eight hundred Norwegians are enroute between Chicago and Sioux City bound for Dakota ... claims are rapidly being taken up in southeastern Dakota." June 8th: "General W. H. H. Beadle, Surveyor-General of Dakota, passed through Sioux City this week. The general informed us that the government land is being settled rapidly by farmers and others who design making permanent homes in Dakota." June 15th: "We learn from parties just returned from up the river that the settlements now extend fifty miles above Fort Dakota." Several correspondents from Elk Point, Vermillion, and Yankton discussed the unparalleled growth and prosperity of the territory.

The census of 1870 gave the total population of Dakota as 14,181, with almost six-sevenths of the number concentrated in the southeastern part of the territory in the Missouri Valley. The counties in order of their population were as follows: Union, 3,510; Clay, 2,623; Yankton, 2,097; Pembina, 1,213; Lincoln, 712; Bon Homme, 608; Minnehaha, 356; Brookings, 163; Deuel, 37; Hutchinson, 37; Todd, 23; Charles Mix, 23; Buffalo, 7. Of the fourteen counties for which returns were given, only seven had been organized, although the boundaries for the others had been defined. There were five forts and two Indian agencies reported with the following number of inhabitants: Fort Sully, 745; Fort Buford, 454; Fort Totten, 243; Fort Stevenson, 151; Grand River Agency, 154; Cheyenne Agency, 134. There were in the territory 3,240 dwellings, 3,201 families and 1,666 farms. There were 5,727 adult males in Dakota, of which 2,522 were engaged in farming.[4]

Although by 1870 the Territory of Dakota had been organized

[4] *U. S. Census Report for 1870,* Volume on Population, pp. 17, 96, 236-41, 328-34, 670-1.

for nine years, the white population was small. It had, however, gone through its hardest test, and there was no longer a tendency

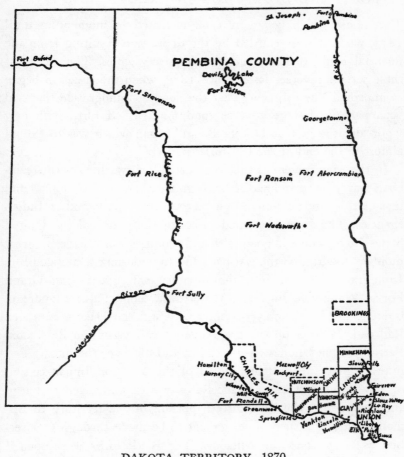

DAKOTA TERRITORY, 1870

Solid lines, counties organized; dotted lines, boundaries defined.

in the East to criticize and decry it. The year 1870 found it in the midst of its first real boom, and Dakota entered its second decade with a reasonable certainty of rapid growth in population and of moderate prosperity.

VI

BOOM AND DEPRESSION IN DAKOTA, 1870-1878

THE BOOM which began in 1868 increased in momentum until 1873, when it was retarded by the depression resulting from the financial panic, drought and grasshopper plagues. The effects of these serious reverses lasted until 1878, when the situation began to improve. The following year the flood of immigration that had been pent up by the adverse conditions rushed forth with new vigor and the "Great Dakota Boom" began which was to extend almost to the end of the territorial period.

In the early seventies the Missouri River swarmed with steamboats carrying merchandise and gold-seekers to Montana, and tens of thousands of tons of goods to military posts and to Indian agencies. The Indians seemed to accept the policy of the United States Government in good faith and promises were made by great numbers to abandon the war-path and to undertake a civilized life. Immigration flowed into the territory through Fargo, Grand Forks, Wahpeton, Bigstone, Watertown, Sioux Falls, Flandreau, Canton, and by the way of Sioux City and the Dakota Southern Railroad. It crept up the grass-covered valleys of the Big Sioux, Vermillion, and James rivers, and spread out over the intervening prairies, practically settling in all of the Yankton Indian cession of 1858. The Northern Pacific Railway was constructed to Fargo and then across the northeastern portion of the territory to Bismarck, causing a strip of settlement to be made through that section as far west as the Missouri. The Black Hills were opened in the middle seventies and drew to that region thousands of experienced miners and husbandmen within a period of twelve months. A fleet of steamboats plied the Red River of the North, furnishing transportation to the growing settlements along its banks which were rapidly extending into the interior. It was estimated that approximately ten thousand settlers came into the territory in 1870 after the Federal census was completed on the first of June.[1]

Governor John A. Burbank in his message late in 1870 emphasized the fact that the Dakota frontier was free from Indian troubles. He pointed out the need of better transportation facilities and the importance of the various railroad projects. He warned prospective settlers of the hardships and suffering that might result from entering the territory without sufficient means to tide over until they could produce a crop. He predicted that settlement would be rapid during the spring and summer of 1871.[2] Several thousand copies of the governor's message were ordered printed in the English language and several hundred in French, German, and Norwegian for advertising purposes. A bureau of immigration was established and James S. Foster appointed as commissioner, and five hundred dollars was appropriated for postage, circulars, and for general promotion purposes.[3]

By the summer of 1871 the government land was taken up for ten to fifteen miles back from the various rivers. Grain and vegetables not used by the settlers were disposed of at the various forts and Indian agencies. Hardly a day passed during the boating season that did not witness the arrival and departure of steamboats from the levees of some of Dakota's older towns that possessed landings. In 1871 actual work was begun on the Dakota Southern Railway, to be constructed from Sioux City to Yankton.[4]

[1] *Yankton Weekly Dakotian*, December 20, 1870, January 6, 1871.
[2] *First Message of Territorial Governor John A. Burbank*, December 9, 1870; *Yankton Press*, January 8, 15, 1871.
[3] *Senate Journal of the Territorial Legislature of Dakota*, 1871, p. 223; *House Journal*, 1871, p. 172. This was the first biennial session of the Dakota legislature as provided by congressional act of March 3, 1869. *U. S. Public Statutes at Large*, XV, 300. The orders for copies to be printed in the various foreign languages was pigeon-holed by the territorial secretary, who claimed that the territory had no funds for printing documents in foreign languages.
[4] A rather remarkable cause of excitement occurred during the summer of 1871. A settler picked up a brilliant or stone resembling a diamond in the glacial drift near Maxwell Mills on the James River about thirty miles north of Yankton. Soon afterwards other stones of like nature were found which led several settlers to draw the conclusion that the James River Valley was a vast

In the winter of 1871 the files of the *Yankton Press* at the territorial capital printed letters from farmers, attorneys, merchants, photographers, physicians, and laborers who expected to migrate to the West during the spring and summer. In the spring various editorials appeared which stressed the need of Dakota for settlers, and an announcement of the Commissioner of Agriculture, James S. Foster's pamphlet, "Outlines of the History of the Territory of Dakota and Emigrants' Guide to the Free Lands of the Northwest," that was to be sent broadcast over the country. The Vermillion Land Office in the southeastern corner of the territory showed the following entries for the spring and summer months of 1871: February, 208; March, 201; April, 211; May, 420; June, 493; July, 213; August, 169.[4]

The construction train of the Dakota Southern Railroad arrived at Vermillion from Sioux City November 25, 1872, and the road was opened to general traffic a few weeks later. The track was completed to Yankton January 25, 1873, and regular passenger service was opened from Sioux City to Yankton ten days later. In the fall of 1872 the Winona and St. Peter division of the Chicago and Northwestern Railroad was completed to Gary, near the Minnesota line, and grading was completed to Lake Kampeska, to which point the steel was laid the following spring.[5] The significance of the coming of the railroad to settlement in southeastern Dakota cannot be overemphasized. The extreme hardships of the lack of transportation facilities were now over, as surplus agricultural products could be marketed and commercial connections established. There was a marked increase in land values. In 1873, land near Vermillion, a railroad town, sold regu-

diamond field. Some of the eastern newspapers talked about it with considerable exaggeration, and this resulted in several small expeditions being made to the valley for the purpose of exploring the supposed diamond district. *Yankton Press*, October 4, 1871.

[4] *Yankton Press*, January to September, 1871; *Clay County Register* (Vermillion, D. T.), same period.

[5] Lake Kampeska is in the central part of Codington County, formerly part of Deuel County. The railroad was not operated until six years later.

larly at fifteen dollars to twenty dollars per acre while ten miles north the same type of land sold for from three to ten dollars.[6]

In the autumn of 1873 the burning of anthracite coal was tested as an experiment in some of the towns of Dakota. An editor at Yankton devoted a whole column to the topic and announced with pride that the office of the newspaper had been supplied with "an anthracite base-burner with windows in it." The use of hard coal was considered the answer to the fuel problem, which had been a serious one away from the wooded river valleys. The existence of a fairly good grade of lignite had been discovered at various points in northern Dakota in 1872 by the civil engineers of the Northern Pacific Railroad, then being surveyed west of the Missouri River. Surveying parties were the first to use lignite coal in their camps and they found it to be a fairly satisfactory fuel where timber was lacking. The railroad company put a great deal of emphasis upon the availability of fuel in their advertising to get settlers.[7]

The population that had come into southeastern Dakota from 1870 to 1873 was fairly well distributed. There had been a steady process of expansion from the older settled areas, making the settlements of that portion of the territory fairly compact. In three years the population of the Big Sioux, James, and Vermillion valleys had increased 300 per cent. While this expansion was taking place in southeastern Dakota, important developments were also occurring in northern Dakota in the valley of the Red River of the North.

In 1869 the directors of the Northern Pacific Railroad had staked the location for the Red River bridge at a place called Elm River and a settlement of town-site speculators gathered at that point. The plans were changed in the spring of 1870 and a line staked to a point not far from the later site of Moorhead

[6] *Clay County Register*, December 4, 1872; *Yankton Press*, December 24, 1873.

[7] *Yankton Press*, November 26, 1873; Kingsbury, *History of Dakota Territory*, I, 591.

which was called Oakport, where a little village of temporary structures soon sprang up. The Lake Superior and Puget Sound Land and Townsite Company was organized, a Northern Pacific auxiliary for the purpose of taking charge of all the valuable town-sites between Lake Superior and Puget Sound. Fargo was decided upon as the crossing-point in the summer of 1871, and the town-site settlers, who had been watching their opportunity and the movement of the company for some time, made a rush for the crossing-point.[8]

A line of stage-coaches established between Fort Abercrombie and Fort Gary in the spring of 1871 also encouraged immigration to the Red River Valley. The company of Blakely and Carpenter of St. Paul were the owners of the new transportation project. The initial trip up the Red River of the steamer *Selkirk*, built at McCauleyville the previous winter, also tended to attract settlers. A post-office had been established at Grand Forks in 1870 for the convenience of those engaged in traffic along the Red River of the North and the Red Lake district, although there were but few settlers then living in that vicinity.[9]

The St. Paul and Pacific Railroad reached the Red River at Breckenridge, Minnesota, during the summer of 1871, and the line opened for traffic to the head-waters of the river. From that time for several years the steamboat industry flourished in the Red River Valley. A rush of immigrants naturally followed, and a new town called Chahinka, or Richville, was founded on the Dakota side of the river by a J. M. Rich. The name was later changed to Wahpeton. Claims were rapidly taken up adjoining the town and the growth of the community resulted in the organization of Richland County early in 1873.

When the news was noised abroad in the fall and winter of

[8] N. K. Hibbard, "Address to the Red River Valley Old Settlers Association," November 26, 1895 (Grand River, N. D., 1897), pp. 1-2; Kingsbury, *op. cit.*, I, 696-7; Lounsberry, *Early History of North Dakota*, pp. 332-4.

[9] George B. Winship, *Forty Years of Development in the Red River Valley* (St. Paul, Minn., 1898), pp. 73-6.

1871-72 that Oakport would be the end of the Northern Pacific Railroad, people hastened there in some numbers to profit by any possible opportunities. Many of them were of a class called in the days of railroad expansion the "end of the track group," which consisted of those who were picking out favorable points and laying out town-sites just ahead of the construction crew. A large number arrived at Oakport, later called Moorhead, on the Minnesota side of the river, and finding that lots had a certain value there, crossed the river to the Dakota side and settled in the timber along the river bank. There they erected tents and log huts and constructed underground habitations for the winter. Some of the settlers had earned money during the summer months on the construction gang, and those without resources engaged in some line of business in a small way, saloons being by far the most popular. Some workmen located with their families, as they expected to continue along the line at some form of construction work as soon as activity opened in the spring. Located on higher ground west of the "squatter settlement" were the headquarters of General Charles Rossers, chief engineer of the Northern Pacific, who with a large corps of engineers lived in tents during the winter months.[10]

The settlement grew rapidly and several saloons and stores were opened that did a considerable business. There was a ferryman there, also, who was waiting patiently for spring to come; three hotels, the Ellsworth House, the Provincial House and the Fargo Hotel; a blacksmith shop; a lawyer on whose shingle was inscribed "Gordon F. Keeney, Esq., Attorney at Law, Notary Public and Land Agent"; numerous gambling-houses; two dancehalls, one named the Pacific, were running full blast, and from thence came the sound of the violin any afternoon or evening in the week. The place was called Centralia, but with the coming of spring and high water it was moved to higher ground and the

[10] G. F. Keeney, "Fargo in the Timber," *Collections*, State Historical Society of North Dakota, I, 318-21.

name changed to Fargo in memory of W. G. Fargo, president of the Wells Fargo Express Company.

In the summer of 1872 Grand Forks contained the following buildings: one sawmill, two saloons, one store, one hotel, one mill, one boarding-house, one stage station and post-office, one boatyard and ferry, five frame houses, and three log cabins. The Northern Pacific reached Moorhead on the east bank of the Red River at the close of 1871, and in June, 1872, crossed to the Dakota side. After the crossing of the Red River at Fargo, attention was next centered on where the railroad would cross the Missouri River.[11]

The Missouri crossing was uncertain during 1872, and a number of towns and trading-points were located on the west side of the river and some improvements made at each. The Lake Superior and Puget Sound Land and Townsite Company located Edwinton back two miles from the river and constructed several log buildings on the town-site. The company sold corner lots for one hundred and fifty dollars and inside ones for one hundred dollars, with the privilege of a free lot in the permanent town-site when it was located. The town of Edwinton grew rapidly. Two other towns were located at prospective crossings, one at Burleigh City about two miles south of Edwinton, and one at Carleton City opposite Camp Greene.[12] Towns were laid out at these points and lots sold. The road was partially graded to Burleigh City, causing a boom in the price of town lots. A sawmill and later a town was located near the mouth of Apple Creek about seven miles below Edwinton. It was estimated that there were about two hundred persons in these various embryonic settlements. Edwinton, however, won the name of the "railroad town."[13]

[11] J. B. Powers, "Bits of History Connected With the Early Days of the N.P.R.R.," *Collections*, Historical Society of North Dakota, III, 337.

[12] Camp Greene was a supply base for the engineers of the N.P.R.R., and was located three miles below the later site of Fort Abraham Lincoln.

[13] Many of the people who located at the various points were really squatters, as the land had not been surveyed and most of them had no idea of making a definite location until they knew exactly where the railroad would cross the river. To protect themselves against claim jumpers the settlers of the Apple Creek district formed an organization called the Apple Creek Settlers'

The railroad was completed to Jamestown in 1872 and reached Edwinton, the name of which was later changed to Bismarck, on June 5, 1873, the road being opened to traffic on June 15th. The stock and franchises of the Lake Superior and Puget Sound Land and Townsite Company were sold to the Northern Pacific Company in the autumn of 1873, and thereafter the railroad company controlled and managed its own town-sites. In the fall of 1873 the Northern Pacific Railroad Company failed, and its bonds, which had been receivable for par in payment for lands within the company's land grant, steadily dropped in price until they reached eight cents on the dollar.[14]

The construction of the Northern Pacific Railroad had attracted a good deal of attention to Dakota and immigration naturally followed. A party of United States deputy surveyors from the Surveyor's Office at Yankton visited the northern part of the territory in the fall of 1871 and laid out several townships along the proposed Northern Pacific line from Fargo, or Centralia, westward, including the fertile Sheyenne Valley. The government expended twenty thousand dollars for land surveys in Dakota Territory in 1872, about half of which was used in the Red River Valley. The total amount of land surveyed in the territory at the close of the year was a little over 6,500,000 acres, leaving more than 90,000,000 acres to be surveyed. In 1872 the work of the surveyors along the line of the Northern Pacific was continued. As the company owned every odd section on each side of the road, it became necessary to make surveys in order that settlers might be able to select their claims on government land, that of the railroad not being on the market at the time.[15]

Association. The association was quite active and adopted a memorial to Congress asking for a prompt survey of the public lands in that locality.

[14] Pamphlet by Jay Cooke and Company, December 25, 1873, pp. 15, 28-9. The name of the crossing-point had been changed at a director's meeting of the company May 1, 1873, from Edwinton to Bismarck, in honor of the Prussian statesman. It is said that the change was made in order to facilitate the sale of bonds in Germany.

[15] *Annual Report of the Commission of the General Land Office,* 1871, pp. 290-7, 1872, pp. 270-7.

Beginning in the spring of 1872 a steady stream of immigration crossed the Red River. While some of them stopped and settled along the river valley, a greater number made preëmption, homestead, and timber claims [16] on the government sections both north and south of the road. A little later, holders of Northern Pacific bonds bought lands from the railroad sections, and many farms both large and small were established there. Three towns along the railroad soon became important points: Bismarck, Jamestown, and Fargo.

Until December, 1870, northern Dakota was a part of the Vermillion Land District, and up to June 1, 1871, only twenty-eight filings had been made in the northern portion of the territory. For the year ending June 1, 1872, there had been sixty-one entries and up to June 1, 1873, the total number of entries on public lands in northern Dakota was 764.[17] Bismarck was the metropolis of northern Dakota at that time and contained some sixty buildings, most of which were constructed of logs covered with earth. The population of the town was about two hundred. There was a military post called Camp Hancock near Bismarck, and across the Missouri River was Fort Abraham Lincoln. The region west of the river was Indian country. In the fall of 1873 the beginnings of a town were noted about twenty miles east of Bismarck near the present town of Sterling. A town named Vincent was located at what is now Lake Eggleston, and Jamestown had increased in size, the box-car formerly used for a hotel having been supplanted by the Goodrich House. The town was ambitious for the land-

---

[16] *U. S. Public Statutes at Large*, XVII, 605. The first Timber-Culture Act became law on March 13, 1873. This bill, "an act to encourage the growth of timber on the western prairies," provided that any person who would plant, protect and keep in a healthy growing condition for ten years, forty acres of timber— trees not more than twelve feet apart—would receive title to the quarter-section of which the forty acres were a part. Only one quarter in any one section could be obtained in this manner, and there was a limit of 160 acres to a person. The law was modified in 1878. *U. S. Public Statutes at Large*, **XX**, 113.

[17] *Northwest Magazine* (Fargo, D. T.), March, 1886, p. 306; *Annual Report of the Commissioner of the General Land Office*, 1870-73.

office and felt certain it would become the capital of the northern part of a divided Dakota. Many homesteaders had taken claims along the railroad between Jamestown and Fargo in 1873 and the latter had developed into a thriving town.[18]

The territorial legislature of 1873, anticipating a rapid influx of settlers, defined the boundaries of seventy counties, fifteen of which were located in the southern portion of the territory. The counties of Stutsmen, Moody, Richland, Kingsbury, Burleigh, and Cass were organized.[19]

The increase in the settlers in northern Dakota was in proportion to that in the southern part. A Dakota editor summarized what had taken place in 1873:

The immigration of 1873 has surpassed the most sanguine predictions and puts to rest the last doubt of the occupation of the prairies of Dakota. While the Sioux, Vermillion and James valleys have swelled their population to treble the number they had when the present season opened, the Red River Valley had done fully as well. The county of Turner now stands at a point of population as far advanced as Union stood in 1871. Settlement has entered the James River Valley to a point eighty miles north of Yankton. The arrival of the Russian-German colonies is one of the most notable immigration events of the year. If they come to Dakota next season as fast as is predicted at present, the problem of how to settle Dakota will be solved.[20]

The period from 1873 to 1878 was one of pronounced economic depression throughout the country. During those years immigration to Dakota was retarded by that and other factors. The years from 1868 to 1873 had been a period of unparalleled prosperity throughout all of the United States. Every line of business had felt the stimulus of war tariffs and prices, and there was over-

---

[18] C. A. Lounsberry, "Early Development of North Dakota," *Collections,* State Historical Society of North Dakota, I, 300-4.

[19] *Session Laws of the Territory of Dakota,* 1872-73, pp. 30-2.

[20] *Yankton Press and Dakotian,* December 24, 1873; *Clay County Register,* August 31, 1873; *Annual Report of the Commissioner of the General Land Office,* 1871-73.

speculation in manufacturing and railroad building. The Homestead Act contributed its full share to the investment craze, and eastern capitalists invested money in Dakota land and property at rather inflated prices. Many pioneers, eager to improve and enlarge their holdings, borrowed money from eastern bankers, mortgaging their property as security. They, like other business men, committed the mistake of sinking in improvements more money than could be made out of their surplus products for years to come. When interest was not paid the creditor often foreclosed and took the land in lieu of payment. The land thus taken over was not readily converted into cash and often became a losing investment. For two years preceding the crisis money was scarce and rates of interest high. The Northern Pacific Railroad Company failed in September, 1873, when a financial panic swept over the entire country. This was not felt in Dakota, however, nearly so much as in the industrial centers. Being an agricultural community, the territory could at least raise its own food. The panic of 1873, therefore, was only one of the contributing causes which checked immigration during the period.[21]

From 1874 to 1876 grasshoppers appeared in enormous swarms in the western region. They destroyed the crops and left many of the frontier farmers destitute. To add to the hardship, the winter of 1874-75, following what is known as the "grasshopper year," was exceedingly severe. It caused a great deal of suffering throughout the territory, and relief was necessary. The moral effect of the grasshopper plague was injurious, and newspaper articles, often supplemented by stories of people who left Dakota, kept many prospective settlers from migrating to the West. Several dry years helped to cause reaction and depression.[22]

Circumstances, however, were not all of an adverse nature, as

[21] E. F. Peterson, *Historical Atlas of South Dakota* (Chicago, Ill., 1904), pp. 58-9. The files of the *Dakota Republican* and *Yankton Press and Dakotian* for 1875-76 are filled with stories of mortgage and sheriff's sales.

[22] "A History of Grasshoppers in Clay County," *Dakota Republican*, May 17, 1877; *St. Paul Press*, July 18, 1874.

certain factors were at work which tended to favor the coming of settlers. After the panic of 1873, the Northern Pacific Railroad Company did everything possible to induce settlers to come to Dakota, and its bonds, which were extremely low, were bought up and converted into lands of the company at par. Foreigners, especially Russian-Germans, were coming to America in large numbers. They were inclined to favor Dakota because of its climate and soil and were encouraged by their fellow countrymen already located there. Those who settled in the southeastern counties were conservative and careful men. They usually had some money with which to begin farming operations. They practised diversified farming and were not inclined to invest in expensive machinery and consequently were not affected by the drought and grasshopper plagues as were the other settlers.

Another factor conducive to an influx of settlers was the establishment of the territorial Bureau of Immigration in 1875, which sent representatives to the East and distributed pamphlets in several languages describing possibilities and opportunities in Dakota. Many of the immigrant folders were sent abroad.[23]

The largest factor, however, that tended to favor immigration was the discovery of gold in the Black Hills. The most direct effect of this was that miners and speculators, as well as people directly or indirectly supported by them, furnished a market for various commodities. The favorably located farmers in the western part of the territory sold produce to the Black Hills population for several years and freighted large quantities of supplies from the railroad termini to the gold region. The total amount of freight received in the Black Hills after 1877 is said to have been at least forty million pounds a year. Most of the oxen and horses used in transporting this freight were raised near-by, and the various Black Hills transportation companies secured many other supplies from the agriculturalists of the region. Goods were also

---

[23] *Session Laws of the Territory of Dakota,* 1875; Visher, "Geography of South Dakota," pp. 143-4.

carried to the Black Hills from Bismarck and Pierre by "farmer outfits" during the winter months, considerable sums of money being earned in this manner by settlers in the counties bordering the Missouri River.[24]

The gold of the Black Hills also influenced the settlement of neighboring areas by attracting thousands of young men to the mining camps. Many of those who went to the gold district did not remain there permanently but, after accumulating a small stake or becoming discouraged, returned to the eastern part of the territory, where they located on farms or entered business in one of the towns observed on their way to the Hills. Indeed, there is considerable evidence that many persons who set out for the mining camps during the gold rush never arrived there, but attracted by opportunities for farming or business in the southeastern part of the territory, remained there instead of making the costly trip to the gold-fields.

The opening of deep gold-mines and the development of other mineral resources gave promise of furnishing permanent employment to many workers. While on a tour of inspection of proposed routes to the Black Hills, Marvin Hughitt, president of the Chicago and Northwestern Railroad Company, became greatly impressed with the possibilities of the area east of the Missouri River and resolved to try an experiment in railroad building. He conceived the idea that by projecting his road into the unoccupied portion of Dakota east of the Missouri he could induce large numbers of settlers to come in and take up land, thereby producing profitable business for the road. The plan was promptly approved by the directors of the company and also adopted by its keen rival, the Chicago, Milwaukee and St. Paul Railroad Company.

[24] E. A. Curley, *The True History of the Black Hills* (Chicago, 1876), pp. 20, 39-40, 80; Tallent, *The Black Hills*, pp. 290-308; Rosen, *Pa-ha-sa-pah or the Black Hills of South Dakota*, p. 117. The territorial legislature defined the boundaries of Custer, Pennington, and Lawrence counties in 1875, the first two being organized on March 5, 1877, and the latter on December 30th of the same year. *Session Laws of the Territory of Dakota*, 1875 and 1877; *Deadwood Daily Champion*, June 21, 28, 1877; *Black Hills Pioneer*, January 16, 1878.

The construction of these proposed transportation lines was one of the factors that made the later settlement of the region possible.

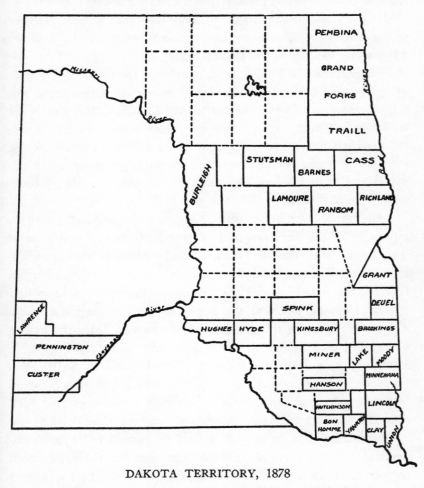

DAKOTA TERRITORY, 1878

Solid lines, counties organized; dotted lines, boundaries defined.

The presence of gold, the excitement created by its discovery, the many encounters with Indians, and especially the exciting times in the mining camps, particularly Deadwood, were described in numerous newspapers, magazines, pamphlets, and books, as

well as by word of mouth. These descriptions and stories advertised the region widely, made Dakota a familiar word throughout
the country and paved the way for the "Great Dakota Boom."

By 1877 conditions began to improve, and families farther
to the east who had been reduced to bankruptcy by the panic of
1873 were looking for a chance to begin life anew. Many saw
their opportunity in Dakota, and, in spite of the discouraging state
of agriculture, began to locate their homesteads in that area. Not
all, of course, who were looking toward Dakota at this time were
bankrupts, as many men with energy and means saw the opportunities there and made ready to avail themselves of them. Young
men just starting in life were the preponderant element in the
movement. Nevertheless, Dakota was to be the salvation of thousands who had failed in the panic of 1873.

Immigration was heavy during the summer and fall of 1877,
especially in the northern and central portions of the territory.
The Sioux Valley was well occupied and a group of men traveling
from Sioux Falls to Lake Kampeska late in May, 1877, reported
that for the first time in their experience they were able to find
regular stopping places at the homes of settlers along the route.
The public lands in the eastern tier of counties, from the mouth
of the Big Sioux River to the international boundary line above
Pembina, were largely exhausted. The Vermillion Valley was
fairly well settled, and the James River Valley had been occupied
to points north of Firesteel and scattering settlements had been
made along the valley both north and south of Jamestown.[25]

The immigration boom, which had its genesis in 1877, developed in volume in 1878. The Winona and St. Peter Railroad,
completed to Lake Kampeska in 1873, had never been operated
and had fallen into disrepair. It was rebuilt in 1878 and opened
for traffic late in the season. The line later known as the Chicago,
St. Paul, Minneapolis and Omaha Railroad, but then called the

[25] *Lincoln County Advocate* (Canton, D. T.), May 7, 14, 21, 28, 1878;
Kingsbury, *History of Dakota Territory*, II, 1033-4.

Worthington and Sioux Falls Railroad, was completed from Sioux City to Sioux Falls during the summer. The Pembina division of the Dakota Southern line was completed as far north as Beloit, two miles below Canton, during the season. Mr. Hughitt, in furtherance of his plans to build a road westward to the Missouri River in southeastern Dakota, made a personal reconnaissance of the field in 1878 and consummated his plans for the extension of the Chicago and Northwestern Railroad to a point on the Missouri River. That year the Hastings and Dakota branch of the Milwaukee Railroad was extended to Montevideo, Minnesota, its southern division to Pipestone, and its southern Iowa division to Sheldon, Iowa. Surveys were completed to Eden and Hudson upon a projection intended to strike Yankton.

The immigration in 1878 was greater than that of 1877, and settlers came into the territory through all gateways from the mouth of the Big Sioux to Pembina in surprising numbers. Thousands of homesteads were taken up, and the importunity of the home-seekers was so determined and persistent that the land and court officials having authority to make out the preliminary papers were frequently routed out of their beds to accommodate parties who felt that a night's delay would give rival claimants an opportunity to file ahead of them. This rush was in evidence at all the land-offices, with the exception of Deadwood and Bismarck. Immigration poured into the territory until it passed beyond the surveyed lands, and in many cases claims were taken in a rather haphazard manner.[26]. Six new counties were organized in 1878 [27] and others followed in rapid succession.

[26] To relieve uncertainty and congestion, Congress enacted a law permitting the claimants to land to deposit a sum of money with the surveyor-general of the territory sufficient to cover the cost of surveying a township, usually about $400, and that official would issue a certificate made receivable in payment of land in case of commutation. They were also transferable to other parties. Under this arrangement thousands of acres of land were surveyed, especially in the northern part of the territory. Congress later found it expedient to repeal the law as unscrupulous parties were taking fraudulent advantage of it. *U. S. Public Statutes at Large*, XIX, 121; *Yankton Press and Dakotian*, May 4, 1878.
[27] *Session Laws of the Territory of Dakota*, 1878.

Some idea of the boom that was developing can be gained from the reports of the various land-offices during these years. For the fiscal year ending June 30, 1877, there were 212,556 acres of land filed upon at the various land-offices in the territory. The report for June 30, 1878, for the six Dakota land-offices showed 1,377,948 acres filed upon, with the Sioux Falls office first with 702,843 acres; Fargo second with 324,384, and Yankton third with 241,837 acres. In June, 1879, 1,657,811 acres were reported, the largest number of filings being made at the Fargo office.[28]

VII

THE EARLY SETTLEMENT OF WYOMING

WHILE soldiers, traders, and trappers had located at various points in the area that was later to become the Territory of Wyoming during the first half of the nineteenth century, and thousands of settlers and miners bound for the Oregon country, Salt Lake City, and the western gold-fields passed through it, few had considered it worth their while to settle there. Permanent settlement of the Wyoming area came with the construction of the Union Pacific Railroad in the late sixties. The first transcontinental railroad was built rapidly across Nebraska in 1866 and by the latter part of June grading had been completed to a point west of Fort Kearney and rails had been laid one hundred and twenty-five miles west of Omaha. In the spring and summer of 1867, when it was rumored that the line would reach Crow Creek that winter, there was a rush of people to the place where the city of Cheyenne now stands.[29]

Although the tentative site for the town had been selected a year before by General Dodge and his party as they surveyed the

[28] *Reports of the Commissioner of the General Land Office*, 1877, pp. 172-3, 1878, pp. 150-1, 1879, pp. 226-9.
[29] *Desert News*, July 12, 1866; *The Latter Day Saints' Emigrants' Guide from Council Bluffs to the Valley of the Great Salt Lake* (Salt Lake City, Utah, 1868), pp. 11-9.

various possible routes, the official history of Cheyenne began with the completion of the town survey by the Union Pacific engineers late in July, 1867. James R. Whitehead, a member of the engineering corps, was made lot agent for the company and was authorized to dispose of lots for one hundred and forty dollars each, one third of which was to be paid in cash. Business was brisk and within a month some of the more desirable locations had been resold for as much as one thousand dollars. During the first few months the greater portion of the buildings consisted of tents, canvas and pole shacks, and dugouts. Mr. Whitehead constructed the first two-story house on the town-site with lumber hauled from Denver by six-horse teams. The first store was opened in August by Morton E. Post, who also speculated on some lots, and was said to have sold in December town lots purchased for six hundred dollars late in the summer of 1867, making a profit of five thousand dollars.[2]

By September 19, 1867, the track of the Union Pacific had been completed to within fifty-five miles of Cheyenne and was expected to arrive there by the middle of October. Toward the latter part of the same month, it was reported that business was booming and that huge heaps of supplies and dry-goods were piled up on the ground waiting for their owners to find a location. On October 10th town lots 22 by 132 feet, that had been purchased a short time before for from $120 to $400 each, were selling for from $400 to $4,000, and two weeks later it was reported that the "Cheyenne fever" was still raging as hundreds of people flocked to the "new boom town in the western portion of the Territory of Dakota."[3]

With the arrival of the railroad in November, lumber came in rapidly and building went on at a lively rate. The sound of saws and hammers could be heard at all hours as the carpenters labored

[2] *Colorado Leader* (Denver, Col.), July 6, 1867.

[3] *Cheyenne Daily Leader*, September 19, October 10, 24, 1867. This region was part of the Territory of Dakota until 1868 when it was organized as the Territory of Wyoming.

day and night in an attempt to keep up with the demand for dwellings and places of business. On November 21st the *Cheyenne Leader* reported that rents were "enormously high" and that real estate had advanced fourfold along the railroad line. The town of Cheyenne was incorporated by the Dakota legislature late in December and by the end of the year there were three thousand buildings in the boom town and a population estimated at from five to six thousand. The *Cheyenne Daily Leader* on July 11, 1867, told in these glowing terms of the rapid growth of the new metropolis:

One of the most remarkable instances of the rapid growth and unexampled prosperity of any city in the world is to be found in Cheyenne. A year ago the town was a boundless prairie, now it is a populous and flourishing city. The metropolis of Wyoming, Cheyenne is the very heart and soul of the plains and judging by her growth of the past year is destined to outstrip Omaha and Salt Lake City. Accessible from any direction any season of the year, it is the seat of the most populous county in the territory. It will soon be the most flourishing town between Missouri and California and now represents a greater population and manufacturing capital than all the other towns in the territory. That the capital of the territory will be located there does not admit of reasonable doubt. A city that supports three newspapers is not to be found in many portions of the country west of the Mississippi River and there are few towns in even Illinois or Indiana that can boast as much. One of the most important adjuncts to the prosperity of Cheyenne is Fort Russell.

Cheyenne remained the terminus of the Union Pacific for passengers and freight until work was resumed the following spring, at which time it was made the beginning of a new construction division. Trains arrived and departed daily, hauling large numbers of passengers and quantities of freight. In addition to the materials used for railroad construction, goods were brought there by rail to be carried to various points by overland freight lines. The streets of the new metropolis, several inches thick with dust, were filled with great creaking wagons hauled by mules and

CHEYENNE IN THE BOOM DAYS

Sixteenth Street in 1868. Courtesy of the Union Pacific Railroad.

oxen, and constantly resounded to the crack of the bullwhacker's whip.[4]

The heterogeneous population consisting of soldiers from Fort D. A. Russell and Camp Carlin close by, railroad workers, trappers, cowboys, cattle rustlers, freighters, prospectors, speculators, promoters, prostitutes, badmen, and loafers was restless and turbulent. The motley crowd, including as it did much of the dregs and scum of society, patronized in a liberal manner the saloons, hurdy-gurdies, gambling establishments, variety halls, and resorts of prostitution. Its fame for notoriousness spread and the new town was often referred to as "the richest and toughest town for its size in the country." Its rapid growth and unsavory reputation caused many to call it "Hell on Wheels," while some of the inhabitants whose sense of civic pride was in evidence, preferred the title "The Magic City of the Plains."

As the Union Pacific Railroad moved westward from Cheyenne in the spring of 1868 land companies preceded the construction gangs, selecting possible locations that were surveyed for townsites in preparation for the boom that was expected. Speculation in town-sites and lots was carried on to the point where it was largely a matter of gambling. Large sums of money were often lost, and high hopes were shattered when the railroad failed to go where it had been expected and many a boom town was left off the rails. Even the towns that sprang up over night along the railroad were often mere flashes in the pan, and with the passing on of the track relapsed into deserted prairies with only the steel rails and scattered debris to remind the traveler of their temporary hopes.

Some few of the boom towns endured after the construction gangs left and of these Cheyenne was the most important. But the future of the Magic City was not certain for a time.[5] When

[4] *Wyoming State Leader* (Cheyenne, Wy.), July 19, 1917.
[5] "Many people wonder about the present importance of the town of Cheyenne," observed a local editor in the fall of 1867. "Some who come here think it is a bubble and will decline." *Cheyenne Daily Leader*, September 19, December 21, 24, 1867.

the railroad moved on in the spring of 1868 Cheyenne quickly shrank to about fifteen hundred inhabitants, but soon settled down and became the largest and most stable town along the line.

During the year 1868 the Union Pacific was rapidly constructed toward the western boundary of the Territory of Wyoming, with three shifts of men working eight hours each. Hundreds of home-seekers were brought in by the railroad and by the close of the year the population of the territory was estimated by enthusiastic boosters at fifty thousand, which was far too high.[6] Early in May as the track arrived at Laramie City a Cheyenne editor made the following comment: "The first train of railroad cars reached Laramie City and there was great rejoicing. Real estate went up and the fluid extract of corn went down. To purchase a lot within sixteen blocks of the *Index* office was a financial impossibility." [7] A few days later an observer wrote in a letter regarding Laramie City: "There are at Laramie City a goodly number of respectable shops and new buildings are being erected. Almost every branch of trade is represented. Many of the dwellers live in tents at present, but the town will soon be built up of logs, boards, and shingles and will be filled with goods and tradesmen. As to what will come of it three months hence? Ask some of the towns along the Union Pacific for an answer." [8] A week later a Cheyenne resident who had gone to Laramie City for business purposes wrote to a home paper: "After two weeks of hard work I am ready to say I should have remained in Cheyenne. There was considerable speculation in real estate here but it is all over now and I congratulate myself that I rented instead of buying. Nobody stops here anymore. The history of the rise, decline, and fall of this place is about written." [9]

[6] *Cheyenne Weekly Leader*, May 5, 1868; *Cheyenne Daily Leader*, July 25, August 21, 1868.
[7] The *Frontier Index* was a newspaper that followed the advance of the track as the Union Pacific advanced westward.
[8] *Cheyenne Daily Leader*, May 5, 1868.
[9] *Ibid.*, June 12, 24, 30, July 6, 20, 24, October 10, 1868.

The early files of the Wyoming newspapers indicated the west-ward advance of the Union Pacific and the development of towns along the way. On June 12, 1868, it was announced that North Platte consisted of one hundred and twenty-five buildings and eighteen days later it was reported that the railroad had been opened to Carbon City, eighty miles west of Laramie City and that freight trains were running daily to the new terminus. On July 20th trains were operating to Benton City, a town on the west side of the North Platte River, and it was announced that the engineers expected the road to reach Green River by fall in spite of the fact that the country between North Platte and Green River was rough, and that if the winter was light it might be able to reach Salt Lake City early the next summer. On October 10th the bridge over Green River had been completed and pas-senger trains were expected to be running to Bryan at an early date. At Green River City every kind of business was lively and booming.

A letter written by an inhabitant of Green River on October 29th to a Cheyenne editor was evidence of the uncertainties of railroad towns along the line of our first transcontinental railroad:

The history of the rise and fall of Green River is ready to be written. Shooting and violence have characterized the short existence of the place, which has been both brief and unpoetic, and is played out. By Monday next there will not be twenty-five persons in the once famous city. The business portion of the community now consists of one house, one whiskey mill, one billiard hall and an outfitting store which is already packing up to leave. Bryan is a little better but has seen its best days and the rush is now for Bear River, alias Gilmer. The end of the track is now beyond Granger, sixty-five miles west of here and going at a lively rate.[10]

But all of the settlement in Wyoming was not along the line of the Union Pacific Railroad, as in May of 1868 there was a con-siderable number of ranches scattered through the Green River

[10] *Ibid.*, October 31, 1868.

Valley, and according to an observer, "That country ere many years shall have passed will become the home of large numbers of Americans." At about the same time thirty-six settlers were said to have erected homes for themselves in the Wind River Valley and several more houses were going up. "The gardens around the ranches are looking well," said an editor, and added the prediction, "We expect to see the Wind River Valley thickly settled by fall." [11]

On November 5th the *Frontier Index* began publication at Bear River and during the last part of the month the town-site of Evanston in the southwest corner of Wyoming, not far from the Idaho line, was in the process of construction in anticipation of the arrival of the railroad. The first issue of the *Evanston Express*, November 27, 1868, stressed the "wonderful future" of the place and spoke of its rapid growth: "Six weeks ago there was not a building here, to-day there are at least one hundred completed and twenty-five more are going up." A week later a well-known Wyoming editor under the heading "Evanston" wrote: "A large number of homes and business places have been lately constructed in this 'Magic City.' They are for the most part substantial buildings. Iron to complete the railroad to Evanston is daily expected. Large stocks of goods are exposed for sale, and business is brisk." [12] On January 19, 1869, the track was finished to Echo City across the Wyoming line and approximately one hundred and twenty miles from Ogden, Utah, where construction was halted because of snow and cold. Work was resumed in March and on May 10, 1869, the Central Pacific and Union Pacific roads formed a junction at Promontory Point not far from Ogden, where the golden spike was driven with full ceremonies and there was rejoicing and celebration throughout the nation.

The building of the railroad across the southern portion of the Territory of Wyoming marked the first step in the settlement

[11] *Ibid.*, May 28, June 1, 1868.
[12] *Wyoming Weekly Tribune* (Cheyenne, Wyo.), December 4, 1868.

of the area. While settlers did not flock to the territory in large numbers, the cattle industry was stimulated and a fringe of permanent settlements was established along the line of transportation. Although the future of many of the Union Pacific towns seemed uncertain during the early years, several of them endured after the construction gangs had passed on and became frontier settlements of considerable importance. With population greatly reduced from what it had been when they were located at the "end of the track," they settled down, "gasped for breath," and became permanent. In 1870 the population of the more important Wyoming towns along the railroad was as follows: Cheyenne, 1,450; Laramie City, 828; Rawlins Springs, 612; Carbon, 244; Bryan, 239; Green River City, 106. Evanston, the last boom town along the line, had been deflated to the point where its population was only 77 in number.[13]

The gold discoveries of the late sixties in Wyoming were widely advertised through the press, and prospectors in considerable numbers tried their luck there, many of them coming in by way of the Union Pacific. For a time, at least, high hopes were entertained by some that Wyoming was destined to become a bullion-producing territory of the first rank. The largest vein of gold was discovered at South Pass just north of the railroad on the southern edge of the Wind River Mountains on the old Oregon Trail. South Pass City boomed and boasted a population at one time of two thousand inhabitants, most of whom left when the gold gave out. Atlantic City, close by, became another gold camp and passed through the same kind of boom and decline. In 1870 South Pass City reported a population of 460 inhabitants, while Atlantic City could muster only 325. Coal-mining attracted some settlers in the early period, the first mine being located about seventy-five miles west of Laramie City. One of the most extensive deposits in the territory was located at Rock Springs, where the Rocky Mountain Coal and Iron Company worked a large seam and at

[13] *U. S. Census Report for 1870*, Volume on Population, 96.

times, shortly after the railroad was constructed, employed as many as four hundred men.[14]

By 1870 there were but a few straggling settlements within the borders of the Territory of Wyoming, most of which were in the southern portion along the railroad. There were five organized

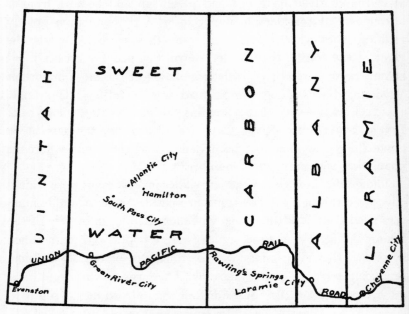

WYOMING TERRITORY, 1880

counties in the territory with a total population of 9,118. Cheyenne, the capital, had less than fifteen hundred inhabitants while Laramie City, the second town in size, had a few more than eight hundred inhabitants.

In spite of the attempts on the part of the Union Pacific Railroad to obtain settlers, and the advertising activities of the local

[14] Strahorn, *Handbook of Wyoming and Guide to the Black Hills and Big Horn Basin*, pp. 52-6; *Cheyenne Daily Leader*, November 2, 1867, October 3, December 3, 1868, October 9, 1869; *U. S. Census Report for 1870*, Volume on Population, 96.

press, few settlers came to Wyoming in the decade of the seventies. Cattle- and sheep-ranching developed rapidly but added relatively few inhabitants to the population of the territory. The very nature of the open-range industry called for exceedingly sparse population. By 1879 stock were being grazed as far north as Johnson County, of which Buffalo was the county-seat.

By 1880 there were seven organized counties in the territory with a total population of 20,789. The bulk of the population still lived along the railroad in the southern part of the territory. The five largest cities were Cheyenne, Laramie City, Rawlins, Evanston, and Rock Springs, whose population numbered 3,456, 2,693, 1,451, 1,277, and 763, respectively, and totaled almost half of the entire population. The early mining towns of Atlantic City and South Pass had declined to almost nothing, one having 82 inhabitants, and the other a total of 27.[15] The rougher elements of population that followed the railroad in earlier years had almost disappeared and the larger towns were cattle centers and points of recreation for cowboys.

VIII

THE EARLY SETTLEMENT OF MONTANA

At the beginning of the Civil War period the Montana area was a frontier wilderness and although the various fur companies had been active there for more than half a century, it had but few permanent settlers. East of the Rockies was Fort Benton, head of navigation on the upper Missouri River, whose rough adobe buildings housed a few white settlers. A Catholic mission by the name of St. Peters was located in the Sun River region, while west of the mountains, a short distance south of Flathead Lake, was the thriving mission of St. Ignatius. At Fort Owen, a former trading-post, had developed a small agricultural settlement.

---

[15] *U. S. Census Report for 1880.* Volume on Population, 375.

The real settlement of the region began in the early sixties with the advance of the gold frontier eastward into Idaho and the discovery of gold at Bannack, which was located within the area that was later to become the Territory of Montana. Within a few months there were several gold-mining camps containing several thousand prospectors scattered over western Montana. Early records indicate that during the winter of 1862-63 there were some 571 inhabitants living in the Montana area, most of which were located in the mining district of Bannack.[1] A traveler from Minnesota arriving at Bannack in April, 1863, estimated the population at that time close to one thousand.[2] When the overland expedition of James L. Fiske reached Bannack late in September of the same year he reported nearly a thousand people living there and stated that in June, before the stampede to the "Stinking Water" mines, the place had boasted of from three to four thousand inhabitants.[3] A Salt Lake City editor in August, 1863, estimated the population of Bannack at five thousand and the following March put it at twelve hundred.[4]

With the discovery of gold in Alder Gulch, the town of Virginia City sprang into existence and in the summer of 1864 it was reported to have almost ten thousand inhabitants. The Territory of Montana was created in 1864 and in the first election for a delegate to represent the new territory in Congress there were 6,230 votes cast, returns from some of the larger settlements being as follows: Virginia City, 338; Highland, 134; Bannack, 27; Deer Lodge, 11.[5] The editor of the *Montana Post* in August, 1865, gave some information on settlement:

Immigration is beginning to arrive from the states and we see many new faces in town. Fifty families have located among us within the last week and the passengers who arrive by overland coaches report

[1] *Contributions*, Montana Historical Society, I, 334-54.
[2] *St. Cloud Democrat*, May 21, 1863; *Deseret News*, July 1, 1863.
[3] *Annual Report of the Secretary of the Interior*, 1863, pp. 132-3.
[4] *Deseret News*, August 16, 1863, March 30, 1864.
[5] *Montana Post*, October 29, 1864.

long lines of "pilgrims" and freighters on the road. Agriculture is looking up and from every valley we hear reports of permanent settlements. Money is now flowing from the sluice boxes and prospectors
will scatter into the gulches in large numbers, and unless some unex-
pected circumstances should arise a lively fall and winter are expected.[6]

The discovery of gold in Last Chance Gulch in 1866 caused
a stampede to that area and within a short time Helena became
an important gold camp and grew rapidly as the rush gained
momentum. The first issue of the *Helena Herald* reported the
laying-out of the town of Copperopolis, sponsored by the Musselshell Mining Company, among the copper lodes in the Musselshell country.[7] At an election in 1867 there were 11,596 votes
cast for a territorial delegate to Congress, which according to the
territorial officials, did not give an accurate picture of the population, as there were few precincts in which all that were eligible
voted. The surveyor-general estimated the population at forty
thousand and predicted that it would reach sixty thousand by 1868
if Indian troubles did not keep emigrants away.[8] J. Ross Browne
in his report on *The Mineral Resources of the States and Territories West of the Rocky Mountains* estimated that in September,
1866, the population of the Territory of Montana numbered
29,500, while another well-informed observer put the number at
32,000 in 1867.[9]

By 1867 settlers had begun to filter into the more fertile valleys of Montana. A traveler from Helena to the Yellowstone
country described the immigration to the Gallatin Valley through
which he passed. Gallatin City was a small settlement with a grist-
mill and a school, in addition to several stores and a saloon. The
population of Bozeman City was estimated at four hundred with

[6] *Ibid.*, August 5, 27, 1865.
[7] *Helena Weekly Herald*, November 15, 1866.
[8] *Annual Report of the Secretary of the Interior*, 1867, p. 388.
[9] *House Exec. Doc.*, 40th Cong., 2nd Sess., No. 202, 487; *House Exec. Doc.*,
39th Cong., 2nd Sess., No. 92, 7.

a church, a school, a large hotel, and two saloons. While the vote cast in the valley that year had numbered six hundred, the observer put the population of the area at thirty-five hundred, which was no doubt a generous figure. X. Biedler, a well-known law enforcement officer of the territory, visited Missoula Mills in the spring of 1867 and reported a rapidly growing town in a flourishing agricultural community with three hotels, one of which was among the best in the territory, a sawmill, a good restaurant, a large flour mill, two mercantile establishments, and a number of other good buildings.[10]

In the fall of 1869 Robert Vaughn located a homestead in the Sun River Valley on the north side of the river about nine miles below the Sun River crossing, not far from the Helena and Benton road. When he entered his claim at the land-office in Helena he was informed that his was the first land taken in Chouteau County. At that time less than two million acres of government land had been surveyed in the territory, of which about 1,600,000 acres had been taken.[11]

The decline of the placer mines and the failure to find new ones of importance in the late sixties caused large numbers of the floating population to leave Montana, while Indian troubles beginning in 1868 tended to keep out new settlers. The census of 1870 reported a total population of 20,580 in the territory, 18,306 of which were whites, with 1,949 Chinese. Eleven counties had been organized, Lewis and Clark ranking first with 5,040 inhabitants; Deer Lodge County second with 4,367; and Madison County third with 2,684. The three counties with the smallest number of inhabitants were Big Horn with 38, Dawson with 177, and Beaverhead, which was accredited with 722. The largest towns in the territory were Helena, the capital, with 3,106 inhabitants;

[10] Helena Weekly Herald, September 5, May 2, 1867.
[11] Robert Vaughn, Then and Now, or Thirty-six Years in the Rockies, 1864-1900 (Minneapolis, Minn., 1900), p. 64.

Virginia City, 867; Deer Lodge, 788; Blackfoot, 499; Diamond City, 460; Bannack, 381; Fort Benton, 367; Beartown, 355; and Butte City, with 241. There were 479 inhabitants in Prickly Pear Valley; 314 in Bitter Root Valley; 176 in Sun River Valley and 144 in Beaverhead Valley. Of the total population, 8,020 were engaged in mining.[12]

IX

IMMIGRATION TO MONTANA, 1870-1880

IN THE DECADE of the seventies the population of the Territory of Montana increased but slowly due to Indian troubles, grasshopper plagues, and, most of all, to the lack of railroad facilities. Large areas of its land were not especially fitted for agricultural purposes, although it had a considerable number of rich river valleys. The cattle industry developed rapidly during the decade, as in the case of Wyoming, but did not bring many settlers to the territory. While the Black Hills gold rush attracted miners from Montana at first, in the long run the advertising and publicity given the West probably helped immigration to Montana. There was some movement of population to the territory, however, throughout the seventies, as immigration activities were carried on by local and territorial authorities.

A Virginia City editor writing in the spring of 1871 on the subject of settlement wondered why immigration was so light to Montana: "Why don't laborers and settlers come out? Crops are good and the fares from Omaha to Corrine, Utah, over the Union Pacific are reasonable, having been reduced to $40 by regular passenger trains and to $30 by immigration train. The farmers of lower Deer Lodge and Flint Creek Valleys are in need of laborers and are offering $60 per month with board." The same editor in August, however, reported that Bozeman was booming,

---

[12] U. S. Census Report for 1870, Volume on Population, 46, 195.

more than fifty business firms having been located there within six months.[1]

A Bozeman editor in August, 1873, reported that a party of immigrants had passed through the town bound for the Yellowstone Valley. "They hail from Oregon. There were five wagons filled with women and children and quite a number of men on horseback driving the stock that belonged to the expedition. They appeared to be a very desirable class of emigrants and had several hundred head of stock." [2] Another party from Minnesota and Wisconsin was reported to have arrived in the valley a week before, some of whom were to settle there, and the remainder were going on to the Yellowstone.

In the spring of 1874 the same editor printed a long article on "Marvelous Montana" which ended with the following statement, "Although the tide of imimgration has not set in, our native population is rapidly on the increase." A few weeks later after describing the movement of settlers westward over the Union Pacific in the spring and summer of 1874, he said: "Of course, very few of these immigrants will come to Montana, because we have no railroads. Montana, however, has many advantages to offer to settlers." [3] At Corrine, Utah, settlers were observed at times on their way to Montana. The editor of the *Daily Mail* in that city in July, 1874, saw a "three-decked outfit pulled by eight large oxen bound for Montana." [4]

In the spring of 1875 the *Benton Record* reported large numbers of prairie-schooners bound westward. On April 25th fifteen were reported in one party, loaded with household goods and children, on their way west. In August a considerable movement of settlers was observed in the fertile valleys of the territory.[5] In the fall of 1875 Butte was booming and there had been more than

[1] *Montanian*, April 13, 27, August 17, 1871.
[2] *Avant Courier*, August 8, 1873.
[3] *Ibid.*, April 10, 17, May 21, 1874.
[4] *Corrine Daily Mail*, July 17, 1874.
[5] *Benton Record*, February 1, April 25, August 14, 1875.

BANNACK, FIRST CAPITAL OF MONTANA TERRITORY

three thousand claims recorded in the district where rich copper lodes had been discovered. The town had five hundred inhabitants, five saloons, one brewery, two butcher shops, two shoemakers, three blacksmith shops, several general stores, and two quartz mills of ten stamps each.[6]

Indian troubles, becoming somewhat serious in Montana as early as 1868, were brought to a head when the Custer exploring expedition was sent into the Black Hills, and was followed by a

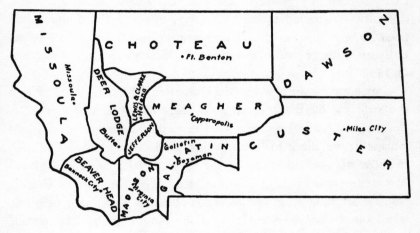

MONTANA TERRITORY, 1879

rush of population to that area in spite of the treaties with the Indians. The Sioux clung tenaciously to their treaty rights, thus placing the military and Indian officials in an embarrassing position. Evidence of fear and nervous tension in the Montana region was shown by the numerous applications for more military protection within the territory. From October, 1873, to October, 1874, the Secretary of War at Washington received nine urgent requests for further military forces by the citizens of Montana, and during the following year five more were sent to the War

[6] *Rocky Mountain Husbandman,* November 25, 1875; *Helena Independent,* December 30, 1875.

Department. The citizens of Missoula County were insistent that they be given a military force for the protection of settlers in the various western valleys. The territorial governor and citizens in the vicinity of Fort Benton, Camp Baker, and Fort Ellis pled with the national authorities for more protection.

The events of the Sioux War culminating in the serious defeat of General Custer at the battle of the Little Big Horn in June, 1876, led to the sending of additional troops to Montana sufficient to curb any possible outbreak that might occur. Although difficulties continued throughout 1877, by 1878 the dangers had been largely eliminated and immigration increased rapidly, especially after the revival of Northern Pacific activities in the summer of 1879.

Grasshoppers were worse than usual in Montana in 1876 and the rush to the Black Hills gold-fields was well under way. A Bozeman editor in February, after reporting a movement of Montanians to the Black Hills and other gold camps, said, "The rush to those gold-bearing sections will be unusually large this year." An attempt was made at this time to establish the town of Carroll below Fort Benton on the Missouri River as a shipping point. It was located thirty-five miles from the mouth of the Musselshell and was more accessible to steamboats after midsummer than was Fort Benton. In 1876 it was a small frontier settlement of about seventy-five inhabitants, consisting largely of wood-choppers, trappers and hunters. By 1878 it was reported to be receiving some freight during low water but had in no way displaced Fort Benton.[7]

During the summer of 1877 there was a gradual revival of immigration and early in June many new-comers were locating in the territory, with the citizens of several towns lustily demanding a more active immigration society.[8] The establishment of Miles City in the eastern part of the territory was largely due to the

[7] *Avant Courier*, February 18, 1876; *Omaha Bee*, January 1, 1876.
[8] *Avant Courier*, June 7, 1877.

advance of ranching activities into that area. The wild and rough life in this "cowboy capital" and the type of population that gathered there brought forth criticism as well as apologies from various editors. One of them, after explaining that other towns that had developed and grown with like rapidity had witnessed just such scenes, added, "Go back to the early history of Bannack, Virginia City, Helena, Bismarck, Bozeman, and the boom towns of the Black Hills, and you have as bad, if not a worse, class of people than to-day are gathered at Miles City." [9]

Immigration gradually gained momentum in 1878, and dozens of covered wagons filled with household goods and women and children were observed moving into the river valleys of Montana. "They are but an advance guard of what is to follow, as settlers will soon be moving into Montana in ever-increasing numbers," was the general opinion. By 1879 strong objections to the type of immigrant known as "floaters" appeared in the *Benton Record*. In May a protest in an editorial on immigration was written as a warning to an ever-moving shiftless population that, in the words of the reporter, "was always active on the frontier." "Montana is no Elysium for idle tramps and idlers," observed the writer, "and it offers few inducements for men without means seeking genteel employment. Incompetent and half-fledged mechanics are not in demand and there is already a surplus of unskilled labor." A Virginia City paper took the same attitude when it printed the following observation:

We venture the assertion that ninety-nine hundredths of the persons who come here without means expecting, as we know many do, that nuggets are lying around loose and gold dust may be scooped up by the handful, will be doomed to have their crop of anticipations rudely smashed and will learn full soon that here, as elsewhere, the favors of fortune can only be secured by patient and persistent labor. But because riches cannot be had for the mere asking, it does not follow that Montana is not a good country to come to. We have seen each

[9] *Ibid., August* 3, 1877.

spring in recent years an ever increasing influx of population to the territory.[10]

Settlers in considerable numbers moved into the Gallatin and Yellowstone valleys in the summer of 1879 and, according to an observer at the territorial capital, seemed to be of the solid, thrifty type of immigrants whose addition would be a benefit to any community.[11]

The Montana boom was only well started when the census of 1880 was taken, which reported the total population of the territory at 39,159. Deer Lodge County ranked first with 8,876 and Lewis and Clark County was second with 6,521, while the next two counties in importance were Madison and Gallatin, with 3,915 and 2,643 inhabitants respectively. Chouteau County had 3,058, while Meagher and Missoula counties come next with 2,743 and 2,537. Dawson County was the most sparsely settled with its inhabitants numbered at 180. Helena, the capital of the territory, was the largest town, with a population of 3,624, and Butte ranked second with 3,363 inhabitants. Deer Lodge had a population of 941, Bozeman had 894, Virginia City 867, and Fort Benton boasted of 367 permanent residents.[12]

X

THE DAKOTA BOOM, 1879-1886

DURING the period 1879 to 1886 much of the Territory of Dakota was settled, and what a few years before had been an almost uninhabited expanse of prairie became a fairly populous farming region, soon to be divided and admitted into the Union as two states. The population of the territory increased from 135,177 in 1880 to approximately 210,000 in 1882, and in 1883 to about 330,000. From the establishment of the first land-office in the

---

[10] *Benton Record*, May 16, 1879; *Madisonian*, May 31, 1879.
[11] *Helena Daily Herald*, August 14, 1879.
[12] *U. S. Census Report for 1880*, Volume on Population, 250.

territory until June 30, 1880, a period of eighteen years, the total number of preëmption and homestead claims filed upon amounted to only 44,122, while the records of the land-office disclose that from the time of the taking of the census in 1880 to December 31, 1881, a period of less than nineteen months, 16,718 claims were entered. The total number of acres filed upon in Dakota prior to the census of 1880 was 7,381,880 acres, while in the succeeding nineteen months 1,029,280 acres were taken.[1] Probably more people moved into this region to make farm homes during any two years of the boom than during the twenty years which followed its collapse. Because of the vital significance of the boom in the settlement and development of the Territory of Dakota, it is desirable to consider in some detail the influences which produced, extended, and terminated it.

Rainfall was a factor of primary importance. Although the irregularity in amount and distribution of precipitation has always been more or less of a climatic handicap in Dakota, the rainfall during the boom period was ample and came at such times as to permit good crops. Had the period from 1878 to 1886 been as dry as the preceding eight years or the eight years that followed, there probably would have been no such rapid increase in settlement. A climatic factor of temporary importance in producing the boom was the "hard winter" of 1880-81. Although the severity of the winter tended to give Dakota Territory a bad reputation because of the blizzards and heavy snowfall, in other respects it promoted settlement. When the first fall came, the ground was practically unfrozen and because of the great depth of the snow, which is said to have averaged more than ten feet,[2] the earth remained only slightly frozen over a large area during the winter.

[1] *Congressional Record*, 47th Cong., 1st Sess., Senate Report 271, 2045-6; Report of the House Committee on Territories submitted in 1882, when reporting a bill for the admission of the State of Dakota.

[2] *Yankton Press and Dakotian*, January 13, 1882; Doane Robinson, *History of South Dakota* (Indianapolis, Ind., 1904), p. 246. This average doubtless applies to the eastern portion of the territory which was most thickly settled at that time.

When the snow melted in March and April, it saturated the soil and subsoil with water, and many of the undrained depressions of the prairies retained more or less moisture for some years after. As a result of the heavy rainfall, the water-table was higher for several seasons, and this residue may well have influenced the crops during those years. Even if the direct result was not very great the snow, by creating thousands of small ponds and lakes, suggested a humid climate, a condition highly attractive to prospective settlers.[3]

In addition to the relatively abundant precipitation of the period, the extension of railroads throughout most of the area was of great importance in starting and maintaining the boom. The early homesteaders remained upon their claims in hope that a railroad would appear and make their land valuable. Without good transportation facilities, or at least the expectation of that desideratum, the boom could not have taken place. During the early years few surplus products could be raised because of the lack of markets, and before the coming of the railroads to the various sections, most of the homesteaders were dependent, in part at least, upon their savings brought from other regions. Even though wheat, corn, and other crops of similar bulk and value yielded exceptionally well, farming could not be profitable if it was necessary to haul the produce many miles to market. Without railroads, necessary articles were bound to be costly and advancement was consequently discouraged. Because of the lack of timber in most parts of Dakota, materials for building and fences, and other bulky and heavy articles, cost so much after being wagoned long distances that most improvements were postponed. It was only with the help of rather extensive fences and buildings that a fairly dense population could support itself by raising stock, which must be driven long distances to market.

But the railroad supplied far more than transportation facilities.

[3] J. P. Finney, *Certain Climatic Features of the Two Dakotas* (Washington, D. C., 1890), p. 25; Visher, "Geography of South Dakota," 147.

It printed pamphlets for free distribution and published advertisements in newspapers and magazines which described the country and enumerated its advantages. It offered many valuable suggestions and in many cases was "explorer, carrier, provider, thinker, heart, soul, and intellect of the settler." A resident of the territory wrote in 1884: "The greatest factor in the upbuilding of Dakota, next to her vast expanse of public lands, has been the railroad. Gradually the fine agricultural lands and immense stock ranges would, no doubt, have been occupied; but without the railroad it would have required a century to accomplish what has been done in five years under its powerful influence."

Another potent factor in influencing the rapid settlement of Dakota was the earlier occupation of much of the more desirable land farther east and its general rise in price. This increase in price was accompanied by a rise in taxes. By 1879 there was little free land in eastern states as desirable for farming as that of Dakota. This caused many people to seek free land in the West, or at least a place where it was cheaper and taxes were lower, and as a result, many came to this territory. The level fields of Dakota gave it distinct advantages over the stony, rugged, stumpy lands to the east. The land of Dakota was ready for the plow, and it was not necessary to clear it of trees, stumps, brush, or stones. The new labor-saving machinery could be used there to better advantage, making large-scale farming practicable. Bumper crops had already established the country's reputation for fertility of soil.

During the years of crop failures and hardship the farmers of Dakota had learned many lessons and had thought out many problems for themselves. Wheat farming carried on alone had been disastrous to many. An occasional crop, even at a dollar a bushel, would not compensate for the losses which came with the lean years. Wheat was easily preyed upon by grasshoppers, and the farmers came to realize that some surer crop must be raised, something that would not be so easily destroyed, and which would furnish food for cattle and hogs. Because of these advantages, corn was slowly displacing wheat as a single crop, and the settlers learned the value of diversified agriculture. This change in farming marked an important epoch in the growth of the territory.[4]

Another factor of an agricultural nature that stimulated settlement and development had to do with the kind of wheat grown. Hard spring wheats were grown in Dakota far more successfully than soft winter varieties. Shortly before this time the invention of a new milling process had made it possible to utilize the hard varieties and to produce as good a grade of flour as by the use of the soft wheats. This raised the price of hard wheat and made wheat-growing in Dakota more profitable than it otherwise would have been. It also increased the demand for land and stimulated settlement.

At this time considerable capital was required for the construction of railroads and buildings, breaking sod, and the putting in and caring for crops, and it was very important that the country be in a prosperous condition. The general financial status of the nation was favorable for these things, as the effects of the panic had been largely overcome, and the abolition of fiat money had greatly improved the country's credit abroad. As a result, there was a strong inflow of capital during the period. The presence of gold in the Black Hills continued to favor settlement at this time by advertising Dakota, while it hastened its general economic development.

While there were many factors favoring settlement and prosperity, there were also certain conditions and influences that worked in an unfavorable manner. Perhaps the outstanding circumstance reacting against settlement during the boom years was the extremely severe winter of 1880-81, with the disastrous flood that followed in the spring, causing extreme hardship. The first snow came on October 15, 1880, so early in the season that the

---

[4] *U. S. Census Reports for 1870 and 1880*, Volumes on Agriculture. In 1870 Clay County in the southeastern portion of Dakota raised 55,612 bushels of wheat and 29,476 bushels of corn. In 1880 there were 8,335 bushels of wheat raised and 375,837 bushels of corn.

settlers were not prepared. There was a shortage of food, and many were forced to use hay and corn for fuel. Several bad storms occurred during the winter, and the damage caused by the flood, especially between Yankton and the Big Sioux River, was enormous.[5]

Another adverse factor was the high rate of interest charged on loans. Although the rate had been fixed at 7 per cent per annum by territorial law, much higher rates were often charged, as the law provided that a higher rate could be fixed by mutual agreement between borrower and lender. Farmers borrowed sparingly under these circumstances, having learned in the previous periods of depression that to attempt to better one's condition by borrowing money on land at high rates of interest was incurring the risk of losing the property through foreclosure. There was money to be had, and opportunties for investment where it could be made, but the high rates of interest made the settler very cautious. The principle generally followed by bankers at this time was that money was worth what it would bring.[6]

With 1879 the flood of immigration increased beyond the wildest hope of the old-time Dakotans. By the end of the year there was scarcely any desirable land left in the Big Sioux Valley that was not occupied and settlers were pouring into the valley of the James River. Immigrants came in large numbers to the Red River Valley and took up homesteads along the Northern Pacific Railway. They even crossed to the west side of the Missouri River and established small communities. In the years 1879 and 1880 there was rapid railroad expansion, which was very essential to settlement and development.

The line of railroad that had been completed from Elk Point to Sioux Falls in the summer of 1878 was extended forty miles to Flandreau in 1879. The Milwaukee Railroad had extended its Hastings and Dakota division as far west as Big Stone, and its

[5] *Yankton Press and Dakotian*, January 13, 1882.
[6] *Dakota Republican*, October 21, 1880.

Iowa division was completed through Canton to Marion Junction. Surveys were made westward from that point to Chamberlain and south to Running Water, both on the Missouri River. The Northwestern, with its restored Winona and St. Peter line resting at Watertown, had projected the Dakota Central division west from Tracy, Minnesota to Pierre, and the line was completed to Volga in Brookings County by the middle of November. Along these new lines towns sprang up over night. Elkton, Brookings, Volga, Goodwin, and Kransburg appeared along the Northwestern soon after 1879.[7] On the Milwaukee road Lennox, Parker, Marion, Mitchel, Scotland, and Tyndall resulted from the building and surveys of 1879, the three latter being laid out by the railroad land company and acquiring a good deal of importance long before the railroad was constructed. It was unquestionably the plan of the Northwestern at this time to push its Pierre extension on to the Black Hills, as it was doubtless the design of the Milwaukee to extend its Chamberlain line to the same terminus. The Worthington and Sioux Falls (Omaha) Railroad extended its line west as far as Salem in 1879, and the Pembina division of the Dakota Southern was built from Beloit to Sioux Falls and the Southern Minnesota reached Flandreau, the first train coming through on January 1, 1880. Within a few months the Dakota Southern and Southern Minnesota passed into the possession of the Milwaukee Railway Company.[8]

In the spring of 1880 the boom in immigration and railroad building continued, and during the year the Dakota Southern division of the Northwestern was constructed from Volga to Pierre, giving rise to the towns of Huron, De Smet, Miller, and Highmore. The road from Egan to Sioux Falls was constructed and the Southern Minnesota extended from Flandreau to Madison. The Milwaukee was extended from Marion to Chamberlain,

[7] *Watertown Times* (Watertown, D. T.), October 6, 13, 27, November 10, 1879.
[8] Andreas, *Historical Atlas of Dakota*, p. 301; Visher, "Geography of South Dakota," pp. 151-2.

causing Mitchell, Alexandria, Plankington, and other towns to come into being. Its Hastings and Dakota division was constructed from Big Stone City to Webster, causing the town of Milbank to be founded. A Grant County editor in February, 1881, emphasized the fact that Milbank was the most prosperous city in the Northwest for its age: "Our town is a little over six months old and has a bona fide population of three hundred and twenty-four souls and a 'hard pan' real estate valuation of $54,120. We venture to say that Milbank will be able to present a showing that will be second to no other frontier town for a genuine healthy growth of less than six months. Although the townsite was laid out in June, 1880, the railroad did not arrive until the middle of August, and trains did not begin running for fully a month." At this writing Milbank had forty-one places of business, which included banks, hardware and drug-stores, general merchandise establishments, three saloons, two laundries, four hotels, two blacksmith shops, a furniture store, a millinery shop, and a newspaper. It also had three physicians, two lawyers, a Masonic Hall, and a brass band.[9]

Early in 1879 the Northern Pacific Railway awakened from its long inactivity and commenced the extension of its line westward from Bismarck. It selected a site just west of the Missouri for the location of its depot, roundhouse, and warehouses, and the town laid out around its buildings was called Mandan. In February, 1879, Chief Engineer Thomas L. Rosser laid the track across the ice and erected a railway boarding-house on the town-site.[10] In July, 1879, the Northern Pacific began its Casselton branch,

[9] *Huron Tribune* (Huron, D.T.), July 24, 1880; *Grant County Review* (Milbank, D. T.), February 10, 1881.

[10] *Bismarck Weekly Tribune*, March 3, 17, April 8, 15, 1880. In the fall of 1878, a few settlers who had crossed the Missouri to make a scattering settlement extending from Fort Abraham Lincoln on the south to Square Butte on the north met and organized Morton County. The county commissioners selected a site about a mile north of the later village of Mandan for county-seat purposes. The location was later shifted to the site located by the Northern Pacific Railroad Company. Kingsbury, *History of Dakota Territory*, II, 1099.

twenty miles west of Fargo. That line was extended to Larimore in Grand Forks County, and from that point to the eastern border of Cavalier County. At the same time the St. Paul and Pacific was building its line from Wahpeton in Richland County to Casselton, which later became a link of the Great Northern system.

While the year 1880 was notable for the progress of railroad building through the territory, it was due, particularly in the northern counties, to the abundant wheat crop. The Casselton branch of the Northern Pacific was completed to Blanchard, thirty miles north of Casselton, and the Fargo and Southwestern Railroad was built from Fargo to the James River, a distance of eighty-eight miles, and La Moure was made its terminus. The towns of Leonard, Sheldon, Lisbon, and Englevale became thriving centers along its route. The Northern Pacific was surveying and constructing its line rapidly westward toward the Montana line.[11]

Since the railways were the real pioneers, preceding the settlements, they as a rule located the stations along the line to suit themselves. Immigration everywhere flowed in the wake of the railroads and not infrequently on the strength of surveys preceding them. Mandan provided an excellent example of the hasty beginning and the rapid growth of a railroad town. Immediately following the construction of the railway boarding-house, the town-site that had previously been located by the Morton County commissioners was moved to the new location, and there came a demand for lots and town property. Buildings sprang into existence with magical celerity, and the embryonic village grew rapidly. By May 1, 1879, the new community consisted of more than one hundred buildings and, according to the census of 1880, had a population of 239. New towns and communities were formed by the score all over the territory, and many new counties were organized. There is no record of the exact numbers who came,

---

[11] This line was expected to tap the Saskatchewan wheat country which joined the northwest corner of Dakota.

A FREIGHT-TRAIN FERRY ON THE MISSOURI

Bismarck, Dakota Territory, 1879. Courtesy of the Northern Pacific Railway.

but the ordinary estimate of the newspapers placed the new arrivals of 1880 at one hundred thousand.

Large beds of lignite coal discovered in various parts of northern Dakota were a great aid to the homesteaders and tended to overcome what was considered one of Dakota's heavy handicaps. Several large veins of lignite were found about thirty-five miles west of Mandan, and a company was formed at Bismarck to open and operate a mine. The "Baby Mine" was opened, and in 1879 the company took out and sold nearly fifty thousand dollars worth of coal.[12]

The census of 1880 disclosed forty-six organized counties with a white population of 135,177, of whom 98,268 resided in the southern portion of the territory. There were twenty-one counties with a population of more than two thousand each, and eight with five thousand or more. The latter were as follows: Lawrence, 13,248; Cass, 8,998; Minnehaha, 8,915; Yankton, 8,390; Union, 6,813; Grand Forks, 6,248; Bon Homme, 5,469; Turner, 5,320; Clay, 5,000. Of the eighty-eight towns and villages reporting, fifty had a population of one hundred or more, and thirteen had five hundred or more inhabitants. Those with a population of a thousand or more were: Custer City, Custer County, 3,777; Yankton, Yankton County, 3,431; Fargo, Cass County, 2,693; Sioux Falls, Minnehaha County, 2,164; Bismarck, Burleigh County, 1,758; Grand Forks, Grand Forks County, 1,705; Lead City, Lawrence County, 1,437; Central City, Lawrence County, 1,008. Of the 57,844 engaged in the various occupations, 28,528 were employed in agricultural pursuits.[13]

Railroad expansion continued in 1881, but during the next year there was relatively little railroad building. It began again in 1883 and continued until 1888. During these years the various main lines were completed and many branch lines were built.

[12] *Bismarck Tribune*, Pageant Number, September 16, 1925; Robinson, *History of South Dakota*, p. 302.
[13] *U. S. Census Report for 1880*, Volume on Population, 52-3, 115-6.

Throughout the period settlement was very closely connected with railroad expansion. While preliminary settlement quickly followed and at times even preceded the building of railways, careful study shows that extensive settlement did not take place in many sections until one, two, or even three years after the coming of the road. This was conspicuously the case in southern Dakota west of the James River.[14] In a good many counties, however, the establishment of train service coincided with widespread settlement. A writer described the situation thus: "Language cannot exaggerate the rapidity with which these communities are built up. You may stand ankle deep in the short grass of the uninhabited wilderness; next month a mixed train will glide over the waste and stop at some point where the railroad has decided to locate a town. Men, women and children will jump out of the cars, and their chattels will be tumbled out after them. From that moment the building begins." [15]

In the years following 1880 immigration was lively, and on June 9, 1881, J. B. Power, land commissioner of the Northern Pacific Railroad, reported, "In this region where five years ago there was scarcely a white man, there is now a thrifty population of nearly 35,000 people, hailing from all parts of the world. There were 273,000 acres of land cultivated on the line of the Northern Pacific Railway last year. Barnes County, which is only four years old, has a population of three thousand, with seven hundred farms." [16]

The rapid increase of population in the Territory of Dakota during the years beginning January, 1880, and ending December, 1881, is nowhere more reliably shown than in the report of the

[14] Visher, *op. cit.*, p. 151. During the height of the boom, 1883 and 1884, railroads often were not built fast enough to keep up with the preliminary settlements, some of which grew quite rapidly. Some land was filed upon far from the completed lines, and some such settlers were not served effectively by railroads for several years.

[15] W. M. Blackburn, "Historical Sketch of North and South Dakota," *South Dakota Historical Collections*, I.

[16] *Valley City Times* (Valley City, D. T.), June 9, 1881.

House Committee on Territories submitted in 1882 when reporting a bill for the admission of the state of Dakota. They estimated
the aggregate increase since the census of 1880 as approximately
seventy-five thousand. The *Watertown Times* during the summer
of 1881 reported unprecedented immigration in the James River
Valley, and added that the plains from Columbia to Belcher's
Ford were dotted with prairie-schooners and new claim shanties.
New towns were springing up, and the editor made the prediction
that all the section east of the upper James River valley would
within five years be cultivated farms supplied with thriving villages and an abundance of railroads. "Villages of 500 to 1000
inhabitants have grown up in twelve months." [17]

Newspapers gave evidence as to the extent of immigration to
Dakota in 1882. The *Chicago Tribune* for April 15, 1882, said:
"The arrival and departure of European and Canadian immigrants during the month has been unusually heavy. Five hundred
trains on the principal trunk lines brought in nine thousand during the past week and one thousand more will arrive tomorrow. It
is estimated that about one thousand of them will remain in
Chicago. The remainder are ticketed for Dakota, with the exception of some eight hundred, who go to Manitoba." The *St. Paul
Globe* for May 4, 1882, reported a great influx of immigrants to
Dakota, and the *Huron Tribune* in July stated that one hundred
and ten teams laden with settlers and materials for shanties were
counted in one day going from the east to the Devil's Lake country. From January 1st to August 1st, four hundred cars of immigrants' goods arrived at Watertown, whose streets were
crowded at times with homeseekers.[18]

In the spring of 1883 two hundred and fifty cars of immigrants'
goods were unloaded at Huron during the month of April. Hurley, in Turner County, reported that four thousand cars loaded

[17] *Congressional Record*, 47th Cong., 1st Sess., Senate Report 271, 2044-45;
Watertown Times, June 18, 1881.
[18] *Watertown Times*, August 20, 1882.

with immigrants' movables had passed through the town during the spring en route to points north and west. A St. Paul paper on April 12, 1883, mentioned the rush to the territory and stated that large groups were going to the wheat-fields of northern Dakota. "Two passenger trains loaded with Dakota settlers left last evening over the Winona and St. Peter Railroad and two trains on the Chicago, Milwaukee and St. Paul." It also stated that a thousand cars loaded with immigrants' stock and movables had been sent west toward central Dakota the preceding week. Sleepy Eye, Minnesota, on the Northwestern line running into southern Dakota, reported on April 17th that one hundred cars of immigrants' goods went through on Saturday bound for central Dakota, about the same number on Sunday, and as many more on Monday. The *Huron Tribune* for May 31, 1883, estimated that the population of the territory was increasing at the rate of one thousand per day. The editor of the *Estelline Bell* of Hamlin County on January 1, 1884, judged that fifty thousand people had actually settled in the Huron land district during 1883 and expressed hope that even more would come in 1884.[19]

The Dakota newspapers continued with such reports throughout the boom period. Various quotations from the *Dakota Republican,* published at Vermillion, gave in a few words the trend of the times. The issue for March 27, 1879, stated: "The spring of 1879 has opened auspiciously for Dakota. There is a general feeling of contentment, courage and confidence which bespeaks prosperity. The grasshopper incubus has disappeared, or at least has lost its terror. Never before was there that spirit of security, of assured success, of the certainty of reward as now animates our people. Real estate has commenced to advance, and there is a general stability of prices." An editorial of April 10, 1879, said: "The outlook is indeed encouraging. Every train brings in new people. Most of them have money in their pockets and a disposi-

---

[19] *Turner County Herald,* May 10, 1883; *St. Paul Globe* (St. Paul, Minn.), April 12, 1883.

tion to remain and set up business. Business prospects for Vermill-lion and Clay County are very bright and encouraging. There never was a better outlook for this section, and the populace are cheerful accordingly."

A year later the following comments appeared: "Every train brings in new people who are examining the country and looking for farms or business locations. The crops are exceedingly good. A boom period has struck us fairly. Never before in the history of the county has there been such prosperity." [20] January 26, 1882: "There is no public land left in Clay County except perhaps an isolated piece here and there. But those intending to make their homes here can find improved farms at reasonable, and in many cases, very low figures." September 8, 1882: "The prosperity of Dakota and Clay County continues. Large amounts of money have been spent during the past year in improvements. The community is largely made up of farmers all more or less prosperous, and many are wealthy. They all owe their prosperity to Clay County soil." On April 10, 1884, another optimistic account of general conditions was printed and editorials appearing August 7, 1885, and June 24, 1886, reported that prosperity still continued.

The reports from the General Land Office during the period give in a concrete way the trend of the boom. The figures showing the amount of land taken in the territory in various years are as follows: 1877, 213,000; 1879, 1,657,000; 1882, 4,360,000; 1883, 7,317,000; 1884, 11,083,000; 1886, 3,075,000; 1888, 1,881,000. [21] The assessed valuation of property in the territory during the period will give some idea as to the extent of settlement and development: 1879, $16,267,000; 1882, $47,701,000; 1885, $106,450,000; 1887, $157,084,000; 1889, $164,200,000. [22] These figures speak for themselves.

[20] *Dakota Republican*, May 10, 1880.
[21] *Reports of the Commissioner of the General Land Office*, 1877-99. The number of acres is expressed in round numbers.
[22] *Ibid.*

The magnitude of the Dakota boom is indicated strikingly by the following comparisons. During the first five years of the territorial government (1862 to 1866) only 100,000 acres were filed upon; by July 1, 1870, less than 500,000 acres had been taken. Nearly two-fifths of the entire acreage filed on in the United States in the year ending June 30, 1883, was in Dakota, where nearly twice as much land (7,500,000 acres) was taken as in Minnesota, Nebraska, and Kansas combined. In 1884 there was nearly a 60 per cent increase over the previous year. During the decade ending June 30, 1889, nearly 42,000,000 acres, or almost half the area of Dakota, were filed on. By 1887 no free land remained in twenty-two counties, and nine others had an area of only 2,500 acres each, most of which was very undesirable. In the more newly organized counties filings were numerous.[23]

The growth in population during this period shows most clearly the magnitude of the immigration. According to the Federal census of 1880, the population of Dakota was 135,177, of which 98,268 were in southern Dakota, including 16,487 in the Black Hills. In 1885 the territory had a population of 415,610, of which 152,199 were located in northern Dakota, with 263,411 in the southern section, of whom 14,842 were in the Black Hills.[24] In 1890 the population of South Dakota was 328,808 and that of North Dakota was 182,719, making a total of 501,527. There were 32,559 in the Black Hills region. The enumeration for 1880 was made after the influx was well started, while that of 1890 was made after there had been an exodus due to two or more crop failures and to many disappointments on the part of town builders and speculators. It is, therefore, impossible to give accurately the total influx to Dakota during the boom. The rapid influx of set-

[23] Visher, "Geography of South Dakota," pp. 151-2; Batchelder, *Sketch of the History and Resources of Dakota Territory*, p. 45; *Reports of the Commissioner of the General Land Office*; Andreas, *Historical Atlas of Dakota*, p. 98; D. H. McClure, *Resources of Dakota* (Aberdeen, 1887), p. 245.

[24] *U. S. Census Report for 1880*, Volume on Population; *Territorial Census of 1885*. The decrease in the Black Hills was produced in part by the almost complete destruction of Deadwood by fire in 1883.

tlers continued for some time after the enumeration of 1885. The
Bureau of Immigration estimated that the increase for 1886 was

DAKOTA TERRITORY, 1885

more than 85,000 and that the population of the territory on the
last day of June, 1887, was 568,477. Allowing a liberal deduction
for overestimation, the percentage of increase over 1880 would
be at least 400 per cent. The increase over the estimated popula-

tion for 1878 would be approximately 750 per cent in about nine years.[25]

Striking as the immigration to Dakota during this period was when considered in its larger aspects, it may be illustrated even more vividly by considering smaller units. Beadle County in 1880 had a population of 1,290; in 1885 it had 10,318. Brown County in 1880 had 353 inhabitants and only 468 acres in farms; by 1885 the population was 12,241 and 248,346 acres were under cultivation. Spink County, with a population of 477 in 1880, had 10,446 inhabitants in 1885. Huron was platted by the railroad company in May, 1880, and the first train arrived late in June. The population in the spring of 1884 was estimated at 3,000. The improvements made during 1883 cost $450,000. The site of Aberdeen was a wilderness prior to June, 1881. The first railroad train arrived on July 6th of that year, and in June, 1882, it had a population of 500. Blunt was first settled in the fall of 1882, and in December of 1883 it boasted a population of nearly 1,000, occupying three hundred buildings. In May, June and July, 1883, real estate transactions amounted to $150,000, and business property advanced 300 per cent in value.[26]

The *Dakota Settler,* a Burleigh County paper published at Bismarck, in its issue of December 8, 1886, gave a description of the rapid growth of Minot in Ward County:

Minot, situated at the end of the track of the westward extension of the Manitoba Railroad in Ward County, is a typical western town. It is now about five weeks since it started, and it has a population of almost one thousand. The first settlers lived in tents and shacks, the latter often partly covered with canvas. Now, at the end of five weeks, a substantial village has been put up. Some of the buildings are two

---

[25] Visher, *op. cit.,* p. 153; *Appleton's Annual Cyclopedia* (1883), p. 268, 1886, p. 269, 1887, p. 217-8, 1888, p. 259; McClure, *op. cit.,* pp. 145, 243; Andreas, *op. cit.,* p. 146.

[26] Visher, *op. cit.,* pp. 153-4; Brenan, *Conditions and Resources of Southern Dakota,* p. 3; McClure, *op. cit.,* pp. 87, 243; *U. S. Census Report for 1880; Territorial Census of 1885.*

story 20 by 60, but the majority are 20 by 40. Nearly every branch of ordinary business is well represented. There are five hotels, three meat markets, a hardware store, twelve saloons, a drug store, three general merchandise stores, a furniture store, a livery stable, a feed store, and a laundry. The company has up the frame of the new depot. Reverend Wirt held Sunday services in the Hope Brothers Hardware Store, and a Sunday School was organized.

Mitchell was another outstanding example of rapid growth. The town, which dates from May, 1878, obtained a railroad in September, 1880. It was incorporated in 1881 and in 1882 had a population of twelve hundred people. With the construction of the second railroad, its growth in 1882 and 1883 was very rapid. At that time several flour and feed mills, an elevator, foundry, machine-shop, and brick-yards were established. Woonsocket was platted in September, 1883. Two months later it had a population of 525 persons and within seven months had more than eight hundred people. Prior to July, 1882, the site of Redfield was an unbroken wilderness, and on November of that year it was reported to have a thousand inhabitants. Brookings, though first settled in 1879, was not recorded as a town by the census of 1880 but had a population of eight hundred in 1882.[27] The editor of the *Devil's Lake Democrat* on December 11, 1884, said: "Two years ago the number of inhabitants in Ramsey County did not exceed twenty, and to-day the county takes rank with the best in the territory. Devil's Lake, eighteen months old, is a city of 1,000 people with a city government, fire department, a United States land-office, and with substantial brick places of business and handsome residences, while the surrounding prairies are dotted with shacks and substantial farm buildings."

With the year 1885 the high level of the boom passed, although it was not realized at that time. It was natural for the settler to believe that this favored land was to advance and be prosperous

---

[27] Visher, *op. cit.*, pp. 153-4; McClure, *op. cit.*, pp. 142, 150, 169; Polk, *Gazetteer for Minnesota and Dakota*, 1881, pp. 926, 1081.

for an indefinite period. That was a part of the western spirit of optimism. But as one reads carefully the newspapers of the times and looks back over the course of events, it is easy to see that by 1886 the best days of the great boom were over and the territory was entering upon a long period of reaction which was to put the settlers to a severe test.

There were various causes for the close of the boom, but the chief one was crop failures. In 1886 Dakota suffered from drought which injured the small grains, producing a shortage of at least a third of the expected yield in wheat and oats. It was local, however, some places having splendid crops while others suffered almost total failures. The weather bureau estimated the shortage at about 50 per cent. In 1887 drought was widespread and severe, and in many counties very little harvesting was done. In 1888 some localities suffered, but the average crop was not a great deal below reasonable expectations. The terrible drought of 1889, which was widespread throughout the central portion of the United States, struck Dakota with great severity, producing much suffering and destitution.[28]

Certain other factors helped to end the boom. Most of the free land east of the Missouri River had been taken by the summer of 1887, and railroad expansion stopped. Dakota was pretty well supplied with transportation facilities at this time, but the failure of the railroad companies to construct various anticipated extensions or branch lines caused many towns and localities to lose hope. Dakota suffered in common with the rest of the country in the general business depression that came in 1886, and the difficulties of the territory became greater after each drought. The financial crisis of 1884 which originated in Wall Street in the failure of several large banking firms hastened and intensified this depression. These failures were caused by dishonest management and

[28] *Annual Report of the Territorial Governor of Dakota to the Secretary* of the Interior, 1886-90; Finney, *Certain Climatic Features of the Two Dakotas,* pp. 28-9; Visher, "Geography of South Dakota," pp. 155-6.

unwarranted speculation rather than by general depression. The stringency of the money market was occasioned largely through the displacement of gold by the newly coined silver and by the sinking of vast sums in western farms and railroads. The large transcontinental roads were not yet on a paying basis, and the interests of agriculture were threatened by falling prices. As time went on, financial conditions had become less and less satisfactory, and by 1886 money was very scarce. Loans were procured with great difficulty, and interest was high. The period of financial reaction had really begun.

While the exodus from Dakota which followed the collapse of the boom was produced primarily by the drought, it was augmented by many disappointments in business and land speculation. To make matters worse, thousands of homesteaders had come to the region with the primary object of securing land while it could be obtained from the government for little or nothing. They had no real intention of making Dakota a permanent home, and after they had received title to their claims, it did not take even a moderate drought to induce them to leave. An urgent demand for statehood had resulted from the great influx of 1879 to 1886, and after many vexations and delays, the Territory of Dakota was divided in 1889 and admitted into the Union as North and South Dakota.

According to the Federal census of 1890 there was a total white population of 511,526 in Dakota, 328,808 of which were in South Dakota and 182,719 in North Dakota. Thirty-two and four-tenths per cent of the total were foreign born, the Norwegian nationality having the most representatives, totaling 80,343. There were 44,698 of these in North Dakota and 35,645 in South Dakota. The German population came next with 17,541 in the northern area and 38,566 in the southern. There was a total of 23,493 Russians, of which 18,363 were in South Dakota. The Irish population numbered 22,238, and there were 19,360 inhabitants of Swedish nationality in North and South Dakota.

XI

SETTLEMENT IN MONTANA AFTER 1880

THE EARLY 1880's were years of peace upon the Montana frontier. More than a thousand Indians from Sitting Bull's band surrendered to Colonel Miles at Fort Keogh in 1880 and in July, 1881, Sitting Bull himself with the last of his followers, numbering sixty-seven men, women, and children, surrendered to the commanding officer at Fort Buford. When General Sherman retired from the command of the army in 1883, in his last annual report he said, "I now regard the Indians as substantially eliminated from the problem of the army." The ranching industry reached its peak in the eighties and there was considerable immigration into Montana on the part of farmers, both being largely influenced by the construction of the Northern Pacific Railroad through the territory.

The town-site of Glendive on the Yellowstone River in the eastern part of the territory developed with the prospect of the railroad's arrival at the point designated by the surveyors as the official crossing. An observer in a Montana newspaper late in December, 1880, wrote:

The new town of Glendive on the Yellowstone at the point where the Northern Pacific reaches the river is situated in a valley twenty miles wide, one of the prettiest and most fertile in the west. The town which has recently been platted is well laid out, the streets being wide and running at right angles with each other. There are twenty-four blocks platted and the longest street is about two miles in length. Several public squares have been laid out, also a grand Esplanade. Several brick blocks and many other business places are to be built next spring as soon as the road reaches the place, when Glendive will have a boom.[1]

It was estimated that at least two hundred and fifty miles of the Northern Pacific would be constructed in Montana in 1881.

[1] *Helena Daily Herald*, December 23, 1880.

In the summer of 1881 various reports indicated that settlers were coming into the territory, and in September of that year Glendive claimed a population of fifteen hundred, when, as one editor said, "there had not been as much as a shanty on the premises earlier than last July." During the autumn more than one hundred and sixty mechanics were in Glendive constructing the machine-shops for the Northern Pacific Railroad.[2] In November it was reported that the railroad had been completed to Powder River and was expected to arrive at Miles City during the season. Fort Benton and Helena were both booming during the fall months. Forty-two buildings had been erected in Helena during the season and Fort Benton claimed she could even beat that. Town lots were in demand although the *River Press* reported serious difficulty in getting the Fort Benton lot-owners to list their property on the assessment rolls. The same editor in November reported that two hundred men were working on the Yellowstone division of the Northern Pacific. "Coulson," read the report, "is one of the places on the Yellowstone where the Northern Pacific has laid out a town, and a boom has already started there. The population of Montana has increased at least 10,000 during the last year." Deer Lodge was reporting a boom with outside parties buying lots and property at a rapid rate.[3] Late in November the tracks of the railroad were within fifteen miles of Miles City, while more than one hundred buildings were erected at that place during the season. During the year ending November 30, 1881, the Helena land-office reported entry and sale of 100,208 acres of land, the largest amount taken in any one year since 1872.[4]

Throughout 1882 the settlers continued to come, especially along the railroad. In January the railroad was tied and ironed to a point twenty miles west of Miles City. The track-layers were up with the grade and could proceed no further during the winter

[2] *River Press*, June 1, July 13, September 21, 1881.
[3] *New Northwest*, November 21, 1881; *River Press*, November 2, 9, 16, 23, 1881.
[4] *Helena Daily Herald*, December 3, 1881.

although the graders were to remain in the field as long as the weather was mild. The winter terminus was to be at Forsyth, a new town already laid out some twenty-two miles beyond Miles City. It had arrived there by February 1, 1882. The town-site of Coulson was still being boomed although it was located 165 miles west of Miles City and the railroad was not expected to reach there until the following fall. There were reported to be at least a dozen movable saloons en route to the "boom city," and immigration was arriving there at a lively rate. In predicting the events of the new year, the various Montana editors were optimistic. One of them on January 18th said, "The tide of immigration to Montana during the year 1882 will be exceedingly large, the new people coming in from all parts of the country." [5]

Immigration was steady during the spring and summer of 1882. Several newspapers printed pamphlets and enumerated the strong points of Montana as against those of the Territory of Dakota which, according to one account, was the best advertised territory in the Union, and as a result was rapidly filling up with settlers for the eastern population seemed to be afflicted with "Dakota fever." "Dakota is a good place to immigrate but Montana has as many advantages," stated the *River Press.* "Our resources are more varied and if our territory were as well advertised as Dakota the Montana fever would claim many victims in the east." Early in March three hundred settlers arrived at Miles City in one day. A westbound Union Pacific train leaving Omaha on April 7th carried six hundred passengers, most of which were ticketed through to Montana. On May 3, 1882, large numbers of settlers were locating in the vicinity of Clark's Fork near Billings, and the secretary of the Billings Townsite Company reported that he had received ten thousand dollars' worth of orders for lots since March 28th. Business lots were selling for as high as five hundred dollars each.[6]

[5] *River Press,* January 18, 1882.
[6] *Ibid.,* March 8, 1882.

Strangers were numerous in Benton in April, 1882, and immigrants were coming from every direction, some of whom stopped while others moved on. The contract for grading on the Northern Pacific from Indian Creek and Helena had been let and active operations were to be started at once. About the middle of May 3,450 men were reported to have been working on the Northern Pacific grade. Butte was overrun with hoodlums and tramps of every description, although the Vigilantes had promised to clean them out. The railroad was to celebrate the Fourth of July at Billings. On September 27th the track was laid thirty-five miles beyond Billings to a new town called Park City which was not more than a week old, but had 110 inhabitants. On November 11th the track was laid to a point thirty-five miles east of Old Wives Lake and in December it was announced that it would reach Bozeman before the end of the year unless cold weather interfered with the work. On December 27th, Livingston was booming, with town lots selling for from $800 to $1,000 and suburban lots at $1.50. Building restrictions in the business sections were required by law to be 24 by 40 feet and two stories high. An observer who no doubt had experienced the rise and collapse of other towns along the track, said, "It will require considerable faith to become a real estate owner in the proposed 'Chicago of the West.' " [7]

In 1883 there had been a considerable increase in the population of the Territory of Montana, and Helena had grown to 6,000 population, with Butte City ranking second with 5,000. Billings was third with 3,000 inhabitants. Bozeman and Miles City were reported to have 2,000 each, while Fort Benton had 1,600; Deer Lodge, 1,200; Missoula, Livingston, and Glendive each had 1,000, and Forsyth, 500. In 1883 population continued to come into the territory, and the Northern Pacific was constructed through the area. Silver Bow County was organized in 1883 from parts of Deer Lodge and Jefferson counties.

[7] Files of the *River Press*, summer and fall of 1882.

In 1884 settlement continued into the fertile valleys as the Bitter Root Valley and the Judith Basin received large numbers of immigrants. Billings was reported to be growing at a rapid rate in July, Fistler's addition having just been included, and lots were being sold at good prices.[8] In August a large group of wagons carrying families and household goods passed through Butte. "This would not have attracted attention," said an observer, "except for the fact that these families started from their homes in southeastern Missouri on April 15th and have crossed the plains in the old-fashioned style. They expect to settle in the Bitter Root Valley." [9]

While the ranching business was coming to its high point in 1885 and 1886 immigration continued into Montana. Settlers came in from all portions of the country and settled along the line of the Northern Pacific or in the various river valleys. While the contemporary newspapers emphasized the cattle industry as the center of interest, there was some evidence of immigration. The New Year's issue of the *River Press* spoke in high terms of "the great Judith Basin, the Wonderland of Montana." In 1885 Fergus County was organized out of Meagher County.

In June, 1887, the *Great Falls Tribune* expressed its objection to the *Butte Miner's* statement that Great Falls was overrun with hoodlums as the Manitoba line was being extended from Minot, Dakota, to Great Falls. The *Butte Miner*, commenting upon the railroad construction to Great Falls, had said, "Great Falls is beginning to realize that there is no rose without a thorn. Nor railroad construction without an advance guard of thugs or worse. No town in Montana has had railroad facilities without being cursed by a horde of hangers-on, camp-followers, tin-horn gamblers, and the scum of the earth. Montana has no need for an increase in that type of population." In August of the same year the graders working on the railroad project were well impressed

[8] *Billings Herald*, July 26, 1884.
[9] *Butte Miner*, August 7 and September 4, 1884.

with the land in the vicinity and were determined to remain there and settle if they could find work for themselves and teams. The track was then about half-way between the two towns, 261 miles from Great Falls.[10]

In December, 1887, it was rumored that fifty miles more of the Missoula and Bitter Root Railroad had been contracted. The railroad was booming Bitter Root Valley. Late in December there were several new-comers to the German colony near Glendive, made up of about forty families, and others were expected to arrive during the winter.[11] In November the *Montana Live Stock Journal* estimated that at least one hundred families had settled in the vicinity of Diamond City, with the idea of establishing permanent homes. Residents living along the main roads complained of the constant movement, night and day, of the population past their homes, an indication that the country was becoming fairly well settled. The onward moving tide of immigration was sweeping over Montana and the story of the Nebraska and Dakota areas was being repeated.[12]

In the spring of 1888 Montana immigration was booming again, and an editor in the western part of the territory observed, in April, "There is a rush of emigration to the Northwest this spring which means a season of prosperity. During February the Northern Pacific carried over twice as many emigrants as during the same month last year and the March aggregation showed an increase about as great. The company sold nearly 90,000 acres of land during the two months." A week later it was announced that during the past month more settlers had arrived in the Gallatin Valley than during the same period for the past ten years.[13] At the same time real estate was booming in Helena and a local editor, worried over the boom tendencies, wrote by way of a warning:

[10] *Great Falls Tribune* (Great Falls, Mont.), June 29, August 20, 1887.
[11] *Montana Live Stock Journal*, December 10, 1887; *Glendive Independent*, December 31, 1887.
[12] *Montana Live Stock Journal*, November 12, 26, 1887.
[13] *Daily Missoulian*, April 14, 21, 1888.

Real estate firms are almost as thick in Helena as the autumnal leaves and the many active and industrious gentlemen who boom the city in season and out are doing a land office business in selling lots. While the business of Helena is good, it is not good enough to warrant or justify paying the prices asked. Prices of lots, residences and rents are all out of proportion to the profits of legitimate business and will work harm some day. We need smelters and factories that will create a demand for labor far more than we need booms in real estate.[14]

Immigration continued in 1889 and in 1890. The total population of Montana was 132,159, showing a gain of almost 100,000 inhabitants in ten years. There were sixteen organized counties, Silver Bow being the largest with a total number of 23,744 inhabitants. Lewis and Clark ranked second with 19,145, while Deer Lodge and Missoula counties came next with 15,155 and 14,479. There were fourteen cities with a population of more than a thousand, Helena being the largest with 13,834. Butte City came next with 10,723; Great Falls with 3,979; Anaconda City, 3,975; Missoula, 3,426; and Livingston, 2,850. Although the frontier period of Montana history was almost over by 1890, settlers continued to come into that state, most of whom were farmers and small ranchers. The population of the area increased to 243,329 in 1900 and to 376,606 in 1910.[15]

XII

SETTLEMENT IN WYOMING AFTER 1880

WHILE the cattle and sheep industries were important in the various territories under consideration, their relative importance in comparison with other occupations was greater in Wyoming than in Montana or Dakota. Except for the towns along the Union Pacific Railroad, practically all of the settlements in Wyoming in the eighties were based on agriculture. While the

---

[14] *Montana Live Stock Journal*, April 28, 1888.
[15] *U. S. Census Reports for 1890, 1900 and 1910.*

final agricultural settlement of both Montana and Wyoming occurred after the arable lands farther east had been taken up,
farmers as well as ranchers began to settle along the Bozeman
trail and in the northern portion of the territory in Sheridan and
Johnson counties on both sides of the mountains in the late seventies and early eighties. Oliver P. Hanna erected a cabin on the
east side of the mountains in the Big Horn Basin late in the
seventies and others took up land along the various streams that
furnished easy water heads for irrigation projects. In 1878 a mail
route was established between Rock Creek on the Union Pacific
and Etchetah, Montana, a distance of five hundred miles. Sheridan boasted a post-office, store, blacksmith shop, saloon, and "large
blowing mill" by 1883, and in March, 1884, the town was
granted a charter of incorporation.

The lands along the various small creeks and rivers across the
mountains in the Big Horn Basin were just as attractive as those
found on the eastern side and a man with a reasonable amount of
capital could construct small irrigation works for his own needs
in the process of reclamation. A few settlers with small herds of
cattle had taken up land along the Wood and Greybull rivers by
1883. Andrew B. Wilson with his wife and daughters settled on
Meeteetsee Creek some five miles above its mouth and these are
supposed to have been the first women to make their homes in the
Big Horn country. Mail service was established to the area in
1883 and Mrs. Wilson became postmistress at Franc, in Wyoming Territory. Other settlers came in and soon there were small
communities scattered through the north central portions of the
region.[1]

Some of the settlers who took land in the northern part of
Wyoming were miners and prospectors who had failed to make a
strike in the Black Hills during the gold rush. Two men by the
names of Hyatt and Morris left the Black Hills in the summer of

[1] *Big Horn County Rustler*, December 23, 30, 1910; *Cody Enterprise* (Cody,
Wyo.), January 14, 21, 1910.

1886 and established themselves on Sage Creek south of Pryor Gap. Their supplies were freighted from Billings, Montana, and Morris, who was ambitious, ran a small herd of cattle and operated a road-house in connection with his farm. When the Burlington Railroad came southward from Billings a few years later, the junction of the Thermopolis and Cody lines was located but a short distance southwest of the Morris cabin.[2]

Settlers continued to come into the Big Horn Basin. A man by the name of J. L. Smith brought his family and household goods by ox team from Nebraska and located his original homestead on the town-site of Shell. He constructed the first irrigation ditch in the area and was soon raising crops of alfalfa and wheat. Other families moved in, and founded homes, some of whom had been following the gold camps during boom times but were now ready to settle down and establish permanent residences. Settlers trekked to the Greybull River area from 1886 to 1890 in considerable numbers. Immigration was small into northern Wyoming in the early nineties, the next appreciable influx occurring in 1893 as the cattlemen began to move out or to reduce the size of their herds.[3] There was some settlement in the various towns in the southern part of the territory in the eighties, but the ranching disaster of 1886-87 did not tend to encourage immigration.

The Mormons of Utah and southern Idaho, attracted by the opportunities in southwestern Wyoming, moved there in large numbers in the late eighties, as many as four hundred families arriving in a period of eighteen months in 1887 and 1888. They acquired property in the form of land, stores, and coal-mines, and built schools and churches. Various Wyoming editors in 1888 and 1889 suggested that the Mormon element was so strong in western Wyoming that it would probably control the vote of that area in the election of 1890.[4]

[2] *Cody Enterprise*, July 11, 1928.
[3] *Thermopolis Record*, May 30, June 7, 14, 1902.
[4] *Billings Weekly Gazette*, August 9, 16, 1888; *Rock Springs Independent*, August 2, 1888.

From 1880 to 1890 six new counties were formed in Wyoming, the first being Frémont County, formed from Sweetwater in 1884. In 1887 Sheridan County was formed in the northern part of the territory from Johnson County, and Converse County was organized from portions of Albany and Laramie counties. In 1890 Weston County was formed from Crook, and Natroma from Carbon, with Big Horn County formed from parts of Frémont, Johnson, and Sheridan. From 1880 to 1890, the population of Wyoming Territory swelled from 20,789 to 60,705. Some of the Wyoming towns increased in population to a marked degree, showing an increase from 3,456 in 1880 to 11,690 in 1890. Laramie City had a population of 6,388 in 1890, Rock Springs, 3,406; Rawlins City, 2,235; Evanston, 1,995; Newcastle, 1,715; Carbon, 1,140, and Buffalo, 1,087. The largest county in point of population was Laramie with 16,777 inhabitants, with Albany ranking second with 8,865, and Uinta third with 7,881.

The decline of open-range ranching in Wyoming in the early nineties opened the flood-gates to an influx of population that continued to pour into the territory for more than two decades. At the end of the period the region was sprinkled with small towns and communities whose primary interests were centered around agriculture as opposed to large-scale ranching, some of the farmers, however, running small herds of cattle and sheep.

Evidence that the line of frontier settlement in the United States was fast approaching the end of arable lands is indicated by the fact that settlers were beginning to penetrate in considerable numbers an area that required irrigation in order to grow a crop. The years of the late eighties and early nineties were dry and this fact, together with the lack of free public lands that were suitable for ordinary farming, gave an impetus to irrigation in various portions of the West. One of the areas where it received a good deal of attention was in the Territory of Wyoming.

In the fall of 1892 a few Mormon scouts visited northern Wyoming to investigate the possibility of a Mormon colony settling there. The report was apparently satisfactory, for the following spring between fifty and sixty families moved in a group and settled in the Big Horn Basin. The movement was not a religious one, in fact, there is evidence that it was disapproved by the Mormon leaders at Salt Lake City. Groups continued to arrive throughout the spring and summer of 1893 and more came in 1894. While there was some coöperation, many of the families came entirely on their own initiative. They made their main settlement at Burlington on the northern side of the river along the flats. Arrangements were made for the irrigation of approximately fifteen thousand acres of land, and as the project was planned large numbers of families selected desirable tracts. The ditch was ready in the spring of 1895 and the first crops were planted.[5] After a successful harvest had proved the project a plausible one, there was another large influx of settlers, many of whom were Mormons from Utah and southern Idaho. The new-comers scattered along the Shoshone, and many established small independent ditches of their own. The settlement of Otto became an agricultural center of some importance below Burlington, and Meeteetse was located just above. The town of Arland, which had become a recreation center for cowhands in the days of the open range, had declined, but was somewhat revived by the incoming settlers. They patronized the dance-halls at Meeteetse and Arland, and social gatherings were held in the homes of ranchers and farmers who lived at central points. The stores and places of business in these inland towns were often inadequate to meet the needs of the settlers, who formed the habit of going to Lander or Billings in the fall and spring for supplies. Billings, located on a railroad, was probably the more popular trading-center.

The town-site of Cody was surveyed and laid out in the winter and spring of 1895-96 on the south side of the Stinking Water

[5] *Frémont Clipper* (Lander, Wyo.), December 27, 1895, January 4, 1896; *Billings Weekly Gazette*, July 15, 22, 1893.

as a part of the project of the Shoshone Land and Irrigation Company, and city lots were put on sale. The names of Richards and Shoshone were considered as possible ones for the new town. The town-site, however, was moved a few miles to the west and the site was named Cody in honor of William F. Cody, one of the promoters of the irrigation scheme. The *Cody Enterprise* began to extol the virtues of the region. Articles appeared in the various Wyoming newspapers, stressing the great opportunities in the Big Horn region for home-seekers, and incidentally telling of the activities of "Buffalo Bill."

Years hence when the name of W. F. Cody shall live in history [wrote the editor], "strangers passing through the Big Horn Basin will gaze with wonder over a vast territory systematically irrigated and covered with prosperous towns and fruitful farms. Already two prosperous colonies have settled in this great basin and two towns, Cody City and Erma, have been platted. By June, 1897, it is expected that 5,000 people will have settled along the canal and in a few more years the number will have increased to 25,000 prosperous, happy citizens.[6]

Other irrigation projects were started, each one attracting additional population to Wyoming. By 1900 the Mormon settlement on the Greybull River had prospered to such an extent that the Church was ready to back a colonization scheme. After an investigating party had visited Burlington in February, a project was organized for the purpose of settlement in the Shoshone River Valley. In April two trains of wagons, one from Utah and the other from southern Idaho, started for the Shoshone Valley in the Big Horn Basin. A Cheyenne editor late in April estimated that there were at least four hundred and fifty people en route to the Big Horn country. Other parties came in and during the fall and winter the colony had separated into three definite communities with town-sites laid out at Byron, Cowley, and Lovell.

The towns of Powell, Ralston, and Garland developed along

[6] *Omaha World-Herald*, July 15, 1896, quoted in Lindsay, *Big Horn Basin*, 189-90.

the Burlington Railroad after 1900 and the question of county division arose as the settlers began coming in. Many of the settlers in the western part of the Big Horn Basin were in favor of a division of the county, but there was much uncertainty as to where the county-seat would be located. The towns of Cody and Garland were both older than Powell, which was anxious to make a fight for the seat of county government. The population along the Big Horn River above Basin was also anxious for the formation of a new county in that area by cutting off a slice from that end of Big Horn County. The town of Thermopolis was the metropolis of this section, due in part to its hot springs, which had been purchased by the United States Government from the Arapahoe and Shoshone Indians in 1896, and were later given to the State of Wyoming.

The early history of Thermopolis was a colorful one and began with the analysis of the springs in the summer of 1875, at which time it was announced by Dr. Thomas Maghee, who was stationed at Fort Washakie, that the water had medicinal properties. A visitor to the place in 1894 found crude bath-houses erected there, and in 1895 the town had been terrorized by a band of desperadoes, sometimes called the "Hole in the Wall Gang," made up of fifty to sixty toughs, who had robbed a store and bullied Thermopolis on election day. A visitor late in 1895 described it thus: "The little city presented a lively appearance. Scores of men with six shooters, strapped to their waists, and not a few carrying winchesters, were seen hurrying in and out or leaning lazily against some convenient building or hitching rack. Some wore a sleepy expression, while others were drowning their sorrows in the bowl." [7]

The town was moved in 1897 to the springs and in 1902 boasted a population of six hundred, increasing in a year to around a thousand. The local editor forecast a rosy future for the place and in his various articles regarding it often spoke of it as "The City of Destiny." When the matter of moving the capital of the state

[7] *Wind River Mountaineer*, December 4, 1895.

from the southeastern corner of the commonwealth was discussed, there was absolutely no question, so far as the local press was concerned, where it would go, for "Thermopolis, of course, would be the best place for it." [8]

In 1910 two additional counties were created and Thermopolis realized her ambition of becoming the county-seat of the newly created Hot Springs County, with Worland becoming the county-seat of Washakie County. In 1910 the population of the Big Horn Basin as reported in the United States census was 13,795, or a little more than three times as great as it had been ten years earlier. The population of Wyoming had increased to 92,531 in 1900, to 145,965 in 1910, and to 194,402 in 1920.

XIII

IMMIGRATION ACTIVITIES

From the time of the arrival of the earliest permanent white settlers, the territories of the Northwest were aware of the importance of immigration and were duly impressed with the necessity of laboring persistently and discreetly to secure it. Settlers were recognized as the very life-blood of the new country, as there could be little progress or development without them. According to the statement of one historian, the real problem of the northwestern frontier after 1850 was "how to put more and ever more men of capacity, endurance, strength, and adaptability into the upper Mississippi, Missouri, and Red River valleys, men who would break up the sod, clear the brush off the slopes, drain the marshes, and do the thousand odd jobs incident to pioneer life." [9] "Immigration is the life of business in a new country," wrote James S. Foster, the first Commissioner of Immigration for the Territory of Dakota. "It gives patronage to railroads; it en-

---

[8] *Thermopolis Record*, files for 1902, January 24, February 1, 8, August 8, 15, 1903, August 6, December 24, 1904.

[9] *Wisconsin Magazine of History*, III (Madison, Wis.), 3-4.

courages manufacturing; it builds up cities and towns, and makes a market for the products of the farmer."

The first organized efforts to obtain settlers for the Territory of Dakota were rather feeble and were as a rule backed by a few Federal officials and local business men. The New York colony of 1864 was secured largely through the efforts of Governor Newton Edmunds, Surveyor-General Hill and W. W. Burleigh. There were no systematic advertising or immigration activities carried out by the territorial legislatures, as they were uniformly adverse to creating any debt against the territory by the sale of bonds and were also anxious to avoid taxation.[2] Frank Bem and James S. Foster were the first authorized immigration agents of the territorial government and were active in various capacities. Bem had been connected with a group of Bohemians who settled in Bon Homme and Yankton counties in 1869. While his status is not clear, he apparently incurred several hundred dollars worth of expenses from September, 1869, to January, 1871, for traveling and publications, which he experienced difficulty in collecting.[3]

In 1870 a commissioner of immigration was created and James S. Foster was appointed to fill the office. After serving as conductor of the New York colony to southeastern Dakota in 1866, he had entered the real estate business in Yankton and devoted much time and energy to promoting the material interests of the area. He wrote hundreds of letters, and had pamphlets and reports printed and scattered broadcast. He attended the national immigration convention at Indianapolis in November, 1870, and visited

[2] When the first territorial legislature convened in Dakota in March, 1862, a bill was presented authorizing the governor to appoint an "emigrant agent" at an annual salary of $100. It secured the sanction of the assembly, but was tabled by the council. In 1866 a law was enacted establishing an "immigration agent" whose duties were specified. Since no money was appropriated to carry on the work, the law was not effective.

[3] Bem presented a bill for $747 to the territorial legislature in 1873 and one for $872 in 1875, making a final effort to collect it in 1876-77. The only record of anything being paid was $100 which was appropriated in January, 1875. *Session Laws of the Territory of Dakota*, 1874-75; *Yankton Press and Dakotian*, January 14, 1875, January 30, 1877.

various cities in the East during the months of November and December, where he spoke to large audiences regarding the resources of Dakota and its inducements to settlers.[4]

With the revival of conditions conducive to settlement in Dakota, there was a demand in the territory for greater efforts to obtain publicity. Early in 1871 at the territorial capital the editor of the *Yankton Press,* in emphasizing the value of advertising, said, "We can just as well build up Dakota in five years as to take a lifetime about it." Foster was anxious for the legislature to appropriate funds whereby pamphlets might be printed in various languages and circulated without cost. Although there were several publications available, they did not meet the needs of the immigration office. A Bureau of Immigration was established by the territorial legislature in January, 1871 and James S. Foster was named as commissioner for two years, the office to be filled by election thereafter. There was no salary connected with the position, but five hundred dollars was appropriated for the purpose of promoting settlement. At the following session of the legislature, an annual salary of four hundred dollars was granted the commissioner.[5]

Foster served as commissioner of immigration until January, 1875, having been elected in the fall of 1872 for a second term. He was quite active during his four years, distributing large numbers of pamphlets and newspapers. He sent out more than two thousand copies of his own publication, three thousand pamphlets in English and five thousand in Swedish between 1871 and 1873. In 1873 a special immigration pamphlet was compiled by the im-

---

[4] *Annual Report of the Commissioner of Immigration of Dakota Territory,* 1871. Foster at this time was also serving as Superintendent of Public Instruction for the territory.

[5] Up to this time three important publications dealing with the resources and possibilities of Dakota were available: Moses K. Armstrong, *History and Resources of Dakota, Montana and Idaho* (1866); James S. Foster, "Outlines of the History of the Territory of Dakota and Emigrants' Guide" (1870); George A. Batchelder, *Sketch of the History and Resources of Dakota Territory* (1870). The latter volume was compiled for free distribution. *Session Laws of the Territory of Dakota,* 1870-71; 1872-73, ch. xiv.

migration office and some five thousand copies distributed. No pamphlet was issued in 1874, as the appropriation had been spent and business men failed to respond when asked for donations.[6] Foster made periodical trips to the East, usually in winter or early spring, at which time he distributed the newspapers and pamphlets of the immigration office, as well as those from his own real-estate office. On his eastern trips, Foster worked toward the organization of emigration societies. He urged prospective settlers to come in colonies or groups, in order to secure railroad rates and to have friends for company on the journey and neighbors when settlement was made. He was responsible for the organization of small groups in Connecticut, New York, and Illinois.

In 1875 the legislature appropriated one thousand dollars toward the erection of a building for the temporary housing of prospective settlers, on condition that the city of Yankton would make a similar grant. A Bureau of Immigration was created, consisting of an elective superintendent, an elective commissioner, and a board of three, one from each of the judicial districts, who were to be elected in joint session of the territorial legislature. A yearly salary of eight hundred dollars was provided for the superintendent and an annual appropriation of three thousand dollars was made to defray expenses. Fred J. Cross of Sioux Falls was chosen as superintendent and Jacob Brauch of Yankton as commissioner. The legislature chose the following as members of the immigration board: S. G. Roberts of Fargo, Cass County; V. P. Thielman of Swan Lake, Turner County; and James M. Wahl of Canton, Lincoln County. Wahl was a Norwegian, while the other two men were Germans. At the organization meeting at Yankton early in February, Roberts, Wahl and Brauch were authorized to go to the seaboard and intermediate points in order to direct migration to Dakota. They were to receive two dollars per day plus expenses. Brauch was given an allowance of eight

[6] Prior to 1875 considerable sums of money for the use of the immigration office were furnished by the citizens of Yankton.

hundred dollars while Roberts and Wahl were to receive two hundred dollars each. Brauch and Wahl assisted Superintendent Cross in the preparation of pamphlets in the German and Norwegian languages. The chief publication prepared under the direction of Cross was a pamphlet of thirty-two pages in 1876, bearing the title "The Free Lands of Dakota." Approximately forty thousand pieces of literature were published in addition to some maps. In the fall of 1875 collections of Dakota products were exhibited at various agricultural fairs in Illinois and Wisconsin, and exhibits were placed in railway stations in Chicago.

There were some who were opposed to the Immigration Bureau, and in spite of the increasing population, its work was not considered by all to be satisfactory. It was contended that little of the increase could be attributed directly to the official activities of the bureau. More than a hundred recent arrivals petitioned the legislature, indicating that they had not been influenced in their coming by the work of the immigration board. The territorial governor was of the opinion that the work of the bureau was cumbersome and expensive. And, although he had approved its creation in 1875, he now recommended that it be displaced by a single immigration official. The local press at Yankton, although keenly in favor of immigration, thought it wise to discontinue the board.[7] After lengthy discussion, no provision was made by the territorial legislature for its continuance, and the board passed out of existence.

The exact influence and results of the early immigration activities are difficult of evaluation. During the Dakota boom, at which time occurred the most rapid increase in population, there was no immigration office. The office was not revived until after the crest of the boom had passed. After a good deal of opposition, the immigration department was revived in 1885, strong criticism still prevailing on the ground that the work could be handled to better advantage by private enterprise. Under legislative action in March,

[7] *Yankton Press and Dakotian*, August 13, 1876, January 18, 1877.

1885, a Commissioner of Immigration was created for two years. His duties were to compile and distribute information and to serve as territorial statistician. His salary was to be two thousand dollars per year and six thousand eight hundred dollars was appropriated to meet the traveling expenses and the cost of maintaining an office. Lauren Dunlap of Huron was chosen for the position. This office employed the same methods as the previous one and was even more enterprising in putting out maps and pamphlets. It printed regular monthly bulletins, seventeen of which were issued.[8] In the meantime, numerous agencies were serving to advertise the various localities, such as town-site companies, real-estate agencies, and emigration departments of the railway companies. During the late seventies the Black Hills gold rush also furnished much publicity for the territory, possibly doing more than any immigration office could have hoped to.

The local newspapers of Dakota played an important part as an advertising medium, their editors receiving thousands of letters from different parts of the country asking about land, climate, and general conditions. They were liberal in sending out copies of their papers to the eastern states and printed boom and immigration editions, of which several thousand copies were broadcast over the country.[9] The editor of the *Yankton Press* in the fall of 1870 stated that he desired to make his paper a publication that would be of value "to send abroad to induce people to come to Dakota." [10] The various papers reprinted pages of material from immigration pamphlets, and their editorials were filled with propaganda. In the news articles the virtues of Dakota and its desirable climate

---

[8] *Biennial Report of the Dakota Commissioner of Immigration,* 1885-90; McClure, *Resources of Dakota;* F. H. Haggerty, *The Territory of Dakota* (Aberdeen, D. T., 1889). McClure and Haggerty are reports of the Commissioner of Immigration, composed largely of statistical material.

[9] The Immigration number of the *Mandan Pioneer,* January 1, 1884, is a good example, of which 6,000 copies are said to have been printed. An illustrated edition of the *Bismarck Tribune* was issued in the summer of 1880; 40,000 copies were printed. *Northern Pacific Times* (Valley City, D. T.), June 3, 1880.

[10] *Yankton Weekly Dakotian,* October 26, 1870.

and "beautiful lands" were set forth in glowing terms. Foster favored newspapers in preference to pamphlets and circulars, since they were more indicative of the progress of the territory. In 1872 he reported the distribution of six hundred copies of newspapers, which included one hundred copies of the *Dakota Republican,* published at Vermillion, and fifty copies of the *Yankton Union and Dakotian,* purchased at five cents each. The others were no doubt donated. In 1873 practically all of the publications in southeastern Dakota were included on the list for distribution. While in charge of the immigration office, Foster wrote regular articles for *Crofutt's Western World,* a monthly magazine which placed emphasis on western matters.[11]

The immigration editions of the newspapers, printed largely for advertising purposes, tried to impress the possible immigrants. Avoiding the mention of such things as blizzards, drought, and grasshopper plagues, much was usually said in behalf of the climate, which was described as "salubrious" and "attractive." The excellence of the soil and reports of forty bushels of wheat and seventy bushels of corn to the acre, with others of various types of vegetables of extraordinary size, were frequently discussed. The papers often warned that some money and equipment were necessary in order to begin farming, even in Dakota. Taking the newspapers into general consideration, they were reasonable and moderate in tone. Practical suggestions were made as to soil preparation, methods of tree planting, and fencing. Considerable emphasis was placed on the possibilities of making money by investing in town-site locations and mill sites. Efforts were made to attract outside capital by stressing the fact that the man with money could obtain high interest rates in the West.

The work of the various immigration bureaus or boards, the local newspapers, and the force of private letters were powerfully supplemented by the efforts of railroad corporations, land and

[11] *Yankton Press and Dakotian,* October 1, 8, 1874; *Biennial Report of the Commissioner of Immigration of Dakota Territory,* 1872.

town-site companies, and steamboat lines, which were always alert to the commercial profit to be derived from the immigrant. The immigrant trade meant a great deal to the railroad companies in profitable traffic, the sale of railroad lands, the settlement of adjacent government land, and the securing of a labor supply. They organized land and town-site companies, colonizing associations, and printed many pamphlets [12] and maps depicting the advantages of the land and its resources. The Northern Pacific Company developed its own mines of lignite coal, a product which it sold at reasonable prices to the homesteaders. The companies made cheap fuel one of their strong advertising points. They took cars of Dakota products on an exhibition tour through the eastern states in an attempt to convince prospective settlers of the advisability of locating in Dakota.[13] The local town-site and land companies were aggressive and were influential through advertisements and maps in getting many settlers to their local towns and counties. Groups of counties often prepared attractive volumes of the history of their locality, including a description of each county and town, with business advertisements.[14] The publicity gained for Dakota by the gold rush to the Black Hills was extremely important, as previously explained, in attracting population not only to the Hills themselves, but to the other portions of the territory.

[12] "The Conditions and Resources of Southern Dakota" by John R. Brenan, published at Sioux City in 1872 by the Dakota Southern Railway Company, was a valuable booklet of this type.

[13] The Chicago, Milwaukee and St. Paul Railroad Company provided a creditable exhibit of Dakota products in the autumn of 1884. It was placed in a passenger-car in charge of W. E. Powell, general immigration agent for the road, assisted by D. H. Moore, the company's immigrant agent. The car was taken to Detroit, Cleveland, and Buffalo, then to the states of New York and Pennsylvania, and to New England. It was also sent through the provinces of eastern Canada. During this trip it was visited by thousands of people who entered their names upon a register prepared for that purpose. Two months later the car was taken to the World's Fair at New Orleans. This was only one of the many Dakota exhibits sent east during the period of settlement.

[14] "The History of Southeastern Dakota," published at Sioux City in 1881, and "The History and Progress of Central Dakota," Chicago, 1882, are good examples of this sort of advertising.

A SETTLEMENT IN THE BAD LANDS

Medora, Dakota Territory, 1886. Marquis de Mores' packing plant at the left. L. A. Huffman photograph.

To properly evaluate the various advertising activities is a very difficult matter. The official territorial efforts must naturally be studied in connection with the work of the railroads, land companies, and other private concerns which sought to attract both American and European immigrants. They must also be considered in connection with European and American conditions which influenced the history of immigration. The operations of the territorial government were efficiently and, on the whole, honorably managed. There can be no question that in many cases the printed documents and pamphlets sent out were too glowing and optimistic, but it is fair to say that there was probably little deliberate misrepresentation. In fact, in many of the official publications there were warnings against too much optimism, and the difficulties and hardships of a homesteader were vividly pictured. Exaggeration was a fault of the private companies to a far greater degree than of the territorial officials. Keen competition no doubt in some instances may have led to unscrupulous methods, and the territorial immigration office at times may have been hampered by politicians, but those cases were few. From the standpoint of advantage to both the territory and to the immigrants themselves, the various advertising agencies employed were of genuine benefit and deserve historical mention. They were extremely effective in the settling of the vacant lands and aiding the economic development of the territorial resources. This competitive advertising added greatly to the strength of the Territory of Dakota and to that of the West in general.[15]

The best proof of the value of the advertising campaign can be shown in the period of the great boom. Had the matter of immigration and settlement been left to chance and the natural factors influencing westward migration and expansion, there is no doubt but that Dakota would have received a fair share of the immigrants from northern Europe and from the eastern states. But it

[15] Herbert S. Schell, "Official Immigration Activities of Dakota Territory," *North Dakota Historical Quarterly* (October, 1935), pp. 5-24.

is certain that deliberate and carefully planned advertising campaigns added greatly to the movement. They resulted in thousands of additional homesteaders from the eastern states and in a greater immigration from Europe.

The territorial officers of Montana were quite anxious to increase permanent settlement in the region and took steps to facilitate it. In 1869 Governor James H. Ashley informed the territorial legislature that he had been very much impressed with the large numbers of German and Scandinavian immigrants that were flocking into Minnesota and other states farther east and that active steps should be taken to get some of them to settle in Montana, which to his mind had as many advantages as the places to which settlers were then going. While he had been in New York City he had thought it wise to employ some one to contact prospective settlers as they landed there, and had engaged a Mr. B. Speyer to act as Commissioner of Immigration for the Territory of Montana. He had instructed Mr. Speyer to prepare circulars that could be easily translated into the German and Scandinavian languages to be sent to Europe by the various railroad companies. The governor requested appropriations to cover the expense of this new type of advertising.[16]

In the early seventies there was evidence of considerable activity on the part of immigrant organizations in Montana Territory. A Salt Lake City newspaper in June, 1871, reported that the newspapers of Helena were coöperating in the printing of immigration pamphlets that were to be widely distributed. A Helena editor on March 30, 1872, printed the proceedings of the Board of Directors of the Montana Immigration Society, whose purpose or objective was defined as that of "obtaining and disseminating reliable information regarding the territory and to afford such as desire it, a reliable exhibit of statistics, resources and advantages offered to immigrants seeking a permanent home." In January, 1873, it was announced that the "Immigration Pamphlet" was

---

[16] *Message of Governor J. H. Ashley*, Sixth Legislative Session, 1869-70.

ready for distribution.[17] Efforts were made by groups of citizens in 1875 to obtain action on the part of the citizens from various parts of Montana to secure a territorial board of immigration to be provided for at public expense.

The people of Bozeman were much interested in immigration, and in December, 1875, a group of citizens met in the sheriff's office to work out some ways and means of encouraging settlers to come to Montana. A series of resolutions was passed, the first being as follows:

Whereas we, the citizens of Bozeman in the Gallatin Valley, Territory of Montana, knowing the great agricultural, mining, and stock-raising facilities of the Big Horn, Yellowstone, and Gallatin valleys and feeling the want of immigration that our natural resources may be developed; and desiring to encourage the surplus population and capital of the east to the settlement of the vast area of rich and inviting country mentioned, and believing that the time has come for systematic action, hereby form ourselves into an immigration society, to be known as the Big Horn and Eastern Montana Colonization Society.

Another resolution expressed their confidence in the ability and integrity of H. N. Maguire and authorized him to become their agent in obtaining immigration to Big Horn and Yellowstone counties. It was also resolved that a committee of correspondence be selected to get in touch with him and with others who might be interested in Montana. It was voted to petition the next territorial legislature asking that a board or bureau of immigration be provided for at public expense and that pamphlets be prepared and circulated telling of the advantages of the territory. Letters were read from Mr. Maguire assuring the people that a colony of one thousand could easily be organized in the vicinity of Chicago.[18]

By studying the advertising methods employed during the period of territorial settlement, one cannot fail to get some idea

[17] *Helena Weekly Herald*, March 22, 30, April 7, 1872, January 18, 1873.
[18] *Avant Courier*, December 16, 1875.

of the optimism, the vigor, and the vision that these pioneers had of the future. It was the spirit that has always characterized the West in its formative periods. These energetic, ambitious, and forward-looking efforts drew into this region large masses of people from the eastern states and from Europe and opened to these groups, suffering under social and economic restraints, the golden door of opportunity on the western prairies.

XIV

COLONIZATION PROJECTS

IMMIGRANTS entered the Territory of Dakota in three ways, by single families, by small groups of two or more households, and by colonies. Down to 1870, with a few exceptions, the first two methods prevailed. During the later period, however, the third method became common, and was especially important during the Dakota boom of the late seventies and early eighties. As a rule, the settlers knew exactly where they were going, since the way had been traveled before their departure and the site of their future homes had been carefully chosen. When a location had once been established in Dakota, whether by a few families or a colony, letters written back home to relatives and friends, together with the stories of those who went back to visit, led again and again to removals to the region described.

The main aim of the various colonization associations was to reduce the cost of investigation and exploration, to obtain cheaper transportation rates, to obviate privation and inconvenience incident to settlement in a new country, and to promote the social, religious, economic, and educational advantages of community settlement. Often groups of friends and neighbors in a certain locality would settle together, and people of the same nationality would locate in groups in order to carry out their own ideals.

The method of organization was about the same in most cases, the association usually being sponsored by a small group of influential men in the local community. A membership fee of from ten to twenty dollars was charged to defray the cost of actual advertising and other expenses incidental to the selection of a location suitable to their needs. Association officers were ordinarily elected to act for the group, but as soon as the colony was located, its members stood on their own feet. After the first or embryonic settlement was made, it often acted as a center around which other groups of the same nationality or from the same locality might settle. The Russian-Germans who located in southeastern Dakota in earlier years followed out this idea of settlement. The first example of a group to migrate to the Territory of Dakota was that of the New York colony in 1866.

The Homestead Act awakened a strong sentiment throughout the United States favorable to the occupation of western public lands. The liberal provisions of the law appealed to the poor man, and soon movements were on foot in various parts of the country to organize groups of people or colonies to migrate in bodies to the West and locate wherever soil, climate, and natural advantages offered the most favorable inducements. Such an organization was formed at Syracuse, New York, March 7, 1863, called the Free Homestead Association of Central New York. The purpose of the association was to get away from the overcrowded East, where farmlands were too high in price for the man of ordinary means to find a satisfactory location, and to settle there in a body.

When first organized, it consisted of about one hundred families and single men, and counting women and children, numbered nearly five hundred. One of the requirements for membership was a moderate amount of money or property, which would enable the group to begin its project under comparatively favorable circumstances. The secretary of the association and one of its leading members was James S. Foster of Syracuse, New York, who was soon in correspondence with various state and territorial officials concerning a possible place to locate. As the Territory of Dakota had no immigration bureau or agent to attend to duties of this character, Governor Edmunds turned the matter over to Surveyor-General Hill, who was an ardent booster for Dakota settlement. He soon got in touch with the organization and informed it through correspondence of the advantages of the territory. He also communicated with another colonizing association that was forming near Ypsilanti, Michigan.[1]

The New York association, having obtained all possible information by correspondence, sent out a delegation in August, 1863, headed by Mr. Foster, to visit and to inspect certain localities in Kansas, Iowa, Nebraska, Minnesota, and Dakota. Governor Edmunds, in his annual message of December 7, 1863, emphasized the importance of fostering and encouraging immigration to Dakota, and concerning the correspondence with the New York association said, "The efforts made by Surveyor-General Hill, though as yet attended with no decided results, would seem to have laid the foundation for a large and flourishing settlement from the Empire state." He asked the hearty coöperation of the settlers in the matter and recommended that a Bureau of Immigration be organized with three commissioners.[2]

W. W. Burleigh, the Yankton Indian agent, while on one of his visits to Washington, stopped at Syracuse in December and gave a talk on Dakota to the organization, and at a meeting held January 16, 1864, the association decided in favor of this territory and recommended Yankton as the best point to locate temporarily until another place could be chosen and a permanent settlement established in the territory. A pamphlet was issued by the organization describing and extolling the wonderful advantages the Territory of Dakota had to offer to "poor men who earn their bread by the sweat of their brow." The plea for new members

[1] "The Free Homestead Association of Central New York" (Syracuse, N. Y., 1863), pp. 1-6, a pamphlet describing the association, membership, etc. Mr. Foster was called Professor Foster, as he had previously been engaged in educational work.

[2] *Annual Message of the Territorial Governor of Dakota*, December 7, 1863, p. 5.

closed with these words, "Persons receiving this circular and sending five dollars to the secretary can rely on receiving a certificate of membership by return mail." [3]

The executive committee in making arrangements for the trip decided at first to go by special train from Syracuse to St. Joseph, Missouri, by way of Chicago and thence by steamboat to Yankton. After some debate it was finally decided to take the "all land route" instead, consisting of travel by train to Marshalltown, Iowa, the terminus of the railroad and the nearest point of approach to Yankton, where equipment was to be purchased for a six weeks' overland journey to Dakota by prairie-schooner. The party left Syracuse April 12th on a special train of twenty cars and arrived at Marshalltown April 17th, where they were met by Mr. Foster, who had been sent ahead to purchase an outfit with which to finish the trip. There were 266 persons in the party, 171 adults and 95 children. [4]

Most of the colonists were ready for the road by May first. Several families, meeting with friends and dreading a tedious overland journey of three hundred miles with ox teams, through miry sloughs and across uninhabited prairies, took up their residence at Marshalltown. The rest of the party headed toward Dakota, but as they proceeded on their way, other families became discouraged with the toil of the journey, and influenced by wild stories concerning Dakota, reported, no doubt, in part by designing persons who wished the colony to settle in Iowa, stopped at Webster City and Fort Dodge. There was some sickness and two deaths on the journey. The main party kept together until it entered Dakota at Pacquette's Ferry. There some of the colonists separated from the group, and going up the Sioux River, settled

[3] "The New York Colony in Dakota Territory in 1864" (Syracuse, N. Y., 1867), pp. 1-3.
[4] The party took with it 51 tons of freight and baggage which was carried the entire distance for $2.05 per hundred pounds. Railroad tickets to Marshalltown cost $15 for adults and $7.50 for children under twelve. Letter from Mrs. Carrie Carney to Doane Robinson, Pierre, South Dakota, November 20, 1923.

at Brule Creek. Twenty-five families are said to have stopped and located between the Big Sioux River and Yankton. They selected farms, erected cabins, and began to put in spring crops. The majority of the party, however, went through to its destination, and located claims around the town of Yankton or in Bon Homme County.[5]

Why they did not carry out the original plan of settling in a compact body and building their own village is not known, but apparently the spirit of individualism was stronger than that of co-operation. As a result of this independent action, nearly every Dakota settlement then existing received an acquisition from this group of Dakota pioneers. The settlers, however, arrived at a very inopportune time, as in July, just as they were well located, the settlements of Dakota experienced their first grasshopper attack, causing some of the new-comers to become discouraged and leave the territory.[6]

The success which had attended the efforts of Dakota to secure immigration, as shown by the coming of the New York colony, created considerable envy and newspaper comment in the sparsely settled sections of Iowa and Nebraska. As already shown, competition in getting settlers was very keen, as every western community fully realized the importance of increasing its population. The coming of the New York colony to Dakota was the subject of an article in the *Omaha Republican*, one of the leading newspapers in Nebraska, in 1864. In an attempt to arouse the Nebraskans to action in trying to get settlers, the editor told the story of how "eight hundred to one thousand population came to Yankton at one time." It continued, "Yankton is about one hundred twenty miles due north of this place, and one hundred eighty miles by the

---

[5] "The New York Colony in Dakota Territory," *op. cit.*, pp. 6-10; *Dakota Union* (Yankton, D. T.), June 2, 1864. Of the one hundred families that started from New York, forty settled in Iowa and the other sixty in Dakota. Visher, "Geography of South Dakota," pp. 21-3.

[6] *Dakota Republican*, May 17, 1877. Visher estimated that by 1870 only about thirty of the original sixty families remained in Dakota.

usual traveled route. It is out of the line of travel, with no particular commercial, agricultural, or stock-raising advantages. Yet we have the foregoing testimony in regard to what that people have accomplished. It is nonsense to blush the fact, and we refer to it not out of a spirit of jealousy, but to induce our leading men to realize their opportunities and to turn their attention a little more in the direction indicated." [7]

In the spring of 1869 a large Bohemian colony from Chicago and vicinity, numbering about five hundred families, was organized for the purpose of migrating to the West in a body. Their agents visited various parts of Nebraska and Dakota in July, 1869, and finally selected a location in Dakota lying mostly in Bon Homme and Yankton counties.[8] The colonists reached Yankton in September, 1869, and began a settlement about twelve miles northeast of that point. Most of the new-comers selected their claims during the fall months and made small improvements. Many constructed sod houses to furnish them with a winter dwelling and to enable them to get at their work early in the spring. Frank Bem was one of the leaders of the group.

The winter of 1869-70 was severe, and there was considerable sickness and suffering among the Bohemian settlers in their hastily constructed sod houses. They were assisted by Yankton citizens, and very few fatalities resulted. In the spring the colonists set to work in earnest. They broke up a fairly large amount of land, built better homes and farm buildings, and raised a quantity of sod crops. The first improvements of these ambitious and hard-working pioneers were crude but substantial.[9]

---

[7] Quoted in Kingsbury, *History of Dakota Territory*, I, 337.

[8] *Yankton Weekly Dakotian*, July 13, 20, 27, August 4, 1869. The tract of land selected embraced a little more than four townships and was located in southeastern Bon Homme and in southwestern Yankton counties. A small portion of the land was near the old town of Niobrara, Nebraska. A few of the Bohemian group settled at the latter place.

[9] *Yankton Weekly Dakotian*, July 26, 1870; files of the *Yankton Weekly Dakotian*, September, 1869 to June, 1870. There is no good evidence available indicating the exact number of families or people who settled in the Bohemian

A new colonization scheme on a large scale was inaugurated in the summer of 1870 by the Peoria Emigration Society of Peoria, Illinois. The organization sent its agents to look up a suitable place for a colony of about two hundred heads of families and single men. After a careful investigation, the representatives decided upon a location on the west side of the Missouri River about seventy-five miles above Fort Randall. They called their town-site Crescent City. Upon making application to file at the local land-office it was discovered that the town-site was on Indian land. They immediately recrossed the Missouri and laid claim to 193 quarter-sections of land and located a town-site some twelve miles below the present town of Chamberlain. The colonizing project did not materialize, as the land on which the town was located was added to the Sioux Reservation by a proclamation of President Grant late in 1870.[10]

James S. Foster, immigration agent and later Commissioner of Immigration for the territory, from 1871 to 1875, directed a good deal of attention to the organization of emigration colonies and at times special agents were authorized to work toward the same objective. In the spring of 1872, a Doctor Lewis of Vermillion was reported to have organized five emigrant societies in Iowa and had departed for Indiana and Ohio, where he planned to continue his work. In April, 1873, the Reverend G. M. Binkley, a resident of Springfield, Dakota, a professional lecturer of considerable ability, was sent to England to speak on Dakota and to distribute literature on the advantages of the territory. The following spring he was reported to be returning with a colony of one hundred families. Other representatives were employed to go to Norway and Sweden to carry on the work of organizing colonies for group migration. The special agents ordinarily served without

settlement. Kingsbury estimates the number at 1,200, which is probably rather high.

[10] A committee was sent to investigate the feasibility of the location. Their report was unfavorable and the scheme collapsed. Robinson, *History of South Dakota*, p. 243; Kingsbury, *op. cit.*, p. 564.

pay, but were allowed the cost of transportation, with a small allowance for postage and incidentals.[11]

During the seventies one of the groups of Europeans interested in migrating to the United States were the Russian-German people of southern Russia. Large numbers of Germans had settled in that area in the eighteenth century under the encouragement of the Russian Government, with liberal concessions concerning language and religion. In the summer of 1871 this government changed its policy and gave those Germans living within its territory ten years in which to adopt the Russian language and religion or to leave the country. A large exodus of the Russian-German groups took place, and during the three years 1872-74 it is estimated that more than one hundred thousand arrived in New York City. All sections of the West with unoccupied lands made every possible effort to secure some of these people and the local press, learning of the movement and its magnitude, worked hard for its own area. Strong immigration organizations in all the states and territories with public lands made their bid for the new-comers. The Union Pacific Railroad, anxious to obtain settlers and extend its activities, was able to locate several large colonies on its lands in Nebraska and, although the competition was extremely keen, Dakota representatives were able to get some of them to settle in the Territory of Dakota.[12]

In the spring of 1873 news came to the Dakota settlements that a large group of Russian-Germans was looking for a place to locate

[11] *Yankton Weekly Press*, April 9, 16, 24, 1872; *Dakota Herald*, April 11, May 28, 1873, November 3, 10, 1874; *Yankton Press and Dakotian*, December 24, 1874.

[12] The so-called Russian-German people are usually referred to in a general way as Mennonites and no doubt far too much emphasis has been placed upon that term. While there were some Mennonites and Hutterites among them, by far the greater number were of the Lutheran and Reformed Church faiths. The Hutterites and Mennonites were most sought after for colonizing projects as their organization in groups under religious leaders made it easy for them to carry on mass migrations. C. H. Smith, *The Coming of the Russian Mennonites* (Chicago, 1927), pp. 75-9; Gertrude S. Young, "The Mennonites in South Dakota," South Dakota Historical *Collections*, X, 485-91.

on lands in the western part of the United States, and the Commissioner of Immigration set about securing contact with them. About one hundred Russian-German settlers with their families arrived in Dakota in the spring of 1873 and settled in Yankton, Bon Homme, and Turner counties. A delegation from Omaha had visited Yankton in April and selected the location. A second committee under the leadership of Jacob Max visited Yankton early in the summer and as a result another group of Russian-German families arrived in the territorial capital early in August, 1873. It has been estimated that about five hundred adult Russian-Germans with considerable money settled in the Territory of Dakota in 1873. On the average, their families were large, some having as many as ten to twelve children, while six or seven were common. "A special train on Sunday," noted a Clay County editor in October, 1873, "brought in 150 Russian-German immigrants with a quantity of children." [13]

Early in 1873 several good-sized Mennonite communities who were planning to come to the United States or Canada sent out an official delegation on a tour of inspection to find a suitable location. After looking over what Manitoba had to offer, they arrived at Fargo accompanied by a Mennonite representative from Indiana and the land agent of the Northern Pacific Railroad. They were favorably impressed with the land about Fargo and after a week of investigation the Northern Pacific offered to sell them land along the railroad at three dollars per acre and to assist them in securing the public land adjacent to their holdings from the government. The arrangement failed, as the government refused to dispose of its lands in this way, since it was inconsistent with its general policy under the Homestead Act. Foster attempted to get the official Mennonite delegation to visit Yankton when it passed through Sioux City, Iowa, but failed to do so. A small group of Mennonites under the leadership of Daniel Unruh settled in

[13] *Yankton Press and Dakotian*, March 13, April 24, July 17, August 7, 1873; *Clay County Register*, October 9, November 28, 1873.

Turner County, north of Yankton. Foster was largely responsible for their coming.[14]

In June a large number of Bohemians came to Yankton directly from their native land. By executive order that month the United States Land Office at Vermillion was removed to Sioux Falls, as most of the land in the vicinity of Vermillion and Yankton had been taken up. During the summer a large colony from Ohio settled on the James River in the north central part of Hutchinson County, about twelve miles below Milltown. Immigration continued during the fall months, and in November a delegation representing a colonizing organization of Effington, Illinois, visited the James River Valley and selected a location not far from Milltown for their colony, where they filed upon a large tract of land for their constituents.[15]

During the winter of 1873-74 several Russian-German delegations visited southeastern Dakota, looked over the country, and picked out land. On March 17, 1874, about five hundred adults of that nationality arrived at Yankton by special train over the Dakota Southern and five or six hundred more were reported to be on their way. On May 27th, one hundred and fifty arrived, accompanied by numerous children. In June, 1874, a delegation headed by Carl P. Meyer visited Yankton and a Dakota newspaper said, "They are from Lancaster, Pennsylvania, looking for land for Russian Mennonites and are well pleased with the region. They have been to Nebraska and had planned on going to Minnesota but gave it up and decided to locate here."[16]

During the summer a colony of about thirty-five families of the Russian-Germans called Hutterians established a communistic settlement a few miles west of the village of Bon Homme, and

[14] *Yankton Press*, July 23, 1873; *Yankton Press and Dakotian*, January 15, 1874; Smith, *op. cit.*, pp. 51-88; *Clay County Register* and *Dakota Herald*, April 14, October 23, 30, 1873, April 14, 1874.
[15] Files of the *Yankton Press* and *Clay County Register*, spring and summer, 1873.
[16] *Yankton Press and Dakotian*, June 18, 1874; *Dakota Herald*, March 17, 1874; *Clay County Register*, May 17, 1874.

another group of these same people, consisting of about forty families, located a colony at Wolf Creek in Hutchinson County.[17] The experience of the Wolf Creek settlers is indicative of the keen spirit of competition and the struggle between the various localities to obtain immigrants. The colony arrived in New York and was induced by the Chicago, Burlington and Quincy Railroad to go to Iowa. Before arriving at Burlington, the superintendent of the train boarded the cars and persuaded them to go to Lincoln, Nebraska. There, according to a story of one of the members of the colony, they were "set upon by a land shark of the railroad and induced to take a large tract of land." After living there for a period of nine months, they communicated with friends in the vicinity of Yankton and decided to move to that locality. Disappointed over the loss of the settlers, the agent of the Burlington Railroad advanced a claim of seven hundred dollars against the group and held their baggage in lieu of payment. The settlers appealed to their friends at Yankton, who intervened and secured a statement from the superintendent of the road that he had promised free transportation for their baggage from Burlington to Lincoln, whether they settled there permanently or not. The baggage was then released. The founders of the second Hutterian colony in Dakota were so well pleased with their location that they did much to secure additional settlers. They worked through the agency of the Lancaster County Society of Pennsylvania and were influential in turning many of the uncertain immigrants toward southeastern Dakota.[18]

In August the coming of the grasshoppers in large numbers

---

[17] Young, op. cit., pp. 490-4; Dakota Herald, August 25, 1874. The Hutterite groups were followers of Hutter and are sometimes called German-Quakers, as they resemble the Quakers in many ways. They were noncombatants, dressed quite plainly, and the members of each colony or association owned all property in common. Another Hutterian colony was established at Elm Creek in Hutchinson County in 1877. The communists were few in number as compared with the other groups of Russian-Germans. Kingsbury, History of Dakota Territory, I, 712-6.

[18] Dakota Herald, August 11, November 3, 1874, June 16, 1879.

stopped general immigration from the eastern states for several years but apparently had little effect upon the Russian-Germans. Late that month a large number of them settled near Chamberlain in Turner County. "The Russians," noted an observer, "are still coming into Dakota, and almost every week brings in additional families. Large portions of our territory are being occupied exclusively by this class of immigration." A large percentage of the Russian-German population that came in during the years 1873-74 settled in Yankton, Bon Homme, Hutchison, and Turner counties, although some of them located in the counties of Spink, Hanson, and Beadle. It is difficult to estimate the increase in population for 1874 in southeastern Dakota. The Commissioner of Immigration in his report of January, 1875, stated that there were at that time at least five thousand Russian-German immigrants in Dakota.[19] The Dakota newspapers and the reports of the Immigration Board showed that they came into southeastern Dakota as rapidly in 1875 as they had the previous year.

A great many of the immigrants who located in Dakota during the boom period came in groups and colonies and that type of settlement was very common during the middle eighties. The Dakota newspapers were filled with accounts of the activity of associations of settlers. The *Turner County Herald* of Hurley in the spring of 1883 mentioned that several colonies of English and Scotch were locating in Yankton County. On June 28th it reported the visit of a delegation from Wales which was looking for a location for a colony somewhere along the Milwaukee Railroad. On April 9, 1884, the same newspaper stated that a colony of five hundred families, the heads of which were mostly former soldiers of the Grand Army of the Republic, was being formed in Cleveland, Ohio, to settle in Morton County.[20]

The *Estelline Bell* on March 23, 1884, reported that a colony of

[19] *Clay County Register*, September 14, 1874; *Yankton Press and Dakotian*, January 8, 1875.
[20] *Turner County Herald*, May 17, June 28, 1883, April 9, 1885.

Rumanians had just arrived in Foster County. They had recently settled in western Canada along the Canadian Pacific Railway but were not satisfied with the location. More were reported to be coming. In the summer of 1885 a German colony settled in Charles Mix County. In April, 1886, the same paper mentioned that a colony of one hundred and twenty families from Fulton County, Pennsylvania, had recently settled in Logan County, many of which were individuals of means. A Methodist colony from Dunn County, Wisconsin, had located near Sterling, Burleigh County. It was also announced that an Irish colony would settle in Stutsman County, and that a colony of Russian Jews would locate in the Devil's Lake district.[21]

The *Mandan Weekly Pioneer* of April 25, 1885, told of the "Lansing Colony" from Michigan arriving at Hoskins in Mc-Intosh County. A Russian colony of fifty families had just settled in Morton County, and more were to follow soon. A group of seventy-five Hollander families had recently located in Emmons County. The *Dakota Settler*, published at Bismarck, reported that a colony from Iowa had located in Logan County in March, 1887. In April notice was taken of three colonies that had just located in Towner County, one from Missouri and two from Canada. On December 8, 1887, a Polish colony of one hundred families was reported as having located at Crystal Springs in the eastern part of Kidder County.

The work of the Northern Pacific Colonization Bureau is worthy of consideration, especially for its influence in the settlement of the region along that railroad west of the Missouri River. The general manager of the bureau was authorized to organize a local board to do colonizing work in any locality where three or more persons signed a call for such an organization and there were rea-sonable prospects of gathering a colony to emigrate to Dakota. Each local board consisted of a president, vice-president and sec-

[21] *Estelline Bell* (Hamlin County, D. T.), May 23, 1884, April 10, 17, 23, 1886.

retary, but one of the officers of the bureau was required to fill one of the offices on each local board. These boards were agents of the bureau. Any person, male or female, of good moral character, was eligible to membership by signing the articles of association and paying a membership fee of twenty dollars. The certificate of membership could be transferred upon consent of the local officers. The central bureau did everything possible to facilitate the location of colonies, recommending locations, obtaining transportation, carefully superintending extensive explorations in search of sites, and giving the local boards all possible information. Each member of the colony had an opportunity to secure government land near the town-site and the Northern Pacific Railroad.

The Northern Pacific Bureau acted only as a central organization in starting the colony and in rendering all possible help in bringing about its establishment. The local organization chose its own site and picked out its own lands. The various colonies detached themselves from the central corporation as soon as the settlement had been made, and the people were left to make their own rules and regulations, and to establish their own local government. This colonization scheme was very successful, and the following towns were located along the Northern Pacific during the early years of the boom: New Salem, twenty-eight miles west of Mandan, by a colony from New England; Glen Ullin, about twenty-six miles west of New Salem; Richardson was located eighty-two miles west of Mandan; Taylor, the county-seat of Stark County, the next station west of Richardson; Gladstone, Dickinson, and Belfield were located west of Taylor. These small colonies or towns were planned to become nuclei around which other groups coming to that part of western Dakota might settle, thus making them the important commercial centers of the region. The plan was entirely successful, as shown by the later influx of immigration to the vicinity of the towns thus established.[22]

[22] *Mandan Daily Pioneer*, Immigration number, January 1, 1885. Dickinson later became the county-seat of Stark County.

Into the great wheat belt along the line of the Northern Pacific came thousands of home-seekers from the villages of New England and the other eastern states. Not only from the crowded East but from Iowa, Minnesota, Wisconsin, Michigan, Nebraska, and Missouri came the land-seekers. They came to till millions of acres that had never known a plow, to make new towns, to redeem the empty places as their fathers had done when they trailed westward to the Ohio and Mississippi valleys from the East in the earlier days. The railroad was the magic key that unlocked this new country. Before the coming of the railroad into this vicinity the prairies were as empty as the open sea. But instead of lonely vessels against the sky-line there were, here and there, miles apart, the low sod shacks of the homesteaders who had come into the country ahead of the railroad. Those pioneers were waiting to be linked with the world beyond that they might expand their farming activities and market their crops. They had been led there by that dearest of incentives to American courage and enthusiasm, the ownership of land and of a place they could call home.

E. R. Steinbrueck, one of the first settlers to arrive at Glen Ullin, described the founding of that place under the auspices of the Northern Pacific Bureau of Immigration, in 1883:

It was on a fair day in May, 1883, when a car arrived on a temporary side track of the Northern Pacific main line in an open country about fifty-four miles west of Mandan. The car was shoved backward onto the siding, and the passenger train puffed away toward its western destination. New settlers came out of the car and scattered over the immediate vicinity. There was land in plenty where the town was to be, but not a house, a shack, or a fence post was to be seen. These first people were compelled to stay in the car and make the best of things until a freight train arrived a few days later with utensils, stock, and tents. Their most necessary baggage had been delayed on the road and was brought by one of the next passenger trains, which dumped the trunks and valises right and left on the prairie.[23]

[23] E. R. Steinbrueck, "The History of Glen Ullin," *Collections*, State Historical Society of North Dakota, I, 197-9.

The first town of Glen Ullin was a canvas town, every one pitching his tent where he found it most convenient. A few days later other settlers began to arrive from Illinois, Wisconsin, Ohio, and Iowa, the majority coming from the State of Ohio. In every one of those states had been established an agency to enlist settlers for Glen Ullin. A. E. Bovay was the trustee for the Northern Pacific Railroad Company, and Isaac Richardson was the Ohio agent at Cleveland, Ohio. Each member had been obliged to pay twenty dollars for a certificate and was entitled to two town lots and to all other concessions, as well as the advice and aid of the agent in getting located. After becoming acquainted with the manner of surveys and locating the corner-posts of the government sections, they all chose their homesteads and on a certain day all went *en masse* to the Bismarck Land Office to file. In the meantime, many had become discouraged and had returned to their old homes.[24]

A St. Paul editor on March 26, 1885, mentioned a boom in immigration, the trains from the East being heavily loaded:

Michigan is sending out a large number of immigrant colonies to Dakota, which are coming from Kalamazoo, Paw Paw, Grand Rapids, and several other points. A company of twenty families arrived yesterday bound west for points on the Northern Pacific. To-day a company of thirty families headed by P. B. Wickham of Athens, Ohio, passed through the city bound for Glen Ullin, Dakota. The west Missouri country in Dakota will receive a very large increase this year, and already several new colonies have gone out. Among these is the Red Wing, Minnesota Swedish colony headed by Frank Bredberg, who have selected a site for settlement west of the Missouri in Morton County. There are fifty families in the colony.[25]

A Mandan editor on April 9, 1885, reported that on Wednesday ten carloads of immigrants' movables had passed through town on their way to New Salem. The next week the same editor

[24] *Mandan Weekly Pioneer,* March 26, 1885.
[25] *St. Paul Globe,* March 26, 1885.

stated that large numbers of Russians were settling in Campbell and McPherson counties: "The prairie schooners, as emigrant outfits are called, are seen in all sections of the territory pointing northward and west. Glen Ullin has secured the great Swedish colony from Goodhue County, Minnesota. The prize consisted of two hundred and fifty families." On April 23rd the same paper reported: "A committee from the colony of one thousand immigrants from Vermont has promised to visit the west Missouri country before deciding upon a location. A small colony of Finlanders recently settled not far from Dickinson." [26]

While there was some settlement in Montana and Wyoming by groups or colonies, this plan was not nearly so popular there as in the Territory of Dakota. This was due in part to the more remote location of the settlements and to the fact that large amounts of the land needed to be irrigated if it were to be used for agriculture. Practically all of the activity in Montana occurred in the eighties after the Northern Pacific Railroad had revived at Bismarck and started westward in 1879. In the fall of 1881, after the railroad had entered Montana, M. L. Halgreen, the Swedish immigration agent for the Union Pacific Railroad, was in Helena gathering statistics as to the merits of this territory as a place for the planting of colonies of his race. He was to return to Sweden in the winter to organize prospective groups or colonies for settlement in the United States, some of which, it was hoped, might be induced to come to Montana.[27]

In 1881 it was reported that a large colony of Germans, mostly in families said to possess from two thousand to three thousand dollars each, would form the settlers of a new town called Landtsheim, five miles west of Glendive, early the next spring. Each colonist was to receive from eighty to one hundred and sixty acres for stock-raising or farming. The town-site proper was to be divided into blocks of six acres each, of which each colonist

[26] *Mandan Weekly Pioneer*, April 9, 16, 23, 1885.
[27] *River Press*, November 9, 1881.

was to receive one for a residence and one for a garden. At that time the Yellowstone Land and Colonization Company owned about half of the town-site of Glendive and was holding its lots at a good price, although sales were not especially numerous.[28]

In January, 1882, the editor of the *River Press* announced that a small colony of English settlers was to locate at Helena and would arrive there during the summer. Thirty families were en route and planned to locate in a body in the Yellowstone Valley. It was also reported that a considerable number of Germans had written for information regarding the Territory of Montana and a large colony of them from the East, numbering between two and three hundred, was to settle near Glendive in the spring.[29] A few weeks later the same editor stated that a colony of settlers from Iowa, headed by Samuel and William Marshall, had arrived in Helena early in February, and that heavy immigration from that state was expected during the spring months.[30] In May a colony from Ripon, Wisconsin, consisting of 115 families, or 506 people, had located on Clark's Fork near Billings. They had brought their household goods, stock, farming implements, and six months' provisions, and according to the editor of the *Billings Herald*, were fully prepared to rough it for a few months until they could harvest a crop. During the eighties several groups settled as colonies along the line of the Northern Pacific Railroad, some of which were sponsored by the Immigration Department of that line, whose activities extended throughout the East and Middle West.[31]

While there is evidence of small groups settling in Wyoming, most of the colonization was connected with irrigation projects in the northern and western portions of the state. An example of a colonization project in Wyoming is that of the Mormon colony incorporated early in April, 1900, as the "Big Horn Colonization

[28] *New Northwest*, January 8, 1881.
[29] *River Press*, January 18, 1882.
[30] *Ibid.*, February 15, 1882.
[31] *Billings Herald*, May 3, 1882.

Company" in Salt Lake City. The company was to be governed by a board of trustees consisting of eight members and was capitalized at one hundred thousand dollars. Abraham O. Woodruff was chosen as its first president. The Morman Church advertised the project rather widely and the report of the men who visited the Big Horn country in February looking for a location had been very favorable toward the region. A goodly number of families made ready in the spring to migrate to Wyoming to establish new homes.[32] By the end of April the vanguard of the colony was moving northward along the old Mormon trail, the families carrying their belongings in covered wagons with enough provisions to last them until supplies could be secured from the railroad in Montana. Freight wagons carried tools and implements, while cattle and other farm animals were trailed with the party.

The Utah and Idaho wagon trains met at Ham's Fork in southwestern Wyoming, where they were organized into companies, each with a captain, two assistants and a chaplain. Instructions were given each party, directing them to their destination. From about the middle of April through May, June, and July companies of Mormons headed northeast toward South Pass. From

[32] The prospective settlers came from two areas: the Bear Lake region of southern Idaho and from the Salt Lake City region of Utah. The settlement in southern Idaho, established about thirty-five years before, had been hard hit by the depression of the nineties, and in addition to that, in the late nineties their settlements were harassed by large numbers of squirrels that destroyed the crops in spite of strenuous attempts to eliminate the animals. Giving up hope of making a success of their Idaho settlements, when opportunity presented itself in Wyoming the group, backed by the Church, was more than willing to move. While economic pressure was not present in Utah as in Idaho, opportunities in the various settlements, many of which were more than fifty years old, were not equal to those offered to a poor man in a new undeveloped area like Wyoming. Then, too, the Mormons were of the true pioneering type. To them, pioneering was a virtue, and it was considered their religious duty to colonize. Just as some of them were "called" to missionary service, there were those who were "called" to "colonize for Zion." If the colony were successful, it would be an economic gain for the Church as well as for the individual settler. "The day will come," suggested President J. F. Smith, on a visit to the infant colony, "when prosperity and riches will come unto this land and this people." Lindsay, *Big Horn Basin*, p. 196.

three to six weeks were required to make the journey, depending upon the type and number of stock trailed. The first companies arrived in the Shoshone River Valley early in May, camp being made on the north side near the mouth of Sage Creek. They found a few settlers scattered along the river in the vicinity of Lovell, where a store and a saloon had been established as early as 1892. A post-office was established upon the arrival of the Mormon colonists.[33]

As the settlers arrived they cut logs for houses and started the construction of their irrigation project. Many of the poorer immigrants worked upon the ditch at day labor. The company or organization furnished a store where the settlers secured provisions, largely on credit. As the irrigation ditch got under way, the community found itself in financial straits. The outlook brightened, however, when it was announced that the Burlington Railroad was contemplating an extension of its line to Cody. Additional settlers came in and the colony gradually divided itself into three main centers of settlement: Byron, Lovell, and Cowley.

XV

COUNTY-SEAT FIGHTS

DURING the period of settlement in the Northwest, the most astute could not foresee which of the many towns platted were to become important cities and chief centers of population, and which were to remain mere way-stations or country trading-posts, or disappear altogether. A curious situation grew up. Ambitious men of ability and determination settled in each of the many villages in about equal numbers, and each group endeavored to

---

[33] While most of the migrating Mormons were fairly young, or at the most, of middle age, there was a considerable number of older people, many of whom came with their children. There were those who had been converted to Mormonism in England and parts of Europe, and some who had pushed handcarts across the plains from the Missouri River to Salt Lake. Some had joined the Church at Kirtland, Ohio, Independence, Missouri, or Nauvoo, Ill. Lindsay, *op. cit.*, pp. 198-9.

make its village the chief one of the section. In consequence, the rivalry between the various towns became intense, resulting in many incidents that were ludicrous, and in many disappointments. No place was so inconsequential that it did not aspire to become the county-seat, and frequently its ambition extended to becoming the capital of the future state. An illustration of this was Ordway in Grant County in the Territory of Dakota, which in after years was only a flag-station, but in the early boom period was supposed by its citizens to possess vast advantages over Aberdeen and Big Stone City, and at that time patronized Milbank as a promising suburb.[1]

Out of these conditions there developed fierce contests for advantage, and county-seat fights were precipitated which in several instances nearly disrupted the communities. In some counties violent possession was taken of the county records. At this time Milbank won the county-seat from Big Stone City, Salem from Bridgewater, and Chamberlain from Brule. In Sanborn County, Letcher contested with Forestburg, which was centrally located, for the seat of county government. Woonsocket secured two railroad lines, and being the only town in the county so favored, began to agitate for the county-seat. The county records appeared there mysteriously and she was successful in retaining them.[2] In Charles Mix County there were several contending towns, and Wheeler, an insignificant place not possessing a railroad, was chosen. Bon Homme, the oldest town and for many years the seat of county government of Bon Homme County, was ultimately succeeded as county-seat by Scotland, a railroad town. The same fate overtook Swan Lake, for many years the chief town and county-seat of Turner County.[3]

In 1884 there occurred in the Territory of Dakota an episode

---

[1] Robinson, *History of South Dakota*, pp. 310-1; Visher, "Geography of South Dakota," pp. 154-7.

[2] *Appleton's Annual Cyclopedia* (1884); Robinson, *op. cit.*, pp. 312-3; Andreas, *Historical Atlas of Dakota*, 169.

[3] Andreas, *op. cit.*, p. 169; Visher, *op. cit.*, p. 154.

commonly known as the "Spink County War." The county-seat was located at Ashton, sometimes called Old Ashton, and Redfield became a good-sized town and a rival for the permanent location of the court-house. The results of an election gave Redfield a majority of votes, but Ashton refused to accept the returns as final. On the night of December 6th, the citizens of Redfield visited Ashton, broke into the vault at the court-house, and carried away the county records. This high-handed procedure inflamed the people of Ashton, and a large body of men, many of them armed, hurried to Redfield to recover the stolen property. Redfield determined to defend the records and, securing an injunction from Judge C. H. Seward of the third judicial circuit, was able to restrain the Ashton party from removing them. After much argument, it was agreed that a joint guard should be maintained over the precious documents until the matter could be definitely decided. A few days later Judge C. M. Smith dissolved the injunction and ordered the records returned to Ashton. When the excitement was at its highest, Governor Pierce ordered a company of militia from Fargo to hurry to Redfield to maintain order and to see that no one was hurt. The trouble was over before the militia arrived. Redfield eventually became the county-seat.[4]

The influx of settlers into the Big Horn Basin from 1893 to 1897 caused the matter of local government to receive attention, since some of the agricultural communities were a considerable distance from the seats of local government for Frémont and Johnson counties. The Wyoming legislature as early as 1890 defined the boundaries of a possible new county which would allow speedy action on the part of the inhabitants as soon as they were numerous enough to warrant its creation. The area that later became Big Horn County was taken from parts of Johnson and Frémont counties that were located in the Big Horn Basin. The requirements as laid down by the legislature were that there must be a minimum population of fifteen hundred within the area and

[4] Robinson, op. cit., pp. 319-20.

taxable property with an assessed valuation of two millions of dollars.[5]

Governor W. B. Richards, a former resident of the region, told the state legislature at its meeting in January, 1895, that action should soon be taken, as population was increasing rapidly and the seats of local government were too distant for practical purposes. The matter was thoroughly discussed in 1895 and 1896, petitions were circulated and various towns considered the possibility of running for the county-seat. The settlement of Otto seemed to be the most promising candidate and a newspaper called the *Otto Courier* was established with Lou Blakesly as editor to advance the cause of the town. Thomas Daggett, editor of the *Rustler* at Bonanza, Wyoming, took his paper to Otto for the purpose of defending its cause in the coming fight for the county-seat of Big Horn County.

Basin City threw its hat into the ring, and since it had no newspaper induced O. T. Gebhart, editor of the *Paint Rock Record* at Hyattville, to move his publication to Basin City in preparation for the fray and to change its name to the *Basin City Herald*. A cowboy from the Embar ranch by the name of Joe Magill was induced to lay aside his saddle and branding-iron to act as editor for the coming campaign. W. S. Collins, a frontier lawyer of some prominence, was reported to have been the man of the hour who headed the fight for Basin City.

The contest over the location of the seat of government in this sparsely settled area of northern Wyoming, many miles from a railroad, was typical of the West both in its general characteristics, as well as in its journalistic extremes. The fight waxed hot in true frontier style, each town belittling the other's chance of success and claiming victory for itself from the very first. The subtle Joe Magill, with his keen powers of observation and clever pen, aroused the editor of the *Courier* and brought forth from that publication all of the rough and ugly aspects of frontier journal-

[5] *Session Laws of Wyoming*, 1890, Section I, chap. xlviii.

ism. In editorials and news articles the *Otto Courier* called the manager of the Basin City publication about all the crude names that came to his mind: "brainless pup," "half-witted cur," "skunk," "lying coward," and others.

In the end Basin City won the election, its victory being somewhat of a surprise. While some observers say that Otto was deserted by its own citizens, the real reason for its defeat was probably the coming into the contest of Cody, a small struggling town on the Shoshone River. With no hope of winning the prize itself, it entered the contest the morning of the election as a surprise candidate, and drawing votes from the Mormons at Burlington, caused the defeat of Otto, which soon assumed a position of minor consequence in the county.[6]

XVI

SOME FORGOTTEN TOWNS

LAND SHARKS and crooks looking for easy money have ever followed the frontier line of settlement, and from the earliest times, town-site promotion was one of the most popular forms of speculation. Town-jobbing schemes followed both the rivers and the railroads in the upper Missouri Valley, where lots costing a few cents each were often disposed of at from one hundred to five hundred dollars. While some of the boom towns became permanent and grew into thriving and industrious settlements, many of them announced without hesitation by their promoters as the "New Chicago" or "the Metropolis of the Plains" disappeared within a few months. The stories of these "ghost towns" are both romantic and pathetic. One of the first boom towns of the Northwest was established at the mouth of the Marias River to become the rival of Fort Benton at the head of navigation on the upper stretches of the Missouri River in Montana.

[6] Manuscript in the State Department of History Library at Cheyenne; *Wind River Mountaineer*, May 27, June 3, 1896; *Big Horn County Rustler*, June 30, 1911; files of *Billings Gazette* for 1895.

On July 14, 1864, the stern-wheeler steamer *Cutler*, with Jim Moore as captain, arrived at the mouth of the Marias River en route to Fort Benton with passengers and miners bound for the gold-fields. Unable to proceed to his destination, the captain stopped and the passengers disembarked and proceeded overland to Fort Benton, from whence they proceeded to the mines. Captain Moore, influenced no doubt by the town-site boom that was going on lower down the river, decided to establish a town or settlement there, twelve miles by land and thirty miles by water, from Fort Benton. He went to Virginia City, where he persuaded twenty men to accompany him to the proposed site of the new village, which was to be called Ophir. He was of the opinion that within a short time the new town would get all of Benton's business, and the town-site was boomed in the most extravagant manner.

The season was too far advanced to allow much building, but a double log cabin was constructed and a few men remained there all winter. In May, 1865, they cut timber for new buildings and their prospects were so good that the promoters claimed that Fort Benton was extremely jealous. The story is told that the group holding down the town-site killed an Indian, which led to an Indian attack in which eleven men were slain. This, according to an account, seems to have been the end of Ophir, as Captain Moore completed repairs on his steamboat machinery and left.[1]

The files of the *Montana Post* give some detailed information as to what was going on. On April 8, 1865, under the heading "Head of Navigation on the Missouri," the editor said:

The name of this new embryo seat of commerce is Ophir. The distance from Virginia City is about 240 miles with a good road passing through Prickly Pear and Last Chance Gulch. There is lots of cottonwood timber close by and located as it is, at the junction of the Marias and Missouri rivers, it is a natural site for a city, with its wharves and warehouses. It is also a good point of supply for Kootenai County.

[1] *Contributions*, Montana State Historical Society, VII (1910), 142-7.

Three weeks later the same editor reported that lots were in demand and large numbers could be disposed of if the owner were inclined to sell.

While some say the building of a large city is quite out of the question, we think it is a necessity and will soon be demonstrated to be a certainty. The American Fur Company steamer will go up to Fort Benton, but no man in his senses will ride forty miles of difficult shallow water to get to a place where there is no fuel or feed, while both are to be had in abundance at Ophir. The climate is excellent. There is little snow. Blacksmiths, bakers, merchants, and mechanics are already there. Lumber is being hauled and a group of men from St. Paul will erect a hotel in the fall, which will be a good inducement to the business men wintering there. A solid and substantial fortune awaits any man of energy who plants his stake at Ophir and no more important service can be rendered to the community than the erection of a town at a point whither heavy goods can be brought by water, thus avoiding the weary journey and the many disadvantages of a pilgrimage across the plains.[2]

On May 29th a letter from Ophir reported the arrival of steamers and that a Mr. William Foster was surveying the town-site and some parties were making adobes with which to build. While there were some short announcements regarding the town during the summer months, nothing more was heard of the place and it passed completely out of the picture.[3]

As the Union Pacific Railroad advanced westward through Wyoming, many towns sprang up, often almost over night. Some of them became permanent towns and others declined rapidly into small villages, or relapsed into a condition of deserted prairie,

[2] The names of the officers of the Ophir Townsite Company were J. W. Moore, president, Mose Clark, secretary, N. M. Burris, treasurer, and E. P. Lewis, captain. *Montana Post*, April 22, 1865.

[3] *Montana Post*, May 29, 1865. In the summer of 1878 an attempt was made to establish Carroll as a shipping-point to displace Fort Benton, whose resident population at that time was said to consist of some 75 wood-choppers, trappers, and hunters. Although the place was boomed with a good deal of energy by various Montana newspapers, the project was not successful. *Helena Daily Herald*, October 22, 1878.

with only steel rails and debris to remind one of brief prosperity. An example of a "ghost town" was Benton City in the Territory of Wyoming. The Union Pacific Railroad was completed to that point toward the last of July in 1868. At that time a large amount of freight for the various western forts was shipped to Benton City, where it was reshipped by wagon train to its destination. During the months of August and September, after the arrival of the railroad, the town presented a lively appearance, which continued until the road was finished to Bryan, Wyoming, about the first of October. The town at that time was composed largely of canvas tents and poles, with a population of at least three thousand, and a tougher set of human beings it would have been difficult, if not impossible, to have found anywhere.

An observer, giving his reactions to Benton City, wrote as follows:

In the worst part of the desert, just west of the last crossing of the Platte, we found Benton City, the great terminus town, 698 miles from Omaha. As far as the eye could see around the town, there was not a green tree, shrub or spear of grass but red hills scorched and bare, while at a distance, to the south and west, spread the gray desert. Drouth and desolation prevailed. Yet here had sprung up in two weeks, as if by the touch of Aladdin's lamp, a city of 3,000 people. There were regular squares arranged in fire wards, a city government of mayor and aldermen, a daily newspaper, and a volume of ordinances, including several on public health. It was the end of the line for freight and passengers and the beginning of a new construction division. Twice daily, immense trains arrived and departed, and stages left for Utah, Montana and Idaho. All goods formerly hauled across the plains came here by rail and were reshipped, and for ten hours daily the streets were thronged with motley crowds of railroad men, Mexicans, Indians, gamblers, saloon-keepers, miners, merchants and mule whackers. The streets were eight inches deep with dust as I entered the city of canvas tents and pole houses.

To look at Benton City with its conglomeration of logs and canvas tents, one would have sworn there was no trade. But in those tents enormous sums of money changed hands and Block and Company, wholesale dealers with whom I lodged in Benton City, in a frame and canvas tent, twenty by forty feet in extent, did a business of $30,000 a month. Others did even better. Ten months afterwards I revisited the site. There was not a tent or a building to be seen. A few rock piles and half destroyed chimneys barely sufficed to mark the ruins. White dust covered everything else and desolation reigned supreme.[4]

Transactions in real estate in the towns along the railroad lines were always more or less uncertain, and although the buildings often looked solid, many of them were a sham. Store fronts of red brick or brownstone, with walls of stucco, were found upon close examination to be flimsy fakes. They were often made to order in Chicago or Omaha and shipped to their destinations in sections. Ready-made houses became popular and common, and were sent out at times in carload lots, boxed, marked, and numbered, and could easily be assembled and erected. Two or three men with hammers and screw-drivers could put up a dwelling in two hours, while a dozen men could construct a block in a day. These buildings were priced to sell and a good stucco house 20 by 40 feet could be purchased for three hundred dollars, and if one's business left him or the town moved on, he could easily take it apart, and ship it to the next town-site.

In a wide portion of the Sheyenne River Valley, in what is now Washburn Township of Griggs County, North Dakota, seven miles northeast of Cooperstown, the town-site of Mardell, long since abandoned, was platted. Its location was ideal and its drainage and environment were excellent. The story of this visionary town-site is typical of the boom periods of western settlement, and, as in many similar cases, had it not been for adverse circumstances, Mardell might have been another Jamestown or Valley City. As expressed by one of its early boosters, "it had good chances for becoming a great metropolis of the west and a rival of Chicago or Omaha."

The location was surveyed and platted in the spring and summer of 1882 by Samuel H. Reynolds. The plat which was filed

[4] Beadle, *The Undeveloped West; or Five Years in the Territories.*

early in July showed plans for an elaborate city with streets running east and west and avenues north and south. The advantages of the town-site, both real and imaginary, were widely advertised by means of a boom map issued and scattered broadcast by the agents of the town-site company. Mardell was indicated in the advertising as a great railroad center, and was shown on the map as the veritable hub of transportation with proposed railroad lines forming the spokes of the wheel. Inhabitants began to come in and business enterprises were established or at least planned. Several general stores, a school-house, blacksmith shop, drug-store, hardware store and a large real-estate office were soon open for business.

A hotel with twenty-four rooms, called the Palace, was erected by the town-site company, where accommodations were provided for home-seekers going north and west, and for those looking for a location. A mail route running between Tower City and Lee, passing through Mardell, was established in April, 1882. From all appearances, the founders of this typical boom town in the northeastern portion of the Territory of Dakota were looking forward to great things for the new metropolis. This was strengthened by the expectation of a coming railroad, or, according to the boom map, of several of them. There was plenty of timber in the immediate vicinity and the first buildings were constructed from logs. But since log buildings would not comport with the ambitions of the town lumber was hauled from Tower City or Valley City for the first business buildings, the round trip taking four days. Planned on a rather elaborate scale, the building program of the company involved considerable time, money, and labor.

Griggs County had not been organized at this time and strenuous efforts were made to locate the county-seat at Mardell. After a hard fight, a town by the name of Hope was made the seat of county government and after an attempt to move it to Mardell had failed, the outlook of the town-site company was not so bright. There was still the chance of getting a railroad, as in the fall of 1882 the Sanborn, Cooperstown and Turtle Mountain Railroad was started north from Sanborn. With the advance of the railroad, the town-site of Cooperstown was established and at once became an aspirant for a location on the line. The only hope for Mardell was the railroad and Cooperstown was soon a strong contender for it, although the Mardell Townsite Company claimed that James J. Hill had definitely promised it to them. It went to Cooperstown, however, and the friends of Mardell were ready to give up the fight. They realized that their hopes and ambitions for the town would never be fulfilled and that the greatness of the place was all on paper.

In the spring of 1883, one by one the buildings were torn down and hauled away by their owners, and in 1885 the town lots were sold for taxes. The post-office was maintained for a time, the school-house was used as a granary by a homesteader, the large and well-built hotel was cut up and made into several farmhouses, and a grain-field soon occupied most of the town-site. Thus ended the story of a visionary town-site that started with great possibilities in the minds of its ambitious promoters and ended in utter failure. It must be recorded as one of the many forgotten towns that came into existence and vanished during one of the boom periods in the advance of the frontier of settlement into the West.[5]

"There is perhaps no more striking illustration of the phenomenal growth of our prairie towns than is furnished by Portland in the northern portion of the Territory of Dakota," wrote a Fargo editor early in 1882, "at present one of the most determined aspirants for metropolitan honors in northern Dakota. Though but a few months old, it is already assuming the air and will soon have the appearance of a busy bustling town. We have before mentioned some of the improvements going on there and are informed that others will rapidly follow." Then followed an

[5] Files of the *Fargo Daily Republican* (Fargo, D. T.), 1882-85; Ole Serungard, "The Story of Mardell," *Collections*, State Historical Society of North Dakota, II, 246-8.

article describing in detail the activities of the town-site company and the construction of buildings, including a large hotel and a flour mill. The rapid rise in value of town property had been almost staggering, with lots that had sold a few months before for less than one hundred dollars then bringing more than two hundred dollars. They were going so fast that the organizers of the town-site company laid out a new addition to meet the demand.[6] Within a year most of the town had disappeared, and the land included in the town-site was purchased by a farmer and plowed under for the planting of crops.

The uncertainty as to the future of towns during the boom in Dakota was illustrated by contemporary gazetteers. Polk's *Gazetteer* for 1881, published at Detroit, devoted only a few lines to Huron, which in three or four years became one of the more important towns in the territory. The same volume gave thirty lines to a discussion of Janesville in Yankton County, a town which soon disappeared. Many other towns which disappeared within a few years were given rather extended notices.

The majority of the settlers who migrated to the plains and valleys of the Northwest during the period of settlement were farmers, who usually went to the frontier to get a free farm and to follow agriculture as their means of livelihood. It was not a country for the weakling, for the pioneer farmer on the frontier of the upper Missouri faced many dangers and difficulties and led a life of almost constant hardship. Fortunately, he saw more often the land of bounteous crops and prosperous towns that existed only in the imagination of town-site promoters and homesteaders, than the area of drought and desolation that only too many years stretched around his crude home. But this vision of a region that could exist was too strong to disappear, and more and more settlers crowded west, dividing the uncultivated land and planting crops, until the Northwest entered upon a new frontier—that of the farmer—which will be the subject of the next and last section.

[6] *Fargo Daily Republican*, December 16, 19, 31, 1881, January 7, 13, 1882.

VI

THE FRONTIER OF
AGRICULTURE

CLOSE in the wake of the miner and the rancher in the Northwest came the farmer. The vast western areas, with their apparently limitless possibilities, had fostered romanticism both here and abroad, and presented one solution for the pressing economic evils of the eastern states and of Europe. Through the pages of the *New York Tribune* Horace Greeley had urged the male youth of the country to go into the new agricultural frontier as small farmers, and hundreds had seized the opportunity to better their circumstances. If the verbal pictures which persuaded more and more of them to turn westward were drawn with a too facile pen, they were often unconscious of that fact because of the high hopes which carried them across the great plains. The frontier of agriculture in the Northwest was an avenue of escape, which promised infinitely more to those who came into it to build rude homes and practise farming than they had left behind.

I

AGRICULTURE IN EARLY DAKOTA

SOME agriculture had been carried on in the Northwest even before the permanent settler came. From time immemorial the various Indian tribes of Dakota practised agriculture, cultivating maize and vegetables and relying upon these products for an important part of their subsistence. Their methods were crude, but by intensive cultivation they secured excellent results. Their chief agricultural implement was a hoe or spade made from the shoulder-blade of a buffalo. They understood the value of fertilizer, using the refuse from their tables, manure from their horses, and buffalo chips gathered from the prairies to enrich the soil. By constant attention to their garden patches, they defeated the destructive efforts of birds and insects. Often children with small willow boughs kept watch to drive out grasshoppers.[1]

During the fur-trading period gardens and small fields were usually cultivated about the trading-posts. At Fort Pierre the traders maintained a considerable tract of land under cultivation upon Farm Island in the Missouri River. Sufficient corn was produced by traders and Indians in the vicinity to support a small mill at the Fort.[2] Farming was pursued in a minor way by the early town-site settlers in the Big Sioux and Missouri valleys, but there was no intensive agriculture conducted in southeastern Dakota until the Indian lands lying between the Big Sioux and Missouri rivers were opened to settlement in July, 1859, and an agricultural population began to occupy them.[3]

Prior to the creation of the Territory of Dakota some farming operations had been carried on by white settlers, Indians and half-breeds in the Red River Valley. An eye-witness told of seeing the Indians and half-breeds, men, women and children, cutting the grain with sickles and binding it with willow withes, while others with horses and ox carts were hauling it in and stacking it. The fields were not fertilized, and both horses and oxen were used in the general farming operations. The methods of cultivation and the implements used were rude and primitive. The grain was sown broadcast by hand labor and the threshing was done with the flail and the tramping of animals. The wheat was made into flour by the use of eighteen windmills and two mills driven by

---

[1] Robinson, *Encyclopedia of South Dakota*, p. 10; Everett E. Edwards, "American Indian Contributions to Civilization," *Minnesota History*, XV, No. 4, 3, 15, 263-4.

[2] "Fort Pierre Journal," South Dakota Historical *Collections*, IX, 69-240 *passim*.

[3] *Sioux City Weekly Journal*, June 3, 1859; *Sioux Falls Democrat*, July 2, 9, 21, August 26, November 8, 1859.

water-power. The census reports for 1860 show that 2,145 acres of land in Dakota Territory were under cultivation in farms, the cash value of which, including implements and machinery, was $4,815. The extent of agricultural activity is further shown by the fact that 517 horses and 412 neat cattle were reported, in addition to 6,260 bushels of oats, 615 bushels of corn, and 1,000 bushels of wheat.[4]

During the first few years of settlement in southeastern Dakota, climatic conditions were generally favorable for agriculture and little care or work was necessary to produce good crops. The fields were not large, a few acres being usually broken with oxen by each pioneer farmer and planted with vegetables, sod corn, and wheat. The crops were raised primarily for home consumption, little attempt being made to raise a surplus as there was no local market for it.

The period from 1862 to 1868 was one of agricultural stagnation in Dakota—the result of drought, grasshoppers, and Indian troubles. During this period the settlers had little to sell and often did not raise enough to feed their families. Very little was done toward improving agriculture during those years, although the raising of stock was increased by the frontier farmers, who found a ready market at the various forts and Indian agencies. The question as to whether the soil and climate of Dakota were adaptable to the successful production of grain and vegetables was frequently and seriously discussed. Many sincerely believed that they were not, as drought and grasshoppers apparently came yearly. In the East many thought that the Dakota area was not a good farming country, and such an opinion was expressed as late as 1868 and 1870. The military authorities seemed to be in opposition to settlement during these early years, and many of the prominent officers openly advised the settlers to get out and give up the land to the Indians. In the face of all of these discouragements, Gov-

---

[4] *U. S. Census Report for 1860,* pp. 1006-7; *Manuscript Journals of Alexander Henry and David Thompson,* ed. Coues, I, 223-31.

ernor Newton Edmunds did all he could to encourage farming, and continued to plow and sow his lands. He introduced live stock and put forth every effort to diversify his crops, encouraging others to do likewise.[5]

The effects of the Civil War left its economic burden upon the Dakota farmers. Although agricultural products brought high prices and labor was well paid, the frontier farmer had nothing to sell and there was little demand for his labor. His condition was aggravated by the high prices which he was compelled to pay for any merchandise he purchased. At Sioux City prices of various commodities based on paper money were as follows: [6]

Commodity	1858	1865
Potatoes per bushel	$0.50 to $0.75	$ 2.50 to $3.00
Flour per barrel	8.00 to 9.00	15.00
Coffee per pound	0.16 to 0.18	.63 to .67
Butter per pound	0.25 to 0.30	.75
Eggs per dozen	0.25	1.00 to 1.50

On January 1, 1868, a territorial legislative Committee on Agriculture rendered a statistical report in which the low status of the farmer was well brought out.[7] The largest area under cultivation by one settler was thirty acres. The main crops were oats, wheat, corn, and potatoes, all of which had suffered from drought and grasshoppers. Another contributing factor to agricultural depression was the unfamiliarity of many of the farmers with the soil and climate of Dakota.

The spring of 1868 was full of promise, and an agricultural boom began which lasted until 1873. After the large crops of 1868 were harvested, glowing reports of the section were sent to the eastern states. Real-estate and land agents became active, and

[5] Questionnaires from early settlers; J. S. Foster, "History of the Territory of Dakota," pp. 26-7.

[6] Sioux City Register, June 12, 1858; Sioux City Weekly Journal, July 3, 1865. This increase in prices was due largely to the substitution of greenbacks for hard money.

[7] House Journal of Territorial Legislature of Dakota, 1867-8, p. 316.

Dakota was widely advertised. Prices of articles bought by the farmer were not high, taxes were low and his products brought a fair price. In 1868 Sioux City was connected with the East by rail, and the raising of a surplus of farm products was now possible. Roads along the Missouri bottom were fairly good in dry weather and the rivers and streams were soon crossed by substantial bridges, as Congress had been liberal in its appropriations.

After Sioux City was reached by a railroad, merchants in the Dakota towns along the Missouri River often bought farm produce which they hauled to Sioux City by team. As they received their merchandise at that point, their wagons carried a load to either terminus, and the cost of transporting the produce was accordingly much less than the cost to the farmer who hauled his produce to market himself. Although this was a marked improvement over previous conditions, wagon transportation as a means of disposing of surplus farm products was still too expensive, and steamboats could not be depended upon.

In 1869 and 1870 crops were exceedingly good, the farmers in many instances raising as many as forty bushels of wheat to the acre. Little winter wheat was planted in the early period, as the spring varieties were considered better adapted to the soil and climate of Dakota.[8] Oats and barley were raised with great success. A considerable acreage of corn was being planted, but corn was not generally considered as certain a crop as the small grains. Excellent vegetables and garden truck were raised.

In the fall of 1869, in the little towns along the Missouri Valley, Elk Point, Vermillion, Yankton, Bon Homme, and even Fort Randall, the stores and market-places were stocked with large squashes and pumpkins, golden corn, wheat, oats, and barley,

[8] Winter wheat did not become popular in southeastern Dakota until the nineties, as it was considered a risky crop because of the uncertain rainfall. It was apt to be killed in winter, as the high winds blew away the surface soil during the comparatively snowless winters. Kingsbury, *History of Dakota Territory*, I, 531. The first record of winter wheat being raised in this area was that of John J. Thompson. He planted forty acres on his farm ten miles east of Yankton in the fall of 1870. *Yankton Weekly Dakotian*, September 23, 1870.

stacks of onions, and pyramids of potatoes. The farmers and gardeners who furnished them declared that what they had left at home far exceeded what they had brought in. Many of them spoke of sending samples of their products to their friends in the East in order to show them what could be raised on the "grasshopper and drought-stricken" Dakota soil.[9]

The grain raised in Dakota in 1870 was as follows: wheat, 170,460 bushels; corn, 133,140 bushels; barley, 4,118 bushels; potatoes, 50,471 bushels; oats, 114,327 bushels. There were two flour mills in the territory, and improved lands in the Missouri Valley were quoted at from $8 to $15 per acre, while unimproved lands sold for from $3 to $10 per acre. Prices received for farm products were good, wheat selling for $.75 to $1 per bushel, oats at $.40 to $.80, corn at $.75 to $1, and potatoes at $.50 to $.60 per bushel.[10]

The Dakota Southern Railway was completed from Sioux City to Yankton in January, 1873, and the great handicap of the early days was over. The most material need of the farmer of southeastern Dakota was now supplied, as ample transportation facilities for surplus agricultural products were now available. The effect of the railroad was shown in the rapid increase in farm products and in the price of land. There were 2,275,000 bushels of wheat produced in the Territory of Dakota in 1872, as compared with 170,460 bushels in 1870. All of this, except 150,000 bushels, was raised in southeastern Dakota. Improved land, which sold for from $8.00 to $15.00 per acre in 1870, sold for from $15.00 to $30.00 per acre in 1872. The influence of the railroad was shown by the fact that the same kind of land sold for $3.00 to $8.00 per acre ten or fifteen miles from the road. According to the Federal census of 1870, there were only two flour mills in the territory. In

[9] *Yankton Weekly Dakotian*, September 14, 1869; *Sioux City Times*, September 21, 1869; Kingsbury, *op. cit.*, I, 531.

[10] *U. S. Census Report for 1870*, Volume on Wealth, 112-3, 180; *Report of the Territorial Governor of Dakota to the Secretary of the Interior*, 1870; Foster, *op. cit.*, pp. 87-93.

1872 there were ten, two others being in the process of construction. This shows the attempt to take care of the surplus wheat raised in the region which could not be shipped out because of the lack of a railroad and the expense of wagon transportation.[11]

The period of prosperity from 1868 to 1873 was followed by five years of hard times for the Dakota farmer. In addition to the financial depression resulting from the panic of 1873, another danger threatened southeastern Dakota after the entering of the railroad from Sioux City in 1872 and 1873. Crops had been good for several years and the farmer settlers had every reason to believe that they would continue to be so. Continued prosperity had brought overconfidence and many of the homesteaders felt it safe to take risks which they would previously have avoided. For several years the wheat yield had been large and prices very satisfactory. A single farmer often raised from five hundred to a thousand bushels and received more than a dollar per bushel. Although some attention was given to corn, oats, barley, and the raising of live stock, wheat had proved the most profitable crop and had become firmly established as the chief one.

The wheat farmer, therefore, felt himself well on the highroad to success. The one handicap to raising a large acreage of wheat was that the old methods of planting and harvesting were tiresome and slow, and became more wearisome as the acreage increased. There had been improvements in farm machinery for taking care of and threshing the grain, and their agents were numerous and active throughout the territory. Many of the Dakota farmers, made reckless by continued prosperity, purchased the improved machinery despite the great expense.[12] Often money was borrowed and a mortgage given as security. The rate of interest paid on the money was usually excessive, and when reverses

[11] *Clay County Register*, November 7, December 14, 1872; *Yankton Press*, December 5, 1872, January 3, February 7, 1873; Kingsbury, *op. cit.*, I, 671.

[12] When binders first came out, they sold for $400 and were down only to $350 by 1880. C. W. Thompson, "The Movement of Wheat Growing," *Quarterly Journal of Economics*, XVIII, 576.

came many of the hard-earned homes were lost by foreclosure and a sheriff's sale.[13]

In 1873 grasshoppers appeared in Dakota, and became such a serious problem that in the fall of 1874 the government found it necessary to investigate the problem. The season of 1875 was a very good one in Dakota, although grasshoppers devastated other areas. In 1876 the early grains were harvested before the appearance of the insects, which came during midsummer in larger numbers than before. Hardships and privations naturally followed. The farmers who had lost their crops were unable to get work, as no one had any work to do or money with which to pay. There was very little wheat or grain of any kind to be sold, and none for food or to feed the cattle during the winter. Corn-bread became the staple article of food, while burnt peas or wheat took the place of coffee. Meat, sugar, tea, coffee, lard and wheat flour became luxuries that few could afford.[14]

Dakota was not bothered by grasshoppers in 1877 and crops were good. The period of boom and prosperity which began in this year developed in volume in 1878 and the new settlers farmed upon a much larger scale than during the earlier period. Conditions were ideal for a man with a little capital to begin farming. By 1878 the Territory of Dakota had passed through all the perplexing problems of frontier agriculture and was able truthfully to announce itself as an excellent farming community. Forest culture had received some attention and many of the farmers had enough cultivated timber for domestic purposes. Various experiments in fruit culture gave gratifying prospects and the agricultural outlook was exceedingly bright.

The status of agriculture in the Red River Valley was about the same in 1870 as it had been ten years before. In December, 1870, there was no wheat, oats, barley, rye, or corn produced for

[13] *Dakota Republican* files for 1870-75; *Yankton Press,* 1871-73; *Yankton Press and Dakotian,* 1873-75.

[14] "A History of Grasshoppers in Dakota," *Dakota Republican,* May 17, 1877.

export in northern Dakota. There was very little raised, in fact, except a few bushels in the settlements about Pembina. There were 3,190 acres of land in farms, 304 acres of which were improved, with a cash value of $10,600. Farm implements and machinery used on the farms were valued at $2,300. In 1870 less than 700 bushels of grain were raised, and 1,515 bushels of potatoes. Some dairying was practised, as 500 pounds of butter were reported.[15]

In the early seventies settlers came into the Red River country in large numbers. At Fort Pembina there was a demand for farm produce, by fur traders and factors, town-site boomers, government and railroad surveyors, railroad employees and builders, stage-coach drivers, transients, and new settlers. J. D. Djuberg settled in Barnes County in 1870, and planted fifteen acres of oats the first season, grasshoppers destroying all except thirty bushels. His first home was a sixteen-foot shed built of lumber, and his stable was constructed of rough lumber covered with sod. He bought a team for $375 and a cow for $65, but was not able to get any chickens until the following year. During the winter months the farmers living near the rivers did a great deal of trapping and sold mink, beaver, muskrat, fox, and coon skins. In the summer, many hauled hay to the forts and stage stations and worked on flatboats when they were not busy on their own farms. The grain was cut with the scythe and threshed with the flail until machinery came in during the later seventies.[16]

The Northern Pacific Railway was completed to the east side of the Red River of the North in the fall of 1871, and in the summer of 1872 was pushing rapidly toward the Missouri River. In the fall of 1871 and the spring of 1872 about five hundred

[15] Lounsberry, *Early History of North Dakota*, p. 234; Kingsbury, *op. cit.*, II, 1028.
[16] Myrtle Bemis, "History of the Settlement of Swedes in North Dakota," *Collections*, State Historical Society of North Dakota, III, 258-9; George Lamphere, "History of Wheat Growing in the Red River Valley," *Collections*, State Historical Society of Minnesota, X, 2-6.

thousand bushels of wheat and five hundred barrels of flour were shipped out of the Red River Valley. Railroad rates were very high at this time, and grain had to be produced at a low cost to warrant shipping to a central market. In 1871 the rate from Moorhead to Duluth was about fifty cents per hundred for grain or thirty cents per bushel.[17] At this period in the evolution of railroad transportation, rates were not uniform from individual to individual, from town to town, from month to month, or from road to road. The farmer was completely at the mercy of the railroad; he knew little of the reasonableness of charges and had not yet taken upon himself the task of demanding fair treatment. The rates from Minneapolis to Chicago and New York varied, as during the season of lake navigation they were cut considerably. Rebates were also given to large shippers.[18]

Northern Dakota suffered as much from the ravages of the grasshopper as did the southern region in the early seventies. But the severely tried farmers of the northern settlements showed the same pluck and endurance as those in the south and few farms were abandoned. Because of high freight rates, distance from a central market and grasshopper ravages, the Dakota farmer of the Red River Valley practised mixed or diversified agriculture down to 1876. There were sheep, cattle, and hogs, and on many farms poultry was important. Vegetables were universal and all varieties of grains were grown.

Agriculture developed rapidly in southern Dakota during the boom period from 1878 to 1886, and although wheat continued to be the money crop in that region, diversified agriculture was the general rule. Newspaper editorials gave a good idea of what was taking place. A Vermillion editor in the spring of 1879 re-

[17] Freight rates were somewhat reduced in 1873, but even as late as 1880 the rate from the Red River Valley towns was $.40 per hundred or $.25 per bushel for wheat. The rates were gradually adjusted during the next few years so that by 1886 the average rates from Red River Valley points to Duluth and St. Paul had been cut one half, leaving them from $.12 to $.15 per bushel. Lamphere, op. cit., p. 103.

[18] Annual Report of the Minnesota Railroad Commission, 1871 to 1877.

ported that there existed in Clay County a feeling of contentment, courage, and confidence that bespoke prosperity; that the
fear of grasshoppers had subsided and a spirit of security, of
assured success, and certainty of reward animated the settlers. The
same editor on October 7, 1880, wrote: "The crops are exceedingly good. A boom period has struck us fairly. Never before in
the history of the country has there been such prosperity." He
again commented upon the agricultural situation in the fall of
1882: "The prosperity of Dakota and Clay County continues. . . .
The community is largely made up of farmers all more or less
prosperous and many are wealthy. They all owe their prosperity
to Clay County soil."

In the spring of 1884 the editor of the *Dakota Republican*
said, "Clay County progress still continues. Vermillion handles
more dairy products than any other town in Dakota. The county
is also strong in corn, cattle and hogs. Mixed farming pays large
returns, while special farming has failed." On August 7, 1885,
the same paper reported: "There are no free lands left in Clay
County, but settlers do not need to stay away on that account, as
much of the land in the county is still lying idle and can be had
at reasonable prices. Land close to Vermillion sells for $10 to $30
per acre, while that further from the railroad sells for less." [19]

During the prosperous period no land that had a free title
could be bought for less than ten dollars per acre, and improved
land sold or was held at from fifteen to thirty dollars per acre.
This price was justified by the crops obtained. General farming
methods were changed in southern Dakota during the period, and
varieties of plants and grain were planted that were better suited
to the soil. The ground was more carefully prepared, and the
custom of burning the stubble and discing in the seed was given
up. The land was usually plowed or double-disced and the planting done with a drill. Rotation and diversification of crops re-

---

[19] *Dakota Republican*, March 27, 1879, April 10, 1880, September 8, 1882,
April 10, 1884, August 7, 1885.

ceived far more attention than in earlier years. Mixed farming, in which stock-raising formed a prominent part, gradually replaced straight or special farming. The "Herd Law," making cattle-owners responsible for damage done to crops whether fenced or not, was passed in 1882. This stimulated tillage, as fencing was expensive.[20]

By carefully reading the territorial newspapers of the late eighties, it is easy to see that by 1886 the best days of the great agricultural boom were over. Dakota was entering upon a period of reaction caused largely by drought. During the years 1887 and 1888 the drought was local and did not affect the different parts of the territory with equal severity. In 1889 the lack of rain was widespread throughout the central portion of the United States and hit Dakota exceptionally hard. The Dakota farmer was also affected by the general business depression of the time. The crop report for 1890 showed a marked decrease in the yield of all farm products.[21]

II

EARLY AGRICULTURE IN MONTANA

THE INDIAN tribes that occupied the area that later became the Territory of Montana paid very little attention to agriculture,

[20] Visher, "Geography of South Dakota," pp. 115-7, 159; *Session Laws of the Territory of Dakota,* 1882, XIV, 150. Most of the fences in southern Dakota prior to 1870 were of posts and boards, or were constructed of rails. Wire fencing was not used extensively until after 1870. It was quite expensive, costing about a dollar per rod. Visher, *op. cit.,* p. 116.

[21] The following table shows the production of the various farm crops in Dakota from 1880 to 1890:

Grain	1880	1885	1888	1890
Wheat	2,830,000	38,166,000	62,550,000	42,940,000
Corn	2,000,000	7,800,000	24,500,000	13,143,000
Barley	277,424	2,166,000	6,400,000	2,272,000
Oats	114,327	2,217,000	43,267,000	13,343,000
Potatoes	2,580,000	3,875,000	5,674,000	3,429,000

U. S. Census Report for 1870, Volume on Wealth and Industry, 234-5, *1880,* 36-9, *1890,* 378-81; McClure, *Resources of Dakota,* pp. 21-9; F. H. Haggerty, *Statistical, Historical and Political Abstract of Dakota Territory* (Aberdeen, D. T., 1889), pp. 31-2.

and the fur traders who were active there had neither the time nor the inclination to raise crops or gardens. The first serious agricultural efforts in Montana were made by Jesuit missionaries who entered the Bitter Root Valley in 1841 and established the mission of St. Mary's. Father De Smet, the leader of the party, after making the choice of a site for the mission, journeyed a distance of three hundred miles to Fort Colville, a post of the Hudson's Bay Company on the Columbia River, where he secured seeds, agricultural implements, and farm animals, returning to St. Mary's in 1842.

In the spring of that year crops were planted, resulting in a bountiful yield. Since it was impossible to make flour with the resources at hand, some millstones were brought in and a crude mill established in 1844. The acreage devoted to crops was gradually increased and attempts were made to interest the Flathead Indians in agriculture. By 1846 there were at St. Mary's twelve houses, a church, a mill, various farm buildings, forty head of cattle, some horses, as well as several thousand bushels of wheat, potatoes, and of other grains and vegetables. In 1850 the mission was abandoned and the buildings sold to Major John Owen, who used it as a trading-post. It soon came to be known as Fort Owen. The Major carried on incidental farming in connection with his trading activities, in 1858 raising 258 bushels of wheat, as well as other vegetables.[1]

The St. Ignatius Mission was established a short distance south of Flathead Lake in northwestern Montana in 1854, and soon developed into a thriving establishment, with fields under cultivation. By 1858 a surplus of three hundred barrels of flour was produced, which was sold to the forts of the American Fur Company along the Missouri River. Some of the Indians were taught to do farming under supervision, and one writer indicated that

[1] Lawrence B. Palladino, *Indian and White in the Northwest* (Baltimore, Md., 1894), p. 37; Vaughn, *Then and Now, or Thirty-six Years in the Rockies*, p. 252.

there were about fifty farms of five acres each under cultivation. The United States Government established an agency for the Flathead Indians in Jocko Valley in 1860 and freighted in seed, plows, and other agricultural implements. Fort Owen became a center for traders and trappers of the region who used it both as a depot and stopping-place, as well as for travelers and road builders. Various wandering traders, half-breeds and squaw-men, all of whom paid some attention to farming, located cabins around Fort Owen, which, by 1860, had become a small settlement. The growing of vegetables and grain received more attention as local demands increased.[2]

Early farming methods in the territory were crude and primitive, the grain being threshed as in ancient times by oxen tramping over the sheaves scattered on the ground within an enclosure. Climatic difficulties were experienced. The dryness of the Montana area caused many of the crops to be planted in the lowest ground available, where they were subject to frost. Crops planted on higher ground escaped frost, but suffered from drought when there was a scarcity of rain. Some accounts gave the impression that it was absolutely impossible to carry on agriculture successfully in a region so far north. Others spoke highly of the agricultural possibilities of the area, even stating that better results had been obtained than in the former homes of the writers in the Middle West.[3]

Range cattle had been driven into the Missoula and Bitter Root valleys from Oregon as early as 1859, and the "Mormon Wars" caused cattle to be driven into the Deer Lodge and Beaverhead valleys from the south to avoid having them killed or captured. By 1862 there were between three and four hundred cattle in the various valleys but there was no local market for them prior to the beginning of gold-mining. Some of them were driven to Cali-

[2] H. H. Bancroft, *History of Washington, Idaho and Montana, 1845-1889* (San Francisco, 1899), p. 604.
[3] William H. Sutherlin, "Montana as an Agricultural Country," *Butte Daily Miner*, Holiday edition, January 1, 1889.

fornia in the early sixties. The price at that time was one hundred dollars for steers and seventy-five dollars for cows.[4] As overland traffic developed through Montana, men settled along the trails to trade in stock and to sell agricultural products to the travelers. Some traffic from the East and from Fort Benton developed as gold was discovered in the Boise and Salmon River areas of Idaho. Captain J. L. Fiske, on his second overland journey from Minnesota, stopped on September 12, 1863, at Morgan's ranch in the Prickly Pear Valley, where he found stock for meat and where he was supplied with vegetables. A large barn and corrals had been built for the purpose of serving the overland trade. Nine days later, the party stopped in the Deer Lodge Valley where it was furnished with supplies at the ranch of John and Richard Grant.

The real development of agriculture in the Montana area came with the discovery of placer gold in its western gulches. Rich deposits were located on Grasshopper Creek, Alder, and Last Chance gulches in 1862, 1863, and 1864, and gold-seekers flocked into the region from all sides, an observer reporting as many as ten thousand miners in Alder Gulch within six months. Food was scarce and expensive, as distances were long, and freight rates high whether it was freighted from the Mormon settlements in Utah or from Fort Benton at the head of navigation on the Missouri River. The mines, however, were located close to rich valleys with agricultural possibilities. The Bitter Root, Prickly Pear, Jefferson, Missoula, and Gallatin valleys contained rich soil, sufficient water for purposes of irrigation, and were low enough in altitude to enable crops to mature without danger from frost. Except for the Bitter Root area, the agricultural valleys were on lands that were not the fixed home of hostile Indian tribes.[5]

[4] Conrad Kohrs, "A Veteran's Experience in the Western Cattle Trade," *Breeders' Gazette* (Chicago, Ill., December 18, 1912); Conrad Kohrs, "Autobiography," dictated in Helena in 1885. Manuscript in the Montana Historical Society Library, Helena. Much of it published in the *Opheim Observer*, April 8, 1924.
[5] The Bitter Root Valley was relatively low in altitude and was well adapted to the growing of garden crops. The Madison Valley was the highest and was

Thomas W. Harris, a former employee of Owen, planted a large garden plot in the Bitter Root Valley not far from Fort Owen in the summer of 1863 and in October was reported to have sold several wagon loads of vegetables, mostly potatoes, turnips, and cabbage in Virginia City and Bannack. The Bitter Root Valley, whose altitude was some two thousand feet lower than the Jefferson and Madison valleys, soon gained the reputation of being an ideal place for the growing of cereals and vegetables for the mining camps. In 1864 a small patch of potatoes, corn, and beans was planted by a station-keeper near the Jefferson River, where the low damp alkaline soil, together with careless cultivation, resulted in poor returns and the report gained headway that it was impossible to grow vegetables in the Jefferson Valley and in some of the areas, as well.[6]

The editor of the *Montana Post,* resenting various implications that Montana was not fitted for agriculture, wrote in the summer of 1864: "Many persons have the idea that our country is not adapted to agricultural purposes. This is not true, as on the Madison agriculture is carried on quite extensively, and large potatoes, onions and turnips are raised in our valley. Crops are also good in the Bitter Root Valley and prices are high. Many homesteads are being taken and large numbers of people are going into farming and stockraising. There are opportunities for young men here and farm boys who come to Montana will be richly repaid for their efforts."[7] Many enthusiastic reports were sent to eastern states, one of which, printed in a Minnesota newspaper, said, "On a little spot of eight acres, with the help of a span of horses, a

better adapted to the raising of potatoes than of wheat. It was close to Virginia City. The Gallatin, which became the most important farming area in early times, was a rich valley, broad and well watered, fifty miles long and thirty-five miles wide, surrounded by high mountains. There was rainfall enough to grow cereal crops without irrigation and the altitude was low enough to be free from frost. It is difficult to imagine a more favorable farming area.

[6] Granville Stuart, *A Historical Sketch of Deer Lodge Valley and City, Contributions,* Montana Historical Society, II, 123; H. A. Trexler, *Flour and Wheat in Montana Gold Camps, 1862-70* (Missoula, Mont., 1918); Sutherlin, *op. cit.*

[7] *Montana Post,* August 27, 1864.

gardener cleared, season before last [1864], the sum of thirteen thousand dollars in gold." [8]

As the influx of miners continued, certain difficulties occurred. The placer mines of the Montana gulches were restricted in area and it was not long before large numbers of the claims were exhausted and many miners were out of work. At the same time, as the stampede continued, many who came were unable to secure claims and were left stranded without employment. With farm products scarce and prices high, many of the new-comers, some of whom had been farmers in their former homes, sought out desirable pieces of land in the valleys and started to raise crops. While the fertile and well-watered valleys were free from Indian dangers, it nevertheless required courage on the part of the pioneer farmers of Montana. They had few farming tools, seed was scarce and expensive, and they were without experience in methods adaptable to the area.

While agriculture was carried on in the various valleys of western Montana, the outstanding farming region to develop in the early period was that of the Gallatin Valley. During the late summer and early fall of 1863 a small number of prospective farmers from Virginia City took up homesteads in the lower end of Gallatin Valley, and the town-site of Gallatin City was laid out. There was little farming in 1864, although settlers continued to come in, and preparations were made for the next year's crops. Land was plowed and irrigation ditches were dug. John Bozeman, a well-known Montana pioneer, writing for a Virginia City newspaper in the fall of 1864, described what was going on in the Gallatin Valley: "The valley is being fast settled with farmers, many of whom came to Montana as a better class of miners and, after a while, quitting their original pursuits, secured 160 acres of land on which they stuck a stake giving the date and name of their claim. They then built their cabins and went to work in true western fashion." [9]

[8] *St. Cloud Democrat*, April 12, 1866.   [9] *Montana Post*, September 17, 1864.

Settlers continued to come into the valley in 1865 and it was estimated that more than 1,500 acres of cereals and garden vegetables were harvested that year, including about 20,000 bushels of wheat produced at an acreage of 25 to 50 bushels. The reapers that cut the grain were shipped in by way of Fort Benton at a cost of about $500 each, and a threshing machine was hauled in from Omaha, arriving in time to do the fall's threshing at $.25 a bushel. A mill that could grind 1,000 sacks of wheat a week was constructed and worked at full capacity most of the winter. Seed wheat for spring sowing was available in the fall for from $4.00 to $5.00 a bushel. The *Montana Post* gave information concerning the trend of events. On August 5th it reported that more attention was being devoted to agriculture "and in two or three years at the fartherest," wrote the editor, "we will be nearly self sufficient. The prospects of the farmers in the Gallatin Valley are very bright. In that area, there are more than fifteen hundred acres under cultivation, some fields of 60 acres yielding as much as 40 bushels to the acre. A grist mill has recently been erected within one-half mile of Bozeman." In September the same editor said, "Starvation is therefore played out, and 'beef straight' is a thing of the past." [10]

In 1866 the influx of miners alone subsided and both gold-seekers and farmers continued to flow into the Gallatin Valley. Acreage increased greatly, as many as six thousand acres being sown to spring wheat. Another mill was constructed and it was predicted that the heavy freighters from Salt Lake City would have little business that year as the home market would be supplied locally.[11] In 1867 high prices for farm products continued and agriculture expanded rapidly. A reliable survey for that year indicated that more than eight thousand acres of wheat were sown and 1,971 acres of oats and barley. The records show that more than three hundred thousand bushels of wheat were threshed,

[10] *Ibid.*, August 5, September 14, 1865, March 3, 1866.
[11] *Ibid.*, January 13, 1866.

which was a goodly increase over the twenty thousand bushels grown three years before. While the other valleys produced wheat, their total probably did not amount to more than one hundred thousand bushels. Farm machinery came into the territory in considerable amounts by way of Fort Benton, and by the end of 1867 there were seven flour mills in the territory.

Prices dropped slightly in 1868 but agricultural production continued. In 1869 the report of the General Land Office was enthusiastic, announcing that the lands of Montana fell into three classes or types which were divided as follows: grazing lands, 69,000,000 acres; agricultural lands, 23,000,000 acres; and mineral lands, 9,200,000 acres. Approximately 23,000 acres of the territorial lands had been surveyed. On the basis of this report and of his own observations, General Hancock recommended that army posts be established in Montana and expressed an opinion that the agricultural development of the territory was such that it could care for its population and for the needs of the army in flour, beef, and horses.[12]

During the sixties stock was ranged in the valleys and foot-hills, and, although nearly every farmer with a family kept cows for milk and butter, the occupations of ranching and farming were ordinarily separated. It was dangerous at this time to range cattle east of the mountains, since they were apt to be attacked by Indians. In 1870 there were 54,863 acres of land under cultivation in the Territory of Montana and the value of the agricultural products of the area was estimated at $1,676,666. The wheat production was put at 180,000 bushels; oats, 149,000; and potatoes, 91,000 bushels. There were 12,863 milk cows accredited to the territory, and out of a total population of 20,505, there were 2,111 males over twenty-one years of age engaged in the pursuit of agriculture. While the census did not take into account the Indians, soldiers, and transient population, there can be no question

[12] *Annual Report of the Secretary of the Interior*, 1869, pp. 162-3; *Annual Report of the Secretary of War*, 1869, p. 63.

that more agricultural products were being produced than the local territorial population was able to consume.[13]

The first attempts at agriculture on the part of the early settlers were often extremely crude, the ground for the first gardens sometimes being made ready with a spade, as the pioneer farmer had neither oxen nor horses. As farming developed, the virgin sod was turned under with a breaking plow to the depth of four inches, which was later increased to about six. It took several yokes of oxen to break the turf for the first time, with a man to drive and another sitting on the beam of the heavy plow to keep it in the ground. Such machinery as plows, harvesting and threshing machines were freighted, while harrows were largely home-made. There were few grain drills, as seeding was ordinarily done by hand. Stubble was plowed in the fall and there was little rotation practised, largely because the land was rich as well as plentiful. Soft varieties of wheat were raised, as the mills were unable to grind the hard types and refused to buy them. Late varieties of oats were raised, and barley was of the malting types. The first potatoes were of a dark variety with a small yield, which was soon changed to the white type, the "Early Rose" becoming popular. All crops in the Montana valleys were irrigated, the grain-fields being flooded three times, as was the common practice among the Mormon farmers of Utah. Native grasses were used for hay. Wheat production ran from thirty to forty bushels per acre and oats from fifty to sixty bushels. Smut was common in wheat and the seed was often chemically treated before planting.[14]

The homes and outbuildings of the early farmers and ranchers in the Territory of Montana were usually constructed of logs, and some of them had roofs of sod. Some of the pioneer farmers con-

[13] U. S. *Census Report for 1870*, Volume on Agriculture; files of the *Montana Post*, 1867-70; Cyrus Thompson, "Report on Agricultural Resources of the Territories," *House Exec. Doc.*, 42 Cong., 2d Sess., No. 326, 269; M. L. Wilson, "The Evolution of Montana Agriculture in its Early Period," *Proceedings*, Mississippi Valley Historical Association, IX (1915-18), 433-4.

[14] Wilson, *op. cit.*, p. 436; Strahorn, *Resources of Montana, passim.*

structed dugouts, which were displaced with log buildings as soon as the timber could be cut. Most of the fields were not enclosed, but there was a growing tendency to construct pole fences. The valleys had plenty of pine timber available, a distinct asset to the frontier farmer. Surveys were made rather slowly, and the first territorial legislature passed laws protecting the rights of the squatter. With conditions and circumstances favoring him at first, certain changes soon occurred that materially changed the status, as well as the outlook, of the early Montana farmer.

As agriculture expanded in western Montana, placer mining declined as the deposits played out, and as early as 1866 there was a rapid increase in quartz-mining that required fewer men and a greater capital investment, some of which went into heavy machinery. The population of the boom mining areas actually declined and with the increase in the number of farmers, as well as in acreage, there was a surplus of farm products. With the nearest railroad more than four hundred miles away, there was no chance of marketing the surplus flour or grain. The price of wheat dropped from $10.00 per bushel in 1865 to $4.00 in 1866 and went on down to $2.80 the following year. In the four-year period from 1868 to 1871 the price was around $2.00 a bushel and in the next four-year period to 1875 went as low as $.50 a bushel and often there was no market at that price. In 1868 a good grade of flour could be purchased at from $8.00 to $15.00 a sack which had formerly sold for $50 to $100 a sack. Potatoes had fallen from the high point of $.80 a pound to where they could hardly be sold for $.02, and barley and oats had dropped from $.30 a pound to $.06.[15]

During the years of overproduction and low prices there came a series of grasshopper invasions that lasted for several years,

[15] Raymond W. Rossiter, "Statistics of Mines and Mining in the States and Territories West of the Rocky Mountains," p. 140; files of the *Montana Post*, 1866-70. Prices prior to 1867 seem excessive but when it is remembered that to practically everything the farmer consumed must be added a freight charge of from six to eight cents a pound, the prices were not out of proportion.

destroying the crops in certain localities. Beginning in 1866, they came again in 1867 and from 1869 to 1875 appeared annually, in some seasons causing a loss of as much as three-fourths of the grain crops of the territory. But even with these serious losses there continued an overproduction that caused wheat at no time to sell above $1.75 a bushel. In the late sixties and early seventies the farmers and business men of the territory were conscious of their isolation from centers of manufacturing and markets because of lack of transportation facilities cheap enough to furnish an outlet for their agricultural products. As the Northern Pacific Railroad extended westward from Duluth, the "Zenith City," across Minnesota, over the Red River and into Dakota, the ranchers and farmers of Montana held high hopes that collapsed completely when Jay Cooke and Company failed in 1873, and the Northern Pacific was held up for six years at Bismarck.

In 1873 the best brand of flour sold in Virginia City and Helena for $1.50 per hundred pounds, although this was a bad grasshopper year and the wheat yield was greatly reduced. The Montana farmers were in distress and were badly discontented, and were loud in their complaints of low prices for their products and the high prices of their supplies. The matter was so serious that late in May, 1873, a great mass-meeting of farmers met at Bozeman, "the old farming capital" of the territory, to discuss possible relief measures for the adverse circumstances under which they were trying to make a living for themselves and their families.[16]

In 1870 the Territory of Montana contained 851 farms, with 84,674 acres of improved land, and by 1880 the number of farms had increased to 1,519. Madison County ranked first with 249 farms and Missoula County second with 211. Farms in the other counties were as follows: Lewis and Clarke, 178; Meagher, 166; Custer, 154; Chouteau, 84; and Beaverhead, 82. Agriculture developed slowly in the territory and by 1889 the total number of farms there was only 5,605. The agricultural development of

16 *Avant Courier*, June 30, 1873.

Montana had been retarded by its arid climate, the average rainfall being 14.7 inches, more than 44 per cent of which fell in May and June. Irrigation has always been necessary for successful crops in most portions of the region, which has been influenced by the location and altitude of the various mountain passes and the resulting water supply. There have been very few large canals constructed, by far the greater part of the irrigation being handled by small independent ditches that furnish water, on the average, to about 225 acres. During the territorial period, the building of ditches and irrigation works was haphazard and temporary, the streams often being diverted into the heads of the ditches by obstructions of logs, rocks, brush, and earth that were replaced after each period of high water.

There were many cases in the western portion of the territory where the ditch or canal-beds were so low that the water would flow without the use of diverting dams. Where the fall was not sufficient to allow the flow of water at all times, high-water ditches were constructed which brought in the water at flood times. Forage crops were usually flooded; small grains were watered by systems of small furrows, while corn, potatoes, and other vegetables were irrigated by allowing water to run between the hills or beds. Hay and small grains were irrigated according to local needs. Where water was not plentiful, some farmers irrigated but half of their land each year. Control of the water was largely in the hands of the farmers themselves, there being but few opportunities by 1890 for the construction of additional small ditches.[17]

III

EARLY AGRICULTURE IN WYOMING

AGRICULTURE was not of very great importance in Wyoming in the early years, even after the building of the Union Pacific Railroad. There were several reasons for this, the most important

[17] *U. S. Census Reports for 1870, 1880, 1890*, Volumes on Agriculture.

being the lack of rainfall, and the rough nature of the soil. The land was far better adapted to cattle-grazing than to the raising of crops, and Wyoming Territory became the center of the cattle industry.

A small agricultural settlement, however, was developing in the valley of the Wind River early in 1868. On February 1st there was a settlers' meeting where resolutions were adopted regulating the size of preëmption holdings and other details regarding home-making on the Wyoming frontier. It was resolved that "a recorder shall be elected by the majority of settlers . . . to record all claims or notices of locations in a book to be kept for that purpose," which shall be "open at all times subject to public inspection." A man by the name of William Whips was elected president and N. Baldwin was chosen as secretary.[1]

The *Cheyenne Leader* of June 1, 1868, described the agricultural settlements in the Wind River Valley: "The gardens on the farms and ranches are doing well. The peas, corn and cabbage and lettuce are well out of the ground. We expect to see the Wind River Valley well settled by fall." The same editor described the construction of an irrigation project started late in May by the Summit Ditch Company, whose four-mile ditch was to be pushed, and was to supply the local Oregon Gulch with sufficient water for agriculture. On May 20th the *Cheyenne Leader* announced to its readers that the valley of the Green River was being settled. These agricultural settlements, however, were not significant enough to be of great importance. In December, 1869, the valley of the Cache La Poudre River in the southwestern corner of the territory, not far from Evanston, was reported to be raising the very finest of vegetables.

According to the Census Reports for 1870 there was less than five hundred acres of land under cultivation in the Territory of Wyoming. There was little advance in the seventies, as by 1880

[1] Account book of N. Baldwin, MS in Library of the State Department of History at Cheyenne, Wyoming.

there were only 457 farms consisting of 83,122 acres of improved land under cultivation. Laramie County came first with 121 farms, the others being listed as follows: Albany County, 101; Carbon, 87; Sweetwater, 62; Johnson, 43; Uinta, 28; and Crook County, 15. While there was some advance in farming in the eighties, by 1889 there were only 3,125 farms listed for Wyoming. There were 1,917 irrigated farms in the territory, that included 61.34 per cent of the improved land. Very little could be grown in Wyoming without irrigation except a scanty crop now and then in spots favored with an unusual amount of summer rain. Irrigation was in its infancy in 1890 as at that time there were few large ditches except in Albany and Laramie counties. Irrigation made rapid strides there from 1890 to 1910, the chief developments occurring in the drainage basins of the Big Horn, Platte, and Colorado rivers and on the tributaries of the Snake, Bear, Powder, and Tongue rivers.[2]

IV

BONANZA FARMING IN THE RED RIVER VALLEY

THROUGHOUT the period of westward expansion and the development of the Middle West, wheat was always an important frontier crop. It was chosen by the pioneer settler largely because it employed most effectively the productive forces involved, namely, land, labor, and capital. On the frontier, land was either free or very low in price, which enabled the farmer to extend the use of a given amount of capital and labor over a large acreage. Wheat-growing as an extensive type of cultivation was therefore very attractive.[3]

In the early seventies a few Red River farmers began to raise

[2] U. S. Census Reports for 1870, 1880, 1890, 1900, 1910, Volumes on Agriculture.

[3] C. W. Thompson, "The Movement of Wheat Growing," pp. 573-6; P. Bigelow, "The Bonanza Farms of the West," *Atlantic Monthly*, XLV (January, 1880), 33-6.

wheat. Charles Bottineau planted fifteen acres in 1871 near Pembina and claimed to have raised fifty bushels to the acre. Two years later Charles Grant, two miles west of Pembina, raised a small field of wheat, which averaged about forty bushels to the acre. With the coming of the Northern Pacific Railway, several settlers started to raise wheat in the vicinity of Moorhead and Fargo, but the acreage was restricted because of the lack of threshing facilities. In 1874 the Hudson's Bay Company brought in a horse-power thresher, and Walter S. Trail, the company's agent at Georgetown, offered to thresh wheat for near-by farmers. This gave a local impetus to the raising of wheat.[2]

The experience of John Holes, who settled on the Red River in 1869, not far from the point which the Northern Pacific Railway was to cross, is a good example of wheat culture by a small farmer. He planted his first wheat in 1874, seeding 15 acres which harvested 20 bushels per acre. The next year his acreage was about the same, but in 1876 he broke 160 acres and in the spring of 1877 he seeded 175 acres to wheat. He secured an average of 27.5 bushels per acre, which he sold for $1.00 per bushel. As the wheat was raised on land worth $5.00 per acre his profit was large. From 1878 to 1889 Holes increased his acreage of wheat until it reached 1,500 acres. His land in 1889 was worth $25 per acre. The poorest field he ever harvested was 10 bushels per acre and the best was 49. Acreage returns varied from year to year, his average always exceeding 10 bushels per acre, but never going over 27½. The price per bushel ranged from $.40 to $1.50.[3]

Henry A. Bruins, one of the earliest merchants at Moorhead, organized a stock company which early in 1874 erected a flour mill. This mill soon demonstrated the fact that Red River wheat

[2] Lamphere, "History of Wheat Growing in the Red River Valley," pp. 13-4; Lounsberry, *Early History of Dakota*, p. 234; C. C. Coffin, "Dakota Wheat Fields," *Harper's Weekly Magazine*, LX, 529, 34.

[3] Lamphere, *op. cit.*, pp. 15-8; John Lee Coulter, "The Industrial History of the Red River of the North," *Collections*, State Historical Society of North Dakota, III, 535-42.

was of superior quality for making flour, as its entry was awarded first premium at the Minnesota state fair for two consecutive seasons. Bruins claimed to have shipped the first carload of wheat from the Red River country to Lake Superior in the fall of 1873. In 1878 the company, seeing the necessity of more storage because of the rapidly increasing production of wheat, erected a large steam-elevator at Moorhead, which had a capacity of 110,000 bushels. It was the first steam-elevator constructed in the Red River Valley.[4]

After the failure of Jay Cooke and Company in 1873, J. B. Power of the Northern Pacific Railway worked out a plan for the selling of the company's land in small lots to actual settlers. His project failed, but he planted the seed of an idea that within a few years developed the so-called "bonanza" wheat farms of the Red River country. In 1875 a number of the bondholders of the Northern Pacific, having determined to save what they could, exchanged their bonds, then worth ten cents on the dollar, for a great block of land in the Red River Valley. George W. Cass, president of the Northern Pacific Railway, through Power, exchanged bonds for a tract of eight sections of land about twenty miles west of the Red River. The amount was later increased to ten sections. E. P. Cheney, prominent in the express business, but also a heavy holder of Northern Pacific securities and a director of that corporation, took over eight sections adjoining that of Cass. Power was authorized to select the land and to have a large area of it prepared for wheat at an early date.

In the spring of 1875, Oliver Dalrymple, an experienced wheat-grower of Minnesota, examined the land and entered into a contract with the owners to take charge. He broke 1,280 acres during the summer, and his first harvest in 1876 yielded 32,000 bushels of choice wheat. As soon as the results of the experiment became known, the Red River region was widely advertised. A St. Paul

[4] *St. Paul Pioneer Press,* September 27, 1877, October 4, 11, 1878; *Yankton Press and Dakotian,* May 17, 1878.

editor, writing in the fall of 1876, spoke in glowing terms of the Red River project, and described in some detail the methods of bonanza farming.[5]

Conditions were ideal in the Red River Valley in 1876 for the development of wheat as a single crop, and a distinct shift from diversified or mixed farming to large-scale wheat production took place. It is not difficult to explain why the new system came into existence. Cheap land was an important factor, and the government, at this time, had reached the most liberal period in its public land policy. The peculiar financial straits of the Northern Pacific Railway had forced it to place its lands on the market at low prices. The composition of the soil, the topography, the precipitation, and the climate were advantageous to large-scale farming. Advertising was a special force, and the Red River country was boomed as the "Nile Valley of the American Continent," and the "Land of Number One Hard Wheat." The railroad companies and the bonanza farms thus placed it in the limelight. After the close of the panic of 1873, large amounts of eastern capital were seeking investment, resulting in excellent transportation facilities and available money for the operation of large wheat farms.

The ever-increasing demand for American flour, especially for that manufactured from hard spring wheat by the new patent process was another factor. The new process, using the middlings purifier, made it possible to produce a fine grade of flour at one grinding. There was also the great influx of immigrants from the agricultural districts of northern Europe who were looking for opportunities to establish themselves. They were ambitious to become farmers and land-owners and were attracted to Dakota and the Red River Valley. A large number of young people from the northern states were moved by like motives. A large supply

<hr />

[5] *Dakota Republican,* July 14, August 21, September 3, 10, 1876, September 16, 1878; *Bismarck Tribune,* April 4, 1878; Lamphere, *op. cit.,* pp. 2-6; *St. Paul Pioneer Press,* September 6, 1876.

A BONANZA WHEAT HARVEST

Twenty-five self-binders at work on the Dill farm, near Fargo, North Dakota, 1897.
Courtesy of the McCormick Historical Association.

of transient labor was a prerequisite for the success of the large-scale wheat farms and was at that time available.

The increasing price of land farther east, the nearness of the region to Lake Superior, with the comparatively low freight rates to wheat centers, made the older wheat-growing districts practically non-competitive, or set the marginal cost of production at such a high point that the profit from wheat in the Red River country was exceptionally large. The fact that the soil in the older districts was depreciating in fertility when compared with the new lands farther west was a potent force. The freedom of the Red River region from grasshoppers after 1875 was another factor. No new enemy to wheat production appeared in the new areas, while in the older districts, the Hessian fly, the chinch-bug, the army-worm, rust, blight, and smut were common. The opportune perfection or invention of time-saving machinery and other equipment necessary to successful large-scale farming, just at a time when the Red River country was reached by the advancing frontier, was a powerful force, the value of which it is difficult to estimate.[6]

In 1877, Dalrymple seeded 4,500 acres of wheat which yielded twenty-five bushels per acre. In the same year the Grandin brothers of Tidioute, Pennsylvania, secured nearly one hundred sections of Red River land and contracted with Dalrymple to manage it. Governor H. Pennington of Dakota Territory in September, 1877, made the following observation on wheat raising: "Along the line of the Northern Pacific Railway west of Fargo for twenty miles or more the wheat fields stretch out on both sides of the road as far as the eye can reach. At Casselton, eighteen miles west of Fargo, we could see eight threshers going in different directions, and were told by Oliver Dalrymple that the yield ran from twenty-five to thirty bushels to the acre. Dalrymple

[6] *Estelline Bell*, January 5, 1884; *Fargo Times*, April 5, 1879; Coulter, *op. cit.*, pp. 594-6; Bigelow, *op. cit.*, pp. 33-6; Coffin, *op. cit.*, pp. 529-35; Thorsten B. Veblen, "The Price of Wheat since 1867," *Journal of Political Economy*, I, 68-75.

and his associates have 7,000 acres in wheat this year and next year propose to have 12,000 acres." [7]

In 1880 there were eighty-two farms in the Red River Valley, each of which contained more than one thousand acres. A large number of them exceeded ten sections. There were 164 farms under one thousand acres, but at least one section in size. The larger farms were of two types: those established by corporations, and those owned by individuals. The Sharon Land Company, with more than thirty thousand acres, north of Casselton, represented the first type; while the farm of J. P. Watson, with twenty thousand acres south of Casselton, was an example of the other. In addition to the Grandin, Cass, and Cheney farms aggregating fifty-five thousand acres and managed by Dalrymple, there were the Lockhart and Keystone farms in Minnesota, and the Dwight, Fairview, Keystone, Cleveland, Downing, and Antelope farms in Richland County, Dakota. Most of the large wheat farms were on the Dakota side of the Red River.

By 1880 the movement toward extensive wheat production had only made a good start. There had been four crops on the Dalrymple farm, while most of the other large units had produced only one or two crops. All of them were as yet in the southern half of the Red River Valley, or within reasonable distance from railroad or river navigation. With the rapid movement of railroad building into the northern half of the valley and the development of lines subsidiary to the Northern Pacific, the opening of large wheat farms continued unabated. By 1885 nearly all of the original large farms had been established. The Census for 1890 showed 323 farms exceeding one thousand acres and 1,253 with over five hundred acres.[8]

[7] *Report of the Territorial Governor of Dakota to the United States Commissioner of Agriculture*, September, 1877, pp. 1-3.

[8] *U. S. Census Reports for 1880, 1890; Bismarck Weekly Tribune*, April 5, 1879, May 11, 1880; *Valley City Times*, March 21, 1881; *Fargo Times*, November 8, 1879; Coulter, "Industrial History of the Red River of the North," pp. 570-5.

. The cultivated land on the large wheat farms was subdivided into tracts of about two thousand acres, each being managed by a superintendent and a foreman, with its own set of books. Each tract had its own buildings, consisting of houses for the superintendent and foreman, granaries, tool-houses, stables, and machine-sheds. To carry on the work of every unit of a large farm required a considerable number of men and horses, and much equipment. The Grandin farm consisted of thirty-eight thousand acres, about twenty thousand of which were under actual cultivation. It was divided into two large farms, which were subdivided into smaller areas, each managed by a foreman. An aggregate of some three hundred men was employed, while three hundred horses, one hundred plows, fifty seeders, seventy-five binders, ten separators, and ten engines were used.[9]

The first operation in wheat-farming was breaking the prairie sod. This work was usually completed before the middle of July in order to give the sod time to become thoroughly rotted for the second plowing, which was begun in September. This backsetting or cross-plowing, as it was sometimes called, was often continued until the ground froze in November. Dalrymple estimated that the breaking cost was about $2.50 per acre, while the second plowing was put at $1.75. During the first few years the single walking plow or the sixteen-inch sulky plow was used on both the large and small farms, but by 1879 the gang plow began to displace the single plow, especially on the larger farms.

After the plowing was completed in the fall, practically all work was suspended until March, when seeding began. Prior to the late eighties the eight-foot broadcast seeder was used almost universally in the Red River Valley. It was drawn by two horses and sowed about twenty acres per day. About eighty pounds of seed were used per acre. After the seeder came the harrow, which was used at least three times before the wheat sprouted. In average years the wheat was ready to cut by the early part of August. The

[9] *Fargo Times*, April 5, 1879; *Valley City Times*, March 21, 1881.

harvester was generally of the Marsh type, with an endless canvas elevator, packers, and wire binder attached. Twine took the place of wire after 1880.

A dozen or more of the binders were superintended on the large farms by a field foreman on horseback. A wagon hauled twine and other supplies, while a machinist with "extras" and other necessary equipment was near at hand. After each brigade of harvesters came the shockers. The grain on the large farms was never stacked, and on the day that the cutting of the grain was finished the threshing began. The first grain cut was thoroughly cured in time to begin operations at once. Steam-engines were used from the first and the separator was the modern combined thresher, separator, and straw elevator. The self-feeder and attachment for cutting bands came in at a later date. Under favorable circumstances a machine would thresh and clean about one thousand bushels of wheat per day, but the average performance was from seven hundred and fifty to eight hundred bushels. The price of a separator was about six hundred dollars, while the engine cost around eight hundred dollars. The typical threshing crew consisted of twenty-three men, under a foreman, and ten teams of horses. This size of crew would clear about fifty acres in a day.

A large part of the wheat crop of the Red River country was marketed soon after it was threshed. This was done for two reasons: it was necessary to realize the proceeds as soon as possible, and there was leisure time for hauling during the autumn months when the roads were usually in good condition. The grain hauled to the railroad was immediately shipped to Duluth or Minneapolis. At that time cars carried about four hundred bushels of wheat. Some grain, however, was stored in granaries or private elevators to await an improved market. The straw was burned, except a few stacks saved for litter. All the teams were then put to plowing the stubble and backsetting or cross-plowing the new breaking. When frost stopped operations or the plowing was completed, the extra men were discharged, a few being retained to do work about the barns and buildings.[10]

Most of the large farmers of the Red River district restricted their crop to wheat and usually purchased their provisions in outside markets.

When I came to Dakota in 1883 [said a Fargo editor], everybody's attention seemed to be directed to the raising of wheat. No cheese, a little butter, and a small percentage of the meat consumed by the settlers and workers was produced west of the Red River. Tons and tons of hams, shoulders and spiced roll, and pork in many forms and canned meats of every kind were shipped in. Tons of cheese, butter and butter substitutes were sold to the large wheat farmers. During the busy season many had their vegetables shipped by express from St. Paul. This importation of foodstuffs was largely concentrated in the "Bonanza Wheat Farm" section and the smaller farmers continued to produce at least enough for their own use, except during harvest and threshing time, when even they bought large quantities of supplies. The hired help demanded good food and lots of it.[11]

Although few of the large farms produced their supplies, the managers of the large enterprises had many advantages over the smaller farmer because their equipment cost much less in proportion to the size of the farm and could be used to better advantage. Lumber was purchased at wholesale rates and machinery was bought directly from the manufacturer. The new equipment for the Grandin farm for 1878 included 38 plows, 35 sets of harness, 17 seeders, 27 binders, 52 wagons, and 5 threshing machines. By direct purchasing a saving of at least a third was made. In most cases horses and mules were bought on the large central

[10] *U. S. Census Report for 1890*, Report on the Statistics of Agriculture in the United States, p. 379; William Allen White, "The Business of a Wheat Farm," *Scribner's Magazine*, XXII, 531-48; letter from A. M. Anson of Cass County, Dakota, dated October 6, 1882, and printed with the title, "Harvesting Wheat in Dakota," *Cultivator and Country Gentleman*, XLVII, 841; Louis Bernard Schmidt, "The Westward Movement of the Wheat Growing Industry in the United States," *Iowa Journal of History and Politics*, XVIII (July, 1920), 396-412.
[11] *Fargo Daily Republican*, November 23, 1883; *Devil's Lake Democrat* (Devil's Lake, D. T.), December 11, 1884.

market at St. Louis, even as many as one hundred in a single year at a total cost of fifteen thousand dollars.[12]

Aside from the first outlay, the largest item of expense in the production of wheat on the large farms was labor. As the Red River wheat-fields were located five hundred miles from Chicago, with railroad fare at five cents a mile, and with the demand for labor limited to a large number of men for a short time, a difficult problem might be expected. During the seeding period in the spring, which lasted about a month, the Grandin farm employed a hundred men to drive seeders and about fifty on harrows. There were extra men to haul seed and do odd jobs. After the seeding period there was a lapse of work, and the number of employees dropped to fifty or seventy-five men. They plowed or made hay until harvest time, which began around August 1st. During the harvest a crew of about three hundred and fifty to four hundred men was needed, and a still larger one was required for threshing. About four hundred men were needed to man sixteen threshing outfits. In 1879 twenty-one machines were used on the Grandin farm. After the threshing, seventy-five to one hundred men were kept through the plowing season.[13]

The employer's big problem was to obtain men when they were actually needed, while that of the laborer was to find employment during the remainder of the year. Many writers of magazine articles and newspaper editors seemed to have the impression that most of the men employed on the large wheat farms were hoboes, bums, and tramps. One editor, commenting on the labor situation, said, "The wheat growing industry employs tramps and hoboes who vanish when the harvest is over, instead of increasing the permanent population." A Fargo editor, in

[12] *Valley City Times*, December 9, 1880, December 28, 1882; *Fargo Daily Times*, November 11, December 16, 1881, June 3, 1882; *Watertown Times*, July 7, 1879; Lamphere, "History of Wheat Growing in the Red River Valley," pp. 21-2; Coulter, *op. cit.*, pp. 585-92.

[13] *Fargo Times*, April 5, 1879; *Pembina Pioneer* (Pembina, D. T.), August 7, 1879; *Northern Pacific Times*, June 19, 1879.

August, 1880, wrote: "For a week or more the streets of Fargo have been thronged with strangers, most of them roughly clad, and having the appearance of vagabonds. Their presence here has caused serious apprehensions of trouble among our citizens, and the city authorities have been urged to take every precaution to prevent trouble. Every mail brings in reports of crimes and outrages committed by tramps in other sections of the country." A Valley City editor on August 24, 1882, under the heading "The Tramp Nuisance," made a plea for additional police protection.[14]

In spite of such reports only a few of the workers were tramps or idle wanderers, and a contemporary observer writing in the summer of 1882 emphasized the point: "Of course with the influx of harvest hands come a large proportion of honest, hard working men, but it cannot be denied that with them come also a few who would not scruple at the commission of crime, and it is of the latter that our city authorities should take notice." Most of the workers were small farmers and homesteaders, or laboring men from the cities who came west for the harvest season only, lumberjacks from the lumber camps of northern Minnesota and Wisconsin, where they were employed during the fall and winter months, and college men out for the summer to earn their way through the next academic year. A conservative estimate is that perhaps 90 per cent of the laborers were honest, industrious working men.[15]

A contemporary writer, describing the harvest period, said:

Harvesting begins about the middle of July, and with it everything takes on new life. Villages, which a month before were almost devoid of activity, are transformed almost by magic. The whir of the harvester and binder is heard on every side. Strangers come in such numbers that the hotels are incapable of providing sleeping rooms. I never

[14] *Northern Pacific Times*, November 25, 1880; *Valley City Times*, August 24, 1882; *Fargo Times*, August 5, 1880.
[15] Letter by J. D., printed under the title, "Dakota as a Farming Country," *Cultivator and Country Gentleman*, XLVII, 46; letter by M. M. F., printed under the title, "Agriculture in Northern Dakota," in *ibid.*, XL, 473.

saw such a mixture of laborers. A man who has outrun the sheriff of his county is pretty sure to be safe while the harvest lasts. The lumbermen from the camps of Minnesota and Wisconsin are enticed by the prospects for fair wages, and prospectors who failed to make their "stake" in the mines of the far west stop to earn enough to carry them back home. Hundreds come from the cities, others from colleges, and perhaps most important of all, hundreds of small farmers and homesteaders and others who would hire out for the season in order to get a small amount of cash to start farming for themselves a little further out, but within range of a market.[16]

The average wage for workers in the wheat-fields was about $18 per month with board, room, and laundry, a foreman or pacesetter receiving $20 to $25. During the rush periods the average monthly wage was as high as $20 to $22, falling to $15 or $16 during the dull period. Daily wages were often as high as $1.75 to $2.50 in rush times, falling to $1.00 or $1.25 per day for fall plowing. Day men were paid only for the actual days worked.[17]

A traveler in the wheat country in the winter of 1880 commented upon the conspicuous absence of women and children upon the large wheat farms. "In no case," he wrote, "was the permanent residence of a family to be found upon them, nor anything that could be called a home. In fact the idea of a home does not pertain to them; they are simply business ventures." Few churches and schools were reported, although religious services were often held on the larger farms. Such a service was held on the Grandin farm, conducted by the bookkeeper.[18]

Although the large wheat farms of the Red River country received a great deal of attention during the eighties, their importance was no doubt overemphasized. While a few made large

[16] *Cultivator and Country Gentleman,* January 19, 1882, pp. 47-9, June 5, 1885, pp. 470-9.

[17] James H. Blodgett, "Wages of Farm Labor in the United States: Results of Twelve Statistical Investigations, 1866-1902," issued by the U. S. Dept. of Agriculture, Bureau of Statistics, as its *Bulletin XXVI.* Also the letters cited in *Cultivator and Country Gentleman,* XLVII, 46 and XL, 473.

[18] Bigelow, "Bonanza Farms of the West," pp. 33-6.

sums of money from bonanza wheat-farming, their big contribution was the advertising that was given to the Red River Valley and to the Territory of Dakota. There were hundreds of farmers in the Red River district who were not satisfied to turn all their land to the production of wheat. In fact, there was far more land owned and farmed by the small farmers than by the large wheat-growers. In 1870 there were 1,720 farms in the Territory of Dakota whose average size was 176 acres. In 1880 Dakota had 17,435 farms which averaged 218 acres. In Cass County, the very center of the bonanza wheat country, the farms averaged 326 acres. By 1890 there were in North Dakota 27,611 farms whose size averaged 277 acres. At that time 8.07 per cent of the farm-land of North Dakota was planted to wheat.

By 1890 the outlook of the large wheat farmer was not so bright as it had been. The drought which was local in 1887 and 1888 became widespread in 1889 throughout the central portion of the United States and hit the Red River Valley with exceptional severity. The crop reports for 1890 show a large decrease in the yield of farm products, that of wheat dropping from 62,500,000 bushels to 43,000,000. The panic of 1893 was disastrous to many of the large-scale farmers because of overexpansion on borrowed capital.[19]

But drought and economic depression were not the only handicaps of the large wheat farmer, in fact, they were only temporary setbacks. The real difficulties went far deeper than that. When large-scale farming began in the Red River Valley, wheat was worth around a dollar a bushel. If a fair yield could be obtained on land worth $5.00 per acre, the profit was large, but, with the increase in the price of land to $20 or $25 per acre and a marked decline in the price of wheat, the business was not so profitable.

A survey of agricultural products in the United States from

1863 to 1867 shows a decided upward trend in prices. From 1867 to 1889 the general trend, especially of wheat, was downward, broken only by an occasional temporary recovery. The year 1867 marked the highest annual price for wheat since its production had become a recognized feature of American agriculture. Number 2 spring wheat averaged $1.43 gold in the Chicago market for the year. From 1868 to 1873 prices averaged from $1.30 to $1.00, while from 1873 to 1876 the price ranged from $1.00 to $.80. From 1876 to 1880 the average was $.79 and from 1880 to 1889 the average was $.66. Between 1880 and 1890 wheat declined in price 29.1 per cent, while corn declined 16.9 per cent. The average decline in ten staples of common use during those years was 15.3 per cent. At the same time there was a rather steady demand for dairy products. While many of the large wheat farmers with capital were able for a time partially to overcome these handicaps by more scientific methods, labor-saving machinery and careful management, a gradual shift from wheat as a single crop to diversified farming was inevitable.[20]

V

GRASSHOPPER PLAGUES

OF THE MANY serious obstacles that beset the pioneer farmers of the Northwest, periodic attacks of grasshoppers were probably the most disastrous. Even during the fur-trading period grasshoppers were a menace at times to the gardens and small cultivated fields about the forts and trading-posts, and only by constant care and attention was it possible to defeat their destructive efforts.[21] In the

[20] Veblen, "Price of Wheat Since 1867," pp. 68-75; Edward W. Bemis, "The Discontented Farmer," *Journal of Political Economy*, XI, 193-8; *Yankton Press and Dakotian*, files from 1876 to 1889.

[21] Grasshoppers were first reported in the Red River Valley in 1819-20. Indian children with long willow boughs were often employed to keep watch and drive away the destructive insects. Robinson, *Encyclopedia of South Dakota*, p. 10; "Fort Pierre Journal," South Dakota Historical *Collections*, IX, 69-224, *passim*.

summer of 1855 they were reported in larger numbers than usual by the various forts and Indian agencies in the Dakota area. They came in great clouds from the north, remaining only long enough to devour the small crops and gardens, and then continued southward. Although a few eggs were hatched in the spring of 1856, and gardens were planted with some misgivings, no grasshoppers came in the summer and autumn.[2]

While agriculture was pursued in a small way by early townsite settlers in the Big Sioux and Missouri valleys after 1857, there was no extensive farming in Dakota until the Indian lands between the Big Sioux and Missouri rivers were opened to settlement in 1859 and an agricultural population began to occupy them.[3] The influx of settlers was rapid and the Territory of Dakota was created in March, 1861. Although there was little actual fighting in Dakota, the outbreak of the Civil War and the Indian uprising of 1862 retarded further settlement for several years.[4]

Accounts of settlers reveal the seriousness of the raids of 1864. G. C. Moody, whose farm was near Yankton, the territorial capital, told of the attack upon a field of promising corn, the ears of which were beginning to form:

The grasshoppers invaded the field like a living river pouring upon it. They literally covered the corn. The stream stretched away to the south and west as far as one could see in either direction and the flutter of their wings created a roaring noise that was almost deafening. Not a ten-thousandth part of the stream lighted in my field, but covered the country for miles and miles. They devoured the tender leaves and

---

[2] "A History of Grasshoppers in Clay County," *Dakota Republican*, May 17, 1877. The females deposited eggs in the sod, and they were hatched early in the spring. As it took several days for the young grasshoppers to develop wings, a great deal of damage could be done before they flew away. *Sioux City Journal*, May 14, 1855.

[3] *Sioux City Journal*, June 3, 1859; *Sioux Falls Democrat*, July 9, 21, August 26, November 8, 1859.

[4] *Yankton Weekly Dakotian*, July 6, August 11, 1861; *Sioux Falls Argus Leader*, June 17, 1919; *Official Records of the War of the Rebellion*, Series I, XIII (Washington, D. C., 1880-1901), 6, 39-41.

newly formed ears of corn and never ceased their feast until the stalks were as bare as tent poles.[5]

A Yankton editor, reporting the disaster, said:

The insects came down at midday upon fields that gave promise of moderate harvests and gardens in fair condition. In a short time all were literally covered by myriads of the voracious insects which devoured and destroyed every green thing, even the leaves on the trees and the grass on the prairies. They ate holes in the family washings hanging in the open air and injured many of the tents in which newcomers had made their temporary homes. The insects remained all night and departed the next morning as abruptly as they came.[6]

General Alfred Sully, encamped between the Missouri and Yellowstone rivers during the summer of 1864, told of the hardships caused by the destructive insects in his report to headquarters at Washington. "The only thing spoken about here is the grasshopper. They are awful. They actually have eaten holes in my wagon covers and in the tarpaulins that cover my stores. A soldier on his way here lay down to sleep on the prairie in the middle of the day—his troop had been marching all night. His comrades noticed him covered with grasshoppers and awakened him. His throat and wrists were bleeding from the bites of the insects."[7]

In the spring of 1865 the eggs deposited the preceding year hatched, but the insects left about the first of June before serious damage could be done. While no small grain was sown, corn and potatoes were planted early in June and a splendid crop was raised. In 1866 much new land was broken and a good grain crop was harvested, but late in the summer another raid nearly destroyed in a single day what had promised to be the best corn crop yet produced in the territory. Although some grasshoppers appeared at various times from 1867 to 1873, they were not a serious menace.[8]

[5] *Yankton Weekly Dakotian*, July 30, 1864.
[6] *Yankton Weekly Dakotian*, July 30, 1864.
[7] *Report of General A. A. Sully to the Secretary of War*, August 13, 1864.
[8] *Dakota Republican*, May 17, 1877.

GRAIN ELEVATORS DOMINATING A DAKOTA LANDSCAPE

A typical farming village on the railroad. Courtesy of the Northern Pacific Railway.

The life of the frontier farmer was of necessity one of hardship, the difficulties being generally increased because most of those who entered it were persons of limited means. Since a newly settled country is compelled to depend almost entirely upon farm products for its subsistence, crop failures were bound to render the pioneers destitute. Those who had lost their crops in 1864 were unable to obtain work and had nothing to sell and no feed for their stock during the winter months. As autumn approached the despondent farmers of the Dakota area drove to the neighboring states of Nebraska, Iowa, and Minnesota to obtain supplies of food and grain until another seed time.[9]

On January 1, 1868, a territorial legislative committee on agriculture rendered a statistical report in which the low status of the Dakota farmer was shown. The largest area under cultivation by one settler was thirty acres and the main crops were oats, wheat, corn, and potatoes. While contributing causes for the agricultural depression of 1862 to 1868 were unfamiliarity with Dakota soil and climate, drought and crude farming methods, the primary cause was grasshopper raids.[10]

The period of boom and prosperity from 1868 to 1873 was followed by five years of hard times, one of the important causes being grasshopper attacks.[11]

While some locusts were reported in various portions of the territory in 1871 and 1872, their attacks were scattered and little serious damage was done. The outlook for crops in 1873 was promising until late in July, when grasshoppers appeared in large numbers in practically all the settled portions of the territory. They destroyed the corn and gardens, but about two-thirds of the grain crop was saved. The prospects were good again in 1874 and

[9] *Yankton Weekly Dakotian,* July 30, August 14, 28, September 4, 11, October 4, November 1, 8, 1864; *Sioux City Journal,* August 20, 1919.
[10] *House Journal of the Territorial Legislature of Dakota,* 1867-68, pp. 316-8.
[11] Visher, *Geography of South Dakota,* pp. 141-2; Kingsbury, *History of Dakota Territory,* I, 504.

the grain harvest had just begun when great clouds of the locusts arrived from the northwest and devoured the crops.[12]

An editor in southeastern Dakota, describing the raids of 1874, said: "Harvesting had barely begun when on August sixth there appeared in the northwest a peculiar looking cloud. By four o'clock that afternoon it had gradually settled and millions of grasshoppers attacked the crops. Attempts were made to continue harvesting but the insects clogged the machinery. When night came, they moved on leaving behind them a scene of desolation, broken hopes and saddened homes." The farmers of northeastern Dakota suffered fully as much as those of the southeast. A St. Paul editor showed the seriousness of the situation: "A vast cloud of grasshoppers entered the state of Minnesota July fifteenth, coming from Dakota where the crops were completely destroyed. They crossed the Red River at Moorhead [Minnesota] where the Northern Pacific bridge is located, moving in a southeasterly direction. The column extended from Moorhead to Mankato, a distance of 225 miles in a straight line, being reported almost simultaneously at all intervening telegraph stations. We can only wait to see what they will do here." [13]

The raids of 1873 and 1874 came at a very bad time for the farmers of Dakota, as the general panic of 1873 had brought to a close in the territory a brief period of overexpansion in agriculture. With the entrance of the Dakota Southern Railroad into southeastern Dakota and the extension of the Northern Pacific from Grand Forks to Bismarck in the early seventies had come a period of rapid development.

Dakota and Minnesota, however, were not alone in the grasshopper misfortunes of 1874, as Iowa, Nebraska, Missouri, Kansas, Colorado, and Montana suffered also. The matter was sufficiently

[12] *Dakota Republican*, May 17, 1877; *Yankton Press*, files for 1870-74; *St. Paul Pioneer Press*, files for 1870-74; *Yankton Press and Dakotian*, August 8, 1874.
[13] *Dakota Republican*, May 17, 1877; *St. Paul Pioneer Press*, July 18, 1874.

serious to cause the United States Government to send out an expert commission in the autumn of 1874 to investigate the problem. The commission passed through the southern portion of Dakota on its tour of investigation, a Yankton editor making the following comment: "The scientific gentlemen who came from Washington have been in the vicinity of the territorial capital for several days and have not slighted their investigation because of any personal privation they might be obliged to endure. They will visit the various Dakota settlements and will use the information gained in a report to Congress." [14]

The winter of 1874-75 was unusually severe, with much stormy, cold weather and heavy snows. Fuel was scarce and expensive, and many poor families were dependent upon prairie hay for heating their homes. During the fall and early winter many of the older and wealthier families were liberal with their aid and were able to supply the needy. But as the winter advanced, destitution became such a common condition that it was apparent that local resources would not be sufficient. Relief societies were formed in every organized county in southeastern Dakota and in many of those in the northeastern portion. The Dakota Southern Railroad organized its own special relief association which did excellent work. In January, 1875, a bill was introduced in the territorial legislature to provide seed grain and assistance to those in need. The bill provided for the immediate issue of twenty-five thousand dollars in bonds, running for ten years at 10 per cent interest. Governor Pennington vetoed the bill on the ground that there was no warrant of law or precedent for the issuance of bonds for such a purpose. The bill was passed over the governor's veto, but no attempt was made to carry it into effect. [15]

The independence and pride of frontier communities is well

---

[14] *Yankton Press and Dakotian*, October 14, 1874; "The Grasshopper and Its Ranges," *Senate Executive Documents* (1875), I, 33-5.

[15] *Session Laws of the Territory of Dakota*, II, 36; *Dakota Republican*, January 28, 1875; *Northern Pacific Times*, January 14, 1875; *Fargo Daily Times*, December 21, 1874.

brought out by the resentment shown in many Dakota counties toward the efforts of the legislature to aid those in want. An editorial appearing in a Clay County newspaper said: "The counties of the Territory of Dakota are neither bankrupt nor helpless and the publication of such a bill to the world is a libel and we enter our solemn protest against it. Does any one pretend that Clay County is unable to care for its poor? Such an idea is simply ludicrous." [16] This statement shows spirit and courage, but it also indicates that many of the people and public officials of the territory did not comprehend the extent of damage and destitution in the farming sections. Long before the winter was over they came to realize that ample help could not be provided by local relatives and friends and county relief. A territorial committee was named by the governor to receive and distribute donations. The committee handled a considerable sum of money and large supplies of food and clothing. It distributed them to the needy judiciously and impartially, keeping an itemized record of all receipts and disbursements.[17]

The United States Government joined the relief forces during the winter and appropriated $150,000 for the purchase of food for the destitute settlers. It was disbursed through the War Department under the direction of General Alfred Terry, Dakota settlers receiving 75,000 pounds of flour and 25,000 pounds of bacon. Money and seed grain were distributed by various relief societies organized in Ohio, Indiana and other eastern states. The Chicago Board of Trade contributed $1,479.50 in cash; the Detroit Chamber of Commerce, $1,020; and the Detroit Relief Committee, $500. By spring most of the needy had been provided with food, clothing, and seed grain, and toward the middle of May the appeals for help ceased. Crops were again planted by the Dakota farmers, who watched and hoped for the best.[18]

[16] *Dakota Republican*, January 28, 1875.
[17] *Ibid.*, February 18, 25, 1875.
[18] Files of the *Dakota Republican, Yankton Press and Dakotian, St. Paul Pioneer Press, Fargo Times* and *Northern Pacific Times.*

The season of 1875 was excellent for crops and although grass-hoppers devastated other areas, very few appeared in Dakota. Many counties in the territory held harvest festivals during the autumn months to celebrate their good fortune. More produce was raised in 1875 than in the previous three years. In 1876 the crops promised splendid returns, and the grain that ripened early was harvested without loss. Late in July the grasshoppers came from the north in even greater numbers than in 1873 and 1874. They devoured the grain, corn, gardens, and most of the potato crop. About one-third of the small grain had already been saved and this, with what was left over from the previous year, was sufficient to keep the settlers from want. The grasshoppers re-mained in some localities for two weeks and left more eggs than ever before. Governor Pillsbury of Minnesota called a convention of the governors of the states and territories suffering from grass-hopper plagues to meet at Omaha, Nebraska. Governor Penning-ton represented the Territory of Dakota, but the convention ac-complished nothing of practical value.[19]

Early in January, 1877, reports came from sections of Dakota that many eggs had hatched during a warm spell and that the grasshoppers had been frozen by the cold weather that followed. The warm spring weather in April, however, showed that the destruction had not been complete and a feeling of great uneasi-ness prevailed. Under these circumstances Governor Pennington issued a proclamation asking that Friday, May 4th, be observed throughout the territory as a day of humiliation, fasting, and prayer. The proclamation was generally observed, banks and busi-ness-houses suspending work.[20] The prairies were ordered burned to destroy as many eggs as possible. About the middle of May a small red bug, first noticed in 1874, is said to have appeared in

[19] *Dakota Republican*, August 19, September 11, 18, 1875, editorial on progress, December 30, 1875; *Yankton Press and Dakotian*, September 4, 1875; *Sioux City Weekly Times*, September 11, 1875.
[20] *Dakota Republican*, January 14, April 24, May 3, 17, 1877; *Bismarck Daily Tribune*, May 15, 1877.

large numbers and destroyed the remaining eggs and the young grasshoppers that were hatched.[21]

The crops of 1877 were good and a report sent out by the territorial governor said, in part, "We are now in the midst of the harvest in Dakota and it is safe to say that the yield for the small grain crops will be far the largest ever gathered in the territory. There has been no damage from grasshoppers." [22] The good crops of 1877 and 1878 paved the way for the "Great Dakota Boom" that occurred from 1879 to 1886 and the farmers of Dakota were not seriously bothered again by grasshoppers during the territorial period.

Attacks by grasshoppers were general throughout the Northwest during the sixties and seventies, and while there were local differences in the seriousness of the depredations, crops in Montana were ordinarily attacked and destroyed in about the same years as in Dakota. While the raids caused some suffering and want in Montana, they were not nearly so serious as in other areas, since that territory was experiencing overproduction in agriculture, with very low prices, due in part to the lack of transportation facilities.

A Virginia City editor early in August, 1866, said, "Grasshoppers came in great numbers and much damage has been done by their raids, to the crops growing in our various valleys. Some men have been totally ruined, while others have not been greatly harmed." On September 9th of the same year another attack was recorded which had played havoc with the late crops. Early in July the following year immense damage was reported to have been done in the Deer Lodge and Jefferson valleys. Gallatin Valley suffered also, but not so seriously. A local editor made this comment: "On Sunday night and Monday the air was filled with

[21] Kingsbury, op. cit., II, 1027-8. Although the appearance of the red bug is reported by several newspapers, its effectiveness in eliminating the grasshopper and its eggs may be questioned.

[22] Report of the Territorial Governor to the Commissioner of Agriculture, July 30, 1877, pp. 1-2.

the migrating scourge so thick that they looked like a snowstorm."
A local ranchman reported them so numerous on his land that
he believed there were as many as ten thousand to the square
foot. A Bozeman editor in August, 1873, said, "Grasshoppers, the
'pesky varmints,' have made their appearance in the Prickly Pear
Valley and our farmers are fearful that the present army will
take the balance of what the first ones left." In the summer of
1875 the Montana valleys were ravaged again and the insect was
reported to be leaving the Prickly Pear Valley late in June "in
great swarms," having almost wholly devoured the vegetable and
grain crops. In the middle of July the following year the grasshoppers were said to have "nearly all left the Missouri Valley
and the farmers are rejoicing in the hope of raising half a crop."
Their hope was a vain one, as a few weeks later the same observer
reported, "Grasshoppers like clouds of smoke fill the air as far as
the eye can reach." [23]

The grasshoppers that inflicted the damage to the crops of
Dakota and Montana in the territorial period were of the grass-
land species and were called migratory or seventeen-year locusts.
They were very different from the ordinary grasshopper, being
darker in color, with a larger and harder frame, and better
adapted to flying. Although lighter in weight the migratory locust
was tough and difficult to kill.[24] The young insects usually passed
over the Dakota and Montana region flying northward in May
and June when the weather was clear with a light wind from the
south. They seldom alighted during this season of the year. Even
the insects hatched from eggs left the summer before were not
especially destructive and usually flew northward as soon as their
wings developed. They seemed to wait for favorable winds.
Whether the northward movement was due to instinct or to the
prevailing currents of wind from the south in May and June was

[23] *Montana Post*, August 11, 29, 1866, July 10, 1867; *Avant Courier*,
August 15, 1873, June 29, 1875; *Rocky Mountain Husbandman*, July 13,
August 3, 10, 1876.
[24] "The Grasshopper and Its Ranges," *op. cit.*, I, 33-4.

a question never definitely decided. In July the "hopper" current seemed to change and the full-grown insects flew southward during the rest of the summer. The locusts did not always alight, their action being partly dependent upon weather conditions. Hot wet weather served to check the plagues while dry weather, either hot or cool, seemed to favor them. A head wind, a calm, clouds, or a storm usually caused them to descend. Only the insects flying southward in July and August ate the crops and laid eggs.[25]

Much time and money were expended in attempts to destroy the destructive locusts and numerous methods were recommended and employed. Several counties paid fifty cents a bushel for the dead insects and those brought in were burned at night in great bonfires in the village streets. The insects were crushed with rollers and other implements or caught in bags or traps during the mating season, at which time they were inactive and stupid.[26] Spots conducive to the hatching of eggs were thoroughly harrowed in the fall, and fields were often carefully burned in the early spring. Loose straw was sometimes placed near the hatching places and was fired at the proper time. Ditches were dug around fields with deep pits placed at intervals. There was a liberal use of tar and oil, while some even resorted to loud noises and yelling to frighten the insects away. Poisoned bait was perhaps the most effective means of checking them. Breaking the sod, the favorite breeding-place, tended to keep down the number while the extension of

[25] "A History of Grasshoppers in Clay County," *Dakota Republican*, May 17, 1877.

[26] Various types of grasshopper machines were patented and placed on the market. W. J. Kinney of Helena, Montana, advertised one that spread coal-tar and was to be drawn by two men. It was reported by the local press to have been used with excellent results. Another machine was advertised in a Montana newspaper as "the best grasshopper catcher ever invented." It consisted of a V-shaped frame six feet apart at the points and about two inches deep, which was pushed along with a wire screen in back to catch the insects. The hoppers thus scooped up could be sold in some of the counties at $.50 a bushel, figuring 70 pounds to the bushel. The price of this patented device was $20. *Helena Daily Herald*, May 25, 1876; *Rocky Mountain Husbandman*, June 7, 1877.

tillage helped reduce the proportional damage done to any unit area.[27]

The grasshopper plagues profoundly affected the growth and delayed the development of the agricultural Northwest. The number of settlers who left the Territory of Dakota during and after the attacks was large as compared with the total population. If funds had been available, the number would have been much larger. As the exodus tended to be selective, the farmers who remained were a hardy group. The proportion of foreign-born was increased, as a large percentage of those who left were native Americans. The plagues also gave the Northwest a bad reputation and discouraged immigration to the farming areas. Eastern newspapers and magazines told colorful stories and often exaggerated tales of the hardships experienced and were inclined to call the insects "Dakota grasshoppers." [28]

The discontinuance of the activity of the locusts was always marked by a rapid influx of settlers. Governor A. J. Faulk of Dakota in his message of December 4, 1866, bemoaned the loss of population and the lack of immigration and made an ardent plea for new settlers. A year later he stated that the population of Dakota had more than doubled during the past year. By December, 1868, it was reported to have doubled again.[29] The records of the Federal Land Office show the decline of grasshopper depredations in the seventies. For the fiscal year ending June 30, 1877, 212,556 acres of land were filed upon at the various Dakota land-offices, while the amount for the following year was 1,377,948 acres.[30]

Another effect of the grasshopper plagues was the impetus they

[27] Visher, *Geography of South Dakota*, p. 118; territorial newspaper files; *Farm and Factory* (St. Paul, Minn.), June 1-29, 1877; *Northwestern Miller* (Minneapolis, Minn.), May 4, 1877, April 19, November 2, 1878.

[28] Visher, *op. cit.*, pp. 157-8; files of territorial newspapers.

[29] *Messages of the Territorial .Governor*, December 4, 1866, December 2, 1867, December 7, 1868.

[30] *Reports of the General Land Office* (Washington, D. C.), 1877, pp. 172-3, 1878, pp. 150-1.

gave to changes in farming methods. Greater care was taken in
the preparation of the land, while varieties of plants and crops
better suited to the climate and less apt to be consumed by the
locusts were planted. Rotation and diversification of crops received greater attention, while mixed farming replaced "pure"
or "straight" farming. More live stock was raised and dairying
became more important than formerly.[31] An eastern observer
writing in 1876 made the following comment: "The only serious
drawback to agriculture in Dakota seems to be the migratory insect or locust that come in swarms in June or early July and
devour the crops. The best protection against these insects is fall
ploughing, early seeding and the cultivation of crops least likely
to be injured by them. Mixed farming with the raising of live
stock and some dairying will assist the Dakota farmer in over-
coming this serious menace." [32]

VI

CLIMATIC HANDICAPS

IN ADDITION to the Civil War, Indian troubles, and grasshopper
plagues of the most devastating type, the frontier farmer of the
upper Missouri country was faced with serious climatic difficulties.
This was especially true in the Dakota area, where irrigation was
not practised. No matter where people live, they are inclined to
tell their friends and relatives residing in other areas of the advantages of their region. That tendency was always strong on the
frontier and the pioneer farmers who settled in the agricultural
sections of Wyoming, Montana, and Dakota often wrote glowing
reports to their eastern friends, each extolling the virtues of his
local community, which was portrayed as a land of wonderful
possibilities, of sunshine, rich soil, and fine crops, whose inhabitants
were prosperous, happy, and honest. The settler was inclined to

[31] Visher, op. cit., pp. 158-9.
[32] Appleton's Annual Cyclopedia (1876), p. 218.

boast that the area was immune from chills and fever or other handicaps of his earlier home and to be silent about, or to gloss over, the fact that this new country was at times subject to severe drought, hot winds, dust and hail storms, and long hard winters often accompanied by blizzards. If the early farmer could be induced to admit that there was something to the stories of his starving contemporaries in "drought-stricken Dakota" and of settlers frozen in blizzards, he did so with reluctance and was quick to explain that those climatic handicaps always prevailed in a new country and would disappear as soon as the area was settled and the land placed under cultivation.

The region under consideration lies almost wholly within the great plains area which is classified by geologists as arid or semi-arid. While the rainfall varies in amount from year to year and there are at times marked differences, the average over a number of years is not sufficient to insure good crops. Variations as to seasonal distribution are much greater than the fluctuations in annual precipitation. Uncertainties in rainfall during the growing season have a marked influence on crop yields. In sections of the Dakota area there might be twice the normal precipitation one month and in the next it might run less than half the normal. At the best, the element of uncertainty was great. Hot winds caused terrible destruction and suffering and fine fields of grain and corn were sometimes destroyed within two or three days. Hail-storms often did great damage to the crops, while the great plains blizzards were vicious in their effects as the high winds, carrying fine snow, covered the farmers' stacks of hay and straw and filtered into the houses and barns through the smallest crevices. Cattle often died by the hundreds and settlers lost on the prairies or even in the vicinity of their own homes froze to death or contracted colds from which they never recovered. Following the blizzards came a period of bitter cold, with snow as much as ten feet on the level.[1]

[1] The details of the winter of 1886-87 have been described in connection with

The frontier farmer of Dakota, faced by these weather handicaps, was at times in serious difficulty. Crops on virgin soil in a new country are always light, as it takes several years to get the land in workable condition ready to produce to its maximum capacity. It must also be remembered that large numbers of the settlers were not experienced farmers, but had come west from the factory and industrial centers and from other walks of life to get free farms and opportunities for economic independence for themselves and their children. They were often with limited financial means, having just enough resources to get to their destination, and to plant a crop of a few acres. If this first attempt at farming failed, the settler and his family were often destitute and had to work for others where this was possible, or to borrow or receive aid from relatives and friends until another seedtime. Moreover, many of the settlers had migrated from the more humid areas to the east and had learned from experience of the bitterest sort that the methods used in regions with more rainfall were not possible in their new home. They learned that plowing must be deeper, plantings must be made more carefully and the crops chosen with great care if the yields were to be at all satisfactory.

Throughout the frontier period there existed the idea that the climatic difficulties were only temporary and that as settlement developed and the land was cultivated, they would disappear and the country would become more uniformly productive. The settlers who had made their homes in the new country hoped for a

the section of the "Frontier of the Cattle-Rancher." Another blizzard that caused much disaster and suffering occurred in 1888. After several mild days, it began to snow and blow very hard on January 12th-13th. Two or three feet of snow fell in an hour or two, after which the temperature sank to 30 degrees below zero and the wind increased its velocity to 40 miles per hour. The snow drifted unusually high as the wind continued, until many buildings were filled with snow which came in through the smallest openings. Railroad and wagon trails were interrupted at many points. For several weeks domesticated as well as wild animals suffered for lack of food and some thousands of the weaker ones died. It is reported that 112 human lives were lost in what is now South Dakota as a result of this storm. Robinson, "Outline of South Dakota's History," *South Dakota Historical Collections*, II, 99.

more humid climate and the fact of variations in rainfall at different times led to the conclusion in the wet years that the climate was changing and that precipitation was becoming greater with settlement. In the years when rainfall was most abundant, new settlers flocked in by the thousands. The moist years were invariably followed by a series of dry ones. Over a fairly long period of five or six decades, scientific experts have shown that there is no real basis for the contention that the climate is changing, and in most cases the average precipitation for one decade to another will vary but little.[2]

Although many an old settler has insisted that the climate of his area has changed, that droughts have become less disastrous and that blizzards are not as severe as they once were, the explanation may perhaps be found in other reasons than the alleged changes of climate. As the country was settled and the pioneers became adjusted to the soil and climate, a better arrangement of crops was worked out, those that were able to withstand the changes and were acclimated taking the place of the poorly adapted ones of the earlier settlers. The later population practised diversified and mixed farming and were not so near the margin of want as they had been in early times. They had food reserves as well as some cash and it took more than a single dry year to render them destitute. Many of them could stand two or three years of failure without as much suffering as had been experienced in one of the earlier years. With better built homes, more adequate fuel and heating facilities, warmer clothing, and improved roads and methods of transportation, the rural population was more favorably situated to withstand the hardships of blizzards and of extended cold weather than in previous years.

The settlers were comforted with the philosophy that rainfall would follow settlement, that breaking the sod would hold the

[2] J. W. Powell, "Reports on the Lands of the Arid Regions of the United States" (Government bulletin: Washington, D. C., 1879); A. J. Henry, "Variation of Precipitation in the United States," *Bulletin of American Geological Society* (March, 1914), pp. 192-201.

moisture and that the growing of crops, the burning of the prairies, and even the smoke from the homes of settlers would somehow cause rain to fall. It was said that the construction of railroad and telegraph lines across the plains would produce rain by means of electrical currents running through the wires. One professed authority on the subject claimed that planting trees would increase rainfall, although he did not explain how soil that could not produce grass could be made to grow trees. These ideas naturally led to the conclusion that humans could in various ways cause rainfall. Ideas of this sort were quite prolific during the seventies and eighties. A civil engineer as early as 1871 had published the thesis that there was a close relationship between rainfall and battles. Daniel Ruggles in 1880 took out a patent on a device whereby rain might be produced by series of explosions among the clouds caused by balloons. When severe drought struck the great plains region in the early nineties, Congress made appropriations of nineteen thousand dollars, of which fourteen thousand dollars was expended in a series of experiments conducted by Major R. G. Dyrenforth under the auspices of the Department of Agriculture.[3]

During the periods of serious drought there were church services and prayers offered to induce rain and some communities resorted to the activities of individuals who claimed they could produce rain. A population heavily in debt while establishing itself on lands that were not producing crops whereby the debt could be retired was ready to listen to almost any sort of a scheme that might solve the difficulty. Rain-makers and fakers were soon taking advantage of conditions that were serious to the frontier farmer. In the fall of 1891 Frank Melbourne, after experiments in rain-making that he alleged to have been successful, appeared at Cheyenne, Wyoming, and entered into a contract with the

[3] George E. Franklin, "The Work of the Rain-makers in the Arid Regions," *Proceedings,* Twelfth National Irrigation Congress, Galveston, Texas (1905); Webb, *Great Plains,* pp. 375-82; Nimmo Report, *House Exec. Doc.,* 48th Cong., 2nd Sess., No. 267, 17.

THRESHING IN THE FIELDS

Near Minto, North Dakota. Courtesy of the Minnesota State Historical Society.

citizens there whereby he agreed to make rain fall "alike upon the just and unjust." Good fortune was with him, as the firm believers and doubting Thomases were forced to seek protection from the shower and those unable to get to shelter were drenched to the skin.[4] The next spring Melbourne printed a pamphlet addressed "to the people of the arid regions" containing testimonials that he had produced rain in Kansas, Utah, Wyoming, and Ohio. "I am ready to enter into contract to produce sufficient rain for crops in any part of the United States on very reasonable terms," announced the author of the pamphlet.

Melbourne received many responses to his advertisement. "Can you come here at once and prospect for rain? Wire conditions," came a telegram from a Nebraska town. "Our money is raised. Name earliest date you can be here and await reply," said another. "Wire your price for an inch of rain," requested still another, continuing, "Don't come until ordered." Melbourne admitted later that the whole thing was a fake. "The American people like to be humbugged," he remarked. "The bigger the fake, the easier it is to work."[5] While there can be no question that human credulity is great, the drought-stricken region of the Northwest was willing to do anything that had even the most remote possibility of giving relief.

VII

CREDIT AND INTEREST

IN ADDITION to the uncertainties of Nature, the frontier farmer of the upper Missouri country was faced with the serious problem of credit. The average settler moving onto an undeveloped farm or homestead usually had sufficient funds to enable him to file on

[4] *Cheyenne Daily Leader,* September 2, 1892.
[5] Letters and correspondence of Frank Melbourne. The catalog and correspondence of Melbourne are in the Wyoming State Department of History at Cheyenne.

his land and to plant a few acres of crops. There were those, however, who lacked the means of subsistence until their first crop
matured and were dependent upon possible employment in the
near-by settlements, Indian agencies, or military posts, until their
first harvest. But work was scarce and if the first crop did not
happen to be successful there was suffering and want. Even after
the first year or two the needs of the pioneer farmer were many
and varied. If he was to do much farming and develop his holdings, live stock, farm machinery, and other supplies were necessary
yet difficult to secure, unless arrangements could be made for
credit.

The main sources of credit for the frontier agriculturalist were
the local bankers, outside mortgage brokers, local implement dealers, manufacturers of farm machinery, and the local merchants.
The bankers and professional money-lenders ordinarily protected
their loans by a mortgage on real estate, while the security of the
dealer in farm implements was apt to be a lien on the chattels of
the farmer. Credit at the local store was usually unsecured and
was often granted while a crop was maturing. The local merchant
played a vital rôle in the life and activities of the frontier farmer
since he was often dependent on the dispenser of merchandise for
supplies long after he had established his farm, and even borrowed small sums of cash from him to tide over emergencies.
At times the local constituency was critical of the merchant because of high prices charged, which were justified by the merchant
as necessary in order to pass on to the community some of the
risks taken. Settlers at times left the country without settling their
accounts or, after getting heavily in debt to a merchant, shifted
their business to a rival.[1]

Money was scarce on the frontier and a system of barter developed whereby wood, corn, wheat, hay, and vegetables were

[1] Herbert S. Schell, "The Grange and the Credit Problem in Dakota Territory," *Agricultural History*, X (April, 1936), 59-83; Lewis E. Atherton, "The
Services of the Frontier Merchant," *Mississippi Valley Historical Review*, XXIV,
153-70.

accepted in exchange for merchandise, editors of newspapers being willing to accept produce instead of cash in payment for subscriptions. An editor at Sioux City, Iowa, writing regarding conditions in the Territory of Dakota in the summer of 1874, said, "There is plenty of trade in all the stores, but little or no money 'till the harvest,' which means, in many cases, until next December, or until the farmer pleases to pay." [2]

Interest rates were always high in a frontier community, and one of the curses of the agriculturist in the upper Missouri area in the seventies and eighties was the excessive rates charged on loans. The ordinary rate for a chattel mortgage was 10 per cent, while those on real estate ran considerably higher, depending to a certain extent on how badly the borrower needed the money. The experience of the Territory of Dakota in this regard is of interest. Starting out in the sixties the legislature fixed the standard rate at 7 per cent, unless some other rate had previously been agreed upon. Because of the keen desire of the territory to attract money the legal rate was changed in 1871 to 24 per cent or 2 per cent a month. After much criticism and discussion the legal rate in 1874 was reduced to 18 per cent. Apparently the law was not carefully observed at first, as in the fall of the same year an editor at the territorial capital told of a court decision declaring a mortgage foreclosure illegal since the rate of interest of the mortgage was 24 per cent, which was excessive and therefore not collectible. [3]

One of the chief reasons for the legal sanction of exorbitant interest rates was the desire on the part of territorial authorities to attract capital to the new areas. James S. Foster, who was in charge of immigration activities in Dakota in the early seventies, in his pamphlets distributed for advertising purposes placed special emphasis upon the fact that interest rates were 2 per cent per

[2] Quoted from the *Dakota Gleaner* (Elk Point, D. T.), July 23, 1874, by Schell, *op. cit.*, p. 62.

[3] *Session Laws of Territory of Dakota*, 1864-65, 1870-71, 1873-74.

month, which might lead men of capital to invest their money there. The interest rate, however, does not tell the whole story. Records show that loans were in many cases discounted, a farmer getting a loan of $500 having the amount discounted 10 per cent, receiving $450 in cash, but being compelled to pay the interest rate agreed upon on the complete amount.

The financial depression of 1873 was especially hard upon the farmers of the upper Missouri country. Many of them were heavily in debt, their loans bearing high rates of interest, and were not able to meet their obligations, and mortgage foreclosures were numerous. There was much sympathy for the farmer and when the territorial legislature of Dakota convened early in December, 1874, Governor J. L. Pennington in his message to the legislative body took a strong stand in behalf of the settler "struggling on a homestead for a subsistence," who could not hope to better himself by borrowing money at from 18 to 24 per cent, since it would, over a period of time, be impossible for him to avoid foreclosure. An editor at the territorial capital attacked the loan system as a complete failure and advocated a change that would to some degree, at least, protect the welfare of the borrower. The popular demand induced the legislature to fix 12 per cent as the legal rate.[4] Mortgage sales continued as grasshopper plagues and crop failures intensified the need for credit. Chattel mortgages ran heavier, especially in Dakota, after 1875.

Another reason for the increased mortgage foreclosures was an emphasis on wheat-growing, which caused a greater demand for machinery.[5] Machinery was sold on the possibility of good crops, and when these failed trouble was unavoidable. Many of the chattel mortgages and some of those on real estate were taken by local implement dealers or machinery manufacturers, who became the leading creditors in the Northwest. Crops were uncer-

[4] *Message of Governor J. L. Pennington*, December 8, 1874; *Yankton Press and Dakotian*, December 10, 17, 1874.
[5] Wheat production in southeastern Dakota increased from 200,000 bushels in 1870, to 2,125,000 bushels in 1872.

tain and the low prices of wheat, the high interest rates, and the shortness of time allowed on mortgages made the situation obnoxious. Prices for machinery were especially high in 1874 and 1875, as reapers sold for from one hundred and seventy to one hundred and ninety dollars on time and mowers were priced at about one hundred dollars. The various manufacturers of farm machinery became the subject of severe criticism. Excessive profits and high commissions to middlemen, it was alleged, caused the farmer to pay from 50 to 100 per cent more than he should for his machinery.[6]

No doubt many farmers who were induced by a few successful crops to purchase expensive machinery on credit used poor judgment. An editor at Virginia City in the Territory of Montana in an editorial on farm machinery, written in the early seventies, said, "If [farm machinery] is bought with good judgment and used with care, I think it will [pay out]. But a small farmer had better hire his work done with machinery than buy it himself." The *Rocky Mountain Husbandman* took about the same point of view and warned farmers continually not to go too deeply into debt in the purchase of farm machinery.[7] The implement dealers answered the various criticisms directed at them by citing the fact that most of the machinery was bought on credit and payments were slow and extended over a long period of time, and reminding their critics that if cash were paid, the price would be much lower.

But all the arguments were not on the side of the farmer and against those who loaned the money, as the dispensers of credit and the holders of mortgages had their troubles, also. Many farmers proved up on their claims as soon as possible, obtained a

[6] Letters of C. H. McCormick to implement dealers in Montana and eastern Dakota, 1873-78, on file in the McCormick Library and Museum, Chicago, Illinois; A. H. Hirsch, "Efforts of the Grange in the Middle West to Control the Price of Farm Machinery, 1870-80," *Mississippi Valley Historical Society Review*, XV, 475.

[7] *Montanian*, November 14, 1871; *Rocky Mountain Husbandman*, August 6, 1873, October 17, 1878.

loan, and moved on. If the loan was held by a local banker, looking after it was relatively easy. Many of the eastern loan companies had loan agents and inspectors in the field to grant loans and to supervise foreclosures. These agents worked on a fee basis, and unscrupulous representatives sanctioned loans that probably could never be repaid in order to collect their fees. Foreclosure was an expensive procedure and loan companies were often unable to get their money back. Mortgage inspectors from time to time caught settlers moving houses and other farm buildings from their mortgaged farms before and after foreclosure. Squatters would sometimes move on a farm after the mortgagee had left the country.[8]

VIII

THE GRANGE IN THE NORTHWEST

AN ASSOCIATION of farmers called the Patrons of Husbandry, but perhaps better known as the Grange,[9] was organized at Washington, D. C., by Oliver H. Kelley in 1867, and by the early seventies had become an organization of national importance. Membership included both men and women. The order was secret and, like lodges of that type, put its members through an elaborate ceremony, in this case consisting of seven degrees. The program of reform it sponsored was designed to improve the condition of the American farmer, and sought to further the agricultural and industrial education of its members, to eliminate or at least reduce the importance of the middleman, to reduce profits and interest, and to lower railroad rates. The organization was non-political and

[8] Samuel Torgeson, "Early Banking in North Dakota," *Quarterly Journal*, University of North Dakota, XIII, 287-8; John W. Scott, "The Pioneer Farmer," *ibid.*, p. 292; Seth K. Humphrey, *Following the Prairie Frontier* (Minneapolis, Minn., 1931), *passim*.

[9] The term "grange," which means barn or granary, was ordinarily applied to the local units or chapters of the organization, whose members were often referred to as Grangers.

the local chapters engaged in social and cultural activities in accordance with their specific needs and desires.[2] The movement was given added impetus by the panic of 1873, the number of chartered granges in the United States increasing from 1,362 in 1872, to 10,029 in 1873.[3]

As has been indicated, conditions in the agricultural portions of the Territories of Dakota and Montana were such in the early seventies as to make an organization like the Grange very timely. Because of the general economic situation, the farmers of those areas were responsive to the campaign against middlemen and monopolies. While conditions of the frontier farmers of the Northwest were in many ways quite different from those in the older settled districts to the eastward, they encouraged its organization and work. The growth and activities of the Grange as a national movement must be kept in mind, but the development of the organization in both Dakota and Montana should be considered in connection with the local needs and conditions in those two frontier territories.

The first subordinate grange to be organized in the Territory of Dakota was in Clay County in the southeastern part, not far from Vermillion, on December 4, 1872. Henry L. Ferry, formerly of Muscatine, Iowa, was instrumental in the formation of the first chapter, which was made up in part of farmers from eastern Iowa, some of whom had been former friends and neighbors of Ferry. He continued his activities for the Grange and was successful in the organization of several active chapters, a county organization being formed in June, 1873, at which time there were six subordinate granges in Clay County. By the fall of 1873 there were twenty-five subordinate chapters in the Territory of Dakota, most of which had been organized by Ferry. In

[2] The reform program of the Grange was well stated at its national convention in 1874 at St. Louis.

[3] S. J. Buck, *The Granger Movement* (Cambridge, Mass., 1913), p. 64; W. A. Pierson, "The Rise of the Granger Movement," *Popular Science Monthly*, XXXII, 203.

November a territorial organization was formed and plans were made for an active drive for additional subordinate units.[4]

The Grange grew rapidly in Dakota and by the early part of 1874 there were forty-four chapters in the territory with a total membership of more than fifteen hundred, which had increased by autumn to fifty-six local lodges whose membership was around two thousand. The membership in Dakota was confined to the southeastern corner of the territory, a large portion of the members residing in Clay, Union, and Lincoln counties. A chapter was formed at Fargo in the northern part of the territory, but apparently did not affiliate with the lodges in the southeastern section.[5]

The local press contained many announcements of meetings and ceremonies which apparently were elaborate and dignified—local picnics, box-suppers, and dances, and other activities. Emphasis was placed on the value of the organization to the individual farmer on the basis of coöperative buying and selling whereby the middleman might be eliminated, plans being made early in 1874 in Clay County for a central purchasing agency. There was much agitation and discussion when various manufacturing concerns refused to sell directly to farmers except at the regular prices charged by retailers. Members were urged not to go in debt for machinery but to use their old agricultural implements or borrow from their neighbors. All forms of credit were to be avoided and unless prices for farm machinery were lowered it was thought better to do the work by hand or at best for several farmers to purchase implements together, paying cash. Attempts were made to obtain supplies from local merchants at reduced prices and certain dealers agreed to meet the demands of the Grange mem-

[4] *Clay County Register,* June 19, 26, July 10, 1873.
[5] The *Bismarck Tribune* told of an attempt to form a unit of a labor organization called the "Patrons of Industry" in Burleigh County late in 1873. The project was disbanded early in 1874 when an attempt was made to organize a chapter of the Grange out of the two local units of the labor association. *Bismarck Daily Tribune,* December 10, 17, 1873, April 30, May 6, 13, November 4, 11, 1874.

bers. While discounts were made by certain firms, it seems that the quality of the commodity was reduced accordingly.[6]

The Grange declined in Dakota, both in members and chapters, in 1875, only forty lodges being represented at the annual territorial meeting in December, 1875, and by July, 1876, the local chapters numbered twenty-six, with a membership of 697. Interest had declined to such an extent that the territory was not represented at the national meeting in December, 1876. Some of the chapters were active locally for some time after the collapse of the territorial organization and attempts were made to revive interest, but the organization was practically extinct in Dakota by 1878. Most of the members in Dakota were settlers of American stock who had moved from the states of the upper Mississippi Valley. The Scandinavian settlers did not take readily to the idea; in fact, the Swedish population refused to have anything to do with the organization. The Scandinavians who did join were Norwegians who were, in most cases, brought into it through the activity and interest created by aggressive leaders. The settlers of French and Irish nationality were enthusiastic, while the German and Russian-German groups were indifferent.[7]

The Granger movement took root quickly in western Montana where the farmers had more difficulties than those of the Dakota area. While they suffered as much as their friends in Dakota from high prices of farm machinery and credit difficulties, they had the additional handicap of no transportation facilities. With the decline of the gold camps, they experienced a badly overstocked market, extremely low prices for everything they sold, and high prices for all incoming commodities, which caused them to complain bitterly.

At the mass-meeting of farmers held at Bozeman on May 30,

---

[6] *Clay County Register*, February 20, 27, 1874; Schell, "Grange and Credit Problem in Dakota Territory," pp. 72-3.

[7] Schell, *op. cit.*, pp. 74-5; *Sioux City Weekly Times*, February 14, 21, March 14, 1874; O. F. Ander, "The Immigrant Church and the Patrons of Husbandry," *Agricultural History*, VIII (October, 1934), pp. 155-68.

1873, called for the purpose of discussing adverse conditions, it was decided some action must be taken. After expressing by resolution their confidence in the local merchants and business men, a committee was appointed to petition the National Grange or Patrons of Husbandry for a charter. The first grange was organized in the Territory of Montana on December 22, 1873, and by spring there were twenty-two subordinate granges in the area with a membership of some six hundred. A Helena editor on January 1, 1874, described the organization: "On Monday evening, December 22, 1873, the first Grange in Montana was formed under the name 'Star of the West,' by H. N. Sutherlin, Deputy of the National Grange. Considerable enthusiasm was evinced and much satisfaction was felt by all. The fact that but thirty charter members are allowed each subordinate grange and that 26 were enrolled may be considered a just estimate of the high appreciation in which the objectives of the organization are held." [8]

One of the objectives of the Montana grange was the building of a railroad at any cost, and it even went so far as proposing that the territorial and Federal governments should construct a branch line connecting with the Union Pacific in Wyoming or Utah to the south. It was critical of local merchants, some of whom it considered sold goods at excessive profits. A Bozeman editor in the spring of 1874 described the activities of the local grange that was holding regular meetings each Tuesday night in its hall in the court-house. "They are working hard on the agricultural problem and as far as they can they mean to better the condition of their class and secure fair prices for what they sell. In this laudable enterprise they have our best wishes for success, for when the farmer is prosperous, all other business is lively." [9]

[8] *Helena Weekly Herald*, January 1, 1874.

[9] *Avant Courier*, April 10, 1874. The farmers and business men of the Gallatin Valley in 1874 organized an armed group sometimes called the Rosebud Expedition. Although the alleged purpose of the expedition was to look for gold, its real objective seems to have been to arouse the Sioux and Cheyenne Indians in the Yellowstone and Big Horn valleys in hope they might become hostile and

The Grange grew rapidly in Montana and much interest and enthusiasm was apparent. On September 22, 1874, the representatives of the various granges met at the fair-grounds near Helena and organized the territorial Grange. There were at that time twenty-three chapters of the organization active in the territory. On June 2, 1875, the first annual session of the territorial Grange was held at Gallatin City, an interesting and active meeting being reported in the press. Several new granges had been added to the directory list and membership had increased to about eight hundred.[10]

One of the territorial officers of the organization, speaking early in 1875, said, "We stand as a unit for our financial security. The merchants denounce us and say we are the curse of the country. We desire self-protection and stand for legitimate trade, legitimate profits and honest and fair transactions." [11] The Montana Grange in 1875 started a movement for collective bargaining in connection with bids on agricultural supplies for the army in that area. They placed bids on hay, oats, and straw contracts and, since their bids were considerably lower than those of the regular post contractors, secured the business. The price for oats was $1.29 per hundred pounds, which was much lower than any of the other bids. Before the crop could be harvested there was a serious grasshopper attack and the price of oats rose to about a dollar higher than the contract price. The granger leaders soon found that the members of the organization refused to fill the contract at the set price and after much haggling and argument the army quartermaster released the grange, which insisted there were no oats available, from the contract. A second bargain, however, was made for oats at $2.50 a hundred which was promptly filled by supplies

cause the government to coerce them, thus opening up those areas for trading purposes and furnishing a market for the agricultural surplus of the valleys of western Montana. E. S. Topping, *Chronicle of the Yellowstone* (St. Paul, Minn., 1883), pp. 101-5.

[10] *Rocky Mountain Husbandman*, January 4, September 22, 1874, June 2, October 5, November 25, 1875.

[11] *Avant Courier*, February 19, 1875.

purchased within a few miles of Fort Ellis. The grangers, apparently, were no different from the group they were attacking when the opportunity for profits was offered. The quartermaster received orders not to take any further bids from local farmers, which put a stop to coöperative activities in the sale of agricultural products.

The Prickly Pear Grange established a school for the benefit of its members early in December, 1875, and in 1876 had it in operation, announcing they expected to make out of it "the best institution of learning in the territory." In August a letter from East Gallatin written to a Bozeman editor explained the status of the granges of the Gallatin Valley. "The granges in the Gallatin area are not getting along very well. The Riverside Grange has not met for six months and the Farmington and East Gallatin Granges have not had a quorum present for two months. A great many members went into the Grange with the expectation of making money out of it. They were of course disappointed and others who had no particular interest, when the novelty of the thing played out, stopped attending the meetings." In 1876 the Grange remained active, although it was gradually losing its membership. In the spring of that year the East Gallatin Grange gave a ball for the purpose of raising money for a library, which netted the chapter $73.25 and "with $52 already subscribed," observed a local editor, "it is sufficient, if judiciously invested, to procure an excellent library." The third annual session of the territorial Grange of Montana was held with the Prickly Pear Grange June 6-7, 1877, twenty-six chapters sending delegates, most of which were from Montana. There was some activity during the year, the Fort Owen Grange opening a new library June 14, 1877, and several chapters holding local fairs or festivals as well as educational institutes in the fall.[12]

While the Montana Grange was gradually losing ground, it

[12] *Rocky Mountain Husbandman*, March 30, June 2, August 24, 1876, June 14, 1877.

did not decline without a struggle, as earnest efforts were made to attract new members. In February, 1878, Sister E. W. Adams of the chapter from Mount Zion, Missouri, read a paper before the territorial chapter at Helena in which the purpose and objectives of the Grange were carefully explained. There was a good deal of emphasis on social activities. "There is need of more social intercourse on the part of the farmer," the lecturer explained. "Our work is laborious and tiresome, and there should be greater opportunities for the social activities of the wives and daughters. We are doing too much physical labor and not enough thinking and the result is retrogression." She reported that the granges of Montana were in a flourishing condition.[13]

In October the Grange Fair held at Helena was well attended, but there is evidence that at that time the organization was weakening. In October the editor of the *Helena Herald* printed a strong editorial on "Maintaining the Grange" in which he appealed for better support for the local chapter as well as for the organization throughout the territory. However, the movement declined quickly after this, no doubt due largely to the accomplishment of one of its strongest motives for existence in Montana, the securing of a means of transportation for produce. When the railroad crossed the Missouri River at Bismarck to the Mandan side in 1879, the death knell of the Montana Grange was sounded.

The benefits derived from the Grange by the farmers of Dakota and Montana were largely social, as little was accomplished in an economic way. The meetings afforded an opportunity for community gatherings, where problems were discussed and plans of action decided upon. The local chapters worked for better schools, repairing school-houses, and purchasing supplies. They aided the destitute, raising nearly a thousand dollars in Dakota in 1874

[13] *Rocky Mountain Husbandman*, February 28, 1878. The next farmers' organization that made itself felt in the territories of the Northwest was the Farmers' Alliance. It developed to some degree in Dakota but gained little headway in Montana.

during the grasshopper plagues. Coöperative buying on any considerable scale was impossible on the frontier because of the lack of capital. Members were granted concessions at times by certain mercantile establishments and some farm machinery was purchased in this way. There could be no escape from the credit system, since farm machinery was a major consideration for most farmers if agricultural activities were to receive normal emphasis. If they were to be expanded, as many of the pioneer farmers were anxious to do, it had to be on future possibilities, in which case credit was inevitable. With the coming of the grasshoppers in the seventies and the drastic curtailment of income, there could be no alternative to credit transactions if purchases were to be made at all. Even while the Grange was largest and most active in its attack on the "grasping implement companies and dealers," the sales of farm machinery increased in both Dakota and Montana, and at times it was difficult for the manufacturers to supply the demand. At the same time the increase in the number of chattel mortgages and foreclosures indicated the helpless financial condition of the frontier farmers.[14]

The conditions and circumstances under which the frontier farmers of the Northwest were obliged to live and labor worked against the success of the Grange and if interest in the organization had not waned in the eastern portions of the country, it could hardly have been successful in the Northwest since the program of coöperation had little chance of functioning there. The very circumstances and conditions that caused the farmers to join the organization reacted against its reform program in the long run. The biggest opportunity for service in Montana and Dakota was along social and educational lines. The Grange plainly failed to

[14] *Clay County Register*, March 13, 20, April 3, 1874; *Sioux City Weekly Times*, March 7, 14, 21, 1874; letters of C. H. and L. J. McCormick to implement dealers in the Territories of Montana and Dakota, on file in the McCormick Library and Museum, Chicago, Illinois. The files of the territorial newspapers contained large numbers of notices of mortgage and sheriff sales. The *Dakota Republican*, published at Vermillion in Clay County, Dakota, contained numerous such notices.

adjust its program to the locality, and overreached itself in placing too much emphasis upon its business activities.[15]

Although the Granger movement subsided in the Northwest, most of the fundamental causes still remained, and in the eighties, when the time was ripe for another agricultural movement, attempts to revive the organization failed. The Farmers' Alliance was formed to take its place and while it was not particularly active in Montana, it spread rapidly in the settled portions of Dakota, many former members of the Grange joining forces with the new movement with high hopes of success.

The remote beginning of the period of agricultural and economic depression which closed the territorial period in Dakota expressed itself in the organization of the Farmers' Alliance late in 1886. The executive committee of the Alliance met at Huron on July 20, 1887, for a two days' session. Representatives were present from nearly every county in the territory and H. J. Loucks presided. It was decided to incorporate the Alliance with a capital stock of two hundred thousand dollars for the purpose of transacting such business as the interests of the members demanded. Provisions were made for the purchasing of articles at wholesale in large quantities, and for the loaning of money to the members on chattels or real estate at greatly reduced rates of interest. Aberdeen was selected as the location of the home or central office of the organization.

It was finally decided to organize a fire and cyclone insurance department in connection with the hail department already in operation. Several thousand dollars were subscribed to the capital stock of the organization and it was resolved to organize the territory into subordinate alliances. It was shown that through the territorial purchasing department already in operation more than a quarter of a million dollars had been saved to alliance members. Prices on farm machinery had been reduced 25 per cent, and all farmers had profited by this whether they were members or not.

[15] Schell, "Grange and Credit Problem in Dakota Territory," p. 82.

This July meeting was the beginning of the rapid growth of the farmers' movement which was to exert a remarkable influence in agricultural circles of the territory and to make its voice heard in political affairs.[16]

The Dakota Farmers' Alliance began its annual session on December 11, 1888, at Jamestown. President H. J. Loucks took charge of the meeting and there were two hundred delegates in attendance. President Loucks in his annual address took official notice of national problems and spoke in favor of government ownership of railroads, telegraph lines, and coal lands. Various resolutions were adopted concerning the regulation of railroads, one being that railroad companies be required to furnish cars for the shipment of grain within three days, and another requiring railroads to build elevators and warehouses adjacent to their tracks.

According to the Hail and Fire Insurance report, there were ten thousand members insured to the amount of six millions of dollars, saving the members nearly a quarter of a million dollars in premiums. With nearly two hundred private insurance companies doing business in the territory, they had succeeded in doing one-sixth of the entire insurance business. Resolutions were passed recommending that the territorial legislature appropriate ten thousand dollars for institute work, indorsing the agricultural college at Brookings, and recommending that generous provision be made for it by the legislature, and advising united and concerted action of the national Alliance, the Grange, Knights of Labor, and kindred organizations.[17]

The beginning of the crusade against trusts on the part of the American farmer is seen in the efforts of the agricultural population of Dakota. At a mass convention of farmers held at Fargo in May, 1888, to consider the attitude of Congress toward agricul-

[16] *Dakota and Burleigh County Settler*, August 4, 1887; *Huron Tribune*, July 22, 1887; *Yankton Press and Dakotian*, July 28, 1887.

[17] *Brookings County Weekly Press* (Brookings, D. T.), December 13, 1888; *Huron Tribune*, December 10, 1888; *Bismarck Saturday Evening Journal*, December 15, 1888.

tural interests, a vigorous platform was adopted against trusts and against the tariff. An expression of thanks was tendered the territorial Farmers' Alliance for its work in protecting, elevating and defending the interests of the farmer, and stated: "It is the duty of all farmers to unite with and help support the organization known as the Farmers' Alliance." [18] Early in January, 1889, there were 740 local alliances in the Territory of Dakota, two hundred of which had been organized in the past twelve months.[19]

The old Farmers' Alliance of both North and South Dakota held its final joint meeting at Aberdeen during the closing days of November, 1889. Provisions were made for the division of the body into state organizations which would act independently. Several joint resolutions were made, and although maintaining that the organization was not a political party, a joint platform or program of social and economic needs was declared by the alliances of North and South Dakota. Division had no effect upon the work of the organization, as the two state alliances coöperated effectively and did everything within their power in the next few years to promote and advance the cause of the Dakota farmer.[20]

IX

THE AGRICULTURAL FAIR

OF THE SOCIAL institutions that have influenced the American farmer, there is none perhaps that has been as significant as the agricultural fair. Originating in Europe, it was transplanted to America, where it followed the frontier of agricultural settlement as it advanced westward across the continent. It was in its "Golden Age" in the United States while the Northwest was being settled and the establishment of the agricultural fair in that region

---

[18] *Fargo Daily Republican*, May 21, 25, 28, 1888; *Grand Forks Daily Plain Dealer* (Grand Forks, D. T.), May 15, 1888.

[19] *St. Paul Pioneer Press*, January 10, 1889.

[20] *Grant County Review*, November 28, 1889; *Yankton Press and Dakotian*, November 21, 28, 1889.

marked one of the first effective efforts to improve the general condition of the frontier farmer. Its objectives were many, some of the more important being educational, as well as for recreation and amusement.[1]

Crops were exceptionally good in Dakota in 1869 after a series of grasshopper plagues, and many saw in the fair an opportunity to stimulate immigration into the territory. A county agricultural organization called the Yankton Agricultural Society and Bureau of Immigration was formed at the territorial capital. Officers were elected and an executive committee appointed. The object of the society was to hold a county exhibit of farm products, if it was thought feasible, and to disseminate among the people of the eastern states reliable information regarding the agricultural resources of Dakota. A fair was held at Yankton each year of good crops throughout the remainder of the territorial period. Clay County also formed a county agricultural organization and held local fairs. Fairs were held in Bon Homme, Clay and Yankton counties in 1871, and Turner County organized a county agricultural society in 1873.[2]

An association was formed at Yankton in the fall of 1875 for the purpose of holding a territorial fair and to make arrangements for an agricultural exhibit at the Philadelphia Centennial which was to be held the following year.[3] A territorial fair was held at Vermillion in Clay County in the fall of 1878 with Governor W. A. Howard as the main speaker. A Dakota editor said regarding the event, "The fair itself was a creditable exhibition of the agricultural and pastoral resources of the territory at that time, except that the northern Dakota settlements were not represented."

[1] W. C. Neely, *The Agricultural Fair* (New York, 1935), *passim;* Earle D. Ross, "The Evolution of the Agricultural Fair in the Northwest," *Iowa Journal of History and Politics,* XXIV, 445-6; *Cyclopedia of American Agriculture,* IV (New York, 1909), 292.

[2] *Yankton Weekly Dakotian,* August 21, 1869; *Dakota Republican,* September 14, 1871.

[3] The Centennial had been authorized by Congress in 1872 and a commission appointed to take charge, made up of two men from each state and territory.

There was an agricultural exhibit of the Northern Pacific Railroad in 1880. A car was arranged displaying the products of Dakota and was taken through the East and Middle West for purposes of display and to advertise Dakota.[4]

At Yankton there was a territorial fair in the autumn of 1884 and Dakota had an agricultural exhibit at the World's Fair in New Orleans in 1884 and 1885. The Milwaukee Railroad Company prepared a baggage-car of Dakota products and, after exhibiting them in various sections of the United States, took them to New Orleans. There was a territorial fair held at Huron in September, 1885, and permanent grounds were established there at that time. A fair was held there each year during the remainder of the territorial period.

In June, 1885, delegates from the counties of the territory met at Mitchell and organized the Territorial Board of Agriculture. The organization was empowered by law to foster agriculture and to hold territorial fairs or "fat stock shows," at such times and places as the board might determine. It was decided that the board would maintain a permanent office at Huron, provided housing facilities were furnished for it by the city without charge to the association. The president of the board was to receive two hundred dollars per annum, while the secretary was to receive one hundred dollars. Officers were elected and the board really functioned as a body to promote annual fairs.

Detailed and definite information regarding specific county fairs is difficult to obtain, although indications show that they were common by 1880. A Grant County editor in June, 1881, said: "The importance and usefulness of county agricultural fairs has not been overrated. They have done more than any other means to awaken the desire for improvements, to awaken ambition to excel, and to furnish tangible evidence that superior culture will

---

[4] *Dakota Republican,* September 8, October 21, 1878; *Yankton Press and Dakotian, September* 13, 1878; *Watertown Times,* April 12, 1881; *Valley City Times,* December 9, 1880.

produce superior products. From small beginnings these farmers' festivals have extended themselves over a great part of Dakota." In 1883 county fairs were held in Aurora, Lawrence, Beadle, Davidson, Kingsbury, Yankton, Clay, and Minnehaha counties. Almost every county in the southeastern part of the territory had a county agricultural association and held fairs from time to time, depending upon the crops and general economic conditions.[5] There is little evidence of fairs or county agricultural organizations in the northern portion of the territory. This was no doubt due to its being a newer country, with a scattered population, and the fact that emphasis was placed upon large-scale wheat-growing. The bonanza wheat farmer, usually well-to-do, was individualistic.[6]

While agricultural fairs were established in both Montana and Wyoming as soon as agriculture developed in those territories, they were never as numerous nor as active there as in the Territory of Dakota. A fair was established at Helena, the territorial capital of Montana, in 1869 and was held each year through the seventies and eighties. It was called the Eastern Montana Agricultural, Mineral and Mechanical Association.[7] In 1875 the Western Montana Agricultural, Mineral and Mechanical Association was formed at Missoula to take care of that portion of Montana. There was coöperation on the part of the two associations and their fairs were held on different dates. Agricultural exhibits were held in local communities when crops were good in the various agricultural valleys, but they were not permanent organizations and only functioned at intervals. The Grange in its days of activity encouraged exhibits of farm products and often held what the chapters called "annual Grange fairs or Grange agricultural ex-

[5] Fair organizations were reported in 23 counties in Dakota Territory in 1886. "Fair Directory," *American Agriculturalist*, September, 1886.

[6] *Devil's Lake Democrat*, September 14, 1884; *Yankton Press and Dakotian*, August 13, October 2, 1884; *Huron Tribune*, June 17, September 24, 1885; *Grant County Review*, June 23, 1881; "Fair Directory," *American Agriculturalist*, September, 1874, September, 1881, September, 1886.

[7] Rural fairs went by a variety of names: Industrial Fair, Horticulture Show, and Cattle Show were some of the more popular.

TRAVELING EXHIBIT CAR OF THE NORTHERN PACIFIC

Equipped to advertise products of the Northwest to prospective homesteaders in the East. Courtesy of the Northern Pacific Railway.

AN EXHIBIT OF NORTHWEST GRAINS

Used by the railroad during the immigration period. Courtesy of the Northern Pacific Railway.

hibits." Except for these local activities there is no evidence of the regular county fairs that were numerous in Dakota farther east. In 1874 there was only one fair held in the territory, and that was at Helena. In 1886 there were three fairs held in the territory, at Helena, Missoula, and a county fair at Billings.

In Wyoming the situation was about the same. There are records of local exhibits at Cheyenne in the seventies, but it did not assume the name of a territorial fair until the early eighties. In 1886 there were two fairs held in Wyoming, one at Cheyenne and the other at Big Horn City in Johnson County in the northern part of the territory.

The early county and local fairs were usually two-day events and sometimes lasted only a single day, while the territorial fairs ordinarily ran for three to five days, sometimes even remaining open a full week. Some of the counties had permanent grounds and buildings, but most of them did not, holding their exhibits in schools or vacant business-houses. It seemed a rather difficult matter to finance the early local fairs and the outcome was so uncertain at times that no cash premiums were offered. Even then there was often a deficit when the event was over. Admission and concession charges were necessarily low.

The exhibits were often meager and not well classified, and the judging, if one accepts the opinion of the local press, was often unsatisfactory. But in spite of many obstacles the fairs were an encouraging sign and meant much to the people both on the farms and in the prairie towns. They served as gatherings where the frontier farmers met their friends and discussed the current topics of the day. They showed the characteristic western spirit of optimism and enthusiasm. Improvements were gradually made and the educational side came to be stressed much as it was in the later farmers' institutes. Agricultural books and pamphlets were often awarded as prizes. Prizes were offered for essays on different phases of farming. There were speakers on agricultural subjects and evening sessions were held with lectures, discussions, and talks. The annual address held a leading place, a local politician or influential man usually giving it at the county exhibit, a territorial leader or well-known outside man speaking at the territorial fair.

It is very noticeable that the amusement features of the fairs were strictly subordinated to the instructional and educational, although some sort of entertainment was usually provided. There were plowing matches, some horse-races, and various athletic contests or feats of strength. At the Clay County fair at Vermillion in 1880 there was a woman's riding contest. There were not many side-shows or gambling devices at first and they were never especially apparent at many of the local and county fairs, most of the amusements being clean and wholesome. There are several cases on record in Dakota where fakers and men with gambling games were asked to leave town.[8] As time went on and the country became more thickly settled and better developed, and money became more plentiful, the larger and more important county fairs and those that were territorial in scope went through a process of evolution, developing certain characteristics that were very undesirable and deviated somewhat from the purposes and ideals of the earlier associations.

Horse-racing, side-shows, and gambling devices were introduced, which tended to thwart the early purpose and objectives of the rural fair. It developed into something very different from what it was intended to be in the beginning,

when [using the words of a writer in an agricultural journal] the treasure of the field and orchard, garden and hot house, sty and stable were temptingly displayed under white tents and rough board stalls. When the very name of fair called to mind long loaded tables of luscious fruits, purple clusters of grapes, plums blushing but rough with powdered blum, crimson apples and great bags stuffed with premium wheat and oats, sleek porkers, and patient sheep, stalls of neighing steeds and smooth rubbed cattle, and, last but not least, great

[8] Ross, "Evolution of the Agricultural Fair in the Northwest," pp. 445-80.

crowds of good natured men, women and children who came happily
from their farms and growing crops to the enjoyment of the festal day.
They looked over the fine exhibits, renewed old ties of friendship and
listened to the lectures of professional as well as practical farmers.[9]

Objections to the change of emphasis were printed in the local
press and in various magazines. An article appeared in a national
agricultural journal in which the writer stated that to his mind
one of the greatest blemishes on state, territorial, and county fairs
were the various side-shows and montebank venders that were
allowed within the grounds. Supposing at first that "such violations of propriety" were due to the weakness and good nature of
the local manager, he was shocked to learn that the regular practice of many of the fair associations was to make a direct appeal
to the proprietors of side-shows and exhibitions of natural curiosities, making every inducement to sell them space on the fair-
grounds. "It is bad enough," said the writer, "to have fat women,
snake charmers and double headed calves outside the grounds and
we think that an association that cannot hold successful fairs without catering to such things had better close up!" [10]

The steps in the evolution or changes that took place were more
or less typical in all areas, and proceeded something on this order.
The fair, conducted as it was at first, placing its emphasis on the
farmer's welfare, hardly paid for itself, and there was usually a
deficit. The first change was to make a broader appeal for the
purpose of taking in more money. It may have started by having
a riding contest for the ladies, or as one editor aptly phrased it,
a "gals' horse-race," followed with a balloon ascension. Then
came side-show concessions with gambling devices, that appealed
more or less to the "livery-stable and grog-house gang" who favored bigger and more numerous attractions. The balloon ascension or whatever new feature was introduced brought out the
crowd and considerable money was taken in at the gate. While

[9] *American Agriculturalist*, September, 1860.
[10] *Ibid.*, October, 1876, p. 394.

many farmers were unable to see any connection between a balloon ascension and farming, they admitted they enjoyed the entertainment and the managers of the fair were contented. They gradually emerged from debt and began to look for possible ways of expansion.

While some of the early fairs tended to emphasize horse-racing, most of them at first did not. In one place racing started by constructing a small track around which the cattle and horses could be led in order to be checked over. This was later enlarged so that the judges could see better. Then with a track available, a few trotting races were introduced. The next year there was a race or two each day, but the competition was restricted to horses from within the county, no outsiders being invited or permitted to enter their horses. The purses for the races, however, grew larger and larger and the fair was in danger of getting in the red again. Then side-shows were added until there was a regular midway with every type of ballyhoo entertainment and gambling game imaginable, and the grounds were filled with spielers and barkers. There was a Ferris wheel, and a merry-go-round, with its tin-pan music; a dog-faced boy, bearded ladies, dwarfs, fat ladies, tall men, perhaps a sword swallower, and an india-rubber man. There were wrestlers and boxers who took on the local "white hope" or "tough guy" of the community and usually "took him," including liberal bets of his friends' money. There was the seductive lure of the oriental dancer or the hula-hula girl, where admission was sold "for men only," as well as the black-face minstrel show with its "plantation singers." There were venders of various types of commodities, including perhaps a salesman of clothing, who carried garments of "marvelous wearing qualities combined with prices equally marvelous in their cheapness." They all paid a liberal license fee to the fair association and reaped a rich harvest from the local community.

With the additional money taken in from concessions, the purses for the horse-races were increased and many outside horses were brought in to compete for them. A regular race-track was operated for a full week and became the outstanding feature of the fair, with all the attendant evils of drunkenness, gambling, and fighting. The race purses were raised as high as possible in order to get better horses in the contests. Even the additional money from the concessions was not enough and many of the fairs closed with a deficit. While most of the fairs in the area of the Northwest assumed the characteristics indicated, the problem of horse-racing developed to a greater degree in Montana than in the other regions. The fairs at both Missoula and Helena were territorial in scope and were held in an area where horse-racing was of considerable importance aside from the agricultural fairs. Everything possible was done for the gambling fraternity, the privilege of handling the racing bets being sold yearly for several hundred dollars. As the race-tracks, side-shows and gambling became more prominent each year, the cattle, sheep, poultry, grain, fruit, vegetables, needlework, canned goods, and other exhibits were crowded into the background and the educational features for the benefit of the farmer were practically eliminated.

The *Rocky Mountain Husbandman,* early in October, 1876, in describing the annual fair of the Western Montana Fair Association at Missoula, said:

The matter of speedy horse races occupied an undue prominence both in the program and on the grounds for a purely agricultural and mechanical association. But it is no worse in this respect than others of its kind. If racing were left out, the fair would be self supporting. There was little at the fair that was of real interest to the farmer.

The following week the same editor was even more critical when he said:

Managers and superintendents of fairs, this article is meant for you. We believe in fairs, town, county, state and national. If conducted as they should be, they are not only good enterprises, but they help farming. The blight that is destroying the otherwise good effect that might result from fairs is the loose management of them. The viper that destroys the fair is the clap-trap resorted to by the management to call the people out under guise of patents, pedlars, prize fights, gambling and horse racing. Large crowds gather each year around these many questionable characters.[11]

In the fall of 1881 another Montana editor wrote critically of the fair at Helena:

At the territorial fair the chief attraction was horse racing, and aside from that the fair amounted to very little. The farmer seems to have been overlooked. The poultry exhibit consisted of a few sickly chickens and other farm exhibits were of the same type. With ten thousand dollars for horse racing, there is little left for the granger. The cattle and sheep industry of Montana are probably ahead of all others and never have been properly looked after by the fair. In the art hall there were some creditable displays of pictures but the chief attraction was horse racing. A Denver party has several horses entered and won several purses. There seems to have been some serious irregularities to which the judge finally "tumbled" in the course of time and the sharpers were ruled out of a few of the races.[12]

X

TOWNS AND SETTLEMENTS

THE AVERAGE western town or agricultural settlement during the early years was a forlorn-looking place with crude and shabby buildings. The houses and business establishments, many of which contained only one room, were often constructed of green cottonwood lumber that shrank and crawled as it dried out, leaving great cracks in the roof and walls. As the towns grew and settled down to permanent existences with stable populations, business blocks were constructed and the homes of the inhabitants were improved. Professional men opened offices, and they and their families took an active part in the cultural life of the town. As there developed a group of citizens with some means, social affairs increased. The

[11] *Rocky Mountain Husbandman*, October 5, 12, 1876.
[12] *River Press*, September 21, October 5, 1881.

territorial capitals of Cheyenne, Helena, and Yankton became social centers of some importance, especially when the legislatures were in session.

Traveling circuses visited the larger settlements, often accompanied by pickpockets and "con men" with their skin games of every possible type. If the devices for obtaining money were too brazen, the disgruntled spectators at times turned upon the operators. If the attack was serious, the cry "Hey, Rube!" invariably brought the circus employees to the rescue and a free-for-all fight ensued, resulting in many heads being broken, the local press often announcing the casualties the next day.

In the summer of 1867, Bartholomew's "Great Western Circus" was making a tour of the western Montana towns.[1] The *Cheyenne Daily Leader* on June 13, 1871, carried the following announcement: "The Olympiad Circus under the management of Madame Lake has come and gone and was well attended and duly criticized by our people. In truth it may be set down as a very fair show. There are better ones traveling but in such features as tumbling and contortionist acts the work of its performers is seldom surpassed. The circus goes from here to Denver on a tour of the western towns." Early in August, 1872, Conkling Brothers' Circus showed at Yankton, in the Territory of Dakota, and was severely criticized by a Sioux City editor who said, "It is most objectionable because it is most unscrupulous and demoralizing. Yankee Robinson, the well-known showman, has allowed his name to be connected with it for one-third of the receipts. The show was scraped up from odds and ends of recently defunct circuses."[2]

Some of the better circuses spent large amounts for local advertising and in addition to a liberal distribution of highly colored hand-bills, considerable newspaper space was devoted to describing the star performers, whose work was usually announced as "stupendous, gigantic, and colossal." In the summer of 1874 the

[1] *Montana Post*, July 6, 1867.
[2] *Sioux City Weekly Times*, August 3, 1872.

James Robinson Company ran a full-page advertisement in the local press that it would hold a "moral show" at Yankton, Dakota, that would include, in addition to the regular tumblers, contortionists, and trapeze performers, "a gigantic menagerie, museum, and the greatest exhibition of animals and curiosities on earth."

The frontier settlers were very fond of exhibitions of real or supposed marvels of all types. They flocked to see "grand menageries of wild animals and rare birds," educated elephants, trained lions and seals, as well as presentations of "curious and extraordinary exhibitions." In one town a rich harvest was reaped by the owner of an educated pig, that, according to an advertisement, could "spell and count with almost human ability." Admission for adults was twenty-five cents, with children under twelve at half price. In another town an exhibition of wax figures, including a "sleeping beauty," as well as historical and romantic personages, was shown with prices of admission at fifty cents for adults and twenty-five cents for children. Agents for liniments and magic oils held "medicine shows," at which small bottles of various types of remedies, guaranteed to cure almost any ailment, were sold to the gullible public at fifty cents to a dollar.

The early towns in the plains area were usually liberally supplied with saloons, dance-halls, gambling-houses and variety halls for public amusement and recreation. A minister arriving in Billings, Montana, early in 1883 counted fourteen saloons on the main business street of the town, and told of his trip over the Northern Pacific Railroad: "In the coach in which I rode, there were passengers representing every type of western life: the cowboy with knife and revolver, the man whose every sentence contained an oath, the man who drank and the gambler whose game captured many a tenderfoot. The wicked woman was there, indulging in smoking, drinking and swearing. Surely her house is the way to hell. A viler atmosphere I never breathed and seeing so much sin in every form was sickening." [3] There were those,

[3] *Billings Herald,* February 24, 1884.

however, who vouched for the morals of the various towns. A book agent reported the sale of $157 worth of Bibles and religious publications in Bismarck in the Territory of Dakota in half a day, which was cited by the local press as evidence of the high moral status of the town. The editor of the *River Press* at Fort Benton in Montana made fun of the claim and was quite sure that the morals of Bismarck were no better than those of the towns and settlements of Montana, and probably not as good.

After the first boom period, many of the towns and settlements lost population, which tended to make them more stable, as those who remained and the new settlers who came in were usually looking for permanent homes. This change in the make-up of a town's inhabitants was well brought out by N. A. Baker, editor of the *Cheyenne Leader,* in the spring of 1871. "The growth of the territory and of Cheyenne during the past two years has been less rapid than before that time, but of a much more healthy character. While the rougher and less desirable class of people, comprising the gamblers, roughs and rascals of the community, have floated on to more lucrative fields, their places have been filled with a more stable population." [4] The stable settlers brought with them the mores of their former homes, and with the coming of economic stability were able to put into practice some of their social and cultural ideas and ambitions.

Each town was proud of its community life and did not hesitate to boast about it. Schools, churches, and lodges were established and often became centers of social activity. There were card parties with prizes, dances, lectures, home-talent plays and entertainments, church socials and dinners. Much emphasis was placed on such holidays as Thanksgiving, Christmas, New Year's, Washington's and Lincoln's Birthday, and the Fourth of July. There were parties and dances, and turkey and chicken dinners at the hotels and in the churches, with elaborate menus. There were private musicales, mixed entertainments, teas and dinner dances, with

[4] *Cheyenne Daily Leader,* May 15, 1871.

flowers and receiving lines; there were oyster suppers, church fairs and bazaars; while spelling, singing, and dancing schools were popular during the winter months. There was both ice and roller skating in many of the towns, where skates were rented and prizes of gold- or silver-plated skates were sometimes given in contests. On one occasion in Dakota the ministers of the town were invited to attend a "skating frolic," probably for the purpose of quieting their opposition by showing them how harmless and pleasant such diversion was.

There were debates during the long winter evenings at the Lyceum and Library Association halls on a wide variety of subjects, including current topics and such themes as: "Which has been treated the better by the United States Government, the Indian or the Negro?"; "Who was the greater General, Julius Cæsar or Napoleon?"; or, "Who was the greater, Columbus or George Washington?" At a local Grange meeting in western Montana, a debate was arranged on the subject, "Resolved, that grasshoppers have been a positive good to civilization." So much local interest was aroused that the debate and discussion were continued at the next regular meeting. Forms and types of government were discussed from time to time, and the virtues of our Constitution were often emphasized.

Early in 1883 the town of Fargo in the Territory of Dakota was called upon to defend the alleged interest and enthusiasm on the part of its citizens for things cultural, which it did in true frontier fashion. It had been announced in the local press that a Miss Maria L. Sanford, Professor of Elocution and Rhetoric at the state university, was to deliver a lecture on "Rome," using illustrated slides. The attendance was very small, which brought from the editor of the *Fargo Republican* the next day the following comment: "It is to be regretted that this intellectual town, which is noted for having more literary talent than any other in the valley, should be so wholly devoted to the buying and selling of real estate as to have no time to give to cultural things. Since notices regarding the lecture were only circulated the day before, we propose to charge the small attendance to the lack of notice rather than to the indifference of our people." [5]

XI

THE THEATER ON THE GREAT PLAINS

As THE VARIOUS types of frontier have moved across the continent, one of the cultural institutions that has kept close to the outer fringe of civilization has been the theater. As the frontier of the cattleman and of the pioneer farmer advanced westward in the sixties, seventies, and eighties, and population poured into the rough railroad, river, and plains settlements despite the rigors of the new surroundings, the cultural life was often vigorous and varied, especially in the larger settlements where it was strengthened by the presence of professional men. The frontier population on the plains was keenly interested in the theater. They supported local dramatic organizations, patronized variety houses, welcomed visiting troupes of all sorts, and later established opera-houses. Every prairie town of any size had its lyceum or library association where mixed programs, essays, lectures, debates, and regular plays were given, often being repeated in the near-by towns.[6] Such entertainments were well advertised and well attended.

Although the southeastern portion of the Territory of Dakota was settled in the sixties, its early population was small and largely rural, and aside from local lyceum programs, there is little evidence of the theater until the arrival of the railroad. Even then, aside from a few of the boom centers, it was never as extensive as in some of the frontier communities farther west. The Dakota Southern Railroad was constructed from Sioux City to Yankton in 1872 and in December of that year a Professor Nickle, "the world-renowned illusionist," was making a tour of southeastern

[5] *Fargo Daily Republican*, February 22, 1883.
[6] *Dakota Republican*, Anniversary edition, April 9, 1931.

Dakota.[2] During the same month the Yankton Ladies' Library
Association gave an entertainment that was described by the local
editor as follows:

Last Tuesday evening the town folks turned out an audience of 250 to
witness the best performance of home talent with which we have so
far been favored. A few of our citizens who have banded together
as a dramatic association put on two plays: *The Spirit of 1776*, and
Cool As a Cucumber, both of which were well executed. The duets on
the piano forte by Mrs. Etter and Miss Jacobs were so well played that
they demanded breathless attention.[3]

Early in January, 1873, the Peck Family of Bell Ringers were
entertaining the people of Yankton and Vermillion.[4]

The Black Hills gold rush in 1876 developed Yankton on the
Missouri River as one of the important points of approach to the
Hills, and a large floating population led to the establishment of
several variety halls and a regular theater presenting legitimate
drama. On October 25, 1877, it was announced by the local press
that Nelson Armstrong, manager of the California Minstrels,
after incurring much expense, had succeeded in organizing an
excellent troupe, for which he had secured the professional services of Messers Beach and Gould of Chicago, the celebrated acro-
batic song and clog dance artists. The troupe was advertised to
offer its first entertainment on Saturday night at Stone's Hall.

In the summer of 1872 the Northern Pacific Railroad crossed
the Red River of the North and moved on westward, reaching
Bismarck on the Missouri River early in June, 1873, the road
being opened to traffic about two weeks later. The company failed
that autumn, but despite the general depression of 1873 to 1878,
Fargo, Grand Forks, and Bismarck became theatrical centers of
some importance. There are records of home-talent entertainments,
variety house bills, and legitimate plays presented at Fargo in

[2] *Sioux City Weekly Times*, December 17, 1872.
[3] *Yankton Press and Dakotian*, November 27, December 11, 1873.
[4] *Sioux City Weekly Times*, January 4, 1873.

the late seventies. In the spring of 1879, which was a typical year, in the month of March there was an advertisement printed in the local paper of a "Literary and Musicale Entertainment" with cards of admission priced at one dollar. On April 5th it was announced by Benjamin Reynolds that he would start a series of variety and combination entertainments at the Music Hall, commonly known as Schey's Opera House, and on April 26th it was advertised that Miss Henrietta Monroe, "brilliant and accomplished dramatic reader, humorist, and impersonator, will pay us another visit en route to Winnepeg." Grand Forks, along with its variety and dance-hall productions, presented also a rather wide variety of legitimate plays. Stock-companies appeared and other theatrical companies paused on tour to present many popular plays. But when a German company gave *The Farmer's Daughter*, the effort was resented, and the *Plain Dealer* made it clear that it would be a long time before another play of similar title got on the boards in Grand Forks.[5]

Bismarck grew rapidly and with the rush of miners to the Black Hills, became the metropolis of northern Dakota. In July, 1873, the *Bismarck Tribune* reported seven concert saloons and dance-halls in operation there, and late in November Excelsior Hall was giving regular variety entertainments to large crowds. Among the more important theaters operating in Bismarck during the late seventies were the Coliseum Variety Hall and Museum, Wallach's Hall, Excelsior Hall, Daly's Theater, and Raymond's Playhouse. The Bismarck Opera House, established in 1878 under the management of A. J. Whiting, became, according to the local press, "second to none west of St. Paul."

On October 9, 1878, "little Etolia, the bewitching little song and dance artist," was at the Bismarck Opera House, and was "filling the audience with delight," while the rest of the troupe was praised for its acting. In December it was announced that Miss Ada Lawrence had made a big hit with the audience with

[5] *Grand Forks Plain Dealer*, files for the early eighties.

the beautiful ballad, "The Man on the Flying Trapeze." On December 30th Miss Mollie Forrest, a contortionist, had consented to extend her engagement at the Opera House, and a walking match was being staged at Raymond's Hall. The Curiosity Pavillion of the Bismarck Coliseum and Museum on Broadway contained, according to an advertisement in the *Bismarck Tribune*, "the largest collection of human oddities ever presented on exhibition, including Chang, the Chinese giant."

The same stock companies and variety troupes played the boards at Bismarck that played the towns along the upper Missouri and the mining camps of the Black Hills and Montana, local newspapers announcing the appearance of the Sawtelle Dramatic Company, of Helena, the Hasenwinkle Company of players, the Katie Putnam Troupe, and others. Late in December, 1878, the Sawtelle Dramatic Company, under the leadership of A. L. Sawtelle, "an actor of considerable merit," played *Rip Van Winkle*, *Handy Andy*, and *Rosedale* to full houses. A few months later the Hasenwinkle Dramatic Troupe on its way to Montana for a tour, pending the departure of the boat for Fort Benton, played *Lena the Madcap* to an appreciative audience.[6]

As towns developed in the agricultural valleys of Montana in the seventies, there is evidence of much theatrical activity. Home-talent plays were staged at Bozeman as early as 1872, while at Deer Lodge it was advertised on August 13, 1875, that Carl Plummer, a fine elocutionist, would give a program of readings at the court-house on Thursday and Friday nights. He was scheduled to appear also in the frontier settlements of Blackfoot, Pioneer, New Chicago, Phillipsburg, and Missoula. The same newspaper carried an advertisement of Betchel's Variety, that, according to the proprietor, "was always crowded, had excellent whiskey and cigars, and an abundance of pretty girls."[7] On June 1, 1876, the Montana Minstrel and Variety Troupe had

---

[6] Files of the *Bismarck Tribune*, 1873-80.
[7] *Avant Courier*, January 20, 1872; *New Northwest*, August 13, 1875.

made the people of Diamond City merry with its "spicy entertainment" for four days, and was moving on. In Miles City in
1877 the Grey Mule Saloon and Theater and the Cosmopolitan
Playhouse were popular places of amusement,[8] and Fort Benton
at the head of navigation on the upper Missouri River was becoming a theatrical center of some importance. The early issues of
the *River Press* carried many announcements of the arrival and
departure of various theatrical troupes who came as far as Fort
Benton by river steamer, often playing a few days before going
on to the mining camps farther west.

A Montana editor writing in 1878 gave a brief description of
one of the variety houses of the combination type in Fort Benton:

On the corner of Casey and Front Streets is a large building seventy
feet long and forty feet wide. The place is full to overflowing. Its
bar keepers are busy and the clink of glasses is set to the music of a
fine string band. On the side of the room opposite the bar are tables
upon which are found almost every type of gambling device. On the
stage in the rear of the building mixed entertainment of songs, dances
and dialogues by professionals and amateurs adds variety, after which
comes the general dance.[9]

Some of the dramatic organizations playing at Fort Benton in the
late seventies and early eighties were the Chapman Stock Company, the Plunkett Dramatic Company, the Katie Putnam Dramatic Troupe, the Leo Theatrical Combination, as well as
numerous variety and specialty organizations.[10]

The *River Press* for June 1, 1881, told about the Hasenwinkle
Dramatic Company, on its way to tour Montana, giving two excellent performances at the school-house. The opening play was
Led Astray and the characters were reported well sustained
throughout. "There are no 'sticks' in the company. On Tuesday
evening *Hazel Kirke*, the greatest of favorites will be played,"

[8] *New Northwest*, June 1, 1876; *Miles City Daily Star*, Golden Jubilee number, May 24, 1934.
[9] *Avant Courier*, January 10, 1878.
[10] Files of the *River Press*, 1881-83.

announced the paper. "To-night they will play *Joshua Whitcomb*. As it is not often that a troupe of such merit comes to the territory, our citizens should take the advantage offered to hear them. They play with an entire change of program every evening of the week."

On August 3, 1881, the Plunkett Constellation was announced to play on Friday and Saturday nights. The play for Friday night was *Black Diamond*. The same issue of the local paper told of the Katie Putnam theatrical troupe leaving for the States on the steamer *Josephine* after a "flat, stale and unprofitable tour of Montana." It was reported as unlikely that they would return again, "for which consolation," said the editor, "Allah be praised!" [11]

Of the many towns and settlements on the plains of the Northwest interested in the theater in the sixties and seventies, Cheyenne, in the Territory of Wyoming, with its early railroad connections, was the most outstanding. The first issue of the *Cheyenne Leader*, in September, 1867, announced the arrival of a theatrical troupe from Julesburg, that, according to the editor, "was making preparations to offer the people of Cheyenne first class entertainment in the histrionic art." A good-sized theater was constructed and on December 3rd James Stark, an actor, was beginning a two days' engagement at Melodian Hall, located on Seventeenth Street, described as "the finest variety hall of the West." Beevais Hall was mentioned a few days later and in February, 1868, the opening of the Model Concert Hall was announced where, according to an advertisement, "every species of innocent amusement may be found in the way of dances, songs, dialogue, impersonations and what is best of all, pretty waiting girls, plenty of lager beer and cigars." In April of the same year the Theater Comique had its grand opening and the two concert-halls, the Oasis and the Union, were opened for business.

[11] *River Press*, June 1, August 31, 1881.

A variety hall of the combination type that was very popular in the early history of Cheyenne was the famous Gold Room, opened on Sixteenth Street in October, 1867, by J. W. Allen, who operated it until 1876. A favorite place of recreation for the soldiers from Fort Russell, it acquired a rather bad name, and as one contemporary very aptly observed, "If Cheyenne lived up to its early reputation and name, 'Hell on Wheels,' the Gold Room was very near the hub." One of its early stars was Joe Wood, whose lugubrious rendition of "Over the Hills to the Poor House" nightly brought tears to the eyes of the patrons in the sentimental stages of inebriation. Allen, the manager, brought his entertainment to a close each night with the gradual unveiling of a female figure, a large crowd collecting to view the ceremony.[12] Complaints in the local press had little effect upon the patronage of the establishment.

During this early activity there arrived in Cheyenne sometime in October, 1867, a man by the name of James McDaniels, who was to become the central figure in that town's theatrical history for the next twelve years. He established a saloon and museum on Eddy Street and soon attracted attention by the uniqueness of his place, newspaper advertising, and excellent variety programs. He described his museum and well-stocked bar in glowing terms. Admission to the museum was free to those who patronized the bar. He alluded to himself as "Professor" McDaniels, and later styled himself "the Barnum of the West." If the Melodian and other variety halls advertised at all, it was usually two or three lines, while McDaniels carried dozens of lines that were flowery and, at times, more or less humorous. On November 9, 1867, part of his ten-dollar advertisement in the *Cheyenne Leader* was as follows: "It is Professor McDaniels' Museum that eclipses every other place of amusement in town. A few days ago Mac made 212 tom and jerries in forty-five minutes. Beat that if you can."

[12] *Cheyenne Daily Leader*, September 19, 28, October 3, 5, 12, 19, 21, December 3, 7, 1867, February 28, April 5, 12, 20, October 5, 1868; *Cheyenne State Leader*, November 24, 1932.

Ten days later he carried fifty-five lines in prose and verse at a cost of fourteen dollars.

Early in January, 1868, McDaniels moved into his new building, consisting of a theater, 60 by 20 feet, with two large additions, one housing "two elegant bars" and the other the museum. He enlarged his museum stock, adding stuffed animals, a few live ones, and Charlotte Temple, the English giantess. In January, 1869, a Cheyenne editor, after telling of McDaniels' return from the East with additional museum stock, said, "The museum is now filled with every description of curiosity, even to a life statue of the Fiji mermaid. No other town in the West can boast such an exhibition." A lecture-room and proscenium were added in March.

McDaniels' Museum Theater and the Theater Comique were the two important amusement centers of Cheyenne in 1869, legitimate productions being interspersed with variety shows at both places. The former theater held the center of attention in 1870 and continued to supply many of the theatrical attractions of the town until the summer of 1872. McDaniels extended and renovated his building in 1871, the central portion being converted into a spacious saloon, which, with its high ceilings, fine paintings, and a superb bar with the most elaborate fixtures possible, was described as being "the finest institution of its kind in the territory." The saloon, museum, and theater were all connected, each, however, having a separate entrance.[13]

During the summer of 1872 a local corporation constructed a new theater, designated at first as the Cheyenne Opera House, but later renamed Recreation Hall. It was evidently sponsored and erected by a group opposed to the free and easy atmosphere of McDaniels' place, and for the next three years was his keenest competitor. Recreation Hall was used for legitimate offerings, lectures, concerts, and home-talent productions, but was not popular after the spring of 1875.[14]

[13] *Cheyenne Daily Leader*, October 17, December 19, 1871.
[14] *Ibid.*, August 27, 1872, July 3, 18, 1875.

VAUDEVILLE ON THE FRONTIER

A variety theater in Cheyenne, Wyoming. *Frank Leslie's Illustrated Newspaper*, 1877.

After the severe fire of 1875, McDaniels began the construction of a new building, moving into the old Planter's House until it was finished. The new establishment, 132 by 48 feet, contained a dozen elegantly fitted boxes, which, together with a dress-circle and a parquet, provided seating facilities for eight hundred persons. When the Gold Room, sometimes called the Bella Union Saloon and Variety Hall, operated by Allen, closed in 1876, McDaniels purchased and refinished it, opening it to the public as the New Dramatic Theater. He operated both places and in June, 1877, began the construction of a three-storied brick building called the McDaniels Block. It was completed in April, 1878, and still stands. Suffering financial reverses, McDaniels sold his property early in 1879 and went to Leadville, Colorado, then a boom town, to engage in the theatrical business.[15]

Although the variety bills of the Cheyenne concert-halls were largely of the common type, some of the presentations were somewhat unusual and attracted more than ordinary attention. Early in January, 1868, a "walkist fad" had swept the town, and concert-halls were holding what would now be called "walking marathons." On January 13th it was advertised that "Jack the Chicken" proposed to walk sixty-five hours without eating, drinking, or sleeping. In February, 1869, a traveling minstrel troupe appeared in Cheyenne for the first time, when the California Minstrels opened for a series of performances at the Orleans Club. During the summer the high points were the California Glass Blowers and the midget, General Tom Thumb, and his company. In June, 1870, the famous P. T. Barnum of New York City lectured at McDaniels' Hall on the subject, "How to be Happy, Healthy and Rich." The Royal Japanese Athletic Company attracted a large audience and the appearance of a tight-rope walker with one leg took the town by storm. In August, 1879, W. F. Cody, popularly known as Buffalo Bill, made his début in Cheyenne, and a few

[15] *Cheyenne Daily Leader*, October 21, 1875, May 18, July 5, August 30, 1876, August 4, 1877, April 1, 1879; *Cheyenne Daily Sun*, May 7, 1881.

weeks later the offerings of the Rentz Female Minstrel Troupe brought from the press the following comment, "The pretty faces of the fair performers were only exceeded by their fine forms, which were untrammeled by superfluous clothing. The living art pictures attracted admiration and received three hearty encores."

While the variety house was the most popular type of theater in Cheyenne in the early period, there was a surprising amount of interest and activity in legitimate drama. The first legitimate production took place on December 6, 1867, at the Melodian, consisting of the play "The Mail Boy" and an afterpiece "The Mischievous Monkey." On February 10, 1868, the C. W. Irwin Stock Company took over the Melodian, and assisted by Madame Schiller and Mr. and Mrs. Waldron, and later coöperating with the J. W. Carter Dramatic Company, presented a wide variety of plays that were well attended. On January 7, 1869, the J. S. Langrishe Dramatic Company arrived and in about a month presented twenty-four plays with numerous afterpieces. Among their repertoire were such plays as *Hazel Kirke, East Lynne, The Lady of Lyons, Camille, The Two Orphans, Richelieu, La Tour de Nesle,* and *Rip Van Winkle.* The actors were assisted by Mr. and Mrs. Waldron and Edward Orpen, a local ballad-singer.

In the spring of 1869 there was much theatrical activity, and there existed a keen rivalry between McDaniels' Museum and the Comique in the presentation of legitimate plays. Both houses advertised a nightly change of program with the best talent available. On March 31, 1869, McDaniels announced that he had engaged the J. W. Carter Dramatic Company to play for him indefinitely, the price of admission being seventy-five cents and one dollar. At this time the Carrie Chapman Company, with Lon McCarty, played for six weeks at the Comique, after which, losing out in competition with McDaniels in legitimate drama, it returned to the presentation of variety bills. From the spring of 1869 until the summer of 1876, legitimate theatrical productions were not especially numerous. About the only legitimate players to appear from 1870 to 1872 were the Langrishes, who played several weeks each year. In the spring of 1872 there was a revival of interest in the drama. The Nathan Dramatic Troupe appeared two weeks in February and on March 9th the Denver Dramatic Company, managed by Phelps and Allen, closed a week's repertoire with the play *The Hidden Hand,* and was held over an extra week because of popular demand. Legitimate theatricals were quiet until the summer of 1876 when the local dramatic scene began to pick up. With the opening of McDaniels' New Dramatic Theater in 1876, with the Langrishe Dramatic Company on the boards, the presentation of legitimate plays increased, reaching its high point in 1878, during which year more theatrical activity was recorded than at any twelve-month period since 1869.[16]

The McDaniels playhouse, under the management of John Chase, was unsuccessful, and variety hall productions gradually declined in importance until the Cheyenne Opera House was formally opened May 25, 1882, and the frontier period of Cheyenne's theatrical history came to a close. In the fifteen years 1867 to 1882, sometimes called the variety-house period, six different theaters offered legitimate productions and seventeen variety halls were mentioned in the local press. Since many of the variety theaters did not advertise in the local newspapers, it is probable that the figure for variety establishments is low. More than three hundred professional productions were staged during the period, and of that number, repertoire companies were responsible for one-half of them. An average of twenty professional productions a year for fifteen years, averaging almost two per month, is an excellent record for a frontier town like Cheyenne, whose population was less than five thousand inhabitants.[17]

When one considers the large number of variety entertainments,

[16] *Cheyenne State Leader,* November 24, 1932.
[17] William Campton Bell, *A History of the Theatrical Activities of Cheyenne, Wyoming* (Master's Thesis, School of Speech, Northwestern University: Evanston, Ill., 1935).

lectures, and home-talent programs, library and lyceum association productions, as well as the legitimate stage offerings, in the towns and settlements on the plains of the Northwest, it is fair to conclude that the area supported the theater in more than a half-hearted manner. While the wide variety of legitimate plays offered included every possible type of dramatic production, the repertoire presented in the plains area very closely approximated that in the gold camps. There seems to have been very little shift in popular tastes, as most of the dramatic companies repeated their offerings again and again in the various towns as the different companies made their circuits from year to year.

In the early period, when the settlements contained a floating and mixed population made up largely of men, the matter of keeping order in the various theaters with their bars in connection was no easy task. The variety houses were the scenes of frequent fights, sometimes between the patrons themselves and at times between the unruly patrons and the management, who ordinarily insisted upon reasonable order. The *Bismarck Tribune* for December 23, 1878, presented a serious complaint that there were far too many roughs attending the theaters of that place and that they were a source of much disorder. Suggestions were made as to how they might be handled. That the theatrical scene was none too wholesome in Cheyenne is evidenced by a paragraph appearing in one of the newspapers in December, 1867: "Under the new management the Melodian Theater appears to be doing a fair business. Ladies may now attend this place of amusement with impunity. The manager is determined to preserve strict order and will not allow dissipated characters admission to the hall." [18] In the spring of 1869 the Theater Comique in Cheyenne advertised that Tuesday and Friday evenings would be designated as "ladies' nights," at which times there would be no drinking or smoking allowed in the theater.[19] Early in 1875 Allen ran an advertisement

[18] *Cheyenne Daily Leader*, December 7, 1867.
[19] *Cheyenne Weekly Leader*, April 18, 1869.

in the local press regarding his well-known Gold Room: "This
theater has been remodeled and refitted and no pains spared to
make it the most comfortable and attractive variety hall west of
Chicago and nothing will be done or said that the most fastidious
cannot witness or hear." [20] The *Cheyenne Daily Sun* in the spring
of 1879 suggested that the theaters in Cheyenne would be better
patronized if "the intoxicated soldiers, Negroes, dregs, and
wantons were separated from the best families." [21]

The variety hall period, with its rough and ready characteristics,
its rapidly changing and often inadequate playhouses, and its lack
of outstanding actors and actresses, came to a close in the Northwest in the early eighties. It was followed by the "opera-house"
period, during which time nearly every town of any size built an
opera-house which its local manager rented to traveling companies
playing one- or two-night stands. This change of emphasis practically eliminated the actor-manager, with his stock-company, who
at times had his own theater. The era in which the opera-house
dominated the theatrical scene, while not as active and colorful
as the frontier period, was marked by a dignity and stability unknown in the earlier years.

XII

LIFE OF THE FRONTIER FARMER

THE LIFE of the pioneer farmer was a hard one, as it was no light
task to make a home and develop a farm from the pathless prairie,
remote from neighbors, and without schools, churches, and many
of the comforts and advantages enjoyed by those living in the
more compact and established settlements. If well done, it was
almost a martyr's life, and it is difficult to estimate properly the
hardships, trials, and discomforts of such an experience without
having passed through them. But in spite of much real suffering,

[20] *Cheyenne Daily Leader*, February 15, 1875.
[21] *Cheyenne Daily Sun*, March 21, 1879.

the average frontier farmer of the upper Missouri country was energetic and courageous, and faced the future with hope and optimism.

The early agricultural settler either took up a claim or bought a quarter-section or more of land, which he usually chose with a good deal of care, often visiting several parts of the region in which he planned to locate before making his decision. If he was a homesteader, and most frontier farmers were, he lived upon his claim five years to perfect his title and obtain his patent, making the required improvements.[1] Gradually the claim shanties of other new-comers dotted the horizon, making his location less isolated. In the early period of settlement it sometimes happened that four families would settle together, each taking a quarter-section as a homestead, and building their temporary dwellings upon adjacent corners so as to be near together.

After locating a desirable piece of land, the first task of the pioneer farmer was the construction of a place in which to live. Often he lived in his covered wagon until his house was finished. The kind of domicile to be built depended on the amount of money available and the materials and labor at hand. If timber happened to be within hauling distance, a log house was constructed, the size of which in many cases depended upon the length of the logs obtainable rather than upon the size of the settler's family. The logs were notched at the ends and at times hewn on the sides so they would fit together more closely. The floor was either the bare ground, or was made of split logs or rough lumber. The roof varied, also, as the pole rafters were covered with slough

[1] There was a fee of $14.00 required on making application, and an additional $4.00 when final proof was made. A shack or shanty must be constructed and ten acres placed under cultivation. It was possible for the homesteader to commute his original entry to preëmption and purchase the land for $1.25 per acre. The Timber Culture Act of the seventies enabled a man to file on a tree claim of 160 acres in addition to his homestead, if he would agree to plant 40 acres of trees and keep them cultivated for eight years. Cottonwood cuttings were ordinarily planted, but it is doubtful if many of those taking tree claims lived up to all of the requirements of the law.

grass, prairie hay, clapboards, or shingles, depending on which was the most convenient.

Where there was no timber and lumber was not to be had, the dugout was often constructed, part of the house being beneath the ground and part of it above. The soil was removed to a depth of a few feet and strips or blocks of prairie sod were used to form the walls. It was common to strip the sod with a prairie plow, the long strips being cut into short lengths for convenience in handling. The walls of the dugout were often from two to three feet thick, and while heavy rains might cause the house to settle, the clay soil kept the inside dry. The sod house was constructed around a frame made of logs or poles, the roof being pitched or with one side slightly lower than the other so the water would drain off. This type of house was better suited to warmer climates as the walls held moisture, making it rather undesirable in the winter.

The more prosperous settlers, where a mill was available, constructed their homes from milled lumber, and even where they were unable to build a substantial dwelling, hauled a few loads of rough lumber from the nearest railroad station or sawmill and constructed a frail little shack which often consisted of only a single room, or, at best, two or three small rooms. The house in many cases looked as if the prairie wind would blow it away, and had it not been for the invention of tar-paper, the flimsy walls with cracks between the boards would not have kept out the wind and snow. Weather-boards were sometimes placed over the walls, which were sheathed with the tarred paper. The inside walls were often whitewashed or covered with newspapers. The barn was usually a nondescript affair with sod walls and a straw roof. Lumber was much too dear to be used for barnyard fences, and there was no enclosure about the house, although a rail or barbed wire fence might have been constructed around the barnyard.[2]

[2] Barbed wire was introduced in the upper Missouri area in the late seventies, and was used extensively in the eighties, as it became cheaper in price. Webb, *The Great Plains*, pp. 309-10.

When the early period had passed and some of the difficulties connected with the establishment of a prairie farm had been overcome, many of the homes were improved. The farm of a "well-fixed" prairie settler often had a house of several rooms, a well-built barn, besides rail stables roofed with fodder, a full-grown orchard, and good fences. Visitors sat down in what was called the "front room," which often contained the spare bed, the newest splint-bottomed chairs and the bureau, in case the family was fortunate enough to have one. There were yellow and scarlet pictures on the walls and on the center table were a few books, including the family Bible.

Just as the type of cabin depended upon the materials at hand, the furnishings often showed the same influence. While many of the settlers brought stoves and, at times, beds or bedding, they made benches, chairs, and tables from logs, and bureaus and wardrobes from boxes that had been brought along packed with the belongings of the family. Some of the settlers had beds, while others slept on the floor or on a "prairie bunk," which was made of poles fastened at one end to the wall and with the other end resting upon a sapling laid across two crotched sticks. Mattresses were almost unknown and feather beds were considered a luxury that few could afford. A tick filled with corn husks was usually laid on the pole bed, which must have been uncomfortable, as the poles worked through the corn shucks. A traveler in the Gallatin Valley in the seventies was directed to a settler's cabin where he was told he would find good accommodations for the night. He slept on a corn-husk tick thrown over a pole bed, and awakened in the morning more weary than when he had retired the previous evening.

Two travelers spent the night in southeastern Dakota with a frontier farmer who lived in a rude log cabin sixteen by eighteen feet in size, plastered with mud. The one room served as a kitchen, parlor, pantry, and for all other purposes. The furniture was rude. It included one rickety chair with a back, with trunks, stools, and boxes serving for additional chairs. The supper consisted of a hearty meal of pork, potatoes, bread and black molasses. There were two beds in the cabin. The settler and his wife occupied one, while the two visitors used the other. The children slept on the floor.

In the Turtle Mountain area in the northeastern part of Dakota, a traveling minister of the Lutheran faith, visiting the settlements and isolated farms, gave a description of a settler's hut near the Antelope Valley settlement, fifteen miles east of Mouse River, in July, 1886:

I got lost and stumbled upon a Norwegian family living in an isolated spot and they seemed to be in great need of a visit from a minister or some one else who had the heart to give them a word of comfort and encouragement. They had recently arrived and had just built a little sod house in which they intended to live their first year, at least. The floor, roof, and walls were of sod. They had no furniture, not even a bench or stump to sit on, and a traveling chest with a flat lid served as a dining table. It was hard to get wood to cook with and food was scarce. The man had an ox team but no plow and it was difficult to find water. He broke down and wept and said he was sorry he had left his happy home in Norway.[3]

The first task of the homesteader in preparation for farming was the breaking of the prairie sod. Since the virgin soil was tough, and it was impossible for an ordinary plow to pass through the long massive roots, the work necessitated a special breaking plow.[4] Since every farmer did not own a plow, it was possible for one who did to sell his services to others for several months out of a year. The price charged per acre for breaking the prairie sod

[3] "A Missionary Journey on the Dakota Prairies in 1886," ed. John H. Blegen, *Minnesota History*, I, 16-29.

[4] The prairie plow was constructed from heavy timbers, the length varying from seven to twelve feet. Because of the weight the forward part of the plow was usually carried on a pair of wheels. The mold-boards of some of the first plows of this type was bound with iron, but later the entire mold-board was made of iron. The share was made from the best grade of steel to enable it to cut through the tough roots of the prairie grass. Oxen were generally used in breaking. They were slower than horses but more steady.

varied from season to season, and in sections of the country. If the breaker employed boarded himself, or, in the words of the pioneer, "found himself," the price per acre was from $2.50 to $4.50. With a twenty-four-inch plow and three yoke of oxen, it was possible to plow about two acres of sod per day. The furrow of the prairie plow ranged from twenty to thirty-six inches.

The prairie land was difficult to work the first year after it was plowed, and was often left idle for a year so the roots of the prairie grass could decay. Sod corn was often a favorite first crop and at times was planted by making a hole in the ground with a spade or ax and dropping the kernel into it. Yields of sod corn varied, and those of ten to twenty bushels to the acre were not uncommon. Wheat was the crop generally planted as soon as the land would produce it, although oats, barley, flax, potatoes, and other vegetables were also planted. As a rule, until markets were available, only a small portion of the land was tilled and little fencing was done. Wild game and fruits contributed liberally to the larder of the early settler. Many pioneer farmers trapped through the winter months, the money secured from the sale of furs often appreciably increasing their income. On the prairie and plains fuel was often a problem, and buffalo chips, twisted hay or straw, corn cobs, brush, and even ear-corn were burned. During the cold months, it often took the full time of one man to supply fuel for heating purposes.

A letter from one of the early settlers to his family, written at Vermillion, Dakota Territory, December 15, 1861, describes some of the conditions of pioneer life:

I will now let you know the whole truth as to our circumstances. It was so late when we got here that I could do little trapping as the river froze over. We have had all we could do to make a living, but have managed to get some provisions for our mules and horses. There is no money here, so we cannot get any for our work. Our claims are all safe. The boys' boots are nearly worn out and no prospects of any new ones. No person gets any credit here at the stores. They have regular hoedowns here every week or two and nearly everybody attends. I will go to Sioux City tomorrow or some day soon, partly for ourselves and others, to get flour. They may want corn meal. The corn cracker has refused to grind corn. We will have pretty hard times here for one or two years until we get to raising enough to live on. Claims are worth little and will be as long as there are any claims vacant. Many have left Nebraska to come over here either for speculation or to make themselves homes. The capital will be located here or at Yankton, but I think it will be here. This will be a big town whether the capital is here or not.[5]

The social life of Dakota at this time was very much like that in any new country. There were parties, corn huskings, quiltings, and various other social events that brought the people together in the informal manner so characteristic of frontier life. These people seemed to have realized that they were engaged in a common struggle and there existed a sympathy and coöperation that tended to lighten the burdens of the individual.[6]

Women were not nearly as numerous as men in the early years of the agricultural frontier, although the disparity in numbers between the sexes tended to disappear as settlement increased. A Montana editor, commenting upon the scarcity of servant girls in the territory in the early eighties, said, "Montana is a sort of paradise for servants of every class. The supply is not equal to the demand and wages are high. This is true in every part of the territory. In Fort Benton girls receive thirty to forty dollars a month and cannot be had at that figure. But girls will be plentiful in a year or two. They will come with the rest." [7] A Missoula editor in the spring of 1883 offered as striking proof that the Mussel-shell Valley of Montana was being rapidly settled, the fact that at a party held there a few days before, sixty women had been present, some of which had come a distance of fifty miles.[8]

---

[5] "A Pioneer's Letter Home," South Dakota Historical *Collections*, VI, 201-2.
[6] *Sioux Falls Democrat*, November 28, December 15, 1859, January 28, 1860.
[7] *River Press*, November 9, 1881.
[8] *Weekly Missoulian*, March 9, 1883.

There were some single or unattached women on the agricultural frontier, but as a rule they did not remain in that condition for any length of time. The demand for women of marriageable age was great and a young woman, or one even fairly young, was almost sure to have plenty of beaux. Young men who had taken claims went back East during the winter months for their sweethearts, and many who had lacked such contacts in their former communities, went East in the fall with the alleged purpose of obtaining a wife. There were, however, exceptions to the rule, as a letter from an unmarried woman at Lake Preston in the Territory of Dakota, published in a Montana newspaper in the summer of 1882, indicated. "I mean business," the communication read. "If there is a young man in this country that has as much sand in him as a pound of plug tobacco, I want to hear from him. I have a tree claim, a homestead, am a good cook, am not afraid of work, and am willing to do my part. If any of you young men with a like amount of land, a decent face and carcass, wants a good wife, I can fill the bill." [9]

The activities and the place of women on the frontier farms have never been recorded as fully nor in the same light as those of men. The success of the frontier farmer and his family depended to a great extent upon the woman of the household. She looked after the family, prepared the food and clothing, and often took her place by the side of her husband as he labored in the fields. The poverty and hardships of life on the western farm, with its monotony and extreme loneliness, bore even more heavily upon the woman than upon the husband. There is no doubt a good deal of truth in the often-repeated story of the young man who, as he was passing through a frontier area, stopped at a homesteader's shack for a drink. Wishing to be pleasant and friendly, he commented to the housewife on the beauty of the country. She answered, "Yes, young man, it is indeed a beautiful country

[9] *Miles City Weekly Press*, July 27, 1882.

for men and horses, but a hard one for women and oxen." A traveler in western Montana was informed by a farm woman that most of her contacts were with men, and that the thing she missed more than anything else in the West was association with other women.

The frontier farm was largely self-sustaining and the preparation of food and clothing took much of the pioneer mother's time. She often made soap for family use by boiling old meat scraps, putrid lard, water, and lye made from wood ashes, in a large iron kettle. One frontier woman in northeastern Dakota was visited by an itinerant minister who, upon making inquiries regarding her children was told that they were always sent to the barn or some other place where they would be out of sight on the approach of a stranger, as they usually did not have enough clothing to make their bodies presentable. The world of the women of the western territories was confined to the wide prairies, or to their rude homes, which, with dirt floors and crude windows and doors, were extremely cold in winter and more than disagreeable in the dry, hot, windy weather of summer, when mosquitoes, flies, and insects poured in through the unscreened openings.

While the needs and desires of the early settlers in the upper Missouri country were satisfied largely by the country stores and business places in the scattered settlements, there is evidence of peddlers or traveling merchants in southeastern Dakota. They went from place to place, visiting isolated farmers and agricultural settlements, traveling by horse and wagon or on foot, mending pots and pans, repairing clocks and carrying with them such items as bolts of calico and gingham cloth, spools of thread, papers of pins and needles, as well as buttons, colored ribbons, silk handkerchiefs, scissors, jews'-harps and mouth-organs for the children, and other odds and ends. They served as a mean of communication, carrying news from one neighborhood to another, and gossiped with the housewives. While, according to their own accounts, they invariably sold their goods at a "ruinous sacrifice," and lost money in every community, they usually returned the next season to be "ruined" again. Contemporary accounts show that the regular profit of these itinerant merchants amounted to at least 200 per cent. But as the population increased and the wants of the settlers became more numerous, and incapable of being satisfied by the transient and periodical supplies of the peddler, rural stores developed at cross-roads and at other strategic points, along with blacksmith shops. The stores carried "large stocks of Yankee goods," and sometimes advertised in the county or local press. While there continued to be tree peddlers and lightning-rod agents, as well as sellers of Bibles and other religious books, the day of the traveling dispenser of general notions was over.

One of the central points of rendezvous for the settlers was the rural or village store. It was a gathering-point, especially on Saturday, and was the headquarters for general information, as well as constituting the meeting-place for the village doctor, blacksmith, minister, and school-teacher. Here the frontier women came to exchange some of the products of the farm for staples, to purchase supplies, and to discuss the news as they waited for their mail. Their buying usually consumed little time, for manufactured goods were expensive, as was tea, coffee, and sugar. Sugar was so high that many of the settlers made their own sorghum at a local molasses mill.

While the women looked over the display of cloth and garments, and wished for better crops in order to have more money for the things they wanted, the men smoked their corn-cob pipes and talked politics. The trips to town did not come often, but were looked forward to with a good deal of pleasure and satisfaction. On those occasions the farmers and their wives gained at least a glimpse of a life broader and more comfortable than that of their isolated farms.

There were doctors in the villages who often traveled on horseback to visit their patients, with their medicine packed in medicine kits. Distances were so long that settlers rarely called for a doctor

THE COUNTRY EMPORIUM

Dry-goods department of the Viking Store, Fessenden, North Dakota. Courtesy of the Minnesota State Historical Society.

except in cases of extreme illness. The settlers were largely dependent upon home remedies and upon those who were experienced in dealing with familiar diseases. Every community had its midwives. Certain diseases, such as diphtheria, smallpox, pneumonia, and typhoid fever, took their deadly toll in the scattered homes every year. In addition to home remedies, such as the prevalent use of sassafras as a spring tonic, and the bag of asafetida hung around the neck for various children's diseases, much dependence was placed in patent medicines. There were traveling medicine agents with liniments, magnetic oils, and general remedies that were guaranteed to cure anything from colds and croup to cancer and rheumatism. Advertisements in the local newspapers of patent medicines were particularly common. They included Dr. Eastman's Elixir of Health, Ayer's Cherry Pectoral, Hostetter's Celebrated Stomach Bitters, Dr. Sweet's Infallible Liniment, Ayer's Sarsaparilla, Paine's Celery Compound, Tull's Pills for Malaria, and Perry's Pain Killer.

One early Dakota newspaper carried lengthy and enthusiastic advertisements of two patent medicines manufactured by J. L. Curtis, the Original Mamaluke Liniment, and his Syrup of Sassafras. The liniment was advertised as a "sovereign remedy for man and beast," which was confidently recommended as an infallible cure for a list of twenty-eight ailments or diseases, including burns, cramps, sore throat, frosted feet, rheumatism, erysipelas, lumbago, bites of insects or reptiles, salt rheum, dysentery, cholera, and cholera morbus. The Syrup of Sassafras was listed as a remedy for consumption, bronchitis, croup or hives, colds, asthma, hoarseness, difficulty of breathing, purifying the blood, whooping-cough, and many other diseases. This medicine was "certain to give more relief in a short time than all the sarsaparillas and other compounds the stomach could bear. It costs only 25 cents per bottle," ran the advertisement, "and every family should be supplied with it at all times."[10]

[10] *Sioux Falls Democrat*, August 26, 1859.

Until common schools were established by law in the agricultural districts, subscription or tuition schools were often operated. The ordinary school term was from four to five months. It was often difficult to get trained teachers and discipline was of vital importance. In fact, the reputation and ability of the prospective pedagogue as a disciplinarian was often more important than the ability to dispense knowledge. Men teachers were in demand and many of them were driven out by the older boys before the term was over. The course of study was limited to the common branches in most cases, and often depended upon the books available. The teacher usually boarded around, the frontier housewife making an effort to have various "extras" the week the master was in her home.

The school-houses were rough buildings, often built of logs chinked with dirt, and with a thatched roof or one of roughly milled lumber. They were poorly lighted and heated and the benches and desks were crudely made. Often the school-house served as a church for the various denominations, who took turns with their services as the traveling ministers arrived. Sunday afternoon camp-meetings were held at times and were well attended. As a rule, the congregations on the agricultural frontier were receptive. Debates, spelling matches, singing-schools, dances and play parties were held in the school-house. These were high spots in the lives of most neighborhoods.

Pioneering on the agricultural frontier had its tragedies, as well as its triumphs, and courage, strength and endurance did not always bring the desired success. Many succumbed to the numerous obstacles and did not live to see their area develop into a thriving and prosperous farming community. The early frontier farmer in the upper Missouri country took many risks and often a gambler's chance. He hoped that he might win, yet he knew that to lose might be his fate, as it had been that of many a better man than he. But win or lose, the chance was worth the risk and, in most cases, he took it willingly.

Nowhere else in our literature has there been so well portrayed the human element in the winning of the agricultural West as in that splendid epic of an age that called for heroic figures, O. E. Rolväag's *Giants in the Earth.* Beret, who could not reconcile herself to the vast lonely acres of the plains, is the epitome of all the alien hearts who either returned home after a brief trial or ended their days in a nostalgic remembering of an older life they could not forget. Not all such were immigrants from Europe, although, it is true, many of them were. From the rocky hills of New England, where small worlds closed in about each individual community, from little Ohio or Missouri or Illinois towns, from southern farms where the woods shut out the stretch of the continent, they came. But here, on the great plains, nothing intervened between the settler and the far horizon.

In the minds of many, the conquest of the fertile fields of the Northwest was a fairy-tale, more real than any they had read or listened to in their childhood. It was so with Per Hansa. But as every fairy-tale must have its dark side, its wicked giant or its ogre, so had this one—Nature. In seasons when the fortunes of thousands depended on her kindness, she seemed deliberately to show her displeasure. Grasshoppers descended in ravenous hordes or dry winds devastated the promising acres. There was no escape from Nature, not even for Per Hansa, at the end.

Fairy-tale or epic, the conquest of the Northwest called first of all for strength, and weakness of any kind, even if it were sanctioned by society, as was Beret's love of the home and mores she had left, could not be tolerated. The true story of western settlement is best told when the broken lives it exacted are recorded, when romanticism and realism run hand-in-hand through the narrative. The human cost of the years from the entrance of white settlers into the great stretches that became first the Territories, and then the States of North and South Dakota, Montana, and Wyoming, and the occupation of the last untilled acres in that region, has yet to be reckoned. In terms of both mental and physical suffering, it was undoubtedly great. Many Berets brooded in their isolated cabins, closing their doors and windows at night against the limitless dark, and watching anxiously by day for passing strangers, in order to reassure themselves that this lonely life was not some punishment inflicted upon them for forgotten sin. Many Per Hansas, on their way to perform kindnesses for other settlers, or to carry out some necessary business of their own, succumbed to the false warmth of the great blizzards and were found when spring had come again.

But even in death Per Hansa faced the West. That was truly symbolic of a nation that, from earliest colonial times, faced the West and relentlessly, in spite of death and fear and the terrible homesickness of women, advanced year by year to the Pacific Coast, and then turned back again into the unknown reaches of the Northwest, here to meet a fresh tide from the East. When towns marked the great plains, and fields lay upturned to the sun, when rails ran wherever man wished to go between East and West, the frontier period was over. The golden days of mining were past, the last buffalo herd had thundered across the level lands, the cattle no longer roamed the unfenced range, and the long strife between cattle and sheep rancher was almost forgotten.

BIBLIOGRAPHY

The materials listed are those that were of most value to the writer and are not intended as a complete bibliography for the area under consideration.

SOURCES

I

FEDERAL DOCUMENTS

Annual Reports of the Bureau of Animal Husbandry, 1880-1890.

Annual Reports of the Commissioner of the General Land Office, 1868-1890.

Annual Reports of the Commissioner of Indian Affairs, 1864-1890.

Annual Reports of the Secretary of Agriculture, 1870-1900.

Annual Reports of the Secretary of the Interior, 1869-1898.

Annual Report of the Secretary of the Treasury, 1836.

Annual Reports of the Secretary of War, 1859-1888.

BROWNE, J. ROSS, *Mineral Resources of the United States* (Washington, D. C., 1868).

CARMAN, E. A.; HEATH, H. A. and MINTO, JOHN, *Special Report on the Sheep Industry* (United States Department of Agriculture: Washington, D. C., 1892).

Census Reports, Eighth to Fourteenth, 1860-1920.

Congressional Globe, 1862-1873.

Congressional Records, 1873-1896.

DONALDSON, THOMAS, *The Public Domain* (Washington, D. C., 1883).

House Executive Documents, 1860-1890. (The specific documents used are cited in the text.)

KAPPLER, CHARLES J., *Indian Affairs and Treaties*, 3 vols. (Washington, D. C., 1904-1913).

Official Records of the War of the Rebellion (Washington, D. C., 1880-1900).

Report of the War Department to the Secretary of the Interior (Washington, D. C., 1858).

RICHARDSON, JAMES D., *Messages and Papers of the President*, 10 vols. (Washington, D. C., 1899).

Senate Executive Documents, 1860-1900. (The specific documents used are cited in the text.)

Stewart, A. S., *Mines and Quarries*, Special Report of the Census Office (Washington, D. C., 1902).

United States Public Statutes at Large, 1860-1890.

Yearbooks of the Department of Agriculture, 1870-1890.

II

STATE AND TERRITORIAL DOCUMENTS

Annual Report of the Commissioner of Agriculture (Helena, Montana Territory, 1870-1888).

Annual Report of the Minnesota Commissioner of Statistics (St. Paul, Minnesota, 1859).

Annual Reports of the Commissioner of Immigration of Dakota Territory, 1870-1889.

Annual Reports of the Minnesota Railroad Commission, 1871-1877.

Annual Reports of the Secretary of the Montana State Board of Livestock Commissioners, Veterinary Surgeon, and Recorder of Marks and Brands, 1890-1900.

Annual Reports of the Territorial Governors of Dakota, Montana and Wyoming to the Secretary of the Interior, 1862-1890.

Annual Reports of the Territorial and State Auditors: Colorado, 1874-1889; Dakota, 1878-1889; Montana, 1866-1888; Wyoming, 1869-1896.

Compiled Statutes of Montana, 1887.

Compiled Statutes of Wyoming, 1887.

House and Council Journals of the Territorial Legislature of Minnesota, 1853-1856.

House and Senate Journals of the Territorial Legislatures of Dakota, Montana, and Wyoming, 1862-1888.

Messages of the Territorial Governors of Dakota, Montana, and Wyoming, 1862-1888.

Report of the Board of Railroad Commissioners of the Territory of Dakota (Fargo, Dakota Territory, 1886).

Session Laws of Minnesota, 1856-1860.

Session Laws of the Territories of Dakota, Montana, and Wyoming, 1862-1888.

Wyoming Board of Immigration Bulletin, 1874.

III

CONTEMPORARY BOOKS, MANUSCRIPTS, AND PAMPHLETS

Allen, J. A., *American Bison, Living and Extinct* (Cambridge, Massachusetts, 1876).

Allen, Lewis F., *American Cattle, Their History, Breeding and Management* (New York, 1881).

Anaconda Standard Almanac (Anaconda, Montana, 1894).

ANDREAS, A. T., *Historical Atlas of Dakota* (Chicago, 1884).

ANDREWS, C. C., *Minnesota and Dacotah* (St. Paul, Minnesota, 1856).

ANONYMOUS, *A Lady's Ranche Life in Montana* (London, 1887).

ANONYMOUS, "The Diary of a Member of the Big Horn Expedition of 1870," Montana State Historical Society, Helena, Montana.

Appleton's Annual Cyclopedia and Register of Events (New York, 1876-1890).

ARMSTRONG, M. K., *History and Resources of Dakota, Montana and Idaho* (Yankton, Dakota, 1866).

———, *Centennial Address on the Territory of Dakota* (Philadelphia, 1876).

BAILLIE-GROHMAN, WILLIAM A., *Campfires in the Rockies* (New York, 1884).

BALDWIN, N., "Account Book of an Early Helena Merchant," MS, Montana State Historical Society, Helena, Montana.

BATCHELDER, G. A., *A Sketch of the History and Resources of Dakota Territory* (Yankton, Dakota, 1870).

BEADLE, J. H., *The Undeveloped West; or Five Years in the Territories* (Philadelphia, 1873).

BENEDICK, GILBERT, "Diary of Life in the Gold Camps of Montana," MS, State Historical Library, Helena, Montana.

BOGART, W. H., *Daniel Boone and the Hunters of Kentucky* (Boston, 1874).

BOND, J. WESLEY, *Minnesota and Its Resources* (St. Paul, Minnesota, 1853).

BOWLES, SAMUEL, *Across the Continent* (Springfield, Massachusetts, 1865).

———, *Our New West* (Hartford, Connecticut, 1869).

Brand Books, Wyoming Stock Growers Association, 1881-1886.

BRENAN, JOHN R., "Conditions and Resources of Southern Dakota" (Sioux City, Iowa, 1872).

BRISBIN, JAMES, *The Beef Bonanza, or How to Get Rich on the Plains* (Philadelphia, 1881).

BURTON, RICHARD F. (ed.), *The Prairie Traveler—A Handbook for Overland Expeditions, By Randolph B. Marcy, Captain, U. S. Army* (London, 1863).

CAMPBELL, J. F., *Six Months in the New Gold Diggings* (Helena, Montana, n.d.).

CATLIN, GEORGE, *The North American Indian* (London, 1876).

Climate, Soil and Resources of the Yellowstone Valley (St. Paul, Minnesota, 1882).

CODY, WILLIAM F., *The Life of Buffalo Bill by Himself* (Hartford, Connecticut, 1879).

COUES, ELLIOTT (ed.), *Manuscript Journals of Alexander Henry and David Thompson*, 2 vols. (New York, 1897).

—— (ed.), *Forty Years a Fur Trader on the Upper Missouri; the Personal Narrative of Charles Larpenteur, 1833-1872*, 2 vols. (New York, 1898).

COUTANT, C. G., "Notes of an Unfinished History of Wyoming," MS, State Historical Library, Helena, Montana.

CRAWFORD, LEWIS F., Personal notes and manuscript material on Dakota Territory, gathered in part through interviews with old settlers and cattlemen, 1925-1928.

CROSS, FRED J., *The Freelands of Dakota* (Yankton, Dakota, 1876).

CURLEY, E. A., *The True History of the Black Hills* (Chicago, 1876).

Deadwood Board of Trade, "The Black Hills of Dakota" (Deadwood, Dakota, 1881).

——, Annual Reports, 1878-1881.

DICKSON, ARTHUR JEROME (ed.), *Covered Wagon Days, A Journey Across the Plains in the Sixties and Pioneer Days in the Northwest*, from the private journals of Albert Jerome Dickson (Cleveland, Ohio, 1929).

DODGE, R. I., *The Black Hills* (New York, 1876).

——, *Our Wild Indians* (Hartford, Conn., 1882).

——, *The Plains of the Great West* (1877).

DUNBAR, SEYMOUR and PHILLIPS, PAUL C. (eds.), *The Journals and Letters of John Owen* (New York, 1927).

EDGAR, HENRY, "Diary," MS, State Historical Society, Helena, Montana.

FISKE, CAPTAIN JAMES L., "The Overland Journey of 1864." MS and photostat copy, Minnesota State Historical Society Library, St. Paul, Minnesota.

——, "Fourth Expedition from St. Cloud, Minnesota, to the Gold Fields of Montana," pamphlet, Minnesota Historical Society Library (St. Paul, Minnesota, 1866).

FLETCHER, R. S., "The Eastern Montana Cattle Range Industry," MS in office of Everett E. Edwards, editor, *Agricultural History*, U. S. Dept. of Agriculture, Washington, D. C.

FOSTER, JAMES S., *Outline of History of the Territory of Dakota and Emigrants' Guide to the Free Lands of the Northwest* (Yankton, Dakota, 1870).

FRANKLIN, GEORGE E., "The Work of the Rainmakers in the Arid Regions," *Proceedings*, Twelfth National Irrigation Congress (Galveston, Texas, 1905).

"Free Homestead Association of Central New York" (Syracuse, N. Y., 1863).

FRÉMONT, JOHN CHARLES. *Memoirs of My Life* (Chicago, 1887), Vol. I.

GREELEY, HORACE, *An Overland Journey from New York to San Francisco in the Summer of 1859* (New York, 1860).

HAGGERTY, F. H., *A Statistical, Historical and Political Abstract of Dakota Territory* (Aberdeen, Dakota, 1889).

HALL, JAMES, *The Romance of Western History* (Cincinnati, Ohio, 1857).

"History and Progress of Central Dakota" (Chicago, 1882).

"History of Southeastern Dakota" (Sioux City, Iowa, 1881).

HUIDEKOPER, A. C., Manuscript on Ranching, office of State Historian, Bismarck, N. D., 1928.

Laramie County Stock Growers' Association: Minute Books (Cheyenne, Wyoming).

LATHAM, HENRY, *Trans-Missouri Stock Raising; the Pasture Lands of North America* (Omaha, Nebraska, 1871).

Latter Day Saints' Emigrants' Guide from Council Bluffs to the Valley of the Great Salt Lake (Salt Lake City, Utah, 1868).

LEE, C. H., *Long Ago in the Red River Valley* (St. Paul, Minnesota, 1880).

List of Members, By-Laws and Reports of the Wyoming Stock Growers' Association (Cheyenne, Wyoming, 1887).

MARCY, R. B., *Thirty Years of Army Life on the Border* (New York, 1866).

MARTIN, EDWARD W., *History of the Grange Movement* (Chicago, 1874).

McCLURE, A. K., *Three Thousand Miles Through the Rockies* (Philadelphia, 1869).

McCLURE, D. H., *Resources of Dakota* (Aberdeen, Dakota, 1887).

McCOY, JOSEPH G., *Historic Sketches of the Cattle Trade of the West and the Southwest* (Kansas City, 1874).

MELBOURNE, FRANKLIN, Catalog and correspondence regarding the matter of rain-making, State Department of History, Cheyenne, Wyoming.

MELINE, JOHN F., *Two Thousand Miles on Horseback* (New York, 1868).

Miners' and Travelers' Guide to Oregon, Washington, Montana, Wyoming and Colorado Via the Missouri and Columbia Rivers (New York, 1865).

Minute Book of the Wyoming Stock Growers' Association, 1881-1886.

Montana Stock Growers' Association: Minute Book of Meetings, 1885-1889. Montana State Historical Society, Helena, Montana.

MORLEY, J. H., "Diary of Life and Events in the Early Gold Camps of Montana," MS, State Historical Society, Helena, Montana.

MORRIS, ROBERT C., *Internal Commerce of the United States* (Bureau of Statistics: Washington, D. C., 1889).

"New York Colony in Dakota Territory in 1864" (Syracuse, New York, 1867).

NIMMO, JOSEPH, *The Range and Ranch Cattle Business of the United States* (Washington, D. C., 1885).

Pamphlet by Jay Cooke and Company, December 25, 1873.

PATTEN, JAMES I., *Buffalo Hunting with the Shoshone Indians in the Big Horn Basin*, Wyoming State Historical Society, Cheyenne, Wyoming.

Polk, R. L., *Gazetteer for Minnesota and Dakota* (Detroit, Michigan, 1881).

Powell, J. W., "Report on the Lands of the Arid Region of the United States" (Washington, D. C., 1879).

Proceedings, Wyoming Stock Growers' Association (Cheyenne, Wyoming, 1915).

Register and Account Book of the California Hotel, Montana State Historical Society Library, Helena, Montana.

"Report of the Black Hills Live Stock Association, 1882-1884." Manuscript used in the office of Lewis F. Crawford, Bismarck, North Dakota, spring of 1928.

Report of the Deadwood Board of Trade (Deadwood, Dakota, 1878).

Report of the Helena Board of Trade (Helena, Montana, 1887).

Richardson, Albert D., *Beyond the Mississippi* (Hartford, Connecticut, 1869).

Richthofen, W. B. von, *Ranching on the Plains* (New York, 1885).

Riter, Mrs. L. D. Woodruff, "Biographical Sketch of John Dwight Woodruff," MS, Wyoming State Historical Society, Cheyenne, Wyoming.

Ross, Alexander, *The Red River Settlement* (London, 1856).

Shepherd, Major William, *Prairie Experiences in Handling Cattle and Sheep* (New York, 1885).

Sheridan, P. H., *Record of Engagements with Hostile Indians Within the Military Division of Missouri, 1868-1872* (Chicago, 1882).

Shinn, Charles H., *Mining Camps; A Study in American Frontier Government* (New York, 1885).

"Sibley Correspondence 1849-1854," MS, Minnesota Historical Library, St. Paul, Minnesota, section for 1851-1852.

Strahorn, Robert E., *The Handbook of Wyoming and Guide to the Black Hills and the Big Horn Basin* (Cheyenne, Wyoming, 1877).

———, *Idaho Territory* (Boise, Idaho, 1881).

———, *Resources of Montana* (Helena, Montana, 1879).

Stuart, Granville, *Montana As It Is* (New York, 1865).

Taylor, Franklin, scrapbooks in personal possession, Vermillion, South Dakota.

Thwaites, Reuben Gold (ed.), *Original Journals of the Lewis and Clark Expedition, 1804-1806*, 8 vols. (New York, 1904-1905).

——— (ed.), "Alexander Ross; Adventures of the First Settlers," *Early Western Travels* (New York, 1897), VII.

——— (ed.), "Bradbury's Travels in the Interior of America, 1809-1811," *Early Western Travels* (Cleveland, 1904), V.

——— (ed.), "Maximilian, Prince of Wied's Travels in the Interior of North America, 1833," *Early Western Travels* (Cleveland, 1915), XXII.

Topping, E. S., *Chronicles of the Yellowstone* (St. Paul, Minnesota, 1883).

TRIGGS, J. H., *History of Cheyenne and Northern Wyoming* (Omaha, Nebraska, 1876).

VILLARD, HENRY, *The Past and Present of the Pike's Peak Gold Rush*, ed. Leroy R. Hafen (reprint by the Princeton University Press, 1932).

WARNER, F. W., *Montana Territory and Business Directory* (Helena, Montana, 1879).

WEBB, W. E., *Buffalo Land* (Philadelphia, 1876).

WEBSTER, N. W., *"Journal,"* MS, State Historical Society, Helena, Montana.

WHITE, JOHN, *Sketches from America* (London, 1870).

WILLIAMS, HENRY T., *The Pacific Tourist, a Complete Traveler's Guide to the Union and Central Pacific Railroads* (New York, 1876).

Wyoming State Board of Live Stock Commissioners: Minute Book, 1889-1906, Cheyenne, Wyoming.

IV

NEWSPAPERS AND PERIODICALS

Agricultural Gazette (London, England), January 29, 1877.

American Agriculturalist, 1860-1880.

Avant Courier (Bozeman, Montana), 1873-1885.

Benton Record (Fort Benton, Montana), 1875-1880.

Big Horn County Rustler (Basin, Wyoming), 1908-1911.

Billings Daily Gazette (Billings, Montana), 1895-1905.

Billings Herald (Billings, Montana), 1880-1884.

Billings Weekly Gazette (Billings, Montana), 1877-1900.

Bismarck Daily Tribune (Bismarck, Dakota), 1873-1886.

Bismarck Saturday Evening Journal (Bismarck, Dakota), 1885-1886.

Bismarck Weekly Tribune (Bismarck, Dakota), 1878-1889.

Black Hills Daily Champion (Deadwood, Dakota), 1877-1878.

Black Hills Daily Times (Deadwood, Dakota), 1878-1880.

Black Hills Herald (Custer City, Dakota), 1877.

Black Hills Journal (Rapid City, Dakota), 1878-1881.

Black Hills Miner (Crook City, Dakota), 1877.

Black Hills Pioneer (Deadwood, Dakota), 1876-1879.

Black Hills Telegraph (Lead City, Dakota), 1877.

Black Hills Telegraphic Herald (Deadwood, Dakota), 1878.

Black Hills Tribune (Crook City, Dakota), 1876-1877.

Black Hills Weekly Champion (Deadwood, Dakota), 1877.

Black Hills Weekly Pioneer (Deadwood, Dakota), 1880-1886; Special Edition, June 8, 1876 (photostat); New Year's edition, 1882.

Black Hills Weekly Times (Deadwood, Dakota), 1877-1879.

Blunt Advocate (Haynes County, Dakota), 1883-1885.

Boise News (Boise City, Idaho), 1863-1867.

Bozeman Chronicle (Bozeman, Montana), 1880-1885.

Breeders' Gazette (Chicago, Illinois), 1881-1890-1915.

Brookings County Weekly Press (Brookings, Dakota), 1880-1886.

Brookings Daily Press (Brookings, Dakota), 1886.

Butte Miner (Butte, Montana), 1879-1889.

Carrington News (Foster County, Dakota), 1886-1887.

Central City Herald (Central City, Dakota), 1878.

Central City News (Douglas, Wyoming), 1894-1895.

Cheyenne Daily Leader (Cheyenne, Wyoming), 1867-1900.

Cheyenne Daily News (Cheyenne, Wyoming), 1875-1876.

Cheyenne Daily Sun (Cheyenne, Wyoming), 1876-1892.

Cheyenne State Leader (Cheyenne, Wyoming), 1930-1935.

Cheyenne Weekly Leader (Cheyenne, Wyoming), 1868-1890.

Chicago Times (Chicago, Illinois), 1880.

Chicago Tribune (Chicago, Illinois), 1884.

Cincinnati Gazette (Cincinnati, Ohio), July 7, 1882.

Clay County Register (Vermillion, Dakota), 1872-1874.

Cody Enterprise (Cody, Wyoming), 1903-1911-1928.

Colorado Leader (Denver, Colorado), 1865-1867.

Corrine Daily Mail (Corrine, Utah), 1874.

Council Bluffs Eagle (Council Bluffs, Iowa), Sept. 14, 1864.

Crook City Tribune (Crook City, Dakota), 1877.

Cultivator and Country Gentleman, 1860-1890.

Daily Independent (Helena, Montana), 1890-1900.

Daily Missoulian (Missoula, Montana), 1874-1878-1916.

Dakota and Burleigh County Settler (Bismarck, Dak.), 1887.

Dakota Democrat (Sioux Falls City, Dakota), August 26, November 8, 1859; February 18, 1860 (photostat).

Dakota News (Watertown, Dakota), 1879-1880.

Dakota Gleaner (Elk Point, Dak.), 1870-1874.

Dakota Republican (Vermillion, Dakota), 1870-1890; 1903. Anniversary edition, April 9, 1931.

Dakota Union (Yankton, Dakota), 1864-1865.

Deadwood Daily Champion (Deadwood, Dakota), 1877.

Deadwood Daily Times (Deadwood, Dakota), 1878.

Denver News (Denver, Colorado), 1874-1875.

Denver Post (Denver, Colorado), 1860-1865.

Denver Republican (Denver, Colorado), November 13, 1909.

Denver Tribune (Denver, Colorado), 1869.

Deseret News (Salt Lake City, Utah), 1850-1890.

Devil's Lake Democrat (Devil's Lake, Dakota), 1884-1885.

Dickinson Press (Dickinson, Dakota), 1883-1886.

Encampment Echo (Encampment, Colorado), December 5, 1935.

Estelline Bell (Hamlin County, Dakota), 1883-1886.

Fargo Daily Republican (Fargo, Dakota), 1881-1889.

Fargo Express (Fargo, Dakota), 1874-1890.

Fargo Times (Fargo, Dakota), 1874-1882.

Farm and Factory (St. Paul, Minnesota), 1875-1877.

Faulk County Times (Dakota), 1882-1889.

Frémont Clipper (Lander, Wyoming), 1887-1895.

Glendive Independent (Glendive, Montana), 1885-1887.

Glendive Times (Glendive, Montana), 1881-1889.

Grand Forks Daily Plain Dealer (Grand Forks, Dakota), 1882-1889.

Grant County Review (Milbank, Dakota), 1880-1889.

Great Falls Tribune (Great Falls, Montana), 1885-1893.

Harper's Monthly Magazine (New York City).

Harper's Weekly (New York City).

Harris Graphic (Dakota), 1887-1888.

Helena Daily Herald (Helena, Montana), 1874-1888.

Helena Daily Independent (Helena, Montana), 1875-1885.

Helena Weekly Herald (Helena, Montana), 1866-1874.

Huron Tribune (Huron, Dakota), 1880-1889.

Idaho Statesman (Boise, Idaho), 1864-1888, May 22, 1932.

Idaho World (Idaho City, Idaho), 1864-1872.

Iowa Register (Des Moines, Iowa), April 12, 1875.

Jefferson City Inquirer (Jefferson City, Missouri), 1858.

Kansas City Daily Times (Kansas City, Missouri), 1880-1885.

Kansas City Star, 1880-1883.

Laramie Boomerang (Laramie, Wyoming), 1880-1885.

Laramie Independent, 1871-1876.

Lead City Telegraph (Lead City, Dakota), 1878.

Lincoln County Advocate (Canton, Dakota), 1876-1883.

Madisonian (Madison, Montana), 1876-1884.

Mandan Daily Pioneer (Mandan, Dakota), 1885-1889-1903.

Mandan Weekly Pioneer (Mandan, Dakota), 1883-1889; Pageant edition,
September 3, 1922.

Medora Bad Lands Cowboy (Medora, Dakota), 1884-1886.

Miles City Daily Star (Miles City, Montana), Golden Jubilee edition, May
24, 1934.

Miles City Weekly Press (Miles City, Montana), 1881-1884.

Miles City Weekly Times (Miles City, Montana), 1882-1889.

Mineral Argus (Lewiston, Montana), 1883-1886.

Missouri Republican (St. Louis, Missouri), 1850-1865.

Montana Live Stock Journal (Miles City, Montana), 1885-1888.

Montana Post (Virginia City, Montana), 1864-1888.

Montana Stockman and Farmer (Miles City, Montana), 1896-1898.

Montanian (Virginia City, Montana), 1871-1875.

Motor Travel (New York City), Aug., Nov., Dec., 1927.

National Live Stock Journal (Chicago, Illinois), 1870-1889.

New Northwest (Deer Lodge, Montana), 1874-1881.

New York Sun (New York City), April 6, 1884.

Niles Weekly Register (Baltimore, Maryland), 1842-1870.

Northern Pacific Times (Valley City, Dakota), 1875-1880.

Northwest Magazine (Fargo, Dak.), 1880-1886.

Northwestern Live Stock Journal (Cheyenne, Wyoming), 1885-1887.

Northwestern Miller (Minneapolis, Minnesota), 1876-1877.

Omaha Daily Bee (Omaha, Nebraska), September 28, 1881.

Omaha Daily Republican (Omaha, Nebraska), February 14, 19, 1880.

Omaha World-Herald (Omaha, Nebraska), July 15, 1896.

Owyhee Avalanche (Silver City, Idaho), 1865-1869.

Pembina Pioneer (Pembina, Dakota), 1879-1880.

Pierre Daily Free Press (East Pierre, Dakota), 1883-1889.

Pierre Weekly Free Press (East Pierre, Dakota), 1883-1889.

Portland Daily Advertiser (Portland, Oregon), June 18, July 9, 1861. July 12, August 7, 1862.

Prairie Farmer (Chicago, Illinois), 1866-1884.

River Press (Fort Benton, Montana), 1881-1907.

Rock Springs Independent (Rock Springs, Wyoming), 1888.

Rocky Mountain Husbandman (Diamond City, White Sulphur Springs, Great Falls, Montana), 1873-1890.

Rocky Mountain News (Cherry Creek, Colorado), 1859-1880.

St. Cloud Democrat (St. Cloud, Minnesota), 1861-1870.

St. Joseph Gazette (St. Joseph, Missouri), 1858-1868.

St. Paul Globe (St. Paul, Minnesota), 1883-1885.

St. Paul Weekly Pioneer and Democrat (St. Paul, Minnesota), 1857-1860.

St. Paul Pioneer Press (St. Paul, Minnesota), 1871-1888.

St. Paul Press (St. Paul, Minnesota), 1874-1875.

Salt Lake City Daily Herald (Salt Lake City, Utah), 1870-1871.

Salt Lake City Daily Tribune (Salt Lake City, Utah), 1878.

San Francisco Daily Bulletin (San Francisco, California), May 19, 1865; June 23, 1866.

Sioux City Eagle (Sioux City, Iowa), 1858-1862.

Sioux City Journal (Sioux City, Iowa), 1914.

Sioux City Register (Sioux City, Iowa), 1858-1862.

Sioux City Weekly Journal (Sioux City, Iowa), 1859-1877.

Sioux City Weekly Press (Sioux City, Iowa), 1859-62.

Sioux City Weekly Times (Sioux City, Iowa), 1869-1879.

Sioux City Weekly Tribune (Sioux City, Iowa), 1861-1878.

Sioux Falls Argus Leader (Sioux Falls, S. D.), June 17, 1919.
Sioux Falls Democrat (Sioux Falls, D. T.), 1858-1860.
Spearfish Record (Spearfish, Dakota), 1884.
Stock Growers' Journal (Miles City, Montana), 1893-1905.
Sturgis Weekly Advertiser (Sturgis, Dakota), 1887-1889.
Sun River Sun (Sun River, Montana), 1884.
Sunset Magazine, July, 1922.
Sweetwater Miner (Sweetwater, Montana), 1868-1869.
The Record (Monthly Magazine: Fargo, North Dakota), 1894-1896.
Thermopolis Record (Thermopolis, Wyoming), 1902-1908.
Toronto Globe (Toronto, Canada), July 9, 1859.
Turner County Herald (Hurley, Dakota), 1883-1886.
Valley City Times (Valley City, Dakota), 1880-1882.
Watertown News (Watertown, Dakota), 1879-1889.
Watertown Times (Watertown, Dakota), 1879-1884.
Weekly Missoulian (Missoula, Montana), 1874-1883.
Western Journal and Civilian (St. Louis, Missouri), n. d.
Western Monthly (St. Louis, Missouri), 1867-1876.
Wind River Mountaineer (Lander, Wyoming), 1887-1897.
Wyoming Daily Sun (Cheyenne, Wyoming), 1880-1884.
Wyoming Industrial Journal (Cheyenne, Wyoming), 1899-1910.
Wyoming State Leader (Cheyenne, Wyoming), 1917.
Wyoming Stock Grower and Farmer (Cody, Wyoming), 1904-1906.
Wyoming Weekly Tribune (Cheyenne, Wyoming), 1867-1874.
Yankton Weekly Dakotian (Yankton, Dakota), 1861—March 11, 1871.
Yankton Weekly Press (Yankton, Dakota), March 18, 1871—November 20, 1873.
Yankton Weekly Press and Dakotian (Yankton, Dakota), November 27, 1873-1890.
Yellowstone Journal (Miles City, Montana), 1878-1886-1904.

SECONDARY WORKS

I

Books

AIKMAN, DUNCAN, *Calamity Jane, The Lady Wildcat* (New York, 1927).
ALDERSON, M. S., *History of Bozeman, Montana* (Bozeman, Montana, 1882).
BAILEY, DANA R., *History of Minnehaha County* (Sioux Falls, South Dakota, 1899).
BANCROFT, H. H., *History of Nevada, Colorado and Wyoming* (San Francisco, 1899).

BANCROFT, H. H., *History of Washington, Idaho and Montana, 1845-1889* (San Francisco, 1899).

BELL, WILLIAM CAMPTON, *A History of the Theatrical Activities of Cheyenne, Wyoming* (Master's Thesis, School of Speech, Northwestern University: Evanston, Illinois, 1935).

BENNETT, ESTELLINE, *Old Deadwood Days* (New York, 1935).

BIRD, ANNIE L., *Boise: The Peace Valley* (Caldwell, Idaho, 1934).

BRANCH, E. DOUGLAS, *The Hunting of the Buffalo* (New York, 1929).

BROSNAN, C. J., *History of the State of Idaho* (New York, 1935).

BUCK, SOLON J., *The Granger Movement* (Cambridge, Massachusetts, 1913).

BUECHEL, FREDERICK A., *The Commerce of Agriculture* (New York, 1926).

CHITTENDEN, HIRAM M., *The American Fur Trade of the Far West*, 3 vols. (New York, 1902).

————, *The History of Early Steamboat Navigation on the Missouri River*, 2 vols. (New York, 1905).

CLAY, JOHN, *My Life On the Range* (Chicago, 1924).

CLEMEN, RUDOLPH A., *The American Livestock and Meat Industry* (New York, 1923).

CONNOR, L. G., "A Brief History of the Sheep Industry in the United States," *Annual Report of the American Historical Association* (1918).

COOK, JOHN R., *The Border and the Buffalo* (Topeka, Kansas, 1907).

COUTANT, C. G., *History of Wyoming* (Laramie, Wyoming, 1899).

CRAWFORD, LEWIS F., *Rekindling Campfires* (Bismarck, North Dakota, 1926).

Cyclopedia of American Agriculture (New York, 1909).

DALE, EDWARD EVERETT, *The Range Cattle Industry* (Norman, Oklahoma, 1930).

DAVIS, JOHN P., *The Union Pacific Railway* (Chicago, 1884).

DICK, EVERETT, *The Sod-House Frontier, 1854-1890* (New York, 1937).

ELLIOT, WALLACE W., *History of Idaho* (San Francisco, 1884).

FARIS, JOHN I., *Seeing the Middle West* (Philadelphia, 1923).

FELTER, MAUDE E., *The Beginnings of the Range and Ranch Business of Montana* (Master's Thesis, University of Iowa: Iowa City, Iowa, 1924).

FILSON, JOHN, *Kentucke*, (reprint of the 1784 edition: Louisville, Kentucky, 1929).

FINNEY, J. P., *Certain Climatic Features of the Two Dakotas* (Washington, D. C., 1890).

FITE, EMERSON D., *Social and Industrial Conditions in the North During the Civil War* (New York, 1910).

FOWLER, WILLIAM W., *Women on the Frontier* (Hartford, Connecticut, 1876).

GILFILLAN, ARCHER B., *Sheep* (Boston, 1936).

GOODMAN, A. T., "Buffalo in Ohio," *Western Reserve Historical Society Tract* (Cleveland, Ohio, January, 1877).

GOETZ, ANNA M., *The History of Yankton County to 1886* (Master's Thesis, University of South Dakota: Vermillion, South Dakota, 1927).

GRIEDER, THEODORE G., *The Influence of the American Bison or Buffalo on Westward Expansion* (Master's Thesis, University of Iowa: Iowa City, Iowa, 1928).

HAGEDORN, HERMAN, *Roosevelt in the Badlands* (New York, 1921).

HAILEY, JOHN, *History of Idaho* (Boise, Idaho, 1910).

HANSEN, J. M., *The Conquest of the Missouri* (Chicago, 1909).

HAZELTON, JOHN M., *History and Handling of Hereford Cattle* (Kansas City, Kansas, 1925).

HIBBARD, N. K., "Address to the Red River Valley Old Settlers' Association," November 26, 1895 (Grand Forks, North Dakota, 1897).

HORNADAY, W. T., "The Extermination of the American Bison," *Annual Report of the United States National Museum* (Smithsonian Institution: Washington, D. C., 1887).

HUMPHREY, SETH K., *Following the Prairie Frontier* (Minneapolis, Minnesota, 1931).

HUNTER, J. M., (ed.), *Trail Drivers of Texas* (Nashville, Tennessee, 1925).

INMAN, HENRY and CODY, W. F., *The Great Salt Lake Trail* (New York, 1898).

JULIAN, RALPH, *Our Great West* (New York, 1893).

KINGSBURY, GEORGE W., *The History of Dakota Territory*, 2 vols. (Chicago, 1915).

LANG, LINCOLN, *Ranching With Roosevelt* (Philadelphia, 1926).

LEYBURN, JAMES G., *Frontier Folkways* (New Haven, Connecticut, 1935).

LINDSAY, CHARLES, *The Big Horn Basin* (Ph.D. Thesis, Dept. of History, University of Nebraska: Lincoln, Nebraska, June, 1930).

LOUNSBERRY, CLEMENT, *Early History of North Dakota* (Washington, D. C., 1919).

MARNER, GRACE LILLIAN, *The Range and Ranch Business in Wyoming* (Master's Thesis, University of Iowa, Dept. of History: Iowa City, Iowa, 1922).

MENDENHALL, W. T., *History of Gold and Silver Mining in Montana* (Helena, Montana, 1891).

The Mineral Resources of Wyoming (Cheyenne, Wyoming, 1929).

NEELY, W. C., *The Agricultural Fair* (New York, 1935).

OSGOOD, ERNEST STAPLES, *The Day of the Cattleman* (Minneapolis, Minnesota, 1929).

PALLADINO, L. B., *Indian and White in the Northwest* (Baltimore, Maryland, 1894).

PEAKE, ORA B., *The Colorado Range Cattle Industry* (Glendale, California, 1937).

PELZER, LOUIS, *The Frontier of the Cattleman* (Glendale, California, 1937).

PETERSON, E. F., *Historical Atlas of South Dakota* (Chicago, 1904).

PICKETT, W. D., *Big Horn Country, State of Wyoming* (1898).

POOR, HENRY V., *Manual of the Railroads of the United States, 1868-1902* (Chicago, 1902).

Proceedings, Red River Valley Old Settlers Association (Grand Forks, North Dakota, 1897).

Prose and Poetry of the Livestock Industry of the United States (Kansas City, Kansas, 1905).

QUIETT, GLEN CHESNEY, *Pay Dirt* (New York, 1936).

QUINN, ARTHUR H., *A History of the American Drama From the Beginnings to the Civil War* (New York, 1923).

———, *A History of the American Drama from the Civil War to the Present* (New York, 1936).

REESE, JOHN B., *Some Pioneers and Pilgrims on the Prairies of Dakota* (Mitchel, South Dakota, 1920).

ROBINSON, DOANE, *Encyclopedia of South Dakota* (Pierre, South Dakota, 1925).

———, *History of South Dakota* (Indianapolis, Indiana, 1904).

ROOSEVELT, THEODORE, *An Autobiography* (New York, 1916).

ROSEN, PETER, *Pa-ha-sa-pah or the Black Hills of South Dakota* (St. Louis, Missouri, 1895).

SANDERS, GEORGE W., *Trail Drivers of Texas* (1920).

SETON, ERNEST THOMPSON, *Life Histories of Northern Animals* (New York, 1909).

SMALLEY, E. V., *The History of the Northern Pacific Railroad* (New York, 1883).

SMITH, C. H., *The Coming of the Russian Mennonites* (Chicago, 1927).

STEINEL, ALVIN T., *History of Agriculture in Colorado, 1858-1926* (Denver, Colorado, 1926).

STEVENS, HAZARD, *The Life of Issac Stevens*, 2 vols. (New York, 1901).

STOKES, G. W., and DRIGGS, HOWARD, *Deadwood Gold* (New York, 1926).

STOUT, TOM (ed.), *Montana, Its Story and Biography* (Chicago, 1921).

STUART, GRANVILLE, *Forty Years on the Frontier*, 2 vols. (Cleveland, Ohio, 1925).

TALLENT, ANNIE D., *The Black Hills* (St. Louis, 1899).

TREXLER, H. A., *Flour and Wheat in the Montana Gold Camps, 1862-1870* (Missoula, Montana, 1918).

TROTTMAN, N., *History of the Union Pacific Railroad* (New York, 1923).

VAUGHN, ROBERT, *Then and Now, or Thirty-Six Years in the Rockies, 1864-1900* (Minneapolis, Minnesota, 1900).

VISHER, S. S., "The Geography of South Dakota," *Report of the State Geologist, 1916-18* (Vermillion, South Dakota, 1918).

WALDO, EDNA LA MOORE, *Dakota* (Caldwell, Idaho, 1936).

WEBB, WALTER PRESCOTT, *The Great Plains* (New York, 1931).

WINSHIP, GEORGE B., *Forty Years of Development of the Red River Valley* (St. Paul, Minnesota, 1898).

WISLACK, FRANK L., *Wild Bill Hickok* (New York, 1926).

WISLIZENUS, F. A., *A Journey to the Rocky Mountains in 1839* (St. Louis, Missouri, 1912).

WISTER, OWEN, *The Virginian, a Horseman of the Plains* (Macmillan: New York, 1922).

WOOD, LOUIS W., *The Red River Colony* (Toronto, Canada, 1920).

WRIGHT, ROBERT M., *Dodge City, the Cowboy Capital* (Topeka, Kansas, 1913).

Wyoming Stock Growers' Association, *Letters from Old Friends and Members of the Wyoming Stock Growers' Association* (Cheyenne, Wyoming, 1923).

II

ARTICLES

ANDER, O. F., "The Immigrant Church and the Patrons of Husbandry," *Agricultural History*, VIII (October, 1934).

ANSON, A. M., "Harvesting Wheat in Dakota," *Cultivator and Country Gentleman*, XLVIII.

ARMSTRONG, W. K., "The Burning Issue of 1859," *Monthly South Dakotan*, IV (Yankton, South Dakota, 1901).

BAKER, R. S., "The Tragedy of the Range," *Century Magazine* (August, 1902).

BAUMAN, JOHN, "On a Western Ranche," *The Fortnightly Review*, XLVII (April, 1887).

BEMIS, EDWARD W., "The Discontented Farmer," *Journal of Political Economy*, XI.

BIGELOW, P., "The Bonanza Farms of the West," *Atlantic Monthly*, XLV (January, 1880).

"The Black Hills," *Motor Travel* (August, 1927).

BROWN, JOHN M., "The Kentucky Pioneers," *Harper's Monthly Magazine*, LXXV (June, 1887).

CLARKE, H. T., "Freighting to the Black Hills," *Proceedings*, Nebraska State Historical Society, Second Series, V (Lincoln, Nebraska).

COFFIN, C. C., "Dakota Wheat Fields," *Harper's Monthly Magazine*, LX.

CRUISE, J. D., "Early Days of the Union Pacific," *Collections*, Kansas State Historical Society, XI (Topeka, Kansas, 1910).

DAVIS, THEODORE R., "The Buffalo Range," *Harper's Monthly Magazine*, XXXVIII (January, 1869).

DUFFIELD, JOHN, "Driving Cattle from Texas to Iowa," 1866, *Annals of Iowa*, XIV (Iowa City, Iowa, April, 1924) No. 4.

EDWARDS, EVERETT E., "American Indian Contributions to Civilization," *Minnesota History*, XV, No. 4.

FINERTY, JOHN H., "Custer's Black Hills March of 1876," *Motor Travel* (December, 1927).

———, "Deadwood in 1876," *Motor Travel* (November, 1927).

GOODMAN, A. T., "Buffalo in Ohio," *Western Reserve Historical Society Tract* (Cleveland, Ohio, January, 1877).

GRAHAM, W. B., "Cattle Ranches of the Far West," *Fortnightly Review*, XXVIII (1880).

HAGER, CHARLES M., "Cattle Trails of the Prairies," *Scribner's*, XI (May, June, 1892).

———, "The Prairie Woman: Yesterday and Today," *Outlook* (April 26, 1902).

———, "Sheep and Shepherds of the West," *Outlook*, LXXII (November 22, 1902).

HANEY, LEWIS H., "A Congressional History of the Railroads," *Bulletin* No. 211, University of Wisconsin Economics and Political Science Series, III, No. 2 (Madison, Wisconsin, 1908).

HENRY, A. J., "Variation of Precipitation in the United States," *Bulletin*, American Geological Society (March, 1914).

HOWARD, R. R., "The Passing of the Cattle King," *Outlook*, XCVIII (May 27, 1911).

JACOBS, JOHN CLOWD, "The Last of the Buffalo," *World's Work*, XVII (January, 1898).

JENNEY, W. R., *Official Geological Report Submitted to the Secretary of the Interior*, Nov. 11, 1875.

KOHRS, CONRAD, "A Veteran's Experience in the Western Cattle Trade," *Breeders' Gazette* (Chicago, Illinois), December 18, 1912.

LAMPHERE, GEORGE, "History of Wheat Growing in the Red River Valley," *Collections*, State Historical Society of Minnesota, X.

LIPPINCOTT, ISAAC, "A Century and a Half of the Fur Trade at St. Louis," *Washington University Studies*, III (St. Louis, Missouri, 1916), Part II, No. 2.

Literary Digest (November 14, 1933). Material on Calamity Jane.

LOVE, CLARA M., "History of the Cattle Industry in the Southwest," *Southwestern Historical Quarterly*, XIX (April, 1916).

MICKELSON, CHARLES, "War for the Range," *Munsey's Magazine* (December, 1902).

MUNSON, LYMAN E., "Pioneer Life on the American Frontier," *Journal of American History*, I (1907).

OGDEN, W. H., "The Toll of the Sheep," *Everybody's Magazine*, XXIII, p. 413.

OLIPHANT, J. ORIN, "The Cattle Trade from the Far Northwest to Montana," *Agricultural History* (April, 1932).

PAXSON, F. L., "The Cow Country," *American Historical Review* (1917).

PHILLIPS, PAUL C., "The Life and Adventures of Calamity Jane," *Frontier and Midland* (Missoula, Montana, Summer, 1936).

PIERSON, W. A., "The Rise of the Granger Movement," *Popular Science Monthly*, XXXII.

ROOSEVELT, THEODORE, "In Cowboy Land," *Outlook*, CIV (May 10, 1913).

———, "Ranch Life in the Far West," *Century Magazine*, XIII (February, 1888).

ROSS, EARLE D., "The Evolution of the Agricultural Fair in the Northwest," *Iowa Journal of History and Politics*, XXIV.

RUSSELL, HAMLIN, "The Story of the Buffalo," *Harper's Monthly Magazine*, LXXXVI (April, 1893).

SCHELL, HERBERT S., "The Grange and the Credit Problem in Dakota Territory," *Agricultural History*, X (April, 1936).

SCHMIDT, LOUIS BERNARD, "The Westward Movement of the Wheat Growing Industry in the United States," *Iowa Journal of History and Politics*, XVIII (July, 1920).

SETON, ERNEST T., "The American Bison or Buffalo," *Scribner's Magazine* (October, 1906).

SNOW, E. P., "Sheepmen and Cattlemen," *Outlook* (April 1, 1903).

STROTHER, FRENCH, "The Last of the Cattle Kings," *World's Work*, XVI (September, 1905).

THOMPSON, C. W., "The Movement of Wheat Growing," *Quarterly Journal of Economics*, XVIII.

TORGESON, SAMUEL, "Early Banking in North Dakota," *Quarterly Journal*, University of North Dakota, XIII.

TREXLER, H. A., "Missouri and Montana Highways," *Missouri Historical Review*, XII.

TRIMBLE, WILLIAM J., "Mining Advance into the Inland Empire," *Bulletin of the University of Wisconsin*, No. 638 (Madison, Wisconsin, 1914).

VEBLEN, THORSTEN B., "The Price of Wheat Since 1867," *Journal of Political Economy*, I.

VOLWEILER, A. T., "Roosevelt's Ranch Life in North Dakota," *Quarterly Journal of the University of North Dakota*, IX (October, 1918), No. 1.

"Where Beef Comes From," *Lippincott's Magazine* (November, 1879).

WHITE, WILLIAM ALLEN, "The Business of a Wheat Farm," *Scribner's Magazine*, XXII.

III

HISTORICAL COLLECTIONS

Annals of Wyoming, I-IV (Cheyenne, Wyoming, 1922-1926).

Collections, State Historical Society of North Dakota, I-VII (Bismarck, North Dakota, 1905-1925).

Contributions, Montana State Historical Society, I-IX (Helena, Montana, 1876-1923).

Mississippi Valley Historical Review, I-XIX (Lincoln, Nebraska), 1914-1936.

Monthly South Dakotan, I-IV (Yankton and Aberdeen, South Dakota, 1898-1902).

Nebraska State Historical Society Collections (Lincoln, Neb.), 2d Series, V, Jan.-March, 1922.

Newsletter, University of North Dakota (Grand Forks, North Dakota, 1925-1928).

North Dakota Historical Quarterly, I-VII (Bismarck, North Dakota, 1926-1933).

Proceedings, Mississippi Valley Historical Association, I-XI (1907-1924).

Quarterly Journal, I-XI (Grand Forks, North Dakota, 1910-1921).

Quarterly Journal, University of North Dakota, XII-XXIII (Grand Forks, North Dakota, 1921-1933).

South Dakota Historical *Collections*, I-XVI (Aberdeen and Pierre, South Dakota, 1902-1932).

South Dakota Historical Review (Pierre, South Dakota, 1936-1937).

Washington Historical Quarterly (Seattle, Washington, 1906-1913).

Wisconsin Magazine of History (Madison, Wisconsin, 1913-1917).

Wyoming State Historical Society, *Miscellanies* (Laramie, Wyoming, 1919).

Wyoming State Historical Society, *Proceedings and Collections*, I-IX, 1920-1936.

INDEX

Aberdeen, Dak., 426
Aberdeen Angus cattle, 263
Abilene, Kans., 198
Academy Hill School, 100
Acrobats, 107
Actor-managers, 108, 109, 110, 111, 112, 581
After-pieces, 112
Agriculture, 6, 66, 370, 390, 436, 439, 484; advance of frontier of, 293-297; in early Dakota, 485-496; in Red River Valley, 492, 493, 509-522; in Montana, 496-507; in Gallatin Valley, 501-503; in Wyoming, 507-509
Agricultural fair, 555-564; in Dakota, 556, 557, 558; in Montana, 558, 559; in Wyoming, 559
Alder Creek, 19
Alder Gulch, 19, 20, 50n, 402, 499
Allen, J. W., 285
Allison Peace Commission, 35
American Fur Company, 59, 148, 149, 153, 155
American Hotel, Idaho City, 99
Antelope, 240
Anthracite coal, used in Dakota, 379
Arapahoe Indians, 275
Aristocracy, in gold camps, 97
Arizona, 3, 76
Arland, Wyo., 291, 292, 440
Arrastra, 48, 48n
Assiniboine Indians, 140
Astor, John Jacob, 147
Atchison, Kans., 64
Atchison, Topeka, and Santa Fe Railroad, 158, 160
Atlantic City, Wyo., 24, 25, 399, 401
Auraria, Colo., 6
Averill, James, cattle thief, 299

Baboon Gulch, 10
Bad Lands, 33, 134, 170, 221, 249, 269

Badger Cattle Company, 223
Bald Mountain, 43, 44, 45
Bald Mountain City, Wyo., description of, 43, 44
Balls, 94, 98
Bands, 96, 108, 111
Bannack City, Mont., 11, 19, 21, 22, 69, 92, 93, 97, 99, 104, 114, 141, 402, 405
Banning's Point, Dak., 364
Baptist Church, 103
Barley, 489, 490, 504
Barnum, P. T., 577
Barter, 540
Basin City, Wyo., 474, 476
Battle of the Little Big Horn, 35, 77, 215, 276, 408
Battle Creek, 27
Bear Butte, 28
Bear River, Mont., 109
Bear River, Wyo., 397, 398
Beartown, Mont., 405
Beaver, 147, 238, 239
Beaver City, Idaho, 13
Beaverhead County, Mont., 14, 138
Beaverhead River, 19
"Bedrock Tom," 88
Beef, demand for, 188-195, 209; price of, 251, 252
Beef-contracts, 194, 195, 250
Bell, Hattie, 105
Bella Union, the, 94, 110, 111
Bell-ringers, 95
Bem, Frank, 444, 459
Benetsee (see also Francois Finlay), 17
Benton City, Wyo., 480, 481
Beret, 593
Berry-Boyce Cattle Company, 222
Big Horn Basin, 23, 25, 42, 43, 219, 437, 439, 440, 441, 443, 475
Big Horn Cattle Company, 219
Big Horn Colonization Company, 471, 472, 473
Big Horn County, Wyo., 475
Big Horn Mining Association, 24

613

Big Horn Mountains, 23, 24, 42
Big Horn River, 57
Big Horn Valley, 23, 24, 25, 68
Big Sioux County, Minn., 352
Big Sioux Valley, 355, 356, 361, 366, 369, 390, 415
Billiard halls, 82, 83
Billings, Mont., 432, 433, 434, 440
Binders, 491n
Bismarck, Dak., 34, 63, 111, 163, 164, 166, 376, 383, 384, 391, 419, 567, 570, 571
Bismarck Land Office, 469
Bismarck Opera House, 571
Bison. See Buffalo.
Bitter Root Valley, 434, 435, 499n, 500
Black Hills, gold in, 25-41; prospecting in, 26; determination to explore, 30; open for settlement, 36; ranching in, 212-215
Black Hills Exploring and Mining Association, 28
Black Hills Live Stock Association, 214, 236, 268, 269, 285
Black Hills Mining and Exploring Association of Sioux City, 31
Blackfeet Indians, 141, 143, 149
Blackfoot, Mont., 104
Blanchard, Reverend Jonathan, 104
Blanchet, Archbishop F. N., 102
Blizzards, 240, 368, 535
Blunt, Dak., 426
Bohemians, 444, 459, 463
Boise City, Idaho, 12, 16, 94, 99, 101, 103
Boise County, Idaho, 99
Boise River Basin, 11, 12, 15, 16, 91, 103
Boise Valley Seminary, 101
Bonanza, Idaho, 12
"Bonanza" wheat farms, 511-522
Bon Homme, Dak., 360, 369
Bon Homme County, Dak., 366
Boom towns, 108, 395, 477-484
Boonville, Idaho, 11
Boston Company, the, 111
Boulder, Colo., 78
Bourke, Captain John G., 39
Bozeman, Mont., 79, 104, 166, 403, 410, 453, 572
Bozeman Trail, 23, 54n
Bradbury, John, 138, 150

Bramble, Miner and Company, 63
Branding, of cattle, 280, 281, 300; of colts, 340, 341
Bread riots, threatened, 66
Brookings, Dak., 427
Brothel, 86, 89, 107
Brown, F., 26
Bruins, Henry A., 510, 511
Buchanan, John, 62
Buffalo, Wyo., 301, 401
Buffalo, uses of, 125, 140-142, 144-146; range of, 125, 126, 127; in the Northwest, 133, 134, 161-172; in folklore, 135; general movements, 135; life of, 135, 136; accounts of, 137-140; and Indians, 140-142, 162, 162n, 177, 178; methods of hunting, 140-142; preparation of skins, 142, 143; robes, 142-144; in early fur trade, 146-149; trading for robes, 150-154; products and steamboat traffic, 154-156; northern and southern herds, 156-158; slaughter of southern herd, 158-161; meat, 161; professional hunters of, 171-176; skinning of, 173; disappearance of, 176, 177; bones, traffic in, 178, 179
"Buffalo grass," 134
Buffalo hunt, Pembina, 130, 131, 132
Buffalo hunters, 163-176
Buffalo Bill (see also William F. Cody), 78, 159, 190
Bull-whacker, 60
Bunker Hill and Sullivan mine, 14
Bureau of Immigration (Dak.), 387, 445, 446, 447
Burleigh City, Dak., 382
Burleigh County, Dak., 385
Burleigh, W. W., 444, 456
Burlington, Wyo., 440, 441
Butte, Mont., 13, 104, 405, 406, 410

Cabin, of miner, 52
Calamity Jane. See Martha Jane Canary.
California, 3, 8, 9, 10, 15, 18, 26, 27, 28, 47, 50, 60, 62, 78, 184
California gold rush, 3, 133, 184
California Hotel, Nevada City, Mont., 70

"California Jack," 88

Callison, Mrs. John, 100

Camp Carlin, 395

Camp meetings, 592

Campbell, Charles T., 63

Camps, gold, in Colorado, 6, 7; in Idaho, 9, 10, 11, 13; East Bannack, 19; in Montana, 22; deserted, 40; food of, 52; routes to, 54, 54n, 55, 56, 56n, 57; trade with, 60, 61; communication with, 63, 64, 65; prices in, 65-71; population of, 71-74; drinking in, 82-84; amusements of, 82-98; education in, 98-102; religion in, 102-107; the theater in, 107-113; justice in, 113-124; in Wyoming, 399

Canal Gulch, 8

Canary, Charlotte, 75, 76

Canary, Martha Jane (Calamity Jane), 75-82, 105

Canary, Robert, 75, 76

Carbon City, Idaho, 13, 397

Cariso mine, 25, 26n

Carleton City, Dak., 382

Carroll, Mont., 408

Carson City, Nev., 8

Cart, Red River, 130n

Carter, Charles, 219

Carter Dramatic Company, J. W., 111, 578

Carver, Frank, 173

Casper, Wyo., 302

Cass County, Dak., 385, 521

Casselton, Dak., 417, 418

Castle Creek, 40

Catholic Church, 103

Catlin, George, 138, 369

Cattle, 54, 436, 437, 439, 508; in early Wyoming and Montana, 186, 187, 188, 190, 192; demand for in mining camps, 188, 189; prices of, 189, 205, 206, 207, 217, 227, 238, 250-253; in early Dakota, 191-195; Texas, 195-226, 245, 259, 261, 263; improvement of, 259-263; round-up of, 271-273; inspection of, 273-274; use of range, 327, 328; in Montana, 498

Cattle associations, need for, 264, 265; types of, 265; organization of,

265-269; work of, 269-274, 285, 286

Cattle boom, 216, 317

Cattle branding, 270, 271

Cattle companies, in Black Hills, 215-226; import blooded cattle, 262; and illegal enclosures, 296; liquidate herds, 304

Cattle drives, 199-203

"Cattle kings," 188, 246, 257, 297

Cattle-ranching, 181-307; frontier of, 181, 182; in Wyoming and Montana, 182-191, 204-211; in Dakota, 191-195, 211-215; in Northwest, 203, 204, 215; in Colorado, 204n; profits in, 205, 206, 211, 217, 227, 250-253; open-range, 204, 209, 211, 215, 220, 242; losses in, 241-246, 251, 252; and Theodore Roosevelt, 246-249; and foreign capital, 253-259

Cattle rustlers, 342, 343

Centerville, Idaho, 11, 103

Central City, Colo., 7

Central City, Dak., 40, 41, 109, 419

Central Overland and Pike's Peak Express, 64

Central Pacific Railroad, 398

Charles Dickens mine, 12

Checker tournaments, 96

Cherokee Indians, 5

Cherry Creek, Colo., 4, 5, 6, 7, 188

Cheyenne, Wyo., 24, 34, 43, 63, 77, 86, 109, 157, 265, 266, 285, 289, 392, 393, 394, 395, 396, 400, 401, 574; theaters in, 579-581

Cheyenne Club, the, 233, 256, 259, 285

Cheyenne Indians, 33, 275

Cheyenne Mining District, 36, 36n

Cheyenne Opera House, 579

Chicago and Northwestern Railroad, 57, 378, 388, 391

Chicago, St. Paul, Minneapolis, and Omaha Railroad, 390

Children, 98, 242, 409, 520

Chinatown, Dak., 37

Chinese, 47, 73, 74, 105, 404

Chouteau County, Mont., 268, 404

Chouteau, Pierre, 151, 153

Chrissman, George, 97

Churches, 20, 102, 520, 592

Circle H Ranch, 223

Circus, 95, 106, 107, 565, 566

Civil War, 28, 53, 161, 163, 197, 349, 366, 371, 488, 523

Claims, on mining frontier, 9, 41, 50; of homesteaders, 297, 298, 582; in Dakota, 374, 391, 411; in copper region, 407

Clark, H. T., 64

Clark's Centennial Express, 65

Clay County, Dak., 361, 366, 423, 528, 545, 556

Clear Creek, 6

Clearwater gold camps, 14

Clearwater mines, 9

Clearwater River, 8, 9

Cleveland, Dak., 37

Cleveland, Jack, 114, 115

Clothing, of miners, 73

Coal-mining, 399

Cock-fighting, 96

Cody, Wyo., 440, 441

Cody, William F. (see also Buffalo Bill), 159, 441, 577

Cœur d'Alene area, 14

Cœur d'Alene Mountains, 13

Cœur d'Alene River, 13

Coliseum Variety Hall and Museum, Bismarck, Dak., 571

Collins, Charles, plan of, 31, 31n, 32

Colonies, New York Colony, 455-458; Bohemian, 459, 463; Russian-German, 461, 461n, 462, 463, 465; Mennonite, 462; Hutterian, 463, 464, 464n; English, 465, 471; Scotch, 465; Rumanian, 466; German, 466, 470, 471; "Lansing Colony," 466; Russian, 466, 469; Hollander, 466; from Missouri, 466; from Canada, 466; Polish, 466; Swedish, 469, 470; in Montana and Wyoming, 470; from Ripon, Wis., 471; Mormon, 471-473

Colonization associations, aim of, 454; organization of, 454, 455

Colorado (see also Territory of Colorado), 3, 4, 5, 8, 18, 28, 31, 34, 44, 53, 54, 56, 135

Columbia River, route to mines, 15

Combination places, 83, 110, 573, 575

Commissioner of Immigration (Dak.), appointment, 444; work of, 445, 446; duties and salary, 448

Communication, in gold camps, 63, 64

Comstock Lode, 8, 11

Concert halls, 571, 577

"Con men," 565

Confederate Gulch, 22n

Congregational Church, 103, 105

Congress, passes bill for colony corporation, 31

Construction camps, demand for beef, 190

Conrad, J. H., 270

Converse County, Wyo., 439

Coöperative buying and selling, 546, 549, 552

Cooperstown, Dak., 483

Copper, 403, 407

Copperopolis, Mont., 22n, 403

Corn, 414, 489, 490

Coronado, 4

Corrine, Utah, 64

Cosmopolitan Theater, 291

Coulson, Mont., 431, 432

Council Bluffs, Iowa, 26, 57, 155

Counties, organization of, in Minnesota, 352; in Dakota, 366, 373, 380, 385, 417n, 419; in Wyoming, 400, 401, 439, 443, 475; in Montana, 404, 433, 436

County fairs, 556, 557, 558, 559

County-seat fights, 473-477

Course of study, 101, 592

Covington, Nebr., 33

Cowan, John, 21

Cowboys, 200, 201, 286-293, 401

Cowtowns, 289-292

Credit, 288n, 539, 540, 552

Cree Indians, 133

Crittenden, J. R., 99

Crook City, Dak., 37, 39, 105

Crook, General, 80

Crooks, Ramsay, 147, 153, 154

Crop failures, in Dakota, 525, 526; results of, 527, 528; in Montana, 530

Crow Indians, 143, 165, 275

Crystal Hotel, Helena, Mont., 71

Cultural life, in mining camps, 92-98; on Great Plains, 567-569

Custer, General George A., 31, 32, 33, 35, 36, 37, 76, 80, 276, 408

Custer City, Dak., 37, 39, 40, 77, 419

Custer County, Mont., 12, 283

Custer expedition, 29, 163, 407

Custer Trail Ranch, 223

Dacotah Lode, the, 19, 48
Dairy cattle, 196, 225, 259, 503
Dairying, 182, 493, 534
Dakota boom of 1878-86, 293, 294, 376, 410-430
Dakota City, Dak., 363, 364
Dakota County, Minn., 349
Dakota Indians, 32
Dakota Land Company, 351, 352, 353, 354, 355, 356
Dakota Military District, 29
Dakota newspapers, and immigration, 448, 449
Dakota Southern Railroad, 377, 378, 391, 490, 526, 527, 569
Dalrymple, Oliver, 511, 513, 514
Daly's Ranch, 91
Daly's Theater, Bismarck, Dak., 571
Dances, 592
Dance-halls, 13, 20, 44, 107, 108, 289, 291, 566
Dancing, 84, 94, 95
Dancing clubs, 94, 95
Dancing schools, 96, 99
Davis, Jack, 333, 334
Davis, Spaulding and Company, 83
Deadwood Gulch, 37
Deadwood, Dak., 3, 37, 44, 49, 69, 70, 75, 80, 81, 82, 86, 88, 94, 100, 104, 105, 106, 107, 110, 389, 391; description of, 38, 39; and Calamity Jane, 77-82
Deep-vein mining, shift to, 41
Deer Lodge, Mont., 18, 104, 268, 404, 410, 431
Deer Lodge County, Mont., 190
Deer Lodge Valley, 60
Deffebach, Erasmus, 213
Deffebach, John, 213
De Mores, Marquis, 228-233, 247, 251, 258, 268, 318
Denver, Colo., 6, 7, 54, 55, 83, 88, 93, 109
Denver Dramatic Troupe, 111
Department of Dakota and the Northwest, the, 30
Desert Land Act, the, 295, 296, 297
Detectives, on cattle ranges, 274
Devil's Lake, Dak., 427
Diamond City, Mont., 404, 435
Dickinson, Dak., 167, 170, 171, 174, 175
Dill, Reverend A. C., Congregational pastor, 105

Dillon, John, 63
Dimsdale, Professor Thomas J., 99, 100
Dinner parties, 97
Diseases of sheep, 325
Diphtheria, 591
Djuberg, J. D., 493
Doctors, 38, 590, 591
Dodge, Colonel Richard Irving, 140
Dodge City, Kans., 158, 158n
Dog fights, 96
Dolliver, Reverend R. H., 106
Douglas, Captain J. H., 26
Douglas, Thomas, 128
Drinking, in mining camps, 82-85, 90; on the range, 292
Drought, 238, 366, 367, 368, 369, 376, 428, 429, 496, 521, 535, 538
Druggists, 38
Dry Creek, 5, 22n, 169
Durham cattle, 259, 260, 261

Eagle City, Idaho, 13, 14
East Bannack, Mont., 19
East Burlington, Dak., 363
East Gallatin Valley, 19
Eastern capital, and large wheat farms, 512
Eastern capitalists, and Dakota, 386
Eastern Montana Stock Growers Association, 268, 277
Edmunds, Newton, 316, 370, 444, 456
Education, on gold frontier, 98-102
Edwinton, Dak., 382, 383
Egan, Captain, 77, 79, 80
Elk, 9
Elk City, Idaho, 9, 10, 11
Elk Point, Dak., 360, 370
Elkhorn Ranch, 223
Elkhorn Valley, 33
Elocutionists, 107
Emanuel brothers, the, 38
Emigrants. See Immigrants, Immigration.
Emigrant Gulch, 22n
Emigration societies, 452, 453, 460, 461, 462, 463
England, 31, 130, 184, 228, 233, 234, 235, 253
English, 256, 339, 465, 471
Episcopal church, 103, 104

Europe, as market for buffalo robes, 154

Evans, Fred, 77

Evanston, Wyo., 398, 401

Excelsior Dancing Club, Helena, Mont., 94

Excelsior Hall, Bismarck, Dak., 571

Exchange Saloon and Gambling House, Helena, 88

Fackler, Michael, 103

Farces, 142

Fare, stage, 55, 57, 58, 64

Fargo, Dak., 163, 363, 376, 380, 383, 384, 419, 568, 570

Farm crops, 488, 489, 490, 496n, 503

Farm products, transportation for, 489, 490, 506; demand for, 493, 499, 500; prices for, 502, 503, 505, 506; surplus of, 505, 506

Farmers, 67, 72, 192, 484, 485; life of, 581-594

Farmers' Alliance, 553, 554, 555

Farming, bonanza, 509-522; diversified, 192, 387, 414, 494, 495, 512, 522, 537; mixed, 315, 496, 534, 537; dry, 336

Farming methods, of Indians, 485, 486; changed, 495, 534; in Montana, 498, 504; in Dakota, 585, 586

Farms, number of acres, in Dakota, 487, 493, 521; in Montana, 506; Wyoming, 509; Red River Valley, 514; bonanza farms, 514, 515

Father De Smet, 16, 26, 184, 497

Father Lonergan, 105

Fences, illegal, 296; in Dakota, 496n

Fenian committee, 31

Fenianism, 97, 98, 98n

Fergus County, Mont., 434

Ferries, river, 356, 357, 371

Finger, Ralph, 171

Finlay, Francois (see also Benetsee), 16, 17

Fiske, Captain James L., 56, 57, 189, 402

Flandreau, Dak., 351, 415

Flathead Indians, 497, 498

Flathead Lake, 17

Florence, Idaho, 10, 11, 67, 68, 70, 99, 114

Flour, shortage of, 66; price of, 185, 505, 506; from hard wheat, 414; of Red River wheat, 510, 511; demand for, 512

Floweree, Dan, 88, 210, 251

Food, of miners, 52, 53; of Chinese, 73; of farmers, 492

Foreigners, 387

Foreclosures, 542, 544, 552

Forest culture, 492

Forsyth, Mont., 432

Fort Abercrombie, 56, 363
    Abraham Lincoln, 31, 384
    Bennett, 161, 195
    Benton, 17, 18, 21, 56, 57, 58, 60, 62, 83, 161, 176, 195, 401, 405, 408, 410, 431, 478, 573
    Berthold, 161, 195
    Boise, 12
    Bridger, 4, 149, 161, 185, 195
    Buford, 161, 195, 430
    Dakota, 369, 374
    D. A. Russell, 76, 161, 194, 195, 395, 575
    Fetterman, 23, 77
    Keogh, 430
    Lapwai, 12
    Laramie, 26, 29, 30, 77, 80, 149, 161, 186, 195
    MacKenzie, 148
    Meade, 77
    Missoula, 161, 195
    Owen, 401, 497, 498, 500
    Peck, 161, 195
    Pierre, 63, 77, 154, 486
    Randall, 161, 195, 356, 360
    Reno, 42
    Rice, 56
    Sanders, 76
    Shaw, 161, 195
    "Sod," 353
    Tecumseh, 154
    Union, 56, 57, 131, 145, 148, 149, 151, 154, 161, 195
    Wadsworth, 56
    Walla Walla, 56
    William, 148

Forts, 183, 194, 289, 368, 371, 374, 377, 497

Fortunatus Mining Company, 43, 44

Foster, James S., 377, 443, 444, 445, 446, 449, 455, 457, 460, 462, 541

Foster, Tom, 95
Fountain City, 37
Franc, Otto, 219, 257
Fraternal orders, 97, 98
Free Homestead Association of Central
    New York, 371, 455-458
Free land, 294, 413, 424, 495
Freight, 15, 16, 21, 54, 58, 60, 61,
    62, 63, 65, 66, 387, 394, 494,
    494n, 499, 513
Freighters, 66, 68, 186
Freighting, 15, 61, 163; companies,
    186
Frémont, Captain John C., 138, 147,
    184
Frémont County, Wyo., 439
Fremont, Elkhorn, and Missouri River
    Railroad, 294
French Creek, 33, 36, 37
Frewen, Moreton, 233, 234, 235, 258,
    262
Frontier farmer, life of, 581-594;
    home of, 582-585
Frontier Index, first issue, 398
Frost, Todd, and Company, 357
Fruit culture, 492
Fuel, 369, 379, 586
Fur-bearing animals, decline in num-
    ber of, 147
Fur trade, 146-154, 146n
Fur traders, 129, 148-153, 182, 185,
    186, 497
Furnishings, of frontier home, 584, 585
Furs, 57, 132, 183

Galena, Dak., 27, 41
Gallatin City, Mont., 403, 501
Gallatin County, Mont., 79, 268, 325,
    340
Gallatin Valley, 501, 502
Gamblers, 13, 39, 72, 88, 89, 106
Gambling, 38, 86, 292, 560; houses,
    20, 82, 84, 89, 90, 107, 566
Games of chance, 86, 87
Gayville, Dak., 37, 40, 41, 360
Gem Theater, 78, 94, 111
General Custer House, the, 95
Georgetown, Dak., 364
Germans, 257, 297, 429, 435, 466, 470
Ghost cities, in Owyhee mining dis-
    trict, 12
Giants in the Earth, 593, 594

Gibson House, the, 83
Girls, 13, 84, 85, 108, 111, 587
Glen Ullin, Dak., 468, 469, 470
Glendive, Mont., 163, 430, 431, 433,
    435, 470, 471
Gold, in California, 3; in Colorado,
    4-8; in Idaho, 8-16; in Montana,
    16-22, 22n; in Wyoming, 22-25,
    41-44; in Big Horn area, 23; in
    Sweetwater district, 23n; in Black
    Hills, 25-41; mining of, 45-50;
    prospecting for, 50-52
Gold Creek, 17, 215, 221
Gold Room, the, 285, 575, 577, 581
Good Templars, 98
Gordon, John, 33, 34
Grand Forks, Dak., 382, 419, 570, 571
Grand Portage, 128
Grange, the, 544-555
Granger farmers, 294, 297, 298, 299
Grasshopper Creek, 19
Grasshopper Gulch, 92
Grasshoppers, 293, 366-369, 376, 386,
    405, 408, 413, 458, 464, 486,
    492-495, 505, 513, 522, 522n,
    523, 524, 525, 526; plague of,
    522-534; machine for catching,
    532n
Great American Desert, 6
Great Falls, Mont., 434, 435, 436
Great Western Museum and Circus,
    95
Greeley, Colo., 161
Greeley, Horace, 5, 186, 485
Green River City, Wyo., 397
Gregory Diggings, 7
Gregory, John H., 6
Grizzly Gulch, 21, 50n
Gymnastic organizations, 96

Hamilton, Reverend H. O., 103
Hamilton, William T., 149
Hancock, Major-General W. S., 30
Hankins, Allen, 88
Hardships, in Idaho gold fields, 10; of
    frontier farmer, 581, 588, 589,
    593, 594
Harvester, 516
Hasenwinkle Company, 111, 572, 573
Hay, necessary, 186; good prices, 195;
    for emergency feeding, 246, 246n;
    for sheep, 317, 325; sold to forts

Hay (con't)
  and stage stations, 493; native grasses, 504
Hayden, Dr. Ferdinand V., 28
Helena, Mont., 21, 22, 52, 62, 63, 64, 67, 69, 71, 83, 84, 88, 94, 96, 97, 98, 104, 109, 110, 333, 403, 404, 410, 431, 435, 436, 471
Helena Weekly Herald, first issue, 119
Henry, Alexander, 127, 145
Hensley, Jack, 88
Hensley, Josephine, 88, 110
"Herd Law," 496
Hereford cattle, 259, 261, 262, 263
Hickok, J. F. (Wild Bill), 77, 79, 80, 88, 105
Highland, Colo., 6
Hill City, Dak., 39
Hill, Surveyor-General, 370, 444, 456
Hinckley's Express, 64
Hogs, 494
Holladay, Ben, 64, 120
Home remedies, 591
Homes, of cattle ranchers, 284, 285; of sheep ranchers, 327; in Montana, 504, 505; of farmers, 582-585, 589
Homestake Mine, 38, 44
Homestead Act, 295, 366, 386, 455
Homesteaders, 297, 298, 372, 385, 412, 419, 429, 491
Homesteads, 249, 297, 390, 391, 415
Home-talent plays, 570, 572
Hornaday, William F., 140, 160, 176, 177
Horse-racing, 96, 292, 560, 562, 563
Horse-ranches, 339-342
Horse-ranching, 338-342; in western Montana, 339-340; in Dakota, 341, 342
Horse thieves, 342-344
Horses, 54, 55, 190, 210, 222
Hot Springs County, Wyo., 443
Hotels, 20, 38, 69, 82, 373, 381, 384, 404, 427
Hough, Reverend A. M., 103
H-T Ranch, 222
Hudson's Bay Company, 17, 128, 129, 149
Huidekoper, A. C., 221, 222, 278, 285, 342
Humboldt River, 27

Hurdy-gurdies, 20, 38, 84, 85, 89, 94, 107, 290
Huron, Dak., 426, 484
Hutterians, 463, 464, 464n

Ice skating, 96
Idaho City, Idaho, 11, 52, 82, 88, 91, 93, 95, 97, 98, 99, 103, 106
Idaho gold camps, 10, 16
Iliff, J. W., 188, 204, 206
Illegal entry on land, 295
Illinois, 18, 34
Illinois Central Railroad, 57
Immigrants, 55, 183, 184, 185, 186, 347, 354, 368, 380, 406, 415, 421, 433, 434, 435, 443-471, 512
Immigration, 41, 367, 368, 369, 370, 373, 376, 380, 383, 384, 385, 387, 390, 391; to Montana, 405-410, 431-436, 470-471; to Dakota, 420-427, 454-470; to Wyoming, 436-443, 470, 471-473
Immigration activities, in Dakota, 443-452; in Montana, 452, 453
Immigration agents, 444
Improvement of stock, 259-263
Independence, Mo., 182, 183
Indian agencies, 192, 193, 211, 212, 374, 376, 377
  agents, 160
  attacks, 15, 36, 58, 181, 274
  dangers to cattle, 274-279
  reservations, 275, 276, 277, 278
  treaty of 1868, 32
  troubles, 56, 57, 405, 407, 534
Indians, 12, 23, 26, 29, 31, 35, 41, 51, 55, 105, 140, 150, 151, 163, 177, 194, 252, 274-279, 350, 352, 353, 354, 359, 360, 376, 405, 430, 485, 486, 487, 496, 503
Inspection of cattle, 273, 274
Interest, 386, 415, 429, 491, 541, 542
Iowa, 10, 18, 34
Ireland, 31
Irish, 31, 32, 429
Irish Literary Society, 32
Irrigation, 437, 439, 440, 441, 471, 473, 501, 504, 507, 508, 509, 534

James River Valley, 390, 415, 421
Jamestown, Dak., 384, 385

Janesville, Dak., 484
Jenny, Walter P., 35
Johnson County, Wyo., 300
Johnson County War, 300-304
Johnston, General Albert S., 187
Judith Basin, 210, 225, 283, 332, 343
Judith Cattle Company, 210
Judith Roundup Association, 262
Junction City, Mont., 20
Justice, in mining camps, 112-124

Kansas, 55, 62
Kansas City, Mo., 32, 149, 207
Kansas Pacific Railroad, 158, 198
Katie Putnam Company, 111, 572, 573, 574
Keel-boats, 182
Kellogg, Idaho, 14
Kelton, Utah, 16
Kent, R., 26
Kent, T. A., 339
Kind, Ezra, 26
King, William, 26
Kingsbury County, Dak., 385
Kingsley, Charles S., 103
Kiowa Indians, 32
Kirwin district, 44, 44n
Kohl and Middleton, 78
Kohrs, Conrad, 189

Labor, in mines, 47; in Dakota, 372; on wheat farms, 518-520
Laborers, needed, 405
Lacon, Dr., 26
Lafayette, Dak., 363, 364
Lake Superior and Puget Sound Land and Townsite Company, 380, 382, 383
Lancaster City, Dak., 41
Land and town-site companies, 348-361
Land-grant railroads, 367
Land laws, 294, 295, 296
Land-offices, 293, 294, 373, 391, 392, 404, 410, 431, 463
Langrishe, J. S., 109, 285
Langrishe Stock Company, 109, 578, 579
Lands, types of in Montana, 503
Laramie City, Wyo., 396, 399, 400, 401
Laramie County, Wyo., 296

Laramie County Stock Growers Association, 266, 275, 315
Larpenteur, Charles, 148, 151
Last Chance Gulch, 21, 110, 403
Lawyers, 38
Lead, 14
Lead City, Dak., 37, 38, 419
Leavenworth, Kans., 55, 158
Lecture club, 93
Lecturers, 95
Legitimate drama, 578, 579, 580
Lemhi County, Idaho, 12
Leviathan Hall, 66, 110
Lewis and Clark, 137, 138, 142, 145
Lewis and Clark County, Mont., 268
Lewiston, Idaho, 9, 12, 113, 114
Library associations, 92, 93, 568, 569
Lignite coal, 379, 419, 450
Lincoln County, Dak., 370, 373
Liquor, in mining camps, 82, 108, 109, 151, 292
Lisa, Manuel, 150
Literary associations, 92, 93
Little Missouri, Dak., 220, 221, 228, 229, 247
Little Missouri Horse Company, 342
Little Missouri River, 222, 223, 242
Little Missouri Stock Growers Association, 239, 269
Little Prickly Pear River, 60
Livingston, Mont., 80, 433
Lodges, 97, 98
Lodging, 69, 70, 71
Long X Ranch, 223
Losses, in cattle, 209, 244; in sheep, 324-326
Lost Horse Gulch, 22n
Lots, town, 38, 69, 348, 382, 393, 395, 431, 433, 434, 441, 477, 484
Lottery, 96
Lovell, Wyo., 473
Lovell, Henry T., 219
Lyceum associations, 92, 568, 569
Lynching, 113, 117, 118, 122, 123, 124, 299

Machinery, mining, 8, 43, 48; farming, 491, 503, 504, 517, 542, 543, 552, 553
Mackinaw boats, 58, 59
Madison County, Mont., 19, 268

Magicians, 95, 107
Magnolia Hall, Idaho City, 94
Mail, 63, 64, 65, 356, 363, 437, 482
Majors, Alexander, 186
Maltese Cross Ranch, 220
Mandan, Dak., 417, 418
Mandan Indians, 137, 140, 143, 144
Marcy, Captain Randolph B., 4
Mardell, Dak., 481-483
Mardell Townsite Company, 483
Markets, 196; for wool, 324
Marriage, on frontier, 588
Marshall, John, 3
Masonry, 97, 98
Matadore Land and Cattle Company, 255
McCall, Jack, 77
McCook, Edwin S., 30
McCoy, J. G., 198
McConnell, Alexander, 105
McDaniels, James, 285, 575-577
McDaniels' Museum Theater, Cheyenne, 576, 578
    New Dramatic Theater, 577, 579
McDonald, Angus J., 219
McKenzie, Sam, 344
Meagher County, Mont., 210, 319, 325
Meals, cost of, 70, 71
Meat-packing enterprise, 228-233
Meckling, Dak., 369
Medary, Minn., 352, 353
Medary, S. A., 351
Medora, Dak., 222, 229-232, 247, 269, 319
Medicine shows, 566
Meeteetsee, Wyo., 292, 440
Melbourne, Frank, 538, 539
Melodian Hall, Deadwood, Dak., 94; Cheyenne, 574
Melodian Theater, Virginia City, 109
Mennonites, 461n, 462, 463
Mercantile establishments, 356, 357
Merchants, 167; rôle of, 540; and Grange, 546, 548, 549
Mesplie, I., 103
Methodist Church, 103, 106, 183
Midway County, Minn., 352
Midwives, 59
Milbank, Dak., 117
Miles City, Mont., 163, 167, 210, 232, 286, 289, 290, 291, 315, 333, 408, 409, 431, 473

Miles City Club, 286
Miles City Dressed Beef Company, 232, 233
Military posts, 56, 161, 183, 192, 193, 194, 195, 195n, 212, 376, 384, 540
Military protection, requests for, 407, 408
Milk River, 137
Miller Creek, 9
Millersburg, Idaho, 9
Mills, quartz, 19, 20, 38, 41, 43, 48, 49; corn, 486; flour, 490, 491, 497, 502, 503, 510, 511
Milwaukee Railway Company, 391, 415, 416, 557
Miners, follow new discoveries, 3-45; in Northwest, 3-124; cabin of, 52; food of, 52; dress of, 73; recreation of, 82-98; attitude toward religion, 106, 107; in Colorado, 188; go into cattle business, 189
Miner's Delight, Wyo., 24
Mining camps, life in, 89-98; liquor in, 82, 108, 109, 151, 292
Mining companies, 8, 44
Ministers, 91, 103, 106, 592
Minnehaha County, Dak., 373
Minnesota, 10, 18, 29, 34, 56, 57, 132, 347, 349, 350
Minnesota massacre, 354
Minot, Dak., 426
Minstrel troupes, 577
Missionaries, 183, 497
Mississippi River, 4
Mississippi Valley, 56
Missoula, Mont., 104
Missoula and Bitter Root Railroad, 435
Missoula County, Mont., 408
Missoula Mills, Mont., 404
Missouri River, 4, 5, 6, 21, 22, 28, 29, 53, 54, 55, 56, 57, 58, 61, 62, 134, 138, 146, 154, 155, 156, 182, 212, 357
Missourians, 73
Mitchell, Dak., 427
Money, on frontier, 540
Montana, Colo., 6
Montana Billiard Saloon, 110
Montana Stock Growers Association, 237, 243, 267, 268, 286, 305, 333

Montana Theater, 109
Montana Wool Growers Association, 315, 328n
Moody County, Dak., 385
Moorhead, Minn., 381, 382
Moreland, Mont., 340
Morley, J. H., 52, 93
Mormons, 4, 184, 187, 438, 439, 440, 441, 471, 472, 472n, 473, 473n, 499
"Mormon Wars," 498
Mortgages, 540, 541, 542, 543, 544, 552
Mortgage inspectors, 544
Mount Lookout, Mont., 26
Mountain City, Colo., 7
Mules, 54, 55, 60, 190, 210
Mullan, Captain John, 17n
Mullan, Lieutenant James, 27
Mullan Road, the, 17n, 60
Murray, Idaho, 13
Murrayville, Idaho, 14
Music-hall, 107
Musical organizations, 96
Musselshell River, 22n, 157
Musselshell Valley, 210
Mutton rams, demand for, 322
Myrtle, Idaho, 13

Natroma County, Wyo., 439
Nebraska, 28, 34, 53, 62, 135
Nelson's Gulch, 21
Negroes, 74
Nester, 282
Nevada, 8, 11, 15, 18, 28
Nevada City, Mont., 20, 70, 85, 95, 99, 104
New Mexico, 3
New York Colony, 444, 455-458
Nez Percé Indians, 141
Nez Percé War, 77
Nineteenth century in United States, 3
Norcross, Reverend L. P., 105
North Dakota, 22, 137, 429
North Deadwood, Dak., 37
North Platte River, 64, 397
Northern Pacific Colonization Bureau, 466, 467
Northern Pacific Railroad, 63, 76, 162, 170, 215, 216, 217, 218, 220, 221, 230, 376, 379, 382, 386, 387, 408, 415, 417, 418, 420, 430, 431, 450, 470, 506, 510, 511, 512, 557
Northwest, 31, 54, 56, 58, 60, 62, 73, 75, 92, 95, 97, 101, 106, 134, 135, 137, 140, 146, 161, 162, 166, 203, 204
Northwest Fur Company, 127, 128, 129, 132
Northwestern Express, Stage and Transportation Company, 63
Northwestern Railroad, 416
Norwegians, 361, 429, 547
Nye, Bill, 80

Oakport, Dak., 381
Oats, 489, 490, 504
Occupancy of Black Hills, opposition to, 29, 30, 32, 34; allowed, 35
Odd Fellows, 98
Ogden, Utah, 398
Omaha, Nebr., 20, 54, 64
O'Neill Colony, 33
Opera-houses, 581
Ophir, Mont., 478, 479
Oregon, 8, 10, 12, 15, 18, 62, 183, 184, 185, 186
Oregon Steam Transportation Company, 15
Oregon Trail, 12, 133, 156
Orem, Con, 95
Orientals, 74
Oro Fino, Idaho, 9, 10, 11
Oro Fino Creek, 8
Oro Fino Gulch, 21
Otis, Johnny, 88
Otto, Wyo., 440, 476, 477
Outfitting points, 6, 33n, 57
Outlaws, 113-123
Owyhee, Idaho, 12, 98
Owyhee Avalanche, first newspaper in Idaho Terr., 12
Owyhee River, 11
O-X Ranch, 222
Oxen, 60, 63, 190, 196, 207, 210, 225

Pack-trains, 9, 10, 16, 60, 67
Panic of 1857, 5
Panic of 1873, 103, 184, 386, 387, 390, 512, 526, 542, 545
Park River, 127

Parker's Hall, 95
Patent medicines, 591
Patrons of Husbandry (see also Grange), 544, 555
Patterson, Professor J. B., 101
Payette Valley, 53
Peddlers, 589, 590
Pembina, Dak., 129, 132, 361, 363, 493, 510
Pembina buffalo hunt, 130-132
Pembina County, Dak., 363
Pemmican, 128, 129n, 132
"Pemmican War," 129
Pennington, Dak., 4
People's Theater, Helena, 110
Peoria Emigration Society, 460
Per Hanse, 593, 594
Pfout's Merchandise Emporium, W. G., 97
Phrenologists, 95
Piano, first in Black Hills, 110, 111
Pickpockets, 565
Piegan Indians, 22n, 177
Pierce, Captain E. D., 8, 9
Pierce City, Idaho, 9, 10
Pierce, Ellis T., 80
Pierre, Dak., 34
Pike's Peak, 4, 5, 10, 54, 188
Pioneer, Idaho, 11, 97, 103
Pioneers, the, 94
Placer mining, 45-47
Placerville, Idaho, 11, 12, 96, 97, 103
Plains, 139, 161, 182, 197, 203
Plains Indians, 135, 141
Platte River, 156
Plays, named, 108, 109, 112, 285, 286, 572, 578
Pleuro-pneumonia, in cattle, 234
Plows, 585, 585n
Plummer, Henry, 113, 114, 115
Plummer gang, 114, 115
Plymouth Gold and Silver Mining Company of Montana, 49
Pony express, 77
Pope, Major-General, 55
Popo Agie River, 24
Population, 19, 22, 40, 51, 55, 71, 99, 293, 294, 365, 366, 374, 375, 379, 384, 394, 396, 399, 402, 403, 404, 405, 407, 410, 418, 419, 420, 422, 424, 425, 427, 429, 431, 433, 436, 439, 443

Portland, Oregon, 9, 10, 11, 15, 60, 64, 103
Post-offices, 366, 380, 473
Poulin, A. Z., 103
Poultry, 494
Powder River, 42
Powder River Cattle Company, 233, 255, 256
Pratt, Chouteau and Company, 147, 153
"Preacher Smith," 104
Preëmption Act, 295
Presbyterian Church, 103
President Benjamin Harrison, 303
Prices, in gold camps, 16, 51, 65-71; for food, 65-68; for meals, 70; for robes, 176; of cattle, 189, 205, 206, 207, 217, 227, 238, 250-253; of wool, 311, 312, 324; of commodities, 488; of land, 413, 490, 495; of farm products, 490; of wheat, 505, 506, 510; of flour, 506; of machinery, 543; for breaking sod, 585, 586
Prichard, A. J., 13, 13n
Prichard Creek, 13
Prickly Pear Valley, 21, 22n, 104
Priests, 103
Princeton, Mo., 75, 76
Prize-fights, 95
Profits, in steamboating, 58; in cattle-raising, 205, 206, 207n, 211, 217, 227, 251; in sheep, 215, 318, 326; in wheat, 521, 522
Promontory Point, junction of Central Pacific and Union Pacific Railroads, 398
Prospecting, 50 et seq.
Prospectors, in Idaho, 10, 14; traces of in Black Hills, 27
Prostitutes, 72, 289
Prostitution, 111; houses of, 103
Protestant Churches, 103
Public Schools, 99, 101

Quartz, 7, 8, 12, 19, 20, 21, 38, 41, 41n, 43, 47, 48, 49
Quartz-mining, 47-50, 505

Race riots, 74
Raffles, 96

Railroad rates, 494, 494n
Railroads (see also railroads listed),
   divide buffalo, 158-160; and settlement in Dakota, 378, 388, 389;
   and town-site speculation, 395;
   and settlement in Wyoming, 396-
   401; services of, 412, 413; as
   pioneers, 418; expansion of, 419;
   and immigrant trade, 450, 450n;
   and immigration, 464, 466, 467,
   468; effect on agriculture, 490;
   boom Red River country, 512
Rainfall, 411, 412; in Dakota, 535,
   537, 538
Rain-makers, 538
Ranches, 180, 219, 220, 221, 222, 223
Ranchers, 180, 181, 182, 189, 242,
   243, 245, 256, 257, 287, 485
Ranch-house, 284, 285
Ranching, on American frontier, 181;
   open-range, 203, 211, 235, 236,
   251
Range, definition of, 264; regulations
   of, 190; wars, 330-336
Rapid City, Dak., 27, 40, 214, 215
Raven City, Mont., 13
Rawlins, Wyo., 42, 69, 289, 401
Raymond's Playhouse, Bismarck, Dak.,
   571, 572
Real estate, 38, 69, 394, 396, 422, 435,
   436, 481
Recreation, 92 et seq.
Recreation Hall, Cheyenne, 576
Red Cloud agency, 35
Red River of the North, 127, 376
Red River carts, 130, 130n, 132
Red River trail, 132
Red River Valley, 128, 361, 363, 379,
   380, 493; bonanza farming in,
   509-522
Redfield, Dak., 427
Refrigerator-car, development of, 228,
   322
Religion, on gold frontier, 102-107
Religious organizations, 101, 102
Rents, in Helena and Deadwood, 69;
   in Cheyenne, 394
Reservations, Indian. See Indian reserva-
   tions.
Richland County, Dak., 380, 385
Riley, Joe, 95
Riverside Ranch, 223
River traffic, 57, 58

Road-agents, 115-123
Road stations, 186
Robbery, 114 et seq., 120 et seq.
Robes, buffalo, preparation of, 142,
   143; types of, 143, 144; impor-
   tance of, 147; trading for, 150-
   154; prices of, 176
Rock County, Minn., 352
Rock Springs, Wyo., 399, 401
Rocky Mountains, 54, 134, 138, 161
Roller skating, 96
Rolvaag, O. E., 593
Roosevelt, Theodore, 222, 223, 246-
   250, 268, 269, 272, 285
Round-up, 271-273
Routes to gold fields, 54, 54n, 55, 56,
   56n, 57
Ruby City, Idaho, 11
Rules for gold camps, 51
Rumanians, 466
Russel, Thomas H., 31, 33
Russell, Majors, and Waddell, 186
Russell, William Green, 4
Russian-Germans, 455, 461, 461n, 462,
   463, 465
Russians, 429, 469
Rustlers, 280, 299, 300, 342, 343

St. Charles, Colo., 6
St. Cloud, Minn., 57
St. Ignatius Mission, 187, 401, 497
St. Joseph, Mo., 54, 57, 60
St. Louis, Mo., 17, 18, 58, 60, 149,
   155, 182
St. Louis and Montana Gold and Sil-
   ver Mining Company, 49
St. Mary's Mission, 497
St. Paul, Minn., 56, 132
St. Paul and Pacific Railroad, 380
St. Peter's Mission, 22n, 401
Salmon City, Idaho, 12
Salmon River, 10
Salmon River mines, 14, 18
Saloons, 13, 20, 21, 38, 44, 82, 83,
   84, 89, 104, 107, 289, 290, 291,
   566
Salt Lake City, Utah, 15, 21, 54, 62,
   68, 75, 93
San Francisco, Calif., 15, 60, 61, 109
Sawtelle, A. J., 110
Sawtelle Dramatic Company, 572
Sawtooth Mountains, 12

Scab, 325
Schools, 99n, 520, 550
School-houses, 592
Scotch, 465; interested in cattle-raising, 254-256
Scott, Daniel, 31, 32
Sedalia, Mo., 198
Selkirk colony, 128, 129, 130
Seminary, 101
Sentinel Butte, Dak., 163
Settlement, frontier of, 347; of Minnesota, 347, 348; in Dakota, 348-361, 372-392, 410-430; along Missouri River, 358; in Red River Valley, 361-366; factors against, 366-370; factors favoring, 370-372; in Wyoming, 392-401, 436-443, 471-473; in Montana, 401-410, 430-436, 470, 471; by colonies, 454-473
Shearers, sheep, 323
Sheep, 309-313, 436, 439; number of, 310, 312, 313, 313n, 314, 316, 318, 319, 320, 321; breeds, 321, 322, 323; shearing of, 323; use of range, 327, 328
Sheep-herders, 329, 330, 331, 333, 335, 337, 338
Sheep-raising, factors favoring, 310, 311; in Northwest, 313 et seq.; on open-range basis, 317, 320; 325; expansion of, 317-322
Sheep ranches, 327
Sheridan, Wyo., 43, 44, 437
Sheridan County, Wyo., 439
Sheridan, General Philip A., 30, 276
Sherman, General W. T., 28, 430
Sheyenne Valley, 383
Shonkin Stock Association, 262, 268, 273, 277
Shorthorn cattle, 259, 263
Shoshone Indians, 275
Shoshone River Valley, 334
Side-shows, 560
Sidney, Nebr., 63, 64
Silver, 11, 12, 12n, 14
Silver Bow County, Mont., 433
Silver City, Idaho, 11, 12
Silver Creek, 22n
Simpson, George, 4
Singing schools, 96, 99, 100, 592
Sioux City, Iowa, 31, 33, 34, 53, 57 488, 489

Sioux City and Pacific Railroad, 371
Sioux Falls, Dak., 350, 351, 353, 354, 356, 419
Sioux Falls Democrat, first issue, 354
Sioux Indian, story of, 29, 30
Sioux Indians, 25, 32, 35, 36, 65, 77, 143, 170, 213, 247, 259, 275, 276, 407
Sioux War, 408
Sitting Bull, 170, 276, 430
Sleighing, 96, 97
Smith, B. M., 28
Smith, Reverend G. J., 103, 104
Smith, Vic, 173
Smoky Hill River, 55
Snake Indians, 141
Snake River, 8, 9
Social life, in Dakota, 587
Society of Montana Pioneers, 62
Sod corn, 586
Southern Colorado Stock Growers Association, 265
South Deadwood, Dak., 37
South Dakota, 22, 429
South Pass City, Wyo., 24, 25, 399, 401
South Platte River, 6
Spanish Merino sheep, 309, 309n
Spearfish, Dak., 26, 38
Special farming, 495, 496
"Spink County War," 474, 475
Spokane, Wash., 14
Stage lines, 15, 21, 55, 63, 64, 65, 230, 372, 380
Stage robberies, 116-122
Stage station, 83, 84
Stampedes, of cattle, 201, 202
Stanley, Colonel D. S., 29
Stansbury, Howard, 156
Staples, Dr. J. M., 350
Steamboats, 5, 15, 17, 18, 54, 59, 60, 83, 155, 156, 376, 380
Steamboat traffic, 154, 155, 156, 367
Steam-elevator, first in Red River Valley, 511
Sterling, Dak., 384
Stevens Company, John A., 111
Stinking Water River, 136
Stock companies, 107, 109, 572, 573, 578
Stock-raising, 6
Stock-yards, 207
Stores, 44
Story, Nelson, 339

Stuart, Granville, 17, 167, 170, 186, 210, 345
Stuart, James, 17, 23
Sturgis, Dak., 77
Stutsmen County, Dak., 385
Subscription schools, 98, 99, 100, 101, 592
Summer of 1886, 238
Summit City, Mont., 85
Sun River, 22n
Sun River Association, 268
Surveys, in Dakota, 364
Swan Land and Cattle Company, 255
Swearengen, Al E., 78, 111
Swedish, 297, 429, 470, 547
Sweetwater area, 23n, 25
Sweetwater River, 24

Tallent, Mrs. Annie, 33
Taxes, 74, 372, 413, 489
Teachers, 99, 99n, 102, 592
Terraville, Dak., 79
Territorial fairs, 556, 559
Territorial legislature of Montana, 64, 190, 257, 260; of Dakota, 221, 306, 306n, 366, 444n, 527
Territorial legislatures, acts of, 264, 270, 282, 444
Territorial organization, changes in, 22
Territory of Dakota, created, 22; gold in, 25-41; buffalo in, 133, 134, 137, 138; early cattle-raising in, 191-195; cattle in, 203, 211-214, 220-224; settlement of, 293, 348-392; horse-ranching in, 341, 342; organization of, 348; divided into states, 429
Territory of Colorado, gold in, 4-8; cattle in, 204n
Territory of Idaho, gold in, 8-16; formed, 22
Territory of Montana, 22, 70, 157, 161, 190; cattle in, 203, 204, 209-211, 225, 226; settlement of, 401-410, 548
Territory of Wyoming, 157, 162, 190, 191, 297; cattle in, 203, 204-208; 218, 219; settlement of, 392-401
Terry, General, 80
Texas, 36, 77, 196 et seq.
"Texas fever," 196, 198, 235

Textbooks, 102
The Virginian, 123
Theater, on mining frontier, 107-112; on Great Plains, 569-581
Theatre Comique, Cheyenne, 574, 576, 580
Theatricals, amateur, 95
Thermopolis, Wyo., 442, 443
Thoen, Lewis, 26
Thoen Stone, the, 26n
Three Sevens (7-7-7) Ranch, 222
Thresher, 510
Threshing crew, typical, 516
Timber, 11, 369, 379, 412, 492, 505, 582, 583
Timber Culture Act, 295, 297, 384n, 582n
Toll-bridges, 64, 185n
Toll-charges, excessive, 64
Tolls, 64
Torrey, Robert A., 219
Town-site agents, 348; companies, 348, 349, 350, 362; promotion, 348
Town-sites, 348, 349, 350, 355, 357, 362, 363, 364, 379, 380, 383, 395
Trade, 59, 61, 62
Traders, 486
Trading posts, 127, 147, 148, 486, 497
Tramps, 518, 519
Transportation, to gold frontier, 5, 15, 21, 53-65; to Dakota, lack of facilities, 366, 377; facilities supplied, 378, 380; and settlement, 388, 389, 412, 428; by wagon, 489; need for cheaper rates, 494, 506
Trapping, 493
Travel, routes of to gold fields, 16; methods of to gold fields, 53, 54; to Montana, 62 et seq.
Traveling medicine agents, 591
Treaty of Traverse de Sioux, 349, 362
Troops, 25, 33, 34, 57, 77, 303, 408
Trusts, crusade against, 554
Tubbs, Alice, 88
Tubbs, W. G., 88
Tuition, 98, 100, 101
Tuttle, Bishop Daniel S., 103, 104, 106
Twine, 516

Umatilla, Wash., 15
Union County, Dak., 366

Union Hall, 103
Union Pacific Railroad, 12, 16, 24, 63, 64, 68, 133, 157, 190, 198, 211, 215, 367, 392, 393, 394, 395, 396, 397, 398, 400, 461
United States Army, 56, 79, 183
United States Government, 12, 34, 35, 64, 132, 141, 162n, 163, 279, 359, 360, 527, 528
Upper Missouri Land Company, 357, 358

Variety bills, 109, 111, 112
Variety Halls, 82, 94, 107, 108, 110, 111, 112, 289, 291, 566, 570, 578, 579
Variety troupes, 107, 109, 572, 573
Vaudeville acts, 108
Vegetables, 52, 53, 188, 489, 494, 500, 502, 508
Ventriloquists, 95, 107
Vermillion, Dak., 360, 365, 366, 373, 495
Vermillion River, 137
Vermillion River Valley, 390
Vigilance Committees, 113 et seq., 282, 283, 433
Vigilantes, 113, 115, 117-124, 433
Village store, 590
Villard, Henry, 5
Vincent, Dak., 384
Virginia City, Mont., 8, 19, 20, 21, 22, 40, 49, 59, 61, 62, 65, 66, 70, 83, 85, 88, 92, 95, 96, 97, 98, 99, 102, 103, 104, 109, 115, 402, 404, 410
Voyageurs, 127, 356

Wages, of miners, 20, 69; for cow-hands, 200; for workers in wheat fields, 520
Wagon-trains, replace pack-trains, 60; from California, 61
Wagoner, C. H., 38
Wahpeton, Dak., 380
Walla Walla, Wash., 8, 10, 15, 60, 64, 67
Wallach's Hall, Bismarck, Dak., 571
Warren, Idaho, 11
Warren, James, 10
Warren, Lieutenant G. K., 28

Washakie County, Wyo., 443
Watson, Ella ("Cattle Kate"), 299
Waugh's Brass and Quadrille Band, W. C., 96
W-B Ranch, 222
Western Ranches, Limited, 255
Western Town Company, 350, 351
Weston County, Wyo., 439
West Port, Mo., 4
Wheat, 413, 414, 486, 489, 489n, 490, 491, 492, 494, 497, 502, 503, 504, 505, 506, 509, 510, 511, 512, 513, 514, 542
Whist tournaments, 96
White, Dr. Elijah, 184
White, John, 18
Whitlatch Vein, 21
Whitman, Marcus, 183
Wholesale liquor houses, 83
Wibaux, Pierre, 221, 229, 245, 248, 258, 285
Wibaux, Mont., 221
Wichita, Kans., 158
Willard, J. H., 42n
Wilsach, Frank J., 80
Wind River Valley, 24, 398, 508
Winona and St. Peter Railroad, 390
Winter of 1880-1881, 236, 411, 414, 415
Winter of 1886-1887, 235-246, 319, 435n, 436n
Witcher, Ephrim, 33, 34
Wisconsin, 18, 34
Wister, Owen, 123
Wolves, menace to cattle, 279
Women, 71, 72, 86, 90, 95, 105, 106, 130, 242, 291, 353, 409, 520, 544, 587, 588, 589, 590
Wood, G. W., 26
Wool clip, 310, 312, 322, 323
Wool production, shifts west, 310, 311
Woonsocket, Dak., 427
Wrestling bouts, 95
Wright, W. H., 41
Wyoming Live Stock Commission, 300
Wyoming Ranch Company, Limited, 255
Wyoming Stock Graziers Association, 266
Wyoming Stock Growers Association, 218, 234, 266, 281, 285, 292, 298, 300, 301, 302, 315
Wyoming Tribune, first issue, 191

Yankton, Dak., 22, 28, 29, 63, 67, 357, 360, 365, 366, 373, 419, 456, 457, 458, 459, 570
Yankton County, Dak., 366
Yankton Indians, 352, 359

Yankton Treaty of 1859, 28
Yellowstone River, 19, 137, 138, 168
Yellowstone Roundup Association, 268
Yellowstone Valley, 22n
Yong Wo Company, 74

(1)

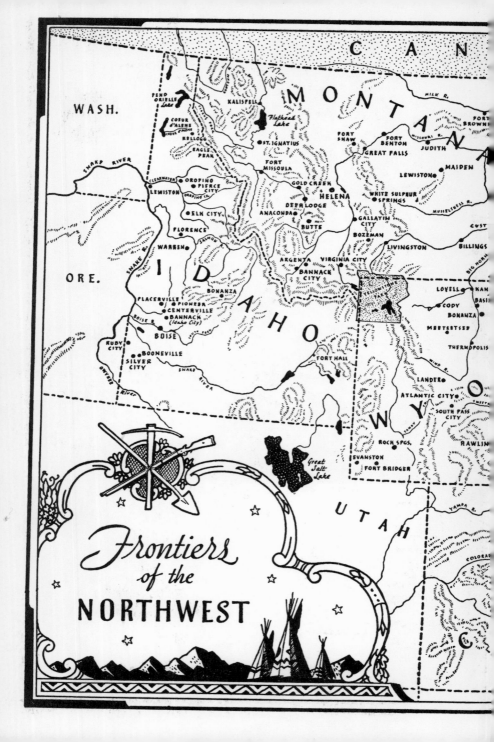

Frontiers
of the
NORTHWEST